EARLY MEDIEVAL IRELAND

LONGMAN HISTORY OF IRELAND

General Editor: Steven G. Ellis

An analytical account of Ireland from early Christian times to the present, the six volumes of this new series are being written by a team of leading historians in Ireland, Britain and America. The volumes (each substantial enough to make a significant contribution to scholarship without becoming unwieldy for the non-specialist) will tackle a common central agenda, including politics, religion, society, the economy and government. The series will be the obvious starting point for anyone – scholar, student or general reader – wanting an authoritative but accessible introduction to Irish history.

The first volume to be published in the series is:

EARLY MEDIEVAL IRELAND 400–1200
DÁIBHÍ Ó CRÓINÍN

EARLY MEDIEVAL IRELAND

IRELAND

400–1200

DÁIBHÍ Ó CRÓINÍN

LONGMAN
London and New York

Addison Wesley Longman Limited,
Edinburgh Gate,
Harlow, Essex CM20 2JE, England
and Associated Companies throughout the world.

*Published in the United States of America
by Addison Wesley Longman Publishing, New York*

©Longman Group Limited 1995

First published 1995
Second impression 1996

ISBN 0 582 015669 CSD
ISBN 0 582 015650 PPR

British Library Cataloguing-in-Publication Data
A catalogue record for this book is available from the British Library

Library of Congress Cataloging-in-Publication Data
Ó Cróinín, Dáibhí.
Early medieval Ireland, c. AD400 – AD1200
p. cm. (Longman history of Ireland)
Includes bibliographical references (p.) and index.
ISBN 0-582-01566-9 (cased). ISBN 0-582-01565-0 (paper)
1. Ireland–History–To 1172. I. Series.
DA930.02 1995
941.503–dc20   94-43307
                                       CIP

Set by 7 in 10/13pt ITC Garamond Light
Produced by Longman Singapore Publishers (Pte) Ltd.
Printed in Singapore

CONTENTS

LIST OF MAPS

ACKNOWLEDGEMENTS

We are grateful to the following for permission to reproduce copyright material: the Royal Irish Academy for the translation by Calvert Watkins of an early Irish verse which appeared in Varia III/Calvert Watkins (*Ériu*, xxix, 1978); Colin Smythe Limited, Publishers for extracts from three (translated) poems which appeared in *Medieval Irish lyrics* by James Carney (The Dolmen Press, 1967); the Governing Board of the School of Celtic Studies of the Dublin Institute for Advanced Studies for translated material from the following works – *Thesaurus palaeohibernicus* by W. Stokes and J. Strachan, *Dicuili Liber de mensura orbis terrae* by J. J. Tierney, and *Old Irish reader* by R. Thurneysen.

LIST OF ABBREVIATIONS

AA	*[MGH] Auctores Antiquissimi.*
AFM	Annals of the Four Masters, John O'Donovan (ed.), *Annala Rioghachta Eireann: Annals of the Kingdom of Ireland by the Four Masters* (7 vols Dublin, 1856).
ALI	*Ancient laws of Ireland* (6 vols, Dublin, 1865–1901).
AU	Seán Mac Airt and Gearóid Mac Niocaill (eds), The Annals of Ulster (to AD1131) (Dublin, 1983).
CCCM	*Corpus Christianorum, Continuatio Medievalis.*
CCF	*Cóic Conairi Fuigill* ('The Five Paths of Judgement')
CCSL	*Corpus Christianorum, Series Latina.*
CMCS	*Cambridge [Cambrian] Medieval Celtic Studies.*
CNRS	Centre National de la Recherche Scientifique.
DIL	*Dictionary of the Irish Language.*
HE	*Historia Ecclesiastica* (usually Bede's).
IER	*Irish Ecclesiastical Review.*
JRSAI	*Journal of the Royal Society of Antiquaries of Ireland* (1848–).
LH	Gregory of Tours, *Libri Historiarum.*
MGH	*Monumenta Germaniae Historica.*
MPL	Jacques-Paul Migne (ed.), *Patrologiae cursus completus, series latina.*
NHI	T.W. Moody, F.X. Martin and F.J. Byrne (eds), *A new history of Ireland* (10 vols, Oxford 1976–).
OE	Old English.
OI	Old Irish.
ON	Old Norse.
OW	Old Welsh.
PLAC	*[MGH] Poetae Latini Aevi Carolini.*
PRIA	*Proceedings of the Royal Irish Academy.*
RIA	Royal Irish Academy.
SRM	*[MGH] Scriptores Rerum Merovingicarum.*
Trans	Transactions.
ZCP	*Zeitschrift für celtische Philologie* (1898–).

PREFACE

Readers of Sellar and Yeatman's classic *1066 and all that* will know about 'The Irish Question' and King John's attempt to solve it by pulling the beards of the aged Irish chiefs, 'which was a Bad Thing and the wrong answer'. This book tries to make good the neglect of Irish history which is thus gently lampooned, offering a different perspective on Britain's nearest neighbour. Most general readers will be vaguely familiar only with the Irishmen mentioned in Bede's *Ecclesiastical History of the English Nation*, with Charles Stewart Parnell perhaps, or with Eamon de Valera, though most will admit that the island of Ireland existed during the First World War, and even during the Second World War (which citizens of the Republic called 'The Emergency'). For the most part, England's involvement in Irish affairs has been seen – in Irish eyes, at least – as baneful and destructive, a verdict echoed by some commentators on the other side of the Irish Sea. Thus, William of Canterbury, writing in the twelfth century, mentions a certain Theobald, who was wounded in the Irish wars, 'and it served him right (said William), or so those thought who saw no reason for the disquieting of a neighbouring nation, who, however uncivilised and barbarous, were remarkable and noteworthy practisers of the Christian religion'.

But most modern readers could hardly be expected to concern themselves with the details of Ireland's history in the early middle ages when the Irish show no great interest in the subject themselves. I am mindful of Maria Edgeworth's comment, in the preface to *Castle Rackrent*: 'Nations as well as individuals gradually lose attachment to their identity, and the present generation is amused rather than offended by the ridicule that is thrown upon their ancestors'. Happy to bask in the afterglow of Ireland's 'Golden Age' (roughly reckoned to have lasted the best part of a thousand years, coming to an end only with the introduction of coalition government in our own time), most Irish people are content that their country's early history should remain embalmed in the state in which it was left by patriotic historians of the early twentieth century. This is understandable enough, since the picture painted is one of almost unsullied brilliance. While the other peoples of Europe grovelled through their 'Dark Ages', Ireland stood alone, a beacon of learning and fountain-head for a steady stream of Christian missionary monks whose tireless labours eventually succeeded in dragging their neighbours out of the darkness and back into the light of civilization. Who would not be proud of such a history?

This book offers a different view of early medieval Ireland. I would like to be able to say that I enjoyed writing it, but that would be a lie. The truth is that the book proved a great deal more difficult to produce than I had anticipated, for reasons as much to do with personal matters as with professional ones. My original intention was to dispose of some of the more intractable material by means of articles which I had been commissioned to write for the first volume of the Royal Irish Academy's *New history of Ireland*, which is devoted to early Irish history and prehistory. Two lengthy articles were delivered, one a detailed narrative of political developments in the period AD400 to 800, the other on Hiberno-Latin literature down to the twelfth century. This should have obviated the necessity for treating these matters in minute detail in this book – something I had deliberately tried to avoid, for fear of intimidating the general reader. Unfortunately, the *New history* was delayed (for reasons that had nothing to do with me), and it now appears that publication – if it happens at all – will follow the appearance of this book rather than precede it. However, those readers who find the level of detailed discussion of political matters in this book inadequate, or who would rather have more on Hiberno-Latin literature, may sate their curiosity by referring to the *New history*, vol. i, when it does appear.

As for the approach adopted in producing this book, I have not tried to be deliberately provocative in what I have written, preferring (where called for) to put our national sacred cows into intervention – thereby ensuring that they can be recycled at a later date – rather than dumping them unceremoniously on the pyre of historical revisionism.

A colleague in the Zoology Department of University College Galway expressed horror in the preface to one of his publications that he might be 'the perpetrator of an improving book'. However, like him, I trust that for school pupils this book would be considered suitable, if not altogether proper reading, and that university undergraduates and their teachers may also find it useful.

It is the custom with books of this kind for the author to thank those who helped in the process of its production. However, since – through my own neglect – none of my colleagues has seen a draft, nor has any real inkling of what is contained in this book, I cannot follow this ritual. Besides, it has always seemed unfair to me that authors should thank a long list of friends and colleagues and then claim all the remaining errors as their own. In my case the claim is thoroughly justified. I can only hope that the faults are so few and so insignificant that none of my colleagues will feel aggrieved at their exclusion. Friends and colleagues in University College Galway and in other institutions have been generous over the years in supplying me with copies of their publications, and for this I am very grateful, as I am to Steven Ellis, who has hovered over me patiently while I laboured with this book. His advice and encouragement kept me going when I was tempted to throw in the towel. In like manner, Longman managed to keep me on course for longer than any must have imagined would be necessary when I began this project.

Last but not least, to my wife Maura I owe special thanks for putting up with me while I was writing this book, and for reading with a critical but helpful eye the various drafts that I produced from time to time. My three daughters, Máiréad, Ionia, and Sorcha, have been curious over the years to know what was in 'The Book', about which they occasionally heard snatches of conversation. Now is their chance to find out.

Dáibhí Ó Cróinín,
Galway,
St John's Eve 1994.

EDITOR'S FOREWORD

In recent years there has been a growing international interest in Irish history. This is reflected in a marked increase in the numbers of scholars and students from outside the island who are engaged in research and study of the subject. *The Longman History of Ireland* is a series of six volumes, written by leading historians of Ireland, which has been devised specifically with this wider audience in mind. Intended primarily for university students of history, it covers Ireland from early Christian times to the present, but it assumes no previous knowledge of Irish history. The aim is to bridge the existing gap between the brief interpretative survey and the weighty collaborative volume which is beyond the pocket of the average student. The series will provide students and teachers alike with a substantial grounding in the subject, an overall interpretation of the period covered, and an assessment of the latest historiographical developments.

There is a further reason for commissioning a new series on Irish history at this time. This relates both to contemporary politics in Ireland and to parallel developments in Irish and British historiography. Inevitably, the growing interest in Irish history reflects in part contemporary concern at the continuing violence in Ireland and the attention which it receives in the news media. The present conflict has a highly developed historical dimension to it which invites the historian's attention, but the writing of history during and about an extended period of civil conflict also presents fundamental difficulties. It is not too much to say that the exceptional circumstances in which the history of Ireland is presently written constitute one of its most salient characteristics and, until very recently, one of the least remarked.

Few countries present the historian with the kind of interpretative challenge offered by Ireland. Its general outlines are of course comparatively familiar – the need to assess the impact of successive waves of colonization; to analyze the endemic unrest, religious strife, and political instability, exemplified in recent times by the partition of the island between rival states; and to evaluate the process of interaction and conflict since the middle ages between two peoples and two cultures, Gaelic and English. In this regard, the principal difficulty lies not so much in recovering and analyzing the concerns and values of past societies – though that task presents problems enough! – but in explaining the relationship between the past and competing versions of the present. The polarization of political opinion means that there is at present comparatively little shared historical sense of community between the island's different traditions. These differences have indeed become institutionalized because, like modern states everywhere, the Republic of Ireland and Northern Ireland, through their respective officials and governmental structures, have attempted to invoke history in order to vindicate contemporary aspirations and values and to promote a unifying sense of national identity among their respective peoples. Overall, therefore, the historiographical difficulties attending the writing of Irish history are such as to raise the intrinsic interest of the subject well above the level which might be suggested by Ireland's geographically marginal position on the world stage.

In view of Ireland's contested history, it is surprising that its historiography is not a subject which has attracted much attention among its professional historians – beyond a desire to debunk popular myths. In the last twenty years, however, our understanding of the subject has been advanced considerably by two related developments. The first is the debate among Irish historians about the character of what is called Historical Revisionism. The other concerns the implications for Ireland of the new British history – the attempt to conceive of the development of the United Kingdom in explicitly multi-national terms. In both cases, the result has been to make historians more conscious in their writings of the differing contexts of explanation and also to revise our understanding of the relationship between nation and state in Ireland.

A particular feature of the present series is the attempt to face up more squarely to this historiographical challenge and to make the subject more intelligible to the non-specialist. This does not mean an uniformity of approach. In fact, the authors of individual volumes in the series come from widely differing backgrounds and bring very different sets of assumptions to their work. Each volume, however, pays particular attention, as appropriate, to these historiographical developments. And the series also attempts to ensure that aspects of Ireland's geography, administrative institutions, and historical terminology, which might be unfamiliar to outsiders, are properly explained. In addition to the main chapters of narrative and analysis, each volume includes a chronological framework of events, an extensive glossary of technical terms, a number of maps or illustrations, tables of officials and institutions, a critical guide to further reading, an extensive bibliography, and a full index. It is hoped that these aids may also prove useful to those more familiar with the subject.

Steven G. Ellis

To Maura, Máiréad, Ionia and Sorcha

FRAMEWORK OF EVENTS

Readers should note that what follows is intended only as a rough guide to the events that occurred during the centuries spanned by this book. For a more detailed chronological survey, see T.W. Moody, F.X. Martin and F.J. Byrne (eds), *A new history of Ireland*, viii (Oxford, 1982), pp. 16–71.

Italicized numbers indicate approximate dates. Items in quotation marks reproduce the wording of the annals.

429   Pope Celestine I, at instigation of deacon Palladius, sends Germanus, bishop of Auxerre, to combat Pelagian heresy in Britain.

431   Palladius sent by Celestine as 'first bishop to the Irish'.

432   'Patrick arrived in Ireland'.

435   Prosper of Aquitaine, in his *Contra Collatorem*, praises Celestine for having restored Britain to orthodoxy and won Ireland to Christianity.

439   'Secundinus, Auxilius and Isserninus, themselves also bishops, are sent to Ireland to assist Patrick'.

441   'Patrick was approved in the Catholic faith'.

444   'Armagh was founded'.

446   Battle of Mag Femin; death of Mac Caírthinn mac Coélboth, Uí Enechglaiss king of Leinster.

447   'Repose of the holy Secundinus in the seventy-fifth year of his age'.

457   'Repose of Patrick the Elder (*Senex Patricius*) as some books state'.

459   'Bishop Auxilius rested'.

467   'Repose of bishop Benignus'.

468   'Bishop Isserninus dies'.

483   Crimthann mac Éndai Cennselaig, king of Uí Cennselaig, killed by Oéngus mac Meic Ercae of Uí Bairrche.

484   Death of Euric, Visigothic king, promulgator of earliest Germanic law code.

485   Death of Findcath mac Dego, Uí Garrchon king of Leinster.

490   Death of Oéngus mac Nad Fraích, ancestor of the Eóganachta.

492   'The Irish say that Patrick the archbishop died in this year'.

495   Death of Froéch mac Findchada, 'king of Leinster'.

496   Storming of Downpatrick, marking rise of Dál Fiatach.

516 Battle of Druim Dergi; Uí Néill victory v. Uí Failgi. 'Thereafter the Plain of Mide was taken from the Leinstermen'.
Death of Gundobad, king of Burgundy, promulgator of *Lex Burgundionum* and *Lex Romana Burgundionum*.

535 Death of Maucteus (Mochta) of Louth, 'a sinner, priest, disciple of Patrick'.

549 'A great mortality'.

561 Battle of Cúil Dreimne; northern Uí Néill victory v. southern Uí Néill.

563 Battle of Móin Dairi Lothair; Uí Néill victory v. Cruithin.
Colum Cille founds monastery of Iona.

565 Diarmait mac Cerrbaill, high-king, killed.

575 'Great convention of Druimm Cett'.

581 Death of Baétán mac Cairill, king of Dál Fiatach.

588 Aéd Dub mac Suibni, king of Dál nAraidi, killed.

597 Death of Colum Cille on Iona.
Bishop Augustine establishes missionary church at Canterbury.

600 Columbanus writes his first letter to Pope Gregory I. *Táin Bó Cuailnge* already in circulation.
'Ussher Gospels' (earliest Irish gospels) written.

601 Pope Gregory the Great sends *Responsiones* to Augustine, archbishop of Canterbury.

603 Battle of Degsastan; Northumbrian victory v. Aédán mac Gabráin, king of Scots Dál Riata.

605 Letter from archbishop of Canterbury to Irish clergy on the Easter question.

610 Death of Mo-Sinu maccu Min, abbot of Bangor, and Colmán, abbot of Lynally.
Columbanus founds monastery of Bobbio in Italy.

611 Death of Colmán mac Lénéni, poet and cleric of Cloyne.

615 Death of Columbanus, founder of Luxeuil and Bobbio.

617 'The burning of the martyrs of Eigg, the slaughter of Tory Island, and the burning of Connor'.

623 Siege of Bamburgh Castle in Northumbria by Fiachnae mac Baétáin, king of Dál nAraidi.
Death of Fergnae Brit, abbot of Iona.

626 Death of Fiachnae mac Baétáin.

628 Pope Honorius I grants exemption from episcopal visitation to Columbanus's monastery at Bobbio.

629 Battle of Dún Ceithirnn; Uí Néill victory v. Dál nAraidi.
Battle of Fid Eoin; Cruithin victory v. Dál nAraidi.

630 Synod of Mag Léna discusses Easter question. Delegation of southern Irish clerics to Rome.

632 Monastery of Lindisfarne founded.

633 Letter of Cummian to Ségéne, abbot of Iona, on the Easter question.

636 Death of Isidore of Seville.

637 Battle of Mag Roth (Moyra); Uí Néill victory v. Cruithin.

638	Death of Aéd Dub mac Colmáin, 'royal bishop of Kildare and of all Leinster'.
640	Synod of northern Irish ecclesiastics to discuss Easter question. Delegation from northern Irish churches in Rome.
641	Pope John IV grants papal privilege to Columbanus's foundation at Luxeuil.
642	Death of Domnall mac Aédo, *rex Hiberniae*.
645	Death of Tocca mac Aédo, king of Cualu. Synchronistic poem *Deus a quo facta fuit* composed.
646	Seventh Council of Toledo.
650	Cummeneus Albus, abbot of Iona, publishes his *Liber de uirtutibus Sancti Columbae*. Anonymous Armagh writer publishes *Liber Angeli*.
652	Death of Chindasuinth, Visigothic king of Spain, promulgator of *Liber Iudiciorum*.
653	Eighth Council of Toledo.
655	Irish Augustine's *De mirabilibus sacrae scripturae* published.
657	Death of Ultán moccu Conchobair, bishop of Ardbraccan.
660	Cogitosus of Kildare publishes his *Vita Brigitae*.
661	Death of Laidcend mac Baíth Bandaig.
662	Death of Cuimmíne Fota, scholar of Clonfert.
663	Death of Guaire mac Colmáin, king of Connaught.
664	Synod of Whitby in Northumbria. Great plague throughout Britain and Ireland.
665	Death of Ailerán 'the Wise', scholar of Clonard.
666	Death of Faélán mac Colmáin, king of Uí Bairrche and Leinster.
669	Death of Cummeneus Albus, abbot of Iona.
679	Death of Cenn Faélad mac Ailella, author of *Auraicept na nÉces*.
680	Fianamail mac Maéle Tuile, king of Leinster, killed.
681	'Burning of the kings at Dún Ceithirnn'.
683	'Beginning of the great plague of children'.
684	Attack by Ecgfrid, king of Northumbria, on Ireland.
687	Adomnán, abbot of Iona, in Northumbria to ransom captives.
688	Battle of Belfast between Ulaid and Cruithin. Death of Ségéne, bishop of Armagh.
690	Tírechán of Armagh publishes his *Collectanea de Sancto Patricio*. Antiphonary of Bangor compiled. Willibrord leaves Ireland for Frisian mission.
691	Death of Crónán moccu Cualne, abbot of Bangor.
692	Death of Conchad, bishop of Sletty.
695	Fínsnechta Fledach mac Dúnchada, king of Síl nAédo Sláne, killed.
697	Adomnán of Iona promulgates *Lex Innocentium*.
700	Death of Aéd, bishop of Sletty. Adomnán, abbot of Iona, publishes his *Vita Columbae*. Muirchú maccu Machtheni publishes his *Vita Patricii*. Anonymous monk of Lindisfarne publishes his *Vita Cuthberti*.

Críth Gablach, law text on status, published.
Ars Malsachani composed.
'Famine and pestilence took place during three years in Ireland, so that man ate man'.

704	Death of Adomnán, abbot of Iona.
709	British mercenaries involved in Battle of Selgg in Leinster.
714	Death of Aéd mac Diarmata, king of Uí Muiredaig and Leinster.
715	Death of Fland Feblae, bishop of Armagh.
716	Iona adopts Roman Easter reckoning.
718	Munich Computus compiled.
725	Death of Ruben of Dairinis, co-compiler of *Collectio Canonum Hibernensis*.
738	Battle of Áth Senaig; Uí Néill victory v. Leinstermen.
739	Fergus Glutt, king of Cuib, dies 'from the venomous spittles of wicked people'.
742	Death of Cathal mac Finguine, first Munster claimant to high-kingship.
743	*Lex nepotis aui Suanaig* promulgated
744	*Lex Ciaráin* and *Lex Brendáin* promulgated.
	Annihilation of Corcu Modruad by the Déis.
747	Death of Cú Chuimne of Iona, co-compiler of *Collectio Canonum Hibernensis*.
753	Whale with three gold teeth cast ashore.
763	Death of Domnall Midi mac Murchada, first Clann Cholmáin claimant to high-kingship.
766	Battle of Sruthair; Uí Briúin victory v. Conmaicne.
767	*Lex Patricii* promulgated.
772	*Lex Commáin et Aédáin* promulgated.
778	*Lex Columbae Cille* promulgated.
	Death of Niall Frossach, northern Uí Néill high-king.
783	Promulgation of Law of Patrick in Connaught.
784	Commutation of the relics of Mac Erccae.
785	Commutation of the relics of Ultán of Ardbraccan.
787	Great fire at monastery of Clonard.
788	Promulgation of Law of Ciarán in Connaught.
790	Commutation of the relics of Kevin of Glendalough, Mochua of Clondalkin, and Tóla of Waterford.
793	Law of Ailbe promulgated in Munster and Law of Commán in Connaught.
794	Commutation of the relics of Trian of Ruscaghbeg.
	'Devastation of all the islands of Britain by the heathens'.
795	'Burning of Rechru [= Rathlin Island?] by the heathens, and Skye was overwhelmed and laid waste'.
800	Reference Bible compiled.
802	Iona burned by Vikings.
806	68 members of Iona community killed by Vikings.

825	Martyrdom of Blathmacc mac Flaind, prior of Iona.
810	Viking fleet of 200 ships appears off coast of Frisia.
811	'A slaughter of the heathen by the Ulaid'.
807	Book of Armagh compiled.
810	*Bóslechta* (Law concerning Cows) promulgated in Munster.
	Viking fleet of 200 ships appears off coast of Frisia.
814	Dicuil publishes his *Liber de mensura orbis terrae.*
821	Vikings carry off large number of women from Howth.
824	Relics of Comgall scattered in Viking raid on Bangor.
	Vikings seize abbot of Sceilg Mhichíl.
837	First Viking fleets on Irish inland waterways.
839	First Irish fleet on Lough Neagh.
841	Vikings establish first *longphort* in Ireland.
843	Death of Donnacán mac Maéle Tuile in Italy.
844	Death of Merfyn Vrych, king of Gwynedd.
	Viking attack on Seville.
848	Battle of Sciath Nechtain; combined Munster-Leinster victory v. Vikings.
	Irish embassy to Emperor Charles the Bald. Sedulius Scottus arrives on the continent (?).
849	Arrival of Danes in Ireland.
851	Vikings winter in England for the first time.
852	Death of Dermait Ua Tigernaig, 'most learned of all the teachers of Europe'.
	Iohannes Scottus publishes commentary on Martianus Capella.
853	First major encounter of Danes and Norse in Ireland.
856	Victory by Rhodri Mawr, king of Gwynedd, against Vikings.
863	Prehistoric tumuli at Dowth, Knowth, and Newgrange plundered by Vikings ('something which had never been done before').
865	Viking army lands in East Anglia.
869	Death of Dubthach mac Maéle Tuile, 'most learned of the Latinists of all Europe'.
871	Vikings brought 'a great prey of Angles, Britons, and Picts' back to Ireland.
873	Death of Ivarr, 'king of the Norsemen of all Ireland and Britain'.
874	Death of Sedulius Scottus (?).
876	First recorded Viking settlement in England.
877	'Sunday Battle' on Anglesey in which Vikings routed Rhodri Mawr, king of Gwynedd, 'who came in flight from the Danes to Ireland'.
888	Death of Cerball mac Dúnlainge, king of Osraige.
891	Anglo-Saxon Chronicle reports arrival of three Irish *peregrini* in England.
902	Destruction of Viking settlement at Dublin. 'The heathens were driven from Ireland'.
917	Dublin Viking settlement re-founded.
919	Battle of Dublin; Viking victory v. Uí Néill high-king, Niall Glúndub, who was killed.

927   Death of Maél Brigte mac Tornáin, abbot of Armagh.
936   Death of Æthelstan, king of England.
937   Battle of Brunanburh; English victory v. the Vikings.
953   Death of Dubinsi, bishop of Bangor.
980   Battle of Tara; Vikings of Dublin defeated and expelled from Ireland.
993   'Great plague of people, animals and bees throughout Ireland'.
1005   Brian Bóraime in Armagh; claims title of 'emperor of the Irish'.
1007   Book of Kells stolen and cover ripped off.
1013   Gilla Mo-Chonna mac Fógartaig, king of Síl nAédo Sláne, dies after a binge.
1014   Battle of Clontarf, in which Brian Bóraime was killed.
1028   Heavy snowfall during Lent.
1030   Gilla Comgáin hanged by community of Clonmacnois for theft.
1034   Death of Ademar of Chabannes, French chronicler.
1056   Marianus Scottus banished from Moville to Germany.
1061   O'Brien fortress of Kincora burned.
1064   Donnchad Mac Briain, Dál Cais king, dies on pilgrimage in Rome.
1066   Battles of Stamford Bridge and Hastings.
1067   Muiredach Mac Robartaig leaves Donegal for Rome.
1072   Death of Diarmait Mac Maíl na mBó, king of Leinster.
1076   Muiredach mac Robartaig founds *Scottenkloster* of Weih-Sankt-Peter in Regensburg, Bavaria.
1082   Death of Marianus Scottus of Mainz.
1086   Death of Toirdelbach Ua Briain, 'king of Ireland'.
1101   Synod of Cashel.
1103   Death of Magnus Barelegs, king of Norway.
1111   Synod of Ráth Bressail.
       Bishop Gilbert of Limerick publishes his *De statu ecclesiae*.
1119   Death of Muirchertach Ua Briain, king of Munster.
1134   Hailstorm in which the hailstones were as big as apples.
1138   Death of Maél Brigte Ua Maéluanaig, scholar of Armagh.
1151   Battle of Móin Mór; Toirdelbach Ua Briain, king of Munster, defeated.
1155   Bull *Laudabiliter* granted by Pope Adrian IV to Henry II of England.
1156   Death of Toirdelbach Ua Conchobair, high-king.
1163   Muirchertach mac Domnaill drowned.
1166   Diarmait Mac Murchada expelled from Ireland.
1167   Diarmait Mac Murchada returns to Ireland.
1169   Arrival of Robert FitzGilbert (Strongbow) in Ireland.
1171   Arrival of Henry II in Ireland.
1172   Death of Diarmait Mac Murchada.
1174   Death of Fland Ua Gormáin, arch-lector of Armagh.
1175   Treaty of Windsor between Ruaidri Ua Conchobair, high-king, and Henry II.
1183   Ruaidri Ua Conchobair deposed.
1188   Giraldus Cambrensis publishes his *Topographia Hiberniae*.
1189   Conchobair Mac Conchobair, king of Connaught, killed.

1198   Death of Ruaidri Ua Conchobair.
1200   Cathal Crobderg Ua Conchobair, king of Connaught, deposed.

INTRODUCTION

Professor Wendy Davies has stated that 'it is not possible to write a history of early medieval Wales that will stand up to the requirements of modern scholarship'.[1] The reason, she added, is that 'the available source material is quite inadequate to resolve the simplest problems'.

It is equally impossible to write a history of early medieval Ireland – but for the opposite reason. There is *too much* material available to the historian of the period, and the difficulty is to decide which sources are to be used and which are to be passed over. Ideally, of course, *everything* should be pressed into service, and that is what historians usually pretend to do. But the bewildering array of documentary and material evidence for the history of Ireland from the fifth century down to the close of the twelfth is almost too much for any one scholar to draw together, at least in a form that would be both coherent and digestible. That is not to say that the attempt should not be made. The historical research which has been carried out in the twenty years since the last specialist studies appeared have led to a thorough reappraisal of the period and a wholesale revision of earlier views in such fields as Irish law, the church, the economy, the structure of society, Irish culture, and the beginnings of the Irish language and its literature. But it would be misleading to exaggerate the amount of work that has been done. Although an American scholar of early Irish history, Professor John V. Kelleher, remarked thirty years ago that 'there is work for all, more than enough for every recruit we can enlist, and for the most part it can be work of sound originality',[2] the fact is that the numbers of Irish university students progressing to advanced research in the field have been strikingly few, and the numbers abroad fewer still. Early Irish history is not for the faint-hearted, and it is not always easy to explain to students what relevance a study of the period could have to our world in the 1990s, but that said, it is still a rueful fact that Ireland in the early middle ages remains a closed book to all but a few.

The reason for this state of affairs has been attributed in the past to the failure of archaeologists, historians and linguists to combine in the writing of

1. Davies 1982a, p. 1.
2. Kelleher 1963, p. 114.

early Irish history.[3] Scholars have done little since then to bring the subject to the attention of a wider public (although the fault is not entirely theirs). The fact that two of the three best modern books on early Irish history, *Ireland before the Vikings* and *Ireland before the Normans* (1972), were allowed to go out of print says much about the attitude of Irish publishers; the third, *Irish kings and high-kings* (1973) – published in Britain – has been reprinted, but without revision or updating. While much has been written in the intervening years, most of it has appeared in specialist journals, and only the rare exception – such as Fergus Kelly's magnificent *Guide to early Irish law* (1988) – has attempted to provide a guide to the material which is accessible to specialist and non-specialist alike.

In general terms the study of early medieval Ireland in the last half century has seen a healthy shift away from the preoccupations that earlier writers had with the church, almost to the exclusion of everything else. The sectarian tone engendered in the writings of the seventeenth-century pioneers of the discipline by the contemporary polemics of Reformation and Counter-Reformation politics set an unfortunate standard for two centuries of Irish historiography, obsessed as it was with the supposed origins of Christianity in Ireland. As recently as 1961 reputable journals were still publishing what one modern scholar has described as 'maudlin flapdoodle' on this theme,[4] and the relentless quest for legitimation of latter-day sectarian viewpoints in the doings of the national saint produced a 'history' of Saint Patrick no less fictional than the one concocted by clerical propagandists in the tenth century (though nothing like as entertaining). But though the study of the early Irish church is still occasionally tarnished by the confessional bias of some of its historians, the trend in the last thirty years in particular – pioneered by Kathleen Hughes's brilliant book, *The Church in early Irish society* (1966) – has been towards a more realistic and less pietistic approach to the subject. Before that, Irish clerical historians had behaved much like the Philosophers' children in *The Crock of Gold*, mesmerized by the shafts of brilliant sunlight beaming down through the forest gloom of the period, leaping in and out of the light to snatch a glimpse of saints and scholars (and occasionally their cats) before scurrying back again to the unlit pagan darkness. Now that more and more of the metaphorical landscape has been cleared, historians are better able to appreciate in their true light the undoubted achievements of the early church and the background developments in Irish society that made them possible.

It is a pity, in the circumstances, to have to say that Irish medieval archaeology has not kept pace with the revolution in historical research. With a few luminous exceptions, Irish archaeologists have preferred to follow the rays of the summer solstice sun down the dark passages of prehistoric tumuli (and speculate endlessly about the 'meaning' of such monuments), rather than excavate and report on the 80,000 or so medieval settlement sites which stand untouched in the Irish countryside. There is nothing in Irish

3. Byrne 1971b, p. 2.
4. Thompson 1985, p. 165.

archaeology remotely comparable to the work of our English, French, and German neighbours. On the contrary, there are ominous signs that the process of shifting from descriptive archaeology to interpretation is in danger of being hijacked by 'New Archaeology' – with consequences that are as depressing as they are predictable.[5] But things are not all bad. The situation has improved dramatically from the time when the great Celtic scholar, T.F. O'Rahilly, could claim as one of the merits of his work that it was 'in no way dependent upon archaeological speculations'.[6] I have tried to integrate the researches of the small band of medieval archaeologists into the documentary narrative of this book, I hope without causing any offence in the process.

Doubtless most readers will bring their own individual expectations to this book, and will be looking for answers to favourite questions. Some of them may be disappointed. I would like to be able, for example, to answer definitively the questions 'When did Patrick come to Ireland?', or 'In what year did Patrick die?' (although these are things that many readers will believe that they 'know' already). Alas! I cannot do so. But there is at least the slight consolation that no one else can answer these questions either. 'Despite our documents and our traditions the fifth century is still all but a lost century in Irish history.'[7] Equally, I would like to be able to state categorically where and when the Book of Kells was written and painted, and by whom, but I cannot do that either. In fact, for all that we have come to know about early medieval Ireland, there is still the uncomfortable realization that few of our earlier doubts have been replaced with certainties. The body of evidence about early Ireland is extraordinarily large, but matching the individual pieces to make up a coherent picture is frustratingly difficult. Since historians do not like to admit what they do not know, this unpalatable state of affairs creates obvious difficulties for anyone who would write a history of the period. The urge to fill up the blank spaces by resort to conjecture is an occupational hazard with historians of all periods, but medievalists need to be especially on their guard against it.

I have tried in this book to face up with honesty to those questions that the average reader would expect to see asked and answered, without sacrificing the truth for the sake of a comfortable lie. I may not always have asked the right questions – I certainly do not claim to have given all the right answers! – but such interpretations as I have offered here are the best that I can produce with the available evidence. There are some things, however, I cannot pass judgement on, such as the fact that an American professor of entomology (the study of insects) has stated as his belief (and offered proof to support the claim) that the position and alignment of the sixty-eight still standing round towers of monastic Ireland can be directly related to the positions of the stars in a map of the northern night sky at the time of the December solstice.[8] These towers are not defensive structures erected to protect monastic

5. See Woodman 1992, p. 38.
6. O'Rahilly 1946, p. vi.
7. Mac Airt 1958, p. 80.
8. Callahan 1984, p. 7.

communities from the depredations of marauding Vikings (a purpose for which, incidentally, they are strikingly unsuited, and which is not borne out by the Irish term *cloigthech* 'bell-tower' used to describe them). Rather, they are nothing more or less than 'magnetic antennae used for concentrating paramagnetic energy' for eco-agricultural purposes.[9] In the face of science the mere historian is reduced to silence.

Even where the evidence gives the appearance of being explicit and relatively plentiful, there are sometimes difficulties. The Annals of Ulster, for example, in the year AD749 report that ships were seen in the air (some said above the monastery of Clonmacnois). Other sources report a similar episode at Teltown,[10] during the reign of Congalach mac Maéle Mithig († AD956), when a ship appeared in the air above the market-fair (*oénach*) and a member of the crew cast a spear down at a salmon below. When he came down to retrieve the spear a man on the ground took hold of him, whereupon the man from above said: 'Let me go! I'm being drowned!' Congalach ordered that the man be released and he scurried back up to his shipmates, 'who were all that time looking down, and all were laughing together'. Well they might. There is no point in trying to explore the Otherworld with the apparatus and outlook of the science laboratory: flying ships are not subject to the laws of quantum mechanics.

Why write a book about early medieval Ireland in the first place? The gullible might follow a recent author, who stated (with unconscious humour) that 'there are reasons to maintain that, in the seventh century in Western Europe, Ireland was the most agreeable country to live in'.[11] A cynic might say that it is because the Irish are obsessed with history, though the only medieval Irish commentator who expressed a view on the matter said quite the opposite, and chided the 'careless Irish nation' (*imprudens Scottorum gens*) for wilfully forgetting their affairs (*rerum suaram obliuiscens*), preferring to read fictions and neglecting to write down the true facts of their own history.[12] The less cynical might suggest that early medieval Ireland offers something unique and interesting to the student of history: the record of a people untouched by the civilization of the Roman Empire. Ireland alone of all the modern countries in Western Europe enjoyed a period of a thousand years and more – until the first Viking raids – during which she evolved and developed an indigenous and unbroken culture different in many ways from any that existed on the continent. Although a revisionist tendency among some modern historians has rendered it unfashionable to make much play of what was distinctive in early Irish society, there is no doubting that contemporaries saw many things in Irish Christianity that struck them as 'counter, original, spare, strange' (to use the words of Gerard Manley Hopkins).

9. Ibid., p. 32.
10. Dillon 1960, pp. 64–76 (p. 73) and Meyer 1908, pp. 1–16 (pp. 12–13).
11. Richter 1991, p. 100.
12. Byrne 1974, p. 137.

A Frankish synod of AD623 chastised the abbot of Luxeuil – Columbanus's successor – because his monks said too many prayers, and in too great a variety.[13] Others remarked that the Irish genuflected too much and were constantly up and down during their prayers. Harmless enough, I suppose, given that the Irish are still fondly remembered on the continent as the nation that led Europe out of its 'Dark Ages'. But even here the pendulum of scholarship has swung away from the view, once not uncommon, that everything worth talking about in the culture of early medieval Europe was contributed by wandering Irish monks. An eminent Swiss authority, Johannes Duft, published an article called 'Iro-mania – Iro-phobia'[14] in which he plotted the course of this shift; since that date there has been a steady trickle of articles (mostly by English authors, it must be remarked), in which Ireland's 'Golden Age' has come under ever more severe scrutiny, to the point where it has been said that, 'measured by patristic or Carolingian standards, . . . the Hiberno-Latin writings of this period were always idiosyncratic, often provincial, sometimes absurd'.[15] There is no getting away from it: 'Ireland was odd in the early middle ages'.[16] To the reader interested in oddities, then, early medieval Ireland is the answer to a prayer.

The chronological limits of this book are, roughly, AD400 to 1200. Within this time-span change was constant, sometimes rapid, and often fundamental. Yet it is a curious fact that the picture of early Ireland that most people have is of a society that was abnormally static, cut off from the great historical events of continental Europe and as a consequence inward-looking and backward. This is an attitude personified by the title of one of Frank O'Connor's books, *The backward look* (1967). True, there is nothing in our period comparable to the Anglo-Saxon invasion of Britain in the fifth century, or to the Germanic invasions of western Europe of the same era. Equally, the Anglo-Norman conquest of Ireland in the twelfth century was by no means so decisive in its effect as the Norman conquest of England. In between, the Viking impact was nothing like so devastating in Ireland as it was in England or on the continent. On the face of it, then, the disruption of society in Ireland during our period should have been less severe than it was in neighbouring countries. That said, there ought to have been more continuity in Irish history than elsewhere in Europe, and therefore all the more reason for an interest in Irish society as a unique opportunity to observe the evolution of a culture which had existed more or less continuously since prehistoric times. Whether or not early Irish society shows obvious traces of such continuity is a matter of hot dispute among scholars of the present generation. The 'seamless garment' of Irish history has been haggled over with a vehemence that onlookers would surely find bizarre, if they were aware of the debate. One of the purposes of this book is to introduce them to some of the arguments and as much of the evidence as I felt they would find useful.

13. Mabillon 1671, i, pp. 320–21.
14. Duft 1956.
15. Brown 1975, p. 248.
16. Hughes 1973, p. 21.

My primary aim, therefore, in writing this book has been to present readers with a glimpse of what early medieval Ireland was like. In doing this I have deliberately avoided the strictly chronological approach, with its catalogue of dates and battles and obscure names, opting instead for a picture of early Irish society in all its aspects. I hope that general readers will find in the narrative things to stimulate further interest in the period. For specialists I have tried to include new interpretations of the material as part of the broader perspective, while at the same time reviewing the years' work in the field during the last two decades. But I am only too well aware of the truth in the remark attributed to William of Baskerville, in Umberto Eco's *The Name of the Rose*, that 'books are not made to be believed, but to be subjected to inquiry'.

CHAPTER 1

THE BEGINNINGS OF IRISH HISTORY

The first reliable date in Irish history is AD431. The source of our information is not an Irish text but the *Chronicle* of Prosper of Aquitaine, a resident of Marseilles and partisan of Augustine in the great controversies surrounding Pelagius and his doctrines that rocked the church in the late fourth and early fifth centuries. Prosper's *Chronicle* records the official introduction of Christianity to Ireland. His words are brief but their significance great:

'To the Irish believing in Christ, Palladius, having been ordained by Pope Celestine, is sent as first bishop'.[1] Historians have linked this statement with an earlier one in the *Chronicle*, AD429:

'The Pelagian Agricola, son of the Pelagian bishop Severianus, corrupts the churches of Britain by the propagation of his doctrines. But at the instigation of the deacon Palladius, Pope Celestine sends Germanus, bishop of Auxerre, in his stead, who overthrows the heretics and guides the Britons to the catholic faith'.[2] Prosper was apparently in Rome when he published his *Chronicle* and his statements must therefore be regarded with the greatest respect. What, then, can we deduce from them? The entry for AD431 leaves no doubt that there were Christians in Ireland already by that date. These Christians were sufficient in number, and apparently far enough advanced in their beliefs, to warrant the despatch of a bishop to oversee their activities and to ensure their adherence to orthodoxy. The bishop sent to them was Palladius, who had been ordained by no less a figure than the pope. So much seems clear enough. But Irish tradition knows of a different bishop whose missionary efforts are indelibly linked with the foundation period of the Irish church, and that man was Patrick the Briton, not Palladius. The resulting confusion – which goes back even to the seventh century, it must be said –

---

1. 'Ad Scottos in Christum credentes ordinatus a papa Caelestino Palladius primus episcopus mittitur'; Mommsen 1892, pp. 384–499 (quotation, p. 473).
2. 'Agricola Pelagianus, Severiani episcopi Pelagiani filius, ecclesias Brittaniae dogmatis sui insinuatione corrumpit. Sed ad insinuationem Palladii diaconi papa Caelestinus Germanum Autisidorensem episcopum vice sua mittit et deturbatis hereticis Britannos ad catholicam fidem dirigit'; Mommsen 1892, p. 472 (quotation). On Pelagius a good recent study is Rees 1988. For recent discussion of the Irish context, see Charles-Edwards 1993a, pp. 1–12.

has generated a vast literature of its own and the controversy about 'The Two Patricks' is as lively now as it was seventeen hundred years ago. The 'Problem of St Patrick', as modern historians have called it,[3] 'bars the very portals of Irish history',[4] but the understandable frustration of scholars at their seeming inability to solve it has led to an unfortunate tendency to gloss over the Palladian mission and concentrate instead on the post-missionary church.[5] But without some attempt to understand the fate of Palladius's mission we can hardly hope to understand the later growth and development of the Irish churches, and the crucial first chapter in Irish history is left untold. In order to see the context within which the Irish missions were organized we must go back a few years, to the churches in Britain and Gaul in the period before the fifth century.

CHRISTIANITY IN GAUL

Although the conversion of the Emperor Constantine to the Christian religion in AD312 undoubtedly accelerated the growth of the church, the extraordinary expansion that took place in the next two centuries, which saw the numbers of Christians grow from roughly half a million in the second century to roughly five million by the end of the fifth, was, in fact, slow and uneven. If Augustine is to be believed, Rome itself was more pagan than Christian until the 390s, when the balance began to change.[6] By the beginning of the fifth century non-Christians still made up a very large minority, perhaps even half the population, to judge by the numbers of centres still awaiting a bishop at that date.[7] The decisive change, therefore, which saw the huge explosion in the number of conversions, postdates AD400.[8]

By the same token, Christianity in Gaul was equally slow in establishing itself. Despite ancient beginnings, at Lyons, for example, in the days of Irenaeus and the second-century persecutions, and later consolidation, due to imperial support, at Arles and Trier, there was no known bishop at Poitiers before Hilary (c. AD365) and Tours had no bishop before c. AD337, no church until c. AD350. Writers like Ausonius (who traced his ancestry proudly back to druids) and Sidonius Apollinaris († c. AD480) show us a society still in the process of gradual Christianization, in which pagan values and traditions were being only slowly replaced.[9] Sulpicius Severus, the biographer and older

3. See, e.g., Carney 1973, a collection of the author's earlier publications on the subject.
4. Byrne 1973, p. 12.
5. The best modern treatment, Hughes 1966, gives only eleven pages to the missionary period and makes only passing reference to Palladius. The same criticism can be made of Sharpe 1984a, pp. 230–70.
6. Augustine, *Conf.* VIII 2,3, cited by MacMullen 1984a, p. 155 n. 34. I am much indebted in what follows to this thought-provoking book.
7. MacMullen 1984a, p. 83.
8. MacMullen 1984a, p. 156.
9. W.B. Anderson, Sidonius's translator, remarks that his subject was no theologian:

contemporary of Bishop Martin of Tours, writes as though paganism still flourished in northern Gaul in the 370s.[10] It is possible, then, to exaggerate the degree of Christianization that had taken place in Gaul in the years immediately preceding the missions to Ireland.

The existence of Christian communities in Britain already by the beginning of the third century can be inferred from Tertullian (AD207),[11] and an organization of dioceses and provinces was apparently in existence by the fourth century. But of the twenty-eight bishoprics associated with Roman *civitates* only three are actually attested in early sources. The oldest written evidence for the existence of dioceses is in the signatures of three British bishops, one priest, and a deacon who attended the Council of Arles in AD318, and they were so poor that they had to accept the payment of their travel costs from public funds.[12] Three further British bishops attended the Council of Rimini in AD359. But to judge from the archaeological evidence,[13] the churches in Britain were, by comparison with the Gallican churches, poor and undeveloped, and in terms of their physical structures they were unimposing. Despite (or perhaps because of) the fact that these churches were capable of producing intellects of the calibre of Pelagius and Fastidius, they seem to have lacked the degree of popular support which ensured the church's survival and growth elsewhere in the West.[14]

But there were two factors at work in the Gallican church after AD370 which were not paralleled in the neighbouring churches of Britain and which were to mark the essential difference between the two: the extraordinary influence of Martin of Tours and the ever increasing expansion of Christianity from the cities into the countryside. Such evidence as survives suggests that the British churches, both officials and members, were predominantly upper-class, though not especially wealthy. But the experience in public affairs and the expertise which many continental prelates like Germanus of Auxerre or Caesarius of Arles brought to their direction of the church seems to have had no obvious parallel in Britain. Nor is there any evidence for the widespread establishment of episcopal schools in Britain as in Gaul, and the bishops did not take over the reins of power in the province after the departure of the Roman legions in AD410.[15] In Britain, political control passed into the hands of local chieftains; the best known of them, the 'tyrant'

'His poem to Faustus shows not only an imperfect knowledge of the Scriptures but a naïve unorthodoxy which would have drawn from a less tolerant ecclesiastic a horrified rebuke'. See Anderson 1963, i, p. xliii.; see also Hanson 1970, pp. 1–10.

10. MacMullen 1984a, p. 155.

11. For good general accounts, see Frend 1968, pp. 37–49; Jäschke 1974, pp. 91–123, and the more recent and comprehensive study by Thomas 1981. The older study, Williams 1912, still makes very valuable reading.

12. Jäschke 1974, p. 122 n. 200 cites the evidence (from Sulpicius Severus, *Chronica* II 41, 3).

13. See especially Thomas 1981. The evidence is far thinner than the book.

14. Frend 1968, p. 143.

15. For the continental developments, see especially Prinz 1973, pp. 1–35.

Vortigern, though Christian in name, consulted soothsayers rather than bishops.[16] Neither these nor the Anglo-Saxon kings who ousted them seem to have felt it necessary to undertake collections of Roman law, such as their contemporaries in Visigothic Spain or in the Burgundian kingdom had done. It appears that the break with the Roman past was sufficiently complete that the survival of a large Roman population was not a problem to be reckoned with.[17]

CHRISTIANITY IN BRITAIN

Christianity failed to emerge in Britain in the first half of the fifth century as the predominant religion of the Romano-British population, and we may assume that the vast majority of the native British population was totally unaffected by it. There is no evidence for the existence of a parochial system and few if any indications that Christianity was making any progress towards becoming the religion of the general mass of Romano-Britons.[18] On the contrary, as MacMullen remarks, 'it is rather useful and necessary to know that there were in fact dozens of British shrines besides that of Nodens [at Lydney Park, Gloucestershire] still active as centres of worship in the latter half of the fourth century'.[19] We do not know why that was so, but it is undoubtedly the case that the British churches left no lasting mark on the countryside in physical terms and little or no impact in terms of a native tradition of learning. Between Fastidius in the fourth century and Gildas in the sixth there is a complete silence.[20] Not a trace remains of the indigenous intellectual activity of British Latin writers in the period before Gildas, and the writings of men such as Fastidius and Pelagius are associated exclusively with their activities on the continent. If the Pelagian bishop Severianus and his son Agricola ever wrote theological tracts as part of their proselytizing efforts, they have not survived. On the other hand, that there were men of good education in Britain in the fifth and sixth centuries is clear from the words of St Patrick and the writings of Gildas, but as Frend remarked: 'The historian is left with the problem of what happened between the end of the "Pelagian" period in Britain, say c. 440, and the implanting of the first Celtic monastic settlements in the far west of the island c. 480'.[21] It is precisely this half-century which is of most interest to us, but unfortunately the first century of Christianity in Ireland has to be studied against the background of a neighbouring church which seems almost to have disappeared.

In AD431, however, there were Christians in Ireland. Who were they, where were they, and how did their conversion come about? Faced with these stark

16. Frend 1968, p. 142.
17. Fischer Drew 1967, pp. 7–29 (p. 22).
18. For this and what follows I am indebted to Frend 1979, pp. 129–44.
19. MacMullen 1984a, p. 81.
20. The best recent survey of the question is Lapidge 1986, pp. 91–107.
21. Frend 1979, p. 143.

questions historians are bound to answer: we simply do not know. But we can make some educated guesses, always mindful of the tentative and sparse nature of our evidence.[22]

It is important to remember that the early church, after St Paul, had no concept of mission; it made no organized or official approach to non-believers; conversion was a matter for the individual.[23] There is ample evidence to show that the post-Apostolic church developed no conscious institutionalized missionary effort or personnel;[24] Christian teachers moved only among the converted, from one Christian household to the next (as they were still doing in Pictland in Columba's time; AD563–AD597). Christians as a rule kept to themselves; conversion was sporadic and individual rather than communal. That being the case, it is clear that the mission of Palladius was never intended to bring the faith to non-believers in Ireland. Palladius was, after all, sent to 'the Irish believing in Christ' (*ad Scottos in Christum credentes*). How, then, did these Irish acquire their Christian beliefs?

CHANNELS OF CONVERSION

It is generally accepted that the fifth-century migrations from the north-east of Ireland to western Scotland were paralleled by similar movements from the south-east to Gwynedd and Dyfed in Wales and to the Devon–Cornwall peninsula.[25] The migrations to Scotland were to have a formative effect on the development of that country in that the Irish colonists were eventually to establish the Kingdom of Scotland. In Wales, on the other hand, the colonists were less successful: there was a dynasty of Irish kings in south-west Wales, perhaps as early as the third century,[26] and they continued to rule there until the tenth century, their genealogy being preserved in both Irish and Welsh sources.[27] They failed, however, to establish in Wales the kind of dominance that was later enjoyed by the Dál Riata and their descendants in Scotland, but they did leave their mark on Welsh place names[28] and an enduring memorial to their presence in the ogam stones, whose distribution matches the extent of their settlements almost exactly.[29] One of these Irish kings is known from the writings of Gildas and it is generally agreed that we have his very tombstone

22. See De Paor 1993.
23. See Thompson 1964, pp. 56–78.
24. MacMullen 1984a, p. 34; Thompson 1964, p. 64.
25. For a good general survey, see Thomas 1972, pp. 251–74. See also Dillon 1977, pp. 1–11, and Ó Cathasaigh 1984, pp. 1–33 (on the literary evidence). The older study by O'Rahilly 1924 still has some value.
26. So Jackson 1953, p. 155, but such an early date is disputed by Lloyd Laing 1985, pp. 261–78 (p. 274).
27. See O'Rahilly 1924, p. 62.
28. See especially Richards 1960, pp. 133–52.
29. Jackson 1953, p. 155 n. 1, points out that the full extent of Irish settlements in Britain cannot be judged entirely from the distribution of the ogams.

in Wales, which reads in Latin MEMORIA VOTEPORIGIS PROTICTORIS ('the monument of Voteporix, Protector') and in ogam VOTECORIGAS.

These Irish settlers were the people known as Déisi (literally 'vassals'), occupying territories corresponding roughly to the present Co. Waterford and adjacent areas of Co. Tipperary,[30] whose ethnic affiliation was with the tribes known as Érainn (whence the modern Irish name for Ireland, *Éire*). It is significant that the various sub-divisions of the Érainn were scattered across southern Ireland in counties Cork, Kerry and Waterford in a band which exactly matches the distribution of the Irish ogam stones.

Little is known about these early Irish overlords in Cornwall and south-west England, but a well-known passage in the *Glossary* ascribed to Cormac mac Cuilennáin († AD908) mentions two of the Irish strongholds in Britain: *Dind Tradui* and *Dind map Lethain* 'in the lands of the Cornish Britons'. The latter site, 'the citadel of the sons of Léthain' doubtless belonged to the Irish Uí Liatháin, a minor branch of the Érainn settled in east Cork and neighbours of the Déisi, and it seems very likely that the Uí Liatháin were part of the same eastward movement that brought the Déisi to Dyfed. A further expansion from Cornwall is suggested by a reference in a later Welsh writer, Nennius, to *filii Liethan* ('sons of Liatháin') as settlers in south Wales. Later Welsh tradition had it that the Irish in north Wales were expelled from there by a Welsh king Cunedda (perhaps at the head of a British force transported by the Romans at the end of the fourth century or beginning of the fifth as *foederati* or mercenaries, with the deliberate intention of subduing or expelling the Irish). At any rate, the Irish presence in north Wales is much less well attested and may perhaps have been less numerous. On the other hand, there is evidence to suggest that the colonists in the south maintained contacts with the homeland until at least the eighth century, and there is even a slight trace of Cornish Christians in Ireland.[31]

It seems very likely that it was through such channels that the first Irish acquaintance with Christianity came about. There is little or no evidence, however, to suggest that the Irish in Britain were themselves Christianized in any significant numbers.[32] Assimilation to the late-Roman culture of south-west Britain need not necessarily have included conversion, and, as we shall see, the evidence – such as it is – points rather to the non-Christian characteristics of these colonists. But they may have provided the channels for the spread of Christian beliefs through their contacts with the homeland.

Another possible means of transmission was through prisoners of war.

30. For what follows see especially Ó Cathasaigh 1984, pp. 1–33; see also Coplestone-Crow 1981–82, pp. 1–24.

31. Some slight trace of Cornish influence in Ireland will be found in the material relating to Cairnech *Bretan*, for which see Kenney 1929, p. 352, and Carney 1955, pp. 407–12.

32. It is difficult to know what significance to attach to the presence of the name Hibernius among the signatories of a report sent to Pope Silvester I following the synod of Arles (AD314); see Munier 1963, p. 4. Jäschke 1974, pp. 117–18, proposed to identify him as an Irish (i.e. Hiberno-British) bishop of York.

Patrick tells us in his *Confession* that he was only one of many thousands (*tot milia hominum*) who were carried off in Irish raids on Britain. Such captives, Christians (in name at least) before they ever went to Ireland, would have brought their faith with them and, if it had survived the shock, they would presumably have retained some at least of their Christian tenets and practices.

There is an exact parallel in the Christianization of the Goths:[33] 'The apostle of the Goths did not convert the Goths to Christianity'.[34] Bishop Ulfilas and his companions found Christianity already sufficiently well-established among the Goths by the mid-third century to enable them to form a self-contained Christian community there. These Christians (clerics among them) were prisoners from the Roman Empire who retained their distinctive character even in captivity. The parallel with the beginnings of Irish Christianity is, indeed, closer still: just as Palladius appears first in a legation to Rome, so too Ulfilas first appears as a member of a legation from the Goths to the Emperor Constantine (or his son Constantius). He was subsequently ordained bishop 'for the Christians in Gothia' (Χειϱοτονεῖται τῶν ἐν τῆ Γετικῆ χϱιστιανιζόντων). Like Palladius, Ulfilas was sent an assistant, Auxentius (compare Auxilius, supposed to have been a member of Patrick's group), who was 'ordained bishop . . . to rule and correct, teach and build the Gothic people' (*Episcopus est ordinatus ut . . . regeret et corrigeret et doceret et aedificaret gentem Gothorum*).[35] These parallels are, of course, coincidental, but it is quite possible, given the evidence, that the first Christians in Ireland were in fact Britons. Whether by intermarriage or example, or both, these first Christians may have influenced some at least of their Irish owners and neighbours and in time their combined numbers would have been thought sufficient to warrant a request for a bishop. It seems strange, in the circumstances, that this first bishop would not have been sought from the British church, but the fact that Palladius, a deacon of Auxerre, was chosen may add further weight to the impression that the British church in the early fifth century was too weak and disorganized to be able to supply such a bishop and the material support necessary to sustain his activities, and the taint of Pelagianism could only have further weakened their case. As we shall see, the condition of the neighbouring Anglo-Saxon church in the mid-seventh century provides an exact parallel.

PALLADIUS AND THE ROMAN MISSION

It matters not a lot whether the 'Irish believing in Christ' of Prosper's account really were British rather than Irish. If they were British they may not have been exclusively so; Prosper might have been simplifying the facts, or been unaware that the Christians seeking a bishop in Ireland were not themselves

33. For what follows see Stockmeier 1981, pp. 315–24.
34. Thompson 1964, pp. 56–78 (quotation, p. 76); see also Thompson 1966.
35. Stockmeier 1981, p. 321.

Irish. At any rate, their new bishop was undoubtedly a man of sound formal training, for Auxerre in the early fifth century was the centre of the Gallican church, a pillar of orthodoxy, and its bishop Germanus one of the leading figures of that church.[36] Palladius was a member of the old Gallo-Roman aristocracy, probably of the *stirps Palladiarum* ('family of the Paladii') that controlled the Auxerre region for generations.[37] Palladius represented the established elite of the Gallican church. Like Constantius, Germanus's biographer,[38] Palladius may have had a rhetorical training, and he was certainly thought suitable to lead a delegation to Rome.

There is nothing in contemporary sources to suggest that Palladius's mission was not sent or that it did not succeed, though some later Irish writers would have us believe that he failed. On the contrary, Prosper, writing some time in the 430s in his polemical tract *Contra Collatorem*, stated that 'With no less care did [Pope Celestine] free the British Isles from that same disease [i.e. Pelagianism] . . . and by ordaining a bishop for the Irish, while he strove to keep the Roman island catholic, he also made the barbarian island Christian'.[39] By erecting an episcopate in a previously non-Christian country Celestine had brought the 'barbarian' (i.e. non-Roman) island, Ireland, within the orbit of the official Christian world. But as James F. Kenney succinctly put it: 'of Palladius or his Irish mission we have no further authentic record'.[40] A remarkable fact, if true. But are there really no traces at all of the Palladian mission to be found?

Palladius and his companions would probably have travelled north-westwards from Auxerre to Nantes, at the mouth of the river Loire, and there taken ship either for Britain or directly to Ireland.[41] We have no documentary evidence to indicate where they might have landed, but there is evidence of another kind which may point to their whereabouts in Ireland. The traditions associated with Patrick include the names of two supposedly continental (not British) clerics, Bishops Auxilius and Secundinus, both of whom are

36. See Levison 1904, pp. 95–175; Atsma 1983, pp. 1–96, and Bardy 1950a especially pp. 39–88, 151–79.

37. The connection with the *stirps Palladiarum* of the Auvergne region was first suggested by Bury 1905, p. 343 n. 3, with reference to Sidonius Apollinaris, *Ep.* VII 9, 24: '. . . Palladiorum stirpe . . ., qui aut litterarum aut altarium cathedras cum sui ordinis laude tenuerunt' (Anderson 1963, ii, p. 356). Paul Grosjean S J suggested that there was another branch of the kindred in Auxerre; see Grosjean 1945, pp. 73–92 (p. 77 ff.).

38. For whom see Bardy 1950b, pp. 88–108.

39. 'Nec vero segniore cura ab hoc eodem morbo Britannias liberavit, quando quosdam inimicos gratiae solum suae originis occupantes etiam ab illo secreto exclusit oceani et, ordinato Scottis episcopo, dum Romanam insulam studet seruare catholicam, fecit etiam barbaram christianam', *MPL* 51, col. 271.

40. Kenney 1929, p. 165.

41. Columbanus, when expelled from Burgundy in AD610, was taken to Nantes, where it was expected that he could be placed on board a ship engaged in trade with Ireland; see Krusch 1905, p. 205: 'Reperta ergo navis, quae Scottorum commercia vexerat' (*Vita Columbani* I 23).

represented as disciples of the saint. The sites which today still bear their names are Killashee (*Cell Auxili* 'the cell of Auxilius') in Co. Kildare, and Dunshaughlin (*Dún Sechlainn* 'the fort of Secundinus') in Co. Meath. Of all our historical evidence, place names are often the most valuable, for they are seldom open to the same manipulation and deliberate tampering that occurs with early medieval written sources. Hence the preservation of these two names, undoubtedly archaic and deriving from an early period of the church in Ireland, suggests that these two individuals made their mark. But the overwhelming weight of evidence, as we shall see, connects Patrick with places in the north-east and north-west of the country, not the midlands or thereabouts.

It may well be the case, then, that Auxilius and Secundinus (and doubtless others who are mentioned in the Patrick dossier) – far from being disciples of Patrick the Briton – were in fact companions of the continental Palladius originally, but were later subsumed into the all-devouring Patrick legend. If that is the case, then it would suggest that the Palladian mission set down on the east coast of Ireland and gradually expanded inland from there. This, of course, is precisely where we would expect to find traces of Christianity at an early date, for it is on the east coast that we find the clearest (if sporadic) traces of Roman influence in Ireland.[42] Several brooches of south-east-British and Gallo-Roman origins were found in a cemetery on Lambay Island in Dublin Bay, dated roughly to the first century AD. There is not sufficient archaeological evidence to support the notion of a thorough-going Romanization of Ireland before the fifth century,[43] but the material that has been found, some of it inland, does add weight to the theory that communications with Roman Britain were closest at this point. The late D.A. Binchy pronounced more than once (though he never cited the evidence) that it was in the east and south-east of Ireland that Christianity first put down its roots.[44] If this was in fact the case, then it may have been following the trade routes of pre-Christian and late-Roman times.

Besides the archaeological and onomastic evidence, however, there is, it is true, little or no visible trace of the Palladian mission. Nothing has survived of the manuscripts, liturgical books, ecclesiastical furniture or altar vessels that must have formed the baggage of the first Gallican missionaries. But one text has come down to us, albeit in fragmentary form, and it affords a precious glimpse of the continental input into the early life of the Irish churches. That

42. See Warner 1976, pp. 267–92, and Laing 1985, pp. 261–78.

43. I do not accept the authenticity of the find at Stoneyford (Co. Kilkenny) and therefore omit it from discussion. On the problem of 'Romanization' generally, see MacMullen 1984b, pp. 161–77.

44. See, e.g., his remarks in Binchy 1962a, pp. 7–173 (quotation, p. 165): 'On a future occasion I hope to write in greater detail about the evidence that considerable areas in the East and South of Ireland had been Christianised by British missionaries before the sending of Palladius'; on p. 166 he talked of 'many other and better arguments' for the existence of pre-Palladian Christian communities in Ireland, but none of these was ever published.

text is an Easter table, which can be associated with Palladius.[45] The Palladian Easter table shows that the first continental missionaries brought with them the doctrines that were current in the Gallican and north Italian churches in the late fourth century: the doctrines of Ambrose and Augustine, of Milan and probably Auxerre. That material survived in Ireland until the early seventh century, but only as an item of antiquarian interest; by that date the Patrick legend had all but buried Palladius and his companions.

Despite the fact that Palladius disappeared almost without trace from the historical record, in Ireland and in his native Auxerre, his formative influence on the earliest Irish Christianity cannot be denied. There can be little doubt that the tentative first steps in organizing the first Irish Christian communities were made by him and his companions. But the apostle of Ireland was Patrick, not Palladius. That, at any rate, is what later generations came to believe. Why? There are two principal reasons: after his mention by Prosper in AD431, Palladius disappears entirely from the historical record. There is no contemporary account of his activities, either in Irish or in continental sources. Irish historians in the seventh century and later made a few guesses about him (some of which may have been correct), but they clearly had no real solid information beyond what they read in Prosper.

PATRICK

The second reason for Patrick's dominant place in Irish history is that two of his own writings have survived, his *Confession* and his *Letter* addressed to the soldiers of Coroticus.[46] The uniqueness of these documents is often overlooked: Patrick is the *only* citizen of the late Roman Empire to have been taken prisoner by marauding raiders, sold into slavery, and who lived to tell the tale in written form. His is an account unparalleled in the history of the West of one man's experience as a captive beyond the frontiers of the Empire. That fact alone would justify the interest which historians have displayed in him over the centuries. Hence *The life of St. Patrick and his place in history* (1905) is the title of perhaps his most famous biography, written not by an early Irish historian but by the foremost authority on the Later Roman Empire in his day, John Bagenal Bury (born in Clontibret, Co. Monaghan). Patrick's missionary career, and the fact that he left an account of it, mark him out as a figure of unique importance in European history.

Who was Saint Patrick? The only reliable information about his life and career is to be found in the saint's own writings; all other accounts are either derivative of these or else entirely spurious. Nothing in the Irish annals, nor in any other Irish source, can be proved to be genuine reminiscence of Patrick or his activities; we are forced to rely on his *Confession* and *Letter* for the saint's own words. These two documents have come down to us in several

45. See Ó Cróinín 1986, pp. 276–83. The comments in Dumville 1993, pp. 85–8, have not advanced the discussion.
46. I have used the edition of White 1905, because it was the one to hand.

later copies, the earliest being the manuscript known as the Book of Armagh, a collection of biographical and related writings compiled by scholars at Armagh in the first decade of the ninth century (c. AD807) as a 'Patrick dossier'. Their survival was not accidental, but reflects the single-minded purpose of the authorities in Armagh from the mid-seventh century on to accumulate as much evidence as possible for the saint's early career – not so much with a view to establishing his history but rather to garner sufficient ammunition to bolster Armagh's later claims to primacy among the Irish churches.[47] One of the difficulties facing the modern historian is that the Armagh propagandists did not baulk at tampering with the text of Patrick's writings, a fact which has its own significance. For the full text of the *Confession* and for our only copies of the *Letter* we are dependent, in fact, on continental manuscripts. The reason for this is that the Armagh propagandists deliberately censored those passages in Patrick's *Confession* which presented him in a less than heroic light, and did so because the genuine humility in the saint's account of his anguished experiences did not fit into the mould of the heroic, all-conquering Christian warrior of later Patrician legend.[48]

A second difficulty for the historian is that Patrick in his writings in fact gives very little detail about himself: his own name (Patricius) and that of his father (Calpurnius) and grandfather (Potitus); his great-grandfather's name, Odissus, is given in a marginal addition to the Book of Armagh, while his mother's (not normally given as part of a late-Roman family name) is quoted by later Irish sources as Concessa, but she does not figure by name in Patrick's own account.[49] His father was a *decurio* (member of a town council) and a deacon of the church; his grandfather was a priest. Patrick also gives the name of the nearest town (Bannaven Taberniae, or variants thereof), but the place has never been satisfactorily identified.[50] His father, a well-to-do landowner, had a small estate nearby (*villula*) with many servants (*servos et ancillas*, Epistola §10) and there Patrick was seized by Irish marauders and carried off to Ireland 'with many thousands of others' (*tot milia hominum*). He was nearly sixteen years old. That is the sum total of Patrick's

---

47. For the manuscripts of Patrick's writings, see Bieler 1952 (1993) pp. 7–31. For a recent survey of some of the problems relating to Patrick's career, see Dumville 1993.

48. The most convincing explanation of the *modus operandi* behind the Book of Armagh copy of Patrick's *Confession* is provided by Binchy 1962, pp. 40–2.

49. Mac Neill 1924–27, in one of his characteristically brilliant contributions to the subject, drew attention to an inscription at Hexham (Northumberland) which mentions a 'Q. Calpurnius Concessinus, praef[ectus] equ[itum], caesa Corontotarum manu'. His suggestion that the Calpurnius concerned might be related to Patrick has not met with favour from subsequent writers.

50. Efforts to identify the site with Carlisle have been made by several archaeologists, particularly Thomas; see, e.g., Thomas 1979, pp. 81–101. The theory has become almost sacrosanct: see De Paor 1986, p. 53: 'On present evidence, Carlisle also appears to be the most likely base of support for the episcopate of St Patrick'. See De Paor 1993, p. 88.

autobiographical information. We are not told whether any other members of his family were seized with him, or killed during the raid.[51] Nor does Patrick give the name of any other individual of the thousands carried off with him into captivity, nor of the Irish among whom he subsequently lived for six years. He mentions none of his earlier companions by name, and none of the British clerics, in Britain or in Ireland, with whom he had dealings. Patrick could hardly have told us less if he had not bothered to write at all. Irish tradition, on the other hand, names many of these people, but that should only serve to warn the reader against accepting anything in Irish Patrician legend at face value.[52]

The story of Patrick's captivity and escape has become something of a national legend in Ireland. His tribulations led, by his own account, to a strengthening of his Christian faith, climaxed by a night vision in which he was told he would return to his homeland. After a rather confused account of his adventures along the way, he was back in his parents' (or relatives') household. It was only after he had spent some years there that he experienced his famous vision of the messenger Victoricus, who had come to him 'as though from Ireland' with letters imploring him to return. At this point (*Confessio* §23) Patrick makes his only mention of a specific place in Ireland, where he seems to have spent his youthful captivity: a wood 'close by the western sea'; unfortunately, this place too has evaded precise identification. The upshot of Patrick's visionary experiences was that he determined to devote his remaining years to preaching the gospel in Ireland. Despite pleadings and blandishments from his family encouraging him to stay, and despite instructions, apparently, from his religious superiors, not to return there (*Conf.* §46), Patrick set out once more for Ireland. He was not sent as a bishop to Ireland; on the contrary, his mission was entirely personal and had no official sanction. In fact, he does not mention any other person by name in this context; his immediate inspiration was from God.

Patrick's writings convey the stark impression of a man at the frontier of the Christian and non-Christian worlds. He states that the Irish with whom he has come into contact have only recently come to the faith (*ad plebem nuper uenientem ad credulitatem, nuper facta est plebs Domini*, Conf. §§38, 41), apparently through his own efforts. It is also clear from what he says that there were many among the British captive population who were not Christians; some are described as freemen, some as Christians, while he adds that 'we know not the numbers of our race that are born (again) there' (*et de genere nostro qui ibi nati sunt nescimus numerum eorum*, Conf. §42). What

---

51. The mention of his return to *parentes* in *Confessio* 43 may mean 'relatives' rather than 'parents', but we cannot be sure.

52. Patrick does mention a letter which has not come down to us, and there were doubtless others which he wrote at various times to various people. The title attached to the copy of his *Confession* in the Book of Armagh is *Libri epistolarum sancti Patricii episcopi*, with plural *libri* ('books'), hence there is a faint possibility that some of the details in later Irish sources derive from such documents now lost; but we have no way of sifting the wheat from the chaff in such matters.

is strikingly different about Patrick's missionary activities is the fact that he went, as he himself put it, 'even to outlying regions beyond which no man dwelt, and where never had anyone come to baptize or ordain clergy, or confirm the people' (*Conf.* §51). There is no obvious reason to doubt the truth of what he writes: whatever else may be said about him,[53] no one questions the patent sincerity of Patrick's words.

But it is precisely this part of Patrick's account that causes difficulty. If, as is traditionally believed, Patrick came to Ireland sometime around the mid-fifth century, why does he give no credit to the work of his most famous predecessor, Palladius? Why is no other missionary mentioned by name, and why is there no reference at all to 'the Irish believing in Christ' to whom Palladius was sent as first bishop in AD431? Here we are faced with another of those curious blanks in Patrick's account: he never mentions a date. We have no idea in what year he was captured nor in what year he returned to Ireland to begin his mission for the simple reason that he himself gives none. Neither do we have a date for his death – none, at any rate, that we can trust. There is no shortage of such information in the early Irish annals, of course (and for good measure the Annals of Ulster give *four* alternative dates for Patrick's death!), but nothing in our native annals can be taken at face value in the period before the mid-sixth century at the earliest; 'despite our documents and our traditions, the fifth century is all but a lost century in Irish history'.[54] The entries for the earlier period have all been added retrospectively and cannot therefore be relied upon.

Archbishop John Healy, writing in 1905, stated categorically that Patrick died in AD493: the date of his death was 'the best attested fact of his entire history'.[55] The truth of the matter, however, is that without Patrick's express information we have no reliable way of knowing when and where he lived and worked in Ireland. Arguments advanced by archaeologists[56] in favour of a mid-fifth-century date unfortunately lack conclusive force. Nor can much be made of Patrick's reference to the practice followed by Gallican ecclesiastics (*consuetudo Romanorum Gallorum Christianorum*, Ep. §14) of ransoming captives from the (still) pagan Franks,[57] since the statement might refer as easily to the mid-fourth century as to the late fifth. Patrick's own references to the Irish who had been converted by him would seem to suggest a period prior to Palladius's mission, and in fact there is nothing in the saint's own account that would rule out a date in the late fourth or early fifth century for his career.[58] The only serious obstacle in the way of such an early dating is in the secondary sources: Adomnán, Columba's biographer, writing *c.* AD700,

---

53. For a startling reappraisal of Patrick's knowledge of Latin and his command of rhetorical skills, see Howlett 1989, pp. 86–101 and Howlett 1994.
54. Mac Airt 1958, pp. 67–80 (quotation, p. 80).
55. Healy 1905, p. 26 (citing J.H. Todd).
56. Based on the supposed period when Roman *vici* are likely to have still existed, and related matters.
57. For general discussion of the practice, see Klingshirn 1985, pp. 183–203.
58. A good case along these lines was made in Esposito 1956, pp. 131–55.

mentions that Columba founded a monastery in Ireland close by another which had been founded by Mochta (Maucteus) 'a certain British stranger, a holy man and disciple of the holy bishop Patrick' (*proselytus Brito homo sanctus sancti Patricii episcopi discipulus.*[59] The name is certainly British, and the annals for AD535 (repeated AD537) record Maucteus's death and preserve the opening words of a letter apparently written by him: 'Maucteus, a sinner, priest, a disciple of holy Patrick, (sends) a greeting in the Lord' (*Mauchteus, peccator, prespiter, sancti Patrici discipulus, in Domino salutem*). Clearly, if the term 'disciple' is here understood literally as one who knew the saint personally, then a date in the 380s or early 400s for Patrick is impossible (unless, as one scholar drily remarked, Patrick had been preaching to babes in arms!).[60] The obvious implication of Mochta's *floruit* is that the Patrician mission followed that of Palladius and his continental colleagues, perhaps by as much as half a century. If that is the case, then Patrick's own words are clear and unambiguous evidence for the fact that Christianity was still only in a fledgling state in Ireland half a century and more after AD431.

THE FIRST CHRISTIANS

This should come as no great surprise to any except the impressionable who believe that Patrick converted the whole country in a long and brilliant missionary career. The progress of Christianity in other parts of Europe was no more rapid, despite the official endorsement and administrative support of the late-Roman state, with all its apparatus of favour and coercion. In Ireland, where there were no such all-pervasive agents of government, the conditions for missionary activity would have been immeasurably more difficult. For the earliest period we are only guessing, but it is reasonable to presume that the organization of Christian communities would have been along the same lines as the organization of Christian communities elsewhere in the West. A structure of dioceses was probably envisaged, doubtless with the intention ultimately of establishing provinces and a regular hierarchy of bishops, priests, deacons, and the other ecclesiastical grades. Unfortunately, there is a large gap in our historical sources between the fifth century and the late sixth/early seventh century, the period of our earliest surviving ecclesiastical legislation, and though the later canon law collections mention bishops and dioceses as apparently established structures and offices, we have no way of knowing how many bishops existed and how they administered the Irish church.

Nor, for that matter, do we have any idea of how the Irish were converted, or what their beliefs may have been. It is reasonable to assume that some early conversions would have come about in the context of mixed marriages, perhaps with members of the captive British population, where the conduct of the catholic partner (then as now) would have been expected to set the

59. Anderson 1961, p. 182.
60. Binchy 1962a, p. 112.

example. In this context, however, it would not be entirely impossible that some conversions took place specifically with a view to obtaining a wife.[61] So also it might be the case that a timely conversion could be the result of material considerations: to repay political debts, to settle old scores, or to ensure advancement (preferment for high office, or whatever), much as Irish people in the last generation acquired a superficial knowledge of the Irish language as a passport to advancement in the civil service. Social climbing could also be a potent cause of conversion, perhaps more potent than either physical coercion or considerations of material gain.[62] Certainly the increase in the numbers of Irish Christians must have been due to conversion, not their birth-rate – despite what some modern propagandists might say! [63]

The stages by which conversion came about, however, are not easily identified, although the assumption has usually been that Christianity was the dominant – if not exclusive – religion already by the sixth century. But there are no documents from Ireland in this period, none of the papyri or parchment records which enable historians of Egypt or the Roman Empire to quantify the numbers of Christians by reference to the numbers and types of documents they produced. We simply have no way of knowing. And because of the church's exclusive control over the publication and dissemination of information concerning church matters, the non-Christian setting of the primitive church, except insofar as it bore directly on church affairs, was studiously ignored in Christian historical accounts.[64] The picture presented in the later hagiography naturally reflects the preoccupations of later Irish ecclesiastical writers and portrays the kind of spiritual community in the process of development that such churchmen knew in their own day. Converts by the hundred and the overthrow of the native, pre-Christian cults are, in general terms, the distinctive features of these accounts. The reality, however, was doubtless very different.

The writings of Patrick – our only contemporary source of information – present an altogether less rosy picture of the first days of the church in Ireland. Several times he remarks on the physical dangers faced by him and his followers and states quite candidly that it was necessary to purchase the goodwill and protection of the local kings and their brehon lawyers (*illi qui iudicabant*, Conf. §53), that body of professional jurists whose remit was the preservation and interpretation of the laws. He claimed in his own defence against detractors that he had expended the price of fifteen men on such things, but even so, he and his followers were in mortal danger on more than one occasion. The Christian message was not everywhere enthusiastically received; many of his flock 'endured persecution and lying reproaches from their parents' (*Conf.* §42). We would dearly like to know what these reproaches were, but Patrick does not elaborate.

---

61. For examples in the early church see MacMullen 1984a, pp. 136–7 n. 31.
62. Early instances again in MacMullen 1984a, p. 145 n. 30.
63. Witness the attitude implied in the remarks of Stanford 1946, p. 26: 'If Unionists would succeed they must breed more children and many poets'.
64. The formulation is MacMullen's, but it has equal application in an Irish setting.

Life was particularly difficult for the women among them: 'they who are kept in slavery suffer especially', he says, and the general impression is one of intense hardship and suffering. Patrick seems to have concentrated particularly on the conversion of women in Irish society, urging a life of celibacy on the unmarried and discouraging remarriage for widows (*Conf.* §42). In this he was, of course, following a pattern established in the early church, and the strictures made on the first Christians were doubtless repeated in the Irish case. From the earliest Christian times it was a constant refrain among anti-Christian writers that the church's doctrines gained credence only with a public unable to tell truth from nonsense; they were believed in only by children, slaves, and especially women.[65] Opponents of Christianity charged that the church's teachings were offered most often to the uneducated and by people of low standing in the community. Patrick refers (*Conf.* §41) to the 'sons of the Irish and daughters of chieftains', and it may well be that his message was addressed principally to the young and to women. He makes specific reference to 'one blessed lady, of Irish birth, of noble rank, most beautiful' (curious that he should add this) who had decided to take the veil. He recounts also how the women converts used, of their own accord, to present him with their little gifts, placing their personal jewellery on the altar (*Conf.* §49), causing scandal in the non-Christian community and also among the Christians, doubtless because some felt that Patrick was abusing his position to make money – a charge which his own strenuous denials prove was widespread.

The three main elements which have been proposed as essential to conversion in Late Antiquity – miracles, money, and coercion – are not easily quantified in an Irish context. If the evidence of the later Irish saints' Lives were to be believed, there was no shortage of miracles. The Patrick epic as recounted by his seventh-century biographer Muirchú is replete with duels and single combats in which the saint is seldom seen without a 'smoking gun'. The latent violence in most Irish saints' Lives, with their constant reiteration of the need to do battle with pagan druids and smash them physically if need be, though not necessarily a genuine record of conditions in the missionary period, certainly reflects the views of Irish Christian writers at the time when they were composed. But the attitude is one which has respectable antecedents in the history of the church: 'the one salient point of difference in Christianity was the antagonism inherent in it'.[66] 'The manhandling of demons – humiliating them, making them howl, beg for mercy, tell their secrets, and depart in a hurry – served a purpose quite essential to the Christian definition of monotheism: it made physically (or dramatically) visible the superiority of the Christian's patron over all others. One and only one was God'.[67] To be fair, Patrick has little or nothing to say about wonder working, but the language he uses when speaking of non-Christian gods makes it abundantly clear how he viewed such things.

65. MacMullen 1984a, p. 39.
66. MacMullen 1984a, p. 19.
67. MacMullen 1984a, p. 28.

TECHNIQUES OF CONVERSION

It would be interesting to know what arguments were advanced by Patrick and his followers in support of the Christian religion and against non-Christian cults and practices. What message did Christianity present to its new audience? What did Irish people know about it (as distinct from what they *thought* they knew about it) before conversion? How much of their new religion did they acquire after – rather than before – they had committed themselves to it? And what, for that matter, did the first missionaries know about Irish pagan beliefs? We have very little in the way of hard evidence for anything that might be classified as pagan religious practices, by contrast with the evidence of traditional customs and beliefs which passed down through the centuries as part of the general body of Irish folklore.[68] 'Celtic religion' in Ireland is still all but a closed book to us.

Patrick could at least boast six years' experience in Ireland, during his captivity, in the course of which he must have come into contact with some at least of the native popular religion. Unfortunately, he offers nothing but abuse and the barest statements about Irish cult practices. He says that the Irish were sun-worshippers (*Conf.* §60) and that they worshipped 'idols and abominations' (*Conf.* §41), a reference presumably to the native pantheon of gods. Herein lay the difficulty. The unique force of Christianity, and its distinctive feature in the period of conversion, was that it denied the character of a god to all other divine powers; it destroyed belief in the old gods while it created belief in the one Christian God. By contrast with pre-Christian cults, which allowed equal rights for all to believe anything about any number of deities and to pay equal respect to all of them so long as none was hostile or aggressive to other beliefs, the Christian God showed no such tolerance but was constantly at war with all rivals.

It was doubtless this exclusiveness that drew down the wrath of non-Christians on the followers of the new religion; after all, their views were a form of heresy in that they denied the gods: 'Christianity presented ideas that demanded a choice, not tolerance'.[69] Furthermore, Christianity defined belief in terms of right and wrong – the series of heresies and sects that were blasted out of existence during the first Christian centuries is evidence enough for the attitude of righteous Christians towards fellow Christians who did not see eye-to-eye with them.[70]

This rigid dogmatism, however, was not known to pagan religions. The whole notion of doctrine, of religion defined as a body of words and verbal

---

68. The best recent survey is Ó Riain 1986, pp. 241–51. See also Ó Cathasaigh 1984, pp. 291–307. The classic discussion of the subject is still Plummer 1910, i, pp. cxxix–clxxxviii: 'Heathen folk-lore and mythology in the Lives of the saints', with exhaustive references.
69. MacMullen 1984a, p. 17 (quotation).
70. For an eloquent description of such developments, see Knox 1950, p. 1 ff.

orthodoxy, transmitted by authorized texts, linked to a special code of symbolic, ritualized actions, was unknown in the non-Judaeo/Christian world; in fact, 'religion' in those terms did not exist before Judaeo/Christianity. Put in those terms, there could be no 'conversion' to paganism, only reversion. Likewise, the idea of a rigid day-to-day service, or even perpetual allegiance to a divinity, had little currency. Supplication was made in time of need; there was no permanent ritual of devotion, either in Antiquity or in the Irish world.

Christianity, on the other hand, defined belief in terms of adherence to prescribed authority. The pre-Christian Irish (like all followers of pre-Christian religions) had their great festival days: Imbolc, Beltaine, Lugnasad, and Samain, but there is no evidence that cults were enforced by kings or that religious guidance was sought from kings. A man might 'swear by the god by whom my people swear';[71] he did not deny other gods, nor would it have occurred to him to do so.

The earliest Christians cannot have been numerous or influential enough to constitute a source of political power; as we shall see shortly, the evidence, such as it is, suggests that kings and aristocracy were conspicuously resistant to the new religion. That is not to say, however, that the Christians were anonymous and unseen. There is no reason to doubt that in Ireland, as in every other country where Christianity was introduced, zealots took to the high-roads and criss-crossed the countryside smashing the symbols of the rival religion and looting its temples: 'There is no such thing as robbery for those who truly possess Christ'.[72] There was ample evidence in the experience of fourth-century North Africa and the Eastern provinces that looting and smashing the physical edifice of all competing cults 'could produce solid results, though not absolutely final ones'.[73] Much of what once existed as the outward and visible expression of pre-Christian religious beliefs in Ireland has doubtless been disfigured or completely destroyed, perhaps on occasion absorbed so successfully into the triumphant religion as to be unrecognizable to us now. The bullauns or indented quern stones commonly found at monastic sites (and frequently referred to in the hagiography in relation to miracle-stories about the saints) may be one such class of artefact. The 'holy wells' that dot the countryside may also mark the sites of pre-Christian cult centres. Apart from these few traces, however, all is lost.

The Life of Patrick by the seventh-century Muirchú maccu Machtheni preserves a remarkable poem of prophecy (rendered into Latin) which is said to have been chanted by druids prior to Patrick's coming. A version of the original Irish text survives in a later Irish Life of the saint and there is no doubt that it has some of the flavour of an early composition. It cannot be a true poem of prophecy, of course, but it must be at least as old as Muirchú's

71. For a discussion of this formula see Ó hUiginn 1989, pp. 332–41. I am not convinced by the underlying argument of the article.
72. The remark made by a leader of Egyptian Christians to whom pagans made suit for compensation after the smashing of their idols, cited by MacMullen 1984a, p. 98 (quotation).
73. MacMullen 1984a, p. 101 (quotation); compare Matthews 1975, pp. 140–3, 157.

day, and perhaps considerably older, and conveys some of the religious atmosphere in sixth-century Ireland:

Across the sea will come Adze-head,
crazed in the head,
his cloak with hole for the head,
his stick bent in the head.

He will chant impiety
from a table in the front of his house;
all his people will answer:
'Amen, Amen'.[74]

'He will utter impiety', Muirchú adds (*incantabit nefas*), which was doubtless the view of non-Christians in the face of demands that they abandon their own gods and adopt the Christian one. The stark reality of the new religion, with its single god who destroyed all others, given to outbursts of divine wrath and prone to vengeance and punishment, may very well have seemed impious to a people more used to a variety of deities and to the toleration of many cults. Muirchú, it may be noted, does not dwell on the subject, but passes on rapidly to other matters: 'enough of these things' (*de his ista sufficiant*). The memory was perhaps a little too vivid.

But for the lowly members of society, unburdened by any sophisticated philosophical attachment to their gods but faithful to them because they had served them well, the new ways must have seemed strange and unsettling. Some inkling of how these people might have felt may be had from another seventh-century source, this time associated with the Irish mission in Northumbria. The Life of Cuthbert of Lindisfarne, composed *c.* AD700, relates an episode about the monks of a monastery at Tynemouth who were returning up-river on rafts with wood for the monastery when a sudden storm swept them towards the sea. A crowd of onlookers along the river bank jeered at the monks because 'they had despised the common law of mortals and put forth new and unknown rules of life' (*qui communia mortalium iura spernentes, noua et ignota darent statuta uiuendi*), and when admonished by Cuthbert for their heartlessness they replied: 'Let no man pray for them, and may God have no mercy on any one of them, for they have robbed men of their old ways of worship, and how the new worship is to be conducted, nobody knows' (*qui et ueteres culturas hominibus tulere, et nouas qualiter obseruare debeant nemo nouit*).[75]

It may well have been their tolerance of the new Christian religion, rather

---

74. Text adapted from Carney 1967, pp. 2–3.
75. Colgrave 1940, pp. 164–5 (*Vita Anon.* §3). I am not persuaded by the different interpretation given to this passage by James Campbell, who thinks that the *vulgaris turba* was a group of Christians 'objecting to changes which were brought about in their worship by the monastery from which the monks came'; see Campbell 1973, pp. 12–26 (quotation, p. 21).

than any inherent weakness, that brought about the destruction of the pre-Christian Irish cults. Patrick, after all, reported how the brehons (*illi qui iudicabant*) allowed him to carry his Christian message wherever he wished (even though they themselves seem not to have believed it). A parallel may be seen in the rivalry between the Arians of Visigothic Spain and their Catholic rivals in the Frankish kingdoms: Gregory of Tours, in his *Books of Histories*, recounts how a visiting Arian royal envoy was happy enough to participate in the Easter ceremonies in the church of Tours, joining the procession from the bishop's house, but drew the line at receiving communion according to the Catholic rite. The legate remarked to him that when he was abroad it was his custom to pay his respects at the shrines of every religion.[76] Such magnanimity was not a feature of the Catholic church, either in Spain or Francia or anywhere else. Hence it is scarcely surprising that not a trace of Arianism survived in those two kingdoms.

There is no evidence to suggest (and no particular reason to believe) that Christianity offered a richer spiritual experience than the native cults: 'there should be, but there is not, evidence to support the view that the non-Christian religions were mechanical, formal, and external only'.[77] Quite the contrary, the frequency with which Christian writers condemn the druids and their ways suggests that Christianity had still to establish complete control even in the seventh century and beyond.[78] The terminology of royal praise poetry could still retain a deference to the old gods as well as the new: the Leinster king Aéd mac Diarmata meic Muiredaich (*floruit c.* AD750 or earlier?) is the subject of one such panegyric, which wishes him, among other things, 'every good of gods or ungods' (*cach maith do dé nó anddae*)[79] and some writers could still be found, in the eighth century, reciting Christian incantations side-by-side with others of starkly non-Christian sentiment against such mundane troubles as a headache.[80] We have no satisfactory way of knowing when Christianity became respectable; we only know that in Patrick's time it clearly still was not.

CHRISTIANITY AND THE OGAM STONES

The only substantial body of contemporary information available for the first centuries of Christianity in Ireland (roughly the fourth to the sixth centuries) is that preserved on the ogam inscriptions, and in this instance the ogam inscriptions preserved in the areas of Irish settlement in Britain are also of

---

76. Krusch 1937, p. 252 (*Libri Historiarum* V 43).
77. MacMullen 1984a, p. 165 n. 9 (quotation).
78. See further below, p. 88.
79. Text and translation in Stokes & Strachan 1913, ii, p. 295.
80. See Stokes & Strachan 1913, ii, pp. 248–9, and Best 1915, p. 100. Besides invocations of God there are others of the pre-Christian deities Goibniu and Dian Cécht; the language is sometimes obscure to the point of unintelligibility.

relevance. In the whole corpus of Irish stones (over 300 in all) [81] there are hardly more than a dozen that show any trace of Christian influence. No stone or inscription contains anything expressive of Christian religious sentiment; [82] no *hic iacet* type funerary formula, no *in pace requievit, pro anima, crux X, in nomine Dei summi*, no prayer for the dead or invocation of the deity. There is no Christian symbolism (chi-rho, cross, alpha and omega, etc), still less the bilingual Irish-Latin inscriptions so characteristic of British ogam stones; no sign, in fact, of any influence from the Christian epigraphical traditions of post-Roman Britain or Gaul.[83]

The Irish stones follow a uniform pattern:[84] the name of the deceased is given in the genitive case ('of X'), followed by the word MAQI ('son') and the father's name, also in the genitive. For MAQI the word AVI ('of the grandson') is sometimes substituted, and the man's tribal affiliation is sometimes also denoted by the word MUCOI. There is never any reference to Christian prayer; the words *óróit do* or *bendacht for* ('a prayer for', 'a blessing on') – so common on the later Christian inscriptions – are conspicuously absent from the ogams.[85]

A comparison with the ogam stones of Britain is instructive.[86] What differentiates the British stones so strikingly from those in Ireland – to which in all other respects they are more or less identical – is the fact that almost all of the British ones have their inscriptions repeated in Latin letters. Jackson's explanation of this phenomenon is that the Irish colonists in Britain 'were anxious to assimilate themselves to the admired culture in which they had come to live, and so they had their names recorded on their gravestones in Latin as well as in Irish'.[87] This is undoubtedly true, up to a point. The remarkable absorption of the Irish colonists into the late Romano-British culture is even better exemplified by the occurrence of Irish names in Latin-letter inscriptions *without* an accompanying ogam inscription.[88] These are found also in areas where ogam inscriptions are rare, such as north Wales, and their features seem to imply that the colonists there did not retain their Irish habits as long as their southern Welsh compatriots did, but were almost totally absorbed into the local culture. But even where Latin-letter inscriptions do occur in Ireland, the earliest examples still lack any trace of overtly Christian sentiment: LIE LUGAEDON MACCI MENUEH ('The stone of Lugáed mac Menb'), on Inchagoill island in Lough Corrib, Co. Galway; LIE

81. Macalister 1945, 1949.
82. See Mac Neill 1909, pp. 329–70, especially pp. 331–2.
83. On the epigraphical formulae of sub-Roman Gaul and Britain see especially Bu'lock 1956, pp. 133–41.
84. For general discussion, see Jackson 1953, pp. 149–93.
85. The word ANM which does occur on some stones is the Irish word for 'name', not 'soul'.
86. For a summary of their basic features see Hübner 1876, p. xvi ff. The best modern discussion is Jackson 1950, pp. 199–213; additional remarks in Jackson 1953, p. 153 ff.
87. Jackson 1950, p. 207 (quotation).
88. Jackson 1950, p. 210.

COLUM MEC GR[. . .] ('The stone of Colum mac Gr . . .'), Gallerus, Co. Kerry.[89] The references to the 'stone' of the individual commemorated clearly echo the ogam tradition.

But it is important to remember, for our purposes, that most of the British inscriptions bear no obvious sign that the person commemorated was a Christian. In some instances, of course, crosses appear on monuments, but the evidence suggests that most, if not all, of these were added much later to monuments erected in the fifth and sixth centuries, monuments which originally bore only inscriptions.[90] Some were undoubtedly Christian in origin, but the British ogams cannot be used to infer an almost wholly Christian society in fifth-century south-west Britain, and still less so in Ireland at the same date. There is no good reason to suppose that ogam stones *per se* were somehow repugnant to Christianity and that the individuals commemorated on them must have been pagans – though there was a strong tendency earlier in this century to argue along those lines, following a lead from Mac Neill.[91] But though the evidence cannot be pushed too far, there is no escaping the fact that the ogam stones reflect a society in which the pre-Christian practice of memorial in stone has remained totally impervious to the influence of Christianity, and this despite the fact that 'the epigraphic habit' is usually believed to have derived from contact with the Roman world.[92] This fact, which has obvious implications for any assessment of the early success of Christianity in Ireland, cannot be put down to mere conservatism on the part of the ogam inscribers. The ogams were not simply a traditional way of recording the names of the dead in a language no longer spoken and in formulae no longer understood, as Jackson put it, 'like Latin names on a modern inscription'.[93] They were erected by men whose living language was Irish and whose funerary practices (and language) must reflect the reality of Irish society in the fourth, fifth, and sixth centuries. When these practices were carried across to Britain they were modified and, in some cases, replaced. But it is surely remarkable that the formulae of late-Roman inscriptions which were borrowed as part of this trend were never re-imported into Ireland by returning colonists. Mac Neill undoubtedly exaggerated when he stated that the Irish tradition was 'pagan to the last',[94] but it is not unlikely that whatever beliefs underlay these memorial stones, and the ritual (if any) that accompanied their erection, were stamped out eventually, like crossroads dances, by an ardent Christian clergy, and some stones were probably 'converted' to the new religion by the later addition of Christian symbols or

89. Stokes & Strachan 1913, ii, p. 288. The two crosses on the Inchagoill stone look like later additions.
90. See especially Nash-Williams 1950, p. 17 ff.; Jackson 1953, p. 165 n. 3.
91. Mac Neill 1909, *passim.* That view has been severely criticized by McManus 1991, pp. 54–60.
92. See the interesting remarks in MacMullen 1982, pp. 233–46.
93. Jackson 1950, p. 210.
94. Mac Neill 1909, p. 333 (quotation); see the criticisms of Mac Neill's views in McManus 1991, pp. 55–7, 81–2.

by the defacement of existing inscriptions. Mac Neill maintained (though he subsequently withdrew the suggestion) that the erasure of the word MUCOI, denoting tribal affiliation, from many ogam stones represented the deliberate vandalizing of these early monuments. The reason, he said, was that the eponymous ancestors who provided the names of these tribes belonged to pre-Christian mythology and were the objects of worship to those who claimed descent from them: 'the violent defacement of eponyms was merely an Irish form of idol-breaking'.[95] This view is no longer defensible, but there is surely some significance nonetheless in the fact that only one solitary ogam inscription in Wales bears the MAQI MUCOI formula denoting tribal affiliation; the formula is otherwise almost entirely absent in the British ogam inscriptions.[96] The ogam inscriptions, therefore, point to an Irish society which, by the sixth century, had still not wholeheartedly embraced Christianity with the fervour that one finds in other regions peripheral to the former Roman Empire.

RELIGION, WORDS AND NAMES

There is another body of information, not normally used by Irish historians, which might help chart, at least in rough outline, the relative progress of Christianity in Ireland in the early period. The evidence is that of names and place-names. It has been remarked that one of the phenomena associated with the Christianization of other countries is the practice of naming children. The proclivity of Christian parents to give special Christian names to their offspring was evident already in Antiquity.[97] Comparison of the position of Christianity in Late Roman Egypt, for example, shows a striking contrast between the practice in the second and third centuries, when distinctively pagan names were the norm, and the practice three and four centuries later. The change is certainly related to the religious conversion of the country. It is natural to ask whether this approach might yield some results for early Christian Ireland.

The Irish evidence is abundant but difficult: there is no prosopography of early Ireland, and no systematic study of the thousands of names that have come down to us in the annals, genealogies, and other literary and funerary sources.[98] In the genealogies, for example, there are thousands of individuals who cannot be identified, other than by their familial connections; they do not appear in the annals and they cannot, therefore, be accurately dated. Nor can we claim to know what names were in most frequent use between the period of the ogam stones and the bulk of the earliest genealogical material, which hails from the seventh and eighth centuries. But even with allowances

95. Mac Neill 1909, p. 334 (quotation).
96. McManus 1991, p. 63 and n. 50.
97. For what follows see Bagnall 1982, pp. 105–24.
98. A beginning was made by O'Brien 1973, pp. 211–36; see also Ó Cuív 1986, pp. 151–84.

made for the intensity of family loyalty in name-giving (and it can hardly be claimed that the Irish were more attached to their traditional, pre-Christian names than were other peoples in Late Antiquity or the early middle ages), it is still remarkable that the patterns found in other parts of the Christian world do not recur in Ireland. The disappearance of pre-Christian names and their replacement by Christian ones, which in Roman Egypt can generally be taken as some indication of how the new religion was progressing, has no reflex in early Irish society, at least among the aristocracy.

Both Old and New Testament names are to be found in the genealogies, but almost always in the pseudo-historical portions which were concocted by monastic literati to fill the gap between the earliest native records and the biblical ancestors to which they were frequently traced back. Even in ecclesiastical circles names like Maél Póil ('devotee of Paul') and Maél Petair ('devotee of Peter') are extremely rare,[99] and names with Gilla ('servant') almost equally so, in the earlier period at any rate. The names of early Christian saints and martyrs are conspicuous by their absence from the Irish records as names for children, and if there were any native martyrs – which the later church denied – their names left no lasting impression on succeeding generations of Irish Christians. Perhaps they should be sought instead among the non-Christians. Though it can be assumed that persecution of the kind described by Patrick might have dissuaded the first Irish Christians from giving their offspring conspicuously Christian names, the same cannot hold true for subsequent generations; there is no evidence of a flood of Christian names coinciding with the supposed period when the church might have felt that it no longer need fear repercussions. If the progress of conversion was widespread and rapid, it did not find expression in names.

The evidence of place-names is more difficult to assess.[100] Irish knows several terms to denote places of ecclesiastical settlement: *andóit* ('founder's church' < Latin *antitas*), *domnach* ('church building' < Latin *dominicum*), *cell* ('church', 'developed cemetery' < Latin *cella*), *tech* ('house'), *eclais* ('church' < Latin *ecclesia*), *dísert* ('hermitage' < Latin *desertum*), *mainistir* ('monastery' < Latin *monasterium*), *tempul* ('church' < Latin *templum*). Of these, *eclais*, *mainistir*, and *tempul* are noticeably absent from the early records, a remarkable fact in itself, given the standard use of the Latin terms *ecclesia* and *monasterium* elsewhere in this period; hence the frequency of names with the element *eccles* in Anglo-Saxon England has no parallel in Ireland.

The commonest forms in the early period are *domnach* and *cell*, the former with a predominantly northern distribution. The antiquity of the *domnach*

---

99. For a rare early dedication to St Peter see the remarkable pillarstone inscription at Kilnasaggart, Co. Armagh: IN LOC SO TANIMMAIRNI TERNOHC MAC CERAN BIC ER CUL PETER APSTEL ('This place, To-Ernóc mac Ciaráin Bic has bequeathed it on behalf of Peter the Apostle'); Stokes & Strachan 1913, ii, p. 289. There is a good illustration of it in Bourke 1993, p. 10.

100. For what follows, see especially Flanagan 1969, pp. 379–88; 1980, pp. 41–5; 1984, pp. 25–51.

form (the Latin term from which it derives, *dominicum*, disappears from use in continental sources in the course of the fifth century)[101] and its complete absence from the areas of Irish settlement in Scotland suggest that the term belongs to the first phase of Christianity, and it appears to have fallen into disuse by the seventh century. The term was associated, in some quarters at least, with the mission of Patrick; hence the *Liber Angeli*, a seventh-century legal document emanating from Armagh, refers specifically to all places everywhere which are called 'domnach' (*et omnis ubique locus qui dominicus appellatur*) and claims a special association for them with the saint (*in speciali societate Patricii pontificis atque heredis cathedrae eius Aird Machae esse debuerat*).[102] The widespread occurrence of *donagh* as an element in modern townland and parish names in the east, and particularly the north-east, of the country could be said to support the other evidence which would locate the Patrician mission in that region, but the argument cannot be pressed too hard. So also the change from *domnach* to *cell* may possibly reflect a shift from a predominantly episcopal church in the earliest phase to a predominantly monastic one in later centuries, but that is a question we shall return to. On the whole, however, the place-name evidence, while supporting the theory of successive phases in the growth of the church in Ireland, cannot be used to plot that growth on a chronological basis; we simply have no way of ascertaining at what date most places acquired their ecclesiastical names. Even as late as the seventh century (and perhaps even later), for example, Muirchú could recall the older name of Ard Macha as Druim Sailech ('the hill of the willow tree')[103] and another writer could write: *Druim Thiprat, áit hi fil Cluain mac Nóis anniu* ('the hill of the well, where Clonmacnois is today').[104] Memories of pre-Christian days must have been equally strong elsewhere, so the onomastic evidence cannot be used to posit an early and widespread reception of Christianity.

Surveyed in general, then, the evidence for the earliest period suggests that the initial progress of Christianity in Ireland was slow and sporadic. This impression is also borne out by an examination of the earliest body of words in the Irish language denoting Christian concepts.[105] The primitive Irish Christian vocabulary contains a remarkable number of terms borrowed from the native pre-Christian religion: *dia* 'God', *cretem* 'belief', *ires* 'faith', *noíb* 'holy', *crábud* 'piety', *érlam* 'patron (saint), founder', originally 'tutelar deity'. These native words, together with some borrowings from Latin such as *domnach* 'church', *cruimther* 'priest' (Latin *presbyter*) and *crésen* 'Christians' (Latin *Christianus*) would have been 'just sufficient to provide a "skeleton service" of Christian terminology'.[106] The fact that so many of the native

101. The word *dominicum* with the meaning 'church building' does not seem to occur in British Latin; this may simply be a quirk of the historical record.
102. Bieler 1979, p. 188.
103. Bieler 1979, p. 108 (Muirchú, *Vita Patricii* I 24 (B II 6)).
104. O'Grady 1892, i, p. 72; cf. Colgan 1645, p. 266.
105. See Ó Riain 1989, pp. 358–66.
106. Binchy 1962a, pp. 7–173 (quotation, p. 166).

religious terms were pressed into service prompts an obvious question: what were the changes brought about by the adoption of Christianity? How much of their pre-Christian experience did converts bring with them into the new Irish church? And how much did they leave behind? Consciously or unconsciously, Irish converts must have brought a great deal of their traditional culture with them, and onto this then were grafted the new concepts of the Christian religion. A striking instance of this process in action is to be seen in relation to Irish methods of reckoning time. The Christian missionaries introduced the Julian calendar and its concept of the seven-day week. This gradually replaced the pre-Christian practice, which reckoned time in terms of three-, five-, ten-, or fifteen-day periods, based on a lunar calendar; traces of this earlier reckoning survive in the Old Irish law tracts,[107] but the seven-day week was entirely unknown. As it happens, however, a list of the oldest Irish names for the days of the week has survived, with names that go back beyond the archetypal seven which, in their modern guise, are still in use in Irish today.[108] The curious mixture of Latin and Old Irish in the names clearly represents the formative period of the church, when native beliefs were interlocking with imported concepts. The names are *Dies scrol, diu luna, diu mart, diu iath, diu ethamon, diu triach,* and *diu satur.* Four of these terms (*Dies scrol, diu iath, diu ethamon,* and *diu triach*) have so far defied explanation.[109] However, the first one, for Sunday, occurs in Cormac's *Glossary* as *Sroll .u. soillsi, unde est aput Scottos diu srol .i. dies solis* ('S., i.e. brightness, whence *diu sról* among the Irish, i.e. Sunday'), and it is interesting to note that the form *diu* (for later *dia*) occurs only in this usage and in these texts. It is surely no coincidence that in Old Welsh too the cognate form *diu/dyw* is used in exactly this construction, whereas Modern Welsh has replaced the older word with *dydd.* The older usage, however, survives in the Annales Cambriae *s.a.* AD876: *Gueith diu sul in Món* ('a battle on Sunday in Anglesey').[110] The linguistic details of our Irish list point, therefore, to a period in the history of the language when the originally Latin names, and the Latin case system, had not yet been fully adapted to Irish practice. In other words, the list is precious evidence for the primitive period of the church, when Irish Christians were still using their inherited pre-Christian terminology to convey ideas in the newer religion.[111]

But the transition involved more than a shared terminology; old habits also died hard. Christianity everywhere is forced, to a certain extent at least, into the mould of local custom. Irish church workers in the Philippines in our own

107. Binchy 1962a, p. 72.
108. See Ó Cróinín 1981, pp. 95–114.
109. See Lambert 1984, pp. 367–8. It is perhaps possible to see in the three forms *diu iath, diu ethamon, diu triach* a repetition of the word *iath* (*triach* = *triath*?), with the meaning 'one iath', 'two iaths', three iaths', with *iath* perhaps another word for 'fasting'; cf. *cétaín, dardaín, aíne* 'Wednesday, Thursday, Friday'.
110. See Phillimore 1888, pp. 141–83 (quotation, p. 166).
111. A different seven-day regimen is preserved in a law text on status; see Binchy 1941, p. 21 (§41); the text dates from *c.* AD700.

day reported seeing an advertisement in Cotobato for cock-fighting 'in honour of the Blessed Virgin Mary, courtesy of Pepsi Cola'.[112] Many of the customs, patterns, and *turasanna* (local pilgrimages) that survived in Ireland until recently were doubtless nothing more than pre-Christian rituals dressed up in Christian clothes.[113]

Unfortunately, we know practically nothing about the religious beliefs of the pre-Christian population, and the 'traces of the elder faiths' which had such a profound influence on writers of the Celtic Revival at the beginning of this century owe more to a misguided Antiquarianism than to any genuine historical research. The entire pre-fifth-century Irish experience has been filtered through the prism of later Christian writers, and those aspects of it which would have been of most interest to the modern student have been irredeemably diluted, if not eliminated completely from the historical narrative.[114] The clergy never tired of condemning such aberrations, not always with success. In a different culture, with a different structure of belief, such forms of worship seemed quite natural; their survival is a useful reminder that we should be on our guard for the occasional glimpse of a popular practice or belief that was relegated by the clergy to the realm of the profane, where its meaning was changed and degraded. The occasional survival of such apparently pre-Christian traces leads us now to discussion of the following questions: what kind of society was it that faced the first Christian missionaries? How was that society organized; how was it governed; how did it function?

112. Reported in the *Sunday Tribune,* 26 October 1986.
113. See Herity 1989, pp. 95–143.
114. For a radical critique of the 'nativist' approach, which would see traces of paganism in a wide variety of later literary sources, see McCone 1990.

CHAPTER 2

KINGDOMS, PEOPLES AND POLITICS, AD400–800

The darkness that shrouds the fifth century in Irish history makes it impossible to say whether the position as it emerges in our earliest sources represents a continuation of the political and social trends that were at work in the decades and centuries before that date, or whether some radically new developments marked off the years after AD400.[1] Some historians believe that cataclysmic upheavals took place on the eve of the documented period: plague and famine, among other things, bringing about the collapse of traditional society. There is no doubt that changes did take place, for example in the Irish language. 'It might be said, indeed, that it changed more during that time than it has ever done since', and the changes can be seen actually taking place on the ogam inscriptions.[2] They are represented in our earliest written sources by the transition from Primitive Irish to Old Irish, a drastic shift in the sound laws of the language which is believed by the linguists to have taken place over a remarkably short period of time. Parallel changes in the physical landscape may have led to the emergence of the new political groupings and dynasties which appear to dominate the historical narrative from this point on. Scholars argue that the older, tribal, 'archaic' structures of society either collapsed or were deliberately dismantled by a new breed of men, more ruthless and dynamic than their predecessors, who rode roughshod over the ancient taboos and tribal customs of the prehistoric period in their drive for power and position.[3]

OLDER POPULATION GROUPS

It is possible that older population groups were gradually ground down and

1. The reader is referred to my chapter on political developments in the forthcoming *New history of Ireland*, i, where a more detailed discussion will be found.
2. McManus 1991, p. 84 (quotation).
3. Byrne 1971a, pp. 128–66 (p. 162): 'Irish history between the seventh and tenth centuries presents us with the spectacle of a tribal society being transformed by the introduction of a dynastic polity to a state wherein territorial lordship replaces hegemony over tribes as a political principle'.

their royal lines allowed to lapse. By the time of our earliest historical sources, tribes like the Ciarraige, Dartraige, Múscraige, and Semonraige were all subordinate to the newer, more vigorous dynastic kindreds, and others like them had disappeared altogether, save for an occasional mention in antiquarian sources.[4] The decline of these ultimately prehistoric population groups can be glimpsed in the subtle change of terminology that creeps into the sources, particularly in the way that the term *moccu*, denoting tribal affiliation, gradually disappears from the annals and genealogies, giving way to newer coinages like *Uí* (Latin *nepotes*) lit. 'grandsons', *Cenél* 'kindred', *Clann* 'family', and *Síl* 'offspring', all of which denoted descent from a known historical ancestor. As Mac Neill pointed out eighty years ago,[5] these types of name appear later in the chronological sequence of tribal name-types and refer in fact to septs and dynastic families, not to tribes in the traditional Irish sense. Some of these later groups, however, demonstrate in their own changing names the slow transition from tribal affiliation to the more expansionist and territorially-centred loyalties of the newer dynasties. The representatives *par excellence* of this phenomenon, the Uí Néill, were descended ultimately from the Connachta who gave their name to the modern province of Connaught.

Ancient tribal boundaries are obscured in the surviving records to the point where it is impossible now to pinpoint the precise extent of the territories occupied by particular tribes or kindreds. Some of the older genealogical material occasionally names the 'cardinal points' of tribal territories, as in the case of the Dál Cormaic in Leinster, whose *ranna* or subdivisions are located by reference to the sites of strategic fords and rivers.[6] The demise of one of these subdivisions, the Uí Gabla Roírenn, is recorded subsequently in the same genealogies.[7] A similar instance is the reference in the annals for AD744 to the annihilation (*foirddbe*) of the Corcu Modruad, a south Co. Clare people, by their rivals the Déis, who subsequently occupied much of their territory. In some cases the names alone survive, and many tribal kingdoms which may at one time have been powerful are known to us only because they left their mark on the political landscape; long after the Eilni, Muirtheimni, and others like them had disappeared, their names 'had much earlier become fossilised in Irish toponomy'.[8] Some were entirely forgotten, mentioned only in passing by contemporary writers, but otherwise unkown, even in the genealogies. Even where dynastic families established a firm grip on more ancient tribal populations, the older traditions stubbornly persisted; in some cases branches of the new overlord dynasty simply appropriated the older name.[9]

4. For what follows, see especially Byrne 1971a.
5. Mac Neill 1911–12, pp. 59–114 (p. 82).
6. O'Brien 1962, p. 34.
7. 'Cellach mac Máel Ottraich meic Cind Fáelad ro báe hi rRáith Dermaige; is reme ro mebaid cath Átha Slabai for firu Muman 7 for hUu Ceinselaig. Is é dano ro ort hUu Gabla Roírenn'; O'Brien 1962, p. 74.
8. Byrne 1971a, p. 165.
9. Byrne 1971a, p. 156.

For the original tribal populations of such areas the change from the older polity to the new may have involved little more than an exchange of rulers. For some, however, the effect was more drastic and was reflected in a shift from the hereditary tribal territories to the less fertile lands on the boundaries and on bogland or mountain upland. Many of these changes were represented by later Irish historians as migrations, and they sought to find evidence for these population movements in the apparent dispersal of related tribes and kindreds such as the Luigni and Gailenga throughout Ireland. In fact, however, the reverse is probably the case, in many instances at any rate; the older, dispossessed peoples were, in many instances, probably the prehistoric inhabitants of these regions whose lands were encroached upon and eventually expropriated by the newer dynastic families. The result was not so much the dispossession and expulsion of whole populations as the displacement of the leading ruling families from the strategic geopolitical centres of the tribal kingdoms, and their consequent relegation to the periphery. Such developments probably involved the political elites rather than the general population; reigning royal families were displaced but the bulk of the population probably remained much as they were, simply exchanging one set of rulers for another.

This was almost certainly the case, for example, with the Airgialla ('eastern subjects/hostages'), a group of tribes located roughly in the area of present-day counties Armagh, Monaghan, and parts of Louth, originally subject to the Ulaid overlords, but that, with the decline of the Ulster kingdom in the early historical period, had shifted allegiance to the rising power of the Uí Néill.[10] Such shifting political sands must have been commonplace and must have had their effect on the morale of the more ancient population groups in particular. One authority[11] has set the first signs of a decline in tribal feeling in the eighth century, but it may be useful in this context to compare the evidence from Irish and British ogam stones. The value of these inscriptions to the historian cannot be overstated, for they constitute unimpeachable early evidence for the situation in southern Ireland and for the presence of Irish settlers in western Britain as far back as the fifth century at least,[12] a period for which we have no native documentary sources whatever.

It is a remarkable fact that the MAQI MUCOI formula denoting tribal affiliation, so frequent in Irish ogam inscriptions, occurs only once in the entire corpus of inscriptions in Wales, and on only two other stones elsewhere in Britain.[13] This has been interpreted by Damian McManus, the most recent scholar to examine the entire corpus of ogam stones, as an indication that traditional Irish naming practices were not as fashionable abroad as they were at home: 'A decline in tribal feeling among the colonists

10. The reciprocal arrangements between the Airgialla and the Uí Néill are recorded in an eighth-century text; see O Daly 1952, pp. 179–88.
11. Byrne 1971a, p. 164.
12. See McManus 1991.
13. McManus 1991, p. 63.

would be an obvious explanation', he remarks, 'together with the influence of patterns of nomenclature among the indigenous [Romano-British] population'.[14] It might well be asked, however, whether this apparent decline in tribal sentiment was restricted to those peoples that migrated to Britain in the fifth century, or if it might not be equally representative of feelings generally among the older population groups in Ireland on the eve of the historical period, a change which the more conservative Irish ogam stones failed to reflect.

We do not know the immediate causes that led to the large-scale movements across the Irish Sea, but one possible impetus might have been a series of political upheavals in the homeland, perhaps in turn sparked by severe outbreaks of plague or some such natural disaster. Here again the ogam stones offer suggestive evidence for the dislocation of society and the dispersal of peoples. Most of the inscriptions are to be found in the areas where the relevant tribes are known to have been located according to the evidence of later historical records. Thus the Corcu Duibne occupied lands in the Dingle and Iveragh peninsulas of Co. Kerry, and in fact they gave their name to the barony of Corkaguiney in Dingle. With just one exception, all the DOVINIAS (= Duibne) stones are to be found in Corkaguiney. By contrast, the Sogain, a Connaught vassal tribe, are located in the documentary period in a roughly midland band across Galway, Meath, and Armagh, whereas a member of the Corcu Sogain (assuming they were related), is commemorated on an inscription in the Bantry area of Co. Cork. Likewise the Luigni are associated mainly with Connaught and Meath, whereas one stone preserves their name in Co. Waterford.

We shall see from other examples (such as that of the Uí Enechglaiss in Leinster) that some at least of these inscriptions can be used to reconstruct a tentative picture of political alignments in the pre-documentary period. For the present, however, we may take them as pointers to a period of disturbance and displacement, when population groups and their rulers were on the move.

When did these movements take place? And what kind of political system preceded them? Mac Neill, the greatest historian of early medieval Ireland, once remarked that the oldest 'fact' in Irish history was the existence of what he called the Pentarchy, the division of Ireland into five provinces (cóiceda), a prehistoric arrangement which has left its mark even on our own times with the use of the Modern Irish word cúige to denote a province.[15] This Pentarchy provides the historical backdrop to the events in the most famous composition of early Irish literature, the epic saga tale called Táin Bó Cuailnge and its related rémscéla ('pre-tales'), collectively known as the 'Ulster Cycle'. The Táin relates the story of how the ancient Ulster kingdom was besieged by the combined armies of the other provinces, led by the redoubtable Queen Medb of Connaught. Only the superhuman powers of the Ulster hero Cú Chulainn saved Ulster from defeat, and the Táin (in its

14. McManus 1991, p. 64 (quotation).
15. Mac Neill 1921, pp. 98–132.

'standard' version, at any rate) recounts the martial deeds of the respective protagonists.

SAGA AND HISTORY

Though some modern historians doubt the value of the *Táin* as 'A window on the Iron Age' (to use the famous description of it coined by one Celtic scholar),[16] there can be little doubting that some memories of an earlier era – however vague – could still have persisted down to the period *c.* AD600 and beyond. Recent archaeological excavations of the large earthworks in south Armagh known as the Dorsey – traditionally believed to be the gateway (Irish *Dóirse*) to the ancient Ulster kingdom – revealed startling new evidence for the construction *c.* 100BC of a massive oak palisade to augment the natural defensive barrier offered by banks and ridges and wet bogland, extending in a linear earthwork along a perimeter of 4.3 km (2.7 miles). Other linear earthworks farther west in south Ulster suggest that they were all built as part of a frontier demarcation system whose purpose was to defend the province at strategically vulnerable points. The obviously defensive character of the Dorsey thus offers confirmation of the *Táin* literary evidence for hostility between Ulster and its southern neighbours.[17] Furthermore, dendro-chronological analysis (tree-ring dating) of the timbers excavated revealed that they had all been felled *in the same year*, and that year coincided with the date of the timbers used in the large wooden structure (possibly a ceremonial building) found in 1960 excavations at the site of Emain Macha (Navan Fort), the ancient royal capital just 27 km to the north. The conclusion is, therefore, that the most intriguing structure of the Ulster royal site at Emain Macha and part, at least, of the Dorsey rampart were constructed at exactly the same time by the same population group. However, precise dating of the timber evidence subsequently revealed that the trees were all felled *a few years after 100*BC. This is long before our documentary period, and therefore between the heyday of the Ulster kingdom and the first historical records there lies a vast and unmarked wasteland of prehistory.

The dynasties that subsequently rose to power over the ruins of Emain Macha and other ancient royal sites all have their origin legends and tribal histories, some of which may be quite old, but hardly older than the sixth century. Between the great days of the Pentarchy and the documentary era there is a hiatus of anywhere up to 500 years. No traditions – however resilient – can survive that long. There are sporadic historical traditions which appear to span some of that gap. The people known as the Corcu Ochae, with branches in different parts of the country but settled chiefly in the region around west Limerick, preserved an origin legend which purported to explain why they had abandoned their original homeland, on the shores of Lough

16. Jackson 1964. For the sceptical view see McCone 1990, *passim.*
17. See Lynn 1982, pp. 121–8; Hamlin & Lynn 1988, pp. 21–4.

Neagh in the distant north-east, and had come to settle eventually in their southern territories.[18]

The story is told in verse in a poem by a seventh-century poet, Luccreth moccu Chérai, and recounts how the Corcu Ochae were descendants of Dubthach Doél or Doélthenga (D. 'the sharp-tongued'), whose people lived in a district called Liathmuine wherein was a well called Lindmuine. The well was guarded by a woman, but it overflowed and drowned all the inhabitants, save four bands of the Corcu Ochae. Their king, Eochu mac Maireda, was drowned, whence the name Loch nEchach ('Eochu's lake').[19] The motif of the covered well that overflows and drowns all around it is a commonplace of folklore, but there are other details in the poem which deserve closer attention from the historian. It is noteworthy, for instance, that the Corcu Ochae are given a descent from Dubthach Doélthenga, for Dubthach is a character from the Ulster cycle. Indeed the poem takes knowledge of this for granted. Another of Luccreth's poems in the same collection, beginning Conailla Medb míchuru ('Medb contracted false oaths') likewise presumes familiarity on the part of its hearers or readers with details and names in the same cycle of tales. As Mac Neill pointed out,[20] the two poems furnish valuable evidence that the Ulster saga belonged to the common stock of Irish literature already by the middle of the seventh century.

If the story of Táin Bó Cuailnge was first brought southwards by migrating peoples such as the Corcu Ochae it would go a long way to explaining some of the peculiarities of the tale. It is interesting to note, for example, that the version of the story told by Luccreth differs markedly from the recension found in later manuscripts. The most curious feature of all in the Táin, however, is the fact that all the events in Emain Macha are related from outside the Ulster kingdom, using the brilliant literary device of the exiled Ulster hero Fergus mac Róich as narrator. Fergus is represented as a king of the Ulaid who was ousted from his throne by Conchobar mac Nessa and driven with his followers into exile in Connaught.[21] As a consequence, several Munster tribes in later centuries traced their origins back to these Ulster exiles.[22] Similar evidence for an early knowledge of Ulster historical traditions in Munster is found in the archaic and obscure law tract on the privileges and responsibilities of poets, part of the Bretha Nemed tract.[23]

The story of the overflowing well provided the literature with a proverbial saying luid Lindmuine tar Liathmuine ('Lindmuine spread over Liathmuine') and was adapted in turn to 'explain' the dindshenchas or place-name lore

18. Text in Meyer 1912, pp. 292–338 (pp. 307–9).
19. For discussion of the story see Mac Neill 1929, pp. 115–21; Bergin 1930, pp. 246–52; Gwynn 1903–35, iv (1924), pp. 58–68 and 389–90.
20. Mac Neill 1929, p. 116.
21. For other early traditions concerning Fergus (alias Fergus mac Léti), see Binchy 1952, pp. 33–48.
22. See especially O'Rahilly 1946, pp. 480–1.
23. Gwynn 1942, pp. 1–60, 220–36.

concerning Lough Neagh and its estuary.[24] An earlier version of the story called *Tomaidm Locha Echach* ('The outburst of Lough Neagh'), now lost, was classed as one of the *primscéla* or principal stories in the repertoire of the early literati. The theme of Lough Neagh overflowing its banks is, of course, far-fetched, though it would be unwise to dismiss the whole migration legend as a fiction. The folklore of Muskerry in West Cork offers an apposite modern parallel in the memories which concern the *Ollthaig* (= *Ultaig* 'Ulster people'), migrant groups that were believed to have wandered southwards as a result either of famine or the clearances that followed the 1641 rebellion. The communities of Ballyvourney and Coolea maintained a very rigid distinction between themselves and the 'newcomers' – despite their presence in the area for over two hundred years. The Corcu Ochae very likely could trace their origins back to Ulster in the fifth or sixth century, and it is not asking too much to believe that they retained some memories, at least, of their homeland down to the seventh century.

The Corcu Ochae may be part of the more general phenomenon which saw the collapse of the old provincial hegemonies before the dawn of the historical era. Hence the saga material embodied in the *Táin* cycle may contain authentic memories of an earlier period when enmity between Ulster and the other provinces was the mainspring of political events. But by the time of our first historical records these were 'Old, unhappy, far-off things/And battles long ago.' The story of the fall of Emain Macha placed those events in the early fourth century, though we have seen from the archaeological evidence that the *floruit* of the site is to be set a good four-hundred years before that date.[25] On the other hand, the collapse of the ancient Ulster kingdom – whatever its cause – was by no means total. As late as the seventh century one of their kings was described in a law tract as *ri Temro*, 'king of Tara', in other words a claimant to the so-called high-kingship of Ireland.[26] In fact, the documentary evidence – such as it is for this period – suggests that the boundaries of the old provincial kingdoms were still quite fluid and this is nowhere more evident than in the case of Ulster. The Ulaid down to the seventh century still nursed ambitions to recover lands as far south as the river Boyne (Co. Louth), the traditional southern limit of their territories. Thus the archaic tract on poets mentioned above has the Ulster poet Athirne lamenting the death of his client Borur, killed in a raid on Connaught (*a crich Connacht*) with the words: 'Woe to the Ulstermen if they be beyond the Boyne'.[27] The usage is doubly significant because it recalls an age when the lands south of Ulster were occupied by the Connachta, before the rise of their offshoot, the Uí Néill, and also when Ulster was at its greatest extent.

---

24. See Gwynn 1903–35, iv (1924), pp. 389–90.
25. Hamlin & Lynn 1988, p. 24; see also Wailes 1982, pp. 1–29 (pp. 8–10).
26. See Kelly & Charles-Edwards 1983, p. 68 (§32).
27. Gwynn 1942, p. 20.

THE KINGDOM OF THE ULAID

By the beginning of the seventh century the dominant power in Ulster were the Dál Fiatach, to the extent that the term *rí Ulad* could mean equally 'king of Ulster' and 'king of the Dál Fiatach'. Their emergence overshadowed their great political rivals, the Cruthin (*Cruithni*), represented principally by the Dál nAraidi of south Co. Antrim and the Uí Echach Cobo of west Co. Down. The term *Cruithni* is the Irish equivalent of the term **Priteni* preserved in Welsh *Prydyn* 'Britons' and denotes the oldest known inhabitants of these islands, more familiar under their Latin nickname *Picti*. Irish authors writing in Latin usually retained a distinction between the Picts of Scotland and their Irish cousins (though the Annals of Ulster record the death of Echu Buide mac Aédáin, king of Scots Dál Riata, in AD629, calling him *rex Pictorum*). On the other hand Adomnán of Iona, for example, in his Life of Columba, uses *Picti* only of the people in northern Britain. He always calls the Dál nAraidi *Cruithini* or *Cruthini populi*. This contrasts with the practice in the vernacular, where the term *Cruthin* is used indiscriminately. It has been suggested that the term was deliberately dropped in the eighth century 'as savouring too much of a foreign "Pictish" origin'.[28] Some Dál nAraidi adherents attempted to cover over these earlier traces by asserting that they were the 'true Ulaid' of antiquity (*na fír Ulaid*), while conceding that the title applied to the Dál Fiatach 'today' – this even after the decline of Dál nAraidi power again in the tenth century, after which the rival Dál Fiatach regained their earlier dominance.

It is perhaps true that in the sixth century the Dál nAraidi controlled lands as far west as Derry, while the territory of Cuib must have extended likewise much farther north than the kingdom of Uí Echach Cobo of Down, since it included (or at least approached) Dún Sobairche (Dunseverick) on the north Antrim coast.[29] The annals record a battle at Belfast (*Bellum Fertsi*) in AD688 between the Ulaid and the Cruithin, while Conchad mac Cuanach, styled by the Annals of Ulster *rex Cobo*, is elsewhere called *rí Cruithne*, as if Cuib were co-extensive with the Pictish kingdom. The term was still used in the annals down to AD773, after which it was dropped in favour of the term Dál nAraidi. In our own time the Cruthin have enjoyed something of a resurgence, as part of the renewed popular interest in early Ulster history, with a political interest manifesting itself in claims by writers of a staunchly Protestant/Unionist disposition who see in the Cruthin a prehistoric reflection of their own present loyalties.[30] The notion that the Cruthin were 'Irish Picts' and were closely connected with the Picts of Scotland is quite mistaken: the Cruthin 'were not Picts, had no connexion with the Picts, linguistic or otherwise, and

---

28. Byrne 1965, pp. 37–58 (quotation, p. 43); cf. O'Rahilly 1946, p. 344.
29. Gwynn 1924, p. 407.
30. See Adamson 1974, and Adamson 1979.

are never called *Picti* by Irish writers'.[31] There is no reason to suppose that they did not speak Irish, or that they practised matrilinear royal succession.[32] On the contrary, the evidence all points the other way.

The emergence of the Dál Fiatach and Dál nAraidi may well conceal the earlier supremacy of other tribes in Ulster. The annals have an enigmatic entry *Expugnatio Duin Lethglaisi* 'the storming of Downpatrick' at AD496 (duplicated AD498) which may well signify an important victory, perhaps for the Dál Fiatach, since they ruled Ulster from Downpatrick for centuries. Their subsequent domination of the famous monastery of Bangor probably resulted from their expulsion of an Uí Echach branch into the isolated Ards peninsula; the founder Comgall belonged to the Dál nAraidi. It is a curious fact that Bangor came to replace Downpatrick as the centre of Dál Fiatach ecclesiastical influence; the shift appears to indicate a northward expansion of their influence into south Antrim.

The rival Dál nAraidi may likewise have supplanted earlier lineages, but they too came under intense pressure from the growing ambitions of their Uí Néill enemies in the west. By the mid-sixth century they seem to have been permanently disabled. This was in spite of some notable victories against the same enemy, especially the defeat of the Uí Néill king Diarmait mac Cerrbeoil at the hands of the notorious Aéd Dub mac Suibni, 'a very bloody man and slayer of many' (according to Adomnán, who was related to Diarmait).[33] That the Uí Néill claimant to the high-kingship should have fallen at the hands of the Cruithin is significant, and Diarmait's son, Colmán Mór, also fell in battle against them, doubtless in a vain attempt to avenge his father's death.

THE BATTLE OF MÓIN DAIRI LOTHAIR

The year AD563 marked a watershed in Cruthin fortunes; the battle of Móin Dairi Lothair was won in that year by a northern Uí Néill alliance against a combination of Cruithin kings, seven of whom were said to have fallen in the battle. The immediate cause appears to have been internal rivalry among the Cruithin themselves. A Cruithin dynast enlisted the Uí Néill as allies against his cousins, promising them the Lee and Magilligan Point as reward. The battle was also remembered by Adomnán who mentions that one of the Cruithin kings escaped in a chariot – one of the latest historical references to the use of chariots in combat (and a useful counter to the notion that chariot-warfare in the *Táin* denotes great antiquity).[34] The account of the battle is also interesting confirmation that the territories west of the river Bann

---

31. Jackson 1956, p. 159 (quotation).
32. On the Pictish language, see Jackson 1956, pp. 129–66.
33. Anderson 1961, p. 280 (*Vita Columbae* I 36).
34. See, e.g., David Greene, in a review of Carney 1955 in the *Irish Times*, 7 April 1956, p. 8: 'It is hard to understand how the pagan system of *gessa*, or the technique of and terminology of fighting from chariots, could have been remembered in 8th century Christian Ireland except through the intermediacy of stories'.

and north of the Moyola river (Mag Dola, in south-east Derry) only came under the control of the Uí Néill in the years following AD563 – long after the date when, according to Uí Néill propaganda, the ancient kingdom of Ulster had collapsed. The loose confederation of Cruithin tribes which had taken the field in AD563 regrouped after their defeat in the territories east of the Bann and consolidated there around the remnants of the Dál nAraidi. Despite the fact that Adomnán portrays Columba, the patron saint of the Uí Néill, and Comgall of Bangor, patron of the Dál nAraidi, as the best of friends, the two antagonists clashed again at the battle of Dún Ceithirnn (Duncairn, a few miles west of Coleraine) in AD629, resulting in a rout of the Dál nAraidi. Their king Congal Cloén escaped, however, and the Dál nAraidi in fact appear again as late as AD681 resisting further Uí Néill encroachment around Derry. On this occasion, however, the Dál nAraidi king and his ally were killed in what the annalists call 'the burning of the kings at Dún Ceithirnn'.

Despite the fact that their king Congal Cloén (alias Congal Caéch) is termed *rí Temro* 'king of Tara' in the seventh-century law tract on bees and bee-keeping[35] – a title which he seems genuinely to have held, if only for a year or two – the Dál nAraidi were never able to break the stranglehold of Dál Fiatach power in the province. Of the sixty-two names in the later Ulster king-lists, only ten belonged to the Dál nAraidi; the rest were Dál Fiatach kings.[36] One of these had good claim to be the most powerful king in Ireland in his time. Baétán mac Cairill reigned for only nine years (AD572–81) and died in unexplained circumstances, but in that short time he did much to restore the military power and prestige of the Ulaid. He is said to have exacted hostages from Munster and to have received tribute from the rest of Ireland and from Scotland at his fortress in Lethet.[37] He is also credited with having 'cleared' the Isle of Man (*et is leis glanta Manand*), perhaps meaning that he had expelled the Conailli Muirtheimne, whose main branch occupied territories in north Louth and south Down and one of whose grandees is commemorated on an ogam inscription in the Isle of Man.[38] Baétán seems also to have taken the opportunity offered by the Dál Riata colonization of western Scotland to force the Dál Riata king to pay homage at Islandmagee, Co. Antrim. There is a hint of these events in the various annalistic references to military activity in this area during Baétán's reign: an expedition (*periculum*) to Man in AD577 by the Ulaid, followed by their retreat (*reuersio*) the following year. The annals also record a victory by the Dál Riata king Aédán mac Gabráin in another Man battle in AD582, the year after Baétán's death. The annalists say that Man was abandoned by the Irish (*Gaídil*) two years after his death, and this doubtless signals the first resurgence of Dál Riata independence after the demise of their principal foe.

Baétán mac Cairill's military campaigns are symptomatic of a wider perspective in the period; the Irish were in close contact with all the other

35. See, however, the comments of Kelly & Charles-Edwards 1983, pp. 123–31.
36. O'Rahilly 1946, p. 347.
37. O'Brien 1962, p. 406.
38. Byrne 1965, p. 56 n. 63.

peoples of the British Isles, Picts, Angles, and Britons. The Annals of Ulster, for example, record a joint expedition to the Western Isles of the southern Uí Néill and the Dál Riata, while a northern Uí Néill prince fought alongside the Irish of Scottish Dál Riata against the northern English kingdom of Bernicia at the battle of Degsastan in Northumbria in AD603 and lived to tell the tale; he died in AD610. Baétán's successes are best judged by the effect they had on his enemies, particularly the Uí Néill and Dál Riata. In order to establish a 'Second Front' against him, Aédán mac Gabráin made an alliance with the Uí Néill; this alliance was forged through the good offices of Colum Cille, whose first-cousin was the northern Uí Néill high-king. The occasion of the agreement was the famous convention of Druim Cett, now Mullagh or Daisy Hill, near Limavady in Co. Londonderry, in AD575; this saw a gathering of kings and clerics from Ireland and Scottish Dál Riata, with Colum Cille and others in attendance. The annals are singularly uninformative about the event, and Adomnán, who mentions it in passing in his Life of Columba, says nothing about its purpose.[39] It seems more than likely, however, that the convention settled the vexed question of the relationship between the Dál Riata and the Uí Néill and cemented the military alliance against Baétán mac Cairill.

The arrangement of Druim Cett survived intact for fifty years, a considerable achievement for the time. Colum Cille's earliest biographer, Cumméne Find, seventh abbot of Iona (AD657–69), depicts the saint strictly warning the Dál Riata against breaking this alliance with the Uí Néill, and for as long as they abided by his warning they were successful. But a shift in their political alignment saw them reverse their previous hostility towards the Ulaid and they joined in alliance with them against their recent allies. The great battle of Mag Roth (Moyra, Co. Down) in AD637 saw the Uí Néill king Domnall mac Aédo meic Ainmirech (the only seventh-century king to be accorded the title *rex Hiberniae* by the annalists) annihilate the Cruithin king Congal Cloén and his Dál Riata allies. The battle marked a turning point for the Ulaid and signalled the end of their hopes of restoring Ulster to its ancient prestige.

Baétán's successor as over-king of Ulster, Fiachnae mac Baétáin of Dál nAraidi, also claimed authority over Dál Riata and, like his predecessor, campaigned also in Scotland. Indeed, a list of saga texts (*prímscéla*) known to the medieval storytellers includes one (unfortunately lost) with the title *Sluagad Fiachna meic Baítáin co Dún nGuaire i Saxanaib* 'The hosting of Fiachnae mac Baétáin to Dún Guaire in the kingdom of the Saxons'.[40] This may be the event recorded in the Annals of Ulster AD623: *Expugnatio Ratho Guali* 'the siege of Ráth Guali', and annals and saga-text apparently refer to an expedition by Fiachnae against the citadel of the Northumbrian kings at Bamburgh Castle (called *Dún Guaire* 'Guaire's Fort' in Irish sources). Whether Fiachnae's campaign was successful is not clear; he himself fell in AD626 and his Dál Fiatach successor followed him shortly after to the grave.

39. For good discussion, see Bannerman 1974, pp. 157–70.
40. Best & O'Brien 1965, iv, p. 837.

Their early deaths brought about a further contraction of Ulaid power to the point where the Isle of Man was occupied by the Northumbrian king Edwin.

THE KINGDOM OF LEINSTER

While political fortunes were waxing and waning in the north, the kingdom of Leinster to the south was also undergoing major changes in the opening decades of our period. Arguably the most powerful of the early provinces, Leinster's importance is perhaps suggested as much by the relative abundance of the evidence as by anything else. By AD800 the province was dominated by two great dynasties, the Uí Dúnlainge to the north and the Uí Cennselaig to the south. Our earliest records, however, paint a very different picture, and it is clear that these two groups were only the most recent ones to emerge from the maelstrom of the fifth and sixth centuries.

The earliest cryptic references in the annals point to a prior supremacy of the Dál Messin Corb, and their principal representatives the Uí Garrchon. Two of their kings are mentioned in the annals as early as AD485 and 495, one of them, Fraéch mac Findchada, being termed *rí Laigen* 'king of Leinster'.[41] As so often in Irish tradition, however, the earlier supremacy of displaced dynasties is better preserved in the ecclesiastical sources. Thus the *Vita Tripartita* (an early tenth-century dossier of historical material relating to Patrick) relates how Patrick encountered an Uí Garrchon king who was allied by marriage to the Uí Néill high-king Loégaire mac Néill; the circumstantial evidence locates the Uí Garrchon of this narrative not in their later lands but around Naas in Co. Kildare – the traditional heartland of political power in Leinster. This association of Loégaire (the saint's *bête noire* in early Patrician saga) with a Dál Messin Corb king is clearly anachronistic, since the sources leave us in no doubt that Dál Messin Corb and the Uí Néill were mortal enemies. It is more than likely, however, that the tribe's prominence is due to their front-line position in the campaigns to stem Uí Néill encroachments on Leinster, and they probably bore the brunt of the fighting. The genealogies provide ample evidence of a wide distribution of this people across north Leinster, while the saints that are claimed as descendant from another sub-sept, the Uí Náir, include Kevin of Glendalough and Bishop Conlaéd of Kildare (contemporary of Brigit), as well as Bishop Éitcheáin of Cluain Fota Baétáin Aba (Clonfad, Co. Westmeath). Early traditions also attached great importance to the old site of Killeen Cormac (*Cell Fine Chormaic*), a few miles west of Castledermot in Co. Kildare. Here Palladius 'first bishop of the Irish' was supposed to have left his books, together with his writing tablet and relics of Peter and Paul.[42] If it were true that the site held relics of the Apostles it would certainly enhance any claim that the Uí Garrchon were the dominant political power in north Leinster until the close of the fifth century.

41. For what follows, see especially Smyth 1974–75a, pp. 121–43, and Smyth 1982.
42. Shearman 1879, pp. 38–54, summarized by Smyth 1974–75a, pp. 130–3.

Later sources, however, place the Uí Garrchon in present-day Co. Wicklow, indicating that they had been ousted from their ancestral lands.

The principal power in north Leinster was probably Dál Cormaic, and particularly their main sub-sept the Uí Gabla. The annals for AD498–503 record a series of battles in which the Leinstermen were worsted by the Uí Néill, and the Uí Gabla were in the firing-line. Their main concentration appears to have been in the Kildare-Leix border area, but pockets of them were also located farther north. The demise of one branch, the Uí Gabla Roírenn, is recorded in the early eighth century, but their fortunes had been decided sometime before that, and the annalists have no further record of them.

Evidence that others besides these groups once enjoyed considerable power in Leinster is furnished by the early king-lists preserved in verse. Names like Fiachu ba hAiccid, Muiredach Mo-Sníthech, Moénach, Mac Caírthinn, and Nad Buidb all belong to tribes that have all but disappeared from the later record. Muiredach Mo-Sníthech, for example, and Moénach belonged to the Uí Bairrche, and Nad Buidb to the Uí Dego, while Mac Caírthinn almost certainly belonged to the Uí Enechglaiss. Muiredach is in fact claimed as a king of Ireland by the poet.[43] Mac Caírthinn's name in the list illustrates how even the flimsiest evidence can still suffice to pull back the veil that covers the fifth century, a 'lost century' otherwise in terms of documentary sources. Although not mentioned in any of the surviving genealogies, he has been plausibly identified with the individual commemorated on an ogam stone near Slane, in the barony of Duleek in Co. Louth: MAQI CAIRATINI AVI INEQUAGLAS '[the stone] of Mac Caírthinn, grandson [or descendant] of Enechglass'.[44] He is perhaps identical with the Mac Caírthinn mac Coélbath who is recorded by the annals as having fallen in the battle of Mag Femin (AD446),[45] probably the area of that name in Brega (where the stone is located). Hence annals and the ogam evidence alike reflect a fifth-century situation in which the Uí Enechglaiss defended the northern frontiers of Leinster in Brega and in the plains of Meath and Westmeath. Mac Caírthinn's memorial stone is eloquent proof that Leinster claims to control once extended as far north as there.

The attrition suffered by the Leinstermen saw many of their once-powerful tribes ground down. The decline of the Dál Messin Corb was followed by that of the Uí Máil (who left their name on the Glen of Imaal in Co. Wicklow), who in turn had replaced the Uí Failgi (whose memory is preserved in the modern county name Offaly).[46] The Uí Failgi genealogies are a sorry mess, which doubtless reflects their weakened position by the end of the sixth century. An eighth-century poem records that they ruled from Rathangan, on the border between Meath and Kildare, and lists each of their kings back to Bruidge mac Nath Í († AD579). Uí Failgi fortunes were already in decline,

43. O'Brien 1962, p. 47.
44. Price 1941, p. 284.
45. See, however, the cautionary remarks of McManus 1991, p. 53.
46. For what follows, see especially Smyth 1974–75b, pp. 503–23.

however, after their defeat by the Uí Néill in AD516. The annalist adds the sombre note that 'thereafter the plain of Mide was taken from the Leinstermen'; and so it was to be. The Uí Failgi therefore probably originally comprised the dominant political overlords in north Leinster up to the mid-sixth century, with territories extending as far as the hill of Usnech in the north-west. The story in Patrician tradition that their ancient inauguration site was cursed by Patrick, and that Failge, eponymous ancestor of the dynasty, died as a result, was merely a later rationalization of the dynasty's political misfortunes.[47]

KINGS AND SAINTS

The only other serious claimants to the over-kingship of Leinster were the Uí Bairrche. As we saw above, two of their kings, Muiredach Mo-Sníthech and Moénach, were numbered among the provincial kings, but we know nothing more about them, so their claims cannot be assessed. The most important Uí Bairrche ruler in our period was Cormac mac Diarmata, who appears to have enjoyed an unusually long reign. The hagiography (saint's lives) associated with rival tribes such as the Uí Cennselaig and Dál Cormaic like to depict him as a harrier of holy men, but the most striking testimony of his success is the fact that later Uí Cennselaig propagandists resorted to the brazen fiction of claiming him as one of their own! Not the least of his claims to distinction is the fact that he died in his bed, after retiring to the monastery of Bangor (Co. Down). The choice of location seems surprising at first, but there are several early connections between Leinster and Ulster centring on the Uí Bairrche. Columbanus, famous missionary saint († AD615), left his native Leinster to join the community of Comgall at Bangor. He may well have encountered Cormac mac Diarmata there, since they were exact contemporaries. In fact Bangor possessed extensive properties in Uí Bairrche territory, granted it is said by Cormac.[48] Traces of such early contacts survive through later centuries and the military and political alliance of Ulster and Leinster kings in the eleventh century, during the reigns of Niall Mac Eochada and Diarmait Mac Maíl na mBó, may well be a continuation of earlier alliances.

A particularly important indication of early Uí Bairrche power is preserved in traditions that the first bishop in Leinster was an Uí Bairrche saint, Fiacc of Slébte (Sletty, Co. Laois). The tradition proved too strong even for the later propagandists to eradicate, and was preserved in the *Vita Tripartita*, which records Uí Bairrche and Uí Cennselaig rivalry. The document records that Oéngus mac Meicc Erca (a brother of the Sletty bishop) slew Crimthann mac Cennselaig († AD483) as vengeance for the exile of his people at the hands of the Uí Cennselaig.[49] That there is some substance to the tradition of animosity is supported by the fact that other traditions of Uí Bairrche expulsion and

47. Mulchrone 1939, pp. 129–30; Smyth 1974–75b, p. 507.
48. See O'Brien 1962, p. 54.
49. Mulchrone 1939, pp. 116–17; Smyth 1974–75b, p. 518.

exile are also found in historical material relating to the Déisi of Munster.[50] By the early decades of the seventh century, however, all this had changed, and with the rise of the Uí Dúnlainge in north Leinster and the Uí Cennselaig in the south the political map was to be redrawn along lines that were to last until the coming of the Normans.

The Uí Dúnlainge traced their origins back to an eponymous Dúnlang, and his sons Illann and Ailill. Bishop Tírechán, in his late-seventh-century collection of local lore about Patrick, relates how the saint's unyielding foe, Loégaire mac Néill, had refused baptism because his father Niall Noí nGiallach ('of the Nine Hostages', so called because of the nine tributary tribes that owed him homage) bade him to be buried in the ramparts of Tara 'face to face with the sons of Dúnlang . . . in the manner of men at war, until the last day'.[51] This notion, that the Uí Dúnlainge enjoyed a monopoly of the kingship as far back as the fifth century is, of course, anachronistic, but it does illustrate nicely how the seventh-century propagandists went about their work. The chief architect of the dynasty's later fortunes is usually stated to have been Faélán mac Colmáin († AD666),[52] but that credit is perhaps more rightly due to his brother Maél Umai. Early sources record how he attacked and routed Deichtire mac Findig, of the Uí Ercáin 'in his fort' (*inna dún*) 'and took his treasure'.[53] The Uí Ercáin are singled out for mention in the *Vita Tripartita* as having been specially favoured by Patrick.[54] Faélán by contrast is represented as having been fostered by several clerics, including Kevin of Glendalough,[55] and if there is any truth to the story it may well indicate that it was Maél Umai in fact who made the first aggressive moves on the road to Uí Dúnlainge expansion, perhaps then being succeeded (due to premature death?) by his brother Faélán.

Unfortunately, a great deal of obscurity surrounds the Leinster regnal succession in the first thirty years or so of the seventh century. Even the date of Faélán's accession is unclear – though the author of the genealogies of saints was able to pinpoint a particular event to 'the fifth year of Faélán's reign'.[56] His brother's assault on the Uí Ercáin, a sub-sept of the Fothairt, an ancient population group in the area around the famous monastery of Kildare, was perhaps intended to establish a grip on that important ecclesiastical site. In this they were singularly successful, establishing their own family in high office there for most of the century. Faélán's brother Aéd Dub († AD638) is described by the genealogists as 'royal bishop of Kildare and of all Leinster'.[57] The same encomium lauds Aéd as a famous man of learning and cites two verses which are among the cleverest pieces of political satire

50. Meyer 1901, pp. 101–35 (p. 106); Meyer 1907a, pp. 135–42 (p. 137).
51. Bieler 1979, p. 132 (§12).
52. See, e.g., Byrne 1973, p. 151.
53. O'Brien 1962, p. 339.
54. Mulchrone 1939, p. 114.
55. Plummer 1910, i, p. 250 ff.
56. Ó Riain 1985, p. 23 (§132.2): 'I cóiced bliadain flatha Faelain m. Colmain ríg Lagen'.
57. O'Brien 1962, p. 339.

in the literature:

> O brother,
> If you follow faith,
> What right have you to compete with Aéd,
> Unless indeed you have drunk henbane?
>
> Are yours the drinking-horns of the wild ox?
> And is yours the ale of Cualu?
> Is your land the Curragh of Liffey?
> Are you the descendant of fifty high-kings?
> Is Kildare your church?
> Is your companionship with Christ?

These are pointed references to all the paraphernalia associated with royal prerogative in Leinster, and served as due warning to any erstwhile rivals to keep their distance.

Faélán in fact sought to bolster the Uí Dúnlainge's position by a series of political marriages with women of the Fothairt and the Déisi, though it is not clear how successful he was in this policy.[58] The genealogists refer laconically to his son Conall as the man 'who was not king' (*qui rex non fuit*), but his descendants, the Uí Muiredaig did in fact retain power after him. Indeed there survives an early eighth-century poem in praise of Aéd mac Diarmata, king of Uí Muiredaig and would-be king of Leinster († AD714?) 'a descendant . . . of the kings of Cualu . . . to whom lovely Liffey belongs'.[59] Despite periodic attempts at resistance by their older rivals, the Uí Dúnlainge and Uí Cennselaig were victors in what might be called the propaganda war. Indeed the Uí Cennselaig could boast of an even better record against the traditional Uí Néill enemy than their northern Leinster rivals and as far back as the sixth century one of their kings, Brandub mac Echach, was successful against them in battle. But despite vague references to 'seven blows against Brega', the Uí Cennselaig failed to press home their victory and they never managed to break out into the rich grasslands of Kildare. They did stage another bid for supremacy in the province in the early eighth century, but they were to fall victim to the power of the Uí Néill.

The convoluted nature of Leinster politics in the first half of the eighth century is well illustrated by an extraordinary entry in the annals for AD738 concerning the battle of Áth Senaig [Ballyshannon, near Kilcullen, Co. Kildare]:

> The battle of Áth Senaig . . . between the Uí Néill and the Laigin was sternly
> fought, and the two kings respectively . . . i.e. Aéd Allán (king of Tara) and Aéd
> mac Colggen (king of Lagen) . . . Then the descendants of Conn [= Uí Néill]
> enjoyed a tremendous victory, when in extraordinary fashion they rout, trample,

58. Byrne 1973, p. 155, is in error when he states that Faélán allied by marriage with the southern Uí Néill. See the chart below, pp. 308–9.
59. Text and translation in Stokes & Strachan 1913, ii, p. 295.

crush, overthrow and destroy their Laigin adversaries, so much so that almost the entire enemy is well nigh annihilated, except for a few messengers to bring back the tidings. And men say that so many fell in this great battle that we find no comparable slaughter in a single onslaught and fierce conflict throughout all preceding ages . . .

Aéd mac Colggen was decapitated with a battle sword, and most of his allies died with him. They included Bran mac Murchado of the Uí Dúnlainge, Fergus mac Moénaig and Dub-dá-Chrích mac aui Cellaig meic Triein, two kings of the Fothairt, Fiangalach mac Maéle Aithchen of the Uí Briúin Cualann, Conall hua Aithechdai of the Uí Cennselaig, the four sons of Flann aui Congaile, probably of the Uí Failgi, and Éladach aui Maéluidir, as well as 'many others, omitted for the sake of brevity'. The annal is a stark reminder of the brutality that accompanied so much medieval political rivalry, and a salutary corrective to the notion that warfare in Early Ireland was little more than ritualistic.[60]

Aéd mac Colggen was the last Uí Cennselaig king to rule Leinster until the revival of their power in the eleventh century; his brother Faélán's death 'unexpectedly and at an early age' set the seal on their misfortunes. From AD738 to AD1042 the Leinster kingship was to be the monopoly of the Uí Dúnlainge. Four sons of Murchad mac Broén Mút produced lineages which alternated in the kingship by a process which Eoin Mac Neill believed to be a 'law' of dynastic succession.[61] Though the evidence is sometimes unclear, there is no denying that the Uí Dúnlainge present a picture of formidable cohesion and it has been suggested that some of this was due to a *modus vivendi* between themselves and the southern Uí Néill. Certainly, the first Clann Cholmáin high-king, Domnall Midi († AD763), seems to have left them undisturbed throughout his twenty-year reign, a policy apparently continued by his successor Niall Frossach until his death in AD778. The fact that hostilities had ceased between these traditional adversaries suggests that their perennial conflict had ceased to be a war of territorial conquest. The stand-off was only temporary, however; when the Uí Néill renewed their attacks in the 780s and 790s they encountered a Leinster opposition fragmented by internal dissension and by the end of the century Leinster's subordinate position was painfully obvious.

THE KINGDOM OF MUNSTER

Sources for the early political history of Munster are more sparing and less reliable than for Leinster or Ulster, though the literary production of the region, particularly in Hiberno-Latin biblical studies, gives the lie to any notion that Munster was somehow less developed in its monastic scholarship. The early history of the province is dominated by the group of families

60. See, e.g., Binchy 1962, pp. 119–32 (p. 128).
61. Mac Neill 1921, pp. 114–43; for differing views see Ó Corráin 1971, pp. 7–39.

known as Eóganachta, with scattered branches throughout Munster occupying the best lands and located strategically among older tribal kingdoms such as the Múscraige (who left their name on the barony of Muskerry in west Cork) and others dispersed across counties Cork and Tipperary. Traces of an older political situation can be found in the sometimes crudely stitched fabric of Eóganachta origin legends, and also – as so often – in the personnel of important churches. Thus the Uí Maic Brócc held control of the monastery of Cork, as did the Uí Selbaig, later hereditary abbots there.[62]

The rise of Cork may have been seen as a deliberate attempt to counterbalance the influence of Munster's most significant early ecclesiastical foundation, Imblech Ibair (Emly, Co. Tipperary). The alternative designation of the site as *medón Mairtine* 'the centre of the Mairtine [tribe]' reflects its former importance as the hub of a widely scattered population group which was apparently pushed out by the Eóganachta. According to the *Triads of Ireland*, Emly was the seat of historical learning, and its bishop heads the list of clerics gathered in council at Mag Léne *c*. AD630 to discuss the vexed question of Easter.[63] The collection of Munster annals known as the Annals of Inisfallen was also closely connected with that church, and our extant copy was probably written there.

EARLY MUNSTER POPULATION GROUPS

The 'synthetic' historians of later centuries present groups like the Múscraige, Ciarraige, Corcu Baiscind, Corcu Duibne, and Fir Maige Féne as vassal peoples of the Eóganachta, connecting them by genealogical fictions to the dominant dynasty of their own times. Lack of evidence makes it well nigh impossible to tease out the earlier position even of the Eóganachta, for between the death-notice of Oéngus mac Nad Fraích – ancestor of most of the Eóganachta – in AD490, and that of his grandson Coirpre in AD580, the Munster annals are a complete blank. However, their expansion in the sixth and early seventh centuries saw them plant settlements in south Connaught and in the Burren area of north Clare. They even established a foothold on the Aran Islands, where Onaght on Inishmore preserves the memory of their name.[64] By the eighth century, however, their power seems to have been already in decline, and with the rise of the group known as In Déis Tuaiscirt (later better known as Dál Cais) in Clare their weakness began to manifest itself.

The looseness of the Eóganacht hegemony in Munster – compared to the cohesion of the Uí Néill in particular – has often been remarked, but as one authority has pointed out, their political documents bear witness to a well-developed institution of kingship.[65] The text known as the 'West Munster

62. See Ó Buachalla 1952, pp. 67–86 (p. 67 n. 8).
63. See Walsh and Ó Cróinín 1988, p. 90.
64. See Byrne 1958, pp. 18–19.
65. Ó Corráin 1980, pp. 150–68 (p. 163).

Synod' exhibits these over-kings exacting levies from their tributary populations, and it may be no coincidence that the earliest example of a genre known as 'Mirrors of Princes', the *De duodecim abusiuis* ('On the twelve abuses' [*inter alia*, of kingship]) is apparently of Munster provenance.[66] That these rights and dues had been more-or-less formalized at a relatively early date is suggested also by the evidence of the texts known as *Frithfholud ríg Caisil* 'The reciprocal rights and dues of the king of Cashel'.[67] An early law tract states baldly that 'supreme among kings is the king of Munster' and the dictum bespeaks a self-confidence which is borne out by the annals. Another law text refers to the special position of the provincial king in terms of his *rechtgae ríg* 'special royal ordinance', 'as in the case of the *rechtgae* of the king of Cashel'.[68] The fatal flaw in their make-up, however, appears to have been the emergence in the mid-eighth century of the west Munster Eóganachta as serious rivals to the monopoly previously enjoyed by their eastern cousins whose centre was at Cashel, Co. Tipperary. In fact, between AD742, with the death of Cathal mac Finguine – the first Munster king to advance serious claims to the high-kingship of Ireland – and AD786 the annals fail to mention any eastern Eóganachta king of Munster. Despite their earlier unanimity of purpose, the Munster kings were, in fact, unable to stem the rising tide of Uí Néill ambitions. The annals seem to indicate a stand-off between the two around the mid-eighth century, but Munster success was to be short-lived. It was not until the reign of Feidlimid mac Crimthainn in the next century that Munster was again to establish a serious claim to the high-kingship of Ireland.

THE KINGDOM OF CONNAUGHT

If the sources for the early history of Munster are meagre, those for Connaught in the centuries before AD800 are almost non-existent. This sparsity of information need not imply, however, that Connaught was a wasteland cut off from the rest of the country and of no consequence. Some of the earliest traditions concerning Patrick, for example, are linked with the region and various other bits and pieces allow some of the jigsaw to be reconstructed. It is true, on the other hand, that Connaught – alone of all the provinces – appears to lack any strong pattern of over-kingship. There is an early law tract which states that 'he is no highest king (*ollam*) who does not magnify the Fifth of Ailill mac Máta'; comparison may be made with the Munster claim *ollam uas rígaib rí Caisil.*[69] Unfortunately, the genealogies make clear that Ailill was in fact a Leinsterman by birth, whose name *mac Máta* shows that he was named after his mother, a Connaught woman who

66. See Kenney 1929, pp. 281–2.
67. O'Keeffe 1934, pp. 19–21; for discussion, see Ó Buachalla 1952, pp. 81–6; Byrne 1973, pp. 196–9; Ó Corráin 1980, pp. 162–3.
68. Binchy 1941, p. 21 (§38).
69. Byrne 1973, pp. 175–6.

had married into Leinster. Hence Ailill's claim to the Connaught throne was from the distaff side (*máthre*).[70]

This may explain why the earliest traditions concerning the *Táin* presume a Tara origin for the campaign against Ulster, and why they depict Medb, Ailill's scheming consort, as having been intensely jealous of the Leinster troops that bore the brunt of the fighting. It is possible also that the (Fir) Domnann, one of the oldest population groups in Leinster, were related to the tribes around Erris (Co. Mayo) which in Irish was called Irrus Domnann. Bishop Tírechán's account of Patrick places the location of the saint's vision 'around the plain of Domnann' (*de campo Domnann*), and yet Tírechán says nothing about a provincial kingship based in Cruachain (Rathcroghan, Co. Roscommon), the traditional centre of the ancient 'Fifth'. In fact, he has a remarkable account of a visit by Patrick to the daughters of Loégaire mac Néill at Cruachain, implying that while Loégaire was high-king at Tara he was also at the same time king of Connaught.

For the period before AD600 we have nothing but a few bare names, and no context for their careers. Tírechán offers some additional snippets for the seventh century, but it is not until the eighth that we see the emergence of the Uí Briúin as the most powerful political grouping.[71] The rival Uí Fiachrach (to whom Tírechán himself belonged) were influential in north Connaught in the seventh century and the later regnal lists claim one of their number as king of the province. But the Uí Briúin began to dominate already by the second half of the seventh century. Cenn Faélad mac Colgen is called *rex Connacht* by the annals, and he is probably the first serious claimant from that dynasty to the overlordship.

Some of the earliest annalistic references to Connaught concern the efforts of its kings to ward off the encroachments of the Uí Néill. That the Uí Néill were in fact an offshoot of the Connachta was still clearly recognized in the seventh century and the oldest texts make a clear distinction between them. Hence the area of Cairpre Droma Cliab might be regarded as belonging to the Uí Néill line of Cairpre son of Niall. It was here, around Drumcliff, Co. Sligo, that the battle of Cúl Dremne was fought between the northern Uí Néill, in alliance with the Uí Briúin, against the southern Uí Néill high-king Diarmait mac Cerrbeoil, probably in AD561. The battle was traditionally believed to have been instigated by Columba, and it is mentioned by Adomnán in his Life of the saint as having occurred two years before his departure from Ireland. The Cairpre took the field in alliance with their Uí Néill kinsfolk, turning their backs on the older tribal affiliation with Connaught.

The best-known seventh-century Connaught king was undoubtedly Guaire mac Colmáin († AD663), of the Uí Fiachrach Aidne. He was the central figure in a cycle of saga tales and acquired the enviable soubriquet of 'Guaire of the bounty'. His career is so thickly encrusted with legend, however, that the best efforts of modern scholars have failed to separate the fact from the fiction. There is no doubting that it was during his reign that the Uí Fiachrach Aidne

70. See the text in O'Brien 1962, pp. 22–3.
71. For what follows, see especially Byrne 1973, pp. 238–40.

acquired their pre-eminent position in the province; indeed, it has even been suggested that their influence extended as far as north Munster.[72] A very confused sequence of annalistic entries suggests that the Uí Briúin Seola were beginning to vie for the kingship towards the end of the seventh century; by the closing years of the eighth they had established themselves not only as the dominant dynasty in the west but as a power to be reckoned with in Ireland as a whole.[73] Indeed the kingdom of Uí Briúin Bréifne, whose expansion from the eighth century onwards was to drive a fatal wedge between the northern Uí Néill and their southern cousins, was carved out from lands which had never been reckoned as Connacht territory at all. Their defeat of the Conmaicne (whose coastal branch, Conmaicne Mara, gave their name to the area of Connemara in Galway) in AD766 marked their consolidation east of the Shannon.

Other lesser tribes still retained some of their earlier power even in the face of these developments. The evidence of Tírechán's account and of the genealogies and annals indicates that all the northern part of Co. Leitrim, before its occupation by the Uí Briúin Bréifne, was Calraige territory. The Book of Armagh preserves a copy of a very interesting tract on the hereditary succession to the monastery of Druim Léas (Drumlease, about two miles north of Dromahaire) which clearly presents the Calraige as rulers still in that area in the seventh century.[74] Tírechán also makes a brief mention of the Uí Maine, whose kingdom must at one time have been very extensive, stretching through all of east Galway and all of Roscommon bounding on Galway. It is clear from Tírechán's account, in fact, that the famous monastery at Clonmacnois – where the Uí Maine kings were buried – was an active and successful rival to Armagh in the greater part of south Connaught generally. It may well be that the Uí Néill kingdom of Cenél Maine was nothing more than an offshoot from the western branch of Uí Maine. Such evidence as there is suggests that there had once existed a single over-kingdom of Uí Maine straddling the Shannon which was then broken up by the emerging dynastic families of the Uí Néill. The earliest annalistic reference to the Uí Maine in Connaught is at AD538, when a brother of the Uí Néill high-king Diarmait mac Cerrbeoil was defeated 'contending for the hostages of Uí Maine Connaught'. The annals in fact make clear that the domination of Uí Maine was essential for any successful claimant to the over-kingship of Connaught.

The years from AD700 to AD723 saw the consolidation of Uí Briúin power in Connaught.[75] The rival Uí Fiachrach supplied only three kings of the province in the eighth century. Having ousted the only other potential rivals, the Uí Ailello, from the threefold alternating kingship, the Uí Briúin eventually occupied the central plains of Connaught from their prehistoric capital at Cruachain. From AD764 on, the kingship was contested between rival branches of their own line. Two decades of sustained aggression against the

72. Ó Corráin 1980, p. 165.
73. Ó Corráin 1980, pp. 165–6.
74. Bieler 1979, p. 172.
75. For what follows, see Byrne 1973, p. 248 ff.

Uí Maine in the south-east reduced them and every other possible rival to submission and by the 780s the final acknowledgement of the Uí Briúin as natural heirs to the provincial title was marked by the visit of Dub-dá-Lethe, abbot of Armagh, to promulgate the Law of Patrick in the province, AD783. In the closing years of the eighth century, therefore, Connaught had emerged from its earlier obscurity and stood on the threshold of becoming a power to be reckoned with in national politics.

The picture that emerges of Irish politics during these years has occasionally been taken to imply conditions of endemic warfare throughout the country, with murder and mayhem the order of the day. In fact, there is nothing to indicate that the conduct of political affairs was any more or less bloody in Ireland than in Anglo-Saxon England or in any of the Germanic kingdoms on the continent. The laconic notices of battles and murders in the annals (proto-chronicles) tend to distort the reality – much as newspaper headlines do today – but we should not assume that the ambitions of rival kings impinged a great deal on the everyday lives of their subjects. True, there are more kings in medieval Ireland than anywhere else in contemporary Europe, but that tended to limit the scope of their activities, rather than expand them.

CHAPTER 3

KINGS AND KINGSHIP

Students of history approaching the subject of early medieval Ireland for the first time usually come to grief in the quagmire of names that faces them almost from the start. The seemingly endless genealogies and tribal histories, stretching in date from the sixth century down to the sixteenth, may be a boon to the historian, but they are the bane of every student's life. Added to this intimidating onomastic barrier are the no less daunting Irish annals containing an equally bewildering litany of names and dates, those 'Tribes and kings in all directions, with their far and near connections' that some balladeer poked fun at. Challenged to make sense of this delirium of information, students often feel much as they would if asked to piece together the course of twentieth-century Irish history using only the evidence of the telephone directory and the death-columns of the national and provincial newspapers.

That much said, we are nevertheless extremely fortunate in the extent and detail of the information that has come down to us – however many gaps there may still be in it. Historians of medieval England, France, Germany, or Italy are often envious (when not entirely ignorant) of the wealth of genealogical and annalistic information from Ireland in the period before *c.* 1200. The first – and so far only – volume of the projected corpus of Irish genealogies[1] lists some 12,000 individual names, and that only covers some of the manuscripts for the period down to *c.* 1100. The other promised volumes should include as many names again and possibly more, and the total corpus – if we include all the personal and tribal names from all the sources up to *c.* 1600 – could amount to something in the region of 30,000 names. Compared to the few hundred names preserved in the Anglo-Saxon genealogies of the same period,[2] and the still fewer names from the Germanic kingdoms of the

---

1. O'Brien 1962.
2. See, e.g., Searle 1899, and Sisam 1953, pp. 287–348. The description of the early Anglo-Saxon royal genealogies as 'a unique collection of semi-mythological materials' by Stanley 1990, p. xi, only serves to show that Irish historians still have some way to go in making their material known to a wider audience.

continent,[3] the historian of early medieval Ireland clearly does not want for raw material.

On the other hand, there are problems with this kind of source material, particularly in the matter of what scholars call prosopography, or the synchronization of data concerning historical individuals. To some extent, the annals and genealogies can be matched one against the other, and where individuals in the genealogies can be securely dated and located it is usually possible to work out where and when they flourished, and perhaps even to hazard a guess at what they were up to. It must be said, however, that in the majority of cases such control cannot be achieved, and we are left with literally thousands of individuals about whom we know nothing save their names and the dates of their deaths. Thus Fergus Glutt, described as *rex Cobo*, king of the small Ulster sub-kingdom of Cuib (roughly co-extensive at one point with the area stretching from mid-Down to Dunseverick, on the north-Antrim coast) died in AD739, according to the Annals of Ulster, 'from the venomous spittles of wicked people'. Clearly, this was an unusual king, with unusual enemies. Unfortunately, Fergus does not appear in the Ulster king-lists,[4] and he is nowhere to be found in the genealogies, so we have no idea what lies behind that curious annal. Similarly, we have a fine praise-poem in honour of Aéd mac Diarmata meic Muiredaich, a Leinster king 'to whom lovely Liffey belongs', preserved in the margin of a ninth-century manuscript on the continent.[5] Aéd was probably an eighth-century king,[6] but we have no means of knowing, since he figures in no king-list or genealogy. These two men were kings, important people; what chance is there then of recovering the histories of less exalted individuals? Forewarned in this way about the potential pitfalls facing the historian we can proceed to a closer examination of the various sources of information concerning Irish kings.

Three questions tend to be asked of all these kings: who were they, how were they chosen, and what kinds of powers did they have? Answers are not all that easy to come by. In some rare cases we can piece together sufficient information from various sources to enable a potted portrait of individual kings, though hardly to the point where we can honestly say that we know what their personalities were like. An example is Aéd Dub ('the Black') mac Suibni – whence the modern Irish surname MacSweeney – a Dál nAraidi

3. Interestingly, the earliest continental king-lists occur in the company of early royal law codes; see Beyerle 1947, described as 'the most systematic and large-scale exposition of Germanic custom that survives from any of the Germanic kingdoms, excluding only that of the Visigoths' by Wickham 1981, p. 36. The earliest Spanish Visigothic king-list (perhaps drawing on even older information) is also found in association with the law promulgated by king Reccesuinth: see Wallace–Hadrill 1971, p. 34. For general discussion, see Dumville 1979a, pp. 72–104.
4. See, e.g., Byrne 1973, p. 287, and Byrne 1984, p. 133.
5. Text and translation in Stokes and Strachan 1901–3, ii, p. 295.
6. Stokes and Strachan 1901–3, ii, p. xxxiv, suggested that he was perhaps the Aéd mac Dermato who is mentioned in the Annals of Ulster at AD714; but it is not stated to what part of Ireland he belonged.

over-king of Ulster who figures prominently in an episode of the *Vita Columbae* written *c*. AD700 by Adomnán, abbot of Iona († AD704). This Aéd – according to Columba's biographer – 'had often stained his hands in human blood and cruelly murdered many persons'.[7] Adomnán's ire was directed against him because he was responsible for the death of Diarmait mac Cerrbeoil, 'high-king' of Ireland, who was slain in AD565 and who also happened to be a close relative of Adomnán's. The biographer records a prophecy of Colum Cille's, that 'Aéd, unworthily ordained, will return like a dog to his vomit, and he will fall from wood into water, and die by drowning. He has deserved such an end much sooner, who has slaughtered the king of all Ireland'. The saintly prophecy is duly fulfilled, and Aéd meets his doom in the manner of Macbeth, a victim of the Threefold Death: *guin, bádud, loscad* wounding, drowning, and burning.[8] Aéd Dub mac Suibni does not figure in any genealogical tract, though his death is recorded in the annals at AD588 (but with no additional detail or comment about the manner of his end). Our knowledge of him, and the undoubtedly important role that he played in the political struggles of the mid-sixth century, is due almost entirely to this one episode in the *Vita Columbae*. Another salutary reminder of how precarious a hold we have even on the important events of the period.

REGNAL SUCCESSION

Much the same kind of difficulty arises in regard to the second of the three questions mentioned above: how were kings chosen? The question leads us into one of the contentious areas of early Irish history: the problem of regnal succession. It was the great Eoin Mac Neill who, over fifty years ago, first formulated the theory which he himself described as the Irish 'law' of dynastic succession.[9] In the intervening period some discussion has taken place on specifically linguistic aspects of the material, in particular those relating to the terminology of regnal succession. The most recent contribution to the debate is concerned mainly with a critique of the earlier literature,[10] so we must crave the indulgence of the reader while we tread gingerly once more across this minefield.

The three tenets of Mac Neill's 'law' were stated succinctly and concisely at the beginning of the chapter on dynastic succession in one of his best-known books, *Celtic Ireland*:

(1) In ancient Irish law, a person eligible to succeed to a kingship (*rígdomna*) must belong to the same *derbfine* as a king who has already reigned.
(2) The *derbfine* was a family of four generations, a man, his sons, grandsons, and great-grandsons.

7. Anderson 1961, pp. 278–82.
8. See Byrne 1973, pp. 97–101, and Radner 1983, pp. 180–200.
9. Mac Neill 1921, pp. 114–43.
10. Charles-Edwards 1993b, pp. 89–111.

(3) Among the persons thus lawfully eligible, the succession was determined by election.

The 'law' is nowhere explicitly stated as such in any early legal document, but was deduced by Mac Neill on the basis of an exhaustive analysis of the annalistic evidence, which, he said, 'covers all the instances found in the *Annals of Ulster* and in the *Annals of Tigernach* for the period preceding the landing of Henry II'.[11] However, we shall see that, in fact, not all the evidence is to be found in Mac Neill's lists, nor did he consider the earliest occurrence of the word *rígdomna* (lit. 'material of a king') which he must have encountered in the *Annals of Tigernach*. On the whole, however, Mac Neill's 'law' of dynastic succession was backed up by a formidable body of evidence. 'In the majority of instances in which the descent has been traced', he wrote, 'a *rígdomna* is son of a king. In a considerable number he is grandson. Instances of *rígdomna* third in succession from a king, but whose father and grandfather are not recorded to have reigned, are not rare, especially in the most important dynasties; and it may be remarked that by far the greater number of the instances belong to the greater dynasties, though these were few in number, so that the designation of *rígdomna* in the case of the numerous petty dynasties was unusual in the annals'.

On the basis of this evidence (which was restricted, it must be said, solely to the occurrence and usage of the term *rígdomna*) Mac Neill concluded that the title of *rígdomna* and the limits of eligibility might extend – in theory at least – to the great-grandsons of a king, that is, four generations including an ancestor who was king. Mac Neill then pointed out that this was the four-generation group which in Irish law is called the *derbfine*, the 'certain kin', the agnatic descendants of a common great-grandfather; in other words, all persons in the male line up to and including second cousins. It was this group which, in Irish law, determined the succession to personal property; they comprise the legal group of joint heirs. Mac Neill then further argued that by analogy with the general law of property, the right to the kingship rested in the *derbfine* of any and all previous holders of the office. In other words, every agnate whose paternal great-grandfather had once been king was himself theoretically entitled to succeed (or at least be considered for succession), even though his immediate predecessor might only have been his second cousin.[12] Not every such person was termed a *rígdomna*, however.[13] Mac Neill was careful (more careful than some of his commentators) to point out that, of all those qualified in theory, only a comparative few are actually called *rígdomnai* in the annals, and those only in the case of their death-notices. Side by side with the individuals so described there are countless instances of men who can be shown to have belonged to royal kindreds and whose descent from kings can be easily demonstrated, but who are not called *rígdomnai*. Furthermore, those that are

11. Mac Neill 1921, p. 116.
12. See Binchy 1970, pp. 25–6.
13. Ibid.

termed *rígdomnai* do not necessarily become kings. On the contrary, in all but a few instances – as Mac Neill pointed out – the term is applied to those who *never* became kings. His conclusion, therefore, was that there must have been a definite recognized limit to eligibility. After all, kingship – unlike property – was indivisible; only one man could become king at a time. But which one?

TÁNAISE RÍG – 'HEIR APPARENT'?

Here Mac Neill ran into his first serious problem. The solution that immediately springs to mind is what later English writers called 'tanistry', the *tánaise ríg* or 'heir apparent'. But Mac Neill stated categorically that the custom of 'tanistry' (preliminary election of a successor before the kingship became vacant) was nowhere in evidence until a time 'considerably later than the Feudal Invasion, and was no doubt a consequence of contact with the feudal regime'.[14] This was in spite of the fact that he had already encountered the term *tánaise ríg* in the early law tract called *Críth Gablach*, which he himself had translated, and which internal evidence dated to *c.* AD700.[15] But Mac Neill maintained that 'the more ancient usage was to decide the succession after it became vacant', adding that it was likely that English writers, finding an Irish custom of tanistry, supposed it to be the universal custom – 'a sort of fallacy common enough when the history of a nation or description of its customs is undertaken by foreigners'.[16] In fact, the real fallacy – one which should serve as a salutary warning to any historian – was Mac Neill's arbitrary dismissal of a vital piece of evidence which told against his theory.

But perhaps Mac Neill was right after all. He had pointed out the fact that the *rígdomna*, in the general run of things, did not become king. The *tánaise*, on the other hand, was certainly expected to succeed to the kingship and, so far as I can see from the evidence, he invariably did. In the law tract *Críth Gablach* the term *tánaise ríg* is explained in this way: 'The *tánaise ríg*, why is he so called? Because the whole tribe looks forward to him for the kingship without dispute'.[17] This can hardly be reconciled with the concept of

14. Mac Neill 1921, p. 115.
15. Binchy 1941. See also Mac Neill, 1923, pp. 265–300. The reason there given for the inadmissibility of the passage in question was 'The want of definite statement as to qualifications in wealth, etc.', which he thought 'may be due to this grade not being of tradition'. He also remarked that the term was found in no other list of grades. His statement in Mac Neill 1921, p. 142, that the title *tánaiste* 'does not appear before the thirteenth century' was countered by Binchy 1956, pp. 221–31 (p. 222), by reference to an entry in AU AD848; but there, interestingly enough, the term is used of a Viking, not an Irishman.
16. Mac Neill 1921, p. 116.
17. The translation is Mac Neill's own: Mac Neill 1921, p. 300. Irish text in Binchy 1941, p. 17 lines 434–5.

rígdomna, which is nowhere taken to imply that the person so called is *expected* to succeed. In fact, however, it can be demonstrated that the two terms – with two separate meanings – existed side-by-side in the early period, and there is a neat illustration of the point – not in an Irish text but a continental one, a collection of miracle stories attached to the *Vita* or biography of Vedastes, patron saint of Arras in France, written in the ninth century.[18] The author of the text remarks that there was an Irishman resident in the monastery for thirty years:

> If any doubting or untrusting person should wish to know how we came by all this, we may reply that a most noble person, by name of Echu, travelling alone, having abandoned his parents and his patrimony, undertook a pilgrimage [here]. For his father was born of royal stock, and was the *secundus post regem* [i.e. *tánaise*] among the nobles (*primordes*) of his kingdom (*prouincia*). Nor have we heard this from him [alone], who according as he was wealthy in possessions wished only to be humble and poor. No, we have heard this from all the people of Ireland, for even today a brother of this Echu holds the noble sceptre of Ireland. Echu, however, having lived most religiously in our midst for about thirty years, ended his life in Christ, and he himself often confirmed this miracle story for us.

The statement in the *Miracula* that the reigning king of Ireland at the time of writing was a *cognatus frater* of Echu's can only make sense in terms of the *derbfine* system of succession. That is not to say that other factors could not or would not have been involved in the determination of succession to the kingship. It is always necessary to recall the strictures of an eminent authority on the subject who wrote that 'some writers appear to give more weight to the dynasty's access to royal ancestors than to their control of more mundane resources, to be more interested in their marital transactions than in their military arrangements'.[19] But in matters such as these – particularly in the early medieval period when records are scarce – one good text is worth a ton of theory, and this text demonstrates, I think, the coexistence of both *derbfine*-type succession and the office of 'tanistry' (in its universal sense, not the restricted one posited by Mac Neill). The *secundus post regem* can be nothing other than the *tánaise ríg*; it is as precise a translation of the Irish as one could possibly wish for.

Furthermore, there is a striking parallel in the Life of Alfred the Great written – significantly enough – by a Welshman, Asser, at the end of the ninth century. On three occasions,[20] Asser uses the word *secundarius* to describe Alfred's position during the lifetime of his brother Ethelred, whom he succeeded in the kingship of Wessex. Stevenson, the editor, noted that this usage was 'otherwise unknown in English sources' and that 'it seems to mean viceroy or almost joint-king'. Binchy, however, suggested that this word *secundarius* was nothing more than a translation of the Welsh word *eil* (=

18. Holder-Egger 1887, pp. 399–402 (quotation, p. 400).
19. Goody 1966, p. 44.
20. Stevenson 1904, pp. 24, 29.

Irish *tánaise*) in the sense of 'heir apparent', and that Asser was simply interpreting this stage in Alfred's career in terms of a Celtic royal office with which he was familiar from his native Wales.[21] If it is accepted that the titles *rígdomna* and *tánaise (ríg)* were originally separate and distinct – with perhaps an additional term, *aiccid* (< *ad-cí/-aicci* ?) parallel to the Welsh usage, which also had three terms – we are still left with the problem of establishing when these terms first came into use and what their original meaning was in the earlier (as distinct from the later) medieval period. It is quite remarkable, when reading through Mac Neill's extensive lists, to note how relatively late the terms *rígdomna* and *tánaise* are actually found in the annals. Mac Neill himself remarked that 'no instance of the term *rígdomna* has been found earlier than AD867, but from that date onward the term appears with great frequency in the annals; there are eleven instances in the period 867–900'. An explanation immediately suggested itself: 'Before this time a Norse kingdom had been established in Dublin, and Norse rulers had been set up in the Isle of Man and the Hebrides. In these early Norse communities lawful succession to the princedom appears to have been in general from father to son, and probably to the firstborn son . . . Possibly the contrast of this law or custom caused the Irish chroniclers to give express recognition to the potential right of succession in Irish dynasties'.[22]

It is a remarkable coincidence in the circumstances – though not one remarked on by Mac Neill – that the earliest annalistic reference to a *tánaise* relates in fact to a Viking leader, Tomrair Erell (jarl), killed at the battle of Sciath Nechtain in AD848, who is described as *tánaise ríg Laithlinne*. It is an even more remarkable coincidence that the earliest annalistic reference to a *rígdomna* occurs in a description of an Anglo-Saxon prince, not an Irish one. The text in the annals of Tigernach AD628 reports the battle of Fid Eoin, where one of the slain was a certain 'Oisiricc mac Albruit rígdomna Saxan'.[23] A good case has been made for accepting this annal as authentic[24] and it therefore raises the question: did Anglo-Saxon *ætheling* precede Old Irish *rígdomna*, and might it have suggested the concept to the Irish?[25] The evidence as it stands, unfortunately, does not allow a categorical answer to this question.

21. Binchy 1956, p. 224. It should be pointed out, however, that Binchy subsequently modified this suggestion in Binchy 1970, pp. 29–30, where he proposed to see influence from the Anglo-Saxon *ætheling*. This revised interpretation has not met with the approval of Dumville 1979b, pp. 1–33.

22. Mac Neill 1921, p. 117. I intend to publish a paper on the *aiccid* elsewhere.

23. Stokes 1896, pp. 199–263 180–1. See Moisl 1983, pp. 103–26; 105 ff.

24. Moisl's discussion supersedes that in Dumville, 'The ætheling', pp. 2–3 n. 5.

25. According to Dumville, 'The ætheling', p. 2 n. 5, 'It is plain that *rígdomna* in this annal renders OE *ætheling*', but there is no other instance of the OE word in Anglo-Saxon sources at so early a date (if his own paper can be taken as providing the full dossier of evidence).

PROCEDURES FOR SELECTING KINGS

Whatever the precise interpretation of the technical terms – which may, of course, have acquired different shades of meaning with the passage of time – the early Irish law tracts are explicit at several points about the procedure for selecting a king. The old law tract *Cóic Conairi Fuigill* ('The Five Paths of Judgement') states that any would-be king must be the son of a king (*mac flatha*) and the grandson of a king. A man whose father ruled before him, but not his grandfather, is called a *flaith medónach* 'a middle-ranking king'.[26] The candidate must also be of good legal standing (*innraic*), be not guilty of theft, and be physically unblemished; he must also be a man of property (*ní bi rí rí cen fola*). The tract follows with a detailed exposition of the number of free and unfree clients the king controls. In effect, the requirements are those specified in relation to the headship (*toísigecht*) of the kindred: the man to be chosen should be son of a principal wife (*cétmuinter*), if possible; if not, then the son of a legitimate second wife; and if not that, then the son of a concubine. Failing all these, the qualification is extended further down the list of female partners.[27] In normal circumstances the eldest son would expect to succeed (or at least have first right of refusal, as he would in the case of land inheritance). On occasions, however – according to legend, at any rate – the youngest could succeed to the *flaithemnas*. If the brothers were of the same age, then they chose by lot (*masa comaes comaith iat, is crannchor aturra uman rígi*).[28]

Once elected the new *flaith* had a portion of the land in the kingdom (*cumal senorba* 'portion of seniority') made over to him. This is additional land, over and above the king's ordinary possessions, which enabled him to carry out certain functions specific to his title, and was made over from the land of the various *gelfines*. In the king's case this meant that he had land for the support and maintenance of individuals who functioned as royal officials.[29]

Fergus Kelly has drawn attention to an interesting passage in the tract known as *Lawes of Ireland*, an early seventeenth-century English account of Irish law, much of which (as he remarks)[30] could equally apply to the seventh or eighth century:

> The chief lord [equivalent to the *rí* 'king' of the Old Irish law texts] had certain landes in demesne which were called his *loughty* [equivalent to *lucht tige* 'household'] or mensall landes wherein hee placed his principall officers, namely his brehon, his marshall, his cupbearer, his phisicion, his surgeon, his chronicler,

26. Qualification: Thurneysen 1926, p. 43 (*CCF* §67).
27. Thurneysen 1926, p. 44 (*CCF* §71).
28. Thurneysen 1925, p. 317 (*Gúbretha Caratniat* §10).
29. See Plummer 1928, pp. 113–14.
30. Kelly 1988, p. 241.

his rimer, and others which offices and professions were hereditary and peculiar to certen septs and families.[31]

The vernacular law texts mention several of these officials: professional jester (*drúth*), sometimes Latinized as *preco*, who is obviously the mimer of the English account; oath-helper (*ara*); keeper of the hounds (*arrchogad*); look-out (*dercaid*); dispenser of drink (*dáilem*), also called cupbearer (*deogbaire*); steward (*rechtaire*); and messenger (*techtaire*).[32] Others mentioned in non-legal sources are the troops or guards (*cliathairi*), and attendants (*fognamthaidi*).[33] This list compares favourably with similar lists of officers at the court of the Merovingian kings of Francia, where mention of the master of the cupbearers (*magister pincernarum*) and the ushers (*ostiarii*) bears out the impression that the Irish lists are not necessarily fanciful.[34] Clearly the maintenance of any number of officials would impose an unbearable burden on the king's personal clients – though the law does grant a king the right to billet a newly-created alien (*deórad*, perhaps a man who has been renounced by his family for some grievous wrongdoing) on any of his clients. But this is no more than the general principle, found everywhere in the medieval world, whereby a stranger is protected by the king. The 'Five Paths of Judgement', besides stipulating the king's title by birth, also states that he must be the owner of three estates (*cundtairsmi*), each of which must have stock of twenty cows and as many sheep, in order to support the king and his retinue while on circuit.[35] These are clearly nothing like the vast royal estates of the Merovingian kings but they do imply nonetheless that an Irish king would be expected to be able to draw on larger resources than the average well-to-do farmer. There is a suggestion also, in the Life of Crónán of Roscrea (Co. Tipperary) that the king was entitled to treasure-trove: the finders of gold regalia (*malum aureum cum duobus cathenis aureis ex se pendentibus*) tried to conceal their discovery from the king, who was deemed to be the rightful owner. But this is not the normal case with treasure-trove in Irish law, which in fact is usually deemed to be either in whole or in part the property of the finder; the king has no rights whatever in such finds.[36]

THE KING'S HOUSE

The king's house is not normally of such grandeur as to distinguish it from those of ordinary mortals. The early tract on the privileges of poets describes the attributes of a typical house: 'I pray for a house roofed, sheltered, shining,

31. Kelly 1988, p. 101 n. 10.
32. Gwynn 1942, p. 23.
33. O'Brien 1962, pp. 25, 49.
34. See Conrat (Cohn) 1908, pp. 239–60 (p. 248–50), and Ganshof 1968, pp. 18–19.
35. Thurneysen 1926, pp. 69–70 (CCF §25).
36. Plummer 1910, ii, p. 30 (*Vita Cronani* §27); cf. Mac Niocaill 1971, pp. 103–10.

well-kept, that shall not be a house for hounds or beasts: a house wherein is honour and welcome. I pray for an abode lofty, rush-strewn, wherein is down fittingly spread'.[37] This is followed by a description of 'a house with a mead-hall' (*tech midchuarta*), apparently synonymous with a king's house:

I wish for a house with a mead-hall,
a song of welcome with honeyed words:
firm and ample its rough-edged ambit,
smooth the beams of its thresholds,
symmetrical its two doorposts
lofty and conspicuous in front of the lintel,
brilliant its light
solid and white its door-valve,
smooth-shaven the spits of its bolts,
well-jointed its high-seat.
  I desire to go into a house, to a king,
  to know him in very truth;
  from house into house I step upon the ground,
  nor shall a great mead-hall be withheld from me.[38]

The most famous royal residence of legend, at Tara, is described in detail in a poem which depicts the king and his entourage of chief poet (*ollam filed*), scholar (*suí*), hospitaller (*briugaid*), doctor (*liaig*), dispenser (*dáilem*), smith (*goba*), steward (*rechtaire*), cook (*randaire*), engraver (*rindaide*), rath- or fort-builder (*ráthbaige*), shield-maker (*sciathaire*) and soldier (*fianaide*), and several more. But the only detail which might be said to imply a more refined comfort for kings is the statement that these royal officials are seated on 'couches that do not burn' (*leptha ná loiscthi lochit*), presumably regular wooden couches, rather than the mere strewn straw which served for the ordinary householder described in the previous text, and which was more prone to damage by fire.[39]

A witty satirist pokes fun at a king whose declining fortunes were obvious in the condition of his house: 'It was no wonder in Crundmaél's slender-wattled house to get salt on bread without butter: it is evident that the flesh of his family has shrunk like the bark on a tree'.[40] The mundane aspects of even a royal household can be nicely illustrated at times: a certain Connaught king who crossed swords with St Finnian of Clonard was struck paralytic when he went outside his royal fort or *dún* to answer the call of nature; only a timely repentance freed him from his embarrassing plight.[41] Elsewhere, in a law text, it is assumed that a *tech coitchenn* or privy was normal. Evidence from the excavations carried out at the Wood Quay/Winetavern Street site of the later Viking settlement at Dublin

37. Gwynn 1942, p. 229 (§40).
38. Text and translation in Meyer 1917, pp. 23–4.
39. Text and translation in Gwynn 1903, pp. 24–5.
40. Meyer 1917, p. 42.
41. Heist 1965, p. 105 (*Vita Finniani* §30).

uncovered a latrine pit which contained residues of various mosses. This would suggest that the more modern resort to sphagnum moss as a cure for nappy rash had a medieval precedent; the moss acts as a neutralizing agent of the acidic chemicals in urine.[42] The sanitation technique was probably not a Viking innovation.

But what were these houses fit for kings? What distinctions – if any – were there between royal residences and ordinary domestic households? How can the modern student identify a royal residential site? The fact is, it is almost impossible to do so.[43] Reference above to the unfortunate Crundmaél's 'slender-wattled house' provides a neat literary parallel for the remarkable house structures uncovered during the archaeological excavations at Deer Park Farms, Glenarm (Co. Antrim) during the 1980s.[44] The site was a raised rath or mound, which the local farmer insisted on bulldozing out of existence, but not before a rescue dig had unearthed a remarkable sequence of settlements denoting continuous occupation at the site from the sixth century down to the tenth. The remains of more than thirty circular dwellings were found at various levels, three or four of which may have stood at any one time. These houses were constructed by means of double- or cavity-walled wicker weavings, the space between the double walls being filled with a mixture of straw, moss, heather, and other organic material. All the houses at Glenarm were double-walled, and in one case a complete door-frame was also found which dendrochronological analysis dated to the year AD648.

Attempts have been made in the past to correlate the literary evidence for house structures with sporadic archaeological finds from various different sites, usually of different dates. There is an astonishing coincidence of archaeological and documentary evidence in the case of the Deer Park Farms houses, as Chris Lynn, director of the dig, has pointed out.[45] He drew attention to the fact that the law tract called *Críth Gablach*, which deals with status and which is usually dated to *c*. AD700, and is therefore roughly contemporary with the date of the early Deer Park settlement, provides a picture of a carefully graded hierarchy of society in which the status of different grades within that hierarchy is represented, among other things, by the size and layout of individual houses. The waterlogged state of the lowest levels at Glenarm meant that it was possible – uniquely for a dry-land site – to uncover the remains of buildings in a remarkably well-preserved condition,

42. Mitchell 1987; see the letter by Seán Ó Ríordáin, *Irish Times*, 9 January 1988. That the circumstances were no different in Carolingian Francia is clear from one of the incidents in Notker the Stammerer's Life of Charlemagne; Thorpe 1969, pp. 128–30: Liutfrid, steward of the palace, 'went out to the lavatory in good health. He was there longer than was necessary, and when we came to look for him we found that he was dead'. Liutfrid's end was, of course, a cautionary tale.

43. See Warner 1988, pp. 47–68, for some very sensible remarks on this subject.

44. Hamlin & Lynn 1988, pp. 44–7.

45. In an unpublished talk given to the 5th Conference of Irish Medievalists, Maynooth 1990.

while the associated organic rubbish or midden layers retained extraordinary quantities of environmental evidence, all of which could be correlated with the documentary evidence from the law text.

ORDINARY HOUSES

For example, *Críth Gablach* describes the house and property of the average 'strong' farmer (*mruigfer*), the highest grade of landowner below the rank of aristocracy whose possessions are itemized in minute detail and whose quantity of stock (20 cattle, 20 sheep, 2 bulls and 6 oxen) is comparable to that which the earlier law tract referred to above stipulated as the proper stock for a king's residence (*cundtairisem*):

> The size of his house: it is larger than a house of rentcharge; for the size of the latter is 17 [metres, in diameter]. It is of wickerwork to the lintel. From this to the roof-tree, a *dit* between every two weavings. Two door ways in it. A door for one of them, a hurdle for the other, and this [hurdle] without [projecting] wattles, without protruberances. A bare fence of boards around it. An oaken plank between every two beds.[46]

This describes exactly the type of house uncovered at Glenarm, down to the minutest detail. The basketry construction of the wattle walls, woven in spiralling sets, formed a solid interlocking weave all around, with the sharp ends of the wattles all facing into the cavity space, leaving the outer- and innermost faces of the interior and exterior walls perfectly smooth. This was no mere finesse: elsewhere in the laws it is stated that injuries caused by the sharp ends of protruding wattles shall be actionable; hence the statement in *Críth Gablach* that the house 'shall be without projecting wattles and without protruberances'. The surviving door-jamb has a mortised groove down one side into which was slotted the wattle wall, the lintel in turn being attached to the two uprights by means of pegged mortise-and-tenon joints.

Chris Lynn has argued against proponents of the 'big house' theory who believe that the houses built for kings must have been considerably larger than the Glenarm type, more like the palatial residences or halls of contemporary Anglo-Saxon or Frankish kings. He points out, however, that in the one excavated and apparently undisputed royal Irish site of our period, the crannóg at Lagore (Co. Meath), the houses were in fact small circular wicker structures of less than ten metres in diameter. A more recent discovery, the house found at Moynagh Lough crannóg (Co. Meath) – though admittedly not a royal site, being apparently a craft centre – also measures ten metres in diameter.[47] Lynn has also pointed out that the mention in the laws of cartloads of wattles or loads of rushes as appropriate fines for damaging parts of a king's house further supports his view that the houses built for

46. Mac Neill 1921, pp. 287–8 (§79).
47. Bradley 1991, pp. 5–26.

kings were little different from those of the lower grades in society.[48] The only obvious contrast might have been in the number of houses on the site, or in the occasional construction of an outer wall or revetment around the outer bank of the rath, giving the mound an impressive appearance of a stone cashel or stone-walled fort. Lynn has made the very plausible suggestion that labour on the construction of such a wall would correspond very neatly to the duty of *drécht giallnai* described in the laws as labour due from a client to his lord. This detail apart, however, there is little or no evidence to suggest that kings lived in the grandeur of latter-day potentates.

KINGS' PROTECTION

Within a king's household protection was offered against violence, called by the law texts 'a place of non-wounding' (*maigen dígona*). Where such a breach of protection occurred (*sárugud*), the perpetrator was liable for the honour-price of the protector as well as for any penalty arising from injury to the victim. The ecclesiastical equivalent of this was called *termann* (Latin *terminus*), but the rights of sanctuary in a king's house undoubtedly predate the influence of Christianity.[49] *Sárugud*, particularly in a king's principal fort (*prímdún*) usually involved assaults on the king himself, or on individuals who were being harboured from assassination or vendetta. The genealogies record that an early Uí Bairrche dynast of Leinster, Rotha mac Oéngusa, was murdered by an otherwise unidentified assailant in spite of protection from Cormac mac Diarmata, who was without doubt one of the most powerful political figures of his time, the second half of the sixth century.[50] Another early Leinster dynast, Cuilenn of the Uí Labrada, slew an Uí Néill man Ciar Cúldub, who was apparently under royal protection ('it was *díguin* of the king' *ba díguin dond ríg*).[51] Interestingly enough, the text goes on to say that Cuilenn was dispossessed of his lands as a result, and these were forfeit to the king. Cuilenn, however, was granted land in recompense by Énda Cennselach, ancestor of the Uí Cennselaig who later came to dominate south Leinster, and this strongly suggests that it was the latter who put up Cuilenn to the murder in the first place.[52]

Both the annals and the genealogies record the slaying of Fianamail mac Maéle-Tuile, an Uí Cellaig king of Leinster, murdered by a household servant (*famulus suus*) at the instigation (*suadente*) of Fínsnechta Fledach mac Dúnchada, king of the Síl nAédo Sláne branch of the southern Uí Néill and

---

48. The problems associated with the house at Lissue (Co. Antrim) have not, to my mind, been satisfactorily resolved; see Bersu 1947, pp. 30–58.
49. For a discussion of ecclesiastical sanctuary, see Doherty 1985, pp. 55–63.
50. O'Brien 1962, p. 52 ('di muin Chormaic ind ríg').
51. Perhaps the text should be corrected to read *Cian* Cúldub, of the Fotharta, another Leinster tribe and perhaps a more likely victim of rising Uí Bairrche ambitions than a distant Uí Néill rival.
52. O'Brien 1962, pp. 31–2.

termed by this text king of Tara (*rege Temoriae*). The assassination was the occasion of a wry poetic composition:

> When Fínsnechta summoned to him all his close relatives, had he been wary of Fochsechán, the son of Maél-Tuile would have been alive.
>
> *In tan con-gair Fínsnechta cucai a choému huile,*
> *affo-menad Fochsechán bid beó mac Maéle-Tuile.*[53]

Fínsnechta was himself assassinated by his rivals, the Fir Chúl of Brega, in AD695. Fianamail's grandfather, Rónán mac Aédo, was ancestor of the Uí Cellaig Cualann who ruled east Leinster in the seventh and eighth centuries. An uncle of his, Tocca mac Aédo, is described as *rex Cualann* in a misplaced obit in the Annals of Ulster (*s.a.* AD477, *rectius* AD645?). Rónán himself, though described by the genealogists as a bishop, was not above murdering his own brother Crimthann, and the death of his son Maél Fothartaig at his hands – another example of *fingal* or 'kinslaying' – became the stuff of legend under the title *Fingal Rónáin*.[54] The vicious struggle for power between the Uí Cellaig Cualann and the Uí Cennselaig even saw the involvement of British mercenaries on the side of the former (according to the annals, AD709).

The king's rights and duties in the legal domain are the subject of some debate. A very old legal text states that 'it is obligatory that a king should have a judge, or that he be a judge himself'.[55] Mac Neill translated the maxim slightly differently ('even though he be himself a judge'), arguing that it implied 'not that a king might be a judge, for the judicial office belonged to every king, but that the king, even if he were himself an expert jurist, ought to have a professional assessor in his court'. It is very likely that in Ireland, as elsewhere, the earliest kings were also dispensers of justice, but by the historical period this function had become almost the sole prerogative of the 'judgment makers' (*brithemain*).[56] This was apparently the position already in St Patrick's time. Hence Binchy interpreted the legal maxim to mean that in every *tuath* the king must have an 'official' judge – 'except in the unlikely event of his being himself learned in the law'.[57] The exception, as Binchy pointed out, was doubtless due to the traditions about certain mythological kings, such as Cormac mac Airt, who are depicted as interpreters of the law and even (as in Cormac's case) credited with the composition of quasi-legal tracts. Indeed, Binchy has described Cormac as the Numa Pompilius of Irish law, and the attribution to him of the gnomic sayings known as *Tecosca Cormaic* ('The instructions of Cormac')[58] is merely an extension or variation

---

53. O'Brien 1962, p. 77; see Radner 1978, pp. 40–1, whose translation differs from mine.
54. See Greene 1955.
55. For what follows, see especially Binchy 1971, pp. 152–68; Mac Neill, 1923, p. 307; Meyer 1917, p. 31; Byrne 1982, pp. 167–9.
56. Binchy 1970, p. 15ff.
57. Binchy 1971, p. 152.
58. Meyer 1909.

of the age-old theme of royal wisdom which is one of the characteristics of the tales known collectively as 'The Cycles of the Kings'.[59] Whether or not any of these traditions reflect a genuine pattern of royal concern with the finer points of the law is difficult to decide, but one scholar – while not denying the possibility – has made the valid point that 'the mediaeval authors who rehandled the native stuff were men of scholarly training, versed especially in Biblical and patristic learning; and it is as well to allow for the influence of their literary studies; their erudition and their patriotism alike tempted them to discover and underline points of resemblance between the culture and history of primitive Ireland and the elder civilizations of Rome and Palestine'.[60]

KINGS' TRUTH

Essential to the king's quasi-judicial status was his 'truth' (*fír, fír flathemon* 'king's truth'). Literature and law texts alike constantly stress the importance of the king's *fír*: if the king is just, his reign will be peaceful and prosperous; whereas if he is guilty of injustice, the natural elements will rise up against him. The seventh-century Hiberno-Latin composition called *De duodecim abusiuis* ('On the twelve abuses')[61] has two sections devoted to kings, the 'lord without virtue' (*dominus sine uirtute*) and 'the unjust king' (*rex iniquus*). The king's truth makes him a force for peace in the kingdom (*pax populorum*), but besides such commonplace notions (possibly derived from the Bible) there are other more elemental boons to be enjoyed by virtue of his good reign: modest climate (*temperies aeris*), calm seas (*serenitas maris*), fruitfulness of the soil (*terrae fecunditas*). But as one commentator has aptly remarked, fundamentally the picture presented in this text is not really Christian at all. 'The writer sees his king as the embodiment of his people's luck and prosperity, not as the holder of a Christian office'.[62] This is an entirely pagan, sacral concept of kingship bound up with fate and taboo, luck and disaster, which continued into the later middle ages, and which modern readers are most familiar with in the Shakespearean play *Macbeth*.[63] The initiation of a king (inauguration is hardly the appropriate term) symbolizes his marriage with the tribal goddess (*banfeis* lit. 'sleeping with a woman'), as it must have done in the centuries before Christianity. Later clerical propagandists tried their best to dust over this older aura by claiming that the good fortune and propitiousness of their kings were inseparable from and guaranteed by the prayers and actions of Christian saints, both living and dead. But the true position is clearly to be seen, and it is no accident that the oldest of the 'Mirror of Princes' type of text represented by the *De duodecim*

59. See Dillon 1946.
60. Gwynn 1903, p. 74; cf. O'Rahilly 1946, p. 284 ff.
61. Hellmann 1909.
62. Wallace-Hadrill 1971, p. 57.
63. See Dillon 1951, pp. 1–36.

abusiuis is in fact a vernacular composition, the 'Testament of Morand' (*Audacht Moraind*),[64] and scholars are agreed that the Hiberno-Latin text took over a great deal of its thinking from the older concepts embodied in the *Audacht*. For its part, the *De duodecim abusiuis* was the model for a great many later Latin compositions on the continent, and it has been claimed – without undue exaggeration, it may be said – that 'the unknown Irish author made a real contribution to the development of European political theory'.[65]

In the realm of jurisprudence (as distinct from moral behaviour) the king's truth had importance as well: his testimony overruled all other testimonies (*do-fuaslaici fír forurchon*) and intervention by the king overruled trial by combat and legal procedure generally.[66] In this sense the king is sometimes called a 'lord of judgment' (*flaith airechta*)[67] whose arrival demands immediate hospitality and therefore the suspension of any legal procedure, even if two individuals are on the point of settling matters with the sword. The implication of the text is that the trial by combat is suspended and the king will adjudicate the matter in dispute between the two parties. It is equally understood, of course, that failure by either party to put in an appearance on such an occasion would render him subject to severe penalty. The further implication appears to be that the king's verdict will be final. It is also understood that the king employs legal officers who act as intermediaries between disputants and the king himself. For example, judgments in Irish law are, strictly speaking, recommendations for resolution of a problem; they are not binding in the way that judgments in our modern courts are, so that any legal judgment passed down by a *brithem* which is not accepted by the disputing parties may be referred by them to one of the king's officers, the *muire*, who in turn takes it to the king. This *muire* or *muire rechtgi* is the marshall referred to in the sixteenth-century English account preserved in 'Lawes of Ireland'. In the normal course of events, the king's subjects may not appear before him to request adjudication; they must first refer to the *muire*, who brings them to the king (*muire rechtgi doda-fet a tegh ríg*). So common was the office in early Irish society that the word denoting it became a common name, Muiredach.

RECHTGE, CÁIN AND ROYAL LAW

The word *rechtge* normally denotes a special ordinance or legal enactment promulgated by the king only in peculiar circumstances, such as war or famine. The evidence of the law texts, however, suggests that the *muire rechtgi* had wider functions as a law officer, different from those of the steward (*rechtaire*), who seems to have presided over the king's property (for

64. Kelly 1976a.
65. Kenney 1929, p. 282. See Anton 1982, pp. 568–617 (with full bibliography).
66. King's testimony: Thurneysen 1928, p. 30 (§80). Ordeal: Thurneysen 1927, p. 222.
67. Thurneysen 1925, p. 333 (*Gúbretha Caratniat*).

example, the administration of his three estates or *cundtairismi*). The *muire* had his own land, *methas*, and could, on certain occasions, act as a warband leader. The *muire* and other royal officials, by virtue of their proximity to the king, appear to have been exempt from legal action arising from any violence caused in the performance of their duties. In some circumstances the king too was immune from prosecution, and could not be held accountable before the law in the normal way. This did not imply, however, that he was above the law. On the contrary, Irish law had devised an ingenious stratagem which allowed a neat balance between maintenance of the king's honour and his accountability before the law. For purposes of legal redress an aggrieved citizen could institute special proceedings against the king, in which case the king was represented by a 'substitute churl' (*aithech fortha*). This was a man of lowly rank dependent on the king and has been aptly described as 'a kind of legal whipping-boy'.[68] In the event of alleged wrong-doing by the king, the plaintiff distrained or impounded some of the property of the *aithech fortha*. By this ingenious means the legal claim could be made against the king without impugning his honour (and thereby rendering him unfit for office). If no *aithech fortha* was available, then 'a churl from the members of his kindred [answers] for his liability, and the whole kindred joins him in levying his indemnity, for it is part of the law of the kindred that each member shall enforce along with the other'.[69]

Binchy has pointed out that the *aithech fortha* was a very ancient institution and represents the earliest attempts to make the state – in the person of the king – amenable to legal proceedings. Failing all other remedy the other, more drastic, alternative was to undertake a ritual hunger-strike against him.[70] In that case, the plaintiff was obliged to give prior notice to the king of his intention to proceed against him in this way. He then fasted against him and impounded the king's calves by locking them away from their mothers. The cattle could not be released until the king undertook to settle whatever matter was in dispute between them. The procedure was probably more a ritual than a serious hunger-strike, but our more recent history suggests that it would be a mistake all the same to underestimate its seriousness, and the consequences for the king if in fact he refused to settle.

The *muire rechtgi* appears to have functioned in regard to royal ordinances relating to traditional or customary law (*rechtge fénechais*), rather than the usual *rechtge*, which involved only emergency action. In the case of the *rechtge fénechais* the *tuath* apparently elected to change the customary law and the king undertook to implement that change.[71] This seems to imply that the initiative for such an ordinance came from the people 'who choose' (*it tuatha dode-gúiset*) presumably at the annual assembly of the kingdom known as the *oénach* (Modern Irish *aonach* 'fair'). The king confirmed such a decision by taking pledges from the various kindred groups for its

68. Binchy 1973b, p. 84; cf. Kelly 1988, pp. 25–6.
69. Binchy 1973b, pp. 80–1, 84–5.
70. Kelly 1988, pp. 25–6.
71. Kelly 1988, pp. 21–2.

observance. The tract on status known as *Críth Gablach* (*c.* AD700), perhaps reflecting a slightly later stage in the evolution of the law, states that

> There are four kinds of *rechtgi* to which a king binds his *tuath* by pledge: What are they? *Rechtge fénechais* in the first place. It is the *tuath* that adopt it, it is the king who binds it. The three other kinds of *rechtge*, it is the king [alone] who enforces them: *rechtge* after defeat in battle, that he may unite his *tuatha* thereafter so that they may not destroy each other; *rechtge* after a plague; and *rechtge* of kings, as the *rechtge* of the king of Cashel applies in Munster [over other kings]. For there are three *rechtgi* which it is proper for a king to bind his *tuatha* to with a pledge: *rechtge* for the expulsion of an invading kindred [*echtarchenél*], i.e. against the Saxons [i.e. Anglo-Saxons]; *rechtge* for agricultural labour (?), and a *rechtge* of religion, such as the Law of Adomnán.[72]

Here the text uses the term *rechtge* to denote ecclesiastical as well as secular law. The usual practice, in fact, is to refer to such an ecclesiastical enactment as a *cáin* (Modern Irish *cáin* 'tax'), which is rendered *lex* in Latin sources – whence Adomnán's code is in fact termed *Lex Innocentium* in the annals of Ulster on the occasion of its promulgation in AD697. The laws list various *cána*: *Cáin Adomnáin* associated with Adomnán of Iona, *Cáin Pátraic* associated with Patrick (and by implication Armagh), *Cáin Diarmata* associated with Diarmait of Killeshin (Co. Leix), and *Cáin Bóshlechta*, which is not associated with a particular saint or monastery but whose co-author, Aduar mac Echind, is named in the annals at AD810; he was of the Osraige.[73] In various literary texts and their accompanying commentaries and glosses there is reference also to other such enactments, particularly the 'Four *cána* of Ireland': *Cáin Pátraic* 'not to kill clerics', *Cáin Adomnáin* 'not to kill women', *Cáin Dair Í Chaillech* 'not to steal cattle', and *Cáin Domnaig* 'not to transgress the sabbath'.[74] The annals occasionally refer to other *cána*: *Lex nepotis aui Suanaig*: AD743, 748; *Lex Ciaráin filii artificis* [= Ciarán of Clonmacnois]: AD744, 788; *Lex Brendain* [perhaps B. of Clonfert]: AD744; *Lex Coluim (Columbae) Cille*: AD778; *Lex Commáin* [= Commán of Roscommon]: AD772, 780, 793; and *Lex Ailbi* [of Emly]: AD793. It is evident that by the latter years of the eighth century every important monastery had promulgated its own *cáin*, with at least a part, if not all, of the proceeds arising from fines accruing to the churches concerned. By this time also the promulgation of such *cána*, or their renewal, seems often to have been marked by the public display of relics and, on occasion, by a formal circuit (*cuairt*) of Ireland or of one or more provinces,

---

72. Binchy 1941, pp. 20–1 (§38); Mac Neill 1923, p. 303. Note that I take the *adannai* of the text, translated by Binchy 'kindles, illuminates', as an intrusive gloss [= Adamnái*n*, with suspension of final -*n*] anticipating (perhaps suggesting) the *recht Adamnáin* of the text.

73. O'Brien 1962, p. 105.

74. Thurneysen 1930, pp. 385–95; Petrie 1837, p. 174; Stokes & Strachan 1901–3, ii, p. 306; Stokes 1905, p. 211; Ó Riain 1990, pp. 561–6.

with a view to exacting a payment or tax on behalf of the patron saint.[75] The practice of the Roman Catholic Church in declaring Marian or Holy Years and the like, without any historical justification, is a close modern parallel.

But *cáin* probably originally denoted any regulation of the law, such as, for example, *cáin aicillne* 'the law of base clientship', later however with particular reference to an ordinance: the difference is that between enacted law and customary law. Hence the frequency with which proclamation of *cána* is marked in the annals by mention of the kings who were responsible for their enactment. The law refers to the king's duties in the *tuath* (*córus fri tuaith*), stipulating that his powers be invoked only in the case of emergency, or if a whale were washed ashore. This latter provision is not at all as fanciful as it may appear. Whales' teeth were highly prized, and there is a note added to the Annals of Ulster at AD753 which reads as follows: A whale was cast ashore in Bairche [= Co. Down] in the time of Fiachnae mac Aéda Róin, king of Ulster. It had three gold teeth in its head, each containing fifty ounces. And one of them was placed on the altar of Bangor in this year, i.e. AD753.[76]

The laws also state that the king is responsible for protecting outsiders who happen to be visiting the kingdom; specific reference is made to merchants (*cendaige*) and the fact that their personal safety is guaranteed by a *cáin*.[77] The law embodies the important principle – doubtless originally the sole prerogative of the king, but subsequently broadened to include every freeman – that the king protects individuals and guarantees their passage through the kingdom unharmed (*snádud*).[78] A natural extension of this function was the administration of a penalty for breaches of such protection. Here the church made an important contribution, urging kings to throw off the milder sanctions of the older law and resort instead to violent means. Anyone who absolved a criminal was, according to the church, to be treated as a criminal himself. The author of an Old Irish poem refers pointedly to the fact that this procedure differed from the earlier practice in Irish law, which worked on the principle that so-called capital offences, such as homicide, could be expiated by the payment of wergild (*éraic*). The remarkable thing about *éraic*, in fact, was that it comprised the same fixed monetary amount (termed *corpdíre*) no matter what the rank of the victim.[79] Our poet, however, was well aware that the new dispensation – which advocated hanging for crimes like homicide or murder – was the doing of those learned in book-law, i.e. the Bible:

I have heard from one who reads books [that] he who absolves a wrongdoer is himself a wrongdoer.

Ro-chuala
la nech légas libru:

75. Kelly 1988, p. 22.
76. For other early references to whales and whaling in Ireland, see Fairley 1981.
77. Thurneysen 1927, p. 195 n. 1; but cf. Kelly 1988, p. 7.
78. Kelly 1988, pp. 140–1.
79. Thurneysen 1925, p. 65 (*CCF* §15); Kelly 1988, pp. 125–31.

int í ances in mbidbaid
iss é fessin as bidbu.[80]

The reference to books is a subtle allusion to the clerical provenance of this new, written law, the *recht littre*, by contrast with the older, unwritten 'natural law' (*recht aicnid*). In one law text a brave defence is made of the older regime: 'the natural law reaches further than the written law' (*ar ro-siacht recht aicnid mar nad roacht recht litri*).[81] The tide was running against such enlightened opinions, however, as the poet made abundantly clear in the rest of his composition:

Moénach of Cashel [† AD662] is a just king, by whom evil people are killed. Munster is at peace through him; may God be good to the good king!

The evil folk have desisted since their fellows have been killed; a blessing upon the king who has hanged them!; they counted their chickens before they were hatched.

Moénach Caisil comdas rí
lasa marbtar drochdoíni.
Atá Mumu lais i ssíd
rop maith Día don dagríg.
Ro-ansat na drochdoíni
ó ro-marbtha a céili;
bendacht for ríg roda-croch,
ba moch canait a séiri.

Clerical enthusiasm for capital punishment is already clearly evident in the eighth century: the Annals of Ulster for AD746 record the violation (*sárugud*) of Domnach Phátraic (or was this a reliquary shrine?), which resulted in six hostages being hanged (*cruciati*). There are numerous later examples also in the annals: in 1030 a certain Gilla Comgáin was handed over to the community of Clonmacnois to be hanged for stealing the monastic treasures. His fate was hardly in question, given that the good monks on another occasion wanted to hang a man for sheep stealing.[82] Doubtless the same treatment would have been meted out to the miscreant who stole the Book of Kells from the sacristy of that church in AD1007, stripping it of its priceless cover and burying it under a sod, where it was found again after eighty days. Another text refers sombrely to the student (*mac légind*) of Monasterboice who, sometime in the late eleventh century, made off with the manuscript known as the Brief Book of Monasterboice, and was never seen again, nor the book either.[83]

Eighth-century Irish lawyers, under strong clerical pressure, tried to have

80. Text and translation in Meyer 1917, pp. 17–18.
81. Meyer 1917, p. 39 = *ALI*, i, p. 16.
82. There is an instructive and amusing account of the hapless Gilla Comgáin's attempts to evade the law in the Annals of Tigernach, *s.a.* 1130.
83. See Best and Bergin 1929, p. 94.

the best of both worlds: a law text, *Uraicecht Becc*, states that 'every judgement of a churchman that exists, it is on the truth and entitlement of scripture that it is based; the judgement of a poet, however, is based on maxims (*for roscadaib*); the judgement of a king, however, is based on them all, on maxims, on precedents, and on scriptural citations'.[84] The doctrine was further fossilized in a third law text, *Córus Béscnai*, which goes back at least as far as the early eighth century:

> Each law is bound. It is in this that the two laws have been bound together. [It is] natural law that was with the men of Ireland until the coming of the faith in the time of Loégaire mac Néill. It is in his time that Patrick came. It is after the men of Ireland had believed in Patrick that the two laws were harmonised, natural law and the law of scripture. Dubthach maccu Lugair the poet displayed the law of nature. It is Dubthach who first paid respect to Patrick. It is he who first rose before him at Tara.[85]

The story in fact links up neatly with some of the earliest elements in the Patrick legend,[86] and the entire episode is a skilful and finely-worked example of the way in which the clerical writers of the seventh century and after had totally absorbed the earlier traditions and reworked them to fashion a new and all-encompassing tradition of their own. It has been argued that, far from being a defence by recidivist secular lawyers against alleged clerical attacks on the native institutions of the pre-Christian era, these texts constitute 'a clerical justification of the church's rather tolerant attitude towards many such institutions'.[87] Having so thoroughly assimilated the respective claims of church and state, it was only natural that ecclesiastical theorists should proceed in tandem with kings and together fashion new concepts of royal prerogative and, eventually, of 'high-kingship'.[88]

There is evidence for such close collaboration already in the seventh and eighth centuries, but it receives what is arguably its most obvious demonstration in the lavish patronage of the church by kings, particularly in the form of ecclesiastical artwork. It is generally assumed – though there is actually no explicit proof of it – that the great treasures of Irish art in the Christian centuries: the Book of Durrow and the Book of Kells, the Ardagh chalice and the Derrynaflan chalice, the Tara brooch, and most of the other masterpieces of book-production and fine metalwork, were all financed by generous donations from kings. This is certainly possible, even likely. But explicit indication of royal patronage is first found in the inscriptions on the

---

84. Text and translation based on Ó Corráin, Breatnach, Breen 1984, pp. 382–438 (p. 386); cf. McCone 1986a, p. 12.
85. Mc Cone 1986a, p. 21.
86. McCone 1986a, pp. 24–6.
87. McCone 1986a, p. 27.
88. For the argument that the Irish were the first to develop a theory of royal anointing at inauguration, see Enright 1985, but bearing in mind also the critique of this book by Dooley and Stoclet 1989, pp. 129–34.

elaborately decorated stone crosses that were erected at churches like Armagh, Clonmacnois, and Kells. Recent research, in fact, has revealed that the Cross of the Scriptures at Clonmacnois and the cross at Kinnity (Co. Offaly) were erected during the reigns of Maél Sechlainn mac Maél Ruanaid († AD862) and of his son Flann Sinna († AD916), who are both mentioned on the cross inscriptions.[89] It is possible that the Ardagh chalice was commissioned as a royal ministerial chalice; if it was so used, the rest of the congregation would presumably have received the sacrament from another chalice. Kings in Visigothic Spain had such an arrangement, which was a good thing in the view of Gregory of Tours (writing in the late sixth century), since it allowed conspirators to poison the royal family without massacring the congregation![90] The Ardagh chalice is a masterpiece of incomparable delicacy, but it had one fault – it leaked. The Derrynaflan chalice, on the other hand, did at least hold whatever liquid was put in it, but it lacks the artistic subtlety of the other.[91]

Kings represented only one stratum, of course, and the fabric of early Irish society was made up of many different strands. It is quite remarkable, however, how much unity appears to have existed within such diversity as we find represented in the wealth of the documentary sources. There may never have been a high-king in the early period, who ruled over the whole country, but that does not necessarily imply that the country was a patchwork of rival kingdoms, forever at each other's throats, and their peoples destined never to enjoy the somewhat dubious honour of being citizens of a unified state. The contrary is, in fact, the case.

89. Ó Murchadha & Ó Murchú 1988, pp. 53–66, and De Paor 1987, pp. 131–58.
90. Krusch 1937, p. 127: 'Erant autem sub Arriana secta viventes, et quia consuetudo eorum est, ut ad altarium venientes de alio calice reges accepiant et ex alio populus minor, veninum in calice illo posuit, de quo mater commonicatura erat'.
91. Some wit remarked that Ardagh must have been made by an artist, whereas Derrynaflan was made by an engineer! For discussion of the background, see Richardson 1980, pp. 92–115; Byrne 1980, pp. 116–26; Ní Chatháin 1980, pp. 127–48.

CHAPTER 4

LAND, SETTLEMENT AND ECONOMY

Writing in the early eighth century, the great English historian Bede remarked on the fact that the climate in Ireland was much milder than in Britain. The Irish never saved the hay in summer, nor did they bother to build stables for winter housing of their stock. Since the snow rarely lasted more than three days on the ground, there was simply no need of such things.[1] Gilbert White of Selbourne, writing just over a thousand years later, remarked that 'the southern counties of so mild an island may possibly afford some plants little to be expected within the British dominions'.[2] The evidence from Irish sources bears out what these observers have to say, at least in general terms. Agricultural practices probably differed from one region to another, and the nature of the landscape, as well as climatic conditions, must have determined the manner in which people worked the land, but such evidence as we have gives the impression that the Irish economy in the early medieval period was not very different from Irish agriculture today, after due allowance is made for regional variations and the effect of elements such as changes in the climate.

THE MEDIEVAL LANDSCAPE

Giraldus Cambrensis, writing in the late twelfth century, remarked how the rich grassland was as green and plentiful in winter as in summer.[3] The observation is doubtless exaggerated (like much else in that writer's account of Ireland), but there may be some slight truth in what he says, for it is a common feature of the calf-skins used to make early Irish manuscripts that they have a greasy texture – a sure sign of overfeeding on grass.[4] The area of grassland in early medieval Ireland must have been far less extensive than it

1. Plummer 1896, i, p. 12 (*HE* I 1); Colgrave & Mynors 1969, p. 18.
2. White 1977, i p. 99 (Letter XLII (March 9, 1775)); the London 2-vol. ed. by R. Bowdler Sharpe 1900, p. 178, gives the year as 1774.
3. O'Meara 1951, p. 34.
4. Ryan 1987, pp. 124–38 (p. 127).

is now, and the woodlands correspondingly more extensive; nevertheless the overwhelming impression from the literary sources and from archaeology is of rolling pasture and a cattle-based economy. This is probably reflected also in the fact that Irish manuscripts are – almost without exception – made of vellum (calf-skin), rather than of the sheepskin which was common in Europe.

An eleventh-century writer maintained that Ireland in earlier times was largely unenclosed: there were no ditches, hedges, or stone walls until the time of the sons of Aéd Sláine (seventh century); the countryside was nothing but a vast stretch of unbroken plains.[5] Indeed a later saint's Life remarked on the unpopularity caused by the stopping up of paths through the construction of fences and the transformation of open plains into narrow fields.[6] The law texts, on the other hand, are quite explicit about the mixed nature of the agricultural economy, and leave no doubt that enclosure was a characteristic part of the landscape. Land was divided into three categories: arable, fenced infield (which could also be grazed after harvest); fenced outfield grassland pasture; and commonage (woodland, mountain upland, bog and wasteland).

The woodland – now disappeared from the Irish landscape – was a source of considerable economic importance in the medieval period, often referred to in saints' Lives and other texts. It supplied wood for heating and lighting, building material for houses, wagons, and household utensils, handles for ploughs and every other kind of implement, and faggots for road-building. Besides the bark which could be stripped and used for tanning hides or for plaiting into ropes, the forest offered excellent grazing ground, with fresh leaves, young shoots, acorns and wood-mast (whose bumper crops are diligently recorded in the annals)[7] and this is graphically illustrated by the legal term 'hospitallers of the forest' (*briugid caille*) – those trees, like the apple, oak, or hazel, which provide wild fruit and vegetables as food for man and beast. The laws go into considerable detail on the subject of fines and penalties for theft and damage in private woods.[8] Apart from certain specified 'immunities of the forest' (*dílsi cailli*) – sufficient wood to light a fire; a handful of ripe nuts when in need, etc. – there were very severe restrictions on the trapping of animals and birds, and very severe penalties for damaging trees, which are classified according to rank as 'noble trees' (*airig fedo*) and 'common trees' (*secht n-aithech cailli*).[9]

There is a long and fascinating account in the Life of Darerca, detailing how smooth planks were fashioned from felled oaks 'in the Irish fashion'.[10] Just as

---

5. Stokes 1897, i, p. 136: 'ni bíd clad na hairbe na caissle im thír in hÉre isind amsir anall, co tanic remis mac nAeda Slani, acht maigi réidi', cited Plummer 1910, i, p. xcvi n. 6.

6. Ibid.

7. The forests could also harbour dangers, of course, and the twilight world of the forest is the setting for many episodes concerning bandits and *díbergaig*, for which see especially McCone 1986b, pp. 1–22.

8. Binchy 1971, pp. 152–68.

9. Binchy 1971, pp. 157–8. On the status of trees, see Kelly 1976b, pp. 107–24.

10. 'Hibernice nationis iuxta morem'; Heist 1965 (quotation, p. 95).

Abbot Suger of St Denis's foresters were doubtful whether the forest of Iveline could produce twelve massive timbers for his basilica,[11] so too Darerca's woodsmen despaired of finding a tree big enough to provide a ridge-beam ('which the Latins call a *spina*'); but one was eventually found and moved miraculously to the building-site. Wood was also necessary for the construction of ships, and the Life of Brendan refers to ship-builders 'who know how to construct vessels of wood' which would be more suitable for the saint's ocean-going travels than something made out of 'the skins of dead animals'.[12] Brendan's advisor seemed to think that such expertise in ship-construction was most likely to be found in the west of Ireland.

The dense woods were also home to foxes, badgers, wolves and deer,[13] while the wild boar was hunted with packs of hunting-dogs;[14] a Life of Ciarán of Clonmacnois recounts how a wild boar gathered branches and grass to provide the wattle for the saint's little cell.[15]

The seventh-century author of the tract 'On the miraculous things in Scripture' (*De mirabilibus sacrae scripturae*) shows a real sense of scientific inquiry, and in the course of his account he gives what is probably the earliest list of Ireland's wild animals:

> Islands [he says] are formed by the action of the sea in separating them from the mainland [instances of which were known to old men whom he knew]. This shows that those wild animals which are enclosed within the confines of islands were not brought there by human agency, but, clearly, were to be found there at that separation of the islands from the mainland. Who, for example, brought wolves, deer, wild boars, foxes, badgers, hares and squirrels to Ireland?[16]

Pigs could feed on the fruit of trees,[17] while sows were fattened on the kernels of nuts.[18] Trees, birds, and forest animals are the constant companions of Irish saints, and occasionally of scribes.[19] One such scribe, pondering on the words of *Félire Óengusso* (a metrical calendar of saints' feastdays), was interrupted by the plaintive call of a bird outside his cell:

> Learned in music sings the lark,
> I leave my cell to listen;
> His open beak spills music, hark!
> Where heaven's bright cloudlets glisten.[20]

11. See Bloch 1966, pp. 7–8.
12. Plummer 1910, i, p. 136.
13. Plummer 1910, i, p. 219.
14. Anderson 1961, p. 384 (*Vita Columbae* II 26).
15. Plummer 1910, i, p. 219.
16. (*De mirabilibus* I 7); *MPL* 35, cols 2149–2200 (quotation, col. 2158). For the term *sesquivolus* (squirrel), see Darcy Thompson 1945, pp. 1–7.
17. 'arboreo saginata fructu' (*Vita Columbae* II 33); Anderson 1961, p. 377.
18. 'scrofa nucum inpinguata nucleis' (*Vita Columbae* II 33); Anderson 1961, p. 378.
19. On the subject of hermit poetry, however, see the cautionary words of Ó Corráin 1989, pp. 251–67.
20. Translation by Flower 1947 (pbck ed. 1978) p. 54: text in Stokes 1905, p. lxvi.

A ninth-century scholar, poring over the rules in Priscian's grammar, was temporarily distracted by the wooded surroundings of his cell:

> A hedge of trees surrounds me,
> A blackbird's lay sings to me –
> Praise which I will not hide! –
> Above my book, the lined one,
> The trilling of the birds sings to me.
>
> In a grey mantle the cuckoo's beautiful chant
> Sings to me from the tops of bushes;
> May the Lord protect me from Doom!
> I write well under the greenwood.[21]

Another ninth-century scholar, best known for his verses about his pet cat, also penned the following curious lines:

> I wish for a wood of *allabair* and *arggatbran*, together with a fire and house;
> I wish for the three lean boars.
> May a spirit come to me with someone's corn
> and a yield of milk, which I increase.
> If this is to be, may it be corn and yield of milk that I see;
> If it is not to be, may I see wolves and deer wandering on the mountain,
>   and bands of *fían*-warriors.[22]

This strange incantation, which invokes no Christian God but seems to be addressed to a more elemental spirit (*siabair*), reflects the modest expectations of an individual who hopes for a small plot of land to grow some corn and raise some cattle. If all goes well, the poet can look forward to reasonable prosperity; the alternative to be hoped against is the shiftless life of the *féne* – the landless youths of the aristocracy who are traditional denizens of the forest. For the average Irishman, then, the expectation was to live out his years on his farm, and the daily routine of life therefore revolved around the cycle of the soil.

The evidence of aerial photography and of recent archaeological discoveries suggests that by the seventh century at least large areas of land were cultivated, and traces of ridge and furrow are frequently to be found to this day as survivals of earlier agricultural practices. There is no particular reason to presume continuity of field systems from the prehistoric period into the medieval centuries, but a legend incorporated into the Life of Gerald of Mayo referred to earlier, which maintained that enclosure took place first in the seventh century, is certainly exaggerated. On the other hand, the banks and ditches associated with the many ring-forts still standing in the Irish countryside may well in many instances have had a prehistoric origin, and

21. Text and translation in Stokes and Strachan 1901–3, ii, p. 290.
22. Text in Stokes and Strachan 1901–3, ii, p. 293; the translation is mine. See also Oskamp 1978, pp. 385–91. I believe the words *allabair* and *arggatbran* are names of (unidentified) wild herbs, not proper names of forests.

remained in more or less continuous use into the later period.[23] Unfortunately, pollen analysis is almost entirely absent from the archaeological evidence, so we have to rely on the literary sources to a greater than usual degree.

LAND AND THE LAW

With partible inheritance a distinctive feature of the law, there must always have been pressure on kin-groups to provide sufficient land to maintain the legal status of their members. The law tract *Críth Gablach* (*c*. AD700) states the problem starkly: 'What is it that deprives a man of the status of *bóaire*? Because there may be four or five men who are the heirs of a *bóaire*, so that it is not easy for each of them to be a *bóaire*'.[24] An older legal poem lays down that if each of the heirs maintains an independent household, legal requirements for *bóaire* status are met; but if the kindred cannot meet the claims of every member, that he should receive as inheritance a holding appropriate to a noble freeman, then (in this early period, at least) the kinsman sinks to the status of a semi-freeman, and the kindred in turn drops in status.[25] In a barter economy, where qualitative variation in lands could be expected to assume a quantitative significance, it is not surprising that the texts pay particular attention to the distribution of land in accordance with quality as well as quantity,[26] and the texts specify land valuation (*mess tíre*) as one of the functions of the law, to be carried out with measuring poles (*forraig*). That the custom was not just an archaic one is borne out by an annal for AD1136 which refers to a cleric of Armagh as *príomh críochaire* ('chief boundary surveyor').[27]

The procedures for dividing up land between members of the same *derbfine* on the death of the father and the sharing out of the land of an extinct *derbfine* among members of the wider kin-group – a much longer and more complicated procedure[28] – are also given in considerable detail. For the first year, the land is shared out among the heirs on a temporary and provisional basis. In the second year, the shares are exchanged; in the third year the shares are assessed, and in the fourth, houseposts (*cletha*) are established in each share as a symbolic gesture to indicate permanent ownership. Finally, in the fifth year, lots are cast among the heirs and the shares are apportioned in that way. In the seventeenth century, justice was sometimes done by making the youngest heir effect the partition and then

23. See Mytum 1992, p. 132.
24. Binchy 1941, p. 6 (§12).
25. For discussion of this difficult text, see Charles-Edwards 1972a, pp. 3–33 (pp. 20–1); cf. Charles-Edwards 1993b, p. 321 f.
26. See Kelly 1988, p. 104.
27. See Ó Cíobháin 1987–8, pp. 365–6, who refers also to the use of the word *críchaire* in an earlier text.
28. Procedure summarized by Kelly 1988, p. 104.

allowing the others to take their choice of his division in order of seniority;[29] the early Irish practice was identical: 'the youngest divides and the eldest chooses'.[30]

A dictum in an archaic legal poem states that 'the land is graded in accordance with quality'[31] and the law made a distinction between arable and roughland when it came to compensation.[32] In the above case, the whole process took five years to complete, involving a rotation of the various land parcels among the heirs in order to establish the relative quality of each plot. Since the shares were finally apportioned by lot, it is more than likely that individuals owned land which was not always contiguous, as is frequently the case today. Where land was bought in by the kindred, the procedure was different again: if the share allotted to one kinsman began to show traces of particular weed infestation – what the law text terms a 'radical disease' (*galar bunaid*): an outbreak of *ditham* (unexplained), *ithloinges* (literally 'corn banishment'), or *máelán muilche* ('bitter vetch' or the like) – then, after a further three years, the land was divided again. With periodic subdivision of lands, and the occasional purchase of additional properties, boundaries must have been subject to change from time to time. In cases of disputed boundaries, one means of deciding the issue was to allow a minor to cast a rod (*bunsach*) and establish the boundary where it fell. A similar procedure is attested for Dublin a millennium later: the franchises of the city were 'perambulated' every three years and the procedure included the delimitation of the maritime boundary by throwing a spear as far as possible into Dublin Bay.[33]

AGRICULTURE

Agricultural practices as depicted in the documentary sources show a heavy emphasis on crop cultivation. Ploughing was carried out with oxen exclusively; only in exceptional circumstances would horses be used – despite the fact that the term in modern Irish for a plough-team is *seisreach* 'six horses', and despite the provision of article 22 of the Irish peace treaty of 1648, by which the natives were promised the repeal of a statute against ploughing with horses by the tail.[34] The plough was usually drawn by four oxen, although some saints' Lives occasionally mention six: the Life of Maédóc of Ferns, for instance, relates how a six-ox plough-team went mad and careered out of control until stayed by the saint's intervention; the animals halted so suddenly that the unfortunate driver was thrown down between the coulter and the plough-share, but without injury.[35] Shares and coulters have come to

29. Andrews 1985, p. 10.
30. 'rannaid osar ocus dogoa sinser'; Kelly 1988, p. 102 n. 15.
31. 'Fo miad grian genithir'; see Dillon 1936, p. 143, and Charles-Edwards 1993b, p. 515 f.
32. Binchy 1955b, p. 70.
33. Andrews 1985, p. 6.
34. See Round 1899c, pp. 137–70 (p. 169 n. 1).
35. Plummer 1910, ii, p. 152.

light in archaeological excavations and one authority has suggested that some of them might have been suitable for ploughing heavy soils (as indeed the use of six oxen would also imply).[36] The first use of the mouldboard in Ireland has been dated to the mid-seventh century[37] and its introduction associated with the growth of ecclesiastical relations between Ireland and England in that period. Pollen traces of sage (*Artemesia*) have also been linked with mould-board ploughing, since the sage rootstock grows deeper than most other weeds, which, when buried under the turned sod, found it impossible to germinate. In Ireland, however, *Artemesia* first becomes common in the pollen diagrams around AD600. Professor Mitchell has remarked that 'it is tempting to see in this a reflection of the introduction of the mouldboard plough.[38]

According to the law tract *Críth Gablach*, the *mruigfer* or highest grade of 'noble freeman' possessed a full plough-team, with all its equipment, whereas the average well-to-do farmer (*bóaire febsa*) had only a half-ownership in a ploughing outfit.[39] The average small farmer (*ócaire*) in turn was expected to have a quarter-share in a wainage: one ox, a plough-share, a goad, and a halter.[40] It is clear, therefore, that only the more prosperous farmers could command a full plough-team; most farmers were obliged to pool their resources for joint ploughing. In some cases, it seems, it was necessary to hire in the entire plough-team: the Life of Maédóc records the saint's practice of ploughing for a neighbouring community of nuns, while in some communities the monks hand-ploughed with hoes. In the early days of Carthach's community, for example, the monks were accustomed to ploughing by hand,[41] while Darerca of Killeevy's hoe and spade were revered as relics. But even when allowance is made for the relatively high mortality rate for the period, with regular subdivision of the land, the plots to be worked must have grown steadily smaller, with the result that many were probably more easily ploughed by hand; hence it would be unsafe to argue from the relative scarcity of plough-finds that crop cultivation was not an important part of early medieval Irish husbandry. Harrowing, which seems to have been almost unknown on the continent, is several times mentioned in Irish sources; the practice of drawing a thorn-bush over the soil, attested as late as the 1950s in the Dingle area of Co. Kerry, may well be a survival from an earlier age. Gilla Mo-Chonna mac Fógartaig of the Síl nAédo Sláne (†AD1013) was reputed to have yoked Danes (*Gaill*) to the plough, 'and he made two of them harrow after them [and sow seed] from their bags'.

Considering Bede's statement about the Irish indifference to hay-saving, and the lack of any regular practice of stock-housing in winter, it must be presumed that winter fodder was scarce, and that measures were taken to

36. Duignan 1944, pp. 128–45 (p. 138).
37. Mitchell 1986, p. 160.
38. Mitchell 1986, p. 162.
39. Binchy 1941, p. 6 (§13): 'leth n-arathair' (*bóaire f.*); p. 7 (§14): 'og n-arathair cona uili chomopair' (*mruigfer*).
40. Binchy 1941, p. 4 (§10).
41. Plummer 1910, i, p. 178.

ensure that the limited supplies were used to maximum effect. Recent research has suggested that the numbers of male calves slaughtered in summer may have been as high as fifty per cent of the total of live births. The sources indicate that after the corn had been harvested temporary fences were erected and the cattle turned out onto the stubble. The laws have elaborate provisions for the proper maintenance of such fences and detailed penalties for any trespass of stock that might result from their neglect.[42] This practice would have served the dual purpose of manuring the land while providing the cattle with grazing, and manuring appears to have been a standard practice, in fact. The laws refer to 'arable with its proper manure',[43] and the term *gert* is sometimes used in the sense of dunghills;[44] both literary and historical sources attest to the use. One of the companions of the Irishman Marianus Scottus († AD1082) entered a note into Marianus's Chronicle recording how the young students in the monastic school at Mainz in Germany (*scolóca manestrech Mauritii*) played a prank on him by dropping him through a trapdoor down onto a dungheap below (*in fundo stercoris*)! He gave thanks to the Lord that he was not drowned in Frankish excrement: *Sed gratias ago, nec mersus sum in stercore Francorum*,[45] and blasted the young students with a curse!

The Lives of the saints give the impression that there may have been a more systematic approach to manuring in the ecclesiastical economy. The evidence is more sparing in the secular sources – although there is a famous scene in the tale *Fled Bricrend* ('Bricriu's Feast') where Bricriu and his wife are tossed from their *grianán* down onto a dunghill in the courtyard of his residence.[46] The laws do, however, mention alternative techniques, such as paring and burning and the use of sea sand and shells;[47] the best land is that 'which does not need the application of dung or shells'.[48] Paring and burning involved turning and drying of the sod, then burning and spreading of the ash; the practice could hardly be good for more than three years, thereafter it would have been useless without manure. The practice was included among the exemptions granted to the Irish by the peace treaty of 1648, mentioned above.[49] Despite the fact that it was frowned on by the lawyers (who made it the subject of a fine), the custom survived down to the last century.[50]

Ploughing and sowing were carried out in spring; the cultivation ridges (*immairi*) are in many cases still visible, as on the hill-top caher or stonefort with drystone wall near Shrule (Co. Mayo), where the furrows have been

---

42. Ó Corráin 1983, pp. 247–51.
43. *ALI*, ii, p. 238.18.
44. Thurneysen 1927, p. 211 ('in ottraig in gerta').
45. Vatican, Bibl. Apostolica, MS. Pal. Lat. 830, f. 67r; text in Mac Carthy 1892, p. 16.
46. Best & Bergin 1929, p. 255.
47. Lucas 1969b, pp.184–205.
48. 'nach eicin do frichnam tuair na slige'; *ALI*, iv, pp. 276–7 (cited in Lucas 1969b, p. 184).
49. See Round 1899c, p. 169 n.1.
50. See Lucas 1970, pp. 99–147.

revealed by bush clearance.[51] The Life of Fintan of Dún Blesci mentions a leper who demanded a loaf of bread from the saint in spring 'as though the corn should have been ripe'. The saint told the man to follow the oxen and sow some seed in the first furrow, whereupon corn instantly grew and ripened.[52] The laws expected a 'strong' farmer to sow sixteen sacks of grain each year, and sacks are frequently listed as part of the average tenant's food render to his lord. The late sixth- or early seventh-century legal poem referred to above describes the kind of farm owned by an average freeman (*bóaire*) and worked by him and his family as an independent unit. This land is valued at fourteen *cumals*, 'the inheritance which feeds a normal freeman'. The acreage under cultivation is impossible to gauge, but comparison with a modern average of about two sacks per acre gives an area of about eight acres for the medieval period – a very small proportion relative to the acreage of pasture. These figures are borne out by excavation results, which record large numbers of animal bones with only the occasional plough-share or quern-stone.

Heavy rainfall makes the harvest time a worry for the Irish farmer today, and the situation was no different in the early medieval period. The hazard is often mentioned in the Lives of the saints and occasions frequent stock miracles. Cainnech of Aghaboe daydreamed about his monks trying to bring in the harvest during heavy rain, while Finán of Kinnitty (Co. Offaly) prayed that the rain falling elsewhere would not fall on his field of ripening corn – a boon granted to him and to Aéd mac Bricc.[53] The depredations of stray livestock represented another danger to the crop: corn trampled by cattle is mentioned frequently; in the Life of Buite of Monasterboice (Co. Louth) the flattened crop was miraculously restored, but not before the errant animal had been corralled by the crop-owner's gilly – a case of what modern lawyers call distress 'damage feasant', and one of the grounds on which early Irish law also allowed the impounding of another man's livestock.

Another problem seems to have been the organization of the harvest-team (*meitheal*). In the Life of Carthach of Lismore (Co. Waterford), there were not enough reapers to bring in the bumper crop, so some of the work was done by angels. The Life of Maédóc of Ferns (Co. Wexford) mentions a *meitheal* numbering 150 men. These had to be fed, and the Life of Kevin of Glendalough (Co. Wicklow) mentions that meat and beer were provided for the harvesters.[54] Against some dangers, however, there was no protection: Fintan of Dún Blesci, angered by the refusal of a local grandee to allow him passage through his lands, invoked the elements, in the form of a lightning-storm, to exact his revenge, and left the harvest a blazing inferno.[55] The corn was always at greatest risk in the fields, and the burning of corn by marauding bands is a constant theme in the annals – just as the summer

51. Mitchell 1986, p. 156 photo 34.
52. Plummer 1910, ii, p. 73.
53. Plummer 1910, ii, p. 92 (*Vita Finani*); i, p. 37 (*Vita Aedani*).
54. Plummer 1910, i, pp. 188–9 (*Vita Carthagi*); i, p. 239 (*Vita Coemgeni*).
55. Heist 1965, p. 191.

newspapers today bring regular accounts of cornfields torched by errant Dublin schoolboys.

After reaping, the sheaves were brought in on wagons and the winnowing and threshing began, although Cainnech's monks at Clonbroney winnowed by hand on the bare flagstones in the open field, and complained that they were hampered in their task by the rain.[56] They had not the services of 'anyone who could construct and operate a kiln' (*artifices et operatores fortes qui possent facere canabam*). The Irish climate made artificial drying a necessity and drying-kilns were probably not uncommon. Some seem to have been fairly elaborate structures: the Life of Ciarán of Clonmacnois mentions one which was constructed on a river-bank and consisted apparently of a recessed circular pit over which was laid a cover (*rota*) of wattle; the grain was strewn on the wattle and a fire below heated the air which dried it.[57] The technique is described as being peculiarly 'western, i.e. British and Irish'. On the whole, however, the law tracts would seem to indicate that only the more substantial farmers had kilns of their own; less wealthy individuals either had shares in a kiln or rented one. English commentators on Irish agricultural habits in the seventeenth century made frequent allusion to a contemporary practice of burning corn in the straw (a practice listed among the more heinous barbarities of the natives); one such writer remarked that 'they burn their oats standing upon the stalk or reeds in the fields and thereby lose the straw which might serve many good purposes'.[58] On the other hand, a reference in Adomnán's Life of Columba to a recessed channel or trench (*fossula excusorii*) in the floor of the threshing house suggests that winnowing, on Iona at any rate, took place immediately after harvesting.[59]

The wet Irish climate would provide little opportunity for piecemeal threshing and winnowing in the open air over the winter and spring months, and the absence of barns for all but the wealthiest, combined with the later evidence of a strong export trade in corn, lead to the conclusion that early Irish farmers carried out their threshing at the end of the harvest.[60] That being the case, grain storage was clearly a problem. Even in storage, however, there could be hazards: the Annals of Ulster, *s.a.* AD787, refer to a great fire which destroyed half the grain-store in the monastery of Clonard; the text adds that the grain was *in ballenio* (lit. 'in a bath/bathing-place'), which presumably means a sunken pit, perhaps a souterrain-type structure.[61] There is no native Old Irish word for barn: *saball* is from Latin *sabellum* (although attested in the laws by AD700), and the modern Irish term *scióból* seems to be unattested in the older literature. The laws, however, state that the 'strong' farmer (*bóaire febsa*) had both a kiln and a barn, together with part-ownership in a

56. Heist 1965, p. 191.
57. Plummer 1910, i, p. 204.
58. O'Brien 1923, p. 33 (cited Lucas 1956, pp. 2–20 (p. 14)).
59. Anderson 1961, p. 368 (*Vita Columbae* II 20).
60. See Lucas 1956, pp. 14–15.
61. Cf. Plummer 1910, ii, p. 19; Heist 1965, p. 231, where a manuscript of the Comgall Life also has the spelling *ballenio*.

mill; the average small farmer (*ócaire*), by contrast, had only a share in all three. It is possible that temporary outdoor grain-stores existed in the medieval period similar to, or identical with, the *fóir* or *síogóg*, an outdoor granary commonly found throughout Co. Cork in the nineteenth century. The structure consisted of a cylindrical body built up layer by layer of superimposed rings of thick *súgán* or straw rope, crowned by a conical cap of straw which was thatched and roped against the elements. The bottom was provided with a damp-proof foundation of dry twigs and branches coated with a layer of carefully laid straw on which the corn rested. The cylindrical base was usually five or six feet in diameter, and the structure rose to an average height of eight to ten feet. Despite its simplicity, the *fóir* provided excellent storage conditions for substantial quantities of grain, while the easy availability of the raw material meant that it could be built by a few hands in a matter of hours.[62] Such granaries would have left no archaeological traces, since they were probably dismantled at the end of every season and built anew. But if there was bulk storage of grain in the early medieval period, then some such granary may well have been in use.

The law tracts list seven different cereals: wheat, rye, siligo, red wheat, barley, oats, and another, unidentified *gráinne ibdaig*, plus peas and beans.[63] In the early tract on sick-maintenance (which offers this list)[64] the size of various wounds is gauged by reference to grain sizes: wheat grain for a provincial king, the lowly bean for a *fer midboth* (dependent son with his own plot). Bread formed a very important part of the diet, being baked by the basketful,[65] and with a generous spread of margarine-like condiment provided the principal food between main meals.[66]

The basic food which a client was expected to provide for members of his lord's entourage comprised one 'proper loaf' daily, with due relish and condiment,[67] while for patients convalescing under the rules of sick-maintenance the doctor prescribed two such 'proper loaves' per day, though where there was no corn 'summer food' (butter and other dairy products) could be substituted.[68] The laws make a distinction – for what it is worth – between bread baked by women ('two fists long, one broad') and loaves baked by men, which were supposed to be twice the size of women's loaves; the commentaries go to bizarre lengths to explain the difference (without much conviction, it must be said). Wheat bread was regarded as a luxury, the food of kings and the aristocracy;[69] wheat hardened in a

62. Lucas 1956, pp. 2–20; Lucas 1958a, pp. 68–77; Lucas 1957, pp. 196–205 (pp. 198–9).
63. See Loth 1924, pp. 193–203.
64. Binchy 1966, pp. 1–66.
65. Plummer 1910, i, p. 111.
66. See the comment of Rudolf Thurneysen: 'Das Brot mit dickem Aufstrich spielt bei der Nahrung der Iren eine große Rolle', Thurneysen 1923, p. 358.
67. Binchy 1938b, pp. 78–134 (p. 112).
68. Binchy 1938b, p. 107.
69. Lucas 1960, p. 5.

corn-oven or kiln is mentioned as part of the annual food render from a client, although malted barley figures much more frequently in such lists of dues. One commentary on a law text refers to 'the soft barley of the isles', apparently an allusion to a kind of barley grown in the Western Isles of Scotland;[70] barley bread seems to have been more penitential than savoury.[71] Oats, on the other hand, were used in various kinds of porridge or gruel, and convalescing children were fed on a diet of egg-yolks, butter, curds and porridge.[72]

Corn was reaped with sickles, and the sickle figures in the list of indispensable farm implements that a farmer deposited with his neighbour overnight as a guarantee that he would return in the morning to carry out joint-farming agreements.[73] The absence of any reference to hay making, and the custom of releasing cattle onto the stubble, suggest that the straw was cut relatively high up on the stalk, as indeed it was in medieval Europe generally. The large numbers of quern-stones uncovered in excavations attest to the practice of grinding the corn by hand; the daughters of small farming families were expected to learn the use of quern, kneading-trough, and sieve.[74] The custom of grinding only what was needed to bake fresh bread for visitors to the monastery also figures frequently in the ecclesiastical literature. The many young students at Finnian's school in Clonard took their turn at grinding the corn by hand, save Ciarán of Clonmacnois, for whom an angel performed the task![75] Fechín of Fore's monks were accustomed to grinding by hand, until an *artifex* was found to construct a water-mill for the community.[76]

MILLS AND MILLING

The literary evidence and the archaeological remains confirm that the horizontal water-mill was the type used by the early Irish; the vertical mill was a later introduction.[77] Several examples have been assigned by Carbon-14 and dendrochronological dating techniques to the period from the seventh century onwards. Literary references indicate that the mill was an elaborate affair which required the expertise of a skilled carpenter for its

70. Binchy 1966, p. 22 gl. 11.

71. *Félire Oéngusso*, Jan. 20 (Stokes 1905, p. 48; a part of Ciarán of Saigir's regimen).

72. Binchy 1938a, p. 42.

73. Thurneysen 1925, pp. 302–76 (p. 315).

74. See Mulchrone 1936, pp. 187–205 (quotation, p. 190): 'bro ocus losut ocus criathrud dia n-ingeanuibh'; cf. ibid., p. 34.

75. Plummer 1910, i, p. 205.

76. Plummer 1910, ii, p. 81.

77. Lucas 1953, pp. 1–36; Lucas 1955, pp. 100–13; Lucas 1969a, pp. 12–22; Fahy 1956, pp. 13–57; Bailie 1980, pp. 62–3. For general discussion, see Bloch 1967b, pp. 136–68; Curwen 1944, pp. 130–46; and for Anglo-Saxon England, Rahtz and Bullough 1977, pp. 15–37. The article by Rynne 1992, pp. 22–3, which purports to describe a vertical watermill, dated *c*. AD630, from Cork, offers insufficient information to show that the mill was, in fact, a vertical one.

construction; the massive hub recovered from the Deer Park Farm excavations in Co. Antrim bears out this impression in a striking way. Besides the wood-working skills required, a stonemason would also have been needed for the manufacture of its 'anvil' and grinding-stone. The mill was usually a small, two-storeyed wooden building, erected on an artificial race or channel into which water was diverted from a neighbouring river or stream. The water was trapped in a pond immediately above the mill, then released through a wooden chute or trough (in one case, two chutes) down to the mill-wheel; the water entered the lower storey at one end and exited through the opposite end. The grinding mechanism consisted of a long vertical wooden shaft to which wooden paddles were attached below, arranged like the spokes of a wheel. An iron spindle attached to the upper end of the shaft passed through an aperture in the floor of the upper storey and through a hole in the lower millstone or 'anvil'; the spindle was so set in the upper or grinding stone that when the shaft revolved the grinding-stone revolved with it. The shaft was turned by releasing the water from the pond by means of a sluice gate. As the wheel, shaft, spindle and grinding-stone formed, in effect, a single unit, the mechanism required no gearing, and the revolution of the shaft produced a corresponding turn of the grinding-stone; the design was simple but effective.[78] Millwrights and rath-builders were highly regarded in society: Mochoémóg's father is described as a craftsman in wood and stone, which may imply that he was a millwright.[79] The Life of Feichín of Fore recounts a story of how a dozing carpenter was caught unawares when water miraculously filled the wheelhouse of a mill which he had just constructed,[80] and a similar incident provided the theme for a famous Middle Irish story.[81]

The legal problems relating to the ownership and sharing of water-mills form the subject of a law tract entitled *Coibnius uisci thairidne* ('The kinship of conducted water')[82] dating probably to the seventh century. The tract enumerates the 'eight parts of a mill' and gives detailed provisions concerning the construction of a mill-race and the subsequent use of the mill. The law lists the ditch or channel formed by the mill-race as one of seven such ditches which are immune from liability should someone injure himself by falling into them, and it also provided for the free passage of water across another's land, if the mill was not already adjacent to a water course. In such circumstances, passage could not be refused, but the farmer across whose land the mill-race was dug received compensation according to the value of the land, or by the grant of a day's free milling at fixed intervals. Once the mill-race was constructed and in use for three generations, the original owner then relinquished all rights of objection arising from the use of his land. The only exceptions were church lands, the area around a *dún* or fort, and the precinct

78. My description is based on Lucas 1969a, pp. 12–22 (p. 22). See also Mac Eoin 1982, pp. 13–19.
79. Plummer 1910, ii, p. 164.
80. Plummer 1910, ii, pp. 81–2.
81. Mac Eoin 1983, pp. 60–4.
82. Binchy 1955b, pp. 52–85.

of a graveyard; these were lands through which it was forbidden to dig a mill-race.

The laws give the impression that mills were usually joint-owned, although mills owned in severalty were certainly to be found. But most men would have rented time at a mill, taking turns to grind their corn, and the partners contributed jointly to its construction and maintenance. Rights of access to the property of neighbours were granted only in certain circumstances, however. These included the right to use a water-mill, to construct a bridge or fishing-weir on or adjacent to a neighbour's land, and rights concerning fruits from trees which fell on neighbours' lands.[83] Early Welsh law refers to a mill, a weir, and an orchard as the 'three ornaments of a kindred' (*tri thlws cenedl*)[84] and much the same kind of thinking can be found in Irish law. Privately owned salmon and other fish-weirs are recognized and protected already in the oldest law texts,[85] while orchards and herb gardens figure frequently in the laws and in the literature, and frequent mention is made both of garden vegetables and of herbs that grow in the wild. Nor was the distinction confined to monastic circles, although the monastic rules do naturally lay particular emphasis on vegetables rather than meat in the communal or penitential diet, and this may perhaps have encouraged a greater degree of specialization in vegetable production on ecclesiastical estates. But the law texts are quite unambiguous about the consumption of a wide variety of root crops and other greens by the general population as well: cabbages, onions, leeks and celery, kale, parsnips, and even nettles and charlock, as well as garlic and a few others which cannot be identified with certainty.[86] The humble shamrock (*trifolium-dubium* – appropriately enough), so beloved of Irishmen at home and abroad, is not a native plant, and the word *seamróg* is first encountered in Edward Llwyd's *Irish–English Dictionary* of 1707.

The early tract on sick-maintenance specifies fresh (wild) garlic and unlimited celery as food which must be supplied to patients of every rank, the celery particularly because of its ackowledged curative properties: 'every person on sick-maintenance in Irish law ... is entitled to celery, which prevents sickness, and does not stir it up; which prevents thirst, and does not infect wounds'.[87] Vegetable plots (*lubgoirt*) seem to have been common, and the law of sick-maintenance also states that patients were normally restricted to garden herbs like leek (*fírchainend*) and celery (*umus*).[88] Edible roots (*meacain*) are also mentioned, including one apparent reference to seakale or beet (*meacain murrathaig*), which Ciarán of Saigir was in the habit of eating as part of a penitential diet.[89] The abundance of wild garlic (*crem*) at the end

83. For the law on fruits, see Kelly & Charles-Edwards 1983, pp. 12–13; general discussion in Kelly 1988, pp. 108–9.
84. See Jones 1983–4, pp. 135–46 (p. 137).
85. Binchy 1955b, p. 82.
86. Lucas 1960, pp. 8–43 (p. 34).
87. Binchy 1938a, p. 36 (§45).
88. Binchy 1938b, p. 108.
89. *Félire Oéngusso*, March 5 (Stokes 1905, p. 38).

of spring gave its name to the season (*crimmess* 'garlic feast' (<*crem* + *feis*)). Where I live myself, Craughwell (Co. Galway), derives its name from *cremchoill* ('garlic wood').[90] The sick-maintenance of a king required three 'foreign' herbs: *sraif, lungait*, and *argadluim* (unidentified),[91] and the author of the St Gall poem mentioned above may have had something similar in mind with his reference to *fid n-allabrach ocus argattbrain*.[92] The laws also refer to apples and 'sweet fruits' (perhaps damson) and stipulate penalties for damage done to fruit trees. The Annals of Tigernach, *s.a.* AD1134 record a hailstorm in which the hailstones were as big as apples. The monks of Tallaght, however, were forbidden to eat even fallen apples on Sunday, so strict was their sabbatarianism. Other fruit types mentioned are strawberries, blackberries, rowan berries, plums, and sloes.[93]

It is clear from all the evidence here reviewed that arable farming was an important part of the agricultural economy throughout the early medieval period. Nevertheless, it is equally clear that crop cultivation was considerably less important than cattle-farming, and dairy-herding in particular. All the evidence underlines the importance of cattle, and cows provided a standard of reference for every manner of transaction and activity.[94] Cattle raids are a stock theme in the heroic literature and figure repeatedly in the annals as well, in the form of the royal 'prey' (*crech ríg*) – the 'inaugural' foray by the newly-chosen king and his braves to plunder the neighbouring people's cattle.[95] The common unit of currency was the milch cow (*sét* = half a milch cow), and the typical farmer is called a 'lord of cows' (*bóaire*). Fines and penalties, dues and renders, the status and honour-price of individuals were all reckoned in terms of milch cows and their values, while the land itself was valued in terms of the numbers of cows it could support: a standard measurement was the extent of land sufficient to feed one cow for a day. One estimate has put the number of acres in an average 'strong' farmer's estate at *c.* 700 (*c.* 280 hectares), which seems very large; the laws reckon on a farm of apparently *c.* 70 acres (*c.* 28 hectares) as the minimum land required to secure the status of an independent farmer. Allowing for the likelihood of less productive stock and lower yields than today's equivalents, the figures seem not impossible. Professor Frank Mitchell (whose figures these are), points out that the first English plantation farms of the sixteenth century ranged in size from 25 to 500 'plantation' acres.[96]

Like the arable plots, pasture land too seems to have been dispersed

90. Royal Irish Academy, *Dictionary of the Irish language* [*DIL*] col. 520, s.v. *crem*.
91. Binchy 1966, p. 26.
92. The first of these two terms is perhaps to be identified with the otherwise unexplained *allabraig n-aí* mentioned in the 'bee-laws', and apparently to be had only in exceptional circumstances. See Kelly & Charles-Edwards 1983, p. 52 (§6), and commentary p. 99.
93. Lucas 1978, pp. 51–66 (p. 55).
94. For a general survey, see Lucas 1958b, pp. 75–87, and Lucas 1989.
95. Ó Riain 1973, pp. 23–30.
96. Mitchell 1986, p. 167.

among the members of the kin, doubtless for the same reason. The procedures which were followed in the allotment of arable plots must have involved some kind of rundale or strip-farming, which allowed every kinsman to share all the various qualities of land, an object best attained by running the farm at right angles to the natural contours and soil boundaries and at the same time allowing easy access to rivers, coastlines, roads and pathways, and to the edges of pasturable bog or mountain.[97] The nett result would have been the system of infield arable plots and outfield pasture which we find reflected in the laws. Any landholder who was deficient in woodland, lake or moorland (*caill, loch, sliab*), open ground (*mag*), or water (*uisge*) had a right to supply the want from wasteland (i.e. unappropriated land), and he enjoyed the further right of easy access to any such extension of his holding, under precise conditions. The laws make detailed provision for the driving of cattle over other men's lands in the absence of roads or droving lanes.[98] They gave a landowner the right to construct a path to moorland and grassland (*rod do sliab ocus mag*) and a roadway to water (*bóthar do uisge*), and when he drove his cattle over these he had to arrange to have them accompanied by three of his own kindred and three kinsmen of the man whose land they passed through. In fact, Irish law numbered the occupation of land where another refused access among the seven forms of possession which could not be claimed against.[99]

The varying proportions of cattle, sheep, and pigs at different sites doubtless reflect differences in the functions of the sites, as well as in the quality of the land and its location. Cahercommaun (Co. Clare), for example, appears to have been a royal enclosure, used as a cattle pound for the royal herd; hence the predominance of cattle bones on the site. The *crannóg* sites, on the other hand, being lake dwellings, present problems of their own in terms of assessing the significance of their archaeological remains. Figures based on bone counts, cited by Professor Mitchell,[100] show the overwhelming importance of dairying, with meats and hide-production apparently side-lines. It is clear, however, that the efflorescence of literary activity in the Irish monasteries of the sixth and seventh centuries, which has been characterized by one authority as 'real mass production',[101] must have required very large numbers of calf-skins for the manufacture of books. One recent estimate, based on a theoretical book size of 140 folios (seventy skins) has produced a figure of 483 adult cattle as the number in a herd required to produce such a manuscript.[102] This estimate assumes that up to fifty per cent of all male calves were culled in summer, the rest being slaughtered in their second autumn, and only the bulls and milch cows being retained. In order to sustain

97. See Andrews 1985, p. 216.
98. Gwynn 1942, p. 33: 'lánimmirce tar tír', in a passage on *Comaithches*.
99. 'Telach fer na-daim cert na sliged do duine', in *Gúbretha Caratniad* (§37 gl.); see Thurneysen 1925, pp. 302–76 (p. 346).
100. Mitchell 1986, p. 168.
101. Bischoff 1967, p. 224.
102. Ryan 1987, p. 135.

the literary output of the monastic scriptoria, therefore, very large numbers of cattle must be presumed, and a significant industry devoted to the mass-production of vellum. The decline in quality that becomes evident in later Irish manuscripts doubtless reflects the changing economic and political circumstances, particularly in the eleventh and twelfth centuries.

Calving took place in spring and the cattle were grazed in both fenced and open pasture, as well as in the harvest stubble. Fenced pasture was of two types: summer pasture and pasture reserved for winter grazing.[103] In some areas, during the summer months, the cows were driven up to mountain pastures (or perhaps onto lowland riverside grazing which was waterlogged in winter) in the practice known as 'booleying', i.e. sheiling or summering. The third Life of Kevin of Glendalough relates how the saint encountered an individual 'on a grazing tour' (*ar cuairt bhuailtechuis*);[104] later evidence suggests that the practice was countrywide, and this may well have been the case also in the early medieval period. References in the laws and in the saints' Lives to herding dogs (*coin buachail*)[105] indicate that both cattle and sheep were guarded against the depredations of wolves. Young boys seem to have been assigned to the task of herding, and the saints' Lives frequently refer to the imposition of such duties as a trial of the youthful saint's obedience.[106]

At night, however, cattle were enclosed in a booley or enclosure (*buaile*). The prose commentary on *Félire Oéngusso* describes Ciarán of Saigir's cattle pen (*lias*) and suggests a fairly elaborate structure: 'Many cattle he had, for there were ten doors to the shed of his kine and ten stalls for every door . . . and there were ten calves in every stall, and ten cows with every calf';[107] but the text has every appearance of being a literary flourish on the writer's part. There is, however, ample evidence for the enclosure of all domestic animals: cattle, pigs, sheep, horses, foals, and hens all have their own specific enclosures and the average farm seems to have had a guard dog (*archû*) as well. The law on sick-maintenance expressly mentions the irritation caused by barking dogs and insists that such animals be kept out of earshot of convalescents.[108] The laws also mention several other kinds of dogs: the yard dog (*cú ottraig*) and the greyhound (*milchû*), which was kept on a chain, perhaps for rabbit or hare hunting. The cat – like the dog, prominent in the decorated pages of the Book of Kells – also figures in the laws, and one was the subject of a famous ninth-century poem, *Pangur Bán*.[109] Other animals, less readily identified, are also mentioned in the saints' Lives (*corona, ludarius*).[110]

103. Charles-Edwards, in Hughes 1972a, p. 62.
104. Plummer 1922, i, p. 157.
105. Binchy 1973b, p. 78; cf. also Plummer 1910, ii, index s.v. *luscicus*.
106. Plummer 1910, i, p. 235.
107. *Félire Oéngusso*, March 5 (Stokes 1905, p. 88).
108. Binchy 1938a, p. 61 (§23).
109. Stokes & Strachan 1901–3, ii, p. 293.
110. Plummer 1910, ii, index s.vv.

Winter housing of cattle seems to have been rare, although the later Irish custom of keeping one or two cows in the domestic dwelling is attested sporadically in the annals towards the end of our period. In AD1028, for example, a heavy fall of snow during Lent kept people and cattle indoors for three days and three nights. The custom of housing cows in the home was common throughout Europe and may well have been practised in Ireland in the medieval period. Cowsheds do not figure among the lists of farm buildings and outhouses in the laws, and the archaeological evidence has not turned up any substantial evidence either. Without hay and other fodder the winter feeding of animals must have been a precarious affair; the annals frequently relate the devastating effects of unusual snowfalls.

Cows comprised *c.* seventy per cent of the stock of a typical independent farmer, according to *Críth Gablach* (*c.* AD700), compared with today's figures of sixty per cent cattle, forty per cent sheep.[111] Most archaeological sites with faunal remains produced figures of about fifteen to twenty per cent sheep, although some had more and others no sheep at all.[112] At Cahercommaun over ninety-five per cent of the bones were of oxen, with only small quantities of sheep, goat, pig, horse, and red deer.[113] At Ballinderry crannóg (I) cattle bones comprised seventy per cent of the remains, while Ballinderry (II) produced a figure of seventy to ninety per cent for cattle. Lough Faughan produced sixty-three per cent cattle, and Lagore (a crannóg) seventy-two to eighty-four per cent.

Sheep are surprisingly small in number, and it is perhaps significant that sheepskin is almost never used in the production of manuscripts; the gospel fragments in Trinity College Dublin, MS. 55 (the 'Ussher Gospels'), which were previously believed to have been made of sheepskin are not, in fact; but the vast majority of Irish manuscripts were made from calf-skin – perhaps a sign of the increasing prosperity of the Irish churches from *c.* AD600 onwards. The Life of Brendan mentions sheep as big as cows, which suggests rather that cows were small. Unlike the other animals, sheep remained on the mountain upland at night and were attended at all times – as Patrick tells us. It was the custom to have a fire burning all night to warm the young herds. The danger was not always from wolves: Kevin of Glendalough's monks wanted to hang a man for sheep-stealing.[114]

Pigs were occasionally rustled or stolen, or they might simply disappear if they were left to graze unattended in the woods. For that reason they were usually penned at night, although it is possible that in winter at least they were left to their own devices in the woods. They provided food in the form of pig-meat and *mucrecht*, a kind of sausage apparently, which occurs in the

111. Mitchell 1986, p. 168.
112. Ibid.
113. For general discussion, with detailed figures from all the sites, see Proudfoot 1961, pp. 94–122.
114. Sheep: Plummer, 1910, i, p. 112; fire: ibid., ii, p. 207; sheep-stealing: ibid., i, p. 239.

lists of additional food payments from clients to their lords. Pig bristles were used, with a lye of potash, to burnish silver.[115]

FOOD AND DIET

The agrarian nature of the Irish economy, allied to the probably low level of population for most of our period, combined to ensure a relatively prosperous existence for most communities.[116] The food supply was probably sufficient, in good times at any rate, and if the annual render of the free client is anything to judge by (one milch cow, or thirty-three per cent of his fief, together with *fobiathad* 'additional foods'), then the average farmer could be expected to do well. There is no reason to suppose that land was in short supply, and what we have seen gives us every reason to believe that the land that was occupied was well maintained. The overall picture is one of a fairly static economy and a stable society. The basic pattern of life must have been pretty uneventful, and most people's lives would have revolved around the daily and seasonal routine of the land. The food renders that formed the annual rent of the average farming families give us a good indication of the typical produce of the time: calves, sheep, and pigs imply a diet of beef, lamb, pork, milk, butter, cream, and what the law tracts call 'summer food': dairy products of all kinds, as well as wheat bread, vegetables, honey, ale and beer, with occasional fruit and herbs. Horsemeat is mentioned occasionally as food, and the finds from the Glenarm excavations conducted by Chris Lynn (on a site dated *c.* AD648) add additional evidence for the domestic consumption of horsemeat. The practice is condemned in ecclesiastical literature, and a reference in the Life of Enda of Aran is clearly intended to bolster that prohibition.[117] However, in the tract on sick-maintenance, included among the three condiments 'which the rule of sick-maintenance forbids' is horsemeat,[118] 'because it causes eyes to water'; the implication, presumably, is that horsemeat would otherwise be expected to form a regular part of the average diet.

For the aristocracy, at any rate, the diet must have been fairly substantial: besides the meat, which seems to have been plentiful, there was a wide variety of 'summer foods': milk, butter, cheese, and other dairy products. Milk was boiled and sweetened, probably by the addition of honey.[119] The term *milsén* (which survives in the modern language with the meaning 'sweet, candy') apparently denotes some kind of thickened butter or quark (called

---

115. Pigs: Plummer 1910, i, pp. 25, 91; woods: ibid., pp. 221–2; silver: Gwynn 1942, p. 58.
116. Mytum 1992, p. 132, has estimates of population (for the aristocracy at least), but the method of assessment is hopelessly inadequate. For general discussion of the problems, see Mac Niocaill 1981.
117. Plummer 1910, ii, p. 73.
118. Binchy 1938a, p. 20 (§25).
119. Thurneysen 1923, p. 358.

'Kochkäse' by Thurneysen) cooked with butter (unsalted) and sweetened with honey.[120] A sour cream of some kind, which was allowed to stand three days and three nights in a tub, is mentioned, and milk is even recommended in certain circumstances as an alternative to ale – a suggestion which might not have appealed to everyone![121] One of the Lives of Kevin of Glendalough describes how women carried different cheeses in the folds of their cloaks.[122]

Without detailed information about the processes involved in their manufacture, however, it is impossible to identify the various types of dairy product named in the sources. But the rich vocabulary of terms and the archaeological evidence for the existence of a wide variety of buckets, troughs, churns, and tubs, as well as other vessels of various shapes and sizes, attest to a considerable skill in cheese-making as well as in carpentry.[123] The wooden bucket, with handle still in place, found at Derreen (Co. Clare) is fashioned from fifteen staves of yew bound by three concentric bronze bands or hoops with fine engraving on them and is a particularly fine example of such workmanship.[124] The oak churn discovered at the rath site of Lissue (Co. Antrim) is also of a very high standard.[125] In fact, it has been suggested that the almost entire absence of potsherds from the island monastery of Iona is due to the prevalence of wood in the manufacture of turned bowls. A four-foot length of oak timber, with a fine mortised grooved slot intended either for fitted planks or wattle, found on the site bears witness to the high standard of carpentry skills available there; the rough-outs for wooden bowls, hewn out of lengths of split log of alder, ash, and poplar, found on numerous Irish sites also suggest the manufacture of wooden vessels on an almost industrial scale.[126] The surviving timbers of horizontal water-mills reveal a workmanship of the very highest standard, in some cases being chutes fashioned from a single piece of oak, and likewise, the occasional wooden troughs for feeding or perhaps for steeping grain in the preparation of malt for brewing also display commendable woodworking expertise.[127]

Both salted and unsalted food (meat and butter) are mentioned in the laws and in the literature, and salt seems to have been relatively easy to come by. Salt-cured fish and meat figure regularly in the lists of food renders and salt, dilesk (edible seaweed), and shallots or leeks (*cainenn*) are named as the standard condiments in *Críth Gablach*.[128] Salt may have been acquired by boiling sea water, or by burning sea-weed; alternatively it could be imported:

120. Thurneysen 1923, p. 356.
121. Binchy 1938b, p. 109; cf. Binchy 1941, p. 16 (*Críth Gablach* §27).
122. Plummer 1922, i, p. 166 §xxii (43): *maothla* and *molcháin*.
123. See, e.g., the variety of buckets described in the commentary on the bee-laws: Kelly & Charles-Edwards 1983, p. 52 (§6 gl.)
124. A colour reproduction in Erichsen & Brockhoff 1989, No. 129.
125. Bersu 1947, pp. 3–58 (pp. 53–4).
126. Lucas 1953–4, pp. 86–9; Lucas 1971, pp. 134–6.
127. Lucas 1975, pp. 13–20 (pp. 16–17).
128. Binchy 1941, p. 6 (§12).

a citation from a now lost law tract concerning 'sea-judgments' (*Muirbretha*) mentions salt among the items that might be expected in the cargo of a trading ship (*barc*).[129] Besides its obvious use for food conservation and storage, salt was also required for baptism and for the consecration of new settlements.[130] Fish figures regularly in the monastic diet, but fishing rights were also the subject of frequent disputes among *seculari homines*.[131] The monks of Bangor apparently thought nothing of making a two-day journey for freshwater fishing (despite having the sea on their doorstep); on occasions the fish could even be scooped out by hand. Besides the fish and domestic animals, the monks of Iona also had preserves of seals.[132] There is no trace in Irish written sources of oysters, such as are mentioned as a delicacy by the author of one of the letters from the first-century AD Roman fort at Vindolanda (Hadrian's Wall) in the north of Britain,[133] but the general impression from the wealth of shell-finds by archaeologists is that seafood formed a significant part of the diet at least in the maritime areas of Ireland.

Beer was drunk, sometimes with gusto: according to the Annals of Ulster, Gilla Mo-Chonna mac Fógartaig († AD1013) died in his sleep after a binge (*iar n-ól*), while Muirchertach mac Domnaill Uí Maél Sechlainn fell off a bridge at Cork in a drunken stupour and drowned (AD1163). Visitors to Crónán's monastery at Roscrea were served (in the manner of the Gothic emissaries in Gregory the Great's *Dialogues*) with miraculously fermented beer and got heartily drunk.[134] The laws cite drunkenness and indolence (*mesca ocus lesca*) as two great failings;[135] but there does not appear to have been a serious problem with drink. Besides, the beer was not always the best: bitter beer could make men sick, according to the Life of Lugaid of Clonfert (Co. Galway); however, on this occasion the king took a hand in the matter, noticed a passing beggar who, for some strange reason carried his shoes in his hands, and when asked why answered that he had been given them by the saint. The king purloined the shoes and dropped them into the beer, miraculously sweetening it.[136] Another wort which failed to ferment properly was saved by having a fragment of the cross of saint Aéd dropped into it.[137] The brewer in Colmán Elo's monastery sought the saint's help with wort that failed to ferment; the result was a gushing geyser of miraculous beer without end![138] The laws refer to a process called 'combing' (*círad*) which involved

129. Thurneysen 1927, p. 409.
130. Plummer 1910, ii, pp. 53–4; i, p. cxxvii n. 12.
131. Plummer 1910, ii, p. 7 n. 6.
132. Anderson 1961, pp. 294–6 (*Vita Columbae* I 41).
133. Bowman 1983, p. 47.
134. Plummer 1910, ii, p. 29; on the Goths, see Momigliano 1955, pp. 207–45, repr. Momigliano 1966, pp. 181–210 (p. 181–2).
135. Thurneysen 1923, p. 343 (§5).
136. Plummer 1910, ii, p. 220.
137. Plummer 1910, i, p. 43 n. 12.
138. Heist 1965, p. 215.

using an unidentified implement to separate fermented malt,[139] but there are, unfortunately, no details of the brewing process from our period.[140]

For connoisseurs of the native brew, the continental beer occasionally left a lot to be desired. A mid-ninth-century Irish pilgrim, passing through Liège on his way to Rome, complained to the local bishop about the conditions in his bed-and-breakfast: 'I cannot live in such misery', he exclaimed, 'with nothing to eat or drink save the most awful bread and the tiniest particle of dreadful beer'.[141] Another Irishman writes of the local beer 'as one who throws his boots at it'.[142] The great Sedulius Scottus regaled his patron, Bishop Hartgar of Liège, with a long list of grievances, including the really horrible beer.[143] If Sedulius is anything to go by, the Irish on the continent preferred to take their chances with the local wine, rather than risk the worst with the beer.

BEES AND BEE-KEEPING

Honey was used, as we have seen, as a sweetening agent in the brewing of ale, and in the manufacture of dairy spreads; both figure regularly in the law tracts. There is an entire law tract, *Bechbretha* ('bee judgments') devoted to the legal intricacies of bees and bee-keeping – an indication of the importance of apiculture in the early medieval economy. The tract lays down detailed regulations concerning swarms and their maintenance, even to the extent of legislating for 'trespass' by bees! Three things are listed as being particularly thorny problems in early Irish law: 'destruction by bees, horses, and pigs', because liability was so hard to establish.[144] Another law text includes bees among the eight categories of livestock, along with cows, pigs, horses, sheep, goats, hens, and geese; a similar classification is found in the sixth-century Burgundian Code.[145] Destruction of bees in large numbers was sufficiently serious to warrant recording in the annals: the Annals of Ulster *s.a.* AD993 record a plague of people, animals, and bees throughout Ireland. Theft of bee-hives figures in the laws and in the saints' Lives, and bee-keeping was sufficiently well established by the eighth century for the ecclesiastical law text *Cáin Domnaig* ('Law of Sunday') to list tracking of swarms as one of the few activities which the church permitted on Sundays.[146] The tract on sick-maintenance, *Bretha Crólige*, mentions honey as a relish or condiment and includes it in a list of three such condiments which should not be administered to the ailing (along with fish or meat cured with

---

139. Thurneysen 1923, p. 350. Something of the kind appears to have turned up in one of the recent digs conducted by the wetland survey unit.
140. The evidence from the laws was collected by Binchy 1982, pp. 3–6.
141. *MGH* Epp. Kar. Aevi, iv, p. 195 (No. 31).
142. Waddell 1927, p. 60.
143. *MGH, Poetae Latini Aevi Carolini* [PLAC], ii/4, p. 169.
144. Binchy 1973b, p. 80 (§11).
145. Drew 1949, p. 24 (*Lex Gundobada* IV 3).
146. Hull 1966, pp. 151–77 (p. 162).

sea-salt, and horseflesh), because honey induces diarrhoea. Elsewhere in the same law tract, however, honey is singled out as being suitable for an *aire ard* ('high lord'), together with fresh garlic and celery.[147] The tract *Bechbretha* obliges the owner of a swarm to supply neighbours with honey in order to satisfy the needs of someone who is suffering from a craving (*miann ngalair*) – perhaps another term for pica, the craving which affects some women during pregnancy (also called *mír méinn* 'the portion of desire').[148] Wheat bread baked in honey figures in the list of food fit for heroes in the saga *Fled Bricrend*, of approximately the same date.[149] Honey was particularly suited to storage and provided much-needed nutrition during the winter months.

Honey bees also produced a second valuable commodity: wax. Wax was used to manufacture candles, especially important in the monastic economy but also listed among the renders of the lay clients. Beeswax could also be used to make wax tablets, frequently mentioned in the saints' Lives as writing material.[150] Compared to other early medieval societies, bees and bee-keeping were probably no more important in Ireland than elsewhere; there are laws on the subject in the Visigothic codes (rewards for finding a swarm, damage done by bees and rights to swarms, theft from hives); in the Burgundian Code, in Frankish law, in the Lombard Edict of Rothar,[151] and closer to home, in Welsh law.[152] But in all these cases the subject of swarms and hives is disposed of very briefly; where Irish law differs is in its lengthy treatment of 'grazing trespass' – a unique concern, not found in any other early medieval legal system – and in its complicated treatment of ownership of swarms.[153] The detailed regulations in the law tract make it quite clear that bee-keeping was a domestic industry and that honey was not simply gathered in the wild. Patrick does mention wild honey (*mel siluestre*), which sustained him and the ship-crew that took him from Ireland,[154] but the evidence strongly suggests that bee-keeping was a significant element, particularly in the monastic economy. In fact, a tradition existed already in the eighth century that honey bees were first introduced to Ireland from Britain by Mo-Domnóc, a seventh-century saint.[155] The linguistic evidence shows the tradition to be impossible, and there can be little doubt that bee-keeping was an integral part of animal husbandry in Ireland from an early date.

147. Binchy 1938b, p. 108.
148. Kelly & Charles-Edwards 1983, p. 52 (§6); pp. 99–100.
149. Best and Bergin 1929, pp. 248.
150. Plummer 1910, i, p. cxv n. 11.
151. Visigothic: *Lex Visigothorum* VIII 6, 1–3; *MGH*, Leges i, pp. 349–50; cf. King 1972, p. 213; Burgundian: see note 144 above; Frankish: *Lex Salica* LIV; *MGH*, Leges i/4 pt 2, p. 222 (theft); Lombard: Drew 1973, p. 114.
152. See Kelly & Charles-Edwards 1983, pp. 192–205, Appendix 7.
153. Kelly & Charles-Edwards 1983, pp. 72–84 (§§36–49).
154. White 1905, p. 241 (*Confessio* §19).
155. See Kelly and Charles-Edwards 1983, p. 40.

POPULATION

The overwhelmingly agrarian nature of the medieval Irish economy, and the high productivity implied by the substantial rents and food renders, give an impression of relative prosperity. For most members of society the level of comfort was probably considerable. True, there are occasional glimpses in the laws and in the saints' Lives of less fortunate individuals, indigents or beggars, like the *sinnach brothlaige* (lit. 'thieving fox'), the character who is compelled by dire necessity to steal for his survival and who is considered exempt from prosecution for that reason (an immunity recognized also in Common Law until Denning). Lords, naturally enough, could expect to enjoy a greater quantity of the agricultural produce than their clients, since they drew most of their annual rents in the form of food renders. On the whole, however, the sources give no reason to believe that there was any widespread or chronic poverty.

It is impossible to make any meaningful estimates of population levels or demographic changes; the occurrence of widespread and devastating plagues in the mid-sixth century and again in the late seventh must have seriously reduced the population, but we cannot tell by how much. There is perhaps a residual folk memory of such traumatic events in the Life of Gerald of Mayo and related literary sources, which report that there was such a burden of population in the years preceding AD664 that there was not sufficient land for all: every *colonus* (the term used in continental sources to denote the bound servant of an estate) received a portion of nine ridges (*iugera*) or seven of flatland (*terra plana*), eight of rough arable (*de aspera*), and another nine of woodland (*de silua*).[156] Such was the burden on the land of this over-population, however, that it occasioned famine (*erat occasio famis*), which provoked disagreement between Gerald and Fechín of Fore concerning the relief measures that should be taken. Fechín advocated a fast by leading clerics and the aristocracy in order to draw down a plague on the lower classes, while Gerald resisted this drastic and elitist solution. According to the commentary on Colmán's hymn – which recounts the same episode in slightly different detail –

> The sons of Aéd Sláne and Fechín of Fore and Ailerán [of Clonard, Co. Meath], and Manchán of Liath Mancháin [Lemanaghan, Co. Offaly], and many others fasted together with the nobles of the men of Ireland for the thinning of the people ... Wherefore the Yellow Plague was inflicted on them, and there died therof in that year the sons of Aéd Sláne and the elders that we have mentioned.[157]

The Life of Gerald states that it was through his intercession that the plague wreaked havoc on the kings and clerics, rather than on the lesser folk

156. Plummer 1910, ii, p. 113.
157. Stokes and Strachan 1901–3, ii, p. 298.

(*populus inferior*), with the result that one-third of the entire population was carried off. The story is apocryphal, of course, but the Yellow Plague (Justinian's Plague) was not. The experience of plague in the neighbouring island, and in the rest of Europe, would lead one to expect a marked drop in the population as a result of these recurrent crises, and there is a sporadic hint of such things in Irish sources. Bishop Tírechán, for example, in his statement of Armagh claims to property, asserts that the rival community of Clonmacnois had taken over several foundations left derelict after the plagues of the 680s (*per uim tenent locos Patricii multos post mortalitates nouissimas*);[158] similar devastation is recorded by Bede in his famous account of the Anglo-Saxons at Rath Melsigi (Co. Carlow), who were almost wiped out by the plague of AD664.[159] Bede reports the plague of that year as 'raging far and wide with cruel devastation and laying low a vast number of people', and the anonymous author of the Lives of the Abbots of Wearmouth-Jarrow has a pathetic account of the annihilation which the plague wrought, leaving none of the monastic community to perform the services save the abbot himself and one young boy.[160]

Survival and subsistence were matters of delicate balance, and incidences of plague – or even less drastic natural disasters, such as heavy snow in winter followed by crop failure in summer – could trigger a series of cataclysmic consequences. The annals occasionally record the forced migrations of peoples as a consequence and there can be little doubt that many, if not most of the movements commemorated in later 'origin legends' have their historical origins in natural disasters of that kind. On the whole, however, early medieval Ireland was a settled community. There is no evidence whatever for pastoral nomadism and large-scale movement of peoples;[161] the general impression is of a people strongly attached to the land.

What conclusions should one draw from this review of the evidence? On the face of it, one might be excused for thinking that early Irish society was rigid and static, conservative in its ways and hidebound by custom and tradition. Very possibly this was indeed the case, though one should beware of accepting at face value the seemingly immutable aspect of Irish society, particularly as it appears reflected in documentary sources. On the other hand, the turmoil that must have accompanied the fifth- and early sixth-century political and social cataclysms – though a thing of the past by the time we reach the seventh century – must have caused after-shocks of disturbance and dislocation long after they had become little more than a memory. However, harmony – not disharmony – is the striking trait that emerges from the later historical sources.

---

158. Bieler 1979, p. 142 (§25. 2).
159. Plummer 1896, i, p. 193; Colgrave and Mynors 1969, pp. 312–14 (*HE* III 27).
160. Plummer 1896, i pp. 388–404 (p. 393 §14). It is generally believed that the young boy was Bede.
161. For evidence concerning transhumance, see Byrne 1971a, p. 140.

CHAPTER 5

LAW, FAMILY AND
COMMUNITY

The most remarkable feature of early Irish society was its homogeneity. From a very early date Ireland could boast of a standard vernacular language, common to all peoples in every corner of the country. Irish in fact preserves the oldest vernacular literature in western Europe, and this literature reflects a uniformity of language throughout the country which still defies adequate explanation. For Ireland was never a part of the Roman Empire and never had to suffer the iron hand of Roman rule. The centralizing structure of Roman civilization, with its official language, law and city-based administrative system, never took root in Ireland, and when, therefore, Ireland eventually did come under the influence of Rome it was, as the Irish missionary saint Columbanus put it, the Rome of Saints Peter and Paul, not that of the Caesars.[1] Although Irish people everywhere shared the same language – in the surviving literature there are no traces whatever of dialect variations, another unique feature in the context of early vernaculars – and although they probably also shared the essentials of common religious cults, the political organization of society, by contrast, presents a very fragmented picture. True, the epic literature, which purports to represent a prehistoric era, describes a country which was a unitary whole, marked off only by the boundaries of the ancient 'Fifths' or provinces (cóiceda < cóic, 'five'), but the picture of society which emerges from the documentary records of the historical period is one in which the country was dotted by myriad small, tribal kingdoms, each separate and independent, and each ruled by its own king. This kind of society has been characterized as 'tribal, rural, hierarchical and familiar',[2] with the emphasis on the local and particular aspects of social organization. By the time of our earliest documentary evidence (law texts, genealogies, and annals), the vision of Ireland as a unitary state, ruled by a 'high-king', had apparently disappeared, to be replaced by a patchwork of local tribal kingdoms, each confident in its own distinctiveness.

1. 'licet enim Roma magna est et vulgata, per istam cathedram tantum apud nos est magna et clara' ('for though Rome be great and famous, among us it is only on that chair [of St Peter] that her greatness and fame depend'); Walker 1957, p. 48 (Ep. 4, 11).
2. The now classic definition of Binchy 1954, pp. 52–65 (quotation, p. 54).

The localized nature of this Irish society is well illustrated by references in Saint Patrick's writings to the necessity of purchasing the goodwill and protection of kings (*regibus*, Conf. §52) in order to carry on his missionary activities in safety. He also refers to the sons and daughters of minor Irish kings (*filii Scottorum et filiae regulorum*, Conf. §41, Ep. §12) who had entered the religious life. The distinction he makes between grades of kings is important, especially as it comes from our only contemporary fifth-century source. Compared with other contemporary barbarian kingdoms in western Europe, such as Anglo-Saxon England or the Frankish realms, where kings were few, or Visigothic Spain and Lombard Italy, where only one king ruled at a time, Ireland is notable for the proliferation of its kings. Where a Lombard ruler in Italy could boast of owning perhaps a tenth of the total land mass of the country,[3] and where the Merovingian kings of the Frankish territories disposed of even greater landed wealth, the multiplicity of Irish kings meant that their kingdoms were correspondingly smaller and less powerful.

According to one early Irish law text, 'that is no kingdom (*tuath*) which has no clerical scholar, no church, no poet, no king to extend contracts and treaties to [other] kingdoms (*tuatha*)'.[4] The word *tuath*, of course, changes in meaning with the passage of time, but the word *rí*, when it occurs in the early laws, usually refers to such a tribal king and it is in terms of his rights and prerogatives that the rights of the ordinary citizen are defined.[5] There is a further distinction in the laws between the minor king (*rí tuaithe*) and the over-king, a man who was overlord of three or four lesser kings (*fuirig < fo + ríg*)[6]. Such an over-king – termed 'great king' (*ruiri*), or 'king of *tuatha*' (*rí tuath*) – might in turn be subject to the most exalted class of king recognized by the laws, the 'king of over-kings' (*rí ruirech*), otherwise described as 'chief of kings' (*ollam uas rígaib*), or 'provincial king' (*rí cóicid*). Such over-kings might exercise power by virtue of personal or dynastic connections, or simply by dint of their strong right arm. The *cairde* mentioned in the early law tract on poets generally involved the negotiation of friendship treaties between neighbouring tribes; the *cor* ('agreement, contract') also referred to might involve a formal conclusion of inter-tribal alliance, which involved the lesser kings in personal pledges of loyalty on behalf of their peoples. But the over-king had no superior rights in law: in theory at least the individual *tuath* was accorded full legal status and its people were recognized as enjoying the same rights as the peoples of other *tuatha*. The law recognized only one jurisdiction, the *tuath*;[7] the petty tribal king and his people were regarded as the norm.

---

3. Wickham 1981, pp. 71–2.
4. Gwynn 1942, pp. 1–60, 220–36 (p. 31); = Binchy 1978, p. 1123: 'Ni ba tuath tuath gan egna, gan egluis, gan filidh, gan righ ara corathar cuir ocus cairde do thuathaibh'.
5. For an excellent synopsis of the legal material generally, see Kelly 1988.
6. The number of lesser kings required of such an arrangement fluctuates; see Kelly 1988, pp. 17–18.
7. Mac Neill 1935, p. 110.

'NATIONAL LAW' OR 'TERRITORIAL LAW'?

It is in this context that the surviving corpus of early Irish law takes on such importance, for despite the seeming multiplicity of kings and loyalties, the edifice of the law stands above all local and regional rivalries as a unified system of custom and practice. Early Irish law is what scholars call 'territorial' law: it applies equally to all citizens in every part of the country. How this came to be the case, we simply do not know. The political map of the so-called 'post-heroic' era (the 'heroic' era being that Ireland which is represented in the stories of the Ulster Cycle) seems too riven by deep-rooted dissensions and enmities to allow for any unanimity of purpose in the promulagation of such a fundamental thing as the law. Perhaps the explanation lies in the solidarity and cohesiveness of the learned order (the druids initially, and then their later offshoots, the poets, lawyers, and priests), a feature that survives down to the end of the Gaelic world in the remarkable unity throughout the country of the bardic order of poets. But does the law itself go so far back as to carry us beyond the threshold of early Irish history? Some scholars have thought so, most notably the late D.A. Binchy, doyen of Irish legal historians, who had this to say:

> For the student of early institutions the Irish law-tracts have a peculiar importance in that they provide lengthy accounts of primitive rules and remedies of which we find only vestigial survivals in the oldest records of other civilisations. There are two reasons for this. First, the introduction of Christianity in the fifth century brought in its wake the art of writing into a society which was still archaic, even primitive. As a result the members of an already powerful and well-organized legal caste were enabled, one might almost say by accident, at an exceptionally early period of social evolution to embody in permanent form the oral tradition that provided the framework of that society. Secondly, the unique 'antiquarianism' of the Irish jurists made them retain among their written sources rules and institutions which had fallen into desuetude long before their own day.[8]

But since Binchy's formulation first appeared in print his views have become matters of controversy and debate. The supposed antiquity of early Irish legal institutions, the 'archaism' of Irish tradition, the influence of Christianity on Irish social and legal developments, the contrast of oral versus written law – all these topics have been placed under the microscope in the last ten years or so by students of early Irish history, sometimes with startling results.[9]

8. Binchy 1973a, pp. 22–71 (quotation, p. 22).
9. The new foundations were laid by Binchy 1978; see the review-article by Charles-Edwards 1980, pp. 141–62.

LAWS AND INSTITUTIONS

Several difficulties confront the would-be student of early Irish laws and institutions, not least the fact that all of our law texts, without exception, are written in Old Irish (i.e. the language as written c. AD600 to c. AD900). This fact in itself is worth remembering, particularly when we come to the question of Christian influences on the law and the interaction of Irish customary law with biblical law. Another difficulty is the fact that a large proportion of the Old Irish legal texts survive only in a fragmentary form, often little more than brief excerpts or maxims from ancient texts accompanied by more-or-less elaborate glosses and explanatory commentaries. At least one-third of the best-known collection, *Senchas Már* ('Great Tradition') survives now only in this fragmentary condition. Irish scholars do not like to talk about 'codes' of law, emphasizing that Irish law contrasts starkly with the formal systems of Roman jurisprudence and shows no trace of ever having been systematically collected, revised and publicly issued in codified form in the manner, say, of the emperor Justinian's *Corpus Iuris Civilis* in the mid-sixth century. Nonetheless, there are collections of Irish law which appear to have their origins in some of the early law schools and which may possibly have enjoyed particular authority, the best known of these being the aforementioned *Senchas Már* and *Bretha Nemed* ('Judgments of privileged persons'), to the contents of which we shall return.[10] Many of the texts bear witness to the practice of expounding and interpreting the laws in schools, as evidenced by the accompanying gloss and commentary. And one modern scholar has made significant advances in the classification of legal texts according to whether they are written in a textbook style or in a more allusive and sometimes quasi-poetic form redolent of earlier days when the transmission of law was supposedly oral.[11] On the other hand, several important tracts (including some of the oldest, such as *Bretha Nemed* and the tract on status called *Críth Gablach*) do not appear ever to have been glossed. This raises the awkward question: what purpose had the Irish law texts in their written form? Were they the work of a class of professional lawmen – *brithemain* 'judges/jurists', whence the term Brehon Law – whose function in society was the preservation of obscure customs from time out of mind, imbued with a reverence bordering on the pedantic for the legal pronouncements of earlier generations? This has certainly been the view of some scholars, Binchy in particular. These early Irish lawyers, described sometimes as a 'mandarin caste',[12] have been frequently portrayed as a group of warped minds, gnawing on the bones of a discarded learning. But so harsh

10. See Breatnach 1989, pp. 1–40. For discussion of these and all the other surviving law texts see especially the judicious treatment of Kelly 1988.
11. Charles-Edwards 1980, p. 146 ff.; see also Charles-Edwards's article on early Irish law in the *New history of Ireland*, i (forthcoming).
12. See, for example, Ó Corráin 1987, pp. 284–307 (p. 285).

a judgement is hardly fair; it derives in large part from a misguided view of medieval law, and Irish law in particular, an attitude unthinkingly superimposed on the early material by scholars conditioned to the view that the law is concerned primarily with crime and punishment, not with compensating the victims of wrongdoing.[13]

EARLY IRISH LAW – ITS NATURE AND ITS LAW-TEXTS

Irish law treated all felonies and misdemeanours as civil offences (as torts, to use the modern legal terminology), i.e. wrongs for which the law prescribed compensation in the form of damages. There was no concept of criminal law, and therefore none of the objects of modern criminal law, such as punishment and retribution, deterrence of would-be wrongdoers, or reform of wrongdoers. There is no evidence that the early Irish thought in those terms, and therefore the liability which men incurred by wrongdoing was strictly a damage liability, not a punishment or penal liability. There were no crimes against society as such (with the exception of betrayal of the *tuath* to an enemy), only injuries done by individuals to other individuals. Modern lawyers, accustomed to an imposing edifice of case-law deriving from copious court records and statute law enactments are understandably bewildered by the early Irish law texts, which present a very different picture of law and society. There are, in fact, almost no surviving records of court procedure for the early Irish period,[14] and the concept of case-law, in which the decisions of particular cases are regarded as binding precedents for similar cases in the future, is entirely absent. Where early Irish lawyers appeal to precedent it is usually to invoke some mythical figure as the source of a particular legal text: thus the laws concerning craftsmen such as blacksmiths, wood-wrights, metal-workers, or physicians are fathered on the pre-Christian deities that were patrons of such activities: *Bretha Goibnenn* ('The judgments of Goibniu'), *Bretha Luchtaine* ('The judgments of Luchtaine'), *Bretha Crédine* ('The judgments of Crédine') and *Bretha Déin Chécht* ('The judgments of Dian Cécht') respectively. There are no judgments attributed to historical personages, whether judges or kings, and only in the so-called 'wisdom texts' are kings depicted regularly as law-givers.

Nor does Irish tradition offer any parallels to the role as law-makers played by the rulers of contemporary barbarian kingdoms in England or Wales or on the continent; there are no Laws of Ine or of Hywel Dda or of Liutprand or the like, for the simple reason that Irish kings did not issue edicts (except in very exceptional circumstances). We have, in fact, none of the charters, diplomas, writs, or wills which characterize the legal systems of neighbouring realms in this era; only towards the end of our period, in the eleventh and twelfth centuries, do such new-fangled instruments appear, and then principally under the influence of feudalizing kings and their legal

13. For some very useful comments, see Jenkins 1988, pp. 89–92.
14. For the exceptions, see Kelly 1986, pp. 74–106.

henchmen.[15] It is precisely the feebleness of what might be termed executive legal power among early Irish kings that explains the large space (excessive, some would say) occupied by the minutest provisions for the conduct of legal suits when parties default on agreements. To that extent the absence of records of court cases should not be taken to infer that formal law was irrelevant: 'The parties to a dispute are most ready to compromise when they realise that the law may not be in their favour'.[16]

The absence of any record of court cases, therefore, and likewise the absence of any concept of a case-law determined by legal precedent, does not mean that there was justice in early Ireland but no law.[17] On the contrary, the most striking aspect of early Irish law is the sheer quantity of texts and the extraordinary variety of topics covered by them – some indeed that are unusual, to say the least, and not found in other contemporary legal systems in western Europe.[18] There is always a danger of overrating both the trustworthiness of written laws and the importance of the matters they deal with, as compared with more mundane matters for which the direct evidence of documents is lacking. This is no different in the case of early Irish law; but the sources themselves make a distinction between the texts of the law (*bélra Féne*) and the matters of purely domestic, everyday concern, what we might call custom and practice (*cumlechta Féne*), which are not considered worthy of discussion in any great detail and which accordingly did not require a judge 'learned in the law' to decide them. To that extent, the surviving law texts may be viewed as a superstructure on a much larger base of custom. The customs and practices of a people within a *tuath* or kingdom (*urradus*) can be changed by agreement at an assembly, and a new regulation (*nós*) introduced as a result, but generally speaking the same practices appear to have applied more-or-less unchanged for generations. Even royal enactments (*rechtge*), which are rare and only arise in cases of emergency, serve only to regulate details outside of customary law, and cannot override individual personal contracts already in existence. The king has no executive power that might make him overmighty.

What, then, do the laws talk about? In summary, they can be categorized under the following headings:

Status and rank Four tracts have survived detailing the various ranks and grades of the aristocracy, with their property-qualifications and entitlements, and their legal rights;

Professional groups Several tracts on the duties of judges, poets, and other 'privileged persons', and (lost) regulations concerning other craftsmen;

Categories of persons Law texts on the subjects of marriage and fosterage, kin-groups and their relationships, clientship and the relations of lord and

15. On the question of early charters, see Davies 1982b, pp. 258–80.
16. Jenkins 1988, p. 90.
17. The formulation is based on Jenkins 1988, p. 90.
18. See Kelly 1988, especially pp. 264–80.

client; maintenance of elderly people, and provisions concerning the mentally ill;

Personal injuries Although there is an abundance of scattered material on the subject, there is in fact no continuous tract on corporal injuries. There are, however, several tracts on the archaic institution of sick-maintenance, with other regulations concerning accidental injuries and injuries suffered in the playing of sports;

Theft and other offences Theft and liability in the case of accessories and relatives of the criminal, arson, and a now lost tract on the subject of poetical satire;

Land-law Tracts on land and its classification, joint husbandry and cooperation of neighbours; laws concerning water-courses and fishing estuaries, 'Bee-Judgments', 'Tree-Judgments', and 'Sea-Judgments' (i.e. the regulation of flotsam and jetsam), and various regulations concerning cats, dogs, deer and deer-trapping;

Contract law By comparison with Anglo-Saxon law,[19] the Irish texts preserve a great deal of information on this subject, which has been collected and analyzed in a recent monograph;[20]

Pledges, sureties, loans and deposits This includes the regulation of personal contracts and agreements between neighbouring kingdoms;

Distraint and legal entry Tracts on the alternative legal procedures available to victims in order to enforce a legal claim. The texts on distraint are particularly interesting, since they provide a detailed description of a procedure which had all but disappeared already by the time of the Twelve Tables (c. 450BC), the oldest surviving documents of Roman Law;

Legal procedure Tracts on the regulation of court procedures, the classification of evidence, and appeal of judgments.

The evidence, therefore – and it is substantial – suggests that the law governed every aspect of daily life and strove at least (if it did not always succeed) to provide a model of normal and acceptable behaviour – an important matter in an era when courts with compulsory jurisdiction were still largely unknown. Because early Irish law was not a fixed code it could not be done away with by decree (royal or otherwise), nor by simply ignoring it. The law had to be reinterpreted, and where changes had come about in social or legal practices, the older rules are often retained beside those which had superseded them. This has an inestimable advantage for the modern student of Irish law because it makes it possible to distinguish successive phases of evolution in the law and to trace the transition from one phase to

19. See Pollock 1893, pp. 239–71 (p. 256).
20. McCleod 1992.

the next. Sometimes these changes must be inferred from linguistic differences such as are found occasionally in composite texts. On other occasions, however, the changes are explicitly pointed out by the authors or compilers of the texts themselves, and these instances are particularly interesting because they graphically illustrate the law in process of evolution and at the same time give the lie to the notion that the lawyers were all unthinking obscurantists, deliberately concealing the cracks in their impressive edifice of monolithic, unchanging, and immutable law.

EVOLUTION, 'UNIFORMITY' AND 'IMMUTABILITY' OF THE LAW

A good example of such change in practice alluded to directly in a law text occurs in the tract on the subject of distraint or *athgabál*, the practice of seizing the property of a wrongdoer and holding it in order to compel him to submit to legal remedy.[21] Writing of the different periods of stay (whether one, three, five, or ten days after seizure of the goods) after which the seized goods become forfeit, the author of the tract has this to say:

> Stays were established on distraints; and there are [now] two [different kinds of] notices for every distraint, notice of five days to a debtor and notice of ten days to a kinsman if it be distress from a surrogate that is being taken. Those people (i.e. the ancients) had a fourfold classification in the notice preliminary to distraint; on the other hand they had neither stays nor delays in pound but simply forfeiture after a single day on every occasion. This was changed afterwards so that now it is [a case of having] four stays and four delays in pound and two notices.[22]

Here the law has clearly advanced from a period when retribution for an injury suffered was immediate and drastic, namely the seizure of the wrongdoer's stock, to a position which mitigated that initial severity, by obliging the injured party to give notice of what he has done. This in turn was changed to an obligation on the part of the client to give advance warning of his intention to distrain, and failing any move towards settlement of his claim before notice expired, the requisite number of stock were impounded. But where earlier these were immediately forfeit the plaintiff now had no more than a lien on them, a 'stay of execution', as it were, during which the stock could still be recovered if the claim were settled. Finally, a second period of stay was introduced so that if the defendant failed to make good the loss, the animals distrained were finally and irrevocably vested in the claimant.

What is noteworthy about the passage is the obvious anxiety of the lawyers to reduce as much as possible the potential for mayhem that existed in such situations. The earliest phase of law must have had, as a result, outbursts of

21. See Binchy 1973a, pp. 22–71 (pp. 63–4).
22. Binchy 1973a, p. 63.

violent conflict between any such rival claimants, for it is easy to understand how an individual who came home to find his cattle gone and no idea of what had happened to them might resort to violence when he discovered that they were distrained by a neighbour, and perhaps even forfeit (if he had failed to locate them or establish the reason for their disappearance within the stipulated period of notice). Even more understandable would be the chagrin of a kinsman (the 'surrogate' of the text) whose stock was removed in lieu of the wrongdoer's cattle. Not only justice but common sense dictated that he at least be accorded the right to be informed as to why his stock had been removed, where they were impounded, and who had acted as agent for the claimant. The obscure and difficult formulaic language used by the law tract in describing the procedure of formal notification suggested to Binchy that here were 'all the characteristics of an ancient ritual', one which could be traced back to the very beginnings of the law.[23]

Another interesting example of the law in process of transformation and adjustment occurs in the tract on status known as *Críth Gablach*, in a passage that discusses the institution called *othrus*. In early Irish law, when someone injured another person, instead of paying a standard rate of compensation (called 'leech fee' or *laecefeoh* in Anglo-Saxon law) he was obliged to undertake the duty of nursing his victim back to health and providing him with medical attendance for the duration of his convalescence.[24] The older term for this obligation in Irish is *folog* 'maintenance' (also called *folog n-othrusa* 'sick-maintenance') but subsequently denoted also by the term *othrus*. With the passage of time, however, the original provisions of the law were diluted: as a first step the obligation to provide a 'safe house' for the injured party's convalescence, and to provide for him (or her) and his entourage during the period of recovery, was changed in favour of an arrangement whereby the patient recuperated at home, and the retinue were no longer supported. Mac Neill, who translated *Críth Gablach* seventy years ago,[25] believed in fact that in the oldest period of sick-maintenance the provision for *snádud co forus tuaithe* ('[the victim's] accompaniment to the *f.t.*') denoted the existence of a public infirmary (*forus tuaithe* can be translated 'resting-place of the *tuath*') in every tribal kingdom, a kind of xenodochium such as is found in other parts of Europe at the same period. Such a secular institution, if it really existed, would be unique in early medieval law, for in other countries such hospices are invariably the preserve of the church in our period.

There may have been good reasons for this change from original practice, for, as Binchy pointed out, 'where one person has injured another of malice aforethought, the prospect for the victim of being nursed back to health by the kin or friends of his aggressor (possibly even in the latter's own house) is not calculated to reassure him'![26] In these new circumstances the injurer's

23. Binchy 1973a, p. 64.
24. See Binchy 1938b, pp. 78–134.
25. Mac Neill 1923, pp. 265–316.
26. Binchy 1938b, p. 126.

liability now consisted in providing the victim in the latter's own home with food, a doctor, a nurse, and a substitute to carry out his manual duties. It was only natural, then, that these obligations in turn would be offset by substituting a single payment to cover all of them. With the establishment of a uniform payment for all victims, whatever their status, Irish law eventually fell into line with other ancient and medieval legal systems. This is the situation reflected in *Críth Gablach*, whose author/compiler (writing *c.* AD700) was familiar with the older state of affairs but who prefaced his discussion of them with the following remark: 'Sick-maintenance does not exist today at the present time, but rather the fee for [= appropriate to] his worthy qualities [is paid] to each according to his rank, including [compensation for] leech's fee and ale and refection, and also the fee for blemish, hurt, or loss of limb'.[27] When due allowance is made for the possibility that the writer's views are not necessarily typical,[28] it is nevertheless clear that the institution of sick-maintenance was an ancient one in Ireland, one that could be traced back a good deal beyond that date, perhaps even into pre-Christian times.[29] It is equally clear that the lawyers were not always driven by a desire to conceal such changes in society as are mirrored in the evolution of sick-maintenance.

Binchy and others have chastised early Irish lawyers for propagating a 'fiction of uniformity' in their presentation of the laws by showing a wilful disregard for the evidence of their own experience, preferring instead to conceal its constant changes under a veneer of pseudo-archaism.[30] The charge raises another closely related question with regard to the laws: the difficulty of establishing what is divergent interpretation on the part of the lawyers, and what is contemporary regional variation. But the criticism – though justified to a certain extent – nevertheless glosses over an important fact: law tracts of different authorship and provenance, and doubtless also of different regional origins, all use the same Old Irish technical terms[31] and treat of the same institutions and customs, even if they do not always handle them in the same way. In other words, Irish law is, as we remarked above, 'territorial' law. This is borne out also by the terminology: the texts refer to *béscnu ínse Érenn* ('the legal practice of the island of Ireland'). In other words there is no 'nationality' in the law, and no distinction made between the laws of the Ulstermen and those of the Leinstermen, nor between any other such provincial or political jurisdiction. It is perhaps possible that there was such a regional or ethnic association in the earliest period, since the oldest Irish law is termed *Fénechas*, i.e. 'the law of the *Féni*' – the same word as *Fianna*, the warrior band later associated with the activities of Finn mac

---

27. Binchy 1938b, p. 128; cf. Binchy 1941, p. 2 (§8).
28. Thurneysen remarked that 'the author of C.G. often goes his own way' ('Der Verfasser des C.G., [der] oft seine eigenen Wege geht'); Thurneysen 1923, p. 344.
29. For striking parallels with ancient Hittite practice, see Watkins 1976, pp. 21–5.
30. See, e.g., Binchy 1973a, pp. 65–6.
31. See Thurneysen 1930, pp. 353–408 (p. 379), where he gives a list of terms (*aidbsen, aire coisrig, aire fine, ánsruth, muire, muiredach*) which all apparently have the same meaning and seem to represent regional variants of the one legal concept.

Cumaill and hence of Leinster origin, like Finn himself. But by the time the laws were committed to writing, the term *Fénechas* is usually taken to represent the customary law of all Ireland in the archaic and pre-literate period; but the names of all the other provinces and their peoples occur without any indication that their law differed in any significant way.[32]

When *Fénechas* is quoted in later texts it seems to be thought of as oral law rather than written text, and preserves archaisms of language and style that are redolent of a time when the law was couched in mnemonic prose or primitive verse to facilitate its memorization in the brehon law schools. 'Furthermore, the early laws appear to think of the secular *brithem* as a man who carried on an un-bookish trade.'[33] Whatever the merits of the argument that Irish law was, from an early date, imbued with much of the spirit of canon law (and this is a subject we shall return to shortly), it is surely reasonable, nonetheless, to believe that there were brehon lawyers in the period down to the fifth century and beyond who practised their trade in the time-worn manner of their ancestors. Saint Patrick, after all, reports how he had to arrange safe passage for himself and his entourage with 'those who gave judgment' (*illi qui iudicabant*).[34] When and how was this law first committed to writing, and who were the men who carried out the task? Why did they write in Old Irish rather than in Latin? What was the motivation for the undertaking, and how did the people involved ensure uniformity in their work? These and other questions have been hotly debated in recent years, as we said above, and though the earlier views of scholars such as Binchy have in some crucial aspects been modified, in many cases it must be said (appropriately enough) that 'the jury is still out'.

THE FIRST LAW-SCHOOLS

The present generation of scholars (with some notable exceptions) seems to have arrived at a consensus regarding the identity of the men who committed the laws to writing: they were, to a man, clerics resident in the monastic schools of the sixth and seventh centuries.[35] The case has been most emphatically and consistently presented by Professor Donnchadh Ó Corráin, who argues that 'in early Christian Ireland, the lawyers, poets, canonists and ecclesiastical scholars formed a single mandarin caste whose legal and other writings, in Latin and the vernacular, are to be seen as the products of a single – though latitudinarian – ecclesiastical culture'. The case rests essentially on the belief that only in the context of ecclesiastical schools (and in the Irish case that is usually taken to mean monastic schools) was there

---

32. Charles-Edwards points out that it can also mean ordinary Irish law as opposed to enacted law (*cáin*) or book-law (*lebair*), i.e. canon law or related ecclesiastical regulations; see Charles-Edwards 1980, p. 146 n. 14.
33. Charles-Edwards 1980, p. 146.
34. White 1905, p. 251 (*Confession* §53).
35. See especially Ó Corráin 1987, *passim*.

access to literacy in the Latin alphabet and the Latin scripts used by Irish scribes when writing both in Latin and in the vernacular. To a certain extent, the ultimate resolution of the debate will rest on the question of when Latin literacy was introduced to Ireland; whether as a result of Christianization (as most scholars have accepted to date), or at a much earlier date, when the ogam alphabet is believed to have been composed.[36] If literacy followed the introduction of Christianity – in the fifth century, or even in the fourth – then the case for the monastic schools is greatly strengthened, for it is difficult to see how otherwise the originally non-Christian brehon law schools could have acquired a knowledge of writing.

ROMAN LAW AND BARBARIAN LAW

There is a marked contrast between the situation in Ireland and that in the Germanic kingdoms of our period. There it can be shown that cooperation existed between Roman noblemen and the newly-established Arian regimes of the later fifth century.[37] For example, the Burgundians under their king Gundobad (d. AD516) issued a law for themselves (*Lex Burgundionum*) in Latin, followed by a separate code for their Roman subjects, the *Lex Romana Burgundionum*. Such legislation would have been inconceivable without the assistance of men familiar with Roman vulgar law, and a very plausible case has been made for identifying just such a likely collaborator in the person of Syagrius (descendant of a Praetorian Prefect and consul for AD381), who was described by Sidonius Apollinaris as being fluent in the Burgundian language and who was, moreover, 'a new Solon of the Burgundians in rendering laws' (*Nouus Burgundionum Solon in legibus disserendis*).[38] Similarly, in Visigothic lands the Arian king Euric (AD466–84) issued the first known codex of Romano-barbarian law, which in turn has been associated with the person of Leo of Narbonne, whom Sidonius compared to Appius Claudius, and who seems to have functioned as official legal advisor to the king. A third example comes from Italy, under the Ostrogoths. The *Variae* of Cassiodorus (head of the Arian king Theodoric's civil service) tell us of Cyprian – comparable to Syagrius as is Cassiodorus himself to Leo – who was apparently grandson of Opilio, Prefect of Rome in AD451–52 and consul in AD453, himself a member of Theodoric's government whose sons grew up in the royal *comitatus* to fight like Goths and speak their tongue. Men such as these, though they may have found the experience initially distasteful, clearly provided the expertise in Roman law and administration without which the Latin barbarian codes could not have been written. Other examples can be found for Frankish Gaul.[39] But there were no such late antique grandees in fifth-century Ireland, and no

36. See further discussion of this question below, pp.190–1.
37. See the important remarks of Wormald 1976, pp. 217–26, especially pp. 222-3 (in a review of John Matthews, *Western aristocracies and imperial court*).
38. Cited from Wormald 1976, p. 222.
39. See James 1982, pp. 81–3.

comparison can be made with continental experience in this regard. There was no 'Late Antiquity' and no late-Roman tradition of law and administration in early Ireland. If early Irish law texts were committed to writing for the first time in the century or so following the introduction of Christianity, then it seems more likely that the process would have involved churchmen, writing down laws *iuxta exemplum Romanorum* in the manner of those clerics who drafted laws (in Anglo-Saxon) for king Æthelbert of Kent at the beginning of the seventh century.[40]

CLERICAL INFLUENCE ON VISIGOTHIC LAW

As it happens, there is an interesting parallel to our Irish situation to be found in mid-seventh-century Visigothic Spain.[41] During the reign of Chindasuinth (AD641–52) there was a concerted drive to reform and revise the older codes of Visigothic and Hispano-Roman law that dated, in some cases, from the fifth century. The result was the work known as the *Liber Iudiciorum* or *Forum Iudicum*, a collection of ninety-eight laws which was subsequently presented to the Eighth Council of Toledo in AD653 for approval by the Spanish bishops, before being declared law by the king. Shortly after Chindasuinth was joined on the throne by his son Recesuinth in AD649 – a move suggested by Bishop Braulio of Saragossa – the heir apparent received a letter from the bishop which describes in fascinating detail how the clerical scholar had been commissioned to revise the ancient legal codes from the original manuscript.[42] The relevant passage reads as follows:

> . . . The deplorable state of the codex, which I have received for correction, has mustered all its forces against my clouded vision, and while I try to conquer them, the very vision which was becoming blind seemed to aid the enemy, and to multiply obscurity to its own detriment. It will be apparent to Your Glory, however, how much labour there is in it, how exacting it is, how many times I have despaired of correcting it, and how many times I have given it up due to various ailments, only to return again to the interrupted task with the intention of fulfilling your request, adding a line here, and deleting letters there; for it is so cluttered up with scribal negligences, that I hardly find a sentence which does not need correction, and hence it would have been quicker to rewrite the whole thing than to correct it. At the command of Your Serenity, however, we desire ardently to recognize the welfare of your kingdom with all our efforts . . .

Is this the kind of activity that Irish clerics busied themselves with in the sixth and seventh centuries? Were they huddled over ancient legal manuscripts, difficult to read and even more difficult to understand? Are the clerical influences in the laws to be explained by such activities, or is the Christianization of the brehon schools a much more deep-rooted and thorough-going affair? Binchy maintained that there was 'ample evidence . . .

40. See Plummer 1896, i, p. 90; Colgrave and Mynors 1969, p. 150 (*HE* II 5).
41. For what follows see especially Lynch 1938, pp. 126–40.
42. Text in Madoz 1941, pp. 171–3; English translation in Barlow 1969, p. 85.

that the law-schools were among the centres of resistance to the new faith'.[43] On the other hand, what one scholar has wittily described as 'the emerging orthodoxy',[44] states that the distinction between secular schools of brehon law and ecclesiastical schools is no longer valid for the period from the early sixth century on, after the triumph of Christianity and its suppression of the older system. 'It is difficult . . . to see how the home-grown traditional lawyers could have stood out successfully against the social prestige and intellectual weight of Christianity and its legal systems and preserved essentially unchanged their inheritances from pre-history'.[45] But there are difficulties with this interpretation, not least because it leaves some basic questions unanswered, and some unasked.

CLERICAL INFLUENCE ON BREHON LAW

All students of the subject now agree that ecclesiastical influence on brehon law was significant, but there is no evidence in Irish sources comparable to the Spanish or Frankish material which might indicate the same degree of involvement by Irish bishops in the civil courts as was clearly enjoyed, for example, by the Hispano-Gothic bishops in Spain. Irish bishops did not sit with local magistrates and preside over secular legal cases; on the contrary, early Irish canon law (sixth-century, or fifth?) specifically warns members of the church against having anything to do with the secular courts.[46] Nor were Irish bishops obliged by canon law to reside at the royal court for a certain period each month to act as advisors to the kings (as the Visigothic bishops near Toledo were obliged to do by the last canon of the Seventh Council of Toledo in AD646).[47] On the face of it, therefore, it does not seem an unreasonable *a priori* proposition that the secular schools held themselves aloof for centuries from the activities of their clerical counterparts. But even if this view is not accepted, is it necessary to adopt the opposite pole of the argument and believe that the brehon lawyers were entirely subsumed into the church and its system?

It is surely significant, for example, that all the Irish law texts, without exception, are written in Old Irish, not in Latin. This striking contrast with the situation in the barbarian kingdoms of Europe surely requires explanation. It cannot be (as one eminent English scholar has claimed) because there was no one with sufficient knowledge of Latin to bridge the gap between local custom and Latin vocabulary,[48] that the Irish, in other words, were incapable

43. Binchy 1966, pp. 1–66 (quotation, p. 4 n. 1). No substantiation of the statement was offered.
44. The term was coined by Harvey 1987, pp. 1–15 (quotation, p. 15 n. 53).
45. Ó Corráin 1987, p. 284 (quotation).
46. Bieler 1963a, pp. 54–8 (p. 56); see the commentary in Hughes 1966, pp. 44–5.
47. Lynch 1938, p. 137.
48. Wormald 1977, pp. 105–38 (p. 115). See also Jenkins's reply to this argument in Jenkins 1981, pp. 323– 48 (pp. 346–7).

of writing good legal Latin; for we know that the Irish schools enjoyed a reputation second to none in terms of their standard of Latin scholarship. Nor is it enough to argue that the Irish held their own language in particularly high esteem, and therefore felt no need to render their laws into an alien tongue. Modern experience provides ample evidence to show that when faced with 'the social prestige and intellectual weight' of a rival civilization, language is usually the first casualty. A third alternative, advanced by an American scholar, is based on the ingenious but not altogether convincing argument that the barbarian codes are written in Latin because if one considers that Latin was likely to have been the language spoken by the majority of the inhabitants of the areas occupied by the Germanic tribes, 'then there is a sense in which all of the barbarian codes were written in the vernacular'.[49] In the one striking instance where it has been demonstrated that a supposedly archaic law text in the vernacular was, in fact, derived directly from a Latin original (in the Irish collection of canon law),[50] commentators have not explained why the Latin text was translated in the first place, and why the archaic rhythmic prose patterns of the oldest *Fénechas*-type laws were imitated in that translation. The answer is, surely, that for law to be accepted as venerable it must appear like the 'good old law', and therefore be written in Irish, not Latin.

This and other evidence would tend to suggest that native Irish law and canon law had already profoundly influenced one another by the latter half of the seventh century at the latest.[51] This is argued to be the case particularly in the prose law tracts, most of which are believed by modern scholars to have been composed in the seventh century and collected together in the eighth. Reference has been made to the parallel activity in the field of canon law compilation, when the materials for the great corpus known as *Collectio Canonum Hibernensis* ('The Irish collection of canons') was assembled by two clerics, Ruben of Dairinis, on the river Blackwater, Co. Waterford († AD725) and Cú Chuimne of Iona († AD747). The impetus to gather together the secular law tracts, it is suggested, 'owe[s] much to the example, if not the labour, of the canonists'.[52] But where there is undoubtedly evidence to show that clerics were concerned with secular law and played a large part in giving it the shape in which we find it, conversely it can be shown that influence flowed also in the opposite direction and that Irish canon lawyers took over many of the institutions and legal concepts of their brehon law peers. Several law texts contrast ecclesiastical and secular law, often acknowledging that aspects of the older customary law embodied features which were not necessarily compatible with God's law but which could be justified in terms of 'natural law' (*recht aicnid*). The distinction could sometimes lead to amusing and instructive attempts by the literati to justify retrospectively

49. Stacey 1991, pp. 39–60 (quotation, p. 43).
50. See Breatnach 1984, pp. 439–59.
51. Ó Corráin 1984, pp. 157–8.
52. Ó Corráin 1984, p. 157. For continental parallels, compare McKitterick 1985, pp. 97–117.

aspects of the pre-Christian code which appeared to run parallel with church law,[53] and it found expression also in legends concerning pre-Christian Irish kings such as Cormac mac Airt, who are said to have foretold Christ's coming. In some instances, it must be said, *recht aicnid* meant not so much old pagan law as common sense, and was invoked in cases where neither customary nor written law (*recht littre*) offered a precedent.[54] Even the heavily Christianized *Bretha Nemed* was prepared to 'render unto Caesar what is Caesar's and render unto God what is God's',[55] while the eighth-century legal tract known as *Uraicecht Becc* ('Small Primer', on rank and status) combined the rival traditions neatly by stating: 'Every judgment of a churchman that exists, it is on the truth and entitlement of scripture that it is based; the judgment of a poet, however, is based on maxims (*for roscadaib*); the judgment of a lord, however, is based on them all, on maxims, on precedents, and on scriptural citations'.[56] There are instances where the disputes that must have taken place between the proponents of the two rival camps can actually be seen in the texts themselves. An example concerns the institution of marriage, and the related question of inheritance.[57]

WOMEN: MARRIAGE, LAW AND PROPERTY

The church's rules concerning marriage, and its prohibition of marriage between members of an ever wider circle of kindred, presented serious problems for lawyers in early Ireland, as indeed they did elsewhere also. Pope Gregory the Great, for example, in his *responsio* to St Augustine of Canterbury (AD601) setting out rules for the newly-converted Anglo-Saxons, forbade absolutely marriage of first cousins, but was prepared to concede that the Anglo-Saxons might marry their second or third cousins, as they were accustomed to do. The directive was controversial, and caused St Boniface in the early eighth century to doubt the very authenticity of the papal letter.[58] When these rules were applied to the circumstances of early Irish society they gave rise to equal controversy. The earliest reference to the matter, in the text known as *Synodus II Patricii* (falsely ascribed to Patrick, but undoubtedly old), states the position bluntly:

> On consanguinity in marriage
> Understand that the law has spoken, nothing more, nothing less. However, they say that they have neither seen nor read what is observed by us, namely that they be separated by four degrees.

53. See especially McCone 1986a, pp. 1–35.
54. Thurneysen 1927, pp. 167–230 (p. 178).
55. Binchy 1976, vi, p. 2214. 34–5: 'Ma eclais, riar eclaisi uime; no riar nime do tabairt do nime; ani bis etar feine imanetar, riar feine uime'.
56. McCone 1986a, p. 12.
57. For what follows I am indebted to Ó Corráin 1984, *passim*.
58. The literature on the Gregorian *Responsiones* is vast; see Meyvaert 1971, pp. 15–33.

De consanguinitate in coniugio. Intellege quod lex loquitur, non minos nec plus: quod autem obseruatur apud nos, ut quattuor genera diuidantur, nec uidisse dicunt nec legisse.[59]

Whatever was meant by this rule (i.e. whether it forbade marriage with first cousins only, or whether it extended up to and included third cousins) is not clear, but what is clear is that the rule cut directly across the established practices of early Irish society regarding inheritance. Donnchadh Ó Corráin has demonstrated how the church's restriction affected particularly the question of female heirs where there were no surviving sons. In those instances, a daughter inherited a life-interest in her father's estate, but this reverted on the daughter's death to her father's surviving kin within specified degrees. The daughter could, however, ensure a continued interest for her children in her father's estate by resort to a legal compromise: by marrying one of the ultimate heirs, i.e. one of her father's cousins. There is evidence in two early Irish sources that this was regarded as the preferred solution. According to the first text, a poem in archaic language, binding sureties are given that the property will not be alienated permanently out of the kindred, and seems to prescribe parallel cousin marriage as the solution to the problem. The second archaic text, *Din Techtugud* ('On legal entry') supports this interpretation with reference to a hypothetical woman 'who sprang from two forks', i.e. an heiress issuing from a parallel cousin marriage. The text says that her *fine* ('family') accepted her taking possession 'because it was a case of reversion' (*fo bíth ba n-adba taisic*).

It is precisely this solution that we find adopted in Irish canon law, where the *Hibernensis* cites a decree of an Irish synod (*Synodus Hibernensis*):

> The authorities of the church have much to add here: that female heirs should give sureties that the property might not be alienated . . . and should they produce sons by their father's relations, these should inherit the patrimony.

> *Auctores ecclesiae hic multa addunt, ut feminae heredes dent ratas et stipulationes, ne transferatur hereditas ad alienos . . . Si peperint filios viris cognationis, hereditas paterna filiorum erit.*

The lawyers sought and found explicit justification for this practice in Old Testament law (Numbers 27: 10–11) but the terminology used is that of Irish law: *ratae* and *stipulationes* are simply calques on the Irish terms *ráth* and *naidm* (which we shall discuss further below).[60]

Given that the existence of such a practice effectively limited the prospects of a church that might otherwise have hoped to inherit property of individuals who failed to produce sons, and given also the strict limits on direct alienation of property to the church expressed elsewhere in the laws,[61]

59. Bieler 1963a, p. 196. My translation differs slightly from his.
60. Ó Corráin 1984, pp. 160–1.
61. See Binchy 1978, pp. 522.33 ff., and 527.20–533.20.

it may be thought that here was good evidence for a stand-off relationship between the church lawyers and their secular peers, or at the least a gentleman's agreement to differ. A similar, and equally significant, difference of legal opinion is found in the laws on the subject of marriage and divorce, but in this instance the brehon lawyers turned the tables very deftly on their canon law rivals. The text known as *Cáin Lánamna* ('The law of couples')[62] is a detailed and comprehensive description of the many different types of marriage (and other) unions that were permitted in Irish law, together with an equally detailed account of the provisions for divorce and the divisions of property resulting on separation. Contrary to the impression often given by modern religious zealots who advocate a return to 'traditional Irish values' in matters of sexual and moral behaviour, early Irish society was unequivocal in its recognition of and support for multiple marriage and divorce. A man could, for example, have a principal wife (*cétmuinter*) in the first form of marriage, and another partner as well. Indeed one text, *Bretha Crólige* (on the subject of sick-maintenance) refers to the possibility of a man having three partners simultaneously. Moreover, the term generally used for the second partner, *adaltrach* (from Latin *adultera*) shows that the secular lawyers were not in the least put off by the contrary arguments of the church, nor by the pejorative tones of the term used by the canon lawyers. The offspring of both marriages would have equal inheritance rights, and the concept of illegitimacy arising from such unions is unknown to the law. The two women would not, of course, have equal status, but in most other respects the arrangement was accepted as normal – at least for the aristocracy. Though there is little or no explicit evidence in the surviving corpus of genealogies which would point to polygyny (i.e. the possession of more than one wife at the one time), as distinct from serial monogamy (wives acquired after the death of a partner, or after separation), the law texts are quite unambiguous on the subject, and the opposition expressed by canon lawyers to the practice serves to copper-fasten its existence. But though the church might intone gravely against this perceived 'abuse' and publish decrees against it ('On not having concubines as well as a legitimate wife', *De concubinis non habendis cum legitima uxore*, in the *Hibernensis* collection, Book 46, ch. 18), the author of the tract *Bretha Crólige* mentioned above neatly trumped the clericalist argument: 'There is a dispute in Irish law as to which is the more proper, many sexual unions or a single one; for the chosen people of God lived in a plurality of unions, hence it is not easier to condemn it than to praise it'.[63] In other words, if the Hebrews in Old Testament times could have many wives, why should not the Irish? Nowhere in *Cáin Lánamna* is there any condemnation of multiple marriage or divorce and in fact the pre-Christian marriage practices of the Irish were to survive right down to the end of the Gaelic world in the seventeenth century.

62. Thurneysen 1936, pp. 1–55. For commentary see Kelly 1988, pp. 70–7, 102–4, and Ó Corráin 1985a, pp. 5–24 (which supersedes in part his earlier article, Ó Corráin 1978a, pp. 1–13).
63. Binchy 1938a, p. 44 (§57).

MARRIAGE AND DIVORCE

It would be wrong, however, to exaggerate the status of women in early Irish society. That society was patriarchal and every aspect of social, legal, political and cultural life was dominated by men, as was the case in every medieval European society. In most such societies women were subject to men, whether to their fathers when young, or to their husbands when married, to their sons if widowed or to the head of their *fine* ('family/kindred') if spinstered, and to the church if they were nuns. Within such constraints, however, women in Ireland appear to have enjoyed a greater degree of independence than in contemporary Germanic kingdoms on the continent.[64] This was particularly the case with regard to marriage and divorce. By the end of the seventh century the normal type of marriage (at least the one about which there is most discussion in *Cáin Lánamna*) was one in which both the man and the woman contributed equally to the marriage goods and the woman is described as 'a woman of joint dominion, a woman of equal lordship'.[65] This form of union entitled the woman to examine and, if need be, object to any of her husband's important contracts in matters such as affected the family farm. Nothing essential to the household economy could be alienated without consultation with the other spouse, but both retained control of their own separate personal and private property (there was no such thing as common marital property). If the marriage were subsequently dissolved each partner then received back what each had contributed to the marriage in the first place, together with any profit that accrued from their joint activities during the marriage. The division of property was in accordance with fixed proportions: one-third went to the partner who provided the land, one-third to the partner who provided the stock, and one third to the partner who provided the labour. In this last instance the woman's work about the farm and in the domestic economy is given full recognition. Such was the arrangement in cases of 'no fault' divorce. If, on the other hand, one or other partner was deemed guilty of misbehaviour which had brought about the separation, then his or her proportion of the family property was reduced accordingly.

Corresponding to the wide varieties of partnership allowed by the law was an equally wide variety of grounds for divorce, and in these provisions the woman's physical well-being and dignity were fully protected. Indeed, a German scholar has remarked that 'the possibility of more or less easy dissolution of marriage will be evaluated differently according to one's outlook but the care which is evident for the individual personality of the woman in Irish marriage law is a widely shining landmark in this early period of western history as compared with the unrespected position of women in

64. See Drew 1977, pp. 17–26; repr. Drew 1988, chapter VIII.
65. For what follows see especially Ó Corráin 1978a, p. 2 ff., and Ó Corráin 1985a, p. 6 ff.

earlier times and in other societies'.[66] When one considers that the penalty for a Burgundian woman who sought to divorce her husband was to be drowned in dung, one can appreciate the strength of the comparison.[67]

Initially, it seems, men in Ireland (as in all ancient and medieval societies) had much wider rights to divorce than women, while women had few, if any. Thus a man could repudiate his wife if she brought disgrace on his honour, by infidelity or constant thieving, by procuring an abortion or by doing away with a newborn child. He could also divorce 'a woman who makes a mess of everything' (*bé loites cach rét*)[68] – which is not as bizarre as it sounds: the glossators of the law text relate it specifically to work with flax and wool, and a woman's importance in terms of spinning, weaving, dyeing and clothes-making, together with all the other activities in her role as housekeeper, were taken very seriously indeed; hers was a vital role in the smooth running of the domestic economy.

However, Irish law also allowed a woman a wide variety of grounds for divorce (fourteen in all), which took account of her physical and psychological needs and protected her physical person. A woman might divorce a man who failed to satisfy her sexual needs, either because of sterility or impotence ('because an impotent man is not easy for a wife'). Likewise in the case of a woman whose husband was either bisexual or homosexual (the woman 'whose bed is spurned'); she was entitled to be paid her bride-price or dowry in addition to a fine in compensation, and to part company with her husband if she wished. Neither could a husband discuss the intimate details of the marriage bed for all and sundry to hear, 'because it is not right for a man who tells of bed to be under blankets'.[69] Such indiscretion was another ground for divorce. Likewise the 'rolling stone' (*fer coirthe*) who abandoned wife and family for a life on the road could also be divorced, since he was no longer in a position to maintain them properly. In addition, of course, should a husband abandon his wife in order to join the church, this too was considered grounds for divorce.

The divorce laws are specific also about the physical abuse that a woman might suffer, and which she could cite as a reason for separation. A husband could strike his wife in order to correct her but if he so maltreated her that a lasting blemish remained, then she could divorce him or not, as she pleased. One is reminded of the touching detail in Gregory of Tours's *Histories*, when a blood-stained handkerchief bore the telltale signs of abuse that led the Frankish kings into war with their Visigothic Spanish neighbours in order to

---

66. Knoch 1936, p. 262 (quotation); translation cited from Ó Corráin 1978a, p. 8.
67. Von Salis 1892, p. 68 (*Liber Constitutionum* 34,1); cf. Drew 1949, p. 45. For comparison with Frankish society, see McNamara and Wemple 1976, pp. 95–124, and Wemple 1985, especially chapters 2–5.
68. Thurneysen 1925, pp. 302–76 (p. 360). This interpretation has apparently been overlooked by Kelly 1988, p. 75 n. 50.
69. This and the previous citation from Kelly 1988, p. 74.

defend their kinswoman's honour.[70] Even if the original face-wound disappeared, a woman was entitled to the equivalent of her bride-price as compensation from her husband. In general terms, therefore, the woman enjoyed considerable protection under early Irish law – in some respects more protection, in fact, than under the present Common Law.[71]

THE LEGAL STATUS OF WOMEN

It has frequently been stated that the influence of the church must have helped to raise the status of women in early Irish society,[72] with reference particularly to their legal capacity. Mac Neill, however, was of a different opinion, preferring to see the change as a natural progression from an earlier law and custom of the pre-Celtic population.[73] From an initial position, in which women enjoyed no independent legal rights whatsoever but were dependent always on the intervention of a male member of their family (father, husband, or whomever) to vindicate their rights, the status of women appears to have risen by degrees to a point where they could act independently in many legal situations, and could even acquire and retain personal property and dispose of it as they saw fit.[74] There were probably always some classes of property which belonged to women and which were deemed to be inalienable even in the earliest period when women's rights were least developed. In the laws concerning distraint, for example, an exception was made to the normal rules in circumstances where the

70. Chlotchilda, sister of the Frankish king Childebert, had married the Visigothic king Amalaric, who tried to induce her to abandon her Catholic faith and adopt the Arian religion. This he did by *inter alia* ordering that dung be poured on her head when she was going to mass. 'Ad extremum autem tanta eam crudelitate dicitur caecidisse, ut infectum de proprio sanguine sudarium fratri transmitteret'. Childebert, *maxime commotus*, led his army into Spain seeking vengeance; Krusch 1937, 106–7 (*LH* III 10).

71. One might compare the current situation in the Republic of Ireland regarding common ownership of the home; as I write there is no legal protection for a wife who is not a co-signatory of the deeds of ownership. A legislative proposal to change the law was struck down as unconstitutional by a recent Supreme Court judgment.

72. Kelly 1988, p. 77, is only the most recent expression of this view. Readers who follow this line would do well to ponder Fr John Ryan's description of Patrick's women converts: 'What service such virgins rendered . . . cannot be accurately estimated, but they were certainly considerable. To provide vestments for the clergy, cloths for the altars, decorative hangings for the walls, and to see to the general cleanliness and beauty of church interiors would doubtless be their chief work'; Ryan 1931, p. 134. One can only add that it is a good thing that Saint Patrick did not field a football team.

73. Mac Neill 1935, p. 66.

74. For a full discussion of the subject, see Thurneysen 1936, which is devoted entirely to the evidence from legal sources. For comparative evidence from a neighbouring Celtic society, see Jenkins and Owen 1980.

defendant was a woman, and the modified rules applied almost entirely to matters connected with the woman's share of household and agricultural labour. Altogether thirty-three cases are enumerated, most of them relating to implements and articles specifically associated with the work of women.[75] This and a similar innovation which is found in the tract on *tellach* (in which women's right to ownership of land is vindicated) are ascribed, significantly enough, to the authority of Brig, a mythological woman-jurist, whose supposed judgment in the matter actually corrected and revised a contrary verdict of her equally mythological jurist-husband Senchae mac Ailella. Such modifications of the law were traditionally traced back to 'leading cases' adjudicated by some legendary jurist, and Brig is introduced here only in connection with the improved status of women; women judges or jurists are otherwise unknown from early Irish sources.

Similarly, there must always have been certain situations in which women could give legal witness, though they were not normally permitted to do so (their evidence being regarded as 'biased and dishonest').[76] Readers who find such a concept difficult to fathom would do well to recall that women in the Republic of Ireland were granted the unrestricted right to sit on juries only in 1962. The notion that the church was instrumental in advancing the cause of women is difficult to reconcile with the evidence on this particular point in the *Hibernensis* collection of canon law, where a bizarre scriptural justification for the ban is offered:

> The testimony of a woman is not accepted, just as the Apostles did not accept the testimony of women about the resurrection of Christ. (Book 16 ch. 3)

> *Testimonium feminae non accipitur, sicut apostoli testimonium feminarum non acceperunt de resurrectione Christi.*[77]

The fact that the women at the sepulchre were right is here studiously ignored. The laws are quite unambiguous also about the validity of female testimony in matters concerning sexual relations and marriage. In a dispute between husband and wife, for instance concerning consummation, female evidence can be called in to settle the matter; this applies equally to cases where the husband is in some way sexually incapacitated: his disability is verified by a physical examination carried out by 'women dignitaries' (*bangráid*), a form of trial by impotence which is found also in other societies.[78] In a case where a woman refuses her husband his conjugal rights either because of her monthly periods, or because she is pregnant and fears that sexual intercourse might harm her child, the law likewise regards her objections as valid, and will allow women to verify her case by physical examination.[79] The law also recognizes the phenomenon of pica, the craving

75. See Binchy 1973a, p. 37.
76. See Kelly 1988, p. 207 for this and what follows.
77. Wasserschleben 1885, p. 46.
78. See Darmon 1985.
79. Binchy 1938a, p. 67, and Thurneysen 1925, pp. 302–76 (pp. 322–4).

(called *mian ngalair* or *mír méinn*) which some pregnant women develop for particular foods and which is best-known in its folktale form in the story of Rapunzel, whose mother developed just such a craving for the winter salad called lamb's lettuce (*Rapunzel* in German, whence the title).[80] The text known as 'Bee-Judgments' requires the owner of a bee-swarm to supply his neighbours with honey gratis should any of their wives require it.[81] The law also held that death in childbirth was an exception to the rule whereby *díre* or body-fine was payable for a person's unnatural death, but this rule applied only if the woman was a recognized wife (*ben aitiden*). The implication appears to be that a woman who became pregnant as the result of a secret liaison was afforded exceptional protection by the law.[82] On the other hand, the law strictly forbade abortion and infanticide, both of which constituted grounds for divorce – though the earliest Life of St Brigit has an unambiguous reference to an abortion miraculously procured by the saint for an errant member of her community.[83]

WOMEN, CHILDREN AND THE FAMILY

The law is also detailed in its provisions relating to women and their role in the upbringing of children. In normal cases a wife was expected to share equally with her husband the duty and expenses of rearing their children. This applied also in relation to the institution of fosterage, in which children were given out to other families to be reared in accordance with a practice which was very old and also very strictly regulated; there is a law tract devoted specifically to the subject (*Cáin Iarraith*).[84] The practice doubtless originated in the necessity to forge alliances beyond the immediate family and kin circles, and there is no doubting the essentially political nature of the institution, nor the strong bonds forged by its observance. In the Old Irish saga text *Táin Bó Cuailnge*, for instance, an added twist is given to the atmosphere of tragic doom by the fact that the narrator, Fergus, was foster-father to the Ulster hero Cú Chulainn, and the famous single combat at the ford between Ferdia and Cú Chulainn is given added poignancy by the fact that the two rivals were foster-brothers. So common was it in Ireland, in fact, that the phrase 'in fosterage with' (*i n-aice le*) came to mean simply 'beside' (as it does still in Modern Irish).[85] A legal text known as *Mellbretha* ('Sport-Judgments') relates how a mythological woman named Fuaimnech 'imprisoned the royal household of Tara without drink or food and without [power] to settle the problems of Ireland until she should be paid

80. See Grimm 1984, p. 104. This topic was the subject of an unpublished paper by Prof. D. Ó Corráin, which I have not seen.
81. Kelly & Charles-Edwards 1983, p. 64 (§25).
82. Thurneysen 1925, p. 356 (§44).
83. See Connolly & Picard 1987, pp. 5–27 (p. 16 §9).
84. See Kelly 1988, pp. 86–90.
85. See also Kelly 1988, pp. 86–7.

compensation for her foster-sons'.[86] The episode seems to refer to an incident in which rival groups of boys engaged in some excessively boisterous game, resulting in the death of Fuaimnech's foster-sons (one thinks of the *macgnímartha* or 'youthful exploits' in *Táin Bó Cuailnge*).

The text of *Mellbretha* offers a fascinating (if only fleeting) insight into the realm of children and their games, and the way in which the law intruded even into this facet of everyday life by carefully assigning liability for injuries incurred in the course of play. The modern trend towards litigation over injuries suffered in school playgrounds obviously has a venerable pedigree! For instance, an obscure passage at the beginning of the tract (set in difficult heptasyllabic verse) states that causing injury to children while playing with slings (*gabulchless*) does not incur the normal legal penalties: 'it is free of penalties save for sick-maintenance until a cry of danger supervenes'. The tract then proceeds with a list of games which enjoy total immunity: hurley, ball, 'boundary pillar', excavating small dwellings (= building sandcastles?), jumping, swimming, wrestling(?), *brandub*, *fidchell*, and *buanfach* (= three boardgames), hide-and-seek, . . . juggling. All these are immune and involve neither sick-maintenance nor penalties.[87] This is followed in turn by a list of more boisterous and dangerous games which involve different legal rules. A careful distinction is made between children's games and those more competitive pastimes that involved youthful vigour and therefore a greater potential for injury. A third classification (*colcluichi* 'guilty sports') covers what might be called 'foul play': one against all, cross-pelting, king-of-the-castle(?) and throwing a wooden javelin into an assembly. The significance of this third group appears to lie in the possibility of injury to innocent third parties. Although the text has survived only in fragmentary form, it is clear that the laws originally dealt in a comprehensive fashion with this aspect of children's lives.

Clearly then, women were afforded considerable protection by the law, both in their capacity as wives but also in their own right as individuals. These independent legal entitlements were doubtless expanded in the course of time, but it is not necessary to assume (nor is there any evidence to prove) that these changes for the better came about due to influence from the church. It is almost impossible to date such innovations. Binchy believed that all the developments in the law of distraint 'must have been completed by the seventh century, possibly earlier'.[88] In regard to the status of women, Saint Patrick is our witness that already in his time women of the aristocracy, at any rate, were free to dispose of their personal jewellery as gifts to the church, though such donations clearly caused murmurings in some quarters (whether among his own flock or among unconverted kindred of the women donors is not clear).[89] By the time of the late seventh- or early eighth-century

---

86. Binchy 1968, pp. 144–54 (quotation, p. 146).
87. Binchy 1968, p. 149.
88. Binchy 1936, p. 65. For criticism of Binchy's views on the stratification of the law, see McCleod 1993, pp. 77, 86–7.
89. White 1905, p. 250 (*Confession* §49).

Additamenta to the Patrick dossier it was clearly acceptable practice for women to possess personal property (including land) and to barter such property on occasions, without recourse to intermediaries.[90] The law texts offer fleeting glimpses of the evolution that took place in the intervening centuries.

It is possible on occasions to see past the all-enveloping veil of clerical bias in the surviving literature to an earlier situation, when the influence of the church was not yet firmly established. Thus in the law relating to lords and their lesser clients (*doérchéli*) it can be seen that under the original regime, when a client absconded from his duties or payments (the possible causes cited are *mesca* and *lesca*, 'drunkenness' and 'laziness') he forfeited half of his land to his lord. This was later emended, doubtless under the influence of the church, so that the division of the forfeited land was now in thirds: one-third to the client's *fine*, a third to his lord, and the final third to the church.[91] A similar example is found in one of the Triads or gnomic statements, which states that there were three men who were deemed ineligible for *othrus*: those who evaded their duties to a lord, a kindred, or a poet.[92] In *Bretha Crólige* this has become the man who evades duties to *fine*, lord, or church. Also significant in this regard is the fact that in the tract called *Coibnius uisci thairidne*[93] which regulated matters concerning water-courses, Sunday is still included as a normal working day. By the time most of our surviving law texts came to be written down, however, such anomalies had been smoothed out and the result is a body of law in which the interests of 'church and state' are rarely distinguishable.

SURETIES

'Law is founded on contracts and legal recognition', states one text, while another states that 'it is part of the law of the kindred that each member shall enforce along with the other'.[94] Where Irish society differed was in the elaborate measures that were developed in order to ensure that the law was enforced without recourse to violence. In most cases, the law required that a contract be formally witnessed and bound by sureties; a contract without sureties was normally unenforceable.[95] To this end Irish law had evolved three different kinds of surety, the enforcing surety (*naidm*), the hostage surety (*aitire*), and the paying surety (*ráth*).[96] Where there was no public

---

90. Bieler 1979, p. 174.
91. See Thurneysen 1923, p. 344.
92. See Meyer 1906, p. 183.
93. Binchy 1955b, pp. 52–85.
94. First citation from Kelly 1988, p. 159: 'Consuiter dliged for coraib bél ocus aititin'; the second is from Binchy 1973b, pp. 72–86 (quotation, p. 80 § 9): 'Is do chórus fine saigid do cách laisin n-aile'.
95. For details, see Kelly 1988, pp. 158–63.
96. Kelly 1988, pp. 167–73, with details of earlier literature.

body to enforce the law the obligation was on sureties to guarantee the fulfilment of legal contracts. Sureties were required for all of the five 'Paths of Judgment' mentioned above, but in the case of the *aitire*, the obligation lapsed on the death of the guarantor, whereas the obligations of the *ráth* passed to his heirs. The law also stipulates that only a member of the aristocracy (*grád flaithi*) could act as an enforcing surety (*naidm*).

The commonest form of surety was probably the *ráth* or paying surety. He guaranteed with his own property that the person for whom he was standing as surety (the principal) would carry out his part of the agreement. If the principal reneged, the other party to the contract gave notice to the *ráth* that he intended to distrain or impound the amount due (plus a fine of one-third its value) from the *ráth*'s property. At this point the *ráth* gave a pledge (some item of personal property) to the injured party, while he attempted to recover the outstanding amount. If the defaulter made good the loss he could redeem the *ráth*'s pledge and pay whatever additional fines he had incurred. If, on the other hand, the principal defaulted again, the consequences for him were very serious indeed and involved him in very heavy fines, which the *ráth* was entitled to sequester from the defaulter's property. The law texts give details about different types of *ráth*, but the underlying principle was that a man could not go surety for a person of higher rank than himself, for the obvious reason that he would not have sufficient property to meet his obligations in case of default. However, where the party to a contract was unable to find a *ráth* of sufficiently high rank to guarantee payment, he was entitled to call on two sureties of lesser rank. On the other hand, the law warns against securing a guarantor of too-high rank, since it was very difficult to enforce a claim against someone of such status.

The enforcing surety (*naidm*) pledges himself to compel the debtor to perform his contractual obligations. Unlike the *ráth*, however, the *naidm* had no financial liability to the other party in the contract, even in the event of the principal's defaulting. In his case, it is his honour that is at stake and Irish law attached such importance to a man's honour that it allowed the *naidm* to use force, if need be, to distrain the defaulter's property or imprison him, and it even allowed him to resort to violence as a last resort. An archaic legal maxim states that 'there are seven blood-lettings in Irish law which do not incur penalties or sick-maintenance, and one of those is the blood [shed] by a man who enforces a binding surety' (*naidm*).[97] For this reason the early church forbade its members from functioning as *naidms*.[98] Only in exceptional circumstances (called *turbaidi*) – such as by attendance at a fair (*oénach*) – could a miscreant escape the *naidm*.

The third kind of surety, the 'go-between' (the literal meaning of *aitire*), functioned as a hostage surety and guaranteed the performance of his client's obligations with his own person and not, like the *ráth*, with his property. This meant that in the case of default the *aitire* surrendered himself to the injured

97. Thurneysen 1925, pp. 302–76 (quotation, p. 325 §17 gl.).
98. Bieler 1963a, p. 54.

party and was kept in custody ('in stocks or in prison')[99] for a fixed period until he is freed, either by the defaulter's agreeing to honour his debt or else by guaranteeing payment of a ransom fee from his own property. The *aitire*-surety was required, for example, to ensure that an accused person appeared in court, but also acted as a go-between in matters affecting neighbouring tribes. Thus an agreement (*cairde*) between two tribes was usually guaranteed by an *aitire*, with perhaps the king himself acting in that capacity (or someone acting in his place, such as a *muiredach*). This procedure differed slightly from that required by a special enacted law (*cáin*), in which hostages were given as pledges for its observation. The hostage (*giall*) was always selected by the kin-group and given by the king, but could buy himself out; the *aitire* became fully forfeit to a claimant in the event of a contract being broken. The consequences of a defaulter failing to make good his debts in such circumstances were, needless to say, enormous. Since the sureties would normally be the kinsmen or lords of the contracting parties, this system encouraged kin-groups to control the activities of their members and encouraged the aristocracy to be responsible for the behaviour of their clients by forcing them to make compensation payments to claimants. Where the burden of repayment was more than any one individual could bear, the responsibility was extended to the next-of-kin, thus broadening the net of social responsibility.

THE LAW: ITS FUNCTION AND WORKINGS

The basic, underlying premise in early Irish law was that individuals (and their families), when they suffered certain injuries under certain circumstances, would, as a matter of routine, seek satisfaction for any injury done, and that they were entitled, if necessary, to use force against the person or persons who had injured them. In other words, the feud was a recognized means of legal redress and was tolerated, at least in theory. Where the injured party was unable to obtain redress by his own efforts he could resort to certain self-help procedures whereby he invoked the assistance of his kinsmen. This was in general a reasonable assumption, and we may take it for granted that in most cases the injured parties were successful in prosecuting their claims peacefully.

The procedures, however, are not always as transparently obvious as we moderns would like them to be. For instance, Irish law laid down, in the case where statements were made on oath, that the man with most oath-helpers would win (*intí is lia lucht fíra*), if the other person's oath-helpers were of equal standing with his own.[100] Readers of Caesar's *Gallic Wars* (*De Bello Gallico* I 4) will recall his anecdote concerning Orgetorix, a recalcitrant leader of the Helvetians, who was called to book by his peers, but who evaded

---

99. In accordance with the oath which he was obliged to swear when the contract was agreed; see Kelly 1988, p. 172; text in Thurneysen 1928, p. 23 (§65 f.).
100. Thurneysen 1926, p. 16 (§3), and cf. p. 37 (§47).

punishment by bringing all his cronies to the assembly and persuading them to swear on his behalf (a process known as compurgation).[101] It is hard for us at this remove to tell how easy it might have been to get oath-helpers, or to persuade (or cajole) them to give false testimony, knowing the severe consequences for them if they were found out; but doubtless such things did happen from time to time. With the oath as the primary mode of proof, assessment of probability in individual cases was seldom sought by forensic investigation of the facts.

The greatest single problem faced by society and the law, then, was how to establish the facts. To that end the law laid down 'Five Paths to Judgment'[102] for each of which specific guarantors were required: 'truth' (*fír*), for instance when the dispute concerned inheritance of office (whether as head of tribe, abbot, or whatever); 'duty' (*dliged*), when the agreement involved a verbal contract (*cor bél*); 'right' (*cert*), where disparities appeared in a contract after its agreement and needed to be emended; 'propriety' (*téchta*), when a dispute involved persons without land; and proper enquiries (*coir n-athchomairc*), when there was doubt about correct legal process. All of these required careful legal consideration and were thrashed out beforehand by the respective lawyers in a process called *airthacra*, akin to the hearing of legal arguments in a modern court case. It was understood, however, that most disputes could be settled before recourse was had to a court, and there is nothing more calculated to upset the equilibrium of everyday life than the wilful flouting of the law: 'There are three periods in which the world is frenzied: when famine is raging, when war is waging, and when verbal agreements (*cor mbél*) are reneged on'.[103]

In certain cases, however, the crime may have been so serious, or the wrongdoer of such a position, that the normal processes of the law could not be followed. If the wrongdoer, for example, was well-connected and could call on the assistance of large numbers of kinsmen (like Orgetorix), attempts to bring him to book were liable to lead to the outbreak of full-scale feuding. In that case Irish law recognized a particular individual in society, the 'nobleman of slaughter' (*aire échta*) whose task was to lead a band of five armed men, designated by the *tuath*, to exact vengeance in neighbouring territories in circumstances which guaranteed them immunity from prosecution for any injury or damage done in the course of their activities.[104] It is quite clear that the action envisaged might include killing one or more members of another *tuath*, and Irish law in fact obliged a victim's kinsmen to carry out a blood-feud against a killer who has not otherwise been brought to justice; *Críth Gablach* seems to imply that for a period of one month after the conclusion of a peace treaty (*cairde*) with a neighbouring *tuath*, the *aire*

---

101. In this instance Caesar states that Orgetorix could call on the help of 10,000 men, who constituted 'omnem suam familiam'!
102. Thurneysen 1926, *passim*.
103. Thurneysen 1927, p. 176 (§7).
104. See Binchy 1941, pp. 14–15 (§25).

échta could lead his posse of avengers into the neighbouring kingdom.[105] The law therefore tried to pre-empt such incidents by obliging every citizen to observe certain legal procedures. This meant, in most cases, that all parties to an agreement were obliged to provide sureties who would guarantee that the provisions of the agreement would be duly carried out.

But despite the absence of any enforcing authority there was no escaping the debt incurred by wrongdoing: if a man could not pay, then his kinsmen had to pay for him; and if the kin could not or would not bear the burden, the wrongdoer was left to the mercies of the injured party. This could mean permanent slavery or death.

Did such sanctions work in practice? Patrick relates how he and his companions were set upon and plundered and himself bound in irons for fourteen days, until he was freed and all that was taken from him restored through the actions of 'near friends, whom we had provided for beforehand' (*quos ante praeuidimus*).[106] Here he is clearly speaking of surety arrangements which he had made with local kings, to whom he had made payments in order to ensure safe passage through their territories. The fourteen-day period is not referred to in any law text, but it must be assumed that Patrick's surety arrangements were the means of his escape.

The intimate workings of this closely-knit society in which rights and duties were laid down in detail and strictly observed is revealed by another fascinating episode in Adomnán's *Vita Columbae*.[107] The story concerns a thatcher(?) named Librán, who arrived at Columba's island monastery of Iona in clerical garb[108] in order, as he put it, to expiate his sins. It transpired that Librán had killed a man in his native Connaught and was consequently held in chains, with the prospect of death. However, a 'very wealthy relative' paid the body-price and he was released into his custody. Despite a binding oath to serve him all his days, Librán absconded and made his way to Iona. Thus far the story illustrates the usual procedures in relation to homicide. The killer was pursued and captured (if not apprehended on the spot). Normally, he could expect to be released if his lord, kin-group, or some other party was willing to assume liability for the 'body-fine' (*éraic*) or *wergeld*, the fixed payment for homicide. It was probably unlikely, in most cases, that the killer in such circumstances was executed. But if, after a certain period of time, the debtor failed to make the *éraic* payment, his temporary bondage became permanent and he became a captive *cimbid*. In such circumstances the family of the victim would have been entitled to flog him,[109] kill him, or sell him as

---

105. Binchy 1941, pp.70–2; McCone 1986b, pp. 1–22 (pp. 7–8); McLeod 1987, pp. 46–50.

106. White 1905, p. 251 (*Confession* §52).

107. Anderson 1961, pp. 420–35 (*Vita Columbae* II 39).

108. Another fugitive, Aéd Dub, also arrived in Iona dressed in clerical garb. Was the wearing of such a form of protection for fugitives?

109. Kelly 1988, p. 222, states that he has found no references to flogging in the Old Irish law texts; see, however, the early gloss in a Turin MS. (Bibl. Naz., F.vi.2) of Matthew 27: 26: 'Ihesum flagillatum' gl. *dilse cimbeto* 'a captive's due'; Stokes and

a slave. In Librán's case, however, a kinsman (of the victim(?), the text is not clear) paid his fine and he entered into debt-bondage with him. Technically, Librán would probably still have been entitled to his freedom had he or his kinsmen been able to pay his fine and redeem the kinsman's ransom payment. The tone of the subsequent narrative, however, suggests that his kinsmen were not willing to do so.

Considering the liability involved, and what appears to be the voluntary manner of its assumption, the kinsman probably gained (temporary) control over Librán and his possessions. In the circumstances, therefore, Librán was being somewhat disingenuous when he 'promised' to remain in his ransomer's service; in fact, he had no choice. It is interesting to see that the debt-bondage was formalized by the debtor's solemn oath (*cum firma iuratione*) that he would remain in his new lord's service. By absconding, therefore, Librán was making an already bad situation even worse, since the ransomer would presumably have been entitled to seek compensation for his loss from Librán's kinsmen.

Librán's flight to Iona could not have solved any of his difficulties. In effect, by seeking out the monastery he was looking for asylum, but Irish law strictly forbade anyone, even members of the *nemed* or privileged classes (which included clerics) from harbouring a homicide.[110] Columba's action in banishing Librán was, therefore, quite in accordance with the law, inasmuch as he did not receive the fugitive into his protection. He first imposed a period of seven years' exile on him and on his return he brought up again the matter of Librán's oath. What follows in the narrative is equally illuminating: Columba gave Librán a sword with inlaid handle, to be given to his ransomer in payment for his freedom.[111] The lord, however, did not accept the sword (as Columba had predicted he would not) but released Librán unconditionally, 'unloosing, according to custom, the captive's belt'

Strachan 1901–3, i, p. 484. The identical gloss, with the same archaic spelling (*cimbeto* for later *cimbetho*) is found in Würzburg, M.p.th.f. 61 (saec. VIII): *signum dilsae cimbeto,* see Bischoff 1954, pp. 206–73 (p. 254). Compare the term *lóg cimbetho* (*lógh cimédha* MS.), the amount required to ransom a captive, in the tract on surety: Thurneysen 1928, p. 24 (§ 67). See also the gloss on 2 Pet 2:9: 'Nouit Dominus pios de temptatione eripere, iniquos uero in diem iudicii cruciendos reseruare' gl. . . .*o (cim)bedo,* perhaps to be read *dílse cimbedo,* as in the other examples above; see Stokes & Strachan 1913, i, p. 714.

110. See Kelly 1988, pp. 9–10, 13, 80, 140; Kelly & Charles-Edwards 1983, p. 74 (§39): 'the seven absconders which exist in Irish law whom the dignitary of neither God nor man protects: bees which escape and a wandering thieving dog and an absconder from the kindred, a man of a blood-stained weapon, a woman who absconds from the law of marriage, and a woman or man who avoids the duty of looking after mother or father' ('.uii. n-éludaig do-chuisin la Féniu na dim nemed Dé na duini: beich to-choislet 7 táidchu foíndil 7 élodach fine, fer airm deirg, ben as-luí a cáin lánamno 7 ben no fer as-luí goiri a máthar no athar').

111. In Anglo-Saxon law, a prosperous wrongdoer had the option of making payment with a slave, a coat of mail, and a sword, rather than the customary 100 shillings; see Riggs 1963, p. 13.

from around his waist.[112] This was not the end of Librán's difficulties, however: 'Your brothers will constrain you to make good the filial service (*debita pietatis*) that you have for so long owed to your father and have neglected'. This is a reference to the Irish concept of *goire* (literally 'warming'), the filial duty owed to elderly parents or relations. The *Vita Columbae* seems to imply that this was the duty of the eldest son, and so much is implied also by the Irish term *macc gor* 'dutiful son'.[113] This duty was regarded as so important that Irish law recognized the right of an elderly man without sons to adopt someone from outside the *fine* whose specific task was to care for his adopted parents in their old age, an arrangement which had to be formalized by agreement (*ráith bráithirse*) with the rest of his kindred because of the potential inheritance difficulties involved.[114] By failing to look after his parents Librán was technically in breach of the law (thereby becoming a *macc ingor* or 'undutiful son') and was therefore classified as an *éludach* ('absconder' [from the law]) who could not be given protection or asylum, even by a member of the *nemed* class.

On his return from Iona, therefore, Librán's brothers compelled him to take care of his parents. When his father died shortly afterwards, that duty transferred to the care of his mother. However, as Columba had prophesied, a younger brother volunteered to release Librán from his obligation (a payment of some kind may have been involved), and Librán was thus free to return to Iona. He handed over the price of his ransom (*pretium redemptionis*) to the saint on arrival and became a member of the Iona community. It may be remarked in passing that his mother was fortunate: one legal commentary remarks that, if a son can maintain both his parents fully, he should do so; if he can merely support them, he should do so; but if he cannot even do that, he should 'leave his mother in the ditch and carry home his father to his house'![115] The only other exception to the duty of *goire* envisaged by the laws is in the case of a son being given away by his father into base clientship.[116]

The picture of Irish society which emerges from the early law texts, then, is one in which the chaotic conditions out of which that society emerged had stabilized and a settled community had come into existence. Their picture of a rural economy, based essentially on the four-generation family household kin-group, probably preserves a true enough ideal pattern for the early period, and the detailed provisions relating to such everyday matters as the sick-maintenance due to injured parties, the sureties required for legal contracts, and so on, very likely preserve some genuinely archaic aspects of

---

112. This is the only evidence I know of that captives or slaves wore such belts.
113. Fergus Kelly, in his commentary on this passage, Kelly 1988, p. 95, suggests that this duty was normally shared by a man's sons, but if that were the case, one might expect the term to be *maicc goir* 'dutiful sons' (plural).
114. Thurneysen 1928, p. 37.
115. Dillon 1936, p. 130.
116. Thurneysen 1925, p. 339 (§30).

the law, some of which can be traced back to Indo-European society.[117] However, the supposedly archaic and ritualistic features of Irish society generally in the early middle ages are more often than not exaggerated, as indeed is the thorough 'archaism' of the Irish laws on which that view is premised.[118]

The law texts depict a settled and self-sufficient rural community engaged in a mixed economy of tillage and pastoral farming. This economic system is based on the interrelationships of lords and clients (*grád flathi* and *grád Féne*). The purpose of the law is to regulate the workings of these relationships, and the Irish texts preserve a mass of information on every aspect of the economic and social activities of this farming community. Their focus, however, is overwhelmingly on the aristocracy and the independent farmers, rarely on the lower classes in society. Their principal concern is to define the property qualifications and the corresponding rights and duties of each grade, and for that purpose a man's rank or status was all-important. Three law texts, dealing mainly with status, have survived, each of which contains detailed classifications of rank.[119] In general, the basic distinction is between those members of society who were privileged (*nemed*) and those who were not; thereafter the distinction is between free (*sóer*) and base, unfree (*dóer*). Early Irish society was, in D.A. Binchy's famous dictum, hierarchical: in all cases a man's rank and status were what determine his legal rights; early Irish law did not know the principle of equality before the law.

CLIENTSHIP AND STANDARDS OF LIVING

The basis of this society is the institution of clientship: the lord (*flaith*) advanced a grant or fief of stock (rarely of land) to his clients (*céli*) and received rents and services in return.[120] The rights and duties of a lord related mainly to these clients and his status was measured by the number of such clients. Hence, the tract on status called *Críth Gablach* ('branched purchase') stipulates that the lowest grade of lord, the 'lord of vassalry' (*aire déso*) should have a minimum of five free and five base clients, while the noble at the top of the scale, the 'lord of superior testimony' (*aire forgill*) was obliged to have forty clients. In return for the grant of stock (or land) made to him, the client gave his lord a food-rent and a variety of other services, depending on the type of clientship involved. The law texts distinguish two types of client, the free client (*sóerchéle*) and the base client (*dóerchéle, céle giallnai*). Free clientship was regarded as an honourable state: one of the legal Triads includes 'serving a good lord' as one of the three virtues (*buada*) of

117. See Watkins 1976, pp. 21-5.
118. See Byrne 1971a, p. 165: 'The tribal society revealed in the law tracts is primarily that of the sixth and seventh centuries'.
119. For what follows, see especially Kelly 1988, p. 9 ff.
120. Details in Kelly 1988, pp. 26–33.

husbandry. The free client held a fief of stock proportionate to his own status from a lord, who may be of the same class as himself. For this he paid a heavy rent: one milch cow (or equivalent) for every three granted for a period of six years; in the seventh year he returned the amount of the original fief and retained the surplus stock for himself. This arrangement also involved the free client in a number of quasi-military duties.

The base client received a similar grant of livestock, land, or farming equipment. In addition to the fief, however, the lord purchased his base client's 'honour price' (*lóg n-enech*), which entitled him to a share of any compensation paid to his client for injuries sustained. In return the base client paid an annual food-rent proportional to the size of the fief. Failure to pay rent drew a heavy fine and obliged the base client to pay his lord double the rent owed. The base client was also obliged to provide winter hospitality (*coé*) for his lord and his entourage (anywhere from twenty to sixty men). In addition, the base client was expected to provide manual labour in his lord's harvest reaping party (*meithel*) and in constructing the rampart fortification (*drécht giallnai*) around his lord's dwelling (*dún*).

A man could be the base client of more than one lord at a time, thereby ensuring for himself the protection of all of them (though whether he could be a free client of one lord and a base client of another is not clear; probably not). The only legal restriction was that the grant from the second and subsequent lords had to be proportionately smaller than that received from the first – a sensible precaution against the possibility that a client might over-extend his resources. The essential difference between the free and base clientships lay in the fact that the free client could terminate his contract without penalty, and his clientship involved no surrender of his independence; the base client, on the other hand, could extract himself from his contract only with difficulty, and in most cases it must have been well nigh impossible for him to do so.

In a tribal economy where wealth was reckoned in terms of land and livestock, the standard of living among the aristocracy cannot have differed very much from that of the ordinary farmer and his family. If a man had surplus stock – as he could expect to have, in the normal course of events – he either sold it or used it to attract and maintain clients. If he had surplus land, he could either sell it or rent it to another who had more stock than his own land would support. With this rented land or stock a man could provide the essentials to maintain a family and, all going well, he could increase his herd and use the surplus to acquire clients of his own. Although the grades in society were rigidly fixed, there was always the possibility of movement between grades: 'a man is better than his people' (*ferr fer a chiniud*), and a man could always better himself. If a typical small farmer (*bóaire*) acquired sufficient wealth to support clients he could rise to a position between that of commoner and lord.[121] Clientship was a mechanism which allowed the aristocracy to acquire loyal followers and a guaranteed food supply. Free

121. Kelly 1988, p. 12.

clientship allowed the lord to invest surplus stock or land in return for personal service; base clientship was the means by which he ensured food-rent and the manual labour of his clients when he needed it.

Both free and base clients were classified as freemen, with full independent legal capacity. Beneath them, however, were lower grades of *fuidir, bothach*, and *senchlethe*, all of them legally and economically dependent on their lord. Just as a successful farmer could better his status by acquiring clients of his own, so it was possible for the less fortunate to decline in status: a *fuidir* or *bothach* whose forbears had occupied the same land for three generations was reduced to the rank of *senchlethe*, the next rank above slavery. Such a person, a hereditary serf, was part of his lord's property, and if the lord sold his land or otherwise transferred ownership, the *senchlethe* and his family passed with the property to the new owner.[122]

FAMILY, KINDRED AND LAND

Given the agricultural basis of the economy, it is clear that the family and not the individual was the important unit in early Irish society. The law tracts underline the fundamental importance of the close kin-group as the basic legal unit for purposes of inheritance, farming, and protection. The term used is *fine* (originally 'friendship'), which has a wider and a narrower connotation in the law texts. It is used like the Welsh word *cenedl* to include all individuals who are legally akin to one another (in Irish law, all male descendants of a given person down to the sixth generation). Every member of such a group is a *brathair* of the rest. In most cases, however, the laws use the term *fine* to denote the narrower circle of kinsmen who are descended from a common great-grandfather (i.e. a man's relatives in the male line down to and including his second cousins); in this case the word frequently used is *derbfine* ('certain, true kin') and every member is a *derbrathair* (Modern Irish 'brother'). Although there are occasional traces of the older system,[123] in the text called *Bretha Comaithchesa* ('Judgments concerning neighbourhood'), the kin-group, for farming purposes, at any rate, had contracted in some areas to the *gelfine*, the male descendants of a common grandfather. But by the late seventh century – the period represented by the bulk of the law texts – the *derbfine* seems to have constituted the primary social, legal, and economic unit. Most farmland was held in common (*fintiu*) and each adult member of the kin-group inherited an equal share, which was fenced and marked and farmed by each member individually, although the other kinsmen retained some control over the eventual disposal of the land.

It is not the case, however, that individuals held no private property in

122. Kelly 1988, pp. 34–5, cites examples of such transfers from the eighth-century *Additamenta* in the Book of Armagh and later texts.
123. Kelly 1988, p. 100 n. 7, where the *iarfine*, the descendants of a common great-great-grandfather, are apparently referred to, significantly, in a text relating to land owned by the kin-group.

land, and that all farmland belonged communally to the kindred. On the contrary, every individual with his own household held land in his own right, and the word used, *orba* ('inheritance'), shows that he could pass on that land to his sons. The law in fact requires that a man possess some land if he is to have full legal status. The *fintiu* ('kin-land') is so called because it could not be alienated (i.e. sold out of the kin-group) without the permission of the rest of the kin. This was a very necessary precaution against the dissipation of the kin's landholding by out-marriage and against the tendency to make donations of land to the church. The Irish adopted several means of ensuring that inheritance of land remained within the close kin-group, while the church, for its part, tried hard to impose regulations which would be to its advantage in the context of potential inheritance from individuals without male heirs.

COOPERATIVE FARMING

The law seems to have envisaged that in the normal state of affairs most clientship contracts would be between kinsmen and that the *derbfine* would function as a cooperative for the purposes of joint farming. The texts refer to a group called the *comaithches* (lit. 'neighbourhood'), comprising those adult members of the *derbfine* who were heads of their own households and who had inherited their share of the *fintiu*. This group was the unit for cooperative farming. Members arranged joint pasturing of their animals and joint ploughing of tillage land. According to *Críth Gablach*, every small farmer (*ócaire*, lit. 'young lord') owned a quarter of a plough-team, and he contracted with three other kinsmen of equal status to make a joint ploughing agreement (*comar*). In a cooperative farming arrangement the partners agreed the terms and guaranteed their performance by means of pledges and sureties; failure to abide by an agreement was punishable by penalties (*smachta*), which were heavy in such cases.

A remarkably detailed account of joint ploughing procedures (*cyfar*) in Welsh law provides some indication of how the Irish arrangements might have worked out in practice.[124] Although considerably later in date than the Irish evidence, the Welsh text clearly describes ancient practice, and allowing for the slightly different circumstances, may be used for purposes of comparison. As in Irish law, the Welsh tract is concerned with the ploughing of land already held in severalty, not land held in common and allocated to individuals after ploughing. Each partner was entitled to have any land of his choice ploughed, whether virgin soil or previously ploughed; the only limit was set by the requirement that the plough-team had to be home by nightfall after every day's ploughing. Ploughing followed the order in which the items of the ploughing unit were contributed; thus the ploughman's land was ploughed first (to set the standard); the second plot was ploughed for the owner of the share and coulter; then came the plots of the men who

124. Jenkins 1982.

contributed the first and second pair of oxen, interrupted (after the plot of the better pair's owner) by ploughing a plot for the driver. The whole tract goes into considerable detail about the equipment used and its proper maintenance and about the rights and duties of the various partners. There is no doubt that similar arrangements must have applied in the case of Irish farmers, and they required considerable legal ingenuity to ensure their trouble-free fulfilment.

The arrangements for common pasturing were equally well regulated, and the law made every effort to protect from mishaps.[125] Joint herding (*comingaire*) involved farmers agreeing to graze their animals together. Each partner contracted to put a certain number of animals into the joint herd, his number depending on the amount of land he was able to contribute; these animals were then grazed on summer pasture from 1 May to 1 November. Since the joint pasturing agreement involved the pasturing of several men's cattle on one man's land at any given time, there are strict regulations concerning the separation of such lands. The law texts are very particular about the proper construction and maintenance of fencing, and 'the great substance of land-law' (*mórmaín mrugrechto*) is defined as 'marking out boundaries, planting of stakes, [and] the law as to points [of stakes]'.[126] Where there was a dispute about title, neighbours were summoned and the dispute was settled by agreement, where possible. In some cases the evidence of boundary stones (perhaps with ogam inscriptions) was held to be binding.[127] Trespass of animals from one property to another arising from neglect of fences invariably led to litigation. In the earlier period joint pasturing, like joint ploughing, was probably restricted to close kinsmen, thereby minimizing the risks of legal action, but one short tract on *comingaire*[128] suggests that this was not always the case; it discusses joint pasturing arrangements between individuals who are partners (*céli*), rather than kinsmen.

The general impression given by the law texts, therefore, is that the everyday existence of the average community was determined by a multitude of debtor-creditor relationships among all members of society and at every level; these relationships helped to stabilize that society by perpetuating contractual arrangements and maintaining a constant balance of lords and clients. The fact that so much of early Irish law is expressed in terms of livestock or its equivalent is accounted for in the same way. Personal liability for wrongs is defined in terms of *cumals* (originally 'female slave') and *séts* (lit. 'jewel, treasure'), cattle or units of precious metals. The descriptions of

---

125. Kelly 1988, pp. 101–2.
126. See Binchy 1971, pp. 152–68 (p. 156): 'mrogad coicríoch, cor cualne, córus rinde'. On the regulations attached to fencing, see Ó Corráin 1983, pp. 247–51.
127. Binchy 1971, p. 157: 'comaithig do garmaim, gaill comlainn, caithigthi astado'. Binchy cites the following from legal manuscripts: 'int ogam isin gollán .i. amal fiadain hé' ('the ogam on the pillar stone is like a witness'), and 'int ogam isin gallán . . . gebid greim tuinide' ('the ogam on the pillar stone has the force [title] of ownership').
128. Binchy 1978, pp. 192.1–33; 576.24–577.24; *ALI* iv, pp. 101.6–103.26; cf. Kelly 1988, p. 274, and Charles-Edwards 1972b, pp. 61–4.

various types of land tenure, fencing duties, impounding of animals, payments for pannage and the value of various types of livestock and chattels all represent attempts on the part of members of a non-centralized political community to standardize and regulate every aspect of the domestic economy. The implication of the myriad rules and regulations seems to be that early Irish society was engaged in a constant struggle to control its members and restrict as much as possible the likelihood of clashes between them. While this may appear to us an excessively rigid and inhibiting structure, it had one great advantage – it worked. How it affected in turn the structures of alien institutions, such as the church, can also be measured.

CHAPTER 6

THE CONSOLIDATION OF THE CHURCH

Between the fifth century, which saw the first formal mission to Ireland, and the seventh century, when the Irish churches emerge for the first time into the full light of history, there is a serious gap in our knowledge. But from that point, *c.* AD600 onward, when the evidence begins to be available in significant quantities, the Irish churches appear to be organized along lines that differ markedly from the church in Gaul. In the century and more leading up to the 'Golden Age', changes came about that worked 'a revolution' in the structures of the Irish churches.[1] From an initially standard administrative system adopted from the western church, in which bishops ruled over dioceses whose territorial boundaries were clearly defined, the Irish churches appear to have been transformed into a quite different but distinctive organization in which most of the important churches are monastic houses, united to lesser daughter houses in a confederation or *paruchia* under the overall control of the abbot of the mother church. In stark contrast to the earlier continental pattern, the *paruchia* was not a territorial unit with fixed boundaries, for the monastic churches comprising it might be widely scattered. This and another distinctive feature marked off the Irish churches as peculiar: administrative power was in the hands of the abbot, not the bishop. Bishops there were still, of course, since the ecclesiastical dignities and sacramental functions of the bishop could never be dispensed with. But his administrative jurisdiction was apparently a thing of the past; that now rested in the hands of the abbot. There was nothing like this on the continent.

The radical nature of this transformation is nowhere better expressed than in the account given by the Anglo-Saxon historian Bede in his *Ecclesiastical history of the English nation*. Writing of the role played by Irish missionary monks in the conversion of his native Northumbria, Bede has cause to dwell at length on the contribution made by the monastery of Iona: 'This island always has an abbot for its ruler, who is a priest, to whose authority the whole province, including its bishops, are subject – an unusual order of things in which they follow the example of their first teacher [= Columba], who was not a bishop, but a priest and monk.'[2]

1. The definition is from Kenney 1929, p. 324.
2. Plummer 1896, i, p. 134; Colgrave & Mynors 1969, pp. 222–4 (*HE* III 4).

An unusual order of things for Bede, perhaps, but not for the Irish. The question is, how did this transformation come about? The usual explanation presents a picture of a first-generation Irish church, established along traditional lines with single bishops ruling over territorial dioceses, but whose structure proved totally unsuited to Irish conditions and quickly gave way in the face of the pressures imposed by the peculiar nature of Irish society. The rigid structures of this territorial church, a mirror-image of its continental counterpart, buckled under the strain and were replaced by a different organization which was better adapted to the nature of Irish society and its institutions.

THE GALLICAN CHURCH IN THE 4TH-5TH CENTURIES

It must be admitted that there is considerable force in this argument. There is no denying the crucial importance of the fact that Ireland was never a province of the Roman Empire and never acquired the apparatus of Late Roman government and administration which has left its stamp on Europe to this day. But even after due allowance has been made for that fact, the fifth-century continental church whose organization is so starkly contrasted with the Irish was not, in fact, quite so rigidly episcopal and diocesan in temperament as is usually portrayed. It is true that in the aftermath of the Empire's decline, during the fifth century particularly, offices in the church emerged as alternative career outlets for the educated young men of the senatorial aristocracy – men who might once have expected to enjoy high office in the imperial civil service. This 'aristocratization' of the Gallican church is perhaps best exemplified in the career of bishop Germanus of Auxerre (c. AD380–448), who also provides an interesting link with the missionary Irish church, for this is the same Germanus who was mentioned by Prosper of Aquitaine in his account of how the Pelagian heresy was suppressed in the British churches in AD429.

Germanus came of a wealthy and distinguished Auxerre family, studied the liberal arts in Gaul and jurisprudence at Rome, and was raised by the Emperor Honorius to the prefecture (perhaps even the Prefecture of the Gauls, which had transferred south to Arles from the imperial capital of Trier).[3] After this meteoric rise in the provincial civil administration Germanus entered the church and was made bishop of Auxerre. Examples of such dual careers could be multiplied without difficulty, but the development involved more than mere opportunism. Many of the fifth-century Gallican bishops shared an interesting feature: prior to their elevation they had undergone periods of intensive monastic training. This was the case particularly with the bishops who formed the 'circle' of Lérins: Honoratus and Hilarius of Arles, Lupus of Troyes (who accompanied Germanus on his second visit to Britain),

3. For this and what follows, see especially Prinz 1965, p. 449 ff.; Prinz 1973, pp. 1–35 (pp. 13–14).

Eucherius of Lyons, Faustus of Riez, Caesarius of Arles, and others. Such men were archetypal representatives of the Late Roman senatorial aristocracy in Gaul,[4] and their vision of the church could not have been anything other than aristocratic. The fifth-century bishop of Clermont, Sidonius Apollinaris, when making the case in favour of an acquaintance who was a candidate for the vacant see of Bourges, cited as a point in the man's favour that his wife was one of the *stirps Palladiarum* (the Palladian family); Palladius, first bishop of the Irish, probably belonged to another branch of the same stock.

Such connections are not to be ignored, but more important from our point of view, however, is that many of these fifth-century Gallican bishops were not only familiar with monasticism, they could be expected to look sympathetically on its practitioners. In this, of course, they were to contrast with most of their sixth-century successors, but for the formative period of the Irish church we can legitimately point to a dual legacy from the church in Gaul, one which need not necessarily have been incompatible with the role that monasticism came to play in the development of the Irish church. It would be mistaken to assume that Palladius – however well-connected socially – was incapable of adapting his experiences as a deacon in the church of Auxerre to the circumstances he encountered in his new mission field. The process of transformation from a rigidly diocesan to a monastic organization need not, therefore, have involved a drastic realignment of thinking among the continental missionaries, nor need the process have been as traumatic as some have supposed.

TRANSFORMATION? . . . ORGANIZATION

The late Kathleen Hughes, in one of many pioneering contributions to the study of the early Irish churches, subjected the evidence to a thorough re-examination and concluded that the transformation from diocesan to monastic was neither as radical nor as rapid as had sometimes been believed.[5] Her judicious remarks are worth quoting:

> Consideration of the ecclesiastical and secular legislation suggests that certain changes in the government of the early Irish church have often been misunderstood and oversimplified. The transition from a church governed by bishops, each with recognizable diocesan boundaries (which seem to be the limits of the *plebs* or tribe), to a church organized in non-territorial monastic *paruchiae* under the control of abbots who were not necessarily bishops, did not happen so rapidly or so uniformly . . .[6]

Working principally from the evidence of synodal activity preserved in the *Collectio canonum Hibernensis* ('Irish collection of canon law'), an

4. For detailed treatments see Stroheker 1948; Matthews 1975; Van Dam 1985.
5. Hughes 1966, pp. 44–54.
6. Hughes 1966, p. x.

eighth-century compilation, and from references in secular law texts, Hughes argued that the monastic system never completely replaced a diocesan one, that bishops were still prominent in the seventh century, and that they still exercised jurisdiction over some Irish churches at that time. By the eighth century, however (she continued), the transition was in large part completed, and the fact that the *Hibernensis* contained canons relating to a church under episcopal control was, she thought, 'inconsistent with Irish developments of the seventh century'.[7] The battle for control had been fought out in the course of the seventh century between two parties within the Irish churches: the *Romani*, who wished to see the Irish churches governed along continental lines; and a nativist group, referred to in the canons as *Hibernenses*, who championed the non-territorial system of monastic *paruchiae*.[8] Hughes believed that the nativist group had won out in this struggle.[9]

Kathleen Hughes's elegant exposition set the tone for all subsequent discussion of the church's development in the period down to AD800 (though her explanations of those changes would not necessarily find favour today).[10] More recent scholarship, however, has approached the subject with renewed enthusiasm.[11] In place of the previous consensus, which saw the Irish church in terms of rival organizations which were vying with each other for control of churches and properties, the 'new orthodoxy' – if it might be so called – offers a much more radical view, namely that there was *no* organization of the early Irish churches:

> Concerning the first introduction of christianity and its subsequent expansion, one may well question whether the Irish church has at any stage the appearance of being organized, after the manner that Gregory suggested Augustine should work towards and Theodore tried to achieve in England, or whether it was not rather the result of disorganized growth. For two centuries, the advance of christianity was probably rather slow – it is only from the seventh century that it shows any really noticeable effect in society; an organized mission might be expected to progress more rapidly. Throughout, however, there is no evidence pointing to a clearly defined hierarchical structure, no evidence for a canonically recognized metropolitan authority; in short, no sign that the growth of the church or its organization were the subject of any form of control. Instead, in the seventh, eighth and later centuries, churches clash with one another in disputes both major and minor without there being any agreed authority to whom recourse might be had.[12]

---

7. Hughes 1966, p. 124 (quotation).

8. Hughes 1966, pp. 125–33; Hughes 1972a, pp. 67–80.

9. For the broader implications of the terms *Romani* and *Hibernenses*, see further below.

10. For a misguided analogy between developments in the church and in native society, see further below.

11. Ó Corráin 1981a, pp. 327–41; Hurley 1982, pp. 297–332; Sharpe 1984a, pp. 230–70; Etchingham 1991, pp. 99–118 [who corrects a fundamental error in Sharpe's article].

12. Sharpe 1984a, p. 241 (quotation).

Whether, in fact, 'an organized mission might be expected to progress more rapidly' in the circumstances pertaining in fifth- and sixth-century Ireland is itself a moot point. Comparison with the Gregorian mission in the neighbouring island is particularly unfortunate, since some recent writers have pointed out that the church established in AD597 at Canterbury had, by the 670s, disintegrated to the point where it was not possible to muster in the whole of England the three bishops required for the canonical consecration of Wilfrid as bishop-designate of York.[13] More difficult still is the theory that the early church in Ireland was devoid of '*any form of control*', and that from the seventh century 'churches clash with one another in disputes both major and minor *without there being any agreed authority to whom recourse might be had*'.[14] The evidence, in fact, suggests a very different state of affairs.

Adomnán, in his Life of Columba, uses the term 'Irish churches' (*ecclesiae*, plural) in reference particularly to the dispute that arose around the question of Easter. There is no implication, however, that the Irish churches were not at one in the essentials of church doctrine and dogma, mindful as they may have been of the noble sentiments and conciliatory words of Pope Gregory the Great (AD591), that 'difference of customs in Holy Church does not destroy the unity of faith'.[15] Nor is there any evidence that their disagreements were somehow the result of 'disorganized growth'. Adomnán, in fact, offers some of the earliest and most interesting evidence for formal organization when he alludes, for example, to a certain synod (*quodam synodus*), held at Tailtiu (Teltown, Co. Meath) in order to pass sentence of excommunication on Columba.[16] This was a large gathering (*congregatio*), brought together in the summer (*aesteo tempore*), doubtless with a view to ensuring that as many ecclesiastics as possible could attend.[17] Despite his biographer's efforts to put a brave face on things, it is clear that Columba was severely censured, and his exile to Iona followed shortly afterwards.[18] The period is therefore around AD563, the year of Columba's departure from Ireland. Already by the mid-sixth century, then, there is unequivocal evidence for the organization of some at least of the Irish churches, an organization which allowed for the referral of disputes to synods for formal discussion and resolution. There is nothing in the evidence to suggest that such organization was confined to only a few churches, or that it was to be found only in the northern half of the country. On the contrary, another text, the famous letter of Cummian to

---

13. See especially Bethell 1981, pp. 36–49 (p. 46); Lanoë 1984, pp. 333–55. Cubitt 1989 does not address this aspect of the problem.
14. Italics are mine in both citations.
15. Ewald and Hartmann 1887–99, p. 57: 'quia in una fide nil officit sanctae ecclesiae consuetudo diversa'.
16. Anderson and Anderson 1961, p. 468 (*Vita Columbae* III 3).
17. Anderson and Anderson 1961, p. 456 (*Vita Columbae* II 45).
18. 'in those same days', Anderson and Anderson 1961, p. 480 (*Vita Columbae* III 3). The *Vita Brigidae* also refers to a synod at Teltown; though impossible to authenticate, it at least suggests that Tailtiu was a customary site for such synods; Healy 1900, pp. 385–99.

abbot Ségéne of Iona on the Easter question, provides confirmation of a parallel organization in the south.[19]

CUMMIAN'S LETTER

Written c. AD633, Cummian's letter offers a unique insight into the procedures followed by a group of southern Irish churches when faced with a major doctrinal problem: it illustrates the manner in which the question was pondered, a synod convened to discuss it, a delegation sent to Rome to ascertain the practice of the universal church, and then a circular letter composed in order to announce the final decision. Cummian's letter is, in fact, a carefully constructed legal document which follows in almost every detail the process prescribed in a canon of Innocent I, a canon which, interestingly enough, is cited verbatim in the *Hibernensis*:

> Innocent says: 'In those cases, therefore, in which the power of absolving or of binding is involved, if the solution is not to be found in the 22 books of the Old Testament or in the four Gospels, or in the writings of all the Apostles, then recourse should be had to those sacred writings which in Greek are called hagiographical; if not in those, then turn to the catholic ecclesiastical histories written by catholic doctors; if not in those, then look in the canons of the apostolic sees; if not in those, look diligently in the known examples of the saints. And if, having examined all these things, the resolution of this question is not clearly to be found, then gather together the senior ecclesiastics of the provinces and interrogate them, for that which is sought by many of one mind is the more easily found. The true *repromissor* says: "If two or three of you come together in my name, whatever you seek will be done" '.[20]

Not only does the Innocentian canon account for Cummian's elaborate discussion of biblical and patristic statements (which some modern commentators, unaware of the precedent, found tedious and irrelevant) but it provides the legal precedent also for the synod which Cummian convened at Mag Léne (somewhere between Tullamore and Clara, Co. Offaly). Cummian actually uses the same words from the Book of Deuteronomy 32:7 that occur in the Innocentian canon, when he reports that he summoned his elders and asked them to tell him what they thought about the issue at hand. Having pondered the question then for a full year before bringing these clerics together, Cummian's hopes of agreement at the synod were rudely shattered by a certain 'whited wall' who sowed discord where previously there had been unison. Far from being stranded, however, 'without there being any authority to whom recourse might be had',[21] Cummian and his colleagues, following precisely the stipulations in a synodical decree (*decretum sinodicum*) decided to despatch a delegation to Rome, which duly returned

19. For text and commentary, see Walsh and Ó Cróinín 1988.
20. Wasserschleben 1885, pp. 59–60; see Walsh and Ó Cróinín 1988, p. 15 ff.
21. Sharpe 1984a, p. 241.

with details of the Easter practices observed in the Holy City. The synodical decree to which Cummian refers laid down that, where there were major disputes (*si causae fuerint maiores*), they should be referred for adjudication 'to the chief of cities' (*ad caput urbium*), i.e. Rome.[22] Cummian's letter is emphatic refutation of the view that the early Irish church was antagonistic toward Rome, but equally emphatically, it also gives the lie to the notion that the Irish churches followed no set procedure in the resolution of important disagreements between them. Indeed, the fact that Cummian cites the synodical decree without further elaboration strongly implies that it was already well known in Irish circles. The southern churches whose representatives came together at Mag Léne adhered consciously to an established protocol, one which had probably received formal status in the canonical decrees of some late sixth- or early seventh-century synod of Irish churches. So much is implied also by the fact that the text of the decree is found in the *Hibernensis*: 'The canons of the Romans say: "A dispute in one province is not to be referred to another; if, however, major disputes should arise, they should be referred to the chief of cities" '.[23] The wording is exactly the same as in Cummian. Hence the letter is not a solitary witness whose testimony might be dismissed; the case for an effective organization of the Irish churches can, in fact, be supported by reference to additional evidence.

The Venerable Bede preserves the text of a letter, dated AD640,[24] addressed by the Pope-elect John IV and three others of the Roman curia to leaders of the northern Irish churches.[25] In the letter John and his curial colleagues state that a letter from Ireland on the subject of Easter and other matters had arrived in Rome sometime previously, addressed to Pope Severinus.[26] Before the contents of the letter could be discussed, however, Severinus had died (August 640), and in the interval between his death and the installation of his successor the Roman see was being administered by three of the curia. There is no need here to go into the contents of the papal letter;[27] what needs to be noted is that the northern Irish clergy – doubtless arising out of a synod similar in kind and purpose to that which Cummian describes for the south in the early years of the same decade – like Cummian, addressed their *maiores causae* to Rome. In other words, the synodal decree referred to by Cummian seems also to have dictated the procedures followed by the northern Irish churches. Hence the evolution of the Irish churches, north and south, in the sixth and early seventh centuries, has all the appearance of being ordered and carefully regulated.

22. See Sharpe 1984b, pp. 58–72. The identification of the *decretum* in the *Hibernensis* was first made in Maura Walsh's M.Phil. (UCD) dissertation, *Cummian's Paschal Letter* (1977) pp. 147–8.
23. Wasserschleben 1885, p. xxxvi and 61 n.(e)
24. Plummer 1896, i, pp. 122–4; Colgrave and Mynors 1969, pp. 198–202 (*HE* II 19).
25. See Ó Cróinín 1985, pp. 505–16.
26. Note that, though Severinus's reign was short (AD638–40), the Irish nonetheless knew his name.
27. See the discussion by Harrison 1984, pp. 222–9.

As a rule, the clerics who attended the synods mentioned in the *Hibernensis* remain anonymous. This is in strong contrast with councils of the churches in Visigothic Spain and in the Frankish kingdoms, whose participants are always named in the records of their proceedings. It is of special significance, therefore, that Cummian's letter and the papal letter of AD640 both list the names of the principal ecclesiastics who presided over their respective deliberations. Equally significant is the order of those names in the two documents. Cummian lists the principal participants at the synod of Mag Léne as 'the successors of our first fathers: of Bishop Ailbe [of Emly, Co. Tipperary], of Ciarán [of Clonmacnois, Co. Offaly], of Brendan [of Clonfert, Co. Galway], of Nessan [of Mungret, Co. Limerick], and of Lugid [of Clonfert-Mulloe, Co. Leix]'. Here it may be noted that Ailbe, a bishop, precedes the other four, who were monastic founders. This in itself need not be especially significant, since bishops invariably precede abbots in contemporary Frankish and Visigothic lists. Besides, there is ample evidence to show that Emly, situated in the heartland of Munster, was a religious site of pre-eminent importance at an early date, when it was known by the older name *Medón Mairtine* ('the centre of the Mairtine'), a tribe whose one-time hegemony in the area is echoed in early saga literature[28] and whose power was eclipsed only with the rise of the Eóganachta in the seventh century.

But given the evidence for a strong monastic church in Ireland already by the 630s, the sequence of names in Cummian's letter may well be significant of a still transitional stage in the evolution of the Irish churches from an episcopal to a monastic system, a stage in which the dignity of bishops was still superior to that of abbots.[29] The list of names in the papal letter of AD640 can be interpreted in an identical fashion. It seems reasonable to assume that the papal notaries – mindful of protocol in such matters – would simply repeat the order of names as they appeared in the original Irish letter to Severinus. It is noteworthy, then, that the sequence is headed by the names of five clerics who were bishops, followed by priests, teachers and abbots. The first name in the list is Bishop Tommianus (Tomméne) of Armagh.[30]

ARMAGH AND ITS CLAIMS TO PRIMACY

Mention of Armagh brings us to the thorny question about primacy in the early Irish churches. Archaeological excavations of recent years at Scotch Street, Armagh city, transected the site called *Na ferta* ('the graves') in early

28. See O'Rahilly 1946, pp. 97, 144.
29. Compare the mid-seventh-century *De mirabilibus sacrae scripturae*, which is addressed, in its Prologue, to 'the most revered bishops and priests of the greater and lesser monasteries' ('Uenerandissimis urbium et monasteriorum episcopis et presbyteris'); *MPL* 35, cols. 2149–50.
30. Sharpe 1982b, pp. 33–59 (pp. 40 and 49), and Sharpe 1984b, p. 66, offers a different interpretation of the names in the papal letter.

documents and referred to as the site of Patrick's earliest settlement there.[31] These excavations uncovered residues in a charcoal- and ash-filled pit which were dateable to the fifth century. Scattered shallow burials on the site suggest a classic example of a 'developed cemetery sequence' (to use Charles Thomas's typology for the earliest Irish churches)[32] which developed subsequently into an established Christian settlement. Confirmation of the antiquity of the burials was found in radiocarbon dating from fragments of oak log coffins, suggesting that the timbers for the coffins were felled in or about the sixth century. As Chris Lynn has pointed out, this site could very well be the 'cemetery of the martyrs' mentioned by Muirchú maccu Machtheni, Patrick's earliest biographer. The discovery of an underground spring at another site in the same area offers an interesting parallel to another literary source, the seventh-century section of the *Liber Angeli* (also from Armagh), which reports Patrick as having baptized people 'at the spring which is hard by the eastern side of the city'. But though these topographical details in the seventh-century literary sources can be related to physical features on the site of Armagh, this is a far cry from proving that Patrick himself was at Armagh in the fifth century (or at any other date). The documentary evidence for an early link has also been re-examined, with results that are not encouraging for those who believe that Patrick was the founding bishop of Armagh.[33]

Although the late Cardinal Archbishop of Armagh, Tomás Ó Fiaich stated that the case for Armagh's primacy was 'very convincing',[34] nothing, in fact, could be further from the truth. The evidence (such as it is) points rather to Downpatrick as the main focus of Patrick's activities, and even Muirchú, the saint's biographer, had to concede that Downpatrick, not Armagh, was the place of Patrick's burial. By the seventh century, however, claims were already being made in support of Armagh's alleged primacy in the Irish church as a whole, based on a supposed link with the missionary saint. The most forthright statement of the case is to be found in the *Liber Angeli* mentioned above. The *Liber* is not a unitary text but a collection of statements which combine a claim to jurisdiction over a territorial diocese (Armagh's *terminus*, Irish *termann*) together with a larger claim to control over a *paruchia* of scattered (monastic?) houses. Armagh, in other words, appears to provide a prime example of an originally episcopal, diocesan church, which, in the course of the seventh century, underwent a transformation to a monastic *paruchia*.

The *Liber* sets out a list of three categories of churches which Armagh's lawyers claimed as part of the *paruchia* of Patrick: (i) every 'free church' (*ecclesia libera*), i.e. every unattached church that had no affiliation to a monastic *paruchia*; (ii) every 'city' of episcopal status (*ciuitas aepiscopali*

31. For what follows see Gaskell Brown and Harper 1984, pp. 109–61, and the summary account of more recent work in Hamlin and Lynn 1988, pp. 57–61.
32. See Thomas 1971, pp. 48–90, 137–44.
33. See Sharpe 1982b, pp. 33–59.
34. Cited Sharpe 1982b, p. 36 n. 9.

gradu), i.e. every ecclesiastical foundation recognized in the seventh century as a *ciuitas* (which in Irish usage implies the seat of a territorial bishopric);[35] and (iii) 'every church, everywhere in Ireland, which is called *domnach*', i.e. every church which nowadays bears the prefix Donough- in its name.[36] This list – though it covered a great many churches – did not exhaust Armagh's claims: Bishop Tírechán, writing *c.* AD700, in his dossier of so-called Patrician properties, did not confine himself to these three categories, but cast his net still wider.[37] Though there are difficulties with the language of these texts, there is no doubting the extent of Armagh's territorial claims, which were now no longer confined to the *termann* or local jurisdiction of the Armagh bishop in the territories of his patron kingdom of Airgialla. Whether these claims were already being advanced in the early seventh century is difficult to establish. The papal letter of AD640, as we saw above, suggests at least the possibility of Armagh precedence over other northern churches in the 630s (whether acknowledged or not is not strictly relevant here).

ARMAGH AND SLETTY

Not all of Armagh's expansionary ambitions in the second half of the century were unwelcome, however, to judge by a famous document preserved in the Book of Armagh (early ninth-century, but containing materials of much earlier date). In the Additions appended to Tírechán's compendium of Patrician churches there is preserved a quasi-legal document which records how the church of Slébte (Sletty, Co. Leix) placed itself under the jurisdiction of Armagh. The text has the appearance of a formal statement of acknowledgement and it is worth citing in full, since it is the only example of its kind:

> Bishop Aéd was in Sletty. He went to Armagh. He brought a testament to Ségéne for Armagh. Ségéne gave back his testament to Aéd and Aéd offered his testament and his kin and his church to Patrick for ever. Aéd left his testament with Conchad. Conchad went to Armagh and Fland Feblae explained its import to him, and Conchad too assumed the abbacy.[38]

The document clearly has reference to events which took place towards the close of the seventh century and seems to describe a process by which Bishop Aéd of Sletty († AD700) negotiated an arrangement with Bishop Ségéne of Armagh († AD688) which established the latter's overlordship, and

35. Compare Binchy 1962a, pp. 7–173 (p. 64), who interprets this as 'every foundation which was supposed to have been originally staffed by a Patrician bishop but later became part of another monastic *paruchia*' – a singularly bold claim, since the number of such bishops would come to *c.* 450!
36. Text in Bieler 1979, pp. 184–91.
37. Bieler 1979, pp. 122–62.
38. Bieler 1979, p. 178. In my translation I have incorporated the suggestions of Byrne 1982a, pp. 167–9. See Doherty 1991, pp. 53–94 (pp. 75–8).

Conchad († AD692), Aéd's successor, renewed that arrangement in turn with Ségéne's successor Fland Feblae († AD715). The legal document incorporating this settlement was deposited in Armagh and in fact formed part of a lengthier dossier containing details of the early history of Sletty and its first bishops. Aéd died at Armagh after several years in religious retirement there. These early Sletty materials preserved a tradition that the first bishop of Leinster was Fiacc of Sletty, an Uí Bairrche saint. The subsequent political eclipse of the Uí Bairrche saw their former glory erased from most of the later historical record, but the Sletty tradition survived down to the time of composition of the *Vita Tripartita* (early tenth century), which records early Uí Bairrche and Uí Cennselaig rivalry in Leinster when it states that Oéngus mac Meic Ercae (a brother of the saint of Sletty) slew Crimthann mac Éndai Cennselaig († AD483) as vengeance for the exile of his own people by the Uí Cennselaig. These traditions are also preserved, in cryptic form, in the *Additamenta* ('Additions') to Tírechán's compendium in the Book of Armagh.[39]

None of the modern commentators on this Sletty/Armagh connection has explained exactly how this ecclesiastical overlordship might have worked in practice. Kathleen Hughes, in an unfortunate comparison with secular concepts of overlordship, pointed to the analogy of an over-king who exercised authority over several lesser kings and thereby enjoyed a position which conferred on him a greater dignity and assured him of increased prosperity.[40] But political overlordship in this sense could only be exercised by kings over their immediate neighbours; the notion that a king in Ulster could exercise such power over another king in Leinster, over a hundred miles distant, is quite impossible for the seventh century. There is no evidence for any such far-flung networks of political power. Yet this is exactly the kind of overlordship, in the ecclesiastical sphere, which appears to be implied by the Sletty/Armagh agreement.

This agreement has been traditionally set against the backdrop of Leinster ecclesiastical politics. Sletty, by the late seventh century, was beginning to feel the chill winds of expansionist claims emanating from its neighbour Kildare; in wishing to forestall incorporation into Kildare's ecclesiastical empire, Sletty opted for a kind of federal status with the *paruchia* of Kildare's great rival Armagh. Certainly Kildare, from the early seventh century, commanded considerable political and economic resources due to its status both as an ancient religious site and an early Christian foundation, but also because it was strategically located in the Liffey plain of north Leinster, the fulcrum of political power in the lands dominated by the citadels of Knockaulin, Naas, and Rathangan. By the 630s the Uí Dúnlainge had emerged as the most powerful of the rival kindreds wrestling for position in this area, and by mid-century they had bolstered their claim to provincial kingship by adding a firm control of Kildare. The true founder of the dynasty's fortunes is

39. See Ryan 1964, pp. 143, 151–2.
40. See Hughes 1966, p. 87. It must be said in mitigation, however, that she was misled in this view by Binchy 1962a, p. 61.

usually said to have been Faélán mac Colmáin († AD666?), but it may well be that their rise should be traced back further, to Faélán's brother Maél Umai, who is credited with military successes which are in stark contrast with Faélán's early fosterage by churchmen. A third brother, Aéd Dub mac Colmáin († AD639) was 'royal bishop (*rígepscop*) of Kildare and all Leinster', while his nephew after him ruled Kildare as abbot. This close connection of the *parvenu* Uí Dúnlainge with Kildare was bolstered by political marriages with the Fotharta (an older tribe from whom Brigit traced descent) – Faélán married Sárnat, a woman of Fotharta origin – and also married Uasal, a daughter of Suibne mac Commáin of the Déisi;[41] this last liaison suggesting a concern to secure the south-western flank of Uí Dúnlainge territory. These developments are reflected also in the hagiography: Cogitosus, author of the oldest Life of St Brigit, speaks in his Prologue of Kildare as 'head of almost all the Irish churches and pinnacle, surpassing all the monasteries of the Irish, whose *paruchia* extends throughout the whole of Ireland and stretches from sea to sea'.[42] Faced with such claims, the church of Sletty to the south, patronized by an Uí Bairrche dynasty now in political decline, must have seen the writing on the wall.

So much can be pieced together from the meagre evidence, but this reconstruction of the historical background cannot explain how Armagh actually protected Sletty from the tentacles of Kildare expansion. It was all very well to claim, as the older section of the *Liber Angeli* did, that the whole of Ireland had been given to Patrick as his *paruchia* 'by an angel of the Lord' (*per anguelum Domini*, whence the title of the collection), and to dress up that claim in quasi-legal terms (using concepts drawn from the native law) by stating that Armagh's bishop had the right, by virtue of his superior status, to 'overswear' the heads of all rival churches and monastic federations in matters of legal dispute, a claim repeated and expanded by Tírechán.[43]

But these extravagant pretensions to privileged status are nowhere recognized except by Armagh propagandists. If the legal claims formulated by the *Liber* (and further elaborated by Tírechán) had really applied 'they would have effectively debarred the head of another monastic federation, or indeed any other Irish ecclesiastic of whatever rank, from bringing a suit against the abbot and community of Armagh'.[44] As it happens, there is ample evidence to show that Armagh in the seventh century did not by any means enjoy an undisputed hegemony, even in the north of Ireland.

41. This Uasal († AD643) has been misidentified by Smyth 1982, p. 57 chart 3. For a corrected presentation of the early Leinster inter-dynastic marriages, see the chart on p. 308–9.
42. Connolly & Picard 1987, pp. 5–27 (quotation, p. 11).
43. Bieler 1979, p. 188; see Binchy 1962a, pp. 61–3.
44. Binchy 1962a, p. 62.

OPPOSITION TO ARMAGH

Despite the best efforts of Armagh propagandists, it was not possible to kick over all the traces of a bitterly contested struggle between Armagh and her rivals, some of whom were in her own backyard. Bishop Tírechán himself, in his catalogue of churches that 'belonged' to Patrick, makes it clear that Armagh in fact did not have control over all of the properties which she claimed. He complains bitterly about rival 'communities' (*familiae*) of monastic churches (and even laymen) who had expropriated Patrician foundations. In one case he reports that the church of Columba at Derry and the church of Ardstraw were competing with Armagh for control of Rath Cungi (Racoon, Co. Donegal);[45] in another he states that the *familia* of Clonmacnois occupied two sites, at Tamnach (Tawnagh, Co. Sligo) and Dumach hUa nAilello (?Shankill, Co. Sligo) 'as they held by force many of Patrick's places'.[46] Tírechán's list by no means exhausts Armagh's catalogue of grievances: Clonmacnois had usurped authority over the church at Caill hUallech, which it later exchanged with Clonard for two other properties; Clonmacnois had also seized churches at Imlech Sescaind and Ailech Mór, as well as the church at Mag Tóchuir, and 'the men of that place are groaning'. These churches laboured under this captivity (*i ndoíri*) until their release by Abbot Nuadu of Armagh († AD812). The *paruchia* of Columba had taken possession of the church at Maigen (Moyne, Co. Westmeath) 'through deception' (*tre fuill*), while Patrick's community grieved over the loss of revenues from certain churches in Airtech, north of Cruachu (Rathcroaghan, Co. Roscommon).[47] Clearly, then, there is some doubt about Armagh's capacity to protect its filiate churches, even those close to hand. Legal claim to such properties does not appear to have been enough, and it is difficult therefore to understand how Sletty could have seen its salvation in an agreement with Armagh.

How was it that Armagh was helpless in the face of rival churches that usurped its properties, and how did it happen that other churches came to acquire those properties? The answer seems to lie in a remark of Tírechán's: in bemoaning the loss of Armagh properties in his native area of Sligo, he adds that these had changed hands 'following the great plagues of most recent times' (*post mortalitates nouissimas*).[48] Ireland had suffered devastating outbreaks of plague before, particularly in the mid-fifth century. The plague that struck in the 660s, however, left a deep scar on the memory.[49] Celestial phenomena seemed to portend disaster in AD664 and the annals record 'darkness on the 1st of May, at the ninth hour' – the solar eclipse of that year

45. Bieler 1979, p. 140.
46. Bieler 1979, p. 142 (quotation).
47. For all these grievances see Mulchrone 1939, pp. 49–51.
48. Bieler 1979, p. 142 (quotation).
49. See above, p. 108f.

– 'and in the same summer the sky seemed to be on fire'. The Annals of Ulster then add: 'The plague reached Ireland on the 1st of August'. Its impact was immediate and devastating, in the south-east initially but soon spreading to the rest of the country. The Ulster annalist begins his account of the years AD665, 667, 668 with the bleak, one-word entry *mortalitas* 'plague'. The Venerable Bede has a graphic account of how the outbreak occurred first in Britain: 'In the same year [AD664] a sudden pestilence first depopulated the southern parts of Britain and afterwards attacked the kingdom of Northumbria, raging far and wide with cruel devastation and laying low vast numbers of people . . . The plague wrought equal destruction in Ireland'.[50] The Lives of the abbots of Bede's own monastery at Wearmouth–Jarrow, composed by an anonymous monk *c.* AD716, records how the plague struck at Wearmouth also, sweeping away the abbot Eosterwine and many of the monks, while at Jarrow 'all those who could read, or preach, or who could chant the antiphons and responses were struck down, except for the abbot Ceolfrid and a solitary youngster'.[51] The pathetic attempts of the abbot to conduct the daily office of psalms and prayers with only the youngster uttering the responses had soon to be abandoned. There is no reason to believe that Bede or the anonymous Wearmouth–Jarrow author were exaggerating: the plague seems to have left devastation everywhere in its wake.

It is more than likely that many ecclesiastical sites in Ireland were equally hard hit, and the impression given by Tírechán particularly is of churches which had lain abandoned after the plague years, their populations wiped out, and these were then subsequently reoccupied by communities of the rival Columban and other *paruchiae*. Mac Neill dated Tírechán's compendium by reference to the three plague years of AD698, 699, and 700, during which 'famine and pestilence took place during three years in Ireland, so that man ate man'.[52] Armagh may have suffered a temporary eclipse following the earlier plague years, and the recurrence in the 680s possibly damaged her position still further. The Columban biographer Adomnán of Iona devotes a separate chapter to the plagues 'that twice in our times ravaged the greater part of the surface of the earth'[53] and adds pointedly that 'two peoples only, that is the population of the Picts and of the Irish in Britain [i.e. Scottish Dál Riata]', were spared these depredations through the holiness of Columba, 'whose monasteries, placed within the boundaries of both peoples, are down to the present time held in great honour by them both'. It would be natural enough for such Columban houses to take over adjacent vacant sites whose inmates had been swept away by disease. Adomnán himself notes that Columba established one of his foundations next door to the church of 'a certain British stranger, a holy man, a disciple of the holy bishop Patrick

50. Plummer 1896, i, pp. 191–2; Colgrave and Mynors 1969, pp. 310–12 (*HE* III 27).
51. Plummer 1896, ii, pp. 392–3.
52. Ryan 1964, p. 139; (AU 700: 'Fama et pestilentia .iii. annis in Hibernia facta est ut homo hominem comederet').
53. Anderson 1961, pp. 458–60 (*Vita Columbae* II 46).

called Maucteus',[54] that is Mochta of Louth. The properties of the two houses were 'separated by the width of one small hedge'. If such sites were abandoned they might become the natural prey for those *paruchiae* lucky enough to escape the ravages of those dark years. In Sletty's case, presumably, the foundation survived the worst of the plague and it was still sufficiently viable as an economic and religious unit to enable it to enter into alliance with Armagh.

AUTHORITY IN THE EARLY IRISH CHURCH

Whether Armagh had ever enjoyed any special prestige (as distinct from status) among the Irish churches before this time is difficult to judge. The papal letter of AD640 might imply such a prestige; the reference to Patrick in Cummian's letter certainly seems to reserve a special reverence for the saint. For in addressing himself to Ségéne – who represented a different federation of churches – Cummian assumes that the abbot of Iona will accept Patrick, as he does, as 'our primate' (*papa noster*). This title is found nowhere else in the entire corpus of Hiberno-Latin literature and is a unique early witness to an honoured position for the saint north and south. The mention of Patrick's name comes almost as an aside: his Easter table heads the list of ten such tables that Cummian consulted, but he does not champion its usage. The occurrence of Patrick's name, therefore, is not at all tendentious and cannot be seen either as propaganda for an Armagh claim to primacy or evidence for its 'Romanist' position in the Easter controversy.[55] It is noteworthy, however, that the synodal decree which dictated Cummian's conduct of his investigation, and which referred major disputes in the churches to Rome for adjudication, is found also in the *Liber Angeli*, but with the wording significantly altered. In the *Liber* version, if disputes arise, they are to be referred in the first instance 'to the see of the Irish archbishop, that is Patrick, and to the examination of that bishop'.[56] Only failing a solution at Armagh is the matter to be referred on to Rome. By the end of the seventh century, in other words, Armagh's lawyers were drawing simultaneously on native and canon law provisions to bolster its campaign for primacy. True, there is another section in the *Liber* which acknowledges the counter-claims to hegemony in Leinster being advanced by Kildare partisans, but this final paragraph of the text is clearly a later addition and signals the fact that by the opening decades of the eighth century Armagh and Kildare had arrived at an understanding whereby each agreed to modify its earlier claims. Kildare, which in Cogitosus's Life of Brigit had once marked out a much more extensive area of interest extending over the whole country bar Ulster, now

---

54. Anderson 1961, p. 182 (Second Preface).
55. Cummian's letter was interpreted in this way by Hughes 1966, p. 115 (wrongly, as I believe).
56. Bieler 1979, pp. 188–90; Hughes 1966, p. 279.

agreed to restrict that claim to Leinster (*paruchia tua in prouincia tua*), while Armagh was given a free hand to push its case elsewhere in the country.

PROPRIETARY CHURCHES

By about AD700, however, the Irish churches had taken on the shape which they were to retain until the great reforms of the twelfth century. As Kathleen Hughes succinctly described it: 'The most revolutionary change which some of the early sees underwent occurred not when the bishop adopted the monastic life but when his church tried to follow the example of the monastic confederations and build up a *paruchia* not limited by the narrow territorial boundaries of the old diocese'.[57] Monastic *paruchiae* were clearly numerous and in the ascendancy,[58] and the principal churches (Armagh, Bangor, Clonmacnois, Kildare, etc.) all claimed jurisdiction over daughter-houses scattered across Ireland, and even in some cases beyond. This monastic church has often been contrasted with the more orthodox and traditional diocesan type of organization in one important feature: the diocesan church is always viewed as being 'territorial', while the monastic federations appear to be quite different. To the extent that episcopal dioceses – at least in the continental church, and presumably also in the fledgling Irish church – were defined by the territorial extent of their boundaries, the distinction is valid enough. But though the monastic *paruchiae* transcended such local boundaries and extended their power over widely scattered houses, they nonetheless incorporated an important territorial principle in their make-up.

The secular law tract known as *Córus Béscnai* ('The regulations concerning proper behaviour') explicitly states that succession to the office of abbot was determined by reference to the family of the founding saint (*fine érlama*).[59] If, for some reason, no suitable candidate could be found from among the founder's kin, then one was sought from the family of the man who donated the site for the monastery. The lawyers elaborated this doctrine and extended the search from the chief church of the monastic federation down through three further types of church, in descending order of rank. Evidence in the later saints' Lives indicates that the rule was applied generally. An interesting early illustration of the law at work is to be found in the Book of Armagh, where the *Additamenta* ('Additions') to Tírechán's compendium describe the provisions made for the succession to the abbacy at Druim Léas (Drumlease,

---

57. Hughes 1966, p. 83.
58. Sharpe 1984a, pp. 243–7 states that 'there is [no] reason to suppose that monastic federations such as that dependent on Iona were the common pattern of ecclesiastical organization in the seventh century'. His parallel argument, that 'there is no contemporary evidence for the early existence of dioceses' is, I believe, equally misguided.
59. For what follows see especially Hughes 1966, p. 160, and Ó Riain 1989, pp. 358–66.

Co. Leitrim), an early foundation, possibly even fifth-century. In this case the founder was Feth Fio (perhaps not a name but a rendering of *episcopus uetus* 'old bishop', as Mac Neill suggested).[60] Two years before his death he made a public declaration before the altar at Drumlease and then a written statement which specified the conditions governing the succession. The text is unique, and worth citing in full:

> This is Feth Fio's public declaration (*coibse*)[61] and written testament (*edocht*) made between the chancel and the altar two years before his death to the monks of Drumlease and the nobles of Callraige; that there is no family right of inheritance to Drumlease for any save the race of Feth Fio, if there be any of the family who is noble (*maith*), devout, and conscientious. If there is not, it should be seen whether such a person can be found from among the community of Drumlease or its church tenants. If that is not possible, an outsider (*déorad*) belonging to Patrick's community should be installed.[62]

It is abundantly clear from this document that the founder (in this case Feth Fio) established ecclesiastical title to the monastery *and its land* for his family by virtue of his role as *érlam*. In these circumstances (as Pádraig Ó Riain has pointed out) it was imperative that the *érlam*'s descent be recorded, 'the result being that Ireland, alone among the nations of western Christendom, possesses a substantial collection of saints' pedigrees'.[63] In each individual case the saint's genealogy constituted a statement of title. Here, then, is the territorial basis of Irish monasticism. No matter how far from his ancestral territory a monastic founder might reside, he brought his title to property with him, and wherever in Ireland his people might eventually reside, they retained their links to him. For example, Carthach of Lismore (Co. Waterford) belonged, according to his pedigree, to the Ciarraige tribe 'from whom the successors of the holy Carthach are always derived'.[64] Such family influence in the succession to high office in the church can be demonstrated in all parts of the country and for every century. Some churches, like that of Darerca (Monenna) of Cell Slébe (Killeevy, Co. Armagh) could boast a continuous record of such hereditary succession back to the time of their founder. In the case of Killeevy, the Life of the foundress contains, besides details of Monenna herself, the names of the second, third and fourth abbesses, and a ninth-century list added to the text provides a chronological sequence for these and all the others up to the fifteenth successor, with name and patronymic in each case.[65] It is clear from the data that the church remained

60. Ryan 1964, p. 122.
61. The word *coibse* is normally used to translate the Latin *confessio* in its original sense of 'public declaration', rather than 'private confession [of sins]'; see Ward 1973, pp. 183–5.
62. Bieler 1979, p. 172; Hughes 1966, p. 160.
63. Ó Riain 1989, p. 360.
64. Plummer 1910, i, p. 188 (§45), cited in Ó Riain 1989, p. 360.
65. See Esposito 1910, pp. 202–51; Esposito 1920, pp. 71–8.

firmly in the hands of the Conaille Muirthemne, rulers of the north-Louth/south-Armagh territory in which Killeevy was situated.

It is worth stressing that such proprietary churches were not unique to Ireland. In neighbouring Anglo-Saxon England, for instance, examples of the phenomenon are easily found. Thus Bede's own house of Wearmouth–Jarrow was established and ruled initially by Benedict Biscop, who, on his death-bed, made a will decreeing that his successor should not be sought from among his immediate family (*secundum genus*) but solely on the candidate's merits as a holy man and teacher.[66] In this case Benedict feared for the well-being of his foundation, since he knew that the practice was to choose from the founder's family. But he pointed to the analogy of Ceolfrid, co-abbot of Wearmouth–Jarrow, whom he had chosen for that office 'although he had a brother of his own . . . in blood indeed very near to him'.[67] In fact, however, Biscop's was a late conversion from the normal practice, for we are told that he had earlier appointed Eosterwine 'a priest and a kinsman of his own' as ruler of Wearmouth.[68] The anonymous author of the Wearmouth–Jarrow *Historia abbatum* also records that the monastery which Ceolfrid first entered when he took up the religious life, Gilling in Yorkshire, was founded and ruled by his elder brother Cynfrid, who handed over the reins of power to a kinsman (*cognatus*).[69] Other examples can be found relating to Beverley, Gloucester, Whitby, and the notorious Withington, where dispute over the inheritance of the church property descended into an unseemly brawl.[70] And the text known as *De abbatibus*, which recounts the early history of an unnamed monastery founded probably in Northumbria in the opening years of the eighth century, shows that two at least of the abbots were succeeded by their brothers.[71] Indeed, that pillar of 'Roman' practices in the early English church, Wilfrid of York, ruled over a federation of houses which his biographer actually calls a *parochia*, using the term in its Irish sense to describe a network of inter-tribal properties. It is quite evident, from the terms of his own will and from the efforts of a Northumbrian synod to nominate new abbots and abbesses over Wilfrid's disputed houses, that Wilfrid controlled the abbatial succession in all of them.[72]

It is clear, therefore, why some of the older diocesan churches saw their future in an alignment with the newer monastic system. The *paruchiae* could call on resources far greater and far more extensive than those of the old territorial dioceses. The old bishopric was limited to a narrow territorial area, co-extensive with the *plebs* or *tuath* ('petty kingdom'); the monastic *paruchiae*, on the other hand, could keep on growing and their steady accumulation of lands and property beyond the boundaries of the *tuath*

66. Plummer 1896, ii, p. 375 (Bede's *Historia abbatum* §11).
67. Plummer 1896, ii, pp. 393–4 (Anonymous *Historia abbatum* §16).
68. Plummer 1896, ii, p. 392 (Anonymous *Historia abbatum* §12).
69. Plummer 1896, i, p. 388.(Anonymous *Historia abbatum* §2).
70. See John 1970, pp. 39–63, especially p. 61 f., and further references there.
71. Campbell 1967, p. xxix.
72. See Colgrave 1927, p. 96 (*Vita Wilfridi* Cap. 47).

meant that the only limit on their growth was the generosity of their benefactors. The *princeps* or abbot of the ruling house controlled an often vast network of monasteries, with their lands, buildings, and tenants. Some of these accessions may have been acquired by force (as the Armagh lawyers would have us believe); but most were probably come by in less contentious circumstances. The Book of Armagh evidence indicates that grants could be made of entire estates, with their tenant populations and labourers; others were made of stock or pasture or both.[73] The Callraige king, for example, granted the fifth part of an estate to Patrick, and the Book of Armagh then lists the boundaries of that land, adding that 'lord and vassal granted all this immediately after baptism'.[74] It may well be that the legal terminology of such transactions – the nearest thing in early Irish sources to the charter formulae so common in Anglo-Saxon and continental sources of the same period[75] – was introduced and developed by the church specifically to deal with such transactions. Thus the Book of Armagh speaks of two women who purchased the site of Óchtar Achid 'together with its estate, in wood, plain, and meadow, with its enclosure and herb-garden'; this they later bestowed on the church.[76] The multiplication of rents which resulted from such grants meant that the church stood to gain financially and there can be no doubt that the church's insistence on written testamentary dispositions (the *edocht*)[77] was a deliberate strategy whose aim was to substitute its own interests for those of the customary heirs. As in Roman law, the written will was an attempt to override the normal rules of inheritance by making separate provision for individuals or institutions not normally entitled to benefit. In the Irish situation this often (perhaps exclusively) meant the church as beneficiary. By encouraging whole families to go over to the religious life, the church circumvented the difficulties involved in alienating land belonging to the kindred; by encouraging a more benign regime which allowed inheritance of property by females (always regarded as a soft touch), and by extending ever wider the degrees of consanguinity within which people could not marry, the church eliminated many of the potential heirs to property.[78] Some of these devices can be seen at work in the Additions to Tírechán's compendium, in the endless list of properties handed over to Patrick. The vast properties accumulated by the monastic *paruchiae* in the following centuries shows just how successful this strategy was to be.

For the traditional diocesan churches, however, the prospects were not so alluring. Someone like Ultán moccu Conchobair, mentor of Bishop Tírechán, was bishop only of the Dál Conchobair (as his name implies); his writ ran no further than the territorial boundaries of that tribe. Initially, the territorial

---

73. See the discussion in Charles-Edwards 1984, pp. 167–75.
74. Bieler 1979, p. 172.
75. See Davies 1982b, pp. 258–80.
76. Bieler 1979, p. 174.
77. I believe that Thomas Charles-Edwards, in describing the *edocht* as 'a solemn *oral* declaration' (my italics) is mistaken; see Charles-Edwards 1984, p. 171.
78. See McCleod 1992, pp. 20, 84–5.

bishops were at no obvious disadvantage, since their churches too could be hereditary – as indeed many continental bishoprics were; Gregory of Tours is a case in point[79] – but the bishop's resources were finite and limited, dependent on the fortunes of his *plebs* or *tuath*. The church canons make it quite clear that considerable numbers of bishops still acted as ecclesiastical administrators throughout the seventh century, and probably beyond.[80] But these were probably in many cases administering their dioceses from monastic residences, the *ciuitates* of the early documents. Once again Bede is a valuable guide to Irish practice, in his description of the Irish monastery and episcopal seat at Lindisfarne:

> And let no one be surprised that, though we have said above that in this island of Lindisfarne, small as it is, there is found the seat of a bishop, now we say that it is the home of an abbot and monks; for it is actually so. For one and the same dwelling-place of the servants of God holds both: and indeed all are monks. Aidan, who was the first bishop of this place, was a monk and always lived according to monastic rule together with his followers. Hence all the bishops of that place up to the present time exercise their episcopal functions in such a way that the abbot, whom they themselves have chosen by the advice of the brethren, rules the monastery; and all the priests, deacons, singers and readers, and the other ecclesiastical grades, together with the bishop himself, keep the monastic rule in all things.[81]

Bede appears to imply with these words that the bishop in this case was not subordinate to the abbot; but between AD664 (when Bishop Colman left the island) and AD678 (when Lindisfarne became a bishop's seat again) the community was ruled by an abbot without a bishop. This is clearly the same Irish system that we encountered at home. The Irish could point to Rome for precedent in these matters: there Pope Gregory the Great ruled as bishop but lived with a monastic community and observed their rule.[82] It was not for nothing that the Irish referred to the pope usually as *abb* ('abbot') of Rome. And it is very likely also that the papal privilege, exempting a house from episcopal visitation, was first conceived in response to the impact of Irish monks on the continent. Pope Honorius I, who granted the first such exemption to Columbanus's community at Bobbio on 11 June AD628, was himself the founder of a monastery and a staunch supporter of Gregorian-style organization.[83] It was the same Honorius who, shortly after his accession in AD625, addressed a letter to the Irish clergy on the subject of the Easter controversy, indicating that he was aware of developments among the *ultimi*

---

79. 'With a certain pride Gregory tells us that, in the long line of his predecessors in the see of Tours, all except five belonged to his family': Dill 1926, p. 309.
80. See Hughes 1966, p. 80.
81. See Colgrave 1940, pp. 206–8 (*Vita Cuthberti* Cap. 16).
82. The literature on Gregory is legion; see Richards 1980.
83. See John 1970, pp. 55–6. I am not convinced by the arguments of Vollrath 1985 (cited Cubitt 1989, p. 23 n. 20) against John's interpretation of the evidence.

habitatores mundi.[84] It is also noteworthy that the only other pope known to have communicated with the Irish at this period, John IV, likewise granted papal privileges of exemption to the Columban house at Luxeuil in AD641 and AD643.[85] It would be a mistake, therefore, to assume that the Irish were at loggerheads with Rome or that Irish and Roman organizations were incompatible. The popes may well have realized better than some modern commentators that the bureaucratic city-based model for the church was not necessarily the best one at all times and in all places.

The 'Irish solution to an Irish problem', therefore, was the tribal church, probably episcopal in organization at the outset but soon converted to a monastic structure, often ruled by a hereditary succession of abbots. Within this system bishops were always necessary and many monasteries had resident bishops (as Columbanus's Luxeuil apparently and Lindisfarne certainly had),[86] but the ruler of the community was the abbot. In certain cases the abbot was a priest (like Columba and his successors) or even a bishop, in which case the community would be more-or-less indistinguishable from a continental episcopal household. Such parochial work as was carried out would have been done so principally by the bishop during infrequent tours of his diocese.[87] The obsession which some modern writers display concerning parochial ministry is at odds with the time. There is no evidence for a truly parochial organization, in the modern (or even late medieval) sense in the early Irish church; such ministering as did take place was largely confined to the monastic communities and their lay tenants.[88] Annual visitations of the diocese by the bishop – if they took place at all – would have been the only occasions for baptism and other sacramental functions.

By the time we arrive at the opening years of the seventh century, therefore, the church in Ireland had long since overcome the initial difficulties posed by the peculiar structures of Irish society. By a judicious combination of self-aggrandizement and innovation, the church adopted some features of social organization which were new and different, and thereby adapted itself

84. See Plummer 1896, i, pp. 122–4; Colgrave & Mynors 1969, pp. 198–200 (*HE* II 19). See also Walsh & Ó Cróinín 1988, pp. 4–7.

85. Eugen Ewig thought that papal privileges were granted to Bobbio and Luxeuil as a result of direct contact between Irish missionaries and Roman prelates; see Ewig 1974, pp. 215–49, especially p. 232 ff.

86. See Columbanus's reference to Bishop Aéd, who blessed the altar in the new foundation; Walker 1957, p. 30 (*Ep.* IV).

87. Compare the vituperative comments of Bede, in his letter to Bishop Ecgbert of York, in which he remarked that he himself had heard, and it was common rumour, that there were many towns and villages in remote parts which had not had the pleasure of an episcopal visitation for many years ('multis transeuntibus annis'); see Plummer 1896, i, p. 410. Bede adds the acid remark that these neglected Christian communities did not escape the exaction of episcopal dues. There is no reason whatever to think that Irish conditions were any different.

88. This is the conclusion also of Eric John for the early English church; see John 1970, pp. 39–63 (p. 56 n. 2). For a recent review of the Irish evidence, see Etchingham 1991, pp. 99–118.

to its new environment, one which differed in several ways from the world of Late Antiquity into which the church at large had been born. It is this peculiar new structure that scholars have come to describe as the 'Celtic' Church. Its triumph and glory were to be the 'Golden Age' of Irish monastic learning, but before we survey that period we must first address ourselves to a preliminary problem, the origins of the Irish schools.

CHAPTER 7

THE FIRST CHRISTIAN
SCHOOLS

Two things mark out the Irish as different in the early middle ages, their language and their script. Ireland boasts the oldest vernacular literature in western Europe, and the richness and variety of the texts in prose and poetry that have come down to us in Old Irish are without parallel in any other European language. Ademar of Chabannes († AD1034), a French chronicler, remarked that 'the Irish have their own language, but use Latin letters' (*propriam linguam sed latinas litteras*).[1] This is itself remarkable, considering that Ireland was never a part of the Roman Empire and never acquired the language and script of empire through conquest, but acknowledged the greatness of Rome (as Columbanus put it) only in terms of her apostles, not her emperors. Through Christianity, therefore, the Irish acquired their knowledge of Latin letters and they developed a variety of the Latin script which came to be regarded by outsiders as uniquely Irish: *libri Scottice scripti* 'books written in the Irish fashion'.[2] The flowering of literature and learning in early Ireland is indelibly linked with the rise of Christian monastic schools, which came to prominence from the second half of the sixth century. But the Latin script used in Ireland is clearly a much older development, and it will be worth our while trying to trace the origins of that script and the beginnings of literacy in Ireland.[3]

ROMAN SCRIPTS AND IRISH BOOKS

In the centuries that followed the break-up of the Roman Empire, scribes copied the Latin classics and the great books of Scripture in two kinds of

1. Chavanon 1897, p. 177 (*Chronicum* III 35).
2. The term was first used in a ninth-century library catalogue for the monastery of St Gall in Switzerland; see Lehmann 1918, pp. 72, 75, 80. For discussion of the usage, see Duft 1982, pp. 916–37 (p. 921 ff.).
3. See especially Harvey 1987, pp. 1–15, and his more recent study, Harvey 1992, pp. 11–26; for a general survey of the literature, see Stevenson 1989, pp. 127–65, and Stevenson 1990, pp. 11–35. Two essays by Eoin Mac Neill are still essential reading: Mac Neill 1922, pp. 13–28, 435–46, and Mac Neill 1931, pp. 39–48, 449–60.

'bookhands', or formal calligraphic scripts, termed uncial and half-uncial. These are the scripts which St Jerome would have known and used in the 380s when he was engaged on the task of revising and retranslating the Bible in order to produce the Vulgate version. Jerome in fact objected in the strongest terms to the extravagant and ostentatious wealth expended by some Christians in the production of de luxe manuscripts written in 'inch-high' letters (*uncia* = inch). Contrasted with these formal hands was the cursive, or rapidly written, script, the everyday handwriting of the educated Roman citizen and the normal medium for recording legal transactions, letters, and public records (occasionally also for literary works).[4] This was the *scriptura franca*, the common script of the later Roman Empire. Scribes who could write in the informal cursive hand would always have far outnumbered those with expertise in the formal calligraphic bookhands used by the book trade, and it must often have been the case that where the calligraphic tradition died out there would still have been one (perhaps many) who knew how to record wills, conveyances, and other formal legal transactions; 'cursive remained even where calligraphy was lost'.[5] This is an important fact when we come to look at the origins of Irish script and the beginnings of literacy.

The oldest surviving monuments of the Irish language, the ogam stones, are evidence for a knowledge of the Latin language at a date which some scholars would now set as early as the second century AD.[6] Whatever the origins of the ogam alphabet, however, the stones offer no clue as to the types of Latin *script* that the Irish came into contact with, since the ogam alphabet is comprised of rune-like strokes, not Latin letters. Patrick is said to have instructed his first converts in letters and given them alphabets (= elements of Christian doctrine) (*babtitzabat cotidie homines et illis litteras legebat ac abgatorias*),[7] but none of these early writings has come down to us – if they ever existed. 'We are still in the dark as to the appearance of the first Bibles and books of devotion which taught the Irish their letters and Christianity'.[8]

The matter should be straightforward enough: 'The script that Palladius, Patrick, and others brought to Ireland would have been an uncomplicated one', writes the foremost modern authority on the subject;[9] but this casual statement conceals a crucial fact: the oldest of the Roman formal bookhands from Late Antiquity, the capitalis (which gave us our 'capital' letters) and the later uncial, were both apparently unknown to the Irish and were never used by them. The Irish script, when first we encounter it, shows no traces of direct continuity from the literary hands of Late Antiquity and the early Christian centuries, nor any affinity with the formal documentary cursive used by officials of the same period, as seen, for example, in the papyri from

4. See Bischoff 1989, p. 62.
5. Lowe 1926, pp. 197–226 (quotation, p. 205).
6. See McManus 1991, pp. 78 ff.
7. Bieler 1979, p. 126 (Tírechán §6).
8. Lowe 1926, p. 209 (quotation).
9. Bischoff 1989, p. 83.

Roman Egypt or from sixth-century Ravenna in Italy. We do not know exactly when it came into being or what were its precise progenitors: its origins are shrouded in obscurity. In other words, there is a 'missing link' between Late Roman scripts and the Irish hand which has baffled the best modern authorities. The great American palaeographer, E.A. Lowe, offered one solution: The Irish – 'probably an impecunious race even in the seventh and eighth centuries' – were forced by the necessity for economy to abandon the more stately capital, uncial, and half-uncial scripts in favour of a smaller, more compact script, in order to cram more into their meagre supplies of vellum. 'It is this forced economy which made the Irish . . . squeeze more writing into a page than a decent regard for the reader's convenience would warrant, or good taste dictate'.[10] The Roman script closest to this requirement in type was the small fifth- and sixth-century Italian cursive half-uncial christened (in jest) 'quarter-uncial'. But the half-uncial which served as a foundation for the Irish must have been a type with considerable admixture of uncial letter forms; it cannot have been the 'canonical' type in use in Italy. The earliest Irish script was then refashioned from something very close to this Italian half-uncial, but with a few characterisitic features (alternative uncial and half-uncial forms for the letters δ/d, N/n, R/r, and S/s; and flat triangular club-shaped tips on the upward strokes of some letters) which produced 'one of the curiosities of Latin palaeography'.[11] The stumpy, flat-topped bookhand that resulted was termed by the Irish 'worn letters' (*litterae affricatae*), or 'shorn letters' (*litterae tunsae*)[12] because of its squat appearance which gave the impression of a letter band that was written between two horizontal lines, just like the old Roman bookhands, capitalis and uncial. Since the particular type of half-uncial which served as a model for the Irish hand cannot have come from Italy, it must have come from Gaul or Britain: 'The evidence of palaeography would seem to confirm the testimony of hagiography, both as to the period and the instrument of Ireland's conversion'.[13]

BEGINNINGS OF IRISH LITERACY

Between the fourth century, however, when Christianity was formally established in Ireland, and the sixth century (the earliest possible date for our oldest written remains) there stretches a no-man's-land of two hundred years, as uncharted terrain in the areas of literacy and literature for which we have no surviving evidence. Within that period Irish scribes developed a variety of script all their own, and employed it in two distinct registers, the majuscule

10. Lowe 1926, p. 204 (quotation). Compare the more practical explanation in Parkes 1982, pp. 16–17 [repr. in Parkes 1991, pp. 93–120 (p. 112)].
11. Lowe 1935, p. xv (quotation).
12. For the terminology, see Bischoff 1934, pp. 461–5. I have accepted the correction (*affricatae* for *Affricanae*) proposed by Brunhölzl 1988, pp. 17–26 (p. 25).
13. Lowe 1926, p. 209 (quotation).

(half-uncial) used for important biblical and liturgical manuscripts, and the smaller, less stately minuscule, which they used for everything else. They also developed a set of new graphic conventions designed to make it easier for non-Latin-speakers to read manuscripts written in that language. This 'grammar of legibility', as it has been called,[14] led them to introduce for the first time word-separation, capitalization of initial letters, and punctuation, together with a system of signs which they used to indicate the grammatical relationship of the words in Latin. By abandoning the *scriptura continua* of antiquity which they found in their exemplars, and by distinguishing also (with superscript dashes) between words written in Latin and words written in Old Irish, they invented the pattern of page-layout such as we still use today. It is generally believed that during these two centuries, when the neighbouring island was experiencing the upheaval of Anglo-Saxon invasion and conquest, the Irish struck out on lines of their own, and being cut off from the general current of events in Britain and the continent (and, because of their history, being less bound by inherited traditions of Roman order), they gave free play to a native bent towards introspection and conservatism. The degree of isolation experienced during these years has probably been exaggerated, but there is possibly some truth nonetheless in this view, particularly in the fact that the Irish retained an antiquated mode of fixing the date of Easter. In the area of literacy it is also curious that the early Irish followed methods different from the continental in almost everything that concerned the techniques of manufacturing books: in the preparation of the skins, in the way they ruled them, in their arrangement of the leaves and their method of making quires, in the punctuation they used, and the abbreviations, in their manner of calling attention to omissions, in spelling and the way they divided words – not to mention the hallmarks of Irish manuscript decoration, such as the use of myriad red dots around initial letters. These are differences which have no obvious parallels in the contemporary scripts of the rest of Europe. There are, however, some pointers to a possible source of influence behind these developments.

It has already been seen how the Irish church in its formative years was closely dependent on (and doubtless influenced by) the church in neighbouring sub-Roman Britain, and the case has been made that 'what was true of the church will have been true of handwriting and books'.[15] In fact it has been as much as suggested that the characteristics of Irish book production were the outcome of 'provincial isolation', a provincialism highlighted by the fact that many of them were not so much innovations as archaisms, features of earlier Roman practice in book-making which had fallen out of use on the continent but which survived in Ireland. As an example one can point to the distinctive Irish quire or gathering, made up of five folded vellum leaves (Old Irish *cín* 'book' (Latin *quinio* 'five')) which was technically primitive compared with standard continental practice of the fifth

14. Parkes 1987, pp. 15–29 [repr. Parkes 1991, pp. 1–18].
15. Brown 1982, pp. 101–19 (quotation, p. 103) [repr. Bately, Brown & Roberts 1993, pp. 201–20].

and sixth centuries, but which was precisely the method followed in some of the oldest Roman books dating from the late fourth and early fifth centuries;[16] Irish habits were simply old. The case has also been made for the survival in the British church of the same period of early Roman, pre-Gregorian liturgical practices, which, together with evidence (admittedly slim) for the use of a peculiar British pre-Vulgate (*Vetus Latina*) version of the Bible in western Britain from the sixth century down to the ninth, suggests that this British church – in liturgical matters, at any rate – was 'conservative in the extreme'.[17] It may well be that the members of this British church were also conservative in their script.

BRITISH INFLUENCE

The evidence for British influence is everywhere to be seen in the early Irish church.[18] Columbanus, writing to Pope Gregory the Great *c.* AD600,[19] reported that he had read the sixth-century British writer Gildas, and adds that a certain Finnian (*Uennianus auctor*) – usually identified as Finnian of Clonard (Co. Meath)[20] – had written personally to Gildas (from Ireland? Columbanus does not say) about the problem of wandering monks, and Gildas had sent 'a most elegant reply'. At every turn the British and Irish are spoken of as being at one, for example, in their practices concerning Easter. In a letter of AD605 to the bishops and abbots of Ireland from the three bishops of the Saxons in England (including the archbishop of Canterbury), the offending Easter practice is impugned as British and Irish. The English bishops had tried reasoning with their near neighbours 'but on becoming acquainted with the Britons, we still thought that the Irish would be better'.[21] Cummian, in his letter to Ségéne, abbot of Iona *c.* AD633, on the same subject remarked sardonically that all the churches of east and west were wrong, 'the Irish and British alone know what is right' (*soli tantum Scotti et Britones rectum sapiunt*).[22] It is hardly surprising then, in the circumstances, that the oldest writings in Latin from the Irish churches of which we have any record are concerned with the Easter question, and three of these texts represent the British and Irish viewpoint in the controversy.[23] Known under the titles

16. For discussion, see Bischoff 1989, pp. 20–1.

17. See Lapidge 1986, pp. 91–107 (quotation, pp. 92–3).

18. For a brief summary of some of the evidence, see Dumville 1984, pp. 17–24.

19. Walker 1957, p. 8 (*Ep.* 1 §6).

20. The evidence for his identification is discussed by Ó Riain 1984, pp. 52–7.

21. 'sed cognoscentes Brettones, Scottos meliores putauimus'; Plummer 1896, i, pp. 87–8; Colgrave and Mynors 1969, p. 146 (*HE* II 4).

22. Walsh and Ó Cróinín 1988, p. 80 (quotation).

23. Mac Neill 1931, p. 450, seems to argue for a British origin for these Paschal forgeries, on the grounds that Latin learning in Ireland was insufficiently advanced to be able to produce such works. On Pseudo-Anatolius, see the important article by McCarthy 1994.

Pseudo-Anatolius, Pseudo-Athanasius, and Pseudo-Theophilus, the works were all in circulation by the early sixth century; the first-named of them, Pseudo-Anatolius, was well known to Columbanus, who quoted it approvingly.[24]

It is not necessary at this juncture to enter into the tangled details of these polemical tracts. Our principal interest here is in the fact that the Irish churches of the sixth century were capable of producing scholars who could debate such matters in Latin. Within a century or so of their first formal introduction to Christianity the Irish had not only come to terms with this new language and its traditions, they had assimilated them to the point where Irish Latin writers were indistinguishable, either in style or in language, from their continental counterparts. How did the Irish schools acquire such a mastery of Latin in a country which had never known Roman civilization? How were they able to train such men as Columbanus to a standard which was as good as, and often better than, anything to be found elsewhere in Europe? The answer clearly must lie in the curriculum developed by these Irish schools, and particularly in the techniques which they developed for teaching Latin grammar.

LEARNING LATIN

'The Irish in the sixth century were in a position unique in the history of western Europe: their conversion to Christianity had forced upon them the necessity for learning a foreign language with which they were not in frequent contact'.[25] Unlike their continental counterparts, who at least spoke Vulgar Latin as their everyday language, the Irish were confronted with an entirely new language: 'an Italian or Spaniard who had studied no grammar would write bad Latin; an Irishman without grammar could write no Latin at all'.[26] A knowledge of Latin was essential for the understanding of church liturgy and ritual, for reading and interpreting the Scriptures, as well as for the day-to-day business of ecclesiastical administration in a church which saw itself as part of the international community of western Christendom. But with the exception of the occasional British clerics they might come into contact with, the Irish had no regular exposure to spoken or written Latin; they had to start from scratch. In these circumstances the only available source of information about Latin grammar was in books.

The acquisition of advanced language skills had formed a central part of the curriculum in Late Roman schools, and numerous grammatical textbooks had survived from Late Antiquity.[27] Reading and writing were learnt (by the sons of the elite, at any rate) at the elementary school, from which the child

24. Walker 1957, pp. 2, 18.
25. Law 1982, p. 30 (quotation).
26. Law 1985, pp. 171–93 (quotation, p. 177).
27. There is a brilliant treatment of the subject in Kaster 1988; see also Kaster 1986, pp. 323–42.

advanced to the school of the *grammaticus*, where the course of study involved reading and analyzing some of the great works of classical literature. Mastery of the great authors required a thorough familiarity with their rhetorical skills, and detailed study of style and literary language presupposed a good grounding in the vocabulary and linguistic components of the *auctores*. In other words, the students acquired the analytical techniques which enabled them to classify and describe the various parts of speech. For the sixth-century Irish – who knew nothing about Latin, still less about the finer points of classical style – the grammatical texts from the Late Roman period were practically useless. Even the most elementary Late Antique grammars took for granted that their users already had a basic command of the Latin language; they concentrated on aspects of linguistic and rhetorical analysis which were already far in advance of anything that a fledgling Irish pupil could have coped with. What was needed in sixth-century Ireland was a description of Latin which concentrated on the basics. There was no such thing (so far as we know) at the beginning of the sixth century. By the end of that century, however, a new kind of Latin grammar, the elementary grammar designed specifically for beginners with no previous knowledge of Latin, had come into being, and the credit for producing it is due in large part to the Irish.[28]

The starting-point in such an undertaking was Donatus, teacher of St Jerome, and by far the best-known and most widely studied grammarian of Late Antiquity.[29] The shorter and more elementary of Donatus's two works on grammar, the *Ars minor*, was a brief summary of the principal features of Latin grammar, arranged in a convenient question-and-answer format. Traditionally it was regarded as the beginner's textbook *par excellence*. The most ancient witness to grammatical teaching in Ireland is to be found in the little manual called *Ars Asporii* (or *Asperi*), the grammar of an unidentified teacher called Asper,[30] whose work is an adaptation of Donatus's *Ars minor*, but with a very different slant. The *Ars Asporii*, in stark contrast to the wholly secular tone of its model, derives from the ascetic world of sixth-century Irish monasticism. The author has everywhere substituted Christian examples for the pagan ones of his original, and the traditional paradigms of the *ars antiqua* are replaced by terms from the vocabulary of monastic life: instead of *musa* 'muse', *ecclesia* 'church' is declined; *scamnum* 'stool' makes way for *ieiunium* 'fast'; in the list of verbs the examples are *ieiunare* 'fast', *orare* 'pray', and *legere* 'read' – as one scholar put it, 'Donatus has undergone a conversion to asceticism'.[31]

The *Ars Asporii* must have seemed to its users a considerable improvement on Donatus; the author himself was not unaware of his achievement: 'It is not out of vanity that I say that you will not find this material more clearly or

---

28. For what follows see especially Holtz 1981a, pp. 135–52.
29. The definitive study of Donatus is Holtz 1981b.
30. See the discussion in Law 1982, pp. 35–41; Holtz 1981b, pp. 142–6; Holtz 1981b, pp. 272–83; Löfstedt 1976, pp. 132–40.
31. Holtz 1981b, p. 144 (quotation).

more rationally expounded anywhere else'.[32] The work established itself rapidly, it seems, for it is quoted approvingly by seventh-century Irish grammarians in terms which suggest that it was a well-known text. But Asper's manual is difficult to date precisely, and Asper himself has been described as 'an utterly enigmatic figure'.[33] The work may, however, have been commissioned by Fergnae Brit,[34] abbot of Iona (AD605–23), an identification which would have added plausibility if the *Anonymus ad Cuimnanum* were addressed to Cummeneus, successor of Fergnae as abbot of Iona (AD657–69); both men would suit admirably the chronology established for the *Ars Asporii* and the *Anonymus ad Cuimnanum* on internal grounds, besides providing the ideal localization on Iona. Whatever his precise dates and location, Asper clearly stands somewhere near the head of the grammatical tradition in Ireland. He knows none of the Late Antique authors whose works are cited in such abundance by later Irish grammarians, and he seems to have based his manual solely on Donatus and a number of unnamed and so far unidentified sources.[35] He represents the state of some Irish schools in the period around AD600, the Ireland of Columba and Columbanus.

COLUMBANUS AND HIS TEACHERS

Asper's grammar represents a fairly rudimentary level of Latin learning. On the other hand, nothing can hide the pursuit of style or the quest for rare and elegant expressions that we encounter in the letters of Columbanus.[36] There is nothing in the monastic rules which Columbanus composed which would suggest an interest in scholarly pursuits; they describe a regime of unremitting and austere asceticism for his monks, with no concessions to the frailty of body and soul. Nothing in the Rules, therefore, can prepare us for the astonishing grasp of Latin language and style which makes his letters such striking documents. His correspondence has a particular importance, being the oldest personal letters of an Irishman that we have: 'part of the very small legacy of original documents which has escaped the annihilation that waited

32. Law 1982, p. 37 (quotation).
33. Law 1982, p. 35 (quotation).
34. The *Anonymus ad Cuimnanum* preserves an allusion to a now lost dedication which stood at the head of his copy of Asper's book when he writes 'Donatus wrote his rules at someone's request, just as Asper is believed to have written his selections at the request of Britus' ('Donatus has regulas quodam postulante ut Asperius putatur scripsisse eglogo uel tritone postulante'), reading *egloge* and *Britone*; the form of *b* in the script of this manuscript could easily be misread as the Irish abbreviation for *uel*. See Bischoff 1958, pp. 5–20 [repr. Bischoff 1966, pp. 273–88]; Holtz 1981a, pp. 141–2 (pp. 144–7); Holtz 1981b, pp. 267–71; Law 1982, pp. 87–90. Bischoff & Löfstedt 1992.
35. Law 1982, p. 35.
36. Walker 1957, pp. 2–59. I do not accept the authenticity of all the poems ascribed to Columbanus, and therefore restrict my discussion to the letters, Instructions, and monastic Rules.

on almost all the records of the early Church in Ireland'.[37] They display a thorough command of Latin, which Columbanus employs in different styles to suit the occasion, and they indicate that he was deeply versed in the Scriptures as well as in the subjects of biblical exegesis and computus.

As it happens we are able to reach back into Columbanus's early years, to the Irish schools in the period before AD600, and catch a glimpse of his first instruction in letters. According to his biographer,[38] Columbanus was born in Leinster and in his early teens, when he evinced an inclination towards the religious life, he travelled north to Ulster, studying first with a certain Sinlanus before entering the monastery of Bangor (Co. Down), then recently founded by Comgall. A brief text has survived which casts an interesting light on this Sinlanus (also known by a familiar form of his name, Mo-Sinu maccu Min) and the nature of the teaching which he must have imparted to the young Columbanus:

> Mo-Sinu maccu Min, scholar and abbot of Bangor, was the first of the Irish who learned the computus by heart from a certain learned Greek. Afterwards, Mo-Chuaróc maccu Neth Sémon, whom the Romans styled doctor of the whole world, and a pupil of the aforesaid scholar, in the island called Crannach of Downpatrick, committed this knowledge to writing, lest it should fade from memory.[39]

Mo-Sinu/Sinlanus, fourth abbot of Bangor, is mentioned in the annals at his death in AD610 and is commemorated in the poem *in memoriam abbatum nostrorum* which survives in the late-seventh-century Antiphonary of Bangor.[40] His pupil, Mo-Chuaróc maccu Neth Sémon, was a Munsterman from the Déisi area of modern Co. Waterford. His title 'doctor of the whole world' will occupy us again later; it is not inconsistent with the sturdy self-confidence which is a hallmark also of Columbanus's writings in his dealings with popes and bishops.

The text illustrates a concern with the computus, or ecclesiastical calendar, which was to be a marked feature of the Irish schools throughout the medieval period. This note, and the six genuine letters of Columbanus, are evidence that the Irish schools, even before the close of the sixth century, were already set in a firm pattern of study: Latin grammar, biblical exegesis, and the ecclesiastical calendar (computus) were the three pillars of the curriculum. Besides the usual texts that one would expect to find in a monastic library of the time (Bible, scriptural commentary, Jerome's catalogue of early Church writers *De uiris illustribus*, and Eusebius's Ecclesiastical History), Columbanus also cites technical tracts on the calendar like the

---

37. Kenney 1929, p. 190 (quotation).
38. Krusch 1902a, pp. 64–152; repr. separately as Krusch 1905.
39. See Ó Cróinín 1982a, pp. 281–95. The note is in a manuscript now in Würzburg, Germany.
40. For connections between the Antiphonary and Columbanus, see Lapidge 1985, pp. 104–16.

Paschal tables of Victorius of Aquitaine and the work of Pseudo-Anatolius. Another brief excerpt on the computus buried in a seventh-century computistical collection is ascribed to 'Palumbus', a name which Columbanus uses of himself in his letters.[41] Columbanus, then, was clearly the product of an intensive schooling, a system which had effectively mastered the techniques of language teaching from the elementary to an advanced level. If he is at all typical of the average monastic teacher (and there is no reason to doubt it) then sixth-century Ireland had every reason for the pride and self-confidence that are mirrored in his correspondence.

MONASTIC SCHOOLS

Columbanus's writings show us the finished product of the Irish schools, the trained scholar. It is not so easy to get behind the texts, however, to discover how monastic novices like him actually acquired their knowledge. How were they taught to read and write the letters of the Latin alphabet? What were their schools like, and where were they situated? How were they provided for? The saints' Lives contain occasional references to the monastic schools, though not as often as one might expect, given the Irish reputation for learning. The *vitae* frequently mention the monastic *nutritor* ('guardian, tutor'), following in a long tradition stretching back to Antiquity in which the tutor took the place of the parent as the source of instruction. The term in Insular texts can mean someone who provides sustenance and may denote not so much the formal status of a teacher as a fosterer,[42] and the institution of fosterage was a remarkably strong one in early Ireland.[43] The texts frequently refer to schools when describing the fosterage of royal sons. When, for example, the youthful Colum Cille and his companion Colum mac Crimthannáin (later founder of Terryglass, Co. Tipperary) produced food for their fellow scholars by means of a miracle, the other boys complained. Their teacher Finnian (of Clonard, Co. Meath – famous for its school) told them not to, because the two boys were sons of kings (*duo filii regum*) and had sacrificed the prospect of worldly rule and plenty for the sake of God.[44] A life of Fintan of Taghmon (Co. Wexford) describes how a king of the Fotharta in Leinster placed two sons in fosterage, one with Fintan and the other with another holy man. When the king arrived with his entourage on a tour of inspection he found one son decked out with royal regalia and a miniature lance, shod in ornate sandals, all very satisfactory. 'Our son is being well fostered here', he pronounced. Fintan's charge, on the other hand, was very poorly got out and had only the tattiest sandals; the king was not amused. There was a moral to the story, of course. The other boy would be murdered (the saint prophesied), while Fintan's foster-son would be an abbot and

41. See Ó Cróinín 1986, pp. 276–83.
42. See especially Kerlouégan 1968–69, pp. 101–46.
43. For the legal material on the subject, see Kelly 1988, pp. 86–91.
44. Heist 1965, p. 226 (*Vita Sti Columbae abbatis de Tír dá Glas* §5).

bishop, an anchorite and a scriptural scholar, and would possess the kingdom of God.[45] Such episodes are not altogether unlikely, it must be said (making due allowance for the self-fulfilling nature of such prophecies). Fosterage of royal sons in monasteries may have had its practical aspects: the child would be reasonably assured of immunity from physical danger (though not from poisoning)[46] should there be complications in the political sphere. In many cases it was probably the second son who was given into the church's hands for care. Thus Faélán mac Colmáin († AD666), later king of the Uí Dúnlainge in Leinster, was apparently fostered with Kevin of Glendalough,[47] presumably because his older brother Maél Umai was the first in line; Faélán seems to have emerged as claimant to the kingship only after his brother's (undated) death.[48] In most cases – though not necessarily in all – such royal offspring might have been expected to enter the church, much as Colum Cille and Colum mac Crimthannáin did according to the latter's *vita*.[49]

The same text describes how the school was maintained: 'In that school it was the custom that each of the twelve boys in turn should provide the food for all the brethren, wherever he could obtain it, either by working for it or buying it or begging for it from others'.[50] This picture is reminiscent of an episode in that curious 'culture fungus of decay', the *Hisperica Famina*,[51] seemingly a seventh-century parody of the question-and-answer or colloquy technique much used by the early Irish schools. Such colloquies had their origin in the bilingual phrase-books of Late Antiquity, their purpose being to inculcate the basic vocabulary of everyday life into young novices who were being taught how to converse in Latin.[52] Hence, the texts usually take the form of conversations in which a few simple sentences can be adapted to suit a variety of circumstances by substituting different words. 'Good morning students: go to the river (or spring, or well) and bring back (or carry back) pure water, so that I can wash my hands (feet, eyes, etc.)'. The author of the *Hisperica Famina* lampoons this kind of teaching by having his troop of pompous pupils beg from the local population for their food using the most highfalutin language: 'Who will ask these possessors to grant us their honied abundance? For an Ausonian chain binds me; hence I do not utter the

45. Heist 1965, pp. 204–5 (*Vita Fintani* §24).
46. See the episode recounted in Plummer 1910, i, pp. 78–9 (*Vita Berachi* §10). One of the positive aspects of life in Ireland, in the view of Giraldus Cambrensis, was that 'the step-son fears no poisoned cup from his step-mother, nor the husband from his enraged wife'; O'Meara 1951, p. 37.
47. A different tradition in the *Vita Berachi* §9 (Plummer, 1910, i, p. 78 and notes) states that Faélán was in fosterage with Caimín (of Inis Celtra, Lough Derg, on the Shannon).
48. For evidence of Maél Umai's career, see O'Brien 1962, p. 339, and the discussion in Smyth 1982, pp. 66–7.
49. For a parallel instance, compare the career of the Northumbrian royal prince Aldfrid, for which see Smyth 1984, pp. 128–31.
50. Heist 1965, p. 225 (*Vita Columbae de Tír dá Glas* §5).
51. Herren 1974.
52. For what follows, see Lapidge 1986, p. 94 ff.

mellifluous Irish tongue'.[53] This is a rather grand way of saying that for the purpose of begging they will have to abandon their 'Ausonian' Latin and resort to the native language (*Scottigenum eulogium*). The example can hardly be serious, but it does allow a glimpse of the elementary techniques used with beginners.

The impression generally, however, is one of solitary study, the master alone in his cell reading his text with the pupil looking over his shoulder, so to speak. The solitary monk is a commonplace of early Irish lyric poetry, so this picture is very likely authentic. At Daiminis (Devenish, on Lough Erne) there was 'a little monastery called a school' (*monasteriolum quod schola dicitur*) in which Daig taught the elements of lettering and the art of manuscript decoration.[54] The text concerning Columbanus's first teacher, Mo-Sinu maccu Min, mentioned that his school was at Crannach Dúin Lethglaise (Wood Island, near Downpatrick, Co. Down), roughly thirty miles from the mother house at Bangor. Columbanus and his teacher both subsequently transferred to Bangor itself, but it may well be that the elementary instruction was confined to the island hermitage. Comgall himself, later founder of Bangor, learned his letters with a cleric who lived *in quadam uilla in rure* ('a rural hamlet'?).[55] A similar inference can perhaps be drawn from the references in Adomnán's *Vita Columbae* to Columba's early schooling; with his foster-father, a priest named Cruithnechán; later with an aged cleric called Gemmán, and of course with 'the venerable bishop Finnio, his master'.[56] In none of these cases is a monastery mentioned by name (though Finnian's is doubtless established by reputation), and it may well be that the saint's early teachers were solitary figures, like Mo-Sinu maccu Min.

The evidence of the texts, such as it is, makes clear that schools and scriptoria were not to be found in every monastery. Indeed, scriptoria – strictly defined as writing centres, not schools – were probably very rare; this seems to have been the case particularly with nunneries. The Life of Ailbe (of Emly, Co. Tipperary) relates how a woman named Scetha, daughter of Mechar, sent to the saint for a scribe 'to write the four gospels'; the scribe was duly despatched, but died in mid-text, was then resuscitated by Ailbe in order to write the remaining two gospels, after which he died a second time! Such absence of writing skills is in marked contrast with the case of the Merovingian nunnery of Chelles, near Paris;[57] there, at the end of the eighth century, nuns copied books on commission for the cathedral church of Cologne and the monastery of Corbie, signing their names to their respective quires. At the Anglo-Saxon nunnery of Whitby also there is archaeological evidence of scribal activity by the nuns in the finds of metal styli and metal

53. Herren 1974, p. 84 (quotation). I have altered the translation slightly.
54. Heist 1965, p. 390 (*Vita Dagaei* §5).
55. Plummer 1910, ii, p. 3 (*Vita Comgalli* §3).
56. See the valuable discussion by MacDonald 1985, pp. 174–5 (quotation, p. 182).
57. See Bischoff 1957a, pp. 16–34, and Bischoff 1989, pp. 42 n. 31, 106–7, 207; Ganz & Goffart 1990, pp. 906–32 (p. 928 ff.).

implements for ruling.[58] Evidence for the education of women is, however, not altogether lacking in Irish sources: the *vita* of Ciarán of Clonmacnois states that a daughter of the king of Tara was placed in the monastery of Finnian at Clonard 'so that she could read the psalms and other texts with the holy man',[59] and she was placed under the personal tutelage of Ciarán who was there at the time (though not without some murmurings about the propriety of such arrangements). The eleventh-century Irish chronicler Marianus of Mainz in Germany reports that there was a famous bearded clerk in Ireland named Aéd who presided over a school for both boys and girls. In AD1053 he directed that the girls should cut their hair in the same way as the boys, whereupon he was expelled from the country.[60] While one can sympathize with Aéd, it must be said that he was somewhat ahead of himself, since the reforms he had in mind have not yet reached the Irish schools.

SCRIBES AND CALLIGRAPHERS

Whatever about ordinary writing, calligraphy was a young person's craft. Maél Brigte Ua Maél Uanaig, scribe of the marvellous gospel-book now in London (British Library MS. Harley 1802) which bears his name, is written in a beautiful Irish minuscule with accompanying gloss and commentary in an even smaller script. Maél Brigte gives his age at time of writing as twenty-eight years. On a small slip of vellum added by him between two folios he has written, in microscopic letters, the boast (in Irish): 'Had I wished, I could have written the whole commentary like this'.[61] The Life of Comgall has a story about a youthful novice whose efforts at writing were like the scratching of a bird's claw.[62] His hand and eyes were blessed by the saint, whereupon he became a veritable calligrapher.[63] Perhaps it was some such youngster of promise, cut off in the early bloom of life, who is commemorated in a simple gravestone at Peakaun (near Aherlow, Co. Tipperary) that bears the sombre words *Finán puer* ('the student Finán').[64]

An important part of the calligrapher's art was the preparation of his script, particularly the drafting of his letter forms on what are called 'motif-pieces'.[65] Excavations at the important early monastic site of Nendrum (Mahee Island, Co. Down) produced some remarkable examples of incised stones, one with

58. See Cramp 1993, pp. 64–73 for the most up-to-date review of the Whitby material.
59. Plummer 1910, i, pp. 205–6 (*Vita Ciarani* §16).
60. I owe the reference to Newton 1972, p. 117.
61. See Kenney 1929, p. 648 No. 483.
62. This adds another meaning to Bischoff's description of Irish minuscule as having a 'claw-like ductus'; see Bischoff 1990, p. 85.
63. Plummer 1910, ii, p. 13 (*Vita Comgalli* §29).
64. I owe my knowledge of this stone to the generosity of Conleth Manning, Office of Public Works, Dublin, who supplied me with a photograph in advance of publication. See Manning 1991, pp. 209–14.
65. For a complete inventory of early Irish motif pieces, with discussion, see O'Meadhra 1979, 1987.

a variety of patterns on both faces, together with a sketch of the body of an annular brooch (and possibly also that of a brooch-pin). These drawings of three-dimensional objects are highly unusual among motif-pieces, which normally bear patterns used typically in two dimensions as surface ornament.[66] A second stone (now unfortunately lost)[67] bore perfectly executed letters in the Irish half-uncial style including uncial and half-uncial **d**, an elaborate initial **b**, with an accompanying frame illustrating the method of its construction, an elaborate **m**, and a perfectly drawn **Et**, ligature – all comparable in quality with the fine calligraphic script of manuscripts like the Book of Kells and clearly the models for some de luxe manuscript that no longer survives. We get a picture of such a scribe at work in a ninth-century Latin poem, *De abbatibus*,[68] from Northumbria in England, in which the author relates the history of a small monastery of which he himself was an inmate and which, in its early years (first quarter of the eighth century), had an Irish scribe, Ultán. This Ultán functioned as both the monastic teacher and a scribe/calligrapher '. . . and he could ornament books with fair marking, and by this art he accordingly made the shape of letters beautiful one by one, so that no modern scribe could equal him'.[69] It seemed to many that 'the creator spirit had taken control of his fingers'. Small wonder, therefore, that his withered hand should be revered as a relic.

Not all scholars were necessarily expert penmen, however, and most of our manuscripts in fact were the work of schoolmasters, not calligraphers. For ordinary purposes it might not even have been necessary to possess parchment. Mention is frequently made in the saints' Lives of the wax tablet used by novices for practising their letters,[70] and there is a very fine example in the National Museum, the Springmount Bog tablets, which comprise six small boards of yew, measuring 21 cm x 7.7 cm, with the four inner leaves hollowed out on both faces in order to receive a layer of beeswax. The two outer leaves are hollowed out on one side only, so that the other faces out and protects the waxed surface when the six leaves are closed and tied with a leather thong.[71] The student carved his letters onto such tablets using the sharp point of a metal stylus. The Springmount tablets, as it happens, are not the work of a novice; their expert script was written by a trained cleric probably around AD600 or before (to judge from the letter forms). Such tablets were in fact often used by established scholars, much as they were in Antiquity, for rapidly written drafts of documents. A case in point is Adomnán, ninth abbot of Iona († AD704) and the author of Columba's

66. See the illustration and commentary in Youngs 1989, p. 177 No. 154.
67. The alphabet stone is illustrated in Lawlor 1925, but it has unfortunately since been lost.
68. Campbell 1967. See Lapidge 1989, pp. 161–78.
69. Campbell 1967, p. 19. See, however, the sceptical comments of Nees 1994, pp. 135–7.
70. See Plummer 1910, i, p. cxv n. 11 for numerous examples.
71. See Armstrong & Macalister 1920, pp. 160–6; Lowe 1969, No. 1684; Wright 1963, p. 219.

biography. A more widely read work of his, however, is the *De locis sanctis*[72] on the holy places of Palestine, in which Adomnán relates how he heard from a visiting Frankish bishop who had spent nine months in Jerusalem 'a faithful and accurate record of all his experiences' around the historical sites associated with the life of Christ, which account he 'wrote down first on wax tablets, then transferred it to parchment' (*primo in tabulis describenti . . . quae nunc in membranis describuntur*).[73] Indeed the bishop, when pressed to describe the appearance of the Church of the Sepulchre and its surrounding chapels, took the stylus in hand himself and drew a rough sketch in the wax for Adomnán's benefit.[74] So common was the practice of writing on wax that the Irish used the word *caraxare* (lit. 'carve') with the meaning 'to write'.[75] The *Hisperica Famina* has a vivid description of a wax tablet, hewn from a branch of oak, 'on which lovely carving has played'. The outside is 'fashioned with various painted designs and has decorated borders';[76] 'the embellished tablet . . . is carried in the right hand of the scholars and contains the mysteries of rhetoric in waxen spheres'.

For writing manuscripts, of course, pen and ink were indispensable – though not always available. Molaissi of Daiminis (Devenish Island) encountered a group of monks on a remote byway who asked to see the book he was carrying in his satchel; one was so taken by what he read that he asked permission to copy it there and then, but he had no pen to hand. The saint raised his arms to heaven, whereupon a passing bird obligingly shed a feather (*penna una*) with which the book was duly transcribed.[77] We are not told what the clerics used for ink, but one can appreciate all the more the triumph of faith over common sense in the anecdote told about Comgall and a visit which the saint paid to a couple of his acquaintance. The woman was barren and the holy man made a pretence of asking for ink, which the woman of the house duly supplied. Comgall then told her to drink the ink, and that would cure her. Needless to say, she did and it did.[78]

GRAMMARS AND GRAMMARIANS

Such sporadic anecdotes apart, the texts, in fact, have little to say about the first steps taken by young recruits to the first Christian schools. As we saw above, initial instruction in Latin grammar may have been the work of British monks labouring in Ireland – though one should not altogether discount the possibility of a continuous tradition from the schools of the fifth-century

72. Meehan 1958.
73. Meehan 1958, p. 36 (Preface).
74. Meehan 1958, p. 46 (*De locis sanctis* I 2,15): 'sanctus Arculfus in paginola figurauit cerata'; Meehan 1958, p. 42: 'cuius mihi formulam in tabula cerata A. ipse depinxit' (I 2, 2).
75. Herren 1982, pp. 273–80.
76. Herren 1974, p. 106 ('De tabula').
77. Plummer 1910, ii, p. 135 (*Vita Lasriani* §18).
78. *Félire Oéngusso*, Nov. 24 (Stokes 1905, p. 246).

missionary period. In a brilliant study, the French scholar Louis Holtz has shown how it is possible to identify no fewer than five grammatical tracts which were composed in Ireland before AD700 or thereabouts; 'Five is a respectable number when one remembers that not a single grammatical manual was written in Merovingian Gaul between the sixth and the eighth century'.[79] These texts demonstrate a progression from the elementary stages of language acquisition to a sophisticated level of linguistic analysis, in the course of which the Irish schools passed from an initially wary and hostile attitude, in the face of the pagan heritage of Late Antique grammatical tradition, to a position in which they revel in the combination of late Roman *ars grammatica* and the Scriptures. In the process, Irish grammarians discovered the wealth of the ancient world as it was transmitted through these Late Roman works.

The two ends of this spectrum are to be seen in the grammars of Asper, some time in the sixth century, and that of the *Anonymus ad Cuimnanum*, in the second half of the seventh.[80] Asper's work is experimental and basic in its technique, but it breathes a very distinctive atmosphere. His manual represents the thinking of that party in the Church at large (and in the Irish churches of the sixth century) which looked on the profane learning of Late Antiquity as something to be avoided. In this rigorously ascetic monastic world all thought was to be directed towards prayer, meditation, and asceticism; any study not directed towards Holy Scripture was regarded as dangerous.[81] There was excellent authority for such a view in the writings of Gregory the Great, who had remarked indignantly in the preface to his *Moralia in Iob* that it was 'wholly scandalous to submit the words of divine revelation to the rules of Donatus'.[82] Between this view and that of the seventh-century grammarians a giant step had been taken; 'the rediscovery of an autonomous and objective culture, finding its rationale in itself and not in any service to the faith'; in other words, between Asper and the Anonymous the Irish discovered all the great grammarians of Late Antiquity: Charisius, Consentius, Diomedes, Pompeius, Priscian, Probus, Servius, and several others as well; indeed, these Irish texts sometimes preserve fragments of otherwise lost works from Late Antiquity. The Anonymous, for example, has two otherwise unknown citations from Pacuvius, while another Irish grammarian of *c.* AD700, Malsachanus, has a citation fom Accius otherwise unknown. Some of these writers also had access to a version of Diomedes more complete than any that now survives.[83]

We do not know exactly when or how this influx of new grammars took

---

79. Holtz 1981b, p. 137.

80. Bischoff & Löfstedt 1992, pp. xxi–xxii, suggests Bishop Cumianus of Bobbio as the dedicatee. His epitaph, inscribed in stone during the reign of the Lombard king Liutprand (AD712–44), was still at Bobbio in the seventeenth century; see Kenney 1929, p. 516. For an alternative dating and location see p. 176 above.

81. Holtz 1981a, p. 142.

82. 'Quia indignum uehementer existimo, ut uerba caelestis oraculi restringam sub regulis Donati', *MPL* 75, col. 516B (cited Holtz 1981b, p. 254 n. 3).

83. Holtz 1981b, p. 146.

place, but it seems to have been at some time around the middle of the seventh century. One of the distinctive features of early Irish manuscripts may offer a clue to what happened: Irish scribes abbreviated far more often than any of their contemporaries and they employed for the purpose a thorough-going and comprehensive system which combined elements of the ancient *notae antiquae* (suspensions), *notae iuris* (legal shorthand), and *notae Tironianae* ('Tironian' notes), all derived from the Late Antique practice of tachygraphy, or shorthand.[84] It would be reading too much into the evidence to suggest that the Irish were in direct contact with such usages in Antiquity (whether via Roman Britain or any other route). It seems much more likely that they acquired their Late Roman abbreviations from the same source as their script, namely in manuscripts containing Late Antique texts. It is perhaps more than a coincidence that the cursive half-uncial script which formed the basis of the later Irish hand – but whose survival on the continent in the seventh century is extremely limited – happens to be the script used in a collection of Late Antique grammars in a manuscript now in Naples but once in the monastery of Bobbio, near Piacenza in northern Italy, founded by Columbanus in AD612.[85] The scribe of the Naples codex uses this same script and the same general type of abbreviations and, what is more, he also employs the 'diminuendo' effect – the enlarged initial letters gradually diminishing in size down to the ordinary letter-size of the text – exactly as the later Irish scribes do. There is perhaps additional significance in the fact that these abbreviations, which are otherwise so characteristic of Irish script, do not appear in the very oldest witnesses to that script: the Cathach psalter of St Columba, the Ussher Gospels, the Springmount wax tablets, and a few others,[86] which can be dated to AD600 or before, whereas they *are* to be found in the manuscript of Isidore's *Etymologiae* in the library of St Gall (mid-seventh century or after) and in all later Irish manuscripts.[87] The ancient Roman *notae* may have come into Ireland with the new wave of interest in Latin grammatical texts, providing the spur for the revolution in Irish schools that took place during the second half of the seventh century.

The delight with which new, better, and sometimes more complete texts were received is clearly to be seen in a letter (probably seventh-century) which survives from a certain Feradach to an unknown compatriot named Calmanus (Colmán).[88] Feradach recounts with unconcealed excitement how he has received from the *Romani*[89] 'many manuscripts of works in which

84. See especially Bischoff 1989, pp. 80–1, 86.
85. See Lowe 1938, No. 397b; Bischoff 1989, p. 76; and Brown 1982, pp. 103–4 [repr. Bately, Brown & Roberts 1993, pp. 201–20].
86. See the accounts of their abbreviations in Lowe 1935, Nos. 266, 271, and Lowe 1971, No. 1684.
87. On abbreviations in the Isidore fragment, see Brown 1982, p. 104.
88. Bischoff 1957b, pp. 121–38 [repr. Bischoff 1966, pp. 195–205 (p. 199)]; Bischoff 1961, pp. 317–44 [repr. Bischoff 1966, pp. 171–94 (p. 181)]; Sharpe 1992, pp. 44–54.
89. Compare the Würzburg note cited above (p. 177), with its reference to Mo-Sinu maccu Min, and its reference to Mo-Chuaróc maccu Neth Sémon 'whom the *Romani* style doctor of the whole world'.

much that has been corrupted in your copies is found corrected', and he goes on to discuss several such texts in detail. The rich vein of Late Roman grammars is turned to best effect in the *Anonymus ad Cuimnanum*, whose work is cast in the form of a commentary on Donatus's larger grammar, the *Ars maior* (Book II). By this time, however, the text of Donatus was so well known in the Irish schools that the teacher could compose his commentary in the knowledge that his students knew the text almost by heart, and therefore that he need quote only the headword or phrase. The Anonymous goes beyond the technicalities of grammatical teaching though, to aim at a higher purpose: he argues for the study of grammar as an autonomous subject, and quotes in his support Jerome's famous reference to Donatus as 'my teacher' (*praeceptor meus*).[90] He is familiar with Jerome's approach to biblical commentary, which sought to apply to the words of Scripture the same techniques of analysis that Donatus applied in his commentary to the words of the classical authors. Like Jerome, his aim is to see that what has been well said by someone should be understood exactly as he expressed it.[91] For this reason the Anonymous's work has been described as 'exegetical' because it applies Jerome's methods in reverse: he treats Donatus's words in a manner analogous to the treatment of the Bible in scriptural discussion. In his preface, for example, he discusses the diversity of languages and relates the fact to the destruction of Nimrod's Tower. In so doing, he remarks that the biblical apocrypha number the offspring of Adam and Eve as fifty-two sons and seventy-two daughters, the latter, of course, corresponding to the number of languages in the world.[92] In the same vein, he asks what the three principal elements are on which study of the Latin language is based and answers with the triad 'on reason, authority, and usage' (*ratione auctoritate consuetudine*). This exactly parallels the Venerable Bede's tripartite division of time *natura consuetudine certe auctoritate*, a notion which his editor thought was innovative but which Bede in fact took over from earlier Irish computists.[93] It is no surprise therefore that the Anonymous should include multiplication tables as an aid to the understanding of number symbolism in the Bible, or that his book shows ample evidence of expertise in the three great subjects of the curriculum: biblical study, computus, and, of course, grammar.

REPUTATION OF IRISH SCHOOLS

Bede knew the reputation of the Irish schools in the second half of the seventh century, but it would be a mistake to think that in the decades before then those schools were significantly poorer. The seventh century in fact

90. The relevant passages are collected by Holtz 1981b, pp. 37–46.
91. '. . . sed quae ab alio bene dicta sunt, ita intelligantur ut dicta sunt', *Comm. in Gal.*, *MPL* 26, col. 400 (cited Holtz 1981b, p. 44 n. 35).
92. For an identical notion in a Middle Irish historical work of c. AD1100, see Ó Cróinín 1982b, pp. 67–9.
93. See Jones 1943, p. 182; Walsh and Ó Cróinín 1988, p. 120 (§6).

opens, almost unheralded, with a flourish in the form of Columbanus's writings, and these are followed shortly thereafter by the famous Paschal letter of Cummian (c. AD633), possibly bishop and scholar (*fer légind*) of Clonfert Brendan, Co. Galway.[94] This is evidence for a quite remarkable range of sources available in a typical southern Irish monastery of the period. Beside the Bible (Vetus Latina and Vulgate versions), Cummian had access also to a wide variety of patristic commentaries by Augustine, Jerome, Cyprian, Origen, Ambrosiaster, and Gregory the Great, as well as other anonymous or pseudonymous works. In addition he could call on collections of canon law, ecclesiastical history, and church synodal decrees – including ones from the councils of Arles (AD314) and Nicaea (AD325) in their original, uncontaminated forms – and a body of synodal enactments from the native Irish churches. The letter is based on excerpts from over forty separate texts (including no fewer than ten different Paschal tracts), an astonishing display of erudition, and one which fully reflects the threefold pattern of study which we have seen established for the Irish schools. This Cummian has been proposed as the possible author of a computistical manual[95] and of a commentary on Mark's Gospel.[96] He is the first in time of a whole group of scholars writing in Latin in the south midlands area of the country whose intense literary activity, particularly in the exegetical field, is only now beginning to be truly appreciated.[97] While it is not possible to speak of a 'school' of exegesis in the sense that they shared a common approach to scriptural interpretation, there can be little doubt that they were intimately familiar with each other's work, and indeed they make explicit reference at times to the differing opinions of others in their circle.

A manuscript once belonging to the island monastery of Reichenau in Lake Constance, but now at Karlsruhe in Germany, preserves the only copy of a seventh-century Hiberno-Latin commentary on the Catholic Epistles; it is the oldest surviving commentary on that book of the bible.[98] Embedded in the text are a couple of glosses which mention several Irish scholars of the period by name: Laidcend mac Baíth Bandaig , Brecannus, Banbanus, and Bercanus filius Aedo.[99] These four formed one circle with the aforementioned Cummian, and with others who are mentioned elsewhere: the anonymous author of the tract 'On the miraculous things in sacred scripture' (*De mirabilibus sacrae scripturae*)[100] mentions two of his teachers, Eusebius and

94. See Walsh & Ó Cróinín 1988, pp. 7–15.

95. The *De ratione conputandi* edited in Walsh & Ó Cróinín 1988, pp. 99–213.

96. See Bischoff 1954, pp. 189–279 [rev. ed. in Bischoff 1966, pp. 205–73 (pp. 213–15, 257–9)]. The case for Cummian's authorship is restated in Walsh 1987, and Walsh & Ó Cróinín 1988, pp. 217–21. For a contrary view, see Cahill 1994, pp. 35–45.

97. For earlier discussions of some of this material, see Kenney 1929, pp. 275–80; Grosjean 1955, pp. 67–98.

98. McNally 1968.

99. See Grosjean 1955 p. 76 ff.; Holder 1907, pp. 266–7.

100. See Kenney 1929, pp. 275–7; Reeves 1861, pp. 514–22; Esposito 1919, pp. 189–207. An edition by Dom Gerard McGinty OSB is in preparation.

Manchianus. Of all these the anonymous author of the *De mirabilibus* (who uses the pen-name Augustine) is the most interesting, for his tract is in marked contrast to the standard allegorical approach to bible exposition in his time. Far more original than Laidcend's epitome of Gregory the Great (which is no more than a rehash of the original), the Irish Augustine tackles the question of miracles in the Bible in a daring way. His thesis is that God ceased all creation on the seventh day of Genesis, and that what appear thereafter as further acts of creation are, in fact, merely God's 'governing' (*gubernatio*) of what already exists. Hence no miracle can involve new creation: it is only the calling forth of some element that normally lies hidden in the depths of nature. Not for him the endless allegorizing about hidden meanings; his approach is to rationalize the seemingly inexplicable phenomena of the Bible miracle-stories by reference to practical observation and a genuinely scientific application of reason. How explain the seemingly miraculous transformation of Lot's wife into a pillar of salt, following the destruction of Sodom and Gomorrah?

> No one who has observed the saltiness of tears doubts that salt is present in the human body, which, coming forth from the gall-bladder, as the medical men say, and flowing from the eyes, prove by their taste the presence of salt . . . And not alone in tears but the presence of salt everywhere in the human body is established also by the phlegm and spittle coughed up from the chest. The powerful Governor of things, therefore, when He desires to turn the part into the whole, spreads what was concealed in the small part through the whole; and for this reason, when he wished to turn the wife of Lot into a pillar of salt, that very slight part of salt which was in the flesh infected the whole body.[101]

One scholar has said of the *De mirabilibus* that the 'reasoning is often childlike, but it is a childishness which has a note of curious originality'.[102] The verdict is hardly fair. Our author is not a simpleton, but has a good grounding in the scientific knowledge of his age. This is nicely illustrated by another passage: to explain the miracle recorded in Joshua 10, 12–13, that the sun and the moon stood still while the Israelites did battle with their enemies, he states that the 'miracle' was no miracle in fact, for there was no dislocation of the celestial movements; sun and moon stood still simultaneously for the duration of the battle then resumed their courses in perfect equilibrium as before. The proof is in the constant recurrence of the lunisolar cycles, which are always in agreement at the end of every term of 532 years. He then gives a brief synopsis of the successive cycles from Creation to the year of writing, in the process revealing the year in which he composed his work as AD655. The passage is a masterful display of computistical skills allied to biblical exposition; it comes as no surprise that the very passage in which he discusses Paschal cycles is borrowed verbatim into the text known as the Munich Computus compiled *c.* AD718.[103]

---

101. *MPL* 35, col. 2149.
102. Kenney 1929, p. 277.
103. See Mac Carthy 1892, pp. 365–6; Ó Cróinín 1983, pp. 74–86 (pp. 81–2).

The Irish Augustine is the earliest medieval writer to discuss the question of tides; he was followed by other Hiberno-Latin writers,[104] and by the Venerable Bede.[105] He gives, in the course of a discussion of the Flood, a very interesting discussion of spring tides and neap tides:

> But some authors say that these kinds of beasts and wild animals were brought forth by the earth itself. They think these animals which are enclosed in islands were produced from the earth itself, and not from the ark ... However, to our mind, that problem remains unsolved, and it is always renewed by the daily flowings and ebbings of the ocean ... For this daily flooding always occurs twice daily from one period to the next through the twenty-four hours, and through alternate weeks the alternation of neap and spring tides takes place. But the neap tide has six hours of flood and the same for the ebb. The great spring tide, however, surges for five hours, and through seven hours uncovers the rocks on the seashores. This shows such agreement with the moon that it always begins three days and twelve hours before the new moon, and is accustomed to last another three days and twelve hours after the beginnings of the waxing moon; likewise it begins three days and twelve hours before the full moon, and thereafter runs its course in the same amount of time ...[106]

The Irish Augustine's style of biblical exegesis did not find general favour in Ireland, however, and the originality which he displayed is not to be found in any other commentary of the period. It was not for want of style; he is a very competent Latinist, for all that modern grammarians might think of him.[107]

LATIN AND THE VERNACULAR

A distinctive feature of the schools, even at this early date, is their use of the vernacular side-by-side with Latin. By AD600 at the latest Old Irish was being written using the letters of the Roman alphabet, and even more remarkable, a standard orthography apparently existed for the literary language already by that date. Furthermore, this written form of the language shows no trace of dialect – a unique feature unparalleled in any other European vernacular in the early middle ages. In other words, despite obvious political fragmentation of the country, and despite the absence of any centalized administration or

104. Díaz y Díaz 1972, pp. 146–50.
105. Jones 1975, pp. 223–5.
106. *MPL* 35, cols 2158–9.
107. See Law's verdict (Law 1982, p. 6): 'the letters and rules of Columbanus, the surviving corpus of biblical exegensis, and miscellaneous compositions [*sic*] like the tract *De mirabilibus sacrae scripturae* are all the work of writers with but a modest education. None of these displays a very high standard of latinity'. Kenney, on the other hand, thought otherwise: 'The literary style of the work seems good; it shows no contamination from the *Hisperica Famina* type of Latinity. Augustinus, though differing widely in thought and diction from Cogitosus, was worthy to rank as a Latinist with that pioneer hagiographer'; Kenney 1929, p. 277.

control that might impose such a standard, Ireland nevertheless had established a uniform literary language which was used in all parts of the country.

How early the Irish began to write their own language in manuscripts is impossible to tell. We can surmise that the circumstances had to do with the necessity of representing Irish names in Latin script, for though Irish scholars had mastered the Latin language at an early date they would still have been faced with the problem of how to render the words and names of their native Irish even when writing in Latin. The problem is vividly illustrated by the author of the seventh- or early eighth-century *Additamenta* to Tírechán's Life of Patrick in the Book of Armagh:

> Here end these few pieces, written imperfectly in Irish. Not that I could not have written them in the Roman language, but these stories are hardly intelligible even in Irish; had they, on the other hand, been told in Latin, one would have been not so much uncertain as at a loss to know what language one was reading and how it was to be pronounced, because of the great number of Irish names which have no established forms (*non habentium qualitatem*).[108]

What follows in the Book of Armagh, the so-called *Notulae*,[109] is a case in point: a series of notes or catchwords comprising Irish names and place-names with just the odd Latin word interspersed, which the medieval editor could not Latinize and his modern successor could not translate. To represent these Irish words in written form the Irish used the Latin alphabet, but the orthography they employed – the phonetic values that they gave to the letters of the Roman alphabet – was an orthography based on the pronunciation of Latin then current. Here is the most remarkable monument to British influence on the early Irish churches, for the Latin that the Irish spoke was Latin they had learned to pronounce in the British manner, with a British 'accent', so to speak. It is in fact demonstrable that a British pronunciation of Latin became established in Ireland at a date preceding the oldest known writings in Irish (the ogam inscriptions excluded), and continued to be used in Ireland until the fourteenth century.[110] The spelling system of manuscript Old Irish, then, was based on this current pronunciation of Latin, but Mac Neill argued that in the ogam stones (which continued to be inscribed sporadically as late as the seventh century) there is a quite different spelling system, which has its own distinctive features. The orthography of the manuscripts, he believed, is not derived from the spelling of the ogams and is not influenced by them. The spelling of the ogams in turn shows no trace of influence from the orthography of the manuscripts.[111] In other words, if Mac Neill were correct, there could be no direct continuity from the Irish of the

---

108. Bieler 1979, p. 178. I have altered Bieler's translation slightly, though without changing the sense.
109. Bieler 1979, pp. 180–3.
110. The formulation is Mac Neill's 1931, pp. 39–48, 449–60 (quotation p. 41).
111. Mac Neill 1931, p. 47.

ogam inscriptions to the Irish of our earliest surviving manuscripts. Since Mac Neill's time, however, considerable work has been done on the question of ogam and the orthography of early Irish, with conclusions which present a startling challenge to the older view.[112] Besides the general argument that Roman letter literacy and ogam script must have coexisted,[113] it has been shown that the distinctions between ogam and manuscript spelling proposed by Mac Neill do not in fact hold good for the earliest manuscript material.[114] Although it is still possible to say that both scripts employed a fixed standard of orthography, that ideal standard in ogam represented a stage in the evolution of the language (Primitive Irish) when the phonemic structure was markedly different from what we encounter in manuscript Irish. There is thus a transition period during which ogam had already begun to take over new spelling conventions from manuscript Irish because, as the sounds of the language changed (as part of its natural evolution), so several symbols of the older alphabet became redundant, and the ogam epigraphers struggled to reproduce these new sounds in an alphabet which was innately conservative and designed to render the now lost sounds of the older language. At the same time some of the earliest examples of written Irish in turn were spelled in the 'ogam' way, before Irish scribes had fully adopted the 'standard' orthography that involved transcribing Irish sounds using Latin letters with their British pronunciation. This process seems to have been in train already by the sixth century.[115]

All the same, there remain two serious difficulties with the theory that ogam and Latin-letter writing were practised side-by-side in Ireland: firstly, there is the fact that Latin-letter inscriptions do not occur on Irish ogam stones as they do in Wales,[116] where (as we saw above, p. 33f) many stones have bilingual inscriptions, with Irish depicted in ogam characters and a Latinized version of the same name(s) alongside it in Roman letters. The explanations offered to date for the absence of Roman-letter material do not seem to me to be adequate.[117] And secondly, if the Irish had preserved a tradition of written Latin (and Irish?) from the second century on, then one should expect to find this reflected in the development of their script, with traces of Late Antique bookhands (capitals and uncial) and cursives (Later Roman, and perhaps even Older Roman cursive, if the Irish were as conservative as some believe them to have been). But no such influence is to be found in even our oldest

---

112. See especially McManus 1986, pp. 1–31.

113. This is the case argued, e.g., by Harvey 1987, pp. 1–15.

114. McManus 1986, p. 11.

115. This appears to be the implication especially of McManus 1986, pp. 12–13.

116. I am aware of the exception in Macalister 1945, i, No. 19, but this exception proves the rule.

117. See esp. Harvey 1987, pp. 13–14. Harvey's analogy with the situation in England after the ninth century, where Anglo-Saxon scribes employ different scripts for different languages (Old English and Latin) ignores the fact that Irish scribes *never* observed such a distinction, but used the Irish script for Latin and the vernacular alike.

Irish manuscripts. Palaeography, therefore, offers no support for the continuity theory.

The circumstances in which Irish began to be written as a literary language, and not just as a medium for recording Irish names (e.g. on gravestones), can only be guessed at, but there is some early evidence which at least points us in one direction. Adomnán in his *Vita Columbae* has a story about a visit paid to the saint while in Ireland by an Irish poet. Columba's companions asked the saint, after the poet and his entourage had departed, why he had not sought his due from the visitor, namely a poem (*aliquod ex more suae artis canticum*).[118] It is, of course, possible (perhaps even likely) that such a poem – an extempore composition? – would have been recited by the poet and committed to memory by the recipient. All the same, there is something in the account which suggests that the work would have been written down, if not immediately then shortly after its recitation. As it happens, there are three poems of an early date which have the Iona saint as their theme, two of probably early seventh-century date (and perhaps by the same author)[119] and a third, the famous *Amra Colum Cille* ('Lament for C.C.') attributed to Dallán Forgaill, a contemporary of Columba. Poetry, by its very nature, can be memorized, of course, and it must be said that there are some doubts still among the philologists about the dating of the *Amra*.[120] But there can hardly be such qualms about the items of occasional verse that survive from the early period, such as the following few lines, recording the loan of a cart:

Will you lend me your cart?
I will, if my cart doesn't break.
Will my cart come back soon?
If your cart doesn't break, it will.

In esser dam to á?
Tó, mani má mo á.
Ara tairi mo á mó?
Mani má to á, tó.[121]

The poem's most recent editor has described this as 'a little tour de force in versification, of the sort that immediately appealed to the Irish listener', pointing to its staccato rhythm, its remarkable language, its archaic vocabularly, and the metrical features which link it with other Old Irish compositions of seventh- or even sixth-century date. 'The poem is surely very old', and who is to say that it could not have been committed to writing in the sixth century? The great Rudolf Thurneysen, doyen of Old Irish scholars, published a masterly paper on the subject of Colmán mac Lénéni, poet and then churchman in later life († AD611), in which he reviewed the evidence for accepting as authentic the fragments of surviving verse transmitted in

118. Anderson 1961, pp. 296–8.
119. See Kelly 1973, pp. 1–23.
120. See especially Greene 1977, pp. 11–33.
121. Text and discussion in Watkins, 1978, pp. 161–5.

Colmán's name.[122] The verdict was positive: internal evidence indicated a date for one of the fragments in the first decade of the seventh century. Given that Colmán had abandoned a professional career as a lay poet in order to enter the church it seems impossible to avoid the conclusion that his surviving compositions (which seem to date from the period of his earlier profession) must be set in the second half of the sixth century.[123] 'It will be seen how the evidence converges in the direction of placing the beginning of writing in Irish somewhat earlier than the beginning of the seventh century'.[124] As it happens, this is around the time when we encounter our first examples of written Old Irish in manuscripts.

SCHOLARS' BOOKS

Irish manuscripts of the early medieval period generally are famous for their glosses. These were sporadic entries, penned by the scribe or by subsequent readers, sometimes between the lines, sometimes in the margins. The practice of making such entries undoubtedly goes back a long way, and usually involves a one-word explanation (in Latin or Irish) of some word or phrase in the Latin text, much as Victorian schoolgoers annotated their Livy. The oldest example of such a gloss in Irish was written with the dry point of a stylus onto a page of the Ussher Gospels (now in Trinity College, Dublin),[125] dateable to around AD600.'[126] The scholar must have been reading the gospels stylus in hand, and when he came to Luke 3:14 he read the word *stipendiis* ('rewards') and added above it *focrici*, the Irish equivalent. All the other glosses in this codex are in Latin; only this solitary Old Irish word has survived. Nonetheless, this one example can be multiplied from other manuscripts, and it can be demonstrated also that the glossing was not confined to biblical studies. In a Paris fragment, for example, written by an Irish hand of c. AD700, there are texts on the Paschal question to which Latin and Old Irish glosses are added with the pen; the Old Irish words are archaic in their phonology.[127] Perhaps the most interesting example of all is the Cambrai Homily,[128] a mixed Latin-Old Irish composition based on passages from Pauline epistles and the homilies of Pope Gregory the Great on the gospels, together with a remarkable Irish excursus on the subject of martyrdom. What is most striking about this text is its fluid Old Irish prose. This is not just glossing, but original composition, and in a plain prose style

---

122. Thurneysen 1933, pp. 193–207.
123. See the discussion of this and related material in Carney 1978–79, pp. 417–33.
124. Greene 1977, p. 14.
125. See the description in Lowe 1935, ii, No. 271.
126. See Bischoff 1954, pp. 189–279 (quotation, p. 197); rev. ed. 1966, pp. 206–73 (p. 211).
127. See Ó Cróinín 1989a, pp. 135–43.
128. See Ó Néill 1981, pp. 137–47, and the edition in Thurneysen 1949, pp. 35–6. The text is in need of a new edition. See further below, p. 203.

which is unique among surviving texts in Old Irish for the extraordinary archaism of its language; the phonological features of the Cambrai text seem to represent a stage of the language older than even the main body of glosses, perhaps *c.* AD650.

From this evidence it should be clear that the practice of writing in Old Irish was thoroughly established by the early seventh century at the latest. Our manuscripts show us Irish scholars still in the process of experimenting with different orthographical systems, an earlier one which is the lineal descendant of the older ogam alphabet, and a later one, based on the British pronunciation of Latin; these British spelling conventions rapidly displaced the older system and became the basis of the remarkably consistent form of the language found in Irish manuscripts from the eighth century onward. It is impossible on the available evidence to determine how exactly this vernacular orthography was disseminated and standardized by the schools. There is a unique early Irish vernacular grammar, the work known as *Auraicept na nÉces* ('The scholars' primer'), traditionally ascribed to Cenn Faélad († AD679), which combines curious information about the ogam alphabet with comparison of Latin and Old Irish linguistic features.[129] Whatever about its dating, however, there is nothing in the work that would stand comparison with the traditional Late Antique Latin tracts *de orthographia*; the *Auraicept* could not possibly teach anyone how to write Irish.

It can hardly be doubted, on the other hand, that writing in Irish was learned in the same schools as writing in Latin; no credence can be given to the notion that writing in the vernacular was the preserve of secular ('druidic') schools independent of the church whose teachers had somehow acquired the art of writing and were functioning parallel to, but separate from, the Christian monasteries.[130] Cenn Faélad is linked in the literature with two archaic legal poems which occur in the law tracts *Míadslechta* and *Bretha Nemed*,[131] both dating from roughly a half-century or so after his death. These compositions clearly betray a familiarity with the church and its learning, and the tradition that Cenn Faélad combined the disciplines of the Latin scholar, the secular poet, and the native (Brehon) lawyer can be traced much farther back than the late medieval versions of his legend. The story relates how Cenn Faélad fought in the battle of Mag Roth (Moyra, Co. Down) AD637 and suffered a wound which destroyed his 'brain of forgetfulness'. He was taken for convalescence to the monastery of Tuaim Drecain (Tomregan, Co. Cavan), where there were three schools: a *scol léigind* of Latin learning, a *scol fénechais* of native law, and a *scol filed* of native poetics. Cenn Faélad memorized the teachings of these three schools by day and wrote them down by night, thereby earning for himself the honorific title *sapiens* ('head of a monastic school') recorded on his death by the annalist. The legend is

129. See Calder 1917 and Ahlqvist 1982 for editions.
130. This appears to be the implication in Mac Cana 1970, pp. 62–78. See, however, the trenchant criticism of this 'nativist' view in McCone 1990, *passim.*
131. For this and what follows, see especially McCone 1990, pp. 23–4.

anachronistic perhaps, but Cenn Faélad's association with the otherwise obscure foundation of Tuaim Drecain lends a certain degree of verisimilitude to the general context, even if the details are not necessarily to be believed.[132] From their first faltering efforts at writing single Irish words such men as Cenn Faélad, the *sapientes* of the monastic schools, advanced to more ambitious things, experimenting as they went along with alternative spelling systems until they had evolved an acceptable standard for the native language. Once launched on this path, the fortunes of the Irish schools, in Latin and in Old Irish, were to see a dramatic rise in the late seventh century and beyond.

132. See McCone's verdict: 'Whatever the proportion of fact and fiction in this narrative, it was clearly intended as a charter for a literate monastic legal tradition applied to society as a whole and believed to combine poetic teaching and practice with ecclesiastical doctrine and techniques'; McCone 1990, p. 23.

CHAPTER 8

THE GOLDEN AGE

Of all the clichés about Irish history none has been more enduring, nor enjoyed such universal popularity, as the 'Golden Age' of early Irish culture. The 'Island of Saints and Scholars' which was a beacon for the rest of Europe when the continental countries languished in their 'Dark Ages', and whose missionary monks brought light to those darkened regions, has left an afterglow that persists to the present day. The picture of native scholars imparting their learning to foreign students free of charge is one of the most oft-cited passages in the Venerable Bede's History of the English Church and People:

> The Irish welcomed them all gladly, gave them their daily food, and also provided them with books to read and with instruction, without asking for any payment.
>
> *Quos omnes Scotti libentissime suscipientes, victum et cotidianum sine pretio, libros quoque ad legendum et magisterium gratuitum praebere curabant.*[1]

And the Irish *peregrini* 'to whom the custom of travelling into foreign lands had become second nature', in the words of the great ninth-century German scholar Walafrid Strabo († AD849)[2] inspired what is perhaps the most brilliant modern evocation of those times, Helen Waddell's *The Wandering Scholars*.[3] The image is an endearing one, but how true is it? How good were the Irish schools, in fact, and did the Irish really carry the torch of learning to Europe in the seventh, eighth, and ninth centuries?

---

1. Plummer 1896, i, p. 192; Colgrave & Mynors 1969, p. 312; Elsewhere (*HE* III 7) Bede mentions Acgilbert, a Frankish cleric, who spent many years in Ireland 'legendarum gratia Scripturarum'; Plummer 1896, i, p. 140; Colgrave & Mynors 1969, p. 234.
2. 'Nuper de natione Scottorum, quibus consuetudo peregrinandi iam paene in naturam conversa est', Walafrid, *Vita Sti Galli* II 46; Krusch 1902b, pp. 280–337 (quotation, p. 336).
3. It is the only fault that I can think of in James F. Kenney's magnificent *Sources for the early history of Ireland* that he dismissed *The wandering scholars* as 'haute vulgarisation'.

MONASTIC RULES AND PENITENTIALS

We may begin with the schools. After the initial phase of conversion and consolidation in the fifth century, Latin learning appears to have wavered in its development, if indeed it did not wither. There are no known Irish writings from the fifth century or the first half-century of the sixth and we have to wait until the mid-sixth century before picking up the trail again. We have seen in an earlier chapter that the hundred years or so of silence concealed important developments in the organization of the nascent Irish churches, changes that are reflected in the new genres of writing that emerge in the sixth century.[4] Distinctive of this phase in Hiberno-Latin writing is the overwhelming monastic influence. The selection of themes is strictly utilitarian and vocational: monastic rules; handbooks of penance (penitentials) or manuals for spiritual confessors; canon law. These texts begin to appear first under strong influence from the neighbouring British church, but the example is taken up enthusiastically by native writers.

Although the rules that governed the monasteries of Columba on Iona and Comgall at Bangor have not survived, they were apparently in circulation on the continent in the ninth century, along with a 'rule of the Irish brothers' (*regula fratrum Hibernensium*) likewise unfortunately lost.[5] The regime at Bangor, however, can be reconstructed on the basis of Columbanus's Rule for his foundation at Luxeuil in Burgundy.[6] This reveals a harsh and unremittingly severe existence for the monks with no concessions to the frailties of body and soul. 'Let him come weary to his bed and sleep walking, and let him be forced to rise while his sleep is not yet finished'.[7] This bleak austerity was the driving force of Columbanus's missionary fervour. Noticeably absent is any mention of scholarly pursuits, and no hint in the *Regula* that studies were encouraged which might result in the astonishing maturity that we find in Columbanus's own writings. He opens the seventh century like a flash of lightning. Even in translation, there is a nobility of language, particularly in his letters, and nowhere more clearly than in the one he addressed to his monks as he awaited deportation back to Ireland:

> I wanted to write you a tearful letter; but for the reason that I know your heart, I have simply mentioned necessary duties, hard of themselves and difficult, and have used another style, preferring to check than to encourage tears. So my speech has been outwardly made smooth, and grief is shut up within. See, the

4. For detailed discussion of the works here under discussion, see especially Kenney 1929, p. 186 ff.; Manitius 1911–31, i, p. 107 ff.; the essays by Mario Esposito collected in Lapidge 1988.

5. All three are mentioned in a ninth-century catalogue from Fulda in Germany: see Lehmann 1925, pp. 1–53 (p. 51).

6. Walker 1957, pp. 122–42 (*Regula monachorum*); pp. 142–68 (*Regula coenobialis*).

7. Walker 1957, p. 140 (*Regula monachorum* §10).

tears flow, but it is better to check the fountain; for it is no part of a brave soldier to lament in battle.

Lacrimosam tibi volui scribere epistolam; sed quia scio cor tuum, idcirco necessariis tantum allegatis, duris et ipsis arduisque, altero stilo usus sum, malens obturare quam provocare lacrimas. Foris itaque aictus est sermo mitis, intus inclusus est dolor. En proruunt lacrimae, sed melius est obturare fontem; non enim fortis militis est in bello plorare.[8]

The reference to a different style was not a conceit on Columbanus's part; in his letters to popes and Frankish bishops he drew on a quite different language, more appropriate – as he felt – to the head of the Church or his local representatives. He opens the first of his surviving letters, addressed to Pope Gregory the Great *c.* AD600, with the following flourish:

To the Holy Lord and Father in Christ, the fairest Ornament of the Roman Church, as it were a most honoured Flower of all Europe in her decay, to the distinguished Bishop, who is skilled in the meditation of divine eloquence, I Bar-Jonah (a poor dove), send greeting in Christ.

Domino Sancto et in Christo Patri, Romanae pulcherrimo Ecclesiae Decori, totius Europae flaccentis augustissimo quasi cuidam Flori, egregio Speculatori, Theoria utpote divinae Castilitatis perito, ego, Bar-Iona (vilis Columba), in Christo mitto salutem.[9]

There is no hint in the stark formlessness of the penitentials that Irish monastic writers could express themselves in a Latin as skilled as this. These strange texts are usually numbered among the genuinely original Irish contributions to medieval civilization, though the honour is a dubious one. 'The penitential literature is in truth a deplorable feature of the medieval Church. Evil deeds, the imagination of which may perhaps have dimly floated through our minds in our darkest moments, are here tabulated and reduced to system. It is hard to see how anyone could busy himself with such literature and not be the worse for it', was the verdict of Charles Plummer, a great scholar and one who knew the early Irish churches better than most.[10] The Irish texts had their distant origins in the penitential practice of the early Christian church, which involved the public separation of penitents from the rest of the community and their exclusion from the sacraments pending absolution of their sins. This regime of sackcloth and ashes was a harrowing experience, and one usually avoided or postponed indefinitely. In the sixth century, perhaps under British influence, a new regime of private penance was introduced into the Irish churches, which allowed frequent confession of wrongdoings to a private confessor or 'soul-friend' (*anmchara*) and with it

8. Walker 1957, p. 30 (*Epistola* IV). Esposito, in a review of Walker's edition (Esposito 1961, pp. 184–203 (quotation, p. 199), remarked that Walker's translation had real literary merit.
9. Walker 1957, pp. 2–3.
10. Plummer 1896, i, pp. clvii–clviii.

came a new practice of spiritual direction and correction, codified in the form of the penitentials. The penitentials assigned penalties for specific sins and were obviously intended as handbooks of penance for confessors, cataloguing every conceivable transgression and apportioning a corresponding remedy for each of them.[11] 'There is no crime which cannot be expiated through penance' intones one text,[12] and there was apparently no crime that could not be thought of: heterosexual and homosexual relations (male and female), the regulation of 'proper' methods of intercourse, aphrodisiacs and potions, physical relations, bestiality (Columbanus has two canons on the subject, one for clerics or monks, the other for laymen), wet dreams, stimulation, abortion, contraception, abstinence from sexual relations, and an endless litany of reprobate behaviour that ranged from drinking in the same house with a pregnant servant woman to keening or wailing the dead.

Columbanus mentions by name two British churchmen, *Uennianus auctor* and Gildas, the former probably the man known in Irish sources as Finnian (either of Clonard, Co. Westmeath, or Moville, Co. Down)[13] whose penitential is probably the oldest example of the genre.[14] Gildas is the best-known writer of the sixth-century British church, and Columbanus had read a 'most polished' letter from him to Finnian, in response to some queries about church matters.[15] Gildas's influence on Columbanus's style has been claimed as strong,[16] but it is not at all clear how much of his work was available in Ireland, nor how widespread was its use.

COLUMBANUS, MAN OF LETTERS

Columbanus, of course, has been claimed as the first great Irish 'man of letters',[17] a claim that rests chiefly on the poems attached to his name. Best-known perhaps is the *Carmen nauale* or 'Boating Song', supposedly composed by him for his monks as they rowed up the Rhine towards Switzerland in AD611. The sweeping rhythm of the poem creates a very effective picture and would do justice as a description of a latter-day Aran currach and its crew:

> See, cut in woods, through flood of twin-horned Rhine
> passes the keel, and greased slips over sea –
> *Heave, men! And let resounding echo sound our 'heave'.*

11. There is a good, brief discussion of the penitentials in Walsh and Bradley 1991, pp. 111–25. For detailed discussion, see Payer 1984, and Brundage 1987.
12. Penitential of Finnian §47: 'quia nullum crimen quod non potest ridimi per penitentiam'; Bieler 1963a, p. 92.
13. Walker 1957, p. 8 (*Epistola* I §7).
14. Bieler 1963a, pp. 74–94. For an important recent study of the genre, see Körntgen 1993, especially p. 60 ff.
15. See Lapidge and Dumville 1984.
16. Winterbottom 1976, pp. 310–17.
17. See especially Bieler 1950, pp. 95–102; Bieler 1954, pp. 213–34.

The winds raise blasts, wild rainstorms wreak their spite
but ready strength of men subdues it all –
   Heave men! And let resounding echo sound our 'heave'.

Clouds melt away and the harsh tempest stills,
effort tames all, great toil is conqueror –
   Heave, men! And let resounding echo sound our 'heave'.

Endure and keep yourselves for happy things;
you suffered worse, and these too God shall end –
   Heave, men! And let resounding echo sound our 'heave'.

Thus acts the foul fiend: wearing out the heart
and with temptation shaking inmost parts –
   You men, remember Christ with mind still sounding 'heave'.

Stand firm in soul and spurn the foul fiend's tricks
and seek defence in virtue's armoury –
   You men, remember Christ with mind still sounding 'heave'.

Firm faith will conquer all and blessed zeal
and the old fiend yielding breaks at last his darts –
   You men, remember Christ with mind still sounding 'heave'.

Supreme of virtues King, and fount of things,
He promises in strife, gives prize in victory –
   You men, remember Christ with mind still sounding 'heave'.[18]

Even without the inclusion of all the poems in the canon of his writings, Columbanus would still rank as a first-rate stylist, and his six surviving letters in particular are evidence that the Irish schools, which even before the close of the sixth century, were already set in a firm pattern of study: Latin grammar, biblical study (exegesis), and the ecclesiastical calendar (computus) had moved beyond the rudimentary initial stages in some instances to a more sophisticated curriculum that was to see its full flowering in the ninth century.

In assessing the extent and quality of Latin learning in Irish schools at the dawn of the seventh century, it is important to guard against the modern trend towards compartmentalization which sees biblical study (exegesis), grammar, and computus as separate disciplines each practised by different teachers. Columbanus – our earliest and best example – handled computus and exegesis with equal facility, and – as we saw – could express himself in a vigorous and expressive Latin of varying styles and registers, to suit the occasion and the audience. His biographer says that he composed a commentary on the Psalms and poems (*carmina*) for instructional purposes.[19] There is no particular reason to assume that Columbanus was an exception in this regard; our seventh-century evidence all indicates that Irish schools, north and south, pursued the same range of interests.

18. Text and translation in Carney 1967, pp. 8–11.
19. Krusch 1905, p. 158 (*Vita Columbani* I 3): 'multaque alia, quae vel ad cantum digna vel ad docendum utilia, condidit dicta'. See Lapidge 1985, pp. 104–16.

CONTROVERSIES

There can hardly be any doubt that much of the impetus towards such studies derived from the controversies that raged through the Irish churches during the sixth and early seventh centuries. Chief among these was the Paschal question. Simply stated, it centred on the problem of how to arrive at the correct date of Easter. But there the simplicity ends. From the second century the church had been trying to devise mathematical tables which would provide such Easter dates in advance, without the necessity of referring each year to Rome. The problem had proved intractable and the level of mathematical knowledge in the West was inadequate to solve it. The centuries up to AD600 are littered with rival tables, tried and found wanting and eventually discarded, replaced each time by a new contender. Columbanus wrote to Pope Gregory that the table being advocated by Rome in his time as the one true and reliable Easter cycle 'has not been accepted by our teachers, by the former scholars of Ireland, by the mathematicians most skilled in reckoning chronology, but has been deemed more worthy of ridicule or pity than of authority'.[20] As one commentator wrily commented, 'it is a letter that would have irked a saint'.[21] Columbanus based his views on the Irish 84-year Easter table and the authority of a tract *De Pascha* by a writer named Anatolius.[22] *De Pascha* is, in fact, one of a group of texts for which modern scholars have coined the rather uncomplimentary term 'Irish Paschal Forgeries'; as it happens, the most recent research has indicated that the 'forgeries' are not the spurious concoctions they were thought to be,[23] while the 'Irish-84' has been shown to derive, in all likelihood, from the fourth- and fifth-century Gallican church.

The Easter controversy inspired one of the most remarkable products of the seventh-century Irish schools: the famous Paschal letter of Cummian and the related text *De ratione conputandi* ('On the method of reckoning [time]').[24] We have seen in the previous chapter the extraordinary range of Cummian's reading, but this instructional manual on computing – which utilises an identical series of biblical, patristic and computistical authorities – offers a much more sophisticated and detailed discussion of Easter and the mathematics involved, and is an extremely impressive witness to the level of scientific knowledge in Ireland at this time. In some respects indeed the author displays a surer grasp of the finer technical points of computus even than Bede, and it can be demonstrated, in fact, that the great English scholar's works on time were directly dependent on Irish predecessors.[25]

20. Walker 1957, p. 6 (*Epistola* I §4). I have slightly changed Walker's translation, but without affecting the sense.
21. Jones 1943, p. 79.
22. Krusch 1880, pp. 316–27; Jones 1943, pp. 82–8.
23. See McCarthy 1994.
24. Walsh & Ó Cróinín 1988 p. ; See also Ó Cróinín 1982c.
25. Ó Cróinín 1983 and 1989, esp. pp. 15–17.

As we mentioned previously, Cummian has also been suggested as the author of a commentary on the Gospel of Mark. This commentary was very influential in Irish circles and one ninth-century fragment, heavily glossed in Old Irish, survives in Turin (Bibl. Naz. F.IV. 1 (No. 7)).[26] Beside displaying many features that are typical of Irish exegesis in this period (for which see further below), the author also refers to skin-covered boats (currachs?) and the penitential practice of *uigilia crucis* (Old Irish *crosfigil*). He displays a keen interest in the Easter question too. Bernhard Bischoff linked these various traits with a reference in an Angers manuscript to a 'recent writer on Mark by name of Cummian' (*nouellum auctorem in Marcum nomine Comiano*), and identified this writer with the author of the Mark commentary.[27]

Foremost among Cummian's contemporaries is Laidcend mac Baíth Bandaig († AD661)[28] who is known principally for his epitome of Gregory the Great's *Moralia in Iob* and for a lorica (or 'breastplate' prayer), a bizarre and strange composition which invokes the Trinity and the heavenly powers for protection of every part of the body (over seventy are listed) with constant repetition of the petition for protection at intervals throughout the text:[29]

O God, defend me everywhere
with your impregnable power and protection.

Deliver all the limbs of me a mortal
with your protective shield guarding every member,
lest the foul demons hurl their shafts
into my sides, as is their wont.

Deliver my skull, head with hair, and eyes,
mouth, tongue, teeth, and nostrils,
neck, breast, side, and limbs,
joints, fat, and two hands . . .

This incantation derives from that twilight zone between paganism and Christianity where the author has advanced little beyond the thought-world of pre-Christian religion, a man for whom the dark forces of the nether world present a very real terror. Yet we have no reason to think that Laidcend was any less sophisticated than his learned contemporaries. He was a scholar at Cluain Ferta Mo-Lua (Clonfert-Mulloe, townland Kyle, Co. Leix) and is mentioned as *auctor Mo-Laggae* in an interesting tract which exhibits in a striking way the fascination that early Irish literati had with their country's prehistory,[30] and the manner in which they wove native and biblical lore through their writings. This juxtaposition of vernacular and Latin learning is a constant theme throughout early Irish scholarship; the Cummian whom we

26. Stokes & Strachan 1901–3, i, pp. 484–94.
27. See Bischoff 1993, pp. xxi–xxii n. 50.
28. See especially Gougaud 1909, pp. 37–46.
29. Adriaen 1969; Herren 1987, pp. 76–89.
30. The text is unpublished; see Byrne 1967, pp. 164–82.

mentioned above may also be the author of a descriptive list of Christ and the Apostles which is found in both Irish and Latin versions.[31] Cummian addressed his letter on the Easter question to Ségéne, abbot of Iona, and a certain Béccán *solitarius* ('hermit'), and this Béccán has been plausibly identified as Béccán mac Luigdech, the author of two Old Irish poems in praise of Colum Cille.[32]

BILINGUAL TEXTS AND GLOSSES

Writing in the vernacular (as we saw in a previous chapter) was certainly established by AD600 and Irish scholars – with just a few exceptions[33] – appear to have encouraged its use alongside Latin. The most striking example from the seventh century is the bilingual text known (from its present location) as the Cambrai Homily.[34] This tract combines excerpts from the Latin text of the gospels, the Pauline Epistles and the homilies of Gregory the Great on the gospels with a sermon in Irish of a very archaic hue; linguistically it is one of the most interesting works in Old Irish, but its theme is also noteworthy. It is the earliest work of Irish Christianity to discuss the theory of 'threefold martyrdom':

> This is the white martyrdom to man, when he separates for sake of God from everything he loves, although he suffer fasting or labour thereat.
> This is the green martyrdom to him, when by means of them (fasting and labour) he separates from his desires, or suffers toil in penance and repentance.
> This is the red martyrdom to him, endurance of a cross of destruction for Christ's sake . . .[35]

The Cambrai Homily is probably mid-seventh-century in date, but the practice of writing prose in Old Irish was clearly well-established by that date.

The earliest extensive appearance of Latin and Irish side-by-side, however, is in the myriad glosses added by Irish scribes to their Latin manuscripts. The habit of marking words or phrases in the Latin with translations in the vernacular seems to have begun at a very early date in the Irish schools, as spontaneous doodles initially, the casual remarks of scholars as they brooded on their texts, pen in hand. Others might be added as teaching aids, reminders to the monastic master of something that needed further explanation. Sometimes, however, the gloss might have nothing at all to do with the text, but simply records the passing whim of the reader: 'Virgil was a

---

31. Ó Cróinín 1989b, pp. 268–79.
32. Kelly 1973, pp. 1–34; Kelly 1975, pp. 66–98.
33. The author of the (?)seventh-century *Additamenta* to the Life of St Patrick by Tírechán apologized for using so many Irish words; see above. p. 180.
34. See Ó Néill 1981, pp. 137–47.
35. Text and translation in Stokes & Strachan 1901–3, ii, pp. 244–7; see also Stancliffe 1982, pp. 21–46.

great poet' (*magnus poeta Virgilius fuit*) remarks the ancient grammarian, twice, to which the Irish reader responded: 'and he is not easy, either!'.[36] The scribe of the Book of Armagh, folio 78′b, remarked at the foot of the page that he had just completed the preceding column of writing with three dips of the pen;[37] another scribe, exasperated by the grammarian Priscian's long-windedness, greeted the close of one exposition with the brusque comment: 'he has made his point at last!'.[38] When pen and ink had got the better of them, scribes occasionally resorted to another liquid on the table, sometimes with dire consequences; one of the readers of the ninth-century St-Gall manuscript of Priscian noted ruefully that he had made too freely overnight and was feeling the effects of a hangover (*lathaeiri*), adding the gloss a second time, in ogam, for good measure.[39] The phenomenon of such talkative scribes was charmingly summed up by Charles Plummer in the opening words of a famous paper on the subject: 'I suppose that everyone who has travelled in Ireland has been struck by the way in which an Irishman will discuss his most intimate private affairs with any casual stranger whom he may happen to meet'.[40] The relief thus found by the modern Irishman in conversation the medieval scribe found by talking either to a neighbour or to himself in the margins of his manuscripts. These glosses and marginalia were liable to be incorporated unthinkingly into a manuscript when a text came to be copied, a phenomenon which Plummer very aptly compared to a humorous example of his own time: in the early copies of a *Blue Book* on China, in the middle of a dispatch, occurred the sentence: 'not very grammatical, but I suppose we must let Sir Claude Macdonald write as he pleases', evidently a criticism which a British civil servant had scribbled on the margin of his proof copy, and forgot to delete before the proof was returned to the printer![41]

We have seen above how the adoption of Latin as the *lingua franca* of the church in Ireland involved the Irish in practical problems which their fellow-Christians on the continent – native speakers of Latin – never had to face, namely the necessity of acquiring this new language from scratch and teaching it as a written rather than a spoken language. Hence the proliferation of elementary grammars, glossaries, and word-lists, extended paradigms to be learnt by rote, and collections of excerpts from the grammarians of Late Antiquity, often strung together without comment.[42] But since Irish was not a Romance language, but has a very different structure, its speakers tended to regard Latin primarily as a written medium of expression,

36. Stokes and Strachan 1901–3, ii, p. 224.
37. Stokes and Strachan 1901–3, i, p. 495.
38. Stokes and Strachan 1901–3, ii, p. 136.
39. Stokes and Strachan 1901–3, i, pp. xxi–xxii.
40. Plummer 1926, pp. 11–44 (quotation, p. 11).
41. Plummer 1926, p. 32 n. 5.
42. Law 1982. See, however, the critical reviews of this book by Herren 1983, pp. 312–6; Ahlqvist 1983, pp. 100–1; Breatnach, 1984, pp. 182–6; and Ó Cróinín 1982–83, pp. 149–56.

to be understood more by the eye than by the ear, and as a result Irish scribes treated the two languages differently when it came to writing them.[43]

Although there is no evidence for conflicts of interpretation among seventh-century writers such as we have for those of the ninth, the literature does reflect some of the controversies and alignments of the period. The rivalry that marked off the two groups of Romani and Hiberni seems to have centred on matters of organization rather than doctrine or belief.[44] And yet there are occasional references to particular interpretations of Scripture that were being proposed by the Romani, sufficient at any rate to suggest that the rift ran deeper than has usually been believed.[45] In the letter of Colmán to an Irish confrère named Feradach, mentioned above,[46] Colmán remarks almost casually that he has acquired a better text of Caelius Sedulius's *Carmen Paschale*, and that he got it from the Romani; Feradach's manuscript (he writes) was faulty and was missing some five pages. We do not know who this Colmán was nor whether he penned his letter at home or on the continent; either is possible. If it is seventh-century in date it demonstrates a remarkable grasp of Latin metrics and the rules of *cursus*, and a very creditable interest on the part of the two correspondents in the finer points of Latin literature.

BIBLICAL INTERPRETATION

The publication in 1954 of an epoch-making article by the great German medievalist Bernhard Bischoff[47] made known for the first time a whole range of Hiberno-Latin biblical commentaries previously unnoticed by scholars. Bischoff's list (which runs to forty titles) revealed an Aladdin's cave of riches which, at a stroke, transformed our understanding of the Irish monastic schools. Most of these commentaries owed their survival to the fact that later medieval copyists thought them to be the work of the Church Fathers, mainly because several of these earlier Irish writers had used pen-names like Augustine, Cyprian, or Jerome. Sometimes, however, the Irish origins of a work were plain to see, even when its author used a patristic pen-name; the Irish Augustine's *De mirabilibus* is a case in point. On the other hand, the commentary on the Gospel of Mark which passed under the name of Jerome has been claimed by Bischoff as a work of Cummian's; but the evidence is not so explicit as in the *De mirabilibus*, and scholars are not unanimous in accepting Bischoff's view.[48] It was the quirks of style and the sources used that enabled Bischoff to suggest Irish authorship for these anonymous texts: a predilection for using a question-and-answer technique, with the answer

43. For this see esp. Malcolm Parkes 1987, pp. 15–29 (repr. in Parkes 1991, pp. 1–18).
44. See McNamara 1984, pp. 283–328; Ó Néill 1984, pp. 280–90.
45. See Hughes 1966, pp. 46 ff., 105 ff., 130 ff.
46. See pp. 185–6.
47. Bischoff 1954.
48. See Walsh and Ó Cróinín 1988, pp. 217–21.

prefaced by the rhetorical exclamation *non difficile* ('not difficult!', translating the Irish *ní ansae*); frequent use of the Three Sacred Languages formula in which particular words of the Bible text are given in Greek, Latin, and Hebrew (with the Greek often home-made and the Hebrew entirely fictitious!); a use of triads is also characteristic, following a pattern frequently encountered in the native literature[49] but also inspired, in the biblical context, by themes like that of the Three Magi.[50] These and other features are not necessarily unique to Irish texts; many, in fact, derive from the writings of the early Church Fathers. It is the sheer frequency with which Hiberno-Latin writers use them, often in combination, that marks their work out as distinctively Irish. Where the Irish do differ significantly is in their choice of sources: biblical apocrypha and uncanonical texts are found in Irish commentaries which had long before disappeared from the rest of the western church under the hammer of anathema.[51]

The Irish are also distinctive in their liking for Pelagius, the 'reluctant heretic'.[52] Best-known for his views on predestination and original sin, Pelagius was the last of the great heresiarchs, doing battle in titanic struggle with Augustine, Jerome, and their followers. Jerome indeed appears to have thought that his arch-rival was Irish, and snorted that Pelagius was 'stuffed with Irish porridge' (*Scottis pultibus praegravatus*). But Pelagius's belief that children are born innocent without the stain of original sin; that baptism is consequently not necessary for salvation, but that man's inherent good nature and reason could lead him to God (so that even pagans might be saved) proved too much for the dour souls of Hippo and Bethlehem. With Pelagius finally succumbing to the combined blows of his opponents, his writings and doctrines were condemned in AD418, but his commentary on the Letters of St Paul was still widely read and highly regarded by Irish scholars, and in fact he retained his popularity in Irish schools from the seventh century to the twelfth;[53] striking evidence of the Irish ability to see the good and useful elements in a work which was doctrinally suspect. Indeed, it is largely due to that fact that knowledge of Pelagius's works survived; other condemned works have disappeared without trace. But it would be a mistake to think that the early Irish church was itself 'Pelagian' in its doctrines.[54] True, there is extant a letter from the Pope-elect John IV and the Roman curia addressed in AD640 to the northern Irish churches in which the Irish are accused of espousing Pelagianism:[55]

---

49. Meyer 1906.
50. See Sims-Williams 1978, pp. 78–111.
51. McNamara 1975.
52. For a good recent summary of his life and career, see Rees 1988.
53. Pelagius is cited by Maél Brigte Ua Maél Uanaig of Armagh in his commentary on Matthew written AD1138; see below, p. 231.
54. The most recent discussion is by Kelly 1978, pp. 99–124.
55. The letter is preserved in Bede; see Plummer 1896, i, pp. 123–4; Colgrave and Mynors 1969, pp. 200–2 (*HE* II 19).

And this also we have learnt, that the poison of the Pelagian heresy has of late revived amongst you; we therefore exhort you to put away utterly this kind of poisonous and criminal superstition from your minds. You cannot be unaware that this execrable heresy has been condemned; and not only has it been abolished for some two hundred years but it is daily condemned by us and buried beneath our perpetual ban. We exhort you then not to rake up the ashes amongst you of those whose weapons have been burnt.

The Roman clergy and most modern commentators have been hopelessly confused by this episode; the letter in fact has nothing to do with Pelagius's ideas but arose out of a misunderstanding in Rome about Irish practice in the matter of Easter observance.[56] But as one fine scholar remarked, 'the doctrine is beguiling and few ordinary English people, still less Americans, avoid being semi-Pelagian, if not full-blooded Pelagians, today'.[57] Among the many more tempting illusions about Ireland's importance in the scheme of things we may, perhaps, number a comparatively harmless belief that this particular heresiarch and believer in mankind's inherent inclination towards good might have hailed from this country.[58]

HISPERICA FAMINA

There is no trace of doubt about orthodoxy in the reputation enjoyed by Irish schools in the seventh century. Such was the good name of Irish teachers, says Bede, that they attracted visiting students not only from Britain but also from Francia.[59] He mentions one by name, a Frank Acgilberct, who – before spending some years as bishop of Wessex and then transferring to Northumbria and eventually back to Paris – spent many years in Ireland in order to study Scripture. Irish sources provide the names of several others, while Bede names no fewer than twelve who were associated with the monastery at Rath Melsigi.[60] He reports them as sometimes having seated themselves behind the shoulders of their Irish masters and studied their Scripture with them; as we saw above, books and board were provided free. This may be the background to one of the most curious of Hiberno-Latin texts (if it *is* Hiberno-Latin), the *Hisperica Famina*.[61] These bizarre 'Western Sayings' have long puzzled scholars, most of whom have tended to see in them the 'culture-fungus of decay'.[62] Composed in an extravagant and tortuous Latin, they seem to be the party-pieces of a group of dotty students whose days are spent trying to outdo one another in verbosity. Where an

56. See Ó Cróinín 1985, pp. 505–16.
57. Bethell 1981, pp. 36–49 (quotation, p. 39).
58. Echoing the view of my namesake, Anthony Cronin, 'Saints, heretics and scholars', *Irish Times*, 14 March 1975.
59. Plummer 1896, i, p. 192; Colgrave and Mynors 1969, p. 312 (*HE* III 27).
60. See Ó Cróinín 1984, pp. 17–49, and Ó Riain 1993.
61. Herren 1974, 1987.
62. The description is Mac Neill's: Mac Neill 1931, p. 457.

obscure word can be substituted for a simple one the scholars never fail to do so, and if perchance they appear to slip into plain vocabulary it usually transpires that theirs is not the normal usage of such words; 'words mean what they want them to mean'. This motley group travels about apparently begging from the local population for their sustenance, to which purpose they must relinquish the bonds of Latin and resort to Irish (*scottigenum eulogium*). The implication in the text seems to be that the group is not Irish, and indeed the evidence of the manuscripts might argue for a Breton origin for the group. But the 'Hisperic' style certainly found favour with the Irish and seventh-century texts are peppered with exotic words of spurious Greek, Hebrew, and even Chaldean derivation. Sometimes even Irish words creep in – though they are not common at any stage in the history of Hiberno-Latin literature. The grammarians coin the occasional word like *orgo* (from Irish *orgaim* 'to kill') and others crop up in works like Adomnán's biography of Columba: *currucus* 'currach', and *tigernus*, from Irish *tigern* 'lord'. Sometimes the syntax is influenced by Irish, but generally the Latin of the time is relatively pure.[63]

HAGIOGRAPHY

The new genre that emerges in the seventh century is hagiography, the Lives of saints. The earliest surviving composition is probably Cogitosus's Life of Brigit of Kildare.[64] It is one of three biographies of the saint that date from this period, the other two being ascribed to Ultán († AD657), bishop of Ardbraccan (Co. Meath), and to Ailerán 'the Wise' († AD665), a scholar of Clonard (also in Co. Meath). Ailerán was also the author of an *Interpretatio mystica progenitorum Domini Iesu Christi*, an allegorical explanation of the names that appear in Christ's genealogy as given in the Gospel of Matthew, setting forth their mystical meaning.[65] He also composed the verses that begin *Quam in primo speciosa quadriga* which present a rhyming list of the so-called Eusebian canons (the parallel columns of chapter and section numbers common to the four gospels). The poem is important as being the earliest Irish evidence for the use of 'beast canon tables', i.e. the canon tables decorated with illustrations of fantastic animals best exemplified by the tables in the Book of Kells.[66]

Pride of place, however, among Irish hagiographers must go to Adomnán, ninth abbot of Iona († AD704), author of a Life of Columba (Colum Cille) in three books.[67] Though the work suffers from many of the faults that disfigure medieval hagiography in the eyes of modern readers, Adomnán's *Vita Columbae* far surpasses all the other seventh-century Irish Lives both as an

63. For the influence of Irish syntax on Hiberno-Latin, see especially Most 1946.
64. McCone 1982, pp. 107–45; *contra* Sharpe 1982a, pp. 81–106.
65. See Kenney 1929, pp. 279–80.
66. See Netzer 1994.
67. Anderson 1961.

authentic portrait of its subject and in its value as evidence for the life of the church in Adomnán's own time. Though not himself a contemporary of the saint, Adomnán did consult many who had known Columba's closest disciples, and he was unusually scrupulous in his use of evidence, both written and oral. There can be few more touching scenes in the whole of medieval literature than the one concerning Columba's horse that shed tears, knowing of his master's approaching death:

> After this the saint left the barn, and returning towards the monastery sat down midway. In that place a cross that was later fixed in a mill-stone is seen, standing at the roadside, even today. And while the saint sat there, resting for a little while, being (as I have said above) weary with age, behold, a white horse came to him, the obedient servant who was accustomed to carry the milk-vessels between the cow-pasture and the monastery. It went to the saint, and strange to tell, put its head in his bosom, inspired, as I believe, by God, before whom every living creature has understanding, with such perception of things as the Creator himself has decreed; and knowing that its master would presently depart from it, and that it should see him no more, it began to mourn, and like a human being to let tears fall freely on the lap of the saint, and foaming much, to weep aloud.[68]

Some of Adomnán's incidental narratives cast interesting light on the everyday aspects of the community life on Iona, while his information concerning contemporary political affairs is extremely valuable.[69] Especially noteworthy is the complete absence of rancour or rivalry in Columba's relations with other monastic leaders of his time; Columba, Comgall of Bangor, and Ciarán of Clonmacnois, and a great many others, are all seen in amicable contact, receiving and visiting one another regularly.

By Adomnán's time, however, the primary position of Iona among the churches of northern Ireland and Scotland had come under challenge as a result of the Easter controversy, but doubtless also for political reasons as well. A sour note had crept into the documents of the time and there was a need to restate the claims of Columba and his successors, and to remind people both in Ireland and in Britain of the seminal role played by the monks of Iona both in the Irish church and also, of course, in the establishment of Christianity in northern Britain.[70] The Columban *paruchia* or monastic confederation was being edged out of its once dominant position by the emergent rival claims of Armagh, and the two Lives of Patrick that appeared towards the close of the century staked out Armagh's claims in no uncertain manner. Compared to the *Vita Columbae*, however, Muirchú's Life of Patrick is a travesty of the man and of the genre. He seems to have known very little about his subject and cared less about the facts concerning him. Even where he draws on Patrick's own writings it is to turn them upside-down. In this he was following the dubious example of his *pater* Cogitosus (author of the

68. Anderson 1961, pp. 522–3.
69. See the analysis by MacDonald 1984, pp. 271–302.
70. See Picard 1982, pp. 160–77.

oldest *Vita Brigitae*) and all the worst elements of that writer's work were shamelessly aped. Muirchú's Life of Patrick is sometimes magnificent literature, but it is not biography.[71]

The hagiographical writings were never more than occasional pieces, composed to suit local circumstances, intended to prove the subject's sanctity by means of miracles worked. 'Each community must be able to demonstrate that its patron was, in this respect, inferior to none other'.[72] Their purpose was generally to enhance the reputation of the founder-saint with a view to attracting popular interest and a corresponding inflow of pilgrims and wealth. Cogitosus's *Vita Brigitae* is a good example; his physical description of Kildare illustrates the genre:

> What eloquence could sufficiently extol the beauty of this church and the innumerable wonders of what we may call its city? For 'city' is the proper word to use, since [Kildare] earns the title because of the multitudes who live there; it is a great metropolitan city. Within its outskirts, whose limits were laid out by St Brigit, no man need fear any mortal adversary or any gathering of enemies; it is the safest refuge among all the enclosed towns of the Irish. The wealth and treasures of kings are in safe-keeping there, and the city is known to have reached the highest peak of good order. And who could number the varieties of people who gather there in countless throngs from all provinces? Some come for the abundance of its feasts; others, in ill-health, come for a cure; others come simply to watch the crowds go by; others come with great offerings to take part in the celebrations of the feast of St Brigit.[73]

Most of these Lives are less than edifying, being little more than a catalogue of miracles and wonders, some of them amusing, most of them ridiculous. Sometimes the miraculous powers of the saint are malign, as with Ruadán of Lorrha (Co. Tipperary) 'who loved cursing'.[74] Like the man who would put his son to studying the law, the church that could boast a good saint 'hath fashioned an engine against its enemies, a machine for its friends'.[75] Despite their incidental value as sources of information for the way-of-life and social and economic conditions at the time they were composed, most of the hagiographies have little claim to strictly historical importance.[76] Most of their authors had access to only the most meagre written sources (lists of founders and their successors, for example) and the oral information that they purvey can never be wholly trusted. Most striking of all, there is no development in the genre; seventh-century texts are practically indistinguishable from twelfth-century ones, and the same tedious formulae recur time after time,

71. Bieler 1974, pp. 219–43.
72. Kenney 1929, p. 299 (quotation).
73. Translation by Liam de Paor, in Almqvist and Greene 1976, pp. 29–37 (quotation, p. 29).
74. According to the poem on the attributes of the saints ascribed to Cuimmín of Condeire; see Stokes 1897, pp. 59–73.
75. I have adapted a phrase in Waddell 1927, p. 132.
76. See the exemplary study by Doherty 1982, pp. 300–28.

often borrowed shamelessly from one Life to another. With few exceptions, the saints' Lives are a dismal swamp of superstition and perverted Christianity, dreary litanies of misplaced reverence and devotion.

HIBERNO-LATIN FLOWERING

The real seventh-century blossoming in Hiberno-Latin writing took place in the three main subjects of the curriculum: exegesis, grammar, and computus. Grammar especially witnessed an astonishing proliferation of texts and a rapidly rising graph of sophistication in their content. Indeed, it is no exaggeration to say that the revolution in Hiberno-Latin grammatical studies – for such it was – paved the way for the remarkable contribution which Irish scholars were to make to the culture of Europe in the age of Charlemagne and after.[77] The impetus for this efflorescence appears to have derived from the discovery by the Irish in the seventh century of a whole new range of grammars from Late Antiquity. Hitherto reliant almost entirely on Donatus, they now had access to Priscian, Charisius (under the by-name Comminianus), Consentius, Diomedes, Probus, Servius, and Papirinus.[78] As well as these, they received anonymous texts from Spain on figures and tropes and another on faults of speech.[79] This embarrassment of riches transformed the Irish schools and revolutionized the format of the standard Hiberno-Latin grammars. A study of the three principal manuals of the period, *Anonymus ad Cuimnanum*, *Ars Ambrosiana*, and *Congregatio Salcani filii de uerbo*,[80] shows the transition from a period when Donatus's *Ars minor* was the basic tool, to a new era in which the teacher could now assume that his students knew the text by heart and therefore needed to cite it only in snippets. The bulk of the teacher's text is now made up of commentary in which Donatus's rules are not only cited but compared with those of other grammarians, frequently criticizing more than one of them.[81] The anonymous author (an Irishman, we need hardly doubt) who addressed his commentary to an unidentified Cuimnanus[82] not only elaborates a sophisticated technique but prefaces his work with a remarkable apologia for the study of Latin grammar as an end in itself.[83] Mindful of the outburst against Donatus made by Pope Gregory the Great, the Anonymous took care to defend his position by

77. The standard survey is Holtz 1981b; see also (though less enthusiastically) Law 1982.
78. Law 1982, p. 29, says that Priscian was not known in Ireland in the seventh century, but she has ignored some important Irish evidence which refutes this; see the reviews cited in n. 42 above.
79. See the brilliant paper by Schindel 1975.
80. On the Anonymous see Holtz 1981b, pp. 267–70, 284–94; Law 1982, pp. 87–90 (who argues for English authorship). On the *Ars Ambrosiana*, see Löfstedt 1982a; Holtz 1981b, pp. 284–94; Law 1982, pp. 93–7. For the *Congregatio*, see Law 1981, pp. 83–97.
81. Holtz 1981b, p. 286.
82. See p. 176 n. 34 above.
83. Holtz 1981b, pp. 267–9; Bischoff 1966, pp. 273–88.

reference to Jerome (who was more than happy to count himself a pupil of Donatus). That he should have felt it necessary to defend himself at all has been interpreted as an indication that Irish schools in the late sixth and early seventh centuries had perhaps witnessed a struggle between those who would rid the curriculum of these grammars (with their profane quotations from pagan classical authors) and have only strictly functional instruction based solely on the Bible, on the one hand, and those on the other side (like the Anonymous) who saw in the study of the ancient authors a means of gaining access to the finer points of Scripture, which were, after all, written in Latin. The eighth and ninth centuries clearly prove that the victory had gone to the more enlightened party, though not without a struggle. The pedantry of the school-masters was, however, sometimes too much to take, and it brought forth a glorious pastiche in the writings of Virgilius Maro Grammaticus ('the grammarian').[84]

Modern scholars do not quite know what to make of Virgil. Is he just a dotty professor, like many of themselves, and therefore to be humoured? Or is he a dangerous lunatic, and therefore to be dismissed? Or is he a comedian, a clever satirist whose bizarre doctrines are a send-up of his pompous colleagues? There is no doubt that some of his statements have raised the eyes as well as the eyebrows of many a modern reader. What is one to make, for example, of his theory that there are twelve kinds of Latin; or his gallery of grammatical 'greats' who rejoice under names like Blastus, Galbungus, and Gurgilius; or the story that two of his grammarians sat up for fourteen days and as many nights debating whether the word *ego* ('I') had a vocative case or not?[85] Computists, too, get the rub: Virgil includes a 'secret code' of letters, each with a numerical value, but how to break the code, and what it all means, no one knows. Such word-games were widely used in the elementary schools to teach youngsters their numbers and the alphabet, and the Venerable Bede says it was great fun.[86] 'In the works of Virgil', one scholar has remarked, 'it is as though in the culture of scholarly Latin one still knew the tune but had forgotten the words'.[87] Virgil, therefore, was undoubtedly poking fun at his contemporaries, who made their students do all kinds of abstruse mathematical calculations using finger-reckoning – like the computist who worked out the number of 'moments' Jonah had spent inside the belly of the whale![88] But it is not all nonsense; Virgil's two

---

84. Polara 1979; on his Irish origin, see Ó Cróinín 1989c, pp. 13–22. I am not convinced by the arguments for Virgilius having been a Spanish Jew offered by Bischoff 1988 [1991].
85. Virgil here borrows from Aulus Gellius *Attic Nights* (Book 14, chapter 5), who recounts a story of two Roman grammarians who all but came to blows over the correct vocative form of the adjective *egregius*.
86. Jones 1943, p. 181; see also Ó Cróinín 1982a, pp. 281–95.
87. Holtz 1981a, p. 316.
88. The author of the unpublished mid-seventh-century Irish computus *De ratione temporum uel de compoto annali* calculated that Jonah was 2,880 moments inside the whale.

compositions in fact contain a great deal of sensible grammatical doctrine, but he was a good teacher who knew full well that large doses of Donatus needed to be washed down with humour; it is not difficult to imagine him (like some latter-day Celtic scholars) holding forth in a pub.[89]

Virgil's jape seems to have started a trend: an unpublished grammar gravely explains – in the Three Sacred Languages, of course! – the names for the strokes in the first letter of the alphabet: 'In Hebrew *abst, ebst, ubst*; in Greek, *albs, elbs, ulbs*; in Latin two oblique strokes and a vertical one above!'[90]

But the best example of all is the hilarious 'Chaldean explanation' of the word *Gloria*: The interpretation of [the word] *gloria* among the Chaldeans: *Gloria* is 'the earth praises the creator'; *glori* is 'the earth magnifies'; *glor* is 'the earth marvels'; *glo* is 'the earth trembles in praise'; *gl* is 'the earth exults in thee, God'; [and] *g* is 'the earth'.[91]

And yet the Classics were not entirely forgotten. There still survives a commentary on Virgil (the classical poet) culled from the (lost) treatises of Gaudentius, Iunilius, and Filargirius; it was very likely compiled – at least in part – by the same Adomnán who wrote the Life of Columba.[92] This is only one instance in which the Irish preserved material otherwise lost; as we saw earlier, they used a text of the grammarian Diomedes better than any that has come down to us, and Malsachanus (or his source) has citations from the poetical works of Accius no longer extant.[93] Some of these rare works may have come via the British connection; others were acquired more recently.

SPANISH CONNECTIONS

One of the reasons for the radical transformation of Hiberno-Latin studies in the seventh century – besides the discovery of the new corpus of grammars – was the arrival from Spain of the works of Isidore of Seville († AD636).[94]

By mid-century his most important writings, the *Etymologiae* ('Etymologies')

---

89. Polara 1993, pp. 205–22.

90. Löfstedt 1982b, pp. 159–64 (quotation, pp. 162–4).

91. Löfstedt 1982b, p. 163. There is a similar 'Chaldean explanation' of the word *Alleluia*, followed by a 'Hebrew' one, in the Psalter of St Maximin; see James 1921, p. 213: 'Expositio Alleluia aput Caldeos: Alleluia est laus tibi soli. Allelui est laus tibi exercituum. Allelu est trinitati. Allel est laus tibi fortis. Alle est laus lucis. All est laus pia. Al est laus. A est labarum. Item apud hebreos: Al est laus tibi benedictus. Le est laus tibi aeternae. Lu est tibi laus lux lucis. Ia est laus tibi inluminatio lucis. Qui nec tempore finiris nec adre noctis nubilo tegeris rex aeternae gloriae'.

92. Thilo 1860, pp. 119–52, especially pp. 132–3; Hagen 1861–67, pp. 673–1014, especially pp. 696–704; Funaioli 1930 [and the review of that book by Lindsay 1936, pp. 336–8]; Beeson 1932, pp. 81–100; there are a number of Old Irish glosses in the text, ed. by Stokes and Strachan 1901–3, ii, pp. 46–8, 360–3.

93. Diomedes: see the note by Bernhard Bischoff in Klotz 1953, p. 4 ff.; Accius: Löfstedt 1965, p. 51. See above, p. 184.

94. For the most recent survey, with full bibliography, see Hillgarth 1984, pp. 1–16.

and *De natura rerum* ('On the nature of things') were in general use by Irish authors – the earliest known use of Isidore outside his native Spain.[95] Isidore's *Etymologiae* especially were a revelation to the Irish, for his encyclopaedic knowledge and detailed descriptions of anything and everything to do with the institutions of the classical world of Roman civilization opened up new vistas to the Irish who had never been citizens of the Empire and whose experience of classical Latin literature derived almost exclusively from the occasional tags quoted by the ancient grammarians. In the same way Isidore's treatise *De natura rerum* provided the Irish for the first time with a compendium of scientific and cosmographical facts previously unknown to them. So highly esteemed were the *Etymologiae* in particular that the Irish coined an epithet for Isidore which expressed their view of him: *Issidir in chulmin* ('Isidore of the summit [i.e. of learning]').[96] Indeed, tradition has it that the Irish literati of the seventh century were unable to recover the full text of *Táin Bó Cuailnge* because someone had swapped it for the Spanish Father's work![97]

The striking advances in computistical studies in this same period were also due, in large part, to the Spanish connection, for besides the Isidorean texts the Irish also received patristic and post-patristic works like the letters of the patriarchs Theophilus and Proterius of Alexandria, the letter of Pascasinus on the Easter question of AD455, and a variety of other works, all relating to Easter.[98] Some of these were ultimately of African origin and Irish computistical collections in the seventh century represent a remarkable continuity of study from the fifth century down to their own time. If they lack the genius for order and conciseness that is the hallmark of Bede's works on time, they are important nevertheless as providing the raw material without which the great English scholar could not have achieved what he did.

HIBERNO-LATIN POETRY

The other distinctive feature of Hiberno-Latin literature in the seventh century is the flowering of composition in verse. There is a large corpus of poems, on a variety of subjects: devotional, hagiographical, computistical and lyrical, some of which may even date from the early years of the century,[99] though the *Altus prosator* – a sort of 'Paradise Lost' ascribed to Columba – is probably not by him, and some of the poems traditionally ascribed to Columbanus are probably not authentic either. But the hymn in praise of

95. See Herren 1980, pp. 243–50. For new evidence of direct traffic from Spain to Ireland with Isidore's writings, see Carley and Dooley 1991. I believe that the dating-clause in Carley's manuscript of the Etymologies can be recovered, and gives AD655 as the year of writing.
96. See O'Rahilly 1926, p. 109.
97. Carney 1955, pp. 165–88.
98. See Ó Cróinín 1982c, p. 407.
99. The most convenient collection is Blume 1908.

Patrick, *Audite omnes amantes*, which is ascribed to a disciple of his, Secundinus, while almost certainly not fifth-century in date, is quite possibly a composition by Colmán Elo (of Lynally, Co. Meath), who died in AD610.[100] The synchronistic verses *Deus a quo facta fuit*, on the Six Ages of the world, are internally dated to AD645,[101] and may be compared to another composition that illustrates nicely the starkly functional nature of the curriculum. This is a versified textbook in ninety lines, which begins:

> The solar year consists of four seasons
> Which complete their cycle in twelve months.
> The year runs its course in fifty-two weeks
> Plus one day and six equinoctial hours.
> In three hundred and sixty-five days
> The sun illuminates the zodiacal course in its circuit,
> But a fourth part of one night and day is not counted,
> By which the solar circuit exceeds
> The calculated cycle of days.
> From this quarter-day, after the completion of twice two years
> Calculators decree a bissextile day has accumulated.
> So great an honour was bestowed on it from regal height,
> For it was named 'bissextus' by Julius Caesar.
> Gaius, in decreeing the end of the year, determined that the
> Five days should go somewhat before the end of the short month of February, etc.

> *Annus solis continetur   quattuor temporibus*
> *Ac deinde adimpletur   duodenis mensibus*
> *Quinquaginta et duabus   currit ebdomadibus*
> *Una die superducta   et sex horis paribus . . .*[102]

Small wonder that Helen Waddell should have said 'it would have been better for literature if this craving for the soil which is the root and ground of Irish poetry had taken seisin of their Latin verse. It is too academic'.[103] But in an age when books were scarce, memorization had an important part to play and if these compositions do not inspire, they are at least instructive. They are not all bad, either; the poems preserved in the Antiphonary of Bangor (before AD692) include the verses *Sancti uenite, corpus Christi sumite* ('Draw nigh and take the Body of the Lord'), a devotional gem which has had an abiding influence in varying Christian traditions down the years. And of the Antiphonary generally it has been said that 'through its pages the general student can receive the voice of the daily worship of God carried across twelve centuries from those famous, but shadowy, monasteries of ancient Ireland'.[104]

It comes as something of a disappointment that the eighth century seems to

100. Lapidge and Sharpe 1985, p. 146 No. 573.
101. See Ó Cróinín 1983, pp. 79–81.
102. See Strecker 1914, pp. 682–6 No. CXIV.
103. Waddell 1927, p. 35.
104. Kenney 1929, p. 712.

have been a period of compilation rather than innovation, though there are occasionally flowers in an otherwise barren landscape. The *Collectio canonum Hibernensis* ('Irish collection of canons')[105] is perhaps the best example of the trend towards standardization. Here, in one compendium, are gathered together the canon law and synodal decrees of over two centuries from the Irish churches, in addition to material from the earlier western church. The two compilers, Ruben of Dairinis († AD725) and Cú Chuimne of Iona († AD747) drew on a wide variety of texts, not all of them ecclesiastical. They cite, for example, from the grammarian Virgil and from computistical tracts. The collection is also remarkable for the fact that it quotes from every single work of Isidore's, bar one.[106]

Whatever about Ruben, his collaborator Cú Chuimne certainly seems to have said more than his prayers, if the words of his obituary-writer are anything to go by:

Cú Chuimne in youth
Read his way through half the Truth.
He let the other half lie
While he gave women a try.

Well for him in old age.
He became a holy sage.
He gave women the laugh.
He read the other half.

Cu Chuimne
Ro legh suithi co druimne,
A lleth n-aill hiaratha
Ro leici ar chaillecha.

Ando Coin.Cuimne ro-mboi,
im-rualaid de conid soi,
ro leic caillecha ha faill,
ro leig al-aill arith-mboi.[107]

We are not told which he preferred, but it has been remarked that Cú Chuimne's name is not included among those of the saints to be remembered in the older martyrologies of the Irish churches.[108] It was doubtless someone like him who had seen enough of the world to know that 'a peck is not the same as a kiss'.[109] Cú Chuimne, however, did not idle away his entire youth;

105. Wasserschleben 1885.
106. See Hillgarth 1984, p. 8.
107. Text and translation in Kelleher 1979, p. 12.
108. Kenney 1929, p. 270 n. 358.
109. Stokes and Strachan 1901–3, ii, p. 100: 'sain poc 7 pocnat'.

we have from his pen the hymn *Cantemus in omni die* ('Let us sing every day'), in thirteen verses, in honour of the Virgin Mary – the oldest such hymn in Latin.

'Let us sing each day, chanting together in varied harmonies, declaiming to God a worthy hymn for holy Mary.

Mary of the tribe of Juda, mother of the mighty Lord, has provided a timely cure for ailing humanity', etc.

Cantemus in omni die
  concinentes uarie,
conclamantes Deo dignum
  ymnum sanctae Mariae.

Maria de tribu Iudae,
  summi mater domini,
oportunam dedit curam
  egrotanti homini, etc.

The poem is a tour-de-force, with rich rhymes, half-rhymes and alliteration, of a kind normally associated with Irish vernacular verse; the whole is a triumph of technique and artistry. It is perhaps the high-point of Hiberno-Latin versification,[110] along with some of the earlier verses from the Bangor antiphonary and the collection preserved in the later *Liber Hymnorum* ('Book of Hymns').[111]

Once in a while there is a flash of genuine poetic inspiration, such as the poem by an unknown Colmán, written on the continent to a confrère, also named Colmán, wishing him a safe journey home to Ireland, the first few lines of which we give below:[112]

The verses of Colmán written for Colmán the Irishman longing for his
  homeland and returning there.

So, since your heart is set on those sweet fields
  And you must leave here,
Swift be your going, heed not any prayers,
  Although the voice be dear.

Vanquished art thou by love of thine own land,

---

110. See Travis 1973, pp. 82–3.
111. On the *Liber Hymnorum* see Kenney 1929, pp. 716–18.
112. Meyer 1907, pp. 186–9; see Rädle 1982, pp. 465–7.

And who shall hinder love?
Why should I blame thee for thy weariness,
   And try thy heart to move? . . .

Give thee safe passage on the wrinkled sea,
   Himself thy pilot stand,
Bring thee through mist and foam to thy desire,
   Again to Ireland . . .

Colmani uersus in Colmanum perheriles Scottigena ficti patrie cupidum
   et remeantem

Dum subito properas dulces inuisere terras
deseris et nostrae refugis consortia uitae, festina
citius, precibus nec flecteris ullis.
nec retinere ualet blande suggestio uocis;
uincit amor patriae: quis flectere possit amantem? . . .[113]

The poet is old, and the thought of that homeward voyage too terrifying; the younger Colmán has had enough of exile, and will return to Ireland. It is the timeless yearning for their native land which seems to follow Irish men and women in every age. A ninth-century Irish codex has a passage from Ptolemy to the effect that a man who has gone into exile can change his sky, but he cannot change his soul. Beside this, in the margin of the manuscript, a scribe has added: 'Cormac always says "So is it with the Irish who die in a foreign land" '.[114] There is something ineffably sad about such occasional sighs. The poem has an added interest because it is one of the earliest such compositions to bear witness to a genuine Irish knowledge of the classics, drawing as it does on first-hand acquaintance with Virgil and Lucan, not just the hand-me-down tags of the grammarians; 'so, in this charming way, the text proceeds, gathering Virgilian flowers and breathing Virgilian fragrance'.[115] It is skilfully wrought, and touching as well.

There are other occasional compositions worth noting, such as those by Cellanus, the Irish abbot of Péronne in Picardy, a pen-friend of the English scholar Aldhelm.[116] Cellanus knew enough of Virgil's panegyric verses to be able to use them as a model for his own in honour of St Patrick, which he then had inscribed on the walls of a basilica at Péronne dedicated to the saint. From about the same period come the hexameter verses penned by the anonymous Irish scribe of the Augsburg Gospels in honour of Laurentius, head of the scriptorium and companion of the Anglo-Saxon missionary Willibrord at Echternach in Luxembourg. The verses are both acrostic and

113. Translation by Waddell 1929, pp. 74–7.
114. 'De Scottis qui moriuntur in aliena regione'; Hagen 1897, pp. xxxix, xlii.
115. Raby 1932, pp. 359–71 (quotation, p. 362).
116. A letter of his to Aldhelm, *c.* AD700, survives; see Traube 1900, pp. 469–537.

telestich, i.e. the first and last letters of every line are written in red ink and when put together read *Laurentius uiuat senio* 'May Laurentius live to old age!'[117] His colleague and fellow-Irishman Vergilius has also left us some stray verses.

The eighth century saw a flourishing industry also in the production of biblical commentaries, and the growing bilingualism of the schools is well illustrated by the famous Würzburg codex of St Paul's letters with glosses in Latin and Old Irish. A wide variety of secondary authors are cited, including Pelagius (over 1,300 times!), but also grammarians and computists.[118] Fragments now in Paris preserve the oldest manuscript corpus of Old Irish glosses, on a computistical text,[119] and other fragments of the period preserve Latin and Old Irish glosses on Bede's computistical works.[120] One of the longest and most sophisticated Hiberno-Latin grammars of the medieval period, the *Ars Bernensis*,[121] probably dates from this time as well. Most impressive of all, however, is the massive 'Reference Bible' of *c.* AD750,[122] which attempted to bring together commentaries on all the books of the Old and New Testaments in one volume. The list of sources is indicative of its range: Josephus, Pseudo-Clemens Romanus, Origen, Pseudo-Abdias, Effrem, Gregory of Nazianzen, Eucherius, Ambrose, Jerome, Augustine, Orosius, Sulpicius Severus, John Cassian, Gregory the Great, and Isidore. True, there is little here that is new, but since originality was never a virtue much practised in the early middle ages the Reference Bible can hardly be faulted on that score. Besides, there are some things in it that might have raised a flutter in continental circles, for the Irish were still using biblical apocrypha and pseudepigrapha long since lost or forgotten in the rest of Europe.

However, after the mid-point of the eighth century Irish methods of biblical exposition were beginning to lose favour and Irish scholars in Europe began to feel a harsh wind blowing against their kind of learning. The writing was perhaps on the wall in the comment of a chronologist at Rome who wrote that 'all are agreed that the Lord will appear at the end of 6,000 years, although the Irish do not agree – they who believe themselves to have wisdom, but who have lost knowledge'.[123] Nevertheless the overall verdict on the Irish abroad was still favourable. They figured in all the areas of contemporary scholarship: the court grammarian Clemens and a companion are immortalized in the opening passage of the famous biography of

117. See Ó Cróinín 1988. For similar acrostic and telestich verses, of roughly the same date and supposedly by the Englishman Boniface, see Burn 1909, pp. 20–1 and pl. XIX.

118. Stern 1910; the Irish glosses are edited in Stokes and Strachan 1901–3, i, pp. 499–712.

119. Ó Cróinín 1989a, pp. 135–43.

120. Stokes and Strachan 1901–3, ii, pp. 10–41.

121. See Holtz 1981b; pp. 301–5, 320; Law 1982, p. 26 denies Irish authorship (but see Ó Cróinín 1982–83, pp. 151–2).

122. Bischoff 1954, p. 225 f.

123. Mommsen 1898, pp. 424–37 (quotation, p. 427).

Charlemagne written by Notker 'the Stammerer', monk of St Gall:

> At the moment when Charlemagne had begun to reign as sole king in the western regions of the world, two Irishmen happened to visit the coast of Gaul in the company of some British traders. These men were unrivalled in their knowledge of sacred and profane letters, at a time when the pursuit of learning was almost forgotten throughout the length and breadth of Charlemagne's kingdom and worship of the true God was at a very low ebb. They had nothing on display to sell, but every day they used to shout to the crowds who had collected to buy things: 'If anyone wants some wisdom, let him come to us and receive it: for it is wisdom that we have for sale'. They announced that they wanted to sell wisdom because they saw that the people were more interested in what had to be paid for than in anything given free. Either they really thought that they could persuade the crowds who were buying other things to pay for wisdom too; or else, as subsequent events proved to be true, they hoped that by making this announcement they would become a source of wonder and astonishment. They went on shouting their wares in public so long that in the end the news was carried by the onlookers, who certainly found them remarkable and maybe thought them wrong in the head, to the ears of King Charlemagne himself, who was always an admirer and collector of wisdom. He ordered them to be summoned to his presence immediately; and he asked them if it was true, as everyone was saying, that they had brought wisdom with them. They answered: 'Yes, indeed, we have it: and, in the name of God, we are prepared to impart it to any worthy folk who seek it'. When Charlemagne asked them what payment they wanted for wisdom, they answered: 'We make no charge, King. All we ask is a place suitable for us to teach in and talented minds to train; in addition, of course, to food to eat and clothes to wear, for without these our mission cannot be accomplished'. Charlemagne was delighted to receive this answer. For a short time he kept them both with him. Later on, when he was obliged to set out on a series of military expeditions, he established one of the two, called Clement, in Gaul itself . . . Charlemagne sent the second man to Italy and put him in charge of the monastery of St Augustine, near the town of Padua, so that all who wished might join him there and receive instruction from him.[124]

It was at the court of Charlemagne that the three traditions, Italian, English, and Irish, came together, and in fact we still have the grammar that Clemens composed.[125] His exact contemporary, Dicuil, was also at the palace school and wrote works on grammar and computus as well as the famous cosmographical treatise *Liber de mensura orbis terrae* ('On the measurement of the earth').[126] The *Liber* tells of voyages by Irish monks beyond the northernmost islands of Britain to a region where the sea turned to ice; their adventures may well have provided the inspiration for some of the later Brendan legends. Irish monks were the first to establish Christianity in Iceland where the sun never set and it was always light, so that a man could pick lice from his shirt in the dead of night. Though Dicuil is more original than most

---

124. Translation in Thorpe 1969, pp. 93–4.
125. Kenney 1929, pp. 537–8; Law 1981, pp. 85–9. See also Gwynn 1952, pp. 57–81, especially pp. 58–9.
126. Tierney 1967; Bergmann 1993, pp. 525–37; for the computus see Esposito 1907, pp. 378–445.

writers of his time, it has been observed of him that the value of his account would have increased a hundredfold had he only put aside the classical authorities like Pliny and Solinus, whose descriptions of natural phenomena he preferred to give rather than his own.[127] As it is, he gives an occasional glimpse into the world of his own experience, and the results are fascinating. He relates, for example, how he heard tell of a brother Fidelis who had an inquiring mind and was much travelled: he measured one of the pyramids (which he took to be Joseph's granaries, as recounted in the biblical story); the measurements he made were quite exact. He sailed also from the Nile to the Red Sea by canal, inspected the spot where Moses crossed it with the Israelites, and asked the boatmen to stop so that he could look for the tracks of Pharoah's chariots in the sand! The boatmen, however, refused – a cause of much grief to Fidelis. He has remarkable descriptions of various marvellous things, like the habits of crocodiles and of the birds on the Faroe Islands. The whole is imbued with the spirit of a thorough scientist, even to the point of mentioning the tides, only to forbear from a detailed discussion (of which he would undoubtedly have been capable) because he was far from the sea (*quoniam sum procul separatus a mare*), and would rather leave such things to those who lived by the shore.

DISCORDANT VOICES

Dicuil's ideas did not all meet with a welcome response, however. The Englishman Alcuin felt it necessary to complain sourly about the Irish teachers and their 'Egyptian boys', whose teachings on computus differed from his own.[128] But Alcuin was mild by comparison with the formidable Visigothic bishop of Orléans, Theodulf. The Spaniard's tendency to irritability and sarcasm is given full rein in a ferocious attack on another Irishman named Cadac-Andreas; written in AD796 to celebrate Charlemagne's victory over the Avars, it describes Charlemagne, the royal family, and the members of the court circle in turn, and the passage devoted to our Irish exile (here referred to, in the usual medieval way, as a Scot) is worth citing:

> Before the Goth and Scot make peaceful pact;
>> For if he wishes peace 'twill be undone.
> If he be whipped or vanish like the wind,
>> Or turn himself to stone, 'tis still a Scot.
> If you subtract from him the letter three,
>> Which happens to be second in his name;
> In 'sky' the first, and the second in 'climb',
>> Third in 'ascent', in 'amicable' fourth,
> He always mouths it, using you instead,
>> Our Saviour's letter, for your Scot's a sot.[129]

127. Laistner 1931, p. 285.
128. See Gradara 1915, pp. 83–7.
129. Translation in Tierney 1967, p. 9. For the controversy and the poems, see Bischoff 1967, pp. 19–25.

But Theodulf's request to Charlemagne that the ignorant Irish oaf be dismissed from court fell on deaf ears. If it was all a joke, the jest has evaporated, and we are left only with the spleen. Cadac was pensioned off with a bishopric, while Theodulf was to suffer a worse fate; imprisoned, suspected of treason, he wrote the hymn *Gloria, laus et honor tibi sit, rex Christe, redemptor* ('All glory, laud and honour to thee, redeemer King') which is still sung on Palm Sunday.[130]

WANDERING SCHOLARS

Such anti-Irish sentiment was the exception, not the rule. Men like Dúngal of St Denis and Bobbio, later bishop of Pavia (the man mentioned by Notker), Donatus of Fiesole, just above Florence, Clemens 'Scottus' and Duncaht all enjoyed good reputations as scholars.[131] The Anglo-Saxon Chronicle in the year AD891 reports the arrival in England of three Irishmen, Dubsláine, Mac Bethad, and Maél Inmuin, who had set out to sea without oar or rudder, following wherever the winds might take them. When they landed on the Wessex coast they headed straight for the court of King Alfred. They were doubtless of the same kind as Notker's Irishmen, who had nothing to declare but their genius.[132] Not all of the Irish on the continent were wandering scholars, though; some were simple pilgrims. Liège is on the route to Rome and there is a manuscript in Leyden which is 'rather like an episcopal post bag',[133] preserving as it does the letters of occasional Irish *peregrini* travelling to and from the Eternal City via Liège. An Irish priest, old and ill, is hindered by the infirmity of his feet and cannot continue with his companions (*cum suis fratribus*) to Rome. He writes devout verses to the bishop requesting assistance and promises daily masses for the bishop's soul. Another, who finds himself in dire straits (*in magnis angustiis coartor*), wails that he has nothing to eat or drink save dreadful bread and the tiniest particle of awful beer: 'I cannot possibly live in such intolerable misery and poverty'. The tone and the prayer (*Christe, faue uotis*) suggest that he was too long among the English.[134] A third pilgrim, returning from Rome, excuses himself with the words 'I am not a grammarian, nor am I learned in the Latin tongue' (*Non sum grammaticus neque sermone Latino peritus*) – an eloquent testimony to the high regard in which his contemporaries were held. He asks no more than bed-and-breakfast and that his letter be returned to him, perhaps because someone else had written it for him to ease his passage. The last

---

130. Waddell 1927, p. 45.
131. See Ferrari 1972, pp. 1–52; Kissane 1977, pp. 57–192; Kenney 1929, pp. 573–4.
132. Keynes and Lapidge 1982, pp. 113–14. This is the oldest dateable occurrence of the name which is better known in its later guise of Macbeth.
133. Waddell 1927, p. 59. The letters were edited by Dümmler 1902–25, pp. 195–206.
134. 'Christe, faue uotis', is supposedly a distinctively English prayer, according to Lowe 1935, p. xix.

letter is from another unfortunate pilgrim returning from Rome who was mugged on board ship near Tongres (*prope hoc monasterium*) by certain miscreants whom he mentions by name (actually, they were the bishop's men). They made off with an alb and a stole and two corporals, a good black cloak worth two *unciae*, and a leather cloak with puttees (*fascioli*) worth two shillings (*solidi*) and a shirt to the same value; four worn Irish garments (*IIII osas Scotticae uestis*) and a heavy skin coat, plus other objects 'small things but necessary to me'. The danger here is clearly from the locals; but there were other hurdles to be crossed closer to home.

We have a letter from a group of Irishmen on the continent addressed by them to their teacher back in Ireland in which they recount how, travelling via Wales, they were entertained on the way by Merfyn Vrych, king of Gwynedd († AD844). At Merfyn's court, however, they met with a strange reception: another Irishman had passed that way before them, Dubthach by name, and had left behind him a riddling text (the famous Bamberg Cryptogram) which the king was urged to use as a test of any would-be scholar that might follow.[135] The Irish party, Caínchobrach, Fergus, Dominnach, and Suadbar, were undaunted by their countryman's cunning challenge, promptly decoding his cryptic message. The letter was a warning to their teacher in Ireland not to let any others cross the Irish Sea without preparing them for what lay in store on the other side. As for Dubthach, the cryptologist, he plied his trade independently on the continent; he is almost certainly the author of computistical verses added in the margin of a Leyden manuscript of Priscian, which are dated by formula to 11 April 838, at 3 o'clock in the afternoon![136] He is doubtless the man whose death is recorded modestly in the Irish annals for AD869: 'Dubthach mac Maél Tuile, most learned of all the Latinists of Europe, died in Christ' (*Dubthach mac Maél Tuile, doctissimus Latinorum totius Europae, in Christo dormiuit*). Irishmen in these years were not overcome with modesty, nor shy to call themselves Europeans; Dermait ua Tigernáin, *heres Patricii* ('abbot/bishop of Armagh') is described in the annals as 'the most learned of all the doctors of Europe' at his death in AD852 (*sapientissimus omnium doctorum Europae*). Indeed, it may be said without too great exaggeration that the medieval Irish had a greater sense of unity with their continental contemporaries than present-day Irish people do.

It is curious, in the circumstances, that some recent scholarship should seem to suggest that the Irish exported all their best teachers while the schools at home went to seed; and furthermore, that the Irish on the continent learned all they knew abroad.[137] A French scholar, Louis Holtz, brilliantly demonstrated how one of these *Scotti magistri* – a man who modestly styled himself Murethach 'most learned of the people' (*doctissimus plebis*) – lay behind three generations of grammatical and biblical study at

135. See Ó Cróinín 1993, pp. 41–52.
136. Lindsay 1910, pp. 36–40 No. 8.
137. Law 1982, p. 98; there is a wry but pertinent rebuke in the title of a paper by Louis Holtz (Holtz 1983, pp. 170-84).

Auxerre, and how in fact he introduced the techniques of textual analysis that were once thought to be the hallmark of the scholastic method in the eleventh and twelfth centuries.[138] A close study of their sources has shown that Murethach and other Irish grammarians of the period all used the same underlying text of Donatus whose uniquely Irish format had been established *before* their departure from Ireland. Far from being the products of some 'nebulous Hiberno-Latin grammatical tradition',[139] these men and their writings bear clear and indisputable witness to a long tradition of development and evolution in the Irish schools.

The Irish group that passed through the court of Merfyn Vrych in Wales left manuscripts wherever they went, so that their footsteps can be traced all across Europe; several of their names recur time and time again in the margins of books which are now in libraries scattered all over Europe. One of them is perhaps the author of the earliest known Irish 'aisling' or vision poem, which survives in a single, incomplete, copy.[140] This and the poem by Donatus of Fiesole that begins *Finibus occiduis describitur optima tellus* are Hiberno-Latin precursors of a genre that, in the Irish language, was to become the characteristic vehicle of expression for Irish political aspirations in the seventeenth century. Donatus's poem in fact was rendered into Irish by the finest Irish poet of that century, Aodhagán Ó Rathaille,[141] and its opening lines – given below – are still recited by many Irish people today:

Inis fá réim i gcéin san iarthar tá,
Dá ngoirid lucht léighinn tír Éireann fialmhar cáil;
Saidhbhir i ngréithribh éadaigh, is mianach breágh,
Ór buidhe, i laochra, aer, is grian, is táin.

An island of fame there is far away in the west,
Which the learned call the land of Ireland, hospitable its fame;
Rich in jewels of cloth, and in fine minerals,
In yellow gold, in warriors, sky, sun, and flocks . . .

There are no serpents in Ireland, the sod is sacred;
They have no wild, ravening monsters nor lions;
But gentle peace, civility, and poets of much dexterity;
Many holy clerics teaching the people.

SEDULIUS SCOTTUS AND IOHANNES ERIUGENA

The ninth century is, above all, the age of Sedulius Scottus and Iohannes Eriugena – the high-point of achievement and Irish reputation in Latin

138. Holtz 1977b, pp. 69–78; Murethach's grammar is edited in Holtz 1977b.
139. Law 1982, p. 74.
140. Traube 1896, pp. 238–40.
141. Dinneen and O'Donoghue 1909 [1911], pp. 34–7. The editors doubt Aodhagán's authorship, though hardly with adequate reason.

scholarship. Sedulius, by his own admission, liked nothing more than to read and teach, but he knew how to enjoy himself as well. He and his companions had arrived at Liège sometime in the 840s (perhaps, as some have suggested, with a legation from the Irish king)[142] and were offered hospitality by the local bishop, Hartgar. His duties were not arduous, providing the bishop with entertainment and the occasional praise-poem in Latin (at which he excelled): 'I eat and freely drink, I make my rhymes, and snoring sleep, or vigil keep and pray'. When the drink ran short, he addressed himself in mock solemnity to the bishop:

> I am a writer, a musician, a second Orpheus,
> I am the ox that treads out the corn, and wish you well;
> I am your champion, armed with weapons of wisdom,
> Muse, tell my lord bishop and father his servant is dry.

> *Scriptor sum (fateor), sum musicus alter et Orpheus,*
> *sum bos triturans, prospera quaeque volo.*
> *sum vester miles sophie preditus armis;*
> *pro nobis nostrum, Musa, rogato patrem.*[143]

The verses he composed mourning the loss of a ram promised him by Hartgar but cut short by a pack of savage hounds are some of the cleverest lines ever written:

> Wherein his guilt – so simple, straight and true?
> Bacchus he shunned, sherbet avoided too;
> not him did liquor from narrow path entice,
> not meal with king, or lesser lord, his vice;
> his solemn feast was grazing on the grass,
> his sweetest drink from brink of limpid Maas,
> nor did he plead that he be vested in
> purple or red – he felt happy with a skin;
> and never did he ride astride a horse
> but steady on his legs he plied a course,
> lied not, nor idle word did say,
> but utterance of depth – just 'baa' and 'beh'.[144]

The serious business of scholarship went on, however; biblical commentaries and treatises on grammar, a *Collectaneum* of rare Greek and Latin works, and the *Liber de rectoribus Christianis*, a Mirror of Princes 'written in a very pure Latin',[145] in which the text alternates between prose and polished verse.[146] All

142. E.g., Kenney 1929, pp. 554–5.
143. Text and translation (here slightly altered) in Waddell 1927, pp. 120–1.
144. Translation by Carney 1967, p. 61.
145. Waddell 1927, p. 62.
146. For a full list of Sedulius's compositions, see Lapidge and Sharpe 1985, pp. 177–80.

in all, a formidable achievement. But Sedulius is also known as a scholar of Greek, and the manuscripts associated with his circle include a pair of bilingual Greek-Latin psalters, the four gospels in Greek, with Latin interlinear translation, and a copy of St Paul's letters in Greek, also with interlinear Latin translation.[147] The sad thing is that we know nothing about him. He may have been the Suadbar who put his name to the Bamberg Cryptogram (adopting the name Sedulius for continental ears); one at least of his companions, Fergus, hailed from Clonard and he too may have been a monk there.[148] He arrived at Liége in the mid-ninth century 'like some uncharted comet',[149] showering the sky with a fireworks-display of scholarship and erudition. He may have fled the Vikings at home, but we cannot tell; he certainly feared them. Nor do we know whether or not the enemy he had come so far to escape found him at last in Liège. The last sure date can be fixed at AD874, in a poem written to celebrate the reconciliation of Charles and Louis; after that we hear no more.

Any nation might be pleased to have a Sedulius in its roll-call of famous men. But there is another who stands head and shoulders above all the scholars of the ninth century, Iohannes Eriugena ('the Irish-born'). Like Sedulius, he appears out of nowhere and of his early background and associations we know nothing.[150] His first appearance came unannounced and arose out of the troubled fortunes of Gottschalk, friend of Walafrid Strabo and reluctant monk, 'condemned for life to the order of St Benedict'.[151] He was committed when a child as an oblate of the monastery at Fulda but found no vocation. At sixteen he sought release and was granted it by a council of bishops, but his superior, Hrabanus Maurus, one of the dullest souls in Christendom but strong on prerogative, appealed the case to the emperor, who decreed that Gottschalk must stay. Gottschalk sought another means of escape, in his books, and the result was a doctrine of predestination that pushed Augustine's interpretation to its logical limits (and that prefigured Calvin's later doctrine): Gottschalk boldly claimed that men were predestined not only to good but also to evil. There was consternation among the bishops and in the ensuing uproar scholars across Europe took sides, some for some against. Faced with the prospect of victory for Gottschalk's party Archbishop Hincmar of Rheims commissioned John, who had been teaching at the palace school, to refute the heresy, but 'before the Irish philosopher could be checked, he had refuted Sin and Hell'.[152] John's treatise *De praedestinatione* ('On predestination') was a dangerous boomerang and John himself became the subject of vilification almost equal to that heaped on the luckless Gottschalk. Prudentius, bishop of Troyes, requested by others to produce a refutation of John's treatise, jeered at this wonder from the west, 'you, the

147. Kenney 1929, pp. 556–60.
148. See Ó Cróinín 1993, especially pp. 47–50.
149. Laistner 1931, p. 251.
150. The standard account is still Cappuyns 1933.
151. There is an evocative account of the entire episode in Waddell 1927, pp. 55–8.
152. Ker 1904, pp. 107–8.

one surpassing all in cleverness, Ireland has sent to Gaul in order that those things which no one could know without your help might be discovered by means of your scholarship'.[153] John, however, appears to have survived the encounter relatively unscathed; Gottschalk was less fortunate. His books went to the flames, burnt by himself after torture. Twenty years later, unceasingly hounded and stretched on his death-bed, he begged the sacrament from which he had so long been barred. Hincmar promised it, and a Christian burial, if he should sign a recantation. Gottschalk refused – 'a worthy end to such a life', said Hincmar (*Sicque indignam vitam digna morte finivit*) – and died, leaving the most beautiful Latin poetry of the ninth century.

If John's patron wondered about his continued usefulness, he did not say so. There followed further writings: a commentary on Luke and another on John, poems in Greek and Latin, a commentary on Martianus Capella and extracts from Macrobius, and finally the great *Periphyseon* ('On the nature of things') – 'the first great philosophical production of western Europe'.[154] Helen Waddell remarked that 'Eriugena belongs to the history of philosophy, not of literature'[155] and this may well be so. But he could also see the lighter side of things. Seated across the table from the emperor Charles the Bald – who seems to have been rash enough to engage in a drinking bout with the Irishman – John was asked blandly by Charles, when the wine was in them both: 'What is there between a sot and a Scot?' 'The width of the table' was John's reply.[156] One manuscript catalogue even claims for him an interest in dogs and ascribes to him a work (now lost), *De compoto et natura canum* ('On the computus and on the nature of dogs').[157] Modern scholars have laboured solemnly to explain the interest, pointing to the touching picture of Odysseus, returned from his wanderings and recognized only by his faithful hound Argos (who promptly expired). But though John was neither the first nor the last Irishman to evince a liking for man's best friend, he must be denied even this frugal comfort; his dogs (like those of St Patrick) have had to be put down – though in the kindest way possible: textual emendation (read *de natura rerum* for *de natura canum*).[158] But Eriugena did know his computus, as is clear from remarks in his commentary on Martianus Capella, which is dated by computistic formula to AD852.[159] Such an interest in the calendar fits well with the picture of Irish scholarship that we have seen to

153. Cited Kenney 1929, p. 577.
154. Kenney 1929, p. 584. See Sheldon-Williams & Bieler 1968–81, and Moran 1989.
155. Waddell 1927, p. 52.
156. 'Quid distat inter sottum et Scottum? Tabula tantum', cited Kenney 1929, p. 589. A scholar of our own time rather spoiled the fun by pointing out that John in fact never used the phrase 'quid distat inter' in his writings, but always 'quid inter est inter', thereby 'proving' that the witticism could not have been his; see Lutz 1956, pp. 32–49.
157. Becker 1885, p. 152 No. 68 (§192).
158. Ó Cróinín 1993, pp. 2–3.
159. The dating 859 x 860 given in Lapidge and Sharpe 1985, p. 189 No. 704(i) is mistaken.

date, for we know that Martin Hiberniensis ('the Irishman'), friend of John's and teacher at the cathedral school of Laon, glossed Bede's works on times with the practised hand of one who knew the subject well.[160] We also have the evidence of a Karlsruhe codex of Bede's *De temporum ratione*, copiously glossed in Irish and Latin, which Bede's modern editor described as the best surviving copy of that work.[161] John was himself compiler of a bilingual biblical glossary with a few difficult words given their Irish equivalents, doubtless as a helpmate to himself and his students. He was not just a dull pedant, either; his pupils seem to have found him inspiring, for his name is mentioned twenty-seven times in the margins of one manuscript.[162] He is mentioned in another work as an authority for the particular pronunciation of a Latin word, and the Karlsruhe manuscript of Priscian's grammar has a gloss which refers to his 'Greek book'.[163] It is as a Greek scholar above all that John's name has been revered through the centuries, and nothing is more enigmatic about this mysterious individual than his remarkable grasp of that language. Nothing like it is known from the earlier Irish schools – despite the fond belief of popular books and the wishful thinking of correspondents to the *Irish Times* – and not even Sedulius and his circle can compare with John. Anastasius, the papal librarian, in a letter addressed to Charles the Bald and dated 23 March 860, remarked: 'It is a wonderful thing how that barbarian, living at the ends of the earth, who might be supposed to be as far removed from the knowledge of this other language as he is from the familiar use of it, has been able to comprehend such ideas and translate them into another tongue: I refer to John Scotigena, whom I have learned by report to be in all things a holy man'.[164]

All in all, though, despite having left so formidable a literary inheritance and despite the fame which he obviously enjoyed during his lifetime, John is a maddeningly enigmatic figure. We know nothing of his personal life, neither his Irish name nor the date or place of his death. Perhaps soured by his experience of the Gottschalk affair, he seems to have fallen out eventually with his patron Hincmar. So much at least is suggested by the biting epitaph which he is supposed to have composed for inscription on the archbishop's headstone:

Here lies Hincmar, a vicious and avaricious thief:
The only noble thing he did was to die!

Hic iacet Hincmarus, cleptes vehementer avarus,
Hoc solum gessit nobile, quod periit.[165]

John's last years are obscure; legend has it that he left France after his

160. See Contreni 1978, pp. 126–8; Jones 1976b, pp. 261–85.
161. Jones 1943, p. 146.
162. Contreni 1982, pp. 758–98 (p. 769).
163. Stokes and Strachan 1901–3, ii, p. 227.
164. Dümmler 1884, p. 430 ff.; translation in Kenney 1929, p. 581.
165. Text in Kenney 1929, p. 587 No. x.

patron's death and taught for a while at Malmesbury in England. The twelfth-century scholar of that monastery, William, says that John was stabbed to death by his pupils with their metal styli 'because he forced them to think'. The story is apocryphal, a literary motif borrowed from the fourth-century writer Prudentius. It seems a sadly inappropriate end to a great career.

THE WANING STAR – THE TENTH CENTURY AND AFTER

After John's departure from the scene the Irish star began to wane in the firmament of European scholarship. It was too much to expect that John's genius could be excelled, or even matched, and the history of Irish scholarship on the continent in the generations that followed him is marked by a steady decline. In contrast to the years that preceded it, the tenth century knows only a few Irish names of note. Best-known perhaps is Israel Scottus, one-time teacher and confidant of archbishop Bruno of Cologne, brother to the emperor Otto the Great. Recent research has revealed that Israel too taught Latin grammar in the time-honoured fashion of Irishmen abroad.[166] The great French scholar, Père Édouard Jeauneau, has also discovered two new tracts by Israel: De anima ('On the soul') and De Trinitate ('On the Trinity').[167] Is he perhaps the same Israel whose name is associated with the fascinating board-game called 'gospel dice' (alea euangelii) copied into an Irish manuscript now in Oxford, Corpus Christi College, but written at Bangor (Co. Down) some time after AD1140? This tenth-century equivalent of 'Monopoly' seems to have been devised with the purpose of teaching students how to master the Eusebian canon tables (or concordance to the gospels). Unfortunately, the scribe of the Oxford manuscript left no playing instructions, and failed to copy his original accurately, but there is a coloured diagram of the board showing the layout of the pieces, together with a note saying that it was learned at the court of King Æthelstan of England († AD936) by Dubinsi, bishop of Bangor († AD953). He acquired the rules there from a certain unnamed Frank and 'a learned Roman, i.e. Israel'.[168] Irish connections with Æthelstan's court are known from other references: the illuminated manuscript known as the Gospels of Macdurnan now in Lambeth Palace, London, was written by Maél Brigte mac Tornáin, abbot of Armagh († AD927) but an inscription before the text states that it was presented to Christ Church Canterbury by Æthelstan,[169] and the manuscript known as 'St Dunstan's Classbook' bristles with Irish symptoms and excerpts from Irish texts;[170] the presence there of Israel Scottus should not, therefore, be ruled out. It has been suggested that Israel may also have been the author of what was

166. Jeudy 1977, pp. 187–248.
167. Jeauneau 1985, pp. 7–71.
168. Byrne 1979, p. 17 No. 8; the board is illustrated in Armitage Robinson 1923; but see also Lapidge 1992.
169. Alexander 1978, pp. 86–7 No. 70.
170. Full facsimile in Hunt 1961.

perhaps the most popular Irish work of the entire middle ages, the *Nauigatio Brendani* ('The voyage of Brendan'),[171] though it must be said that little solid evidence supports the theory. There is, on the other hand, no doubting the appeal of the *Nauigatio*; it took on the stature almost of a European epic and enjoys an undying popularity to this day, directly inspiring the intrepid voyage of Tim Severin and his crew in their successful attempt in 1976 to sail an Irish currach, or leather boat, to America.[172]

Not till the end of the eleventh century do we encounter any other Hiberno-Latin writers of note. Perhaps the best-known is Marianus Scottus of Mainz, who was banished from his monastery of Moville (Co. Down) in AD1056 and spent the remainder of his years in exile in Germany.[173] Marianus's Chronicle of World History is the earliest and one of the most important examples of a genre which became popular after his time, and his own compilation was very influential among both English and continental writers. The Chronicle, in fact, follows closely in the long-established Irish tradition of chronological studies and it parallels in Latin a tradition of World History chronicling which is a dominant theme also in Irish during the tenth and eleventh centuries.[174] The bilingualism of the Irish tradition is in fact illustrated by the many Irish verses added in the margins of Marianus's own manuscript autograph in the Vatican Library.[175] His namesake and contemporary Marianus of Ratisbon (now Regensburg in Bavaria) had the Irish name Muiredach Mac Robartaig and came probably from Donegal stock (McGroarty is still a common Donegal name). With two companions, Iohannes and Candidus, he set out on pilgrimage to Rome in AD1067 but on their way they were persuaded by another Irishman, Muirchertach, an *inclusus* of the monastery of Ratisbon, to remain there permanently. Later Iohannes himself became an *inclusus* at Göttweig in Lower Austria, while Muiredach in AD1076 built the monastery of St Peter at Ratisbon commonly known as Weih-Sankt-Peter, one of a number of Schottenklöster or Irish monasteries which were to remain important in the ecclesiastical life of southern Germany and Austria until the Reformation. Marianus was the subject of a biography written about a century after his death by another Irish monk at Ratisbon and it is one of the most interesting and valuable sources of information for the history of Irish monasteries on the continent in the eleventh and twelfth centuries and their close contacts with home.[176]

With the close of the eleventh century almost the last is heard of Hiberno-Latin scholarship in Europe. But there is some evidence from native

171. Selmer 1950, pp. 69–86; see Selmer 1956.
172. Severin 1978.
173. Mac Carthy 1892, pp. 3–7.
174. See especially Mac Airt 1953, pp. 255–80; Mac Airt 1955–56, pp. 18–45; Mac Airt 1958–59, pp. 98–119.
175. Mac Carthy 1892, pp. 20–8; Ó Cuív 1990.
176. Breatnach 1977; see also Ó Riain-Raedel 1982, pp. 220–4; Ó Riain-Raedel 1984, pp. 390–404.

manuscripts to indicate that the traditional subjects of the *Artes* were still being taught and studied:[177] a fragment of Clemens Scottus's *Ars grammatica* and of Bede's *De temporibus*,[178] versions of Eriugena's *Periphyseon*,[179] and a copy of the *De ratione metrorum* of Lupus of Ferrières.[180] But there is evidence also of influence from the schools of scholastic philosophy in France. Bernard of Chartres's *Glosae super Platonem*, the very existence of which had been doubted by previous scholars, were discovered in the same manuscript that contains the epitome of Eriugena's *Periphyseon* and other Irish texts.[181] Fland Ua Gormáin, arch-lector of Armagh, who died in AD1174, is described in his death-notice as 'having been twenty-one years learning among the Franks and Saxons and twenty years directing the schools of Ireland'; through such channels the new learning was doubtless introduced into Ireland. On the other hand, the gospel commentary of Maél Brigte Ua Maél Uanaig († AD1138), compiled at Armagh in the generation before Fland, has recently been shown to derive entirely from the earlier Irish exegetical tradition, combining patristic and seventh-century Hiberno-Latin material only; no sources later than Bede appear to have been used.[182] The marginal references in that manuscript to the teachings of Peter Comestor († AD1179) and Geoffrey Babion (*fl.* AD1096-1110) are actually written in a thirteenth-century hand and are not contemporary.[183] Similarly, the tract *De statu ecclesiae* ('On the structure of the church') by Bishop Gilbert of Limerick (*c.* AD1111), far from being a contemporary blueprint for structural reform in the Irish church, in fact derives almost entirely from earlier Frankish models.[184] Only one twelfth-century text shows any influence from the continental schools: a Life of Flannan of Killaloe was composed by a man who had been through the schools and liked to show off his superior learning, but it is a very modest erudition.[185] All in all, the twelfth century was a sad end to a once great and vibrant tradition. William of Malmesbury remarked sourly that in his time the Irish 'were less than safe guides to the formation of Latin words and the proper speaking of Latin'.[186] The 'crowded hour of glorious fame' that was Irish scholarship in Europe between the seventh century and the ninth was now 'an age without a name'.

The newly-founded Anglo-Norman colony of the twelfth and thirteenth centuries produced little that could be classified as literature, and there is no

---

177. 'Es gab in Irland im XI.–XII. Jahrhundert noch klösterliche Schulen, in denen ebensolche Artes-Studien wie in guten festländischen und englischen Schulen betrieben wurdern' – the verdict of Bieler and Bischoff 1956, p. 220.
178. Bischoff and Bieler 1956, pp. 216–20.
179. Sheldon-Williams 1956, pp. 1–20.
180. Oskamp 1977, pp. 191–7.
181. Dutton 1984.
182. Rittmueller 1983, pp. 185–214.
183. Flower, 1926, p. 429.
184. Kenney 1929, pp. 763–4.
185. Ó Corráin 1982, pp. 213–31.
186. Stubbs 1874, p. 257.

evidence for any continuity of Latin learning from the pre-Norman period into the new era. The leading luminaries of the new elite, men like Richard FitzRalph of Armagh or Thomas of Ireland, were products of the intellectual world which embraced England and western Europe.[187] There is nothing distinctive either in their Latin or in their thought which marks them out as characteristically Irish, and the fact that Peter of Ireland – to take just one example – taught Thomas Aquinas at Naples is interesting but hardly much more than that. If he had not been called 'of Ireland' we would never have guessed his Irish origin. From the twelfth century on, native Irish men of learning turned increasingly to their native language and became increasingly marginalized, physically and intellectually, as a result. Pushed inexorably westward by the advancing Anglo-Norman conquerors, Irish learning appears to have lost contact with the rest of Europe and become ever more inward-looking. The stream of thought from Europe which earlier had been the lifeblood of Irish Latin scholarship gradually seeped away in stagnant and muddy lowlands.

187. Scott, in *New history of Ireland*, vol. i (forthcoming).

CHAPTER 9

THE VIKING AGE

On the eve of the ninth century Irish society gave the appearance – in the annals, at any rate – of having achieved a happy equilibrium. Apart from the occasional outrage, such as the 'dishonouring of the staff of Jesus and relics of Patrick by Donnchad mac Domnaill [southern Uí Néill claimant to the high-kingship] at an assembly in Ráth Airthir', recorded in AD789, church and state had arrived at a *modus vivendi* which suited both well. The more important churches enjoyed the privilege of seeing their respective 'Laws' (*cána*) promulgated in their own provinces and sometimes beyond, while they and their humbler sister-churches were able to take the relics of their founders on circuits, thereby raising the consciousness of their flocks and some much-needed financial contributions as well. The 'commutation' *(commotatio)* of relics is recorded in the Annals of Ulster in AD784: the relics of Mac Erccae (patron of Ardstraw, Co. Tyrone) 'arrived at the city of Tailtiu' (Teltown, Co. Meath); in AD785: Ultán's relics were on circuit from Ardbraccan (Co. Meath); in AD790: those of Kevin of Glendalough and Mo-Chua of Clondalkin (Co. Dublin) were taken about; the lesser relics of Tóla, from the Déisi in Waterford, on circuit in the same year; in AD794: there was commutation of the relics of Trian (perhaps Mo-Thrianóc of Ruscaghbeg, Co. Offaly). During the same period several 'Laws' were promulgated or renewed: AD783: Cáin Pátraic in Connaught, pronounced by the abbot of Armagh Dub-dá-Lethi and Tipraite mac Taidc, king of Connaught; AD788: Ciarán of Clonmacnois's *cáin* also in Connaught; AD793: the *cána* of Comán, of Roscommon, in Connaught, and Ailbe of Emly in Munster. This latter occasion marked the apex of church–state collaboration with the first recorded ordination of an Irish king: 'The Law of Ailbe in Munster and the ordination of Artrí mac Cathail as king of Munster' (*Lex Ailbhi for Mumain 7 ordinatio Artroigh m. Cathail in regnum Mumen*).

Individuals so inclined, though, might have seen cause for worry in the occasional unusual event recorded around the same time in the annals: AD788 the moon appeared blood red in the night of 26 February, while the following year saw deep snows on 29 April. The supposedly sophisticated modern reader would do well to pause before scoffing: early in 1938, on the eve of the Nazi Anschluss of Austria, an intense aurora lit up the sky so that in many districts fire alarms were sounded. Plague birds appeared on the streets of Vienna, albino sparrows with red splotches like dried blood on their wings.[1] The penultimate entry in the Irish annal for AD794 has an equally ominous ring about it: 'Devastation of all the islands of Britain by the heathens' – the Vikings had arrived.

The standard image of the fierce and savage Viking enjoys hallowed status in the Irish historical imagination. Wild hordes of bloodthirsty and merciless savages cascade from their dragon-ships in search of defenceless women and children, church treasures, and a well-known Irish lager. The television lager commercial has one native character dismiss the Vikings contemptuously as 'tourists!', but that is probably as far as any would-be revisionism has come, in the public mind, at any rate. One of the first attempts, some twenty years ago,[2] at a considered review of the Viking period in Ireland provoked an outraged letter to the *Irish Times*, protesting at 'the move on foot at present to whitewash the Vikings and play down their depredations'.[3] Similar outrage was expressed at the notion that the archaeological remains of Viking Dublin might be worth preserving. The old image of the heathen raiders, eager to put their Christian Irish victims to the sword and their churches to the torch, survives still in popular art, along with that other Viking trademark, the horned helmet, which has no historical basis whatever.

Vikings did, of course, raid, steal, murder and burn (though they were by no means the first to do so), and we have ample evidence of their activities recorded, particularly in the Irish annals, but in other sources as well. In the margin of a famous ninth-century Irish manuscript, the St Gall copy of Priscian's Latin grammar, the scribe added the following verse:

> The bitter wind is high to-night
> It lifts the white locks of the sea;
> In such wild winter storm no fright
> of savage Viking troubles me.[4]

> *Is acher in gáith innocht,*
> *fo-fuasna fairggae findfolt.*
> *Ni ágor réimm mora minn*
> *dond láechraid lainn ua Lothlind.*

THE EARLIEST VIKING ATTACKS – FIRST AND SECOND PHASES

The first specific reference in the annals to an attack on Ireland reports, AD795 'the burning of Rechru by the heathens, and Skye was overwhelmed

1. Zückmayer 1966, cited by Moore 1989, p. 333.
2. The Merriman Summer School, held annually in Co. Clare, had for its theme 'Ireland and the Vikings' in 1971.
3. A letter from M.M. Ireland, *Irish Times*, 7 September 1971.
4. Irish text in Stokes and Strachan 1901–3, ii, p. 290; English translation by Flower 1947, p. 38.

and laid waste'. There can be no doubting their initial impact, which was as ferocious as it was sudden and unexpected. And for the decade or so after that first onslaught the attacks persisted with a devastating effect that forced the monks of Columba's monastery on Iona, for example, to abandon that hallowed site and flee, with the remains of their founder, back to Ireland. The monastery was burned in AD802, and in AD806 sixty-eight of the community were put to the sword. Another attack on Iona in AD825 saw the violent death (*martre*) at Viking hands of Blathmacc mac Flaind (apparently prior of the monastery in the absence of Abbot Diarmait, who had removed with most of the community to Kells), an episode recorded in a metrical panegyric of Blathmacc composed by the great Walafrid Strabo, scholar and abbot of Reichenau, in Lake Constance.[5] The hexameter verses describe Blathmacc as of royal stock (*regali de stirpe*), 'the hope of his homeland, fortune of his patrimony, and a future king of his people', who had renounced a political career (he was *patriae princeps*) in order to seek out the religious life. He was on Iona when a marauding band of Vikings (described, probably wrongly, as Danes by Walafrid) arrived, 'threatening cruel perils to the blessed men'. The sacred relics of the founder Columba, contained in a casket of precious metal (*arca . . . preciosa metalla*), had been buried by the monks in a trench, but Blathmacc refused to reveal its whereabouts, and the raiders – lacking the more sophisticated weaponry of modern raiders: metal detectors – did him to death. It was at Kells (Co. Meath) that the monks of Iona re-established their main house, and Kells thereafter was to remain the chief monastery in the Columban federation.[6] That is why the famous illuminated manuscript of the gospels known as the Book of Kells received its name, because it was preserved at Kells in later centuries and was presented, after the Restoration, to Trinity College, Dublin, by Henry Jones, bishop of Meath.

Our principal source of information about Viking activities is the annals, but here a problem immediately arises. The annals derive exclusively from the scriptoria and writing schools of the Irish monasteries, penned by clerics whose fear and loathing of the Vikings is evident even in the terminology they use. These new raiders are termed *geinti* 'heathens/pagans', and the annalists catalogue a long series of sackings and lootings in which they showed no quarter to their Irish enemies, nor any respect for ecclesiastical sanctuary. On the contrary, the Vikings sought out the monasteries precisely because they were considered as places of safe-keeping for royal treasure, as well as monastic property. Cogitosus, the seventh-century biographer of St Brigit of Kildare, described an 'ornate altar' and sarcophagi 'adorned with a refined profusion of gold, silver, gems and precious stones with gold and silver chandeliers hanging from above', and how the wealth and treasures of kings were in safe-keeping there.[7]

It is hardly surprising that the records made by inmates of such monasteries

5. Dümmler 1884, pp. 297–301.
6. For details of Iona and its later history, see especially Herbert 1988, p. 68 ff.
7. *MPL* 72, cols 775–90 (Cogitosus, *Vita Brigidae* §32); translation in Connolly and Picard 1987, pp. 5–27 (quotations, p. 25).

have left a vivid picture of Viking depredations, and some of the scribes at least may have had cause to fear the Vikings from first-hand experience. Nevertheless, modern historians are obliged to treat such annals as they would any other source of information, and make allowances for the (sometimes understandable) bias of their authors. Taken at face value, such apparently relentless slaughter conveys an impression of almost permanent mayhem. The reality may have been somewhat different.

An examination of the Annals of Ulster for the two decades AD800–810 and AD811–820 gives a total of only seven years in which any Viking activity of any kind is recorded. For the first decade there are only three relevant entries, the two relating to Iona previously mentioned, together with an attack on Inishmurray, off the Sligo coast, and another on Roscommon (or Roscam, near Oranmore, on the Galway coast; an inland attack on Roscommon at so early a date is suspicious). For the second decade of the ninth century Viking activity is no greater: an unlocalized defeat in Ulster (*strages gentilium apud Ultu* 'a slaughter of the heathen by the Ulaid') in AD811, followed the next year by a reverse at the hands of the Fir Umaill around Clew Bay (Co. Mayo); this setback appears to have been avenged the following year, when the Conmaicne (presumably the Conmaicne Mara of the Connemara coastal region in Galway) and the Umaill were slaughtered by the Vikings. However, an attempted advance by them into Munster was rebuffed. These sporadic incidents apart, there is no annalistic evidence of any widespread or concerted Viking attacks for these years. Only in the third decade of the century do they appear to have mounted sustained campaigns on coastal monasteries in the north-east and south-west, with the first on the eastern coastal site of Howth in Dublin Bay. An attack there in AD821 saw the raiders make off with a large number of women captives (*praed mor di mnaibh do brid as*; was this a nunnery?). An attack on Bangor in AD823 was repeated the following year, when the relics of Comgall, the monastery's founder, were scattered from his reliquary shrine. In the same year an attack on the remote Kerry coastal monastic site of Sceilg Mhichíl saw the Vikings make off with its abbot(?) Éitgal, who died shortly afterwards from hunger and thirst. The attack on Sceilg is a tribute to Viking seamanship, if nothing else.

For the opening decades of the ninth century, therefore, the extent of Viking activities is anything but overwhelming. The Annals of Ulster open with six entries, three of which concern attacks outside Ireland. There is a gap in coverage between AD813 and AD821, after which the details of raids become steadily greater. But it is not until AD833, with a raid on Lismore (Co. Waterford) and south Munster generally, that AU records any significant Viking activity beyond Ulster and Leinster. In AD835 attacks took place on Mungret (Co. Limerick) 'and other churches of West Munster' (*ala n-aile cheall Irmumen*) and another attack on Clonmacnois was dated precisely by the annalist to 6 March. The unfortunate community at Clonmacnois had two years previously suffered an attack from the Munster king Feidlimid mac Crimthainn, whose fervent Céli Dé sympathies did not inhibit his ardour against fellow Christians: he slaughtered half the inmates and torched the monastic lands up to the door of the church, paying scant heed to the monastery's traditional rights of sanctuary; for good measure he repeated the dose in Durrow the same year. Clonmacnois had hardly recovered from the fury of the Munster king when a third part of the monastery was put to the flame by the Vikings. The year AD836 in fact saw a crescendo of Viking activity, particularly in the west, which saw 'a most cruel devastation of all the lands of Connaught by the heathens'. The annalist notes particularly a victory won by them over the Déis Tuaiscirt; it is ironic that this minor group, under its later and better-known name, Dál Cais, was to emerge eventually as the most formidable opponents of the Vikings in the centuries to follow.

With the mention in AD837 of the first Viking fleets on the rivers Liffey and Boyne a new phase of activity begins, centred now on the midlands region. The Boyne and Liffey fleets are said to have numbered sixty ships each; with a crew of thirty men in each longship, that would mean a fighting force of three thousand men – formidable opposition for even the strongest Irish king.[8] They also extended their raiding to secular settlements: churches, forts, and homesteads (*cealla, dúne, treba*). AD837 also marks the first occasion when southern Uí Néill forces did battle with the raiders, killing 120 of them in an initial encounter, but suffering heavily in a set-piece battle at Inber na mBarc (the Boyne estuary at Drogheda?) 'in which an uncounted number [of Uí Néill] were slaughtered' – though the kings escaped (*sed primi reges euasserunt*). It is in their account of this battle that the annals for the first time coin a phrase that was to become a leitmotif in Viking affairs: warfare 'from Shannon to the sea' (*ó Shinaind co muir*). It is also the first time that they mention a Viking leader by name: Saxoilbh (Old Norse Saxólfr), *toísech na nGall* 'chief of the foreigners', who fell at the hands of the Cianachta. In AD839 another new development is seen: a Viking fleet on Lough Neagh, from which attacks were launched against targets all over the north-east. The same fleet was active for the next two years, and the annal for AD841 opens with the words: 'The heathens still on Lough Neagh'. But Viking activities were not confined to the north: they won a battle (*bellum*) against the men of Connaught in AD838, while Ferns (Co. Wexford) and Cork in the south both suffered attacks in AD839. By this date the pattern of Viking raids was all two clear: swift, sharp attacks, hit-and-run, with secular and ecclesiastical settlements equally likely as targets. Those that were not put to the sword were taken away to be ransomed, as was the case with the important clerics of Louth in AD840. This steadily rising graph of activity parallels the situation in neighbouring England, where it gradually became clear that the Danes were set on colonization: from AD835 onwards barely a year passed without some account of a Viking raid.

8. Sawyer 1982, p. 93, reckons on a maximum capacity of fifty men for short distances. He estimates the Viking armies generally as numbering hundreds rather than thousands.

THE FIRST *LONGPHORTS*

The year AD841 saw another new development: the establishment of naval camps (*longphort*) by the Vikings at Linn Duachaill (Linns, Co. Louth) and Dublin (*Duiblinn*) from which they directed their attacks against the midlands and Leinster as far as the Slieve Bloom Mountains on the Laois-Offaly border. This consolidation of their positions has all the appearance of a coordinated plan by the Vikings to establish permanent bases, either with a view to settlement or as staging-posts for further attacks against other targets along the length of the Irish Sea. A large set-piece battle had taken place in Scotland already in AD839 against the men of Fortriu, in eastern Scotland, in which casualties were very high (*alii pene innumerabiles ceciderunt*). In fact the first recorded Viking attack anywhere in the British Isles was on the Columban daughter-house of Lindisfarne, off the Northumbrian coast, which was burned and looted in an orgy of violence as unexpected as it was severe. It so stirred the imagination of the Anglo-Saxon Chronicler that he remarked on portents which had preceded the calamity: whirlwinds, lightning, fiery dragons in the air, and a severe famine.[9]

The following year, which marked the first attack on Ireland, at Rathlin Island, also saw a Viking raid on Skye, and from then on they were active in the Western Isles, the North Channel, and the Irish Sea. Though neither Orkney nor the Shetlands are directly mentioned, the Vikings sailing south from Norway cannot have missed the Northern Isles, and it is a safe assumption that they too felt the impact of Viking raids from the beginning. Another Irish monk, Dicuil, writing around the same time as Blathmacc's demise (and perhaps, like Blathmacc, also a monk of Iona at one time) tells of islands two days' sailing to the north of Britain which had been inhabited by Irish hermit monks for nearly a hundred years, but which were now abandoned 'because of Norse robbers' (*causa latronum Normannorum*).[10] Whether Dicuil was referring to the Shetlands or the Faroes is not crucially important; what is worth noting is the fact that the remoter islands off the north British coast were apparently occupied by Vikings at a very early date. How early is difficult to establish: Dicuil says that his information came from an Irish priest (*aliquis presbyter religiosus*) who had himself visited one of these remote islands. His information on Thule (presumably Iceland) was derived from conversation with clerics who had lived there for six months, from February to August, and whom he had interrogated thirty years earlier. It is possible, therefore, that the 'Norse robbers' had appeared in the Shetlands or Faroes before AD793, the earliest recorded date for their arrival in the British Isles.

---

9. *Anglo-Saxon Chronicle* (DEF) AD793. For what follows I am indebted especially to Wainwright 1962, pp. 117–62.
10. Tierney 1967, p. 76 (VII 15).

EARLIER RAIDS?

Some authorities have speculated on the possibility of an even earlier Viking incursion, perhaps at the end of the sixth century or the beginning of the seventh.[11] They point to the annal for AD617 which records 'the burning of the martyrs of Eigg [explained in a note as a massacre of the community of that island monastery off the western coast of Scotland along with its founder Donnán], the slaughter of Tory [another religious community, presumably, on that island], and the burning of Condeire [Connor, Co. Antrim]'. The great nineteenth-century German scholar Heinrich Zimmer – 'the Ishmael of Celtic studies, whose hand was against every man's'[12] – was the first to suggest that these early raiders might be Scandinavians, and his view was taken up by subsequent writers.[13] The Norwegian scholar Alf Sommerfelt argued from linguistic evidence – particularly the fact, as he saw it, that the Old Norse name for the Picts, *Péttar/Pettar* must have arisen before AD700 – that the Vikings must therefore have sailed the northern seas long before the Viking Age. The most recent examination of the evidence, on the other hand, has come down categorically against this view: 'It was far too early in the seventh century for [Donnán's] assailants to have been Vikings, and unthinkable, even given the violent conditions of the age, for so many monks to have been butchered by Christians'.[14] This touching tribute to Christian sentiment says more about the modern historian than about his seventh-century subjects; in fact, a battle-roll of Ulster achievements against her enemies says 'Luckily came the Ulstermen on a raid, a warlike venture, when Tory was sacked against a third of the men of Fálga'.[15] The unfortunate monastic communities at Eigg, Tory, and Connor would appear to have been victims of the dangerous political games being played out around Ireland and Scotland in the early seventh century.

CHARACTER OF THE VIKING IMPACT

Whatever the earliest date at which they appeared, it is important to remember that the character and duration of Viking raids, and the date and extent of their earliest settlements, differ considerably in the various regions

11. See Chadwick in Ó Cuív 1962 (repr. 1975), pp. 13–42: 18, 21.
12. The formulation is in Kenney 1929, p. 77.
13. Bugge 1904–06, i, pp. 136–7; Marstrander 1915, pp. 1–3; Sommerfelt 1958, pp. 218–22.
14. Smyth 1984, pp. 107–9 (quotation, p. 108).
15. See Gwynn 1926, pp. 92–4 (quotation, p. 93 (§6)): 'Sén dollotar Ulaid i réim, fechtas n-ágda,/dia ro-toglad Torach [for] triun fer Fálga'. It should be noted that the large number of martyred monks referred to by Smyth derives from a later addition to the text of the Annals of Ulster.

of the British Isles, reflecting different Viking ambitions and strategies.[16] In terms of their activities in Britain alone, the Viking Age could be said to have extended from AD794 to AD1066 (the battle of Stamford Bridge, not Hastings; it is worth noting that the Irish annalists record the first, but not the second, which took place three weeks later). In Ireland, on the other hand, the first Viking raid (as we saw) occurred in AD795, but the period of Viking influence lasted well into the twelfth century. In England the first settlements are not attested before AD876, some eighty years or more after the first raids, although attacks had been rising in a crescendo which climaxed in AD866 with the Danish capture and occupation of York, where they installed their own puppet king (an Englishman) on the throne. The Anglo-Saxon Chronicle for that year records that 'Healfdene shared out the land of the Northumbrians, and they proceeded to plough and support themselves'.[17] In Scotland, on the other hand, there is fairly good evidence for settlement in the first half of the ninth century, and in some parts of Scotland, both mainland and the Isles, settlement may well have been established from the start. In Orkney and Shetland, for example, virtually every feature of the landscape has a Scandinavian name, and very few pre-Scandinavian place-names survive.[18] In fact, the native speech of these islands disappeared entirely and was replaced by a Scandinavian dialect which was still spoken by a few islanders down to the eighteenth century and, in the ballad of Hildina, was still sung in 1774 on the island of Foula in the Shetland group.[19] This would appear to suggest a native population so small that the Vikings were able to establish permanent hold there from the start; elsewhere in the British Isles and in Normandy they and their descendants learned the native language, English, Irish (in Ireland and Scotland), or French.

In Ireland the Vikings settled in much more limited areas than in England or Scotland, and they had lost most of their independent political power by the late ninth century, becoming, in effect, just another factor in the tangled web of native Irish political alliances. The Viking towns of Dublin, Limerick, Cork and Waterford enjoyed no meaningful autonomy after the tenth century. On the other hand, Norse power was finally broken in the Western Isles of Scotland only in AD1263, when the islands were restored to Scottish rule (although Norse earls in fact continued to hold sway in the Isles until AD1331). The earliest Viking activities in the Isle of Man are recorded as having occurred during the ninth century and later, but the Kingdom of Man was founded by Godred Crovan, a Viking survivor of the defeat at Stamford Bridge in AD1066, whose successors for two centuries also claimed authority throughout the Hebrides under the overlordship of the Norwegian kings. In fact, Orkney and Shetland remained under Norwegian control until AD1468–69. The Vikings left their mark on Man not only in place-names but also in graves and runic inscriptions, some of which commemorate

16. For what follows, see especially Wilson 1976, pp. 95–113.
17. Whitelock 1979, p. 79.
18. For this and what follows, see especially Sawyer 1982, pp. 100–1.
19. See Chadwick 1962, p. 20 n. 24.

individuals with Irish-style names, demonstrating that intermarriage between the Vikings and the native population must have been common.[20] Godred Crovan's epithet is in fact Irish (*Crob bán* 'white hand') and a later king, Godred Don, derived his epithet from the Irish word *donn* meaning 'brown haired'. The independence of Man was ended only in AD1266 by the treaty of Perth, which transferred Man and the Western Isles to the Kingdom of the Scots.[21]

Within this time-scale the Vikings clearly had ample time to leave their mark and it is disappointing from that point of view that the evidence for the earliest settlements, in Scotland, is so meagre. From historical sources alone it is impossible to establish, even by implication, a secure date for the first Scandinavian settlements in the Northern Isles. It is true that one Irish source, the so-called Fragmentary Annals,[22] states that a certain Ragnald and his sons visited Orkney in the mid-ninth century, and that Ragnald and one son remained there while the two other sons went elsewhere. These intrepid raiders are said to have brought back black slaves from North Africa, 'and those black men remained in Ireland for a long time' (*As fada dna ro badar na fir ghorma sin i nEirinn*).[23] The episode is not quite the confection that it seems: a Moorish embassy sent to Ireland after a Viking attack on Seville in AD844 'most probably was directed to a Norse court in Ireland'.[24] It is quite possible that Scandinavian settlements were already in existence in Orkney and the Shetlands before the end of the eighth century, either as temporary bases from which to launch attacks on the Scottish mainland or elsewhere in Britain and Ireland, or as places of refuge for displaced Vikings. This latter interpretation is the one suggested by native Scandinavian sources as represented by the Old Norse sagas. In Snorri Sturluson's *Heimskringla* collection of kings' sagas it is said that Harald Finehair attempted to impose his rule over Norway, driving his rivals into exile as he did so. These then harried and raided their homeland until Harald set out to subdue them. We are told that Harald then gave Orkney and Shetland to Ragnald, Jarl of Møre, and that Ragnald then gave them to his brother Sigurd, who thus became the first earl.[25] This would place such settlements about the middle to second half of the ninth century, but as we saw above, the historical evidence strongly suggests that, in fact, the earliest of them were almost a hundred years earlier than the Old Norse sagas would have us believe. This should warn us against accepting any of the sagas as authentic historical records of the Viking period.

20. Sawyer 1982, p. 111.
21. Barrow 1981, p. 120.
22. Radner 1978. This problematical text has generated a literature all of its own, without yet resolving the many difficulties which it still presents.
23. Radner 1978, p. 120.
24. Shetelig 1954b, p. 122, citing Steenstrup 1876, p. 113.
25. See Wainwright 1962, pp. 127–8.

ARCHAEOLOGICAL EVIDENCE – DUBLIN

The archaeological evidence – such as it is – both for Ireland and the Northern Isles, agrees reasonably well with the date suggested by historical sources, but for the early period, apart from the Dublin cemetery finds, only some ten or eleven Viking graves are known from Ireland as a whole, and all of these are on the coast. It is also true that the information to be gleaned from these sites is disappointingly meagre, with the possible exception of Dublin, which in fact provides the only clear archaeological evidence in western Europe for Viking settlements in this early period.[26] The Dublin finds, at Islandbridge–Kilmainham, not far from the main Dublin railway station for west-bound trains, comprise both men's and women's graves, indicating a settlement site.[27] They show a remarkable homogeneity and appear to date almost exclusively from the ninth century. Unfortunately, the main part of the cemetery was destroyed in the course of railway construction in the mid-nineteenth century, so that it is impossible to estimate with any accuracy what the total number of graves might have been. Neither are there any records as to the association of the objects which are preserved from the cemetery, so that the contexts of the finds are now irrevocably lost. It is likely also that a great part of the grave goods passed unnoticed by the workers and were consequently dumped. It has also been remarked that 'the cemetery of Kilmainham and corresponding finds in the city of Dublin suggest that similar remains undoubtedly must have been met with also in other parts of Ireland, which were exposed to the Norwegian invasions, but have in most cases been neglected as not deserving serious notice.[28] But comparison has been made with other important Viking towns such as Hedeby in Schleswig and Kaupang.[29]

The predominantly military nature of the finds is their most obvious feature: the National Museum collection in Dublin includes some forty swords, thirty-five spear-heads, twenty-six shield bosses, with some axe-heads and arrow-heads as well. Evidence of more domestic activity is offered by the finds of various articles such as knives, smith's tools (forge tongs, pincer and hammers), weighing scales with lead and bronze weights, and other implements; the women's graves, here and from other sporadic sites like Aylesbury Road in Donnybrook (south Dublin), Three-Mile-Water (at the mouth of the Avoca river, Arklow, Co. Wicklow), and Ballyholme (Co. Down) produced pins, brooches and beads, buckles, needle-cases, keys, as well as a spindle whorl and fragment of bone comb, tortoise brooches with silver

---

26. Sawyer 1982, p. 84.
27. Bøe 1940, pp. 12–25; for a useful summary see Smyth 1979, ii, pp. 192–6, 212–13, 215, 237–8.
28. Shetelig 1954a, p. 86.
29. See Foote and Wilson 1970, p. 218.

chain, and two other brooches and a bowl containing fragments of wool.[30] Evidence for an artistic side to this early Viking settlement is to be found in the toy axe made of bronze (144 mm long, head 44 mm long) and a fine animal-shaped mounting, and also in the game pieces (bone draughtsmen).

There can be no doubting that the existence of the Kilmainham–Islandbridge cemetery outside the walls of the later Viking town of Dublin (it is some two miles upriver from the Woodquay–Winetavern Street site) indicates that the Vikings settled originally in that area. The site is enclosed by the junction of the river Liffey with its tributary the Cammock, thus providing an ideal location for reasonably well-defended settlement. There can be no doubting either, despite arguments to the contrary,[31] that this was the site of the original Viking settlement of Dublin. Dublin was in fact founded twice over, in AD841, when the Vikings established a *longphort* there, which developed into the first settlement and which came to an end with its capture and destruction in AD902 by the kings of Brega, an event marked by the Annals of Ulster with the statement: 'The heathens were driven from Ireland, i.e. from the fortress of Dublin; . . . and they abandoned a good number of their ships, and escaped half dead after they had been wounded and broken.' Dublin was apparently deserted for fifteen years, until Sitriuc son of Imar re-entered it in AD917. The second settlement was two miles downstream, where the Dublin civic offices now adorn the skyline at Woodquay, a *monumentum aere perennius* to the final triumph of Irish culture over the pagan Viking horde.

That Dublin in fact owes its importance – if not its origin – to the Norse settlement may be inferred from the almost total silence of native sources regarding it in the years preceding AD841. The Irish name for the site was *áth cliath* 'ford of the hurdles', a descriptive term which in fact was used of other Irish river-fords as well (e.g. Clarinbridge, Co. Galway). There may have been some kind of small settlement there in pre-Viking times (whence the *baile* of the modern name *Baile Átha Cliath*), but its development as a town is due entirely to the Norse. They had their *Thing* or meeting-place at the junction of Church Lane and Suffolk Street, nearly opposite the present church of St Andrew, and not far from Trinity College, where it was still to be seen in the seventeenth century, a massive mound of earth forty feet high and 240 feet in circumference.[32] This mound is referred to in a document of 1647 as 'the fortified hill near the college', but in 1685 it was levelled to the ground and the earth used in the building of Nassau Street. Even after the mound was demolished it was the practice for the mayor and city fathers of Dublin to erect a pavilion on the site where they observed the annual military review which dated from Norse times. 'The customs of a people frequently survive their dominion', as Haliday says, and the ancient mound was still used as a site for pageants and miracle plays down to the seventeenth century. All along College Green, called Le Hogges (which survived until the eighteenth

30. Bøe 1940, *passim*; Shetelig 1954a, pp. 83–4.
31. Smyth 1979, ii, pp. 238–9.
32. For this and what follows, see Haliday 1881, p. 162 ff.

century in the name of Hog Hill) and later Hoggen Green, the Norse had their barrows (ON *haugar*). The name *Dublinn* (ON *Dyflin*) apparently refers to the Liffey anchorage just below Christchurch Cathedral.[33] By the end of the ninth century, and again during the tenth century, the Kingdom of Dublin – called by the Norse *Dyflinarskiri* – had become one of the most important in western Europe.

WESTWARD FROM THE CONTINENT TO IRELAND

The course of the Viking era before *c.* AD920 can therefore be summarized as follows: after an initial stage, when the attacks were random and apparently uncoordinated, comprising hit-and-run raids followed by swift withdrawal, the Vikings established bridgeheads on certain strategic headlands and islands where they built fortified *longphorts*; in these they began for the first time to winter over in Ireland. The raiders that established their base on Lough Neagh in AD840 did not withdraw in the winter of that year, and the first permanent coastal bases were set up in AD841. These initial settlements may have been the result of set-backs suffered by the Vikings elsewhere in Europe, at the hands particularly of the Frankish kings. Charlemagne had already ordered – *c.* AD800 – the construction of coastal defences and a fleet as a result of attacks along the Gallic Sea, 'which was infested at that time with pirates' (*quod tunc piratis infestum erat*).[34] Threats in AD808 from a Danish army against the Abrodites, north of the Saxon frontier, were also repulsed, but not before the Danes had destroyed some market towns in the region.[35] Further skirmishing with the Danes continued down to AD810. In that year a Viking fleet allegedly numbering two hundred ships (*classem ducentarum navium*) appeared off the Frisian coast, but the assassination of the Danish king Godred, and the succession of his nephew Hemming, led to a negotiated peace with the Franks.[36] There followed a period of bloody internal feuding among the Danes until AD820, when a fleet of thirteen ships was repulsed from Flanders and the mouth of the Seine,[37] but not before they had burned some farms and carried off their cattle. By the 830s, however, the political situation in the Frankish kingdoms had deteriorated after the deposition of the emperor Louis the Pious – a fact which the Vikings were quick to seize upon. In AD834 they attacked the great Frisian market town of Dorestad, some 80 km from the open sea, and they repeated the raid in the following year. In AD836 Dorestad was raided for the third time and so too were other coastal towns at Antwerp and on the Meuse. In that year the monastic community of St Philibert at Noirmoutier, on the Seine in

33. This is the interpretation of Smyth 1979, ii, pp. 268–9; but Smyth's argument for the identity of the older *Áth cliath* and the later *Dublinn* is not conclusive.
34. Pertz and Kurze 1895, p. 110.
35. Pertz and Kurze 1895, pp. 125–6.
36. Pertz and Kurze 1895, p. 133.
37. Pertz and Kurze 1895, p. 153.

Normandy, abandoned their foundation and sought shelter in the Loire valley, suggesting that Viking raids were now more serious and threatening.

The restoration of Louis in AD836 saw a programme of fort-building as part of an effort to shore up the Frisian defences. Louis also took personal command of military operations against the Vikings, taking the field against them in AD837 after another attack on Dorestad. He had abandoned a pilgrimage to Rome to hurry back to Nijmegen, where he supervised the defensive operations from May of that year 'so that by his presence the sort of damage that occurred in previous years because of the pirates' savagery and our peoples' fecklessness might now be avoided'.[38] It may have been the determined resistance organized by Louis that deflected the Vikings' attacks towards the British Isles; their appearance in the Bristol Channel in AD836, after a raid in the Thames estuary the previous year, indicates that they were making exploratory forays similar to those reported by the annals for Ireland. In AD840 thirty-three ships attacked Hamwih (unidentified) and the same fleet may have also attacked Portland in Dorset in the same year. In AD841 there were attacks on Romney Marsh and elsewhere in Kent, East Anglia and Lindsey. The following year Hamwih was attacked again, as were London and Rochester. In AD844 the Northumbrians suffered a severe defeat and by AD851 the Vikings were wintering in England for the first time.[39]

From AD841, with the construction of the first *longphort* at Dublin, the Vikings began to gain a firm foothold along the coastline. Norse colonies established themselves along the east and south coasts, founding proto-towns at Vikingaló (Wicklow), Veigsfjörthr (Wexford), Vethrafjörthr (Waterford), Cork, and Hlymrekr (Limerick). These early settlers appear to have come from Norway; the Irish word for their place of origin *Lothland* represents Rogaland,[40] and the great Norwegian Celtic scholar Carl Marstrander maintained that most of the Norse loan-words in Irish could be traced to a dialect in south-western Norway.[41] This is borne out also by the archaeological evidence.[42] The metalwork from Norwegian graves numbers 122 specimens from 110 graves, with one from Finland, four from Denmark, and six from Sweden (including a bucket from Birka).[43] The finds in all from Norway number over five hundred, and most of these (about a third of the total) come from Rogaland and Sogn og Fjordane in the area around Bergen; it would seem from the archaeological evidence that these were the two main centres of Viking enterprise. It is clear, however, that they sailed west from all

38. From the *Annales Sti Bertiniani*, cited by Sawyer 1982, p. 83.
39. This section is based on Sawyer 1982, p. 83.
40. Marstrander 1911, pp. 250–1; but see also Greene in Almqvist and Greene 1976, pp. 76–7.
41. Marstrander 1915, p. 56 ff. For an earlier discussion, see Bugge 1900.
42. Petersen in Shetelig 1940–54, v; summary in Wainwright 1962, pp. 144–6. See also the addendum in Shetelig 1940–54, vi, p. 243, and Alenstam-Peterson 1951–52, p. 233 f., which gives a list of finds of Irish metalwork in northern Europe other than Norway. There is a more up-to-date discussion in Wamers 1983, pp. 277–306.
43. Shetelig 1940–54, vi, p. 243.

the seaboard fylker of south-west Norway (Rogaland, Hordaland, Sogn og Fjordane, Mømre and Trømndelag) and from even farther north.[44] As we have seen, the importance of this Norse element is attested also by the place-names evidence of the Inner and Outer Hebrides.

The second phase of Viking activity in Ireland is sometimes associated with the activities of the Viking leader Turgéis (either ON Thórgestr or Thórgils). Turgéis's identity is, unfortunately, otherwise unknown, though some Scandinavian texts provide him with a fictitious origin. The *Haraldssaga* would identify him with Thórgils, son of Harald Finehair, who allegedly accompanied his father and brother on an expedition to Ireland.[45] The similarity between this account and the equally unreliable accounts in some Irish sources has been pointed out.[46] The work known as *Cogadh Gaedhel re Gallaibh* ('The war of the Gael with the Foreigners')[47] is a case in point: this extravagant concoction, composed in the twelfth century as propaganda for the Ua Briain dynasty of Munster, describes Turgéis as the leader of a 'great royal fleet' (*ríglonges adbalmór*) who 'assumed the sovereignty of Ireland', plundering widely with fleets stationed on Lough Neagh in the north and Lough Ree on the Shannon.[48] The Annals of Ulster report that in AD845 Connaught and Meath were attacked from his fortress (*dúnad*) on Lough Ree and that Clonmacnois, Clonfert, Terryglass, Lorrha, and other monastic cities (*alaile cathracha*) were all burnt. The *Cogadh* goes one better[49] by stating that Turgéis drove out the abbot of Armagh and usurped his title (though in fact the annals make clear that the attack on Armagh in that year was carried out by Limerick Vikings). His wife Ota (ON Authr) took possession of Clonmacnois and disported herself in the most unseemly fashion there, giving out oracular responses (*a frecartha*) from the high altar! This latter was a clever touch by the Irish author, playing on the similarity of the high altar to the *seidr-hjallr* or 'incantation platform' on which the Norse magicians performed their magical rites.[50] Turgéis's activities came to a sudden and permanent stop when he was captured by the Uí Néill king Maél Sechlainn and drowned in Lough Owel (Co. Westmeath). Even in death, however, Turgéis enjoyed something of a reputation, and his end became the subject of myth-making. In his *Topographia Hiberniae*, which was first read publicly in or about AD1188, the Welsh writer Giraldus Cambrensis describes the Norse king's death in this way:

> But in the reign of this Feidlimidius the Norwegians put in at the Irish shores with a great fleet. They both took the country in a strong grip and, maddened in their hatred, destroyed nearly all the churches. Their leader, who was called Turgesius,

44. Wainwright 1962, p. 144.
45. See the passage cited above, p. 241.
46. Walsh 1922, p. 2.
47. Todd 1867.
48. Todd 1867, p. 224.
49. Todd 1867, p. 224.
50. Chadwick 1962, p. 23.

quickly subjected the whole island to himself in many varied conflicts and in fierce wars . . . Turgesius ruled the kingdom of Ireland for some time in peace, until he died deceived by a trick about girls . . . Turgesius happened at the time to be very much enamoured of the daughter of Omachlachelinus (Maélsechlainn), the king of Meath. The king hid his hatred in his heart, and, granting the girl to Turgesius, promised to send her to him with fifteen beautiful maidens to a certain island in Meath, in the lake of Lochver. Turgesius was delighted and went to the *rendezvous* on the appointed day with fifteen nobles of his people. They encountered on the island, decked out in girls' clothes to practise their deceit, fifteen young men, shaven of their beards, full of courage, and especially picked for the job. They carried knives hidden on their persons, and with these they killed Turgesius and his companions in the midst of their embraces.[51]

The fact that no corroborating evidence for this story exists in any Irish or Scandinavian source should not surprise us;[52] Giraldus's reputation generally leaves something to be desired on that score. But Turgéis's death may be regarded as a fitting end to such a life, though it was hardly the ritual killing that one author has proposed to see in it.[53]

IRISH RECOVERY; CAPTIVE IRISH

Whatever Turgéis's origins, his death appears to have marked a turning point in the fortunes of the Norse in Ireland. Doubtless because after AD841 they were no longer 'moving targets', Irish kings began to record their first real military successes against them. In AD848 Turgéis's nemesis Maél Sechnaill won a smashing victory in which seven hundred Vikings allegedly fell; and a second reverse, at the hands of the Munster king Ólchobur mac Cinaéda (who combined his title with the abbacy of Emly) and his Leinster ally Lorcán mac Cellaig, at Sciath Nechtain, (near Castledermot, Co. Kildare) saw a further two hundred Vikings dead. In that battle the annals record the fall of jarl Thórer (*Tomrair erell*), who is described as 'tanist of the king of Lothland' (*tanise righ Laithlinne*).[54] The victory by Maél Sechnaill was the occasion for an embassy to the West Frankish King Charles the Bald, announcing the victory and requesting a free passage for pilgrimage to Rome:

> The Irish, falling upon the Northmen, with the help of Our Lord Jesus Christ were victorious, and drove them from their country. Whence the king of the Irish [*rex Scottorum*] sent legates with gifts to Charles in the interests of peace and amity, requesting him to grant passage to Rome.[55]

51. Translation by O'Meara 1951, pp. 102–3 and 104–5, cited by Stewart 1970, p. 47.
52. I discount, of course, the passage in Geoffrey Keating's History of Ireland, which is taken directly from Giraldus; see Dinneen 1906 [1908], iii, pp. 176–82.
53. Dalton, cited by Stewart 1970, p. 56 n. 26.
54. For a discussion of this term (the earliest dated instance of its occurrence in the annals), see above p. 67f.
55. Latin text (from the *Annales Bertiniani*) cited by Chadwick 1958b, pp. 101–2.

This episode has been connected with the arrival at Liège in Belgium about the same time of the Irish poet and scholar Sedulius Scottus, who may have been a member of this royal mission.[56] Among the poems by Sedulius that have survived, three have a particular relevance to these years.[57] One is a panegyric addressed to a certain *Roricus* who apparently erected an altar to honour relics of the saints.[58] This Roricus has been identified with Rhodri Mawr, son of Merfyn Vrych, ruler of the Welsh kingdom of Gwynedd (AD844–78). The first of the poems, however, celebrates a famous victory over the Norsemen – either the Irish victory of AD848 or, as seems more likely, an emphatic victory by Rhodri against the Danish leader Horm (ON Gormr) in AD856;[59] the Welsh triumph was reported in the Irish annals, for Horm had appeared in Irish waters three years previously, when he routed a Norse fleet in Carlingford Lough.

Sedulius has long been seen as the central figure in a circle of Irishmen on the continent in the mid-ninth century, some of whose manuscripts still survive in continental libraries.[60] Particularly important among these are a manuscript of Horace now in Bern, a Greek psalter in Basel, and codices with bilingual texts of the gospels and epistles of St Paul now in St Gallen in Switzerland and in Dresden. All the manuscripts of this group have the names of individuals belonging to the 'Circle of Sedulius' in the margins of many pages and some have poems in Irish added to blank pages or margins; an example is the composition on the subject of pilgrimage to Rome which has sometimes been ascribed to Sedulius himself:[61]

> To go to Rome –
> great labour, little profit!
> The king that you seek there,
> if you do not bring him with you,
> you won't find him.

> *Teicht do Róim*
> *mór saído, becc torbai,*
> *In rí chon-daigi hi foss,*
> *mani mbera latt, ní fogbai.*

The sentiments might not be inappropriate to an Irishman who had made that pilgrimage to Rome in AD848. Another ninth-century Irish manuscript in St-Gall, the famous codex of Priscian, though not usually reckoned among the manuscripts of Sedulius's circle,[62] contains the verses quoted at the

---

56. The suggestion was first made by Traube 1892, p. 342; Kenney 1929, p. 555, was sceptical, but see the comments by Chadwick 1958b, p. 102 n. 1.
57. Traube 1896, pp. 208–9 (*Carmina* XLV–XLVII).
58. *Carmen* XLVII.
59. See Davies 1982a, p. 106.
60. For this, see especially Bischoff 1977, pp. 39–54 (especially pp. 45–6).
61. Text in Thurneysen 1949, p. 41.
62. See Bischoff 1977, p. 45.

beginning of this chapter about the 'bitter wind' as protection against the Viking terror. The Priscian codex did, however, follow the same route as Sedulius and was at one point in Wales (*do Inis Maddoc dún .i. meisse 7 Coirbbre* 'we are on the island of Madoc, Coirbre and I')[63] and the scribe at one point remarks on King Rhodri's presence (*Ruadri adest*).[64] The Fergus whose name also occurs in the margin is almost certainly the same Fergus *grammaticus* who accompanied Sedulius and who, with his three companions Blandus, Beuchelus and Marcus, made up a 'four-horse chariot of God'. Liège is far inland and the Vikings still plied their trade in the Seine and Loire, and against the monasteries of northern France. By the time of Bishop Hartgar's death, however, the Vikings have come a little nearer.

One scholar has noted thirteen references to *Nordmanni* in Sedulius's poems, and the conclusion has been drawn that Sedulius and the other Irish scholars on the continent in the ninth century were refugees from the Viking terror.[65] Perhaps. There is certainly evidence to suggest that several were unwilling guests of that inhospitable people before they arrived. One of the most detailed accounts – a Latin text with Old Irish embedded in it – casts interesting light on the *modus operandi* worked out between the Vikings and the Irish. It concerns Findan, a Leinsterman whose *floruit* is around the mid-ninth century. His sister was taken prisoner in a Viking raid, along with other women (*inter alias feminas*), and Findan's father instructed him to go to the Vikings and ransom his sister, which he duly did, with the aid of an interpreter. The Vikings, however, clapped him in chains and bore him off to their ship. There he remained for two days without food or drink, until the *Nordmanni* held a conference to decide his fate. 'Some, whose attitude was more reasonable . . . argued that people coming from Ireland for the purpose of ransoming others ought not to be forcibly detained', and their counsel won out. Findan was released (and so, presumably, was his sister), and lived to see another day – though he only barely survived a second brush with the Vikings. On his third encounter with them he was less lucky, but the episode offers another interesting view of Irish–Norse relations at this time: a fierce dynastic feud in his native Leinster saw Findan's father and brother murdered, though Findan himself fought his way to safety. His enemies, fearing revenge for the death of Findan's kith and kin, arranged a banquet for him 'in a place near the sea'. Findan was invited, the *Nordmanni* arrived and seized him from the midst of the guests, as they had contracted with his enemies to do, bound him in the closest bonds and carried him off'. Findan was sold and resold but made his escape by hiding from his captors during a stopoff on the Orkney Islands, and eventually made his way to the continent, where he made a pilgrimage to Rome and on his return journey he stopped off at the monastery of Rheinau, on an island in the Rhine near Schaffhausen in Switzerland. There he spent the remaining twenty-six years of his life and

63. Stokes and Strachan 1901–3, ii, p. xxi. The traditional association of this entry with the Irish saint Maédóc is impossible on linguistic grounds.
64. Stokes and Strachan 1901–3, ii, p. xx.
65. Murphy 1928, pp. 39–50, 229–44.

died in AD878. His *Vita* was composed not long after his death and clearly preserves a great deal of interesting historical detail.[66]

There is another remarkable account (this time in Latin verse) which recounts the similar adventures of another Irishman called Murchad (Moriuht), married with a daughter, who was captured by Viking raiders and taken to Corbridge in Northumberland. There he was sold as a slave to a nunnery, where he charmed his way into the beds of more than one of the inmates, transformed the nunnery into a brothel, and was finally expelled. His punishment was the classic Irish penalty of being cast adrift in a boat with no oars (*ingreditur parvam cum nullo remige cymbam*). Recaptured by the Vikings, he was sold again, this time at a Saxon market (perhaps Hamburg or Bremen, or even Hedeby) where he was bought by a widow with counterfeit money. Our hero promptly seduced her too, and the story gets even more complicated thereafter. Murchad is eventually reunited with his wife and embarks on a new career as a Latin grammarian! The entire poem is a wonderful pastiche of all the clichés about the Irish at the time (including a skit on the 'traditional' Irish form of dress, the kilt), but underneath it all there appears to be a strong element of historical fact. The Irish may have suffered grievously at the hands of the Vikings, but in many cases (we are asked to believe) it all came good in the end.

DANES, NORSE, IRISH, BRITONS

The second half of the ninth century saw serious developments for the Norse: for the first time a fleet of Danes arrived in Irish waters. The Annals of Ulster at AD849 state that 'a naval expedition of seven score ships of adherents of the king of the foreigners (*righ Gall*) came to exact obedience from the foreigners who were in Ireland before them, and afterwards they caused confusion in the whole country'. These were the *Danair* or *Dub-Gaill*, whose mark survives still in the personal names Doyle and Mac Dowell and also in the place name Baldoyle (*Baile Dubgall* 'the settlement of the Dubgall'). The activities of this new force were directed more against the Norse than against the Irish: in AD851 they attacked and sacked Dublin, and followed this up with another attack on the Norse *longphort* at Linn Duachaill (Linns, Co. Louth). In AD853 the Danes and Norse clashed in a great naval battle in Carlingford Lough which lasted three days, before the Norse were routed and abandoned their ships.

It has been suggested that these Danish attacks were the result of a strategic alliance between them and the Irish, who are supposed to have enlisted the aid of the Danes against their deadliest rivals.[67] The suggestion is

66. Holder-Egger 1887, pp. 502–6. See Kenney 1929, pp. 602–3, and Christiansen 1962, pp. 137–64 (especially pp. 147–64).
67. See Bugge 1900, p. 8 f., following Steenstrup 1876–82, ii, pp. 76–82; see also Walsh 1922, pp. 12–13. Chadwick 1962, was wrong in stating (p. 24 n. 32) that this theory was dependent on the 'uncertain testimony' of the Fragmentary Annals.

not impossible, since the annals record just such an alliance as early as AD842, when the abbot of Linn Duachaill was killed and burned 'by heathens and Irish' (in this case, presumably, Norsemen). The notion that the Irish formed alliances for or against the Vikings indiscriminately, concerned only with their own local political ambitions – though it might shock the general Irish reader – can be amply demonstrated from the sources, as we saw above.

It is just about this time, in AD853, that the Annals of Ulster record the arrival in Ireland of Amlaíb (ON Oláfr) 'son of the king of Lochlann' (*mac righ Laithlinde*). The annalist adds that 'the foreigners of Ireland (*Gaill Erenn*) submitted to him, and a tribute (*cis*) was paid to him by the Irish'. This Oláfr is generally identified with Oláfr the White, famous in Norse tradition.[68] Having gained possession of Dublin he allied with another Viking leader, Imar (ON Ivarr)[69] to make Dublin and the Irish Sea area the principal sphere of Norse activities in Scotland, the Isle of Man, and England. Ivarr's name dominates the account in the annals for ten years after his arrival, until his death in AD873. In AD859 the two Norse[70] leaders led an army into Meath (Mide) in alliance with Cerball mac Dúnlainge of Ossory and laid waste southern Uí Néill territory, perhaps while Maél Sechnaill mac Maéle Ruanaid was still *en route* back from his foray into Munster the same year.[71] The Munster Annals of Inisfallen in fact state that it was Cerball mac Dúnlainge who led the attack against Maél Sechnaill, and this may be borne out by the outcome of a 'royal conference' (*righdhal*) shortly thereafter which saw the relinquishing of Munster claims on Ossory and the recognition of its (presumably limited) autonomy under the overlordship of Meath; 'Maél Guala, king of Munster, warranted the alienation'. The fact that Cerball appears to have abandoned his Norse allies in the process would doubtless explain why they killed the acquiescent Munster king Maél Guala, in pique. In AD862 a northern Uí Néill army led by Aéd mac Néill appeared in Meath in reply to a sally northwards by their southern Uí Néill rivals the previous year. The attack on Meath was carried out in alliance with the Norse kings (*co riga gall*) and Flann mac Conaing, the brooding king of Brega, whose brother Cinaéd had been drowned in a pool by Maél Sechnaill in AD851 'in spite of the guarantees of the nobles of Ireland, and the successor of Patrick in particular'. The following year, AD863, saw the most shocking development yet: the ancient prehistoric tumuli of Knowth, Dowth, and Brug na Bóinne (Newgrange) itself were rifled by Amlaíb, Ivarr and a third Norse king, Auisle

68. See especially Hunter Blair 1939, pp. 1–27; repr. in Lapidge and Hunter Blair 1984, chapter 1.
69. Imar has been identified with Ivarr Beinlaussi ('the boneless'), son of Ragnarr Lodbrók, but the matter is controversial. See Ó Corráin 1979, pp. 283–323.
70. The case for Ivarr's supposed Danish origins advanced by Smyth 1975, p. 16 f. is dependent on his identification with Ivarr Beinlaussi, which has already been rejected. Besides, the Annals of Ulster refer to Amlaíb and Imar as *duo reges Norddmannorum* in AD870.
71. For this and what follows, see especially Byrne 1973, pp. 264–5.

(perhaps the Eowils of the Anglo-Saxon Chronicle, AD911) – 'something which had never been done before' (*quod antea non perfectum est*).

Between AD863 and AD871 Amlaíb and Auisle appear to have directed their attention to Britain. They and Ivarr campaigned separately, the former against western Scotland and the Strathclyde kingdom of the Britons, while the latter concentrated on attacks in England. Auisle was assassinated treacherously by his allies in AD867 (*dolo 7 parricidio a fratribus suis iugulatus est*). The campaigning in England seriously weakened the Viking settlements in Ireland; the northern Uí Néill king Aéd mac Néill sacked all their strongholds in the north in AD866, making off with their flocks of sheep and their herds of cattle, as well as twelve score of their heads. In the following year Amlaíb's *dún* ('fort') at Clondalkin in Dublin was burned to the ground and a great slaughter of the Viking leaders (*airechaibh*) ensued. Amlaíb seems to have avenged himself against Armagh in AD869, from which he allegedly took 1000 prisoners and caused untold damage to boot. In AD870, however, Amlaíb was back in north England, and he and Ivarr combined in a four-month-long siege of the north English stronghold at Dumbarton Rock, in the Forth of Clyde, which fell eventually and was plundered by them. In the following year they returned to Dublin 'bringing away with them into captivity to Ireland a great prey of Angles and Britons and Picts' (as the annalist records).

The activities of the Dublin Vikings in Scotland and north Britain are difficult to explain. They may have had a tactical motivation, directed against a too powerful concentration of rival Danish forces in those parts. It has been suggested that the arrival of Amlaíb and his men in Dublin in AD853 and their activities during the decade that followed reflected a determination to eliminate the incipient Danish threat that had appeared with the arrival of *Dubgaill* in the late 840s, a threat that was all too evident with their decisive naval victory in Carlingford Lough in the same year, when the two leaders of the Norse fleet, Stain (ON Steinn) and Iercne (ON Járn-kné) were routed, and the latter beheaded. While making due allowance for the possibility that there were several independent bands of Vikings in Irish waters during these years, it would be unwise to exclude the alternative possibility, namely that Norse activities centred on Dublin were part of a policy of consolidation intended to bolster the gains of Turgéis and his ilk earlier in the century. For the forty or so years following Ivarr's death in AD873 there are no more large-scale Viking invasions of Ireland; this is the period described by the *Cogadh Gaedhel re Gallaibh* as the 'forty years' rest'. On the other hand, it has been argued that the activities of Amlaíb and Auisle in Scotland and Strathclyde may have been due to 'the failure of the Irish Vikings to possess themselves of sufficient lands and treasure'.[72] The destruction of Norse *longphorts* and other semi-permanent settlements may have encouraged them to look elsewhere for booty, and a parallel can be seen in the contemporary activities of their Danish brothers.

In the 860s Danish raiders began to appear in English waters.[73] In the

72. Ó Corráin 1979, p. 313.
73. For what follows, see Sawyer 1982, p. 90 ff.

autumn of AD865 a Viking army landed in East Anglia and took advantage of a civil war in Northumbria in the following year to seize York. This army was apparently reinforced at that point by Viking ships from France, where they had established a permanent control of the lower Loire region. In AD867 these Danes repulsed an attempt to oust them from York and they were subsequently able to establish a Scandinavian kingdom centred on that city. From there they conquered eastern Mercia and East Anglia, but their efforts to add Wessex to their gains were frustrated by Alfred 'the Great'. The activities of what the Anglo-Saxon Chronicle terms the 'Great Army'[74] saw the establishment of a formidable Viking presence in England and by AD876 the same source could report that one of their kings, Healfdene, having stayed through the winter, divided out the lands of Northumbria among his followers. In an earlier annal (s.a AD871) Healfdene and Bagsecg are named as two leaders of the Great Army, and the names of five Danish earls are also given. In the annal for AD875, besides Healfdene the annal mentions 'three kings, Guthrum, Oscetel, and Anwend [who] went from Repton to Cambridge with a great army and stayed there a year'.[75] It has been suggested that the attacks by the Dublin Norse kings Ivarr and Amlaíb in north Britain were intended as the essential preliminary to a large-scale occupation of Galloway and Cumbria.[76] Whether this was the intention, or whether the attack was a cautionary measure directed against the rival ambitions of Danish kings in Northumbria, cannot be deduced from the meagre information at our disposal. But it may be significant that in AD875 Healfdene, the Danish ruler of Northumbria, harried both Strathclyde and Galloway overland from the Tyne, and may also have led the Danish forces that inflicted a severe defeat on the Picts. Welsh annals for the same period record the famous 'Sunday battle' fought in Anglesey in AD877 (*ueith diu sul in Món*),[77] followed by the expulsion of the Gwynedd king Rhodri Mawr (patron of Sedulius and his circle) who 'came in flight from the *Dubgaill* to Ireland'. The following year the Irish and Welsh annals record his death (and that of his son, Guriat, according to *Annales Cambriae*) at the hands of the Saxons, doubtless in an ill-starred attempt to recover his kingdom.[78] There was little consolation in the fact that a Welsh victory at Conway in AD880 is described in the *Annales Cambriae* as 'vengeance for Rhodri from God' (*digal Rotri a Deo*). The Vikings appear, in fact, to have controlled the waters around Pembrokeshire and Cornwall; a Cornish king, Dungarth (Old Cornish *Doniert*) was drowned in AD875, doubtless at the hands of the Vikings whose fleet of twenty-three ships, led by 'the brother of Ivarr and Healfdene', wintered off Dyfed and Devon between AD875 and 877.[79]

74. See Stenton 1947, pp. 243–6.
75. Ó Corráin 1979, p. 317.
76. Chadwick 1962, p. 29.
77. Phillimore 1888, pp. 141–83 (quotation, p. 166).
78. For a good, general account of Viking activities in Wales, see Charles 1934.
79. For discussion of the difficulties surrounding the identity of this unnamed brother, see especially Ó Corráin 1979, *passim*.

THE VIKINGS OF DUBLIN, AD873–902

Tha Annals of Ulster at AD873 record the death of Ivarr of Dublin, describing him as 'king of the Norse of all Ireland and Britain' (*rex Nordmannorum totius Hiberniae et Britanniae*). His brother-in-arms, Amlaíb, apparently survived him by over twenty years, though his death-notice at AD896 is perhaps misplaced (if it is he, and not a grandson of Ivarr's, he is named Amlaim hua Imair). The history of the Dublin kingdom during this period is confused and confusing. A succession of sons and grandsons of previous Viking leaders figure in the subsequent chronicle of events, but their doings are obscure. The Danish king Healfdene of Northumbria, who disappears from the Anglo-Saxon Chronicle around this time, has been identified as the individual who figures twice in the Annals of Ulster at AD875 and 877 as Alband (cp. Alpthann mac Gothbrith, AU AD926), who is said to have been killed by an otherwise unidentified Oistin (ON Eysteinn) son of Amlaíb, *rex Norddmannorum*; this Alband was in turn killed in an encounter with the Norse at Loch Cuan (Strangford Lough) two years later.[80] The supposed title to the kingdom of Dublin which this Alband was allegedly seeking to reclaim is highly uncertain.[81] There is no further record of Danish activity in Dublin or anywhere else in Ireland until the second settlement of the town in the tenth century. What clashes do occur appear to have involved only Norsemen, such as Otir, son of Auisle, who died in AD882 apparently through some stratagem involving a rival named Eloir mac Iercne (Halldór son of Járn-kné) and the daughter of Maél Sechnaill (*o mac Iergni 7 o ingain Mael Sechnaill*). This Eloir is possibly identical with Eloir, son of Barith, mentioned in the annals AD888, a son of Barith 'the great Norse tyrant' (*tirannus Norddmannorum magnus*) who was killed in AD881 through the agency of Cianán of Duleek, whose oratory Barith had destroyed. In AD893 the annals report 'a great dissension among the foreigners of Áth Cliath', with the result that they divided their forces in two, one party siding with the son of Ivarr, the other with Sichfrith Ierll (ON jarl Sigfridr). Ivarr's group apparently left Dublin as a result, but returned the following year. The bloody internecine struggle undoubtedly weakened the Dublin Vikings and in AD902 the town fell once more into Irish hands: 'the heathens were driven from Ireland, i.e. from the fortress of Áth Cliath . . . and they abandoned a good number of their ships, escaping half-dead after they had been wounded and broken'.

80. For the identification, see Smyth 1975, i, p. 16 ff.; but see the critique by Ó Corráin 1979, esp. pp. 319–23.
81. Besides the critique by Ó Corráin cited *supra*, see also Rory McTurk, 'Ragnarr Lodbrók in the Irish annals?', in Almqvist and Greene 1976, pp. 93–124.

DUBLIN ABANDONED AND REGAINED

The collapse of Dublin appears to have precipitated a large-scale exodus of Vikings from Ireland. [82] The Welsh annals record the arrival of Hingamund (ON Ingimundr) in Anglesey (*Igmunt in insula Món*). This Ingimundr became the subject of an Irish saga preserved in the so-called Fragmentary Annals.[83] The narrative gives a vivid and detailed account of the arrival of a warband led by Ingimundr first in Anglesey, where they were resisted and driven out, and then, with the consent of Æthelflaed, queen of Mercia ('because her husband Æthelred was ill at the time') they settled on land near Chester. The story has more than a grain of truth behind it.[84] The expulsion from Dublin probably also explains the Viking colonization of north-western England which also dates from this period.[85] The place-names of Cumberland have been shown to reflect settlement by Norwegians whose speech had been modified by previous contact with Irish-speakers,[86] while the coastal strip of Lancashire and Morecambe Bay from the Dee to the Solway and Cumberland again was also densely settled very early in the tenth century, as were the Wirral and other Cheshire districts. In the early years of the tenth century, however, the Vikings of the Danelaw suffered a series of major defeats, culminating in the famous Battle of Brunanburh in AD937, in which the Danes lost five kings and seven earls. The battle became the subject of an Anglo-Saxon epic poem[87] but it also made a great impression on the Irish annalists. The Annals of Ulster described it as 'a great, lamentable and horrible battle . . . between the Saxons and the Norsemen, in which several thousand Norsemen, who are uncounted, fell, but their king, Amlaíb, escaped with a few followers. A large number of Saxons fell on the other side, but Athelstan, king of the Saxons, enjoyed a great victory'. It is not clear where the Norse who had been expelled from Dublin were now located, but the annals report various skirmishes between rival bands in the waters and on the shores around the Irish Sea. A particularly large naval battle took place off the Isle of Man in AD914 in which Ragnall, grandson of Ivarr, routed the forces of Bárdr, son of Ottarr; this was apparently a clash between Waterford Vikings and the Dublin dynasty of Ivarr. The next two years saw a massive build-up of Vikings in Waterford, and the rival forces of Ivarr's dynasty brought reinforcements to Dublin and the Leinster coast. The annals open the account for AD917 with an ominous report of portents and omens reminiscent of those

82. For what follows, see the summary by Chadwick 1962, pp. 27–31.
83. Radner 1978, pp. 166–73.
84. See Wainwright 1948, pp. 145–69; but see also Smyth 1975, pp. 61–2 and 71–2 nn. 9, 10.
85. The Scandinavian settlement of north-western England was dated on linguistic grounds to the period after AD900 by Ekwall 1910, p. 95.
86. Dickins 1952, p. xiii.
87. Campbell 1938.

that marked the first Viking attack on Lindisfarne in AD793:

> Snow and extreme cold and unnatural ice this year, so that the chief lakes and
> rivers of Ireland were passable, and causing death to cattle, birds, and salmon.
> Horrible portents also: the heavens seemed to glow with comets, and a mass of
> fire appeared with thunder in the west beyond Ireland, and it went eastwards over
> the sea.
>   Sitriuc, grandson of Imar, landed with his fleet at Cenn Fuait on the coast of
> Leinster. Ragnall, grandson of Imar, with his second fleet moved against the
> foreigners of Loch dá Chaéch. A slaughter of the foreigners at Neimlid in Munster.

The annal for that year – AD917 – closes with the laconic statement: 'Sitriuc, grandson of Ivarr, entered Áth Cliath'. The Vikings were back with a vengeance. Not since the 870s had they appeared in such numbers in the Irish sea, and the next few years were marked by fierce warfare with Irish kings. The campaign began with the arrival of what the annals call the grandsons of Ivarr (curiously, their fathers are nowhere named) and seven such grandsons in all are named (suggesting almost that the name has become a surname, Ua hImair). Between AD918 and AD927 three kings, Ragnall (?ON Rögnvaldr), Sitriuc (ON Sygtryggr) and Gothbrith (ON Górödr), appear to have commanded Viking forces. On 14 September AD919 they defeated the combined forces of Niall Glúndub, northern Uí Néill claimant to the high-kingship, and his allies in the battle of Dublin (*bellum re ngentibh occ Duiblinn*), killing Niall and five other kings 'and many other nobles' (*alii nobiles multi*). The relationship of these Viking kings to their ninth-century predecessors is not at all easy to work out, but it is clear that Amlaíb and Ivarr were regarded by the Irish annalists at least as the founders of Norse power in Dublin, and the activities of the next fifty years saw them reclaim their patrimony and consolidate their hold on the sea-port towns.

THE SECOND DUBLIN SETTLEMENT

The second Viking settlement of Dublin was located two miles downstream from the first *longphort* site of AD841, doubtless because they had learned from their experiences of AD902 and felt that a site closer to the sea would be more prudent. Hence there is no continuity between the first and second settlements. But whereas nothing is known of the form or layout of that first Viking town, nor indeed any trace of ninth-century habitation in the area around Islandbridge, the second Viking town of Dublin has produced extraordinarily rich environmental, structural and artefactual evidence which enables a detailed reconstruction of the physical extent of the town and its economy, especially for the tenth and eleventh centuries.[88] In the course of

88. For the archaeological remains of Viking Dublin see especially the several papers by Wallace 1982, pp. 129–43; 1984, pp. 112–33; 1985a, pp. 103–45; 1987a, pp. 271–85; 1987b, pp. 200–45; 1988b, pp. 123–60, and his *magnum opus*, Wallace 1992.

twenty years' excavation of the area around High Street, Winetavern Street, Christchurch Place, Woodquay, Fishamble Street, and John's Lane an unprecedented quantity of preserved organic remains was uncovered; the waterlogged environment ensured that, in some cases, for example, bedding materials and waterfront vegetation were still green.[89]

More importantly, the excavations at Fishamble Street have shown that the earliest levels of this second Dublin site, c. AD925, commenced with an ordered layout of streets, houses, and properties of different type and structure in accordance with a preconceived plan which continued in use almost without alteration until the twelfth century. Most remarkable of all, the origins of this town-concept are not to be found in the Viking homelands of Scandinavia – where no earlier towns occur – but appear to mark a completely new and innovative development by the Dublin Vikings.[90]

There is some debate between historians and archaeologists as to whether the Woodquay site evolved from an earlier, pre-Viking nuclear Irish settlement at Áth Cliath flanked by an ecclesiastical site called by the Irish Dublinn ('black pool') – whence the modern (and Viking) town derived its name[91] – or whether its beginnings as a town are due entirely to the Vikings. The defended area of the town covered roughly twelve hectares, spreading from a core area in the west and expanding eastwards during the eleventh and twelfth centuries along High Street. The Fishamble Street site already had houses and plots laid out along a street plan in the tenth century, following the natural contours of the site, with the houses fronting onto the street, and individual properties separated by wooden fences. This apparently curved streetscape contrasts with the grid pattern of other Viking towns, particularly in England but also in Scandinavia (e.g. Haithabu),[92] and doubtless was determined by the defensive requirements of the settlement. Its somewhat congested appearance within a surrounding earthen bank was an unavoidable consequence of the same need for self-protection; the original defensive rampart was modified and enlarged in four stages culminating in the construction of a stone wall c. AD1100.

Within the town the positions of houses and sheds occasionally shifted, but the boundary lines of each plot remained constant, with access being provided to each individual property and from each property down to the waterfront. The regularity of house structures, their layout, and the provision of a rudimentary drainage system for some houses all indicate a well-regulated and ordered urban life 'in which property was respected and its regulation possibly controlled by the legal force of an urban authority'.[93]

89. Wallace 1985b, p. 81.
90. For a brief general estimate of Dublin's importance as a town, see Bradley 1987, pp. 321–70, especially pp. 332, 355–63.
91. For the arguments in favour of the earlier proto-town, see Clarke 1977, pp. 29–51; the case for a later origin was made by Wallace 1982, p. 139, and has been endorsed by Bradley 1987, p. 356.
92. Wallace 1985, p. 112.
93. Wallace 1984, p. 115.

Within the town all the buildings were of wood and wattle. The buildings comprised houses, workshops, sheds and latrines, and there may also have been a ceremonial platform at Christ Church Place.[94]

Four different house types have been identified, some with single and some with double post-and-wattle walls, indicating that some at least had cavity insulation as in modern houses. It has been suggested that the Dublin house design might also be innovative, since the house types there do not correspond in shape or construction to other Scandinavian types in England or in the Viking homelands.[95] Objects found in the excavations show clearly that Viking Dublin was a town of merchants and craftsmen, the range of artisans including carpenters, coopers, turners, shipwrights, carvers, black-smiths, metalworkers, comb-makers, and weavers. Dublin's location on the western shore of the Irish Sea at a point where the northern trade routes passed from Scandinavia, the Faroes, and the Northern Isles down to England and the continent ensured it a pivotal role in the development of Viking trade and commerce in the tenth and eleventh centuries, and the discovery of silks there shows that its trading network was expanding eastwards all the time. The wines, silver, wool and other goods that the Vikings obtained in England and on the continent were traded northwards to the Scandinavian homelands in return for ivory, furs, amber, resins and, of course, slaves.[96]

The population of Viking Dublin probably numbered thousands,[97] and the very size of the town meant demands in terms of providing foodstuffs, which cannot have been acquired by trade alone. The extensive farmland, pasture and woodland needed to provide food and building materials would in itself suggest that the occupants had control over a fairly large area of territory in and around Dublin.[98] The actual boundaries and extent of Dyflinarskiri (the 'shire' of Dublin mentioned in several Icelandic sagas) are, of course, unknown, though valiant efforts have been made to track them down. Haliday believed the territory extended from Arklow in the south to the river Delvin, near Skerries (Co. Dublin), and from the coast westwards as far as Leixlip (ON Laxlöb) in an area equivalent to the later dioceses of Dublin and Glendalough. The proliferation of Scandinavian place-names along the eastern seaboard (Skerries, Holmpatrick, Lambay, Ireland's Eye, Howth (ON Hofud), Bullock (ON Blowick), Wicklow and Arklow) is further evidence for Viking settlement.[99] A distinction must be made, however, between lands settled by the Vikings and territory controlled by them;[100] the archaeological

94. Murray 1983, especially pp. 43, 203.
95. Wallace 1985, pp. 127–9.
96. Wilson 1976, p. 110. On the slave trade, see Holm 1986, pp. 317–45.
97. Wallace 1985, p. 133, says 'possibly several thousands'.
98. For this and what follows, see esp. Wallace 1987b, p. 204 ff., and Bradley 1988b, pp. 49–78, especially pp. 56–60.
99. Haliday 1881, pp. 138–40.
100. Bradley 1988b, pp. 58–9.

and historical evidence is, to a certain extent, difficult to reconcile. For example, the annals refer frequently to the numbers of cattle extracted by neighbouring Irish kings from the Dublin Vikings by way of tribute, and the analysis of bone remains from the town showed clearly that cattle provided about 90 per cent of the meat weight consumed by the inhabitants.[101] But the same analysis revealed that the number of calves was low, indicating that the Dublin Vikings did not graze herds on the grasslands around the town but bought in their cattle from native farmers in the hinterland, or else carried them off as plunder (AU AD951: 'the foreigners of Áth Cliath plundered Kells and Downpatrick ... and a great spoil of cattle and horses and gold and silver was taken away'). The discovery that 57 per cent of the cattle represented were over four years old likewise indicates that mature steers were driven in from the countryside and were not normally kept in the town.[102] This contrasts with the evidence for pigs, sheep and goats (55.8 per cent, 24.8 per cent and 10.7 per cent of bones respectively) indicating relatively low consumption of pork/bacon and even less of mutton (the latter figure, 1.6 per cent, being about the same as for horsemeat). Pigs were almost certainly reared within the town but the comparatively small number of sheep bones found suggests that they were being raised for their wool rather than for their meat.

Within the town of Dublin (and doubtless also in Waterford, Cork, and Limerick, though the evidence has yet to be unearthed) there was large-scale manufacturing by leather-workers, shoe-makers, bone-workers and comb-makers, and a variety of different craftsmen and tradesmen engaged in building and tool-making.[103] A reference in the twelfth-century Life of Patrick by Jocelin of Furness[104] records a tribute in iron knives, shoes, gloves, and combs paid by the inhabitants of Dublin to the archbishop of Armagh, and this is probably a good snapshot of the small industrial activities in Dublin during the eleventh and twelfth centuries. Many of these manufactured goods were traded with the Irish kingdoms on whose periphery the Norse towns had their existence. In fact, the evidence of the annals shows that commercial and cultural contacts, intermarriage, and the spread of Christianity among the Norse made mutual relations easier with the Irish. The Annals of Ulster in AD921 reported that Gothfrith, grandson of Ivarr, attacked Armagh, but 'the prayer-houses with their complement of Culdees and sick he spared from destruction, and also the monastery, save for a few dwellings which were burned through carelessness'. Times had changed since Turgéis's wife had disported herself on the altar at Clonmacnois. It was during the reign of Amlaíb Cuarán (AD945–80) that Dublin became an important player in the

---

101. Bone analysis, by Finbar McCormick, in Reeves-Smith and Hamond 1983, pp. 253–68, cited by Wallace 1987b, p. 204.
102. For this and what follows, see the personal communication by Finbar McCormick reported in Wallace 1985, pp. 133–4.
103. For the remarkable bone 'trial-pieces' of this period from Dublin, see especially O'Meadhra 1987, pp. 39–55.
104. See Szövérffy 1957–60, pp. 6–16.

Irish political scene. He was the recipient of encomiastic verses from Irish poets who clearly enjoyed his patronage.

> Amlaíb, chief champion
> of Dublin in the east
>   of many-territoried Ireland;
> good king of Dublin,
> eager for strong,
>   noble patrimony.[105]

> *Amlaíb airchingid*
> *Átha airtheraig*
> *   Érenn iathaige;*
> *dagrí Duiblinde,*
> *déne dúthaige*
> *   tréne triathaige.*

He had been baptized and his daughter and grandson bore Irish Christian names – Maél Muire and Gilla Ciaráin.[106] Amlaíb himself abandoned his kingship in the last year of his life, following a defeat at the hands of the Uí Néill king, Maél Sechnaill mac Domnaill, in which 'very great slaughter was inflicted on the foreigners' and Amlaíb's son, Ragnall, was killed. Amlaíb ended his days 'after penance and a good life' on Iona. The victor of AD980, Maél Sechnaill, captured Dublin on three separate occasions between AD980 and AD993 but despite the annalist's claim that 'foreign power was ejected from Ireland' (*roladh nert Gall a hÉrinn* AU AD980) he in fact made no attempt to destroy the city nor expel its occupants. For the next century and a half Irish kings preferred to see the 'foreigners' of Dublin as a source of wealth and tribute, and the success of the various pretenders to the 'high-kingship of Ireland' can be gauged by the effectiveness of their control over the city.[107]

THE VIKING ACHIEVEMENT

In general terms the Viking impact on Ireland has been greatly exaggerated. In a famous essay entitled 'The passing of the old order', delivered to the First International Congress of Celtic Studies in Dublin in 1959,[108] the late D.A. Binchy set the pattern with his remarks about the Viking impact on Irish society:

105. Cited by Ó Cuív 1988, pp. 79–88 (quotation, pp. 87–8). Note, however, that Ó Cuív suggests identification with a ninth-century Amlaíb, known in Icelandic tradition as Oláfr inn hvíti.
106. Chadwick 1962, p. 35; note, however, that her reference to the Annals of Inisfallen *s.a.* AD944 as stating that 'it was about this time that the Norsemen began to be baptised' is mistaken.
107. Byrne, *Irish Times*, 22. April 1975.
108. Binchy 1962b, pp. 119–32.

I am convinced that the coming of the Norsemen had a profound – one might even say a shattering – effect upon native Irish institutions. Indeed, the title of this lecture has been deliberately chosen to suggest that the old order of Goidelic society, as mirrored in the Irish law-tracts, was drastically altered by the events of the ninth and tenth centuries.

Binchy's classic definition of this pre-Viking Irish society as being 'tribal, rural, hierarchical, and familiar (using this word in its oldest sense, to mean a society in which the family, not the individual, was the unit)'[109] set the tone for much subsequent discussion, but in fact his interpretation of the laws in this way would now be seen by most historians as too rigid and narrow, and the Viking impact on it mostly chimerical. The 'old order' which Binchy believed to be in existence down to the ninth century is now felt to have effectively disappeared by the end of the seventh century.[110] The supposedly archaic aspects of that society are likewise viewed by sceptical modern historians with a jaundiced eye, and nowhere more obviously than in regard to the violent impact of the Vikings:

> In pre-Norse times, [wrote Binchy] all wars, inter-tribal and inter-provincial alike, followed a curiously ritual pattern. They were hedged around with taboos: one did not continue the fight after one's king had been slain; one did not annex the enemy's territory or confiscate any of his lands; one did not dethrone the 'sacred' tribal dynasty; one refrained from attacking a number of 'neutral zones' on enemy soil – the monastic settlements, the property of the learned castes (*áes dána*), and so on. Now, however, the Irish found themselves faced with an alien foe who respected none of the traditional conventions. Hence war as waged by the invaders was more 'total', to use a modern term; ancient taboos were ignored; no holds were barred. Before long the native kings themselves were using these ruthless and efficient fighters as allies in their own quarrels, and, inevitably, came to adopt the new tactics.[111]

This picture calls to mind G.K. Chesterton's clever lines:

> The great Gaels of Ireland
> are the men that God made mad;
> for all their wars were merry
> and all their songs were sad.

Save for the observation that Irish kings frequently employed the Vikings as allies, Binchy's quaint picture has no supporting evidence whatever to sustain it. On the contrary, the annals indicate all too clearly that before, during, and after the Viking period more churches were plundered and burned and more clerics killed by the Irish than by the Norse.[112] When it came to murder and

109. Binchy 1962b, p. 121.
110. See, e.g., Ó Corráin 1972, pp. 82–6.
111. Binchy 1962b, p. 123.
112. See esp. Lucas 1966, pp. 62–75, and idem 1967, pp. 172–229.

mayhem, the native Irish needed no instruction from anyone. The larger-than-life Vikings of the popular imagination, barbarous, savage and heathen, contrasted with the cultured Christian and peace-loving Irish, are the stuff of medieval and modern legend as best exemplified by the twelfth-century *Cogadh Gaedhel re Gallaibh*:

> There was an astonishing and awfully great oppression over all Ireland, throughout its breadth, by powerful azure gentiles, and by fierce hard-hearted Danes, during a lengthy period and for a long time, namely, for the space of eight score and ten years . . . The whole of Munster became filled with immense floods, and countless sea-vomitings of ships, and boats, and fleets, so that there was not a harbour, nor a landing-port, nor a fort, nor a fortress, nor a fastness, in all Munster without fleets of Danes and foreigners; . . . and they ravaged her kingdoms and her privileged churches, and her sanctuaries; and they rent her shrines and her reliquaries and her books . . . [113]

This rousing narrative is about as good a source of information on the Vikings as 'Star Trek' is for the American space programme.[114] There is of course some element of truth behind it all, but the modern historian must look beyond the literary hyperbole and dynastic propaganda to the contemporary facts. There are house-shrines and other Christian artefacts in Scandinavian museums which undoubtedly came from Ireland during the period of Viking raiding,[115] and it would be taking revisionism too far to say – as at least one Scandinavian archaeologist has done – that the majority of these objects were not looted but were acquired by Norsemen 'having been sold second-hand as precious jewellery in the market-places of Scandinavia' or handed over as 'gifts or bribery'.[116]

The finds of Viking buried silver and coin-hoards from this period – they were the first to mint coins in Ireland – show starkly that in the first half-century of their involvement the Vikings were raiders and not traders,[117] and the notion that ecclesiastical and secular metalwork was traded by the Irish because 'as merchandise they can hardly have had much value'[118] is stretching credulity beyond reasonable limits. Most of these fine objects were forcibly removed intact from Ireland and subsequently broken up or refashioned as jewellery for Viking women (though the evidence of the recent Blackwater finds in Co. Armagh would suggest that some looted ecclesiastical treasures may have been subjected to such crude handling even before they left the country).[119]

These things, however, need to be set in context. Initially, of course, the

113. Todd 1867, pp. 2, 41.
114. The formulation is due to De Paor, *Irish Times*, 15 September 1971.
115. See Wamers 1983, pp. 277–306; O'Meadhra 1979, pp. 3–5.
116. Blindheim in Andersson and Sandred 1978, pp. 166–76 (quotation, p. 176, cited Wallace 1987b, p. 223).
117. Graham-Campbell, in Almquist and Greene 1976, pp. 39–74.
118. Blindheim, loc.cit. p. 176.
119. See Bourke 1991, pp. 103–6, and Bourke 1993, pp. 24–39.

Vikings must have had a traumatic effect on their victims, but their raiding was never so prolonged, nor their activities so widespread throughout the country, that they can have brought about the collapse of the Irish social system. Nor were they totally isolated from their Irish neighbours once they had established their towns. The conversion of the royal house of Dublin is perhaps the most obvious proof of the growing sympathy between the two peoples, but there is evidence also from Norse runic inscriptions in Scotland and the Isle of Man not only for the early christianization of the Vikings there, but also for a mixed population of Hiberno-Norse stock. The famous Hunterston brooch found in 1826 on the estate of Hunterston, West Kilbride, in Ayrshire is regarded as second only to the Tara brooch in terms of its delicate mastery; a long runic inscription on the back of it shows that it was owned at one point by a Viking who had an Irish name: *Melbrigda á stilk* ('Maélbrigde owns this brooch').[120] Several Isle of Man inscriptions commemorate individuals of obviously mixed origins: 'Thorstein erected this cross after Ofeig, son of Crínán'; 'Thorleif knakki erected this cross after Fiac his son'; 'Druian Dubgall's son erected this cross'; 'Melbrigdi, son of Athakan the smith, erected this cross'; 'Maél Lumkun erected this cross after his foster-mother Maél Muru, Dufgal's daughter';[121] altogether forty-four names are preserved on the Manx inscriptions, thirty-three of them Norse and eleven Irish.[122] On one piece of rough slate-stone the names of three Irish saints are invoked: 'Christ, Malachi, and Patrick, Adamnán', the first-named presumably the archbishop of Armagh who died in AD1148.[123]

There is ample evidence for intermarriage and fosterage from as early as the ninth century. The most famous example became the subject of a witty epigram preserved in the genealogies:[124]

> Three buck-leaps were made by Gormlaith
> which no other woman shall do until Doomsday:
> a buck-leap into Dublin, a leap into Tara,
> a leap into Cashel, the plain of mounds above all.
>
> *Trí lémend ra-ling Gormlaith,*
> *ní lingfea ben co bráth:*
> *léim i nÁth Cliath, léim i Temraig,*
> *léim i Cassel, carnmaig ós chách.*

Gormlaith was the daughter of Murchad mac Find, Ua Faéláin king of Leinster, and the genealogists record that she was first married to Amlaíb Cuaráin, Viking king of Dublin, then to Maél Sechnaill mac Domnaill, Uí Néill

---

120. Olsen in Shetelig 1940–54, vi, pp. 151–232 (quotation, p. 171).
121. Olsen, loc.cit., pp. 190, 193, 209, 216. The name Maél Muire is elsewhere attested as a woman's name in the case of Amlaíb Cuaráin's daughter, whose death is recorded in the annals (AFM) at AD1021.
122. Olsen, loc.cit., p. 231.
123. Olsen, art.cit., pp. 202–5; see also McManus 1991, pp. 130–1.
124. O'Brien 1962, p. 13.

high-king, and finally to Brian *Bóraime* alias Brian Boru. She bore a son, Sitriucc, to Amlaíb, and another son, Donnchad, to Brian. According to the *Landnámabók* many distinguished Icelanders traced their descent from Cerball mac Dúnlainge (Kjarval), king of Ossory († AD888). His grandson Dubthach (Dufthak) was the founder of an Icelandic family, and three of his daughters, Gormflaith (Kormlöth), Frithgerth, and Rafarta married Norsemen.[125] The interchange of family and personal names which took place during the Viking period also points to close connections between the two populations.[126] Indeed, it is notable how frequently the Irish annalists and saga-writers refer to Viking leaders by name: a summary inventory compiled by the great nineteenth-century Celtic scholar Whitley Stokes listed over a hundred such individuals.[127]

By the eleventh century such contacts had ensured that Scandinavian styles in art are everywhere to be seen in Irish metalwork and in the stonework of the high-crosses. Indeed, it has been remarked[128] that Irish art, which had been moving towards a measure of conformity with west European styles, was, in the course of the eleventh and twelfth centuries, diverted by this Scandinavian impact back into old channels. In Irish metalworking in particular, Scandinavian patterns begin to exert a strong influence and two of these patterns are especially important: the 'Ringerike' and 'Urnes' (so called from the names of the places where specimens were found). The Ringerike style is characterized by a pattern of loose interlace and spirals with many free-flowing tendrils, curling into lobes of stylized leaves. The patterns sometimes incorporate animal shapes as well and the style makes its appearance in the Dublin archaeological finds, not only on finished objects but also on bone 'trial-pieces' or 'motif-pieces' (O'Meadhra's term) – an important fact, since it proves that the metalwork was not imported from Scandinavia but produced in Dublin by resident Viking craftsmen. More importantly, the style appears also on objects originating from native Irish contexts. For example, the beautiful inlaid bronze crozier from Clonmacnois[129] and the shrine made for the 'Cathach' or psalm-book of St Columba in the eleventh century[130] display the Ringerike animal ornament clearly. Although made for a northern patron, the Cathach shrine was actually manufactured by a Viking or mixed Irish-Viking craftsman, almost certainly at Kells between 1072 and 1098, who signed his name to the object as Sitric Mac Maec Aeda. A bone trial piece found in Dublin bears a Ringerike-style pattern almost identical with that on the shrine.[131] A similar comparison has been

125. Walsh 1922, pp. 14–15. For more complicated marriage alliances, see ibid., p. 17.
126. Ó Cuív 1986, *passim.*
127. Stokes, *The Academy* No. 959 (20.9.1890), pp. 248–9.
128. De Paor, *Irish Times*, 9 July 1974.
129. See Cone 1977, pp. 185–6 No. 59; there is a very fine colour reproduction of the crozier on the front cover of the book. For general discussion, see also Shetelig 1954b, pp. 113–50.
130. Cone 1977, p. 188 fig. 36.
131. Cone 1977, p. 149.

made between patterns on the earlier Kells crozier (dated *c.* AD950) and another bone trial-piece found at a tenth-century level of the Dublin excavations.[132]

The slightly later Urnes style takes its name from the decoration in a church in western Norway which has wooden panels carved in high relief depicting four-footed animals entwined in the loops of wiry serpents. Although the term 'Urnes' in fact covers a wider range of decorative features than are found in the small church after which it is named, there is a constant theme in the various manifestations of the style: fantastic four-legged beasts struggle in the coils of snakes which have distinctive ovoid-shaped heads with prominent ears and bulging eyes, modelled almost invariably as if viewed from above. The style found great favour in Ireland and clearly appealed very strongly to Irish artistic tastes in the period from *c.* 1090 down to the end of the twelfth century, and beyond. It is the style of the magnificent processional Cross of Cong (dated by its inscriptions to *c.* 1125)[133] and the shrine of St Patrick's Bell, produced for Armagh *c.* 1100,[134] and recurs in many other handsome shrines of the period manufactured for the great ecclesiastical centres of the time. The Urnes style made a powerful impression on Irish stone sculptors as well: its appearance on the superbly decorated sarcophagus in the chapel built by Cormac Mac Carthaig between 1127 and 1134 on the famous Rock of Cashel in Co. Tipperary heralds a phase in which the decoration advanced from a subsidiary to a dominant position on the carved high crosses and Romanesque doorways and chancel arches of numerous twelfth-century Irish churches. A striking eleventh-century instance of the two traditions at work side-by-side is the fragment of a cross now built into a wall of the cathedral enclosure at Killaloe (Co. Clare) which has a runic inscription that reads 'Thorgrim erected this cross', and an ogam inscription in two lines that reads 'A blessing on Thorgrim' (*bendacht for Torogrim*).[135] A good late example is a window on the church of Annaghdown (Co. Galway) carved between 1190 and 1200, in which the body of the monstrous beast forms the moulding around the window itself. The influence of the style is also to be seen even in the more conservative realm of manuscript decoration: the elaborate interlacing of the larger initials in the twelfth-century missal now in Corpus Christi College, Oxford, shows the development at its best; the style of the decoration is remarkably close to that on the Cross of Cong.[136] The evidence of artistic work in stone, metal, and manuscripts offers, therefore, a useful balance in any assessment of the Viking impact in Ireland. It is one of the most remarkable – even if long unremarked – witnesses to the positive and enduring contributions which the Scandinavians made to our cultural history.[137]

132. Ibid.
133. Cone 1977, pp. 214–15 No. 63, with plates.
134. Cone 1977, pp. 213–14, with plates.
135. Olsen 1954, pp. 181–2; see also McManus 1991, p. 130.
136. For the twenty or so manuscripts of the period, see especially Henry and Marsh-Micheli 1962; the Corpus Missal is discussed at pp. 137–40.
137. De Paor, *The Irish Times*, 9 July 1974, p. 8.

THE BATTLE OF CLONTARF

No account of the Vikings in Ireland, however, can close without making reference to the most famous episode in that period of Irish history; the Battle of Clontarf. The clash of Irish and Viking armies on Good Friday, 1014, is perhaps the most vivid image in the otherwise hazy modern conception of medieval Irish history. The details of the encounter have come down to us in the florid prose and poetry of Irishmen and Vikings alike as one of the most picturesque battles in medieval Europe: Brian Boru, gallant leader of the Irish Resistance Movement,[138] too old and feeble to lead his troops, is slain in his tent, kneeling on a cushion with psalter in hand, while Sitriuc, Viking king of Dublin, watches the battle from the ramparts of his city; Sidurdr, earl of Orkney, carries his magical banner into the fray, guaranteeing victory and death to him who bore it; all against the background of terrible visions and dreams and hideous portents in the sky throughout the Celtic world. The battle reaches its apotheosis with Brian's death:

> Brodir could see that King Brian's forces were pursuing the fugitives, and that there were only a few men left to man the wall of shields. He ran from the woods and burst through the wall of shields and hacked at the king. The boy Tadhg threw up an arm to protect Brian, but the sword cut off the arm and the king's head. The king's blood spilled over the stump of the boy's arm, and the wound healed at once. Then Brodir shouted, 'Let the word go round that Brodir has felled King Brian.[139]

It matters little that the Norse saga-text was composed long after the event, nor that the Irish equivalent, *Cogadh Gaedhel re Gallaibh*, is equally high-flown in the understandable eagerness of its O'Brien author to show the ferocity and wickedness of the enemies whom his ancestor had defeated, saving Ireland in the process.

But despite the fact that these stereotypes of medieval propaganda still exert a strong influence on modern writers of pseudo-historical fiction, with Brian in the role of 'Lion of Ireland',[140] the commonly-held view among historians is that the battle of Clontarf owes its prominent place in Irish history mainly to its literary prestige; they are almost unanimous in the verdict that the encounter was of no real political significance.[141] The alignments on

138. The term is actually used by Chadwick 1962, p. 31.
139. Magnusson and Palsson 1972, p. 45.
140. Llewelyn 1980. The fact that the book is a rattling good read has, of course, contributed to its obvious success.
141. For a valuable critical re-assessment of the battle, see Ryan 1938, pp. 1–50. See also Goedheer 1938, p. 108: 'The facts force us to reject the conception of the battle of Clontarf as a national victory over the Norsemen', and Young 1950, pp. 11–33 (quotation, p. 20): 'The great battle was really little more than an incident', and ibid., p. 31: 'The battle of Clontarf was more of a spectacular episode than a decisive

the eve of the battle reveal that Brian was opposed by the Norse of Dublin and the men of Leinster, while the Uí Briain were in fact aided by the Limerick Vikings. Brian himself was married to the mother of Sitric 'Silkenbeard' (Sigtryggr Silkiskeggi), and there is a possibility that he gave his own daughter to Sitric in marriage.[142] Far from being a pagan ogre, Sitric of Dublin was a paragon of Christian virtue: the coins minted in Dublin during his reign (AD989–1036) – the earliest known Irish coinage, of high quality and based on the pennies minted by contemporary English kings – bear the sign of the cross;[143] his daughter – with a distinctively Irish name, Caillech Finnén – was apparently a nun (her death is recorded in the Annals of Tigernach at AD1042), while he himself is known to have visited Rome on pilgrimage at least once (AD1028); he is also credited with the foundation of Christ Church cathedral, Dublin.[144]

The fact is that the Viking trading towns and their populations were gradually absorbed into the political and social system that surrounded them. The two significant defeats of Viking power in Dublin, in AD980 and again in 1014, ensured that the Dublin kingdom remained within the orbit of Irish political affairs, while Wexford, Waterford, and Limerick likewise came under the control of native Irish overlords. From the late eleventh century the O'Brien kings of Thomond and Munster actually resided in Limerick, and they held the city successfully against the Normans until the end of the twelfth century. Similarly, the Mac Carthaig kings treated Cork as the capital of their south-Munster kingdom of Desmond, where in fact Norse town and native monastic settlement flourished side-by-side. Waterford came under the overlordship of Munster and like Limerick appears to have retained its own Norse dynasty throughout this period. The first known bishop of Waterford was an Irishman, Maél Isu Ua hAinmire (Latinized as Malchus); Limerick's early bishops, on the other hand, were mostly of Norse blood; most of Dublin's bishops, beginning with Dúnán (possibly recipient of the endowment at Christ Church supposedly made by Sitriuc), were Irish.

As centres of accumulating wealth, these Norse towns came to be regarded as sources of income and power, not as the citadels of foreigners to be sacked. When Maél Sechnaill mac Domnaill captured Dublin in AD989 after a twenty-day siege 'they gave him whatever he wished for as long as he was king: an ounce of gold from every garth (garda) on every Christmas Eve for ever'.[145] These garths (whence the Modern Irish word garrdha) were doubtless the rectangular allotments characteristic of the street-plan uncovered in the Dublin excavations; it has been pointed out that Russia was known to the Norse as Gardhariki 'the land of towns'.[146] A twelfth-century

landmark in the history of the Scandinavian occupation of Ireland'. For an alternative view, see Chadwick 1962, p. 37.

142. Chadwick 1962, p. 36.
143. Chadwick 1962, p. 36.
144. See Walsh 1922, p. 55.
145. Stokes 1895–8, p. 346 (Annals of Tigernach, s.a. AD988).
146. Byrne, Irish Times, 22 April 1975.

Irish poet boasted that 'three ounces of the tax were left in the gardens (*a ngarrdaib*) of the Foreigners; Dublin is thrice plundered on account of it by the Irish of the bright shields'.[147] In fact, so thoroughly absorbed into Irish life had the 'foreigners' become by the twelfth century that they received the ultimate *imprimatur* of native scholarship: their mythical founder-king of Dublin was converted to Christianity by St Patrick himself.[148]

VIKING INFLUENCE AFTER 1014

The Viking period in Ireland was not, then, an unremitting catalogue of desecrations and disasters. After the initial phase of raiding and harrying, when Norsemen first began to settle and establish towns, the Viking presence changed from a baneful influence to one which contributed in significant measure to the development of Irish social, political, and cultural life. In the political sphere their native practices have been proposed by one eminent scholar as the inspiration for a significant innovation in the institution of Irish kingship.[149] Certainly, in the field of warfare – at sea and on land – their impact was immense, in the development of both weaponry[150] and tactics. In response to the Viking raids Irish kings put fleets of ships into battle; the first recorded use of such a fleet by the Irish is mentioned in AU *s.a.* AD912. Ocean-going ships were not new in Ireland: *Scottorum commercia* with the continent is already attested *c.* AD600,[151] while the first documented out-of-sight-of-land voyages anywhere in north-west European waters for two consecutive nights are those described by the Irish writer Dicuil in the early ninth century (recording journeys to the northern islands in the eighth century).[152] Nor was the use of a mainsail a Viking innovation, since the famous Broighter boat model in gold (from a find in Co. Londonderry), whether prehistoric or not – there is disagreement among archaeologists on the subject[153] – clearly shows that sail and oars were both used in early Ireland. But there was nothing in Ireland (or anywhere else in western Europe) remotely comparable to the wonderful technological achievement that was the Viking longship, and the secrets of its construction appear to have remained in Viking hands.

A less savoury influence attributed to the Vikings is the growth of slavery and a slave-trade, particularly in the tenth and eleventh centuries.[154] Again it must be remarked that slaves were not unknown in early Irish society, but

147. Text and translation in Dillon 1962, pp. 116–17.
148. Ibid.
149. Mac Neill 1921, p. 117.
150. Rynne 1962, pp. 181–4.
151. See above, p. 21 n, 41.
152. McGrail 1987, pp. 280–1.
153. See Warner 1982.
154. See Holm 1986, pp. 317–45. For the comparative evidence for England see also Pelteret 1981, pp. 99–114.

those that existed were most likely prisoners of war or the unfortunate victims of debt-bondage.[155] There is, on the other hand, no evidence for a trade in slaves in the pre-Viking period in Ireland – though there is for England and its continental neighbours.[156] It is perhaps useful in this context to recall that Willibrord of Rath Melsigi, who established the Anglo-Saxon mission in Frisia in AD690 from an Irish base, also attempted to undertake missionary work in Scandinavia and for that purpose brought back from Denmark thirty Danish boys whom he had presumably bought there at a slave-market, with the intention of establishing a seminary for future mission workers.[157] 'The problem with the Vikings was not that they practised slavery – every self-respecting aristocrat did that – but that they did not follow the rules of society and that they had the foreigners' ambition to carve out a piece of land for themselves'.[158] Although the Irish show signs of having adopted the practice themselves, they appear to have restricted its use to Viking prisoners of war, 'an act of defiance and humiliation' visited only on their Viking enemies.[159] The institution of slavery, and its concomitant, a slave economy, remained alien to the Irish way.

CULTURAL AND ECONOMIC INFLUENCE

The cultural and economic interaction which characterized Irish-Viking relations for three centuries and more after AD800 is best seen in such areas as commerce and language. The Norse element in the Irish language has been much discussed by philologists,[160] who are unanimous in the view that the area of profoundest influence was that of shipbuilding and seafaring. Many of the Middle and Modern Irish nautical terms go back to Norse words borrowed into the language during the Viking period: e.g., *accaire* ('anchor' Old Norse *akkeri*); *accarsoid* ('harbour' ON *akkerissaeti*); *achtuaim* ('a brace' ON *akraumr*); *bád* ('boat' ON *bátr*), etc. But the influence extends also to military matters and the terminology of everyday urban life; e.g., *sráid* ('a street' ON *straeti*) and terms describing domestic houses:[161] *fuindeog* ('window' ON *vindauga*); *garrda* ('a garden' ON *garthr*); *halla* ('a hall' ON *höll*); *sparr* ('a rafter' ON *sparri*); and *stól* ('a stool' ON *stóll*). The Irish word for 'market' *margad*, which derives from ON *markaðr*, is a good example of the influence which the Vikings exerted on the native Irish as merchants and traders. The two languages, Old Norse and Middle Irish, were of course very different and mutually unintelligible, but with the passage of time, and with the increasingly frequent phenomenon of inter-marriage, bilingualism must

155. Kelly 1988, pp. 95–7.
156. Besides Pelteret 1981, see also Levison 1946, pp. 5, 8–10, 51.
157. Levison 1946, p. 64.
158. Holm 1986, p. 326 (quotation).
159. Holm 1986, pp. 329–30 (quotation, p. 329).
160. See especially Walsh 1922, pp. 78–9 for the literature.
161. Walsh 1922, pp. 39–41, has useful lists.

have come about fairly rapidly, at least in those small pockets where the Vikings had settled – though it should be remembered that the numbers of Viking settlers in Ireland was always relatively small, by comparison, say, with those in Scotland, the Hebrides, and the Isle of Man, where the Norse impact on Scottish Gaelic and Manx was a great deal more profound.[162] There are far more Norse borrowings in the Gaelic of Scotland than in that of Ireland, and very many more place-names, testifying to the significantly different degree of Viking settlement and assimilation in Scotland.[163]

The most remarkable Viking achievement in Ireland, however – and in the British Isles as a whole – was their introduction of towns. There were proto-towns of a kind already in existence, of course, represented by the larger monastic settlements like Armagh, Clonmacnois, and Kildare.[164] What is striking, though, about the Viking input is precisely its innovative character. Town life was not something that the Vikings brought with them fully-fledged from Scandinavia to their newly-conquered territories. They were essentially an agricultural people, and settlement sites at home such as Birka in Sweden, Haithabu in Schleswig, or Bergen in Norway were themselves as much a product of the new age of Viking mercantile and political expansion as was the founding of Dublin, Limerick, and Waterford (or of Kiev and Novgorod in Russia). Most of these settlements were defensive in nature at first, fortified encampments that then developed into small towns, while places like Dublin, Limerick, and Waterford eventually progressed to become quasi city-states. Viking mastery of the high-seas and their control of strategic commercial land-routes in Europe brought them a massive wealth which was to outclass the resources of most native Irish kings.

It was for this reason that claimants to the high-kingship of Ireland from the 980s onward saw the 'Foreigners' of Dublin in particular not as an enemy bridgehead to be driven back into the sea but as a potential source of wealth and tribute. In fact the success of various pretenders to the high-kingship can be gauged by the effectiveness of their control over that city, which came to be regarded abroad (if not yet at home) as the capital of Ireland. Despite everything that has been said in later Irish histories, Dublin in fact survived the battle of Clontarf unscathed, and in the eleventh and twelfth centuries enjoyed a position of unrivalled importance both as an emporium for the entire Atlantic trade of the north-western world, and also as the base of a powerful fleet which could be hired out as a mercenary force in England and Wales to contestants on either side of the political divide. During those years the activities of the fleet were most in evidence, in fact, when the city was under the control of Irish kings. Hence when Diarmait Mac Murchada hired it out to King Henry II of England for a six-month campaign in Wales in AD1165, he placed the king in his debt – a debt he was able to call in the following year, when he himself was expelled from Ireland. This direct involvement of Irish kings in the affairs of Dublin and the other Norse towns

162. See Jackson 1962, pp. 8–10.
163. For a general survey of the Scottish evidence, see Crawford 1987.
164. Doherty 1985.

came to an end, of course, with the Anglo-Norman conquests in the twelfth and thirteenth century, but by that time the Vikings had left their mark on almost every facet of Irish life.

CHAPTER 10

Ireland 1014–1200

'The history of Ireland in the eleventh and twelfth centuries is the history of a race evolving its monarchy, and is therefore likely to prove a valuable contribution to European history'.[1] Standish Hayes O'Grady's words, just quoted, might be thought reason enough to study the political and social history of Ireland in the period from the battle of Clontarf in 1014 down to the coming of the Anglo-Normans in 1169, but his benign view has not been the hallmark of all historical scholarship on the subject; far from it. Historians have differed considerably even in our own time in their judgements concerning the evolution of medieval Irish institutions, and not all of them have been complimentary. The great English historian, John Horace Round, in an essay apparently provoked by O'Grady's earlier contribution, saw things in a radically different light. He wondered 'whether Ireland, if left to herself, would even yet [in 1899!] have emerged from the tribal stage of society', and came out against the likelihood, which, he added, 'becomes doubtful when we contemplate the persistence of the *mores Hibernici*'.[2]

For writers like Round, weaned on stories of Empire and the Raj, the contemporary squabbles over Irish Home Rule were just another tedious reminder of the incorrigibility of Irish ways. 'We went to Ireland [in 1169!] because her people were engaged in cutting one another's throats; we are there now because, if we left, they would all be breaking one another's heads'.[3]

RULE BRITANNIA

In the face of such attitudes it comes as no great surprise that the great historian of Anglo-Norman Ireland, Goddard Henry Orpen, writing in 1911, should have seen twelfth-century Ireland as still in 'a tribal state'.[4] To him and

1. O'Grady 1889, pp. 286–303 (quotation, p. 287).
2. Round 1899c, pp. 137–70 (quotation, p. 168).
3. Round 1899c, p. 169.
4. Orpen 1911–20, i, p. 20.

others like him Ireland was a patchwork of warring tribes ruled by a bizarre and perverse law which was more anarchy than government, and hence the Irish lacked any claim to self-rule and any right to self-determination. To quote Round's ringing phrase: 'Claiming to govern a people when they cannot govern themselves, they clamour like the baboo of Bengal against that pax Britannica, by the presence of which alone they are preserved from mutual destruction'.[5] The reason for this state of affairs in Ireland was clear to Orpen:

> Until the coming of the Normans – and then only partially – Ireland never felt the direct influence of a race more advanced than herself. She never experienced the stern discipline of Roman domination, nor acquired from the law givers of modern Europe a concept of the essential condition of a progressive society, the formation of a strong state able to make and, above all, enforce the laws.[6]

Eoin Mac Neill, whose familiarity with the vernacular source material allied to a patriotic disposition made him a historian more sympathetic to the pre-Norman Irish, sought to rebut Orpen's arguments by emphasizing the role of kings and high-kings in the formation of a nascent Irish state and by pointing out the various laws and institutions through which they and their lesser vassals ruled and governed.[7] The motivation for both parties to the argument was clearly to be found in the political preoccupations of their own time and the received ideas of their own milieu.[8] It is ironic, therefore, in the circumstances (as the late D.A. Binchy pointed out) that Mac Neill and Orpen, the two chief protagonists, 'started from precisely the same suppressed premise, that law and order were impossible in any society where the state had not substantially the same functions as [in] the late Victorian era in which they both grew up'.[9] This led Orpen, on the one hand, to exaggerate the allegedly static nature of early Irish society, and Mac Neill, on the other hand, to exaggerate the degree to which the social, political, and legal organization of an earlier age had evolved into 'national' institutions centred on a 'high-kingship' of all Ireland.

AFTER CLONTARF – NEW KINGS?

The century or so after 1014 may be said to mark the period in which Irish power politics began to take on a life of their own. The annals record the

5. Round 1899c, pp. 169–70. The attitude is not exclusive to the nineteenth century; writing of the Anglo-Irish 'ascendancy class' Lyons 1982, p. 22, had this to say: 'If they were arrogant it was because it had been their fate to govern a people which, for much of its history, had shown little capacity to govern itself'.
6. Orpen 1911–20, i, p. 105.
7. Mac Neill's critique of Orpen appears in Mac Neill 1935, pp. 91–118; the lectures on which the book is based were delivered in New York in 1931. See also his earlier essays in Mac Neill 1919 and Mac Neill 1921 (repr. Cork 1988).
8. See the comments in Ó Corráin 1978b, pp. 1–35.
9. Binchy 1954, pp. 54–5. It might be pointed out, in the light of the passage cited above, that Orpen's premise, at least, was anything but suppressed.

partition of minor kingdoms, the expulsion of their ruling dynasties and the imposition of puppet kings in their place. This growth of an ever more powerful kingship manifests itself in the increasing militarization of Irish society, the appearance of castles and bridges, naval fleets and cavalry units, and of something akin to standing armies; even in the evolution of what, for want of a better term, might be described as military strategy. Doubtless some of these developments arose out of the torrid period of Norse attacks, when merely local defence proved woefully inadequate to counter the hit-and-run tactics of the first raiding-parties and the more formidable fleets and armies that followed them from the mid-ninth century. But not all of these were necessarily new developments, nor were their causes to be laid, in every case, at the door of the Vikings. The rulers of petty kingdoms were clearly subordinated already in the eighth century as is shown, for example, in instances of kings of vassal peoples being referred to occasionally by the inferior title of 'lord' (*dux*); in AD756 the king of Delbna Ethra is so termed.[10]

In AD771 and 796 the same title is used of the kings of Luigne and Ciarraige, while in the ninth century, the term becomes even more widely used. In these instances minor kings were being reduced to the status of dependent lords and the growth of ever more forceful over-kingship further reduced their powers to the point where, by the twelfth century, the rulers of such one-time independent kingdoms are referred to in the annals as *tigerna*, *toísech*, or *toísech dútchais*, all of which may be translated as 'lord'.[11]

Warfare takes on the appearance of being more bloody and prolonged, with armies in the field for months on end – something which would have been difficult to sustain in previous centuries. Toirdelbach Ua Conchobair, King of Connaught from 1106 and claimant to the high-kingship of Ireland up to his death in 1156, carried out no fewer than twenty-three long-range military actions which took him from his native area (present-day Co. Galway) as far afield as counties Waterford and Wexford, Cork and even Tory Island off the northern coast of Donegal.[12]

Casualties too appear to have been correspondingly higher in number. Unfortunately, the economic expansion on which such developments were based is all but invisible in the historical documents. We have no indication of increased agricultural productivity for the period; no hint of how the land was worked while the menfolk were away on campaign. Clearly, though, the kings who undertook such ambitious campaigns were in a position to draw on economic and military resources which were unknown to their predecessors. This in turn meant that Irish kings could acquire powers and prerogatives which were new and different; they now exercised a degree of control and authority in their own provinces which none of their predecessors had enjoyed. 'But will Irish stability and royal authority stand comparison with that of either of the first two Henrys'?', as Kathleen Hughes

10. Ó Corráin 1978b, p. 9.
11. Ó Corráin 1978b, pp. 9–10.
12. Lucas 1989, pp. 195, 197–9.

rather pointedly asked.[13] The question is perhaps not so straightforward as it might seem, nor the answer so self-evident.

Comparison with the neighbouring kingdom in the period of late Anglo-Saxon or early Norman rule may appear superficially unkind to the state of Irish development in the eleventh or twelfth centuries, but the smaller island may not have been so backward as is sometimes thought. It is true that the late Anglo-Saxon rulers of England, building on the foundations laid by the West Saxon kings Alfred, Edward, and Æthelstan, and their reconquest of the Danelaw, did introduce a remarkable series of innovations which enabled them to extend their control to quite a remarkable degree.[14] The creation of the shire system, and the introduction of the hundreds and the burghal hideage, produced a system of assessment which enabled kings to levy taxes on the entire country. The same system was used to provide military and naval service and enabled kings to raise troops for royal campaigns.[15] These innovations, dating in some cases back to the tenth century, created new administrative units and the suppression of old ones. The shires in fact mostly survived on the map until 1 April 1974. There are, however, parallels to all this in Irish society during the same period. In fact, it is worth pointing out that no instance is known before the tenth century of the word 'hundred' in Anglo-Saxon documents, or of any word, in English or Latin, meaning a numerical hundred, used to denote a unit of government or jurisdiction. In Irish sources of around the same time, however, the term *trícha cét* occurs,[16] first with the meaning of 'military muster', then subsequently (i.e. from the eleventh century on) to denote a geographical area. In fact, it is used in the Annals of Ulster 1106 as a unit of assessment, when the bishop of Armagh, on a circuit of Munster, levied dues of 'seven cows and seven sheep and half an ounce [of silver] for every cantred in Munster' (*secht mbae 7 .uii. cairigh 7 lethunga cech fuind tricha cet i Mumain*). The antecedents of the English system are usually sought in earlier Frankish custom, where indeed the *centena* is to be found. But military levies based on administrative territorial units are clearly present in the Irish world also from an early date; we need only refer to the text known as *Senchus Fer nAlban*[17] for an instance of such units (in this case naval levies) on the island of Iona in the seventh to eighth century. It has also been suggested that the elaborate body of genealogies which preserve such an abundance of detail concerning Irish aristocratic families from the seventh to the twelfth centuries[18] may have served as a form of rent-roll for purposes of taxation.[19] The same system could have functioned as a means of levying military service. It is true that no Irish word for 'army' occurs in these sources – though Latin prayers for the Irish king

13. Hughes 1972b, pp. 190–3 (quotation, p. 193).
14. For what follows, see especially Campbell 1986a, pp. 155–70 (pp. 157–8).
15. Campbell 1986b, pp. 171–89 (p. 172).
16. See Hogan 1920, pp. 148–235.
17. See Bannerman 1974, pp. 27–156.
18. See especially O'Brien 1962.
19. See Ó Cíobháin 1987–88, pp. 364–6 (p. 366).

and his army (*ut regem Hibernensium et exercitum eius conseruare digneris*) are to be found in the Missal at Corpus Christi College, Oxford, dated *c*. 1145 (based ultimately on Frankish models but perhaps more directly derived from Winchester)[20] – so we need set no great store by the absence of a native word. There are words aplenty denoting ships and fleets, hosts and battalions, footsoldiers (*ceithernn*) and cavalry, and all their stock-in-trade, including swords and bows, quivers and slings, and even castles (*caisléin*).

There is no denying that the native Irish were erecting substantial earthen fortifications before the Anglo-Normans ever set foot in Ireland; the only question is of their precise nature and shape.[21] Unfortunately, none of the *caisteoil* erected by Toirdelbach Ua Conchobair at many sites along the perimeter of his kingdom is known to have survived (or at least been identified), though some nineteenth-century topographical information suggests that they may have looked something like the 'platform motte'-type of structure usually associated with the invaders. Whatever its nature, however, the native Irish castle must have been identical in function with the later Anglo-Norman fortifications, and indeed it has even been suggested that the 'typical' motte-and-bailey sites in fact represent a secondary phase of colonizing activity,[22] following on a phase of ringwork construction which marked their first line of advance. In many cases, it can hardly be doubted, the Anglo-Normans probably built their castles atop earlier Irish fortifications.

There was no shortage of lethal weaponry, nor of kings ready and willing to use it, men with ruthless ambitions who rode roughshod over the ancient rights of tribes and dynasties in their pursuit of Orpen's heady dream: 'a strong state able to make and, above all, enforce the laws'. The annals for the years after 1014 bear brutal witness to the extent and duration of those ambitions.

The battle of Clontarf, far from being the high-point of patriotic endeavour, was a disaster for Brian Boru and his eponymous descendants, the O'Briens (Uí Briain). The frightful casualties suffered by Brian and his relatives in the battle very nearly brought about their political extinction. As it happened, the O'Briens only barely managed to hold on in Munster; their national ambitions disappeared with the tide at Clontarf and did not recover for the best part of a century.[23] From 1014 until 1022 then, Brian's bitter rival, Maél Sechnaill of the southern Uí Néill, recovered his former position as most powerful king in Ireland and Brian's son, Donnchad, managed little more than to hang on to the remnants of his father's claims in Munster in the face of serious internal rivalries. In 1061 the O'Brien fortress at Kincora and the neighbouring monastery of Killaloe were burned to the ground. Two years later his principal stronghold at Limerick fell to the combined army of Leinster and his own nephew, Toirdelbach (Turlough) O'Brien. The defeated Donnchad went to Rome on pilgrimage and died there in 1064. The accession of Turlough

20. See Warren 1879; Kenney 1929, p. 706; Gwynn 1964, pp. 47–68.
21. Nicholls 1982, pp. 370–403 (pp. 389–92).
22. Nicholls 1982, p. 389.
23. See especially Ryan 1941, pp. 141–52; 1942–3, pp. 1–52, 189–202.

marked an upturn in the dynasty's fortunes, however, for he showed a ruthlessness and a matching ability above the ordinary that were to make him the most able candidate for the elusive title of 'king of Ireland'.

TURLOUGH O'BRIEN

Turlough doubtless learned much from the example of his former ally and erstwhile claimant to the high-kingship, Diarmait mac Maíl na mBó, king of Leinster between 1042 and 1072. In one annalistic account of his death Diarmait is described as 'King of the Britons and the Isles and of Dublin and the Southern Half [of Ireland]', which was not as extravagant as it seems, for he controlled not only Dublin but also the Norse town of Wexford and its prosperous trade with Bristol. During his reign there was a steady flow of exiled princes into his domains from England and Wales, and the Viking fleet of Dublin saw frequent service in the internecine wars of the Welsh princes, and also in the Hebrides and in western England. In 1046, for example, thirty-six Viking ships from Ireland sailed up the Severn and allied with Gruffudd ap Llywelyn; this followed on a similar alliance with Hywel ab Edwin two years previously. In the year 1055 Ælfgar, son of the rebellious Earl Leofric and himself an earl, first of East Anglia then of Mercia, was exiled to Ireland and Wales, where he sought the aid both of Gruffudd and of the Hiberno-Norse in Dublin. In fact, Ireland became a refuge for English and Welsh exiles during these years: Harold Godwinesson in 1051, Ælfgar in 1055, Hywel ab Edwin probably in 1044, Rhys ap Tewdwr in 1088, Gruffudd ap Rhys in 1093, Gruffudd ap Cynan and Cadwgan ap Bleddyn in 1098, Hywel ab Ithel, perhaps in 1099, and probably others as well.[24] After the battle of Hastings in 1066 the sons of Harold fled to Diarmait, who led the Dublin fleet to the coasts of Devon and Somerset in 1068 and 1069 in an attempt to restore them to the English throne. Among the treasures which Turlough O'Brien obtained from Diarmait on his expedition to Leinster in 1068 was the sword left by his father at Clontarf and the standard of the Saxon king (claideb Briain 7 mergge ríg Saxan), a reference presumably to a trophy won by the Welsh from Edward the Confessor.[25] Later writers described him politely as rí Érenn co fressabra ('king of Ireland with opposition'), and he had much of it. The title was a new one, coined by the learned of the period to denote kings who were paramount in the greater part of the country but who failed to impose their authority on the whole island.[26] The other annalists are more grudging in their estimate of Diarmait, content to describe him merely as rí Laigen 7 Gall ('king of Leinster and of the Foreigners [i.e. Dublin Vikings]'). The reality was more impressive: with his ally Niall mac Eochada of the Ulaid he raided in Connaught and Meath (Mide); he installed his own son, Murchad, as king of Dublin and he

24. See Maund 1991, p. 181.
25. Byrne 1973, p. 272.
26. Ó Corráin 1972, p. 137.

established Turlough O'Brien as a puppet king in Munster. Only his unexpected fall in battle against his Meath rivals brought an end to a promising career.

Within a year of Diarmait Mac Maíl na mBó's death all that he had gained was in the hands of his erstwhile puppet Turlough O'Brien. Besides asserting his new-found authority over Dublin, Turlough marched north as well and reduced that province to submission. In Leinster he dismantled his precedessor's power-centre by the favourite tactic of divide-and-rule. By 1075, with his son Muirchertach installed as king in Dublin and his Leinster rivals successfully fragmented, he was in complete control of the province. In Connaught he pursued the same policy, setting the rival dynasties against one another. In this he was greatly assisted by the fierce rivalry of the three main Connaught political families, the O'Connors, O'Rourkes, and O'Flahertys (Uí Conchobair, Uí Ruairc, and Uí Flaithbertaig). Rory O'Connor killed Aéd O'Flaherty in 1078, which prompted an expedition into Connaught by Turlough to unseat him. Similar tactics were used to deflect the rising power of O'Rourke, but he proved a more elusive target. When Turlough marched north to Meath in 1084 O'Rourke launched a counter-attack in the Munster rear, plundering and burning many monasteries and making off with considerable booty. This success was their undoing, however; an O'Rourke attack on Leinster in October of the same year, with Cennétig O'Brien, a bitter Munster rival of Turlough's, was crushed at the battle of Móin Cruinneoice in which O'Rourke and Cennétig fell along with many others (one annalist numbered the dead at 4,000). The Munstermen brought O'Rourke's severed head back to Limerick as a trophy. This put paid to Uí Ruairc ambitions for the moment and when Aéd O'Rourke died in 1087 the kingship of Connaught passed to his great rival, Rory O'Connor, whose family was eventually to emerge as the most powerful in the province.

It is noteworthy that Turlough O'Brien made no hostings into the north. This was no doubt due in part to the fact that he was struck gravely ill in 1085 (and lost his hair), but there were political factors involved as well. The Cenél nEogain of the northern Uí Néill were riven by dynastic faction-fighting which reduced their strength and influence drastically, and it was only with the accession in 1084 of Domnall O'Loughlin (Ua Lochlainn) that they began to regain their former power. The situation in the kingdom of the Ulaid, on the other hand, was slightly different. The Annals of Ulster report that Dondsléibe Ua hEochada, a claimant to the Ulster kingship, went to Munster 'with the nobles of Ulster to pay homage' (*ar cenn tuarustail*). He had evidently been ousted by a close relative, Aéd In Méránach Ua hEochada, who in turn was deposed and drowned in Limerick in 1083. Turlough appears to have been acting as king-maker in Ulster, playing the rivals off against each other, and retaining each in turn at his Limerick stronghold, 'keeping him as a card up his sleeve'[27] should the other prove too ambitious. The policy was soon tested. An attempt by Dondsléibe to recover some of the lost Ulaid claims in 1084 saw him hosting into Louth, where he exacted the

27. See Ó Corráin 1972, p. 141.

submission of Donnchad O'Rourke. But the death of O'Rourke and the arrival on the scene of O'Loughlin brought Dondsléibe's ambitions to a halt. 'The fact that Turlough could play such an influential role in the politics of Ulaid without moving outside Munster, and the fact that the king of Ulaid actually travelled to Munster to make repeated acts of submission, bears striking witness to his power and influence'.[28] When he died in 1086, in the seventy-seventh year of his life and after twenty-two years as king, even the Annals of Ulster, not normally given to encomium of Munster kings, saluted him as *rí Érenn*, 'King of Ireland'.

MUIRCHERTACH O'BRIEN

With Turlough's departure from the scene Munster was divided between his three sons, Muirchertach, Diarmait, and Tadc, who died within a month of his father. Muirchertach banished his brother Diarmait and assumed the sole kingship, and the quarter-century that followed was dominated by Muirchertach's attempts to emulate his father's achievements. The opening years of his reign, however, were anything but auspicious. An attempt in 1088 to subdue Connaught with a three-pronged attack, using a fleet on the river Shannon and another on the west coast, was routed by O'Connor. A combined army of O'Loughlin and O'Connor then marched on Limerick, which they burned, together with the territory for miles around, including the O'Brien stronghold of Kincora, while in the following year Munster was devastated by the Ua Maélechlainn king of Meath in alliance with O'Connor 'so that it is doubtful if they left a beast or a human being in all that space'. Undaunted by these setbacks, Muirchertach set about exploiting the internal rivalries of Leinster to seize control of Dublin. A strategic submission in 1090 to O'Loughlin helped stabilize his position, but sporadic hostilities between Munster, Connaught, and Meath continued for a further two years. In 1092 O'Connor was treacherously blinded by his foster-son O'Flaherty, who seized the Connaught kingship. Two years of relentless attack enabled Muirchertach to impose his will on the rival Connaught factions and soon he was presenting a renewed threat to O'Loughlin power in the north. Between 1097 and 1113 Muirchertach marched north against O'Loughlin no fewer than ten times:[29] in 1097, 1099, 1100, 1101, 1102, 1103, 1104, 1107, 1109, and 1113 the near annual ritual took place and on every occasion he failed to compel O'Loughlin to acknowledge his claim to be high-king. On most of these expeditions his efforts were frustrated by the intervention of successive abbots of Armagh, whose peace-making efforts ensured a stand-off between the rival armies. Despite plundering his rival's Cenél nEogain kingdom in 1102 and razing his fortress at Ailech, Muirchertach failed to deliver the knockout blow. After yet another year's truce, arranged by the abbot of

28. Ó Corráin 1972, pp. 141–2.
29. See Candon 1991, pp. 1–25.

Armagh and secured by the giving of hostages from O'Brien and O'Loughlin, the two came face-to-face once more at Armagh in 1103 and encamped outside the city for a week confronting each other. With Muirchertach's men tiring of the confrontation (*ro batur toirrsigh imorro fir Muman*), he entered Armagh and placed an offering of eight ounces of gold on the altar, with the promise also of eight score cows, if the abbot would take his side. But where a similar gesture had secured the support of the Armagh clergy for his great-grandfather Brian in 1005, Muirchertach on this occasion failed to move the abbot, Domnall (perhaps because the offering fell far short of the twenty ounces of gold which Brian had donated). Restiveness appears to have set in among his men and he made the disastrous strategic decision to split his forces, leading one contingent on a search for booty while the other faced O'Loughlin's army in the area near Newry (Co. Down). When O'Loughlin fell upon the weakened rearguard at the battle of Mag Coba he inflicted a crushing defeat on them, and the annals record a long list of the dead (who were mostly from Leinster). O'Loughlin made off with Muirchertach's tent and the royal standard (*pupoll rígda 7 in chamlinne*) amidst his other spoils.

The battle should have proved fatal to Muirchertach's ambitions; as it transpired, he was back in the north the following year. But he never again succeeded in pressing his claims to the high-kingship and in fact was ousted from his own kingship in Munster as a consequence of an illness which disabled him in 1114 and from which he never really recovered. Even though he regained his throne in 1116 he was clearly a spent force, and the balance of power in the country had already shifted away from Munster again before his death in 1119.

It is remarkable how Muirchertach O'Brien has enjoyed such a good reputation with historians, given his manifest failure to impose his authority for any length of time on his rivals. Such temporary dominance as he achieved could hardly compare with his father's military successes, and he certainly brought about no new innovations in political institutions. Credit should perhaps be given him, however, for originality in military strategy: he employed ships on the inland waterways in a manner which had not been seen since the Viking campaigns of earlier centuries, and he also allied himself with forces outside the country. In 1102, following a failed attempt by the king of Norway, Magnus 'Barelegs', to reassert Norse influence in the Isles and in Ireland (in the course of which he raided the O'Brien monastery of Inis Cathaig in the Shannon estuary in 1101), Muirchertach made a marriage alliance with him, giving to his son Sigurd a daughter called by Old Norse sources Bjadmunju.[30] He married off another daughter, 'Lafracoth' [= Lebarcam?], to Arnulf de Montgomery, at the request of Arnulf's brother, the rebellious Robert de Belesme, head of the Montgomery family and Earl of Shrewsbury.[31] According to the chronicler Orderic Vitalis, Arnulf had

30. See Hudson 1979, pp. 92–100. The name 'Bjadmunju' (or 'Biadmynia') is close to the form Bébinn which occurs as the name of a daughter of Cennétig O'Brien who was wife to Domnall O'Loughlin, king of the northern Uí Néill, and who died in 1110.
31. See Curtis 1921, pp. 116–24.

conceived the plan as a means of acquiring Ireland for his family (*Ernulfus filiam regis Hiberniae nomine Lafracoth uxorem habuit per quam soceri sui regnum obtinere concupivit*);[32] the example may not have been lost on Diarmait Mac Murchada (Dermot Mac Murrough) a half-century later, when he married his daughter to the Anglo-Norman Strongbow. Muirchertach sent his daughter with a fleet of ships to assist the rebels against Henry I, but the Montgomeries's plans came unstuck and Henry captured their castles in England and Wales. Robert de Belesme was banished to Normandy and Arnulf spent the rest of his days aimlessly between Normandy and Ireland. William of Malmesbury remarked that Muirchertach 'from some unknown cause acted for a short time rather superciliously towards the English, but soon after, on the suspension of navigation and foreign trade, his insolence subsided'.[33] In a letter addressed to Anselm, archbishop of Canterbury, *c.* 1105(?), Muirchertach thanked the archbishop for his prayers 'on my behalf, a sinner, and also because you have intervened [with Henry I] on behalf of my son-in-law Arnulf'.[34] But whatever plans Muirchertach may have had to forge a grand alliance spanning the Irish Sea and the Isles finally came undone with the death of Magnus 'Barelegs' on 24 August 1103, shortly after his own disastrous defeat at the battle of Mag Coba.

Muirchertach is chiefly remembered not for his military successes (which were few) but for his activities as a would-be reformer of the Irish church; but in this also his interest was as much political as it was devout, and followed along lines laid down by his father before him. Turlough O'Brien had involved himself closely in the appointment of bishops to Dublin and Waterford, and had corresponded with Pope Gregory VII and with Lanfranc, archbishop of Canterbury, on these and other matters of ecclesiastical administration.[35] His son Muirchertach continued this pattern and in the year 1111 he presided over 'a great assembly of the men of Ireland, both clerics and laity, at Ráth Bressail, including . . . the eminent bishop of Ireland and the coarb of Patrick, and the nobles of Ireland generally, and they enacted discipline and law better than any made in Ireland before their time'.[36] Both Muirchertach and his father had been urged by successive Canterbury archbishops to take in hand the reform of the church, and the synods which they convened clearly reflect that policy. What most impressed observers (then and since) was Muirchertach's gift of the Rock of Cashel to the church at the synod of Cashel in 1101.[37] The gesture was not quite the political master-stroke it appears to be, for the O'Briens apparently controlled the

32. Cited in Curtis 1921, p. 118 n. 5.

33. Bethell 1971, pp. 111–35 (quotation, pp. 121–2); see also Candon 1989, pp. 397–415.

34. Ussher 1632, p. 526, No. XXXV. See also Southern 1963, pp. 133–4, on Anselm's friendship with Arnulf.

35. See especially Gwynn 1941a, pp. 481–500; pp. 1–15; 1941b, pp. 97–109 [repr. in Gwynn 1992, pp. 68–83, 84–98].

36. Mac Airt 1951, *s.a.* 1111.

37. See, for instance, Ó Corráin 1972, p. 149.

territories around Cashel by the end of the eleventh century, and there is even a suggestion that Muirchertach maintained a house there.[38] There must, however, have been a considerable psychological significance in the fact that Muirchertach handed over the ancient capital of his family's enemies to the church in perpetuity, though not even the Munster annalists thought fit to remark on the deed. They preferred to recall 1101 as 'the best year for milk, corn, and good weather'.

TURLOUGH O'CONNOR

The techniques developed by Muirchertach O'Brien – combined military and naval operations, the partition of kingdoms with the expulsion of their ruling dynasties, and their replacement by puppet kings – were all carried further by Turlough O'Connor and his son, Rory, 'who achieved a supremacy over Ireland never equalled by O'Brien'.[39] From Muirchertach's forced retirement in 1114 to 1116 the pendulum of power swung decisively towards the west. The first clash came in 1114, when Turlough led a combined army of the north and the west, with the men of Meath, against Munster and routed the southern army in a cavalry encounter. But he refused to press home the victory ('against the wishes of the northerners', as the annalist put it), preferring to see O'Brien survive as a useful counterweight to his northern rival O'Loughlin. Turlough was lucky to survive an attempted assassination the following year, in which he was seriously wounded, but he recovered and soon consolidated his position. From this point he became a serious contender for the elusive high-kingship and laid the foundations for an O'Connor dominance which only barely fell short of seeing them establish a single, unified kingship over all Ireland.

O'Connor, more than any of his predecessors, set about the military preparations for his campaigns with a will. In 1120 he constructed a network of strategic bridges (*trí prímdrochaid*) across the Shannon at Athlone and another further south, with a further one at Dunlo, near Ballinasloe, and in 1124 he built three castles (*trí caisdeoil*), one at the mouth of the Corrib in Galway, another at Coolooney, near Sligo, and a third at the bridge of Dunlo, whose remains were still to be seen in the nineteenth century.[40] These, and other fortifications mentioned in the annals, secured his defensive position at home. In the following year he then ranged north and south, reducing O'Rourke and his kingdom of Conmaicne to submission, banishing the Ua Maélechlainn king of Meath into Munster and chastising the men of Ossory 'so that they gave him his full award in respect of the revolt which they had made against him'. He spent a night in Dublin, signifying his authority over the Norse city, and left it in the hands of his vassal king of Leinster. The

---

38. Candon 1991, p. 9. It should be noted, however, that the annalistic evidence is far from clear on this point.
39. Ó Corráin 1972, p. 150.
40. Nicholls 1982, p. 389.

annals for 1126 have a long list of Turlough's further construction activities and expeditions, describing the year as a 'great storm of war in Ireland'. In 1127 he was in a position to put 190 ships into a campaign in Munster. He had already taken the trouble of securing his spiritual rear in 1123: a relic of the True Cross was encased in the shrine known as the Cross of Cong. Similar largesse had seen him donate three treasures to the church of Clonmacnois: a goblet of silver, a cup of silver with a golden cross over it, and a drinking-horn inlaid with gold. In 1127 he consolidated his position with a grand gesture to the archbishop of Tuam in the form of a large grant of land and established the family of Uí Muiredaig as perpetual office-holders there. It was perhaps a reflection of the changed times, however, that the church of Clonmacnois was plundered in 1129 and Turlough's treasures looted. The hapless culprit, a certain Gilla Comgáin, attempted to escape from the country by seeking ship in turn at Cork, Lismore and Waterford, each time without success; St Ciarán, founder of the monastery, blocked his departure every time. Gilla Comgáin then tried to 'fence' his ill-gotten goods to the Limerick Norse but was handed over to Conchobar O'Brien, king of Munster and extradited back to the community of Clonmacnois, who had him hanged.

The decade from 1121 to 1131 saw O'Connor as unrivalled power in the country. The following decade saw him faced with an unprecedented combination of foes. By 1133 the allied armies and fleets of his enemies north and south saw him reduced to a shadow of his former greatness, forced to sue for peace on all sides. His castles were burnt and he was faced also with internal rivalry, one party apparently seeking to replace him with his son Rory (who survived only through the intervention of powerful clerical forces). By 1139, however, O'Connor was on the way back: he built huge earthworks on the river Suck, linking two large turloughs to the river Inny and Lough Ree, using a muster of Connaught labourers for the task (*robaí tinól Connachtach ac dénum an gníma sin*). In 1140 he threw another wicker bridge across the Shannon at Athlone and renewed hostilities against Meath. All the time, however, there were rumblings at home, with the party favouring the young Rory still pressing their case. Turlough appears to have handed over the boy to Tigernán O'Rourke for safe keeping, but a large clerical delegation, numbering twelve bishops and 500 priests, led by the archbishop Ua Dubthaig, apparently fearing for the boy's safety – doubtless with good reason – insisted that Turlough release him. The king bought time by promising his return on the next May Day. Turlough's plans were dealt a fatal blow, however, when his favoured son, Conchobar (who was named by the annalists as co-conspirator in the plot to remove his brother Rory) was killed by the men of Meath, over whom he had been placed as king by Turlough. Massive retaliation ensued and Turlough hosted into Meath to avenge his son's death, inflicting a slaughter 'like the Day of Judgement'. The annals, after their account of this campaign, add cryptically that 'another son of Turlough's, Tadc, the most beautiful, the best, and the most spirited crown-prince that dwelt in Ireland', was spirited away (*do thesdáil*). There is perhaps a link between this curious episode and another great gathering of clerics and lords at Roscommon, including the archbishop of Armagh, again seeking the release of the young Rory. On this occasion their petition appears to have been successful. Shortly afterwards, Turlough and his main rival, Turlough O'Brien of Munster, met in a great conference (*móirthinól*) and peace was agreed between them. In 1145 the annals report that the Tadc who had disappeared the previous year was dead; how, or in what circumstances, we are not told.

MUIRCHERTACH MAC LOUGHLIN

At this point a new candidate for the high-kingship appeared from the north in the person of Muirchertach Mac Loughlin, king of Cenél nEogain. O'Connor's position was already weakened by the defection of Tigernán Ua Ruairc, and of the rising young hope of Leinster, Dermot Mac Murrough. The increasingly brutal nature of the conflict is evident in an attack by O'Rourke on O'Connor's territory as far as Lough Long in which he burned O'Connor's ships, including the womenfolk and crews on board. Turlough himself narrowly escaped death when the wicker bridge at Athlone was sabotaged and collapsed under his retreating army. He gained his revenge, however, two years later, when O'Rourke barely escaped a murder plot arranged by O'Connor when they met at the Shannon. By 1150 Mac Loughlin's leading position was acknowledged by O'Connor, who came to terms with him. Before Mac Loughlin could turn this arrangement to good effect, however, events took a dramatic turn in the south. A combined army of O'Connor and O'Rourke, Ua Maélechlainn of Meath and Dermot Mac Murrough of Leinster clashed with a hopelessly outnumbered Turlough O'Brien of Munster at Móin Mór, near Glanmire in Cork, in one of the bloodiest battles of the twelfth century. 'Until sand of the sea and stars of the heaven are numbered,' the annalist remarked, 'no one will reckon all the sons of the kings and chiefs and great lords of the men of Munster that were killed there'. The battle dealt a mortal blow to O'Brien's ambitions and eliminated them from the contest for high-kingship.

Though O'Connor tried hard to make good the losses of the preceding few years by capitalizing on his success at Móin Mór, it was Mac Loughlin who emerged as the dominant force in the ensuing power struggle between them. By the time of his death in 1156, aged sixty-eight, Turlough had ruled for half a century and was still laying plans for the future. That future, however, was to be beyond his power to control, and probably beyond the imagination of his son Rory to comprehend.

For a decade after Turlough's death the dominant influence in Irish politics was Mac Loughlin,[41] but throughout his brief reign he seemed never quite secure. These years did, however, see a strategic shift in power alliances, with Mac Loughlin cultivating Leinster and Dermot Mac Murrough, while Rory O'Connor effected a reconciliation of sorts with O'Rourke. O'Connor had

41. For what follows see especially Ó Corráin 1972, p. 164 ff.

secured his own position in the time-honoured fashion of blinding his brother and chief rival; it was hardly surprising, given the dubious circumstances in which his older brother Tadc had met his end eleven years previously. But a combined attempt with O'Rourke to unseat Mac Loughlin in 1159 proved premature, and met with a military defeat from which they did not recover until 1166. To compound his woes, O'Connor also lost a son at the bridge of Athlone to a slingshot from a sharp-eyed enemy. Mac Loughlin, on the other hand, set the stamp of his authority on Meath by billeting two battalions (*dá chath*) there for a month. But his success could only be provisional and temporary so long as he failed to secure the submission of his chief northern rivals, the Cenél Conaill to the west and the Ulaid to the east. This he tried to do by negotiating a settlement with Eochaid Mac Duinnsléibe which was guaranteed by the taking of hostages from every important family of the Ulaid, secured by the solemn oaths of the archbishop of Armagh and a long list of important figures. In 1166, however, Mac Loughlin – for reasons not now clear – took captive and blinded Mac Duinnsléibe. The reaction was as sudden as it was surprising: all his former allies turned against him and he was soon facing a united front of enemies. Faced with attacks from all directions his defences crumbled and he himself fell along with sixteen of his closest followers 'by the miracles of St Patrick' in retribution for his treachery.

DERMOT MAC MURROUGH

The sudden fall of Mac Loughlin had implications not just for Rory O'Connor, it also gravely prejudiced the position of his chief ally, Dermot Mac Murrough. He had attempted to come to terms with O'Connor during the campaign of 1166 but to no avail; in the face of his advancing enemies he torched his own house at Ferns in Wexford and gave four hostages, but 'got no glory but the corpses of Uí Cennselaig'. Since his emergence as king in 1132 Mac Murrough had manœuvred cleverly to maintain position in Leinster and to control the strings of power in neighbouring Ossory and Meath. 'His massacre of the rival Uí Dúnlainge princes without engaging them in battle was indicative of his power and his determination to be a real king of Leinster rather than a *primus inter pares*'.[42] Despite several reverses at the hands of O'Connor and Mac Loughlin, he retained his precarious hold and managed to avoid the frequent depositions that were the fate of his Ua Maélechlainn rivals to the north. By 1166, however, Mac Murrough had run out of allies, and Rory O'Connor had tired of his endless manœuvrings. The Annals of Inisfallen for that year report that Mac Murrough was 'banished eastwards across the sea after the foreigners of Dublin and the Leinstermen had turned against him'. Another, more partisan, observer expressed himself ·differently:

'O Mary! It is a great deed that has been done in Ireland on this day, the 1st of

42. Byrne 1973, p. 271.

August: Dermot Mac Donnchad Meic Murchada, king of Leinster and of the foreigners, to have been banished by the men of Ireland over the sea eastwards! Woe, woe, O Lord! What shall I do?'[43]

Abandoned by his own people, he had nowhere else to turn to but the Angevins in England. The previous year Henry II had hired the Dublin fleet (then under Mac Murrough's control) for his six-month-long campaign in Wales. Dermot had thereby established a debt which he was to reclaim with interest. The annal for the year closes with the laconic statement: 'Rory O'Connor took the kingship of Ireland'. But while Rory was powerful enough to isolate Mac Murrough from any hope of assistance in Ireland his strengths and weaknesses were essentially those of all the other 'high-kings with opposition' that had gone before him. He might build a 'huge castle' (caislén ingantach), as he did at Tuam in 1164, and take himself on triumphal circuit through all the other provinces, smashing down the last bastions of resistance to his ambition, but in the final analysis there was little that distinguished his achievement from that of previous high-kings. It was true, of course, that he had established a military supremacy never before equalled and no rival could take the field against him with any hope of success. He had emerged from the maelstrom of twelfth-century provincial rivalry as the man who took the spoils and had established a supremacy for Connaught which, on the face of it at least, compared with that of any other contemporary king in Europe. In the process he had ridden roughshod over older loyalties and provincial boundaries which the murder of puppet kings showed were not yet entirely forgotten.[44] He had not yet succeeded in establishing his family as hereditary custodians of a national monarchy – though there is some reason to think that the O'Connor dynasty might have emerged in such a role, had circumstances taken a different course.

On the eve of the Anglo-Norman invasion, however, O'Connor was doubtless blissfully unaware of the threatening clouds beyond the horizon. When he summoned a great royal council in Athlone he demonstrated his overwhelming power by granting lavish tuarastal to all the other kings in Ireland. He was hardly to realize the significance of the event recorded in the solitary Annals of Inisfallen entry for 1167: 'Dermot Mac Murrough returned from overseas and Uí Cennselaig was taken by him'. Like his ancestors of old, Dermot was about to reclaim his Leinster heritage and make one last pitch for even greater things. While the elements appeared to signal a propitious reign for the new high-king, with 'a great nut-crop in this year, and wealth and abundance of every good thing bestowed by God on the kingship of Rory O'Connor' in 1168, the annals recorded in the following year that 'a large body of knights came overseas to Mac Murrough'.

43. Best, Bergin, O'Brien and O'Sullivan 1954, i, p. xvii.
44. See especially Byrne 1973, pp. 270–1.

THE ANGLO-NORMANS AND HENRY II

The arrival in 1170 of Richard FitzGilbert (the nickname 'Strongbow' is first attested in a charter for Tintern Abbey of 1223)[45] marks a new era in Irish history, though contemporaries could scarcely have seen it that way.[46] His attack on Waterford immediately after landing indicated that he and his ally Mac Murrough were intent on seizing the initiative, and their advance on Dublin thereafter made clear that they knew well where the nub of power lay. O'Connor led an army to repel the invaders from Dublin, but after a three-day standoff the city was 'struck by lightning' and O'Connor retreated. The reality is more likely that Mac Murrough and FitzGilbert plundered and sacked Dublin, and that the annalist was putting a brave face on the high-king's vacillation. Mac Murrough's further incursion northwards into Meath made clear that he intended to extend his power beyond Leinster in that direction also, ousting his long-time rival and bitter enemy, Tigernán O'Rourke. Nearly twenty years previously Mac Murrough had been involved with Turlough O'Connor in an attack on O'Rourke in which Tigernán had been defeated and Mac Murrough made off with his wife, Derbforgaill, 'with her wealth'. Though Derbforgaill made good her escape the following year, the episode had clearly rankled and it was O'Rourke who supposedly insisted that Rory O'Connor banish Mac Murrough in 1166.[47] It has been suggested, however, that the mutual enmity may have been occasioned less by Dermot's abduction of Derbforgaill than by the long-standing rivalry between the two as to who controlled the plains of Meath, of which Derbforgaill, daughter of Murchad Ua Maélechlainn and sister of another of the 'unfortunate and ephemeral Ua Maélechlainn kings' was perhaps the symbol.[48] But the reality is probably that O'Rourke and Mac Murrough had equally little time for sentiment. The brutal murder of Mac Murrough's hostages by O'Connor in 1170 was, according to one annalist, carried out at the instigation of O'Rourke, 'for O'Rourke had pledged his conscience that Rory would not be king of Ireland unless they were put to death'. Little wonder, then, that one contemporary writer saw Tigernán, not Diarmait, as the villain of the piece, describing O'Rourke as 'the source and origin of all the ill that befell Ireland'.[49] His treacherous killing in 1172 at the hands of the newcomers was

45. Round 1899d, p. 310.
46. The entry in the Annals of Tigernach which begins: 'The beginning of Ireland's evil, i.e. Richard FitzGilbert came into Ireland' has a retrospective ring to it.
47. Byrne 1973, p. 273.
48. Byrne, loc.cit.
49. See Ní Bhrolcháin 1982, pp. 61–81 (quotation, p. 81), citing a mixed Irish-Latin passage from the prose *Banshenchas* ('Lore of Women'), which is exactly contemporary with the events mentioned: '[Tigernán Ua Ruairc] qui fuit fomintum omnium totsi fere Hiberniae mesariae .i. triana hindarba Diarmada acidit. A triall air dain tar muir co tug-sidi Galla leis a nÉirinn' ('Tigernán Ua Ruairc, who was the

in some eyes perhaps a fitting end to such a life. But by then Mac Murrough too had passed away and the stage was occupied by a new and formidable figure: the Angevin king of England.

When Henry II landed at Waterford in 1171 he was, in ecclesiastical law, fulfilling the terms of a papal grant which had been given to him 'in obscure circumstances some sixteen years before'.[50] This was the famous document called *Laudabiliter* (from the first word of its Latin text) which purported to cede to Henry the right to conquer Ireland in order to reform her church, a right derived from the spurious Donation of Constantine, a forgery dating from the eighth century,[51] which claimed for the Pope the right to control all the islands of the world. Though *Laudabiliter* has loomed large in the modern historiography of the period, in fact it was only one of many reasons given for the Anglo-Norman invasion. One source was quite specific in laying the blame squarely on the shoulders of Ua Andocc and Ua Cellchín of Kilmore, hUa Sluaisti of Cúil Ua Sluaisti, and Ua Glesáin, because 'it was they who stole the horses and mules and asses of the cardinal who came from Rome to Ireland to instruct them in the time of Domnall Mór Ua Briain, king of Munster († 1194). That is why the successor of Peter [i.e. the Pope] sold the tax and tribute of Ireland to the Saxons. And this is the right and claim that the Saxons follow today upon the Irish. For until then the tax and tribute of Ireland used to go to the Pope in Rome'.[52] Contemporaries, however, were in no doubt that the king's true purpose was to assert control over the territories which had been conquered by his vassals, the Anglo-Norman adventurers who had sailed to Ireland in 1169 and 1170. His interest in reforming the Irish church – if it existed at all – was surely a secondary motivation for his actions.

That Henry believed the activities of his vassals in Ireland to be something more than mere individual enterprise is clear both from the fact that he appointed royal constables to their castles in the Welsh Marcher lordships, as a sign of his displeasure, and from his subsequent measures against private war and private peace in Wales.[53] At the council of Gloucester in 1175 he extended that ban to their activities in Ireland. Already by 1172 the Pipe Roll recorded assessments of the scutage (payment made by a vassal to his lord in lieu of military service) for Ireland (18 Henry II), while the scutage for Arundel assessed only those 'who had not gone to Ireland' (*qui nec abierunt*

---

instigator of all [or] nearly all the misery of Ireland, i.e. it came about through the expulsion of Diarmait Mac Murchada. He crossed the sea thereafter and brought [back] foreigners with him to Ireland').

50. Frame 1982, p. 1.
51. The literature on *Laudabiliter* is legion. For good summary of previous discussion see especially Richter 1974, pp. 195–210, and Flanagan 1989, pp. 7–55. Earlier discussion which is still useful will be found in O'Doherty 1933, pp. 131–45; O'Doherty 1938–39, pp. 154–7; Bethell 1971, pp. 111–35.
52. Text and translation in Bergin 1914, p. 244.
53. Davies 1979, pp. 41–61 (pp. 55–6).

in Hybernia).[54] Clearly the undertaking was a massive one and the newcomers were able to put several hundred fighting men into the field.[55] By 1177 the *Gaill glassa* ('grey foreigners', so-called from the fact that they wore armour, a novelty for the time) had advanced as far as Cork and Waterford, and to Limerick, though not without fierce resistance from the Irish. The reversal suffered by O'Connor in 1171 when FitzGilbert broke the siege of Dublin appears to have unnerved him and he compounded the initial error by failing to put up a united front against the advance of the invaders. The arrival of Henry in Ireland in October 1171 appears to have had the intention of disciplining his over-mighty subjects, actuated principally by 'fear of the consequences of a too complete success of his barons in Ireland'.[56] But the peace thus achieved was short-lived and a renewal of hostilities was only brought to an end by the mediation of Laurence O'Toole (Lorcán Ua Tuathail), archbishop of Dublin, who persuaded the parties to come to terms. The treaty of Windsor signed on 6 October 1175 saw O'Connor acknowledge Henry's title to the territories conquered in the east of the country – the lands held of him *in capite*, i.e. by vassals of the crown (the former kingdoms of Meath and Leinster), and those held in demesne, i.e. under his own direct control (the towns of Dublin, Waterford, and Wexford); in these areas the full feudal system of administration and government was established along the same lines as in England.[57] O'Connor was to remain king of Connaught and over-king of all the other territories not conquered by the Anglo-Normans, conditional on his payment of an annual tribute to Henry.

There is no good reason to believe that Henry was anything other than sincere in his intention that the treaty of Windsor should work, but the truce thus brought about proved ineffective and Henry himself was either unable or unwilling to rein in the activities and ambitions of his subjects.[58] In the summer of 1176 they launched campaigns northwards and against Rory's own kingdom of Connaught. Only a scorched earth policy by the natives in the west, and Rory's belated military response, brought a stop to de Cogan and his troops, while Henry recalled his chief barons to England (with the exception of de Courcy, who was still fighting in the north).

RORY O'CONNOR DEPOSED

In 1183 Rory O'Connor was ousted from the kingship after 'great war' with his son Conchobar, and went on pilgrimage. It was an ignominious end to a career which had brought him to the pinnacle of political achievement; but

54. Round 1899b, pp. 125–36 (pp. 131 and 134).
55. The Annals of Inisfallen *s.a.* 1174 report a rout of the Anglo-Normans in which they suffered 700 losses.
56. O'Doherty 1937, p. 603.
57. See O'Doherty 1937, pp. 623–34 and Dudley Edwards 1938, pp. 135–53 (pp. 136–7).
58. See especially Flanagan 1989, pp. 229–72; 312–13.

his failure to maintain his position as overlord of the Irish territories accorded him by the treaty of Windsor had fatally undermined his authority. The promise of renewed vigour in the Irish resistance signalled by Conchobar's accession was cut short, however, by his assassination in 1189, though the man who eventually emerged to succeed him, his younger brother Cathal Crobderg O'Connor, almost succeeded where others had failed before him. In 1195 Cathal levelled all the Norman castles of Munster, 'and everyone expected that he would destroy all the foreigners in that expedition; and he arranged to come again, but he did not'. The plaintive note in the annalist's account matches the mood of the events. It was to be the last real opportunity for the Irish. When the aged Rory O'Connor died at Cong in 1198 he was unmourned and almost forgotten (the annalist was not even sure of the correct date of his death), and the deposition of his son Cathal from the kingship in 1200 saw the departure of the last great leader from the Irish side.

A great Hope fell
You heard no noise
The ruin was within.

THE INEVITABLE ANGLO-NORMAN TRIUMPH?

Perhaps the triumph of Anglo-Norman arms was inevitable; certainly J.H. Round thought so. In a lyrical passage which he devoted to their activities in Ireland he described the invaders – 'that marvellous people' . . . driven only by 'their boundless ambition and their love of native enterprise' (for which others might have substituted the words 'murder' and 'treachery') – in the following terms:

Conquerors, courtiers, or crusaders, they were always lords in the end; the glamour of lordship was ever present above the Norman horizon. Ireland alone knew them not, and thither they had now begun to cast their eager eyes. The wave that had spread itself over England and Wales had now gathered up its strength anew, and the time had come for it at last to break on the Irish shore.[59]

Orpen, too, thought that, 'had Dermot never been expelled, or had he never invoked Norman aid, we may rest assured that the ultimate result would not have been very different'.[60] His conviction, of course, rested on the belief that Ireland's fate was brought upon her by what he perceived to be the primitive condition of Irish society. Another more recent authority has seen the failure of the Irish to develop strong provincial governmental units like the French duchies as a fatal flaw in the country's political make-up, preventing the establishment of a hierarchy of authorities, which, as in France, could have

59. Round 1899b, p. 140.
60. Orpen 1911, i, p. 20.

led eventually to the advantage of the national king.[61] But there is something curious, surely, about the criticism of Irish kings for being too powerful.

FEUDALIZATION IN IRELAND, c. 1000

It is true that in the eleventh and twelfth centuries Ireland had no public or private administrative records; no memoranda or estate lists; no stock inventories or *descriptios*; no central writing office or chancery; no equivalent of the Northamptonshire Geld Roll; no burghal or county hideage; no Domesday; no coinage and no royal mints – conspicuously ignoring the example given them by the Vikings of Dublin when they issued their own coinage – nothing, on the face of it, which might give grounds for comparison with the royal powers of neighbouring Anglo-Saxon or Anglo-Norman kings. But even after allowance is made for the fact that elaborate administrative systems are possible without the use of written records (as is clearly the case in many modern African societies), the fact is that the apparatus of state was neither so large in England nor so small in Ireland as would appear at first sight. Henry I had a chancellor, as did William Rufus before him; but the institution seems not to have been much older than them.[62] Brian Boru, on the other hand, caused an entry to be made in the Book of Armagh in 1005, on the occasion of an expedition to the north, in which he was described as *imperator Scottorum* by his secretary Maél Suthain, who appears, on the surface at least, to have functioned much as a chancellor.[63] Exaggerated claims have sometimes been made for the innovative nature of Brian Boru's contribution to the development of Irish kingship, and these have been rightly questioned,[64] but there is no denying that changes came about in Irish society during the eleventh and twelfth centuries which might, with some justification, be described as a parallel to the feudal system that had evolved in England and on the continent. Kings were now levying taxes and promulgating laws, endowing churches with lands by the instrument of written (Latin) charters, and granting and regranting territories confiscated from defeated adversaries. These territories were being granted in return for loyalty and the promise of military services.[65] Parallel to the rise of this royal authority was the emergence of new royal office-holders: the *rechtaire* ('steward, bailiff', glossed *praepositus* and *villicus*); *taísech luchta tige* ('head of the [king's] household'), also called *taísech teglaig*; and military office-holders such as *taísech marcslúaige* ('commander of the [king's] cavalry'), and *taísech an coblaig* ('commander of

61. Barlow 1994, pp. 237–9 (p. 238).
62. See Campbell 1986b, p. 177.
63. See Gwynn 1978, pp. 35–50.
64. Ryan 1967, pp. 355–74 (pp. 368–89).
65. Ó Corráin 1978b, p. 22 f. For discussion of some parallel developments see Flanagan 1989, p. 273 f., and Berg 1987, p. 246 f.

the [king's] fleet').[66] By the year 1196 O'Connor of Connaught was even putting a company of archers (*rúta sersenach*) into the field.

Faced with developments such as these Standish O'Grady was undoubtedly correct when he wrote that 'there is no trace of tribal warfare in the history of these centuries. All the wars are of dynastic kings warring upon kings to assert dominion or retain independence . . . Tribes and nations had ceased to count'.[67] If these developments had not yet led to the emergence of a centralized monarchy they were not far short of doing so, and the authority of the great twelfth-century kings over their vassals, though often transitory, was greater than at any previous time. But the development of royal government, and its expression through laws and institutions, is a subject fraught with dangers. It assumes many things, both about native Irish society and about the Anglo-Norman state. For those – like Orpen – who believed that crime was rife and went unchecked because Irish kings were too weak, civilization naturally presumed an active and continuous interest on the king's part in the eradication of violence. This could only be achieved by the growth of centralized monarchy with an executive arm of government and by the emergence of kings prepared to control and discipline the aristocracy and lesser officials through a system of feudal administration and law enforcement. The emergence of a unified state, ruled by a king whose powers reached into every corner of the land, had its parallel in England in the evolution of the doctrine that all aristocratic titles and liberties derived from the king.[68] But though English kings might claim supreme authority, the extent to which contemporaries accepted the rightfulness of that claim (and the degree to which any such claim could be enforced in practice) are matters for debate. To many indeed, kings would have been the problem. Irish kings, for their part, would not have understood the claim in the first place, and the attempt by one of them to import the precepts of their neighbours across the water had disastrous consequences. But as another scholar has written: 'Had he been successful the name of Diarmait na nGall [*alias* Dermot Mac Murrough] might yet be revered as that of the true founder of the national monarchy'.[69] Fortune, however, dictated otherwise and the prospect – which loomed large on the horizon by the mid-twelfth century – of a single, united Irish kingdom, ruled over by a hereditary family of high-kings, was destined to become just another of those might-have-beens of Irish history.

66. Ó Corráin 1978b, pp. 28–30.
67. O'Grady 1889, p. 291.
68. See the pertinent remarks of Clanchy 1974, pp. 73–8.
69. Byrne 1973, p. 274.

GLOSSARY OF TERMS

abb abbot.

adaltrach second wife, concubine (<Latin *adultera*); may have replaced an older, native word *airech*.

aiccid heir-apparent to kingship.

aice fosterage; **i n-aice le** in fosterage with.

aicillne service or fief of base-clientship.

aire any noble, freeman, or commoner of independent legal status; occasionally used to mean 'a noble' (its usual meaning in the literature) **a. ard** lit. 'high lord', one of the noble grades; **a. déso** 'lord of vassalry'; **aire échta** lit. 'lord of vengeance' whose function was to lead a small band of warriors from his own into a neighbouring kingdom in order to avenge a wrongdoing not otherwise redressed; **a. forgill** lord of superior testimony; **ócaire** small farmer; **airig fedo** nobles of the forest, the most valuable trees in Irish law.

airthacra fore-pleading in court.

aithech churl; originally perhaps 'rent-payer'; later denotes an ordinary commoner (as opposed to a nobleman); **a. caille** one of the least valuable trees in Irish law.

aithech fortha substitute churl; a man who accepts legal accountability on behalf and instead of his king.

aitire an 'in-between' surety, who guarantees the performance of a legal contract by offering his own property as bond.

alea evangelii gospel-dice; a board-game.

allabar an unidentified herb

andóit founder's church (<Latin *antitas*).

anmchara lit. 'soul-friend', confessor.

annal record of an event in a given year; pl. **annals** proto-chronicle.

arca casket (for relics).

argadluim a 'foreign' herb, listed in law tract on sick-maintenance.

arggatbran an unidentified herb.

arra oath-helper.

asperum rough ground or arable land; pl. **aspera**.

athgabál seizure of property in distraint.

auctor Latin ecclesiastical writer; pl. **auctores** Latin classical authors.

audacht written testamentary disposition (also **edocht**) .

aurchogad keeper of hounds.

baile settlement, town.

banfheis symbolic marriage of king with tribal goddess.

Banshenchas historical lore concerning famous women (title of a text).

barony modern division of an Irish county, usually based on an earlier territorial division.

bélra language; **b. féne** lit. 'language of the Féne', legal language.

ben woman, wife; **b. aitiden** recognized wife (who is not a **cétmuinter**).

béscnae lawful behaviour (cf. **córus béscnai**) .

bóaire originally the only grade recognized among freeholders (cf. **grád féne**); used generally to mean any economically self-sufficient farmer; **b. febsa** b. of substance.

bothach lit. 'one who lives in a hut', cottier.

bóthar road, pathway, track.

brandub a board-game.

brehon law the law as interpreted by legal experts called **brithemain** (cf. **brithem**) .

breth legal judgment; **b. comaithchesa** 'Judgments concerning Neighbourhood'; **mellbretha** 'Judgments concerning games and sports injuries'; **muirbretha** 'Sea-judgments' (titles of law tracts).

brithem legal expert, lawyer; later used generally to mean 'judge'; pl. **brithemain**.

briugu hospitaller; **b. caille** lit. 'hospitaller of the forest', a term for fruit-bearing trees.

buad virtue, benefit; pl. **buada**.

buaile enclosure, byre.

buailtechas seasonal movement of animals and herds to winter/summer pasture (cf. **cuairt**) .

buanfach a board-game.

bull solemn papal document.

bunsach rod; used as a measuring-stick.

caill wood, forest.

cáin edict or ordinance; usually denotes enacted law (as opposed to traditional or customary law); **c. aicillne** the law of base clientship; later used to mean 'tribute'.

cainend leek; **firchainend**, lit. 'true leek'.

cairde lit. 'friendship'; a legal arrangement between two or more neighbouring kingdoms guaranteeing mutual recognition and enforcement of legal claims.

caislén (also **caisdeol**) castle; pl. **caisléin** (**caisdeoil**) .

capite, in lands held in c. = lands held by vassals of a king.

ceithern footsoldier.

céle originally a client of a lord; used generally with the meaning 'companion'; **céle giallnai** unfree client, also called **doérchele**; **soérchéle** free client.

Céli Dé clients of God (anglicized as 'Culdees); an ascetic or anchoritic movement of the eighth- and ninth-century Irish church.

cell church, developed cemetery (<Latin *cella*).

cendaige merchant.

cenél family, kindred, aristocratic descent-group; used generally to denote a race or people; **echtarchenél** invading people (cf. OW *cenedl*).

cert right.

cétmuinter head of the household, chief spouse; usually denotes the principal wife in a normal marriage.

chancellor officer in the king's household, head of the royal secretariat, and keeper of the royal seal.

chancery royal writing-office or secretariat.

charter formal document issued (usually by a king) granting rights, privileges, or exemptions.

cimbid captive, unransomed criminal.

cín book (<Latin *quinio*).

ciniud ascendants, tribe, people.

círad combing; process in beer manufacture.

ciuitas seat of a tribal bishop.

clann, Clann family, sept (<Latin *planta*).

cless trick, feat; **gabulchless** game played with slingshots.

cleth house-post.

cliathaire soldier, guard; pl. **cliathairi** troops.

cluiche a game, **colcluichi** games involving foul-play.

coé winter hospitality.

cognatus kinsman; **c. frater** brother.

cóiced lit. 'a fifth'; usually denotes a province.

coir n-athchomairc proper enquiries.

colonus serf.

comaithches neighbourhood relations (cf. **bretha comaithchesa**) .

comar joint ploughing.

comingaire joint herding.

commotatio circuit of relics.

computus study of the ecclesiastical calendar.

constable keeper of a royal castle.

cor a verbal contract (also **cor bél**) ; the equivalent in early Irish law of the Roman *stipulatio*.

córus béscnai 'The regulation of proper behaviour' (title of a law tract).

crábud piety.

crannchor lot-casting.

crannóg artificial fortified lake-dwelling.

crechríg royal expedition for plunder, usually associated with the inauguration of a new king.

crem garlic.

cresén a Christian (<Latin *Christianus*)

cretem religious belief

críochaire boundary surveyor

cruimther priest (<Latin *presbyter*).

cú hound; **cú glas** lit. 'grey hound'; in the laws, denotes an exile from overseas; **c. ottraig** yard dog; **milchú** greyhound.

cuairt circuit; **c. buailtechais** transhumance.

cumal lit. 'a female slave'; used generally as the highest unit of value in ordinary commerce.

cumlechta Féne customs and practices not regulated by law.

cundtairisem royal estate; pl. **cundtairismi**.

currucus small boat made with hides (renders OI *currach*).

dáilem dispenser of drink (cf. **deogbaire**) ; a royal official.

debitum duty; **debita pietatis** filial duty to parents.

decretum a synodal decree.

decurio member of a Roman town council.

demesne, in lands held **in d.** = lands held personally by a king.

deogbaire cup-bearer; a royal official.

deorad outsider, alien, exile.

derbfine see **fine**.

dercaid look-out, sentry.

dia god, God.

díbergach bandit, brigand.

díguin violation of protection, legal and physical (cf. **maigen dígona**) .

díles immune from legal challenge; **dílsi caille** fruit of the forest which an individual may take without being liable for theft.

diminuendo practice of beginning a line of text with enlarged letters, gradually diminishing the following letters down to normal size.

dindshenchas historical lore concerning place-names.

díre lit. 'honour-price'; the monetary valuation of an individual's legal status.

dísert hermitage (<Latin *desertum*).

ditham an unidentified disease of the soil.

diu day, in names of the week-days.

dliged duty.

doér unfree, base, dependent.

doíre captivity, bondage.

Domesday Book record of land-survey of England carried out by royal commissioners for William the Conqueror in 1086.

domnach church building (<Latin *dominicum*).

drécht giallnai labour due to a lord from his client.

drochad bridge.

drúth professional jester (renders Latin *preco*).

dún fort; **prímdún** principal fort.

eclais a church (<Latin *ecclesia*).

éludach absconder from justice, fugitive.

enech honour (cf. **lóg n-enech**) .

eponymous relating to an eponym, an ancestral figure from whom a descent-group traces its origin.

epscop bishop (<Latin *episcopus*); **rígepscop** royal bishop.

éraic 'wergild'; the fixed penalty for homicide.

érlam patron saint, church founder.

exegesis exposition of the Bible.

familia family, monastic community (renders OI *munther*).

felony criminal offence carrying the death penalty.

fénechas traditional or customary law; originally orally transmitted.

Féni originally denoted all freemen, without distinction of rank, who possessed legal status or capacity (cf. **grád féne**) .

fer coirthe vagrant.

fer légind scholar.

fer midboth semi-independent son living on father's land.

fianaide soldier (cf. **Fianna**) .

Fianna legendary warrior-band associated with activities of Finn mac Cumaill, a Leinster prehistoric figure.

fidchell a board-game (usually rendered as 'chess').

fili poet.

fine an agnatic kindred group; the basic social unit of early Irish society; **f. érlama** family of a founding saint; **derbfine** descendants in the male line of a common great-grandfather; **gelfine** descendants in a the male line of a common grandfather.

fingal kin-slaying, parricide, fratricide.

fintiu kin-land, land owned in common by a **fine**.

fír truth, oath-helper; **f. flathemon** king's truth.

flaith authority; also denotes a king or lord.

flaithemnas rulership.

fobiathad additional foods (besides stock) paid as food render by client to lord.

foederati Germanic warriors in Roman army on foot of a treaty (<Latin *foedus*).

fognamthaid attendant, a royal official; pl. **fognamthaidi**.

fóir temporary outdoor granary made of straw rope.

foirddbe annihilation.

folog maintenance, support; the obligation on a guilty party to provide a person who has been seriously injured with medical attention and maintenance; also called **f. n-othrusa** sick-maintenance; later called simply **othrus**.

forrach measuring pole; pl. **forraig**.

forus infirmary(?); **f. tuaithe** public infirmary(?).

fosterage custom of placing children of aristocratic families into care of other families in order to form political alliances.

frithfholud reciprocal rights, benefits.

fuidir tenant, semi-freeman.

gaill foreigners, Vikings (later Normans); **Dubgaill** Danes; **g. glassa** Normans.

galar disease; **g. bunaid** a disease of the soil.

garda garth, garden; habitation allotment in Viking towns.

geinti heathens, Vikings.

Geld Roll the Northamptonshire Geld Roll is a record of the collection of a geld (general land-tax) made between *c.* 1068 and *c.* 1083.

gelfine see **fine**.

genealogy text illustrating direct descent of an individual or group from an ancestor.

giall hostage.

goba blacksmith.

goire filial duty; in the laws, the obligation on an eldest son to maintain his parents in old-age.

grád grade, rank, status; **g. féne** freemen of plebeian origin (as opposed to **g. flatha**) ; **grád flatha** freemen of aristocratic origin; the noble grades; **bangráid** women dignitaries.

gráinne ibdaig unidentified type of grain.

grianán solarium, sun-room.

guin wounding; in ritual formulation; **g. bádud, loscad** wounding, drowning, burning.

heres heir, successor as abbot.

Hibernenses a party or faction within the early Irish church which favoured adaptation to native Irish practices and social customs.

hideage Anglo-Saxon land assessment; **Burghal H.** assessment of land required to support garrisons for royal fortifications during reign of Edward the Confessor; **county h.** distribution of hides in counties for purposes of tax-assessment.

historiography historical research, writings about history.

idpart offering, grant to church; pl. **idparta**.

immaire cultivation ridge (cf. **iugerum**) .

inclusus person walled up in solitary confinement in a monastery.

innraic of good legal standing.

ires religious faith.

ithloinges some kind of weed infestation.

iugerum ridge (renders OI *immaire*) ; pl. **iugera**.

iuratio solemn oath.

Landnámabók 'Book of Settlements'; collection of historical information about earliest Icelandic settlers.

Laudabiliter bull granted by Pope Adrian IV to king Henry II of England, authorizing the invasion of Ireland.

lebar book; book-law (as opposed to **fénechas**).

liaig doctor, physician.

lias cattle-pen.

literatus learned scholar; pl. **literati**.

loch lake.

lóg n-enech honour-price, payment due for dishonouring a person.

longphort Viking fortified settlement.

Lothlaind Rogaland (Denmark); later OI name for Scandinavia.

lubgort vegetable plot.

lucht tige see **toísech**.

lungait a 'foreign' herb, listed in law tract on sick-maintenance.

mac(c) son; **m. gor** dutiful son; **m. ingor** undutiful son; **macgnímartha** youthful exploits (associated with boyhood of Cú Chulainn in saga-text *Táin Bó Cuailnge*); **m. légind** student.

maélán muilchi a weed (poss. bitter vetch).

mag a plain.

maigen dígona sanctuary (cf. **díguin**)

mainistir monastery (<Latin *monasterium*).

máithre maternal kin.

March border territory.

martre violent death, martyrdom.

meacain edible root; **m. murrathaig** sea-kale, beet.

meithel cooperative harvest team.

memorandum short written summary of property.

mescae drunkenness; **mescae ocus lescae** lit. 'drunkenness and laziness', indolent behaviour.

mesne king an intermediate-rank king, subject to an over-king.

mess measurement; **m. tíre** surveying, land-valuation.

methas land held by **muire** by virtue of his office.

miann ngalair craving for particular food (cf. **mír méinn**) .

milsén thickened butter, quark.

mír méinn pica; craving developed by pregnant women.

misdemeanour minor criminal offence (as opposed to a **felony**).

mruigfher a 'strong farmer'.

mucrecht a kind of sausage.

muirchorthe castaway, ship-wrecked person.

muire(dach) lord, marshall; **m. rechtgi** intermediary between king and subjects in legal disputes.

naidm binding surety; a surety who guarantees the performance of a contract by the use of force, if necessary.

nemed sacred place; dignitary, member of privileged class.

noéb holy.

nós new regulation.

nutritor guardian, tutor (renders OI *aite*).

oblatio offering, grant to church (renders OI **idpart**).

oénach regular (often annual) assembly of people in one or more kingdoms, presided over by king(s) for the transaction of public business (e.g. introduction of new ordinances or regulations); also occasions for leisure, sporting and commercial activities.

ogam early Irish runic-like alphabet.

ollam expert, master, the highest rank of scholar; **o. filed** master of the art of poetry.

origin-legend legend or tradition which purports to explain the origin of a tribe or dynasty.

palaeography dating and classifying of ancient and medieval scripts.

papa bishop (used to denote special reverence).

paruchia confederation of monastic houses under the overall control of the founder's monastery.

Pelagianism doctrine attributed to the heresiarch Pelagius (*c.* AD360–*c.* AD420), that salvation could be achieved by man's own efforts and God's grace, and not by grace alone.

peregrinus a wandering scholar or cleric.

peritus learned scholar (renders OI *senchaid*); pl. **periti**.

pipe-roll enrolled accounts of annual royal income.

plebs tribe (renders OI **tuath**) .

polygyny having more than one wife or partner.

pretium payment; **p. redemptionis** ransom.

princeps leader, abbot of principal monastery in a monastic *paruchia*; **p. patriae** member of royal family, king.

provincia (ecclesiastical) province.

randaire lit. 'carver of meat', cook; a royal official.

rann subdivision of tribe or territory; pl. **ranna**.

rata surety (Latinization of OI *ráth*); pl. **ratae**.

ráth surety; someone who guarantees the performance of a contract by providing his own property as bond; **r. bráithirse** formal agreement between members of a kindred to allow adoption of outsider into the *fine*.

ráthbaige fort-builder.

recht law; **r. aicnid** natural (unwritten) law; **r. littre** written law, scriptural law; **mruigrecht** land-law

rechtaire royal steward or bailiff (rendered in Latin as *praepositus* or *villicus*).

rechtge an ordinance or regulation usually enacted in times of emergency or natural disaster.

regula a monastic rule.

rí a king; any ruler of a small kingdom; **fuiri** sub-king; **ruiri** lit. 'great king', an over-king; **rí ruirech** lit. 'king of over-kings'; usually denotes a provincial king or **rí cóicid**.

rígdamna lit. 'materials of a king'; a man who by virtue of his lineage qualifies as a candidate for kingship.

rindaide engraver.

Romani a party or faction within the early Irish church which favoured adoption of Roman/orthodox practices in church administration and liturgy.

rúta company, troop; **r. sersenach** company of archers.

saball barn (<Latin *sabellum*).

sapiens scholar, head of a monastic school (renders OI **fer légind**) ; pl. **sapientes**.

sárugud violation of protection or of a holy place.

scél story, tale; **rémscéla** stories recounting events prior to *Táin Bó Cuailnge*; **prímscéla** principal tales.

sciathaire shield-maker; a royal official.

scioból barn

scol school; **s. légind** school of Latin learning (as opposed to **s. fénechais** s. of native law, or **s. filed** s. of native poetics).

scolóc student, pupil.

scutage lit. 'shield payment'; in feudal society, the commutation of military service due from a vassal to his lord, in return for financial payment.

seisreach plough-team of six horses.

senchléthe hereditary serf.

senorba lit. 'inheritance of seniority'; portion of land granted to new king as royal patrimony.

sesquivolus squirrel.

sét lit. 'a valuable'; denotes a unit of value usually reckoned as the equivalent of a heifer or half a milch-cow.

siabar an elemental spirit.

síl, Síl seed, descendants.

silva woodland.

sinnach brothlaige lit. 'fox of the cooking-pit'; vagrant, down-and-out.

síogóg straw-rope, granary.

sliab mountain, moorland.

smacht fine, penalty; pl. **smachta**.

snádud protection, safe-passage.

soér noble, free, independent (cf. **céle**).

soérléicthe someone released from family duties.

solitarius hermit.

sraif a 'foreign' herb, listed in law tract on sick-maintenance.

stipulatio surety (renders OI *naidm*); pl. **stipulationes**.

súgán straw-rope

suí scholar.

supernus leader, chief.

tánaise heir-designate to kingship; anglicized as 'tanist' (rendered in Latin as *secundus post regem*).

tech house; **t. coitchenn** privy; **t. midchuarta** lit. 'house with a mead-hall', synonymous with a king's house; **tech** also occurs in eccl. place-names.

téchta propriety.

techtaire messenger; a royal official.

tellach legal entry.

tempull church (<Latin *templum*).

termann sanctuary (<Latin *terminus*).

Thing Scandinavian assembly or court.

tigern(a) a lord; later used to replace **rí** as a title for lesser kings; **óchtigern** young lord, lowest grade of aristocracy; Latinized as **tigernus**.

tinól hosting, gathering; **mórthinól** conference.

toísech lit. 'first'; a lord or leader; **t. luchta tige** head of a [king's] household (also termed **t. teglaig**) ; **t. marcsluaige** commander of [king's] cavalry; **t. an coblaig** commander of a [king's] fleet; **t. dútchais** lord; **toísigecht** headship of a kindred.

transhumance seasonal movement of cattle and people to new pastures.

treb homestead; pl. **treba**.

trícha cét lit. 'thirty hundreds'; a military muster; later a territorial division.

troscud fasting as a legal procedure.

tuarastal fee paid by a king to a subordinate in return for service or tribute.

tuath people, kingdom; the primary political unit in early medieval Ireland; usually a small territorial area ruled over by its own king.

turas pilgrimage-round; pl. **turasanna**.

t(a)urbaid postponement or stay of legal action.

uisce water.

ummus celery.

urradus traditional or customary law; citizenship.

vassal in feudal society, a man who enters into a personal relationship with a lord, to whom he pays homage and swears fealty, in return for protection and/or a fief, grant or benefice of land or stock.

MAPS AND GENEALOGICAL TABLES

Map 1 Ecclesiastical foundations mentioned in the Annals of Ulster

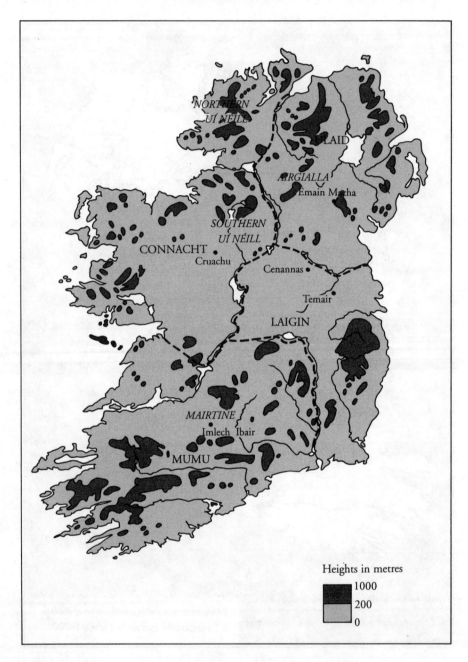

Map 2 Provincial boundaries and principal power-groups *c.* AD500

Map 3 Principal dynasties and population-groups *c.* AD700

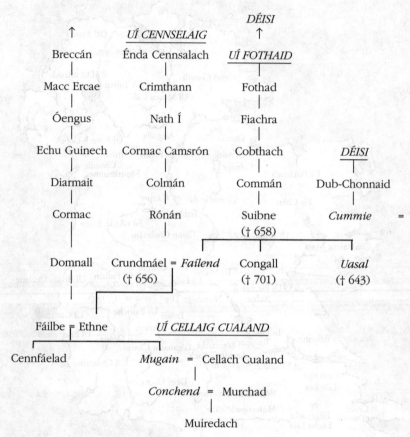

Principal Leinster tribes and their marriage alliances, *c.* 550–*c.* 700 (note: names of women are italicized)

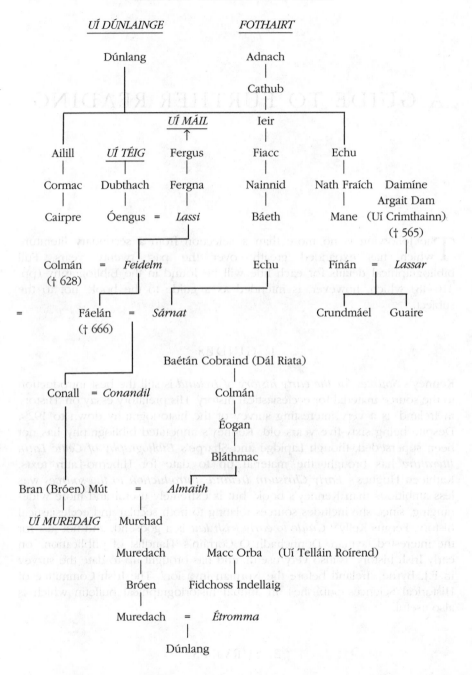

A GUIDE TO FURTHER READING

The following is no more than a selection from a secondary literature which has expanded greatly over the past twenty years. Full bibliographical details for each title will be found in the Bibliography (pp. 316–48) which, however, is intended as a guide to the book, not to the subject.

1. GUIDES

Kenney's *Sources for the early history of Ireland* is still the best introduction to the source material for ecclesiastical history. His prefatory essay on 'History in Ireland' is a very interesting survey of the historiography down to 1929. Despite being sixty-five years old, Kenney's annotated bibliography has not been superseded, though Lapidge and Sharpe's *Bibliography of Celtic Latin literature* has brought the material up to date for Hiberno-Latin texts. Kathleen Hughes's *Early Christian Ireland: introduction to the sources* was less ambitious than Kenney's book, but is extremely useful and more wide-ranging, since she includes sources relating to both secular and ecclesiastical history. Fergus Kelly's *Guide to early Irish law* is a godsend, and not just for the interested layman. Donnchadh Ó Corráin's 'Handlist of publications on early Irish history' is also very useful, and has brought up to date the survey in F.J. Byrne, 'Ireland before the Norman invasion'. The Irish Committee of Historical Sciences publishes an annual historiographical bulletin which is also useful.

2. SURVEYS

There were no good general surveys of early Irish history until Gearóid Mac Niocaill and Donnchadh Ó Corráin published their studies of *Ireland before the Vikings* and *Ireland before the Normans* in 1972, and Francis John Byrne published his *Irish kings and high-kings* in 1973. These three volumes revolutionized the study of the period. Michael Richter's *Medieval Ireland*

(1988) is no substitute. It now looks as if the long-awaited first volume of the Royal Irish Academy's *New History of Ireland* will finally appear in 1996 and should provide additional reading-matter (though its long gestation means that the material will not all be new). For the later period Orpen's *Ireland under the Normans* is still indispensable, but readers should also consult James Lydon's *Lordship of Ireland in the middle ages* and the reprint of A.J. Otway-Ruthven's *History of medieval Ireland*, which, though devoted exclusively to the post-twelfth-century era, also has a very useful introductory essay by Kathleen Hughes on the early period.

3. POLITICS

The volumes by Mac Niocaill, Ó Corráin and Byrne provide the essential details of political developments down to 1172. The raw material is notoriously difficult and intimidating and the only criticism one could justly level at those books is that they are perhaps unduly concise and provide no footnoted references to the sources. The *New History of Ireland*, vol. i, will include updated surveys of political developments, broader in scope and more detailed than was possible in this book. Much of the material is discussed by earlier scholars such as Eoin Mac Neill in articles scattered throughout the specialist journals of history and Celtic Studies. Some of his best studies are collected in his *St Patrick*, a valuable book both for the material in it and for the insight it gives into Mac Neill's working methods, which set the standard for all subsequent research.

4. THE CHURCH

By far the greatest bulk of the literature on early Irish history has been devoted to the study of the church. Still the best one-volume treatment of the subject is Kathleen Hughes's *The church in early Irish society*. Ryan's *Irish monasticism* and Gougaud's *Christianity in Celtic lands* – both recently reprinted – are worth looking at, though now dated in many respects. Walsh and Bradley's *History of the Irish church, 400-700 AD* is a very useful introduction, though somewhat pious in places. A useful recent survey is Lisa N. Bitel's *Isle of the saints*. The Late Antique background to the early church is brilliantly treated in MacMullen's *Christianizing the Roman Empire*, which is essential reading. The same author's various essays on Romanization and kindred topics are also valuable. For the Patrician period D.A. Binchy's 'Patrick and his biographers' is still essential reading. The article is hopelessly disorganized but useful as a piece of destructive criticism and an antidote to the 'maudlin flapdoodle' that preceded it. Denis Bethell's 'Originality of the early Irish church' is iconoclastic but thought-provoking. The reinterpretation of the early period offered by Sharpe, 'Some problems concerning the organization of the church', is vitiated by a sometimes wilful use of the evidence. The material discussed by him is treated more succinctly in Corish's 'The pastoral mission in the early Irish church'. For the developments in the Irish church in the eleventh and twelfth centuries, Aubrey Gwynn's various essays are now conveniently reissued in one volume, *The Irish church in the eleventh and twelfth centuries*. A radical reappraisal of the subject is offered by Ó Corráin in his 'Dál Cais – church and dynasty', which contrasts with the pious (but still useful) 'The church of Armagh under lay control' by the late Cardinal Tomás Ó Fiaich.

5. LAWS AND INSTITUTIONS

The pioneering studies of early Irish law by the great Swiss scholar, Rudolf Thurneysen, must still be sought out in the various specialist journals. Translations of one or two have appeared in English, e.g. in Jenkins, *Celtic law papers*, and Charles-Edwards, Owen and Walters, *Lawyers and laymen*, but there is still no collected edition of his papers, which are in German. D.A. Binchy's valuable editions and commentaries are likewise uncollected, but they are at least in English, for those who are willing to seek them out. Binchy's *Corpus Iuris Hibernici* is a six-volume diplomatic edition of the principal texts, but without translation, index, summary, or word-list. For many texts, therefore, the much maligned nineteenth-century editions in the *Ancient laws of Ireland* (described by the great Whitley Stokes as 'a curiosity of official scholarship') are still the only printed versions available with translation. For those not initiated into the secrets of Old Irish (particularly legal Old Irish) Kelly's *Guide* is a godsend and supersedes Mac Neill's disappointing *Early Irish laws and institutions*. Charles-Edwards's *Early Irish and Welsh kinship* is a monumental study of the material on that subject. His review of Binchy's *Corpus* offers a very useful brief guide to the nature of the Irish laws, while his chapter in the forthcoming *New History of Ireland* promises to provide a comprehensive survey of the subject. The material on marriage is collected and discussed in Binchy, *Studies in early Irish law*, on which Donnchadh Ó Corráin has provided useful commentaries, especially his chapter in *Marriage in Irish society* (edited by Art Cosgrove). Specialist studies have recently appeared relating to contract law and the system of sureties: Neil McLeod, *Early Irish contract law*, and Robin Stacey Chapman, *The road to judgement: from custom to court in medieval Ireland and Wales*.

6. ECONOMY AND SOCIETY

The best brief summary is Ó Corráin's *Ireland before the Normans*, chapter 2, which brings together all the earlier published work scattered through the archaeological and historical journals. There is, unfortunately, nothing yet for Ireland to compare with H.P.R. Finberg's *Agrarian history of England and Wales* (which is unreliable in its treatment of early medieval Ireland). Where the earlier literature tended to concentrate almost exclusively on the archaeological and legal evidence (e.g. Proudfoot's 'Economy of the Irish rath' – a pioneering study), more recent studies have tried to integrate the material and present it in more coherent form, e.g. in Doherty's 'Aspects of hagiography as a source of Irish economic history' and Gerriets, 'Economy and society: clientship according to the Irish laws', and 'Kingship and exchange in pre-Viking Ireland'. The only systematic thematic study to date is Lucas's *Cattle in ancient Ireland*.

7. SCHOOLS AND LEARNING

The question of Christian and pre-Christian learning in Ireland has been attracting considerable scholarly attention in the last few years, with diametrically opposite views being expressed, sometimes with vigour. The most radical re-evaluation of the earlier position is that offered by McCone, *Pagan past and Christian present*, which seeks to demolish the more conservative views of scholars such as Kenneth Jackson, whose *Oldest Irish tradition: a window on the Iron Age* is perhaps the best representative of the older school of thought. The case for the survival of pre-Christian schools of law and poetry into the Christian era is argued by Charles-Edwards, in his review of Binchy's *Corpus*, but is roundly dismissed by Ó Corráin, Breatnach and Breen in 'Laws of the Irish' and Breatnach's 'Canon law and secular law in early Ireland'. Fundamental to the whole question still is Mac Neill's 'Beginnings of Latin culture' and 'A pioneer of nations', for their clarity and conciseness. The question of literacy has been discussed in several important articles by Anthony Harvey; Stevenson, 'The beginnings of literacy in Ireland' and 'Literacy in Ireland: the evidence of the Patrick dossier' add nothing new to the argument, but the first is a useful survey of the earlier literature. Though there are several guides to the material (e.g. Kenney, Lapidge and Sharpe, and Esposito's essays) there is, strange to say, still no satisfactory one-volume survey of the topic. Douglas Hyde's *Literary history of Ireland*, though interesting, is now badly dated.

The study of Latin grammar in the Christian schools has, curiously, attracted most scholarly attention in the last twenty-odd years. Following (and in part revising) Löfstedt's pioneering *Malsachanus*, Vivien Law has provided a useful guide to the material in her *Insular Latin grammarians*, though her treatment is rather tendentious and underplays the importance of the Irish contribution in this field. Holtz's monumental *Donat* has a comprehensive introduction, and his various articles are all very valuable. The crucial role of grammar in the curriculum is brilliantly conveyed by Kaster, *Guardians of language*.

Biblical studies has enjoyed almost as much popularity as grammar, with Kenney's *Sources* providing the early inspiration. Bischoff's ground-breaking 'Wendepunkte' re-opened the field with its appearance in 1954, and most research since then has centred on his catalogue of Irish and Irish-related texts. Chief contributor in this field has been Martin McNamara, whose publications have set the standard. The various essays collected together in the 'Ireland and Europe' series of publications (e.g. Löwe, *Die Iren und Europa*, and the follow-up volumes edited by Ní Chatháin and Richter) offer a useful panorama of the material. A handy bibliography of the last twenty years' work is Kelly's 'Catalogue of early medieval Hiberno-Latin biblical commentaries'.

Still indispensable in the field of computistics is Jones's *Bedae opera de temporibus*, with its brilliant introductory survey of the material. My own researches have, I hope, advanced the study of the material on various points, particularly the articles on 'Mo-Sinu maccu Min' and 'The Irish provenance of Bede's computus', while the central text has appeared in a new edition by Maura Walsh and myself, *Cummian's letter 'De controuersia paschali'*, with an introduction that brings the discussion up to date.

For the Irish contribution abroad Gougaud's *Christianity in Celtic lands* is still handy, though Helen Waddell's famous book, *The wandering scholars* is by far the most evocative account. Bieler's *Ireland: harbinger of the middle ages* (which appeared originally in German) is an excellent general survey.

8. KINGS AND KINGSHIP

Byrne's *Irish kings and high-kings* is essential reading on this subject, along with Ó Corráin's 'Nationality and kingship'. I have deliberately steered clear of the vast literature in Old Irish discussed by Myles Dillon, *The cycles of the kings*, since it has provided little more than a happy hunting ground for mythologists and folklorists. For the legal and technical rules relating to kingship Mac Neill's 'Ancient Irish law: the law of status or franchise' provides an English translation of the basic text, which is edited (without translation, but with a very useful glossary) in Binchy, *Críth Gablach*. On the vexed question of royal ordination, Enright's *Iona, Tara and Soissons* has generated some controversy. On regnal succession, Ó Corráin's 'Irish regnal succession: a reappraisal' reopened discussion, which had been more-or-less dormant since Mac Neill had discussed the subject in a famous paper in his *Celtic Ireland*.

9. KINGDOMS AND PEOPLES

Byrne's 'Tribes and tribalism' is an excellent introduction to this subject, and elaborates on some of the material in his *Irish kings and high-kings*. The same author's 'Ireland of St Columba' is a model treatment of the evidence for the sixth century. The raw material is contained in O'Brien's *Corpus genealogiarum* and other (often unpublished) manuscript collections, and still awaits systematic treatment that would be accessible to the non-specialist reader. A start was made by Ó Corráin with 'Irish origin legends and genealogy' but there is much still to be done. Byrne's '*Senchas*' is also helpful. A bold attempt to integrate historical and genealogical material with a geographical approach was made by Smyth in *Celtic Leinster*. His earlier papers in *Études Celtiques* were a 'dry-run' for the book. The older studies by Liam Ó Buachalla relating to political developments in the south-west of Ireland deserve credit for what they produced from very unpromising and scanty material.

10. THE VIKING AGE

As I write these words Poul Holm's 'Vikings in Irish and Scandinavian history' has just appeared, with its very interesting review of historiography in Scandinavia and Ireland. The Vikings have tended to be curiously neglected in modern Irish historiography, following a period when they were the *bêtes noires* of Irish history. The first attempt at a reasoned and dispassionate account of their impact is Ó Corráin's *Ireland before the Normans*, chapter 3, though it must be said that the path was laid by the pioneering studies of Lucas: 'Irish-Norse relations: time for a reappraisal?' and 'The plundering and burning of churches in Ireland' (the latter marred, however, by a too indiscriminate use of statistical evidence). Walsh's 1922 study of *Scandinavian relations with Ireland during the Viking period* was really excellent for its time. The more sympathetic treatments by Scandinavian scholars have not always received the attention they deserved from Irish historians. Smyth's several books on the Vikings in Britain and Ireland have received mixed reviews; Ó Corráin's 'High-kings, Vikings, and other kings' is a particularly severe critique of Smyth's use of evidence. Still useful is the collection of essays in Ó Cuív, *The impact of the Scandinavian invasions*, which review the Viking influence on language, art, and literature, as well as politics. Sawyer's *Kings and Vikings* is an excellent modern treatment which presents Viking activity against its Scandinavian and European background and sets their Irish impact in context. Analysis of the material remains of the Viking presence in Ireland has been revolutionized by the excavations of the Viking Dublin settlement at Woodquay, for which Wallace's various essays and his two-volume study are essential reading.

11. POST-VIKING IRELAND

The eleventh and twelfth centuries have tended to be seen as a new Dark Age in Irish history, with Ireland a 'trembling sod' under the marching feet and tramping hooves of rival armies in a never-ending cycle of wars and military campaigns – though whether warfare was, in fact, any more 'endemic' in Ireland at that time than, say, in Stephen's England, is debateable. The situation has been redressed somewhat by Ó Corráin's *Ireland before the Normans* and Byrne's *Irish kings and high-kings*, and also

Byrne's splendid essay in the *New history of Ireland*, vol. ii. The concentration in the past has been almost exclusively on politics and ecclesiastical affairs, to the neglect of nearly every other aspect of Irish society at the time. However, the flourishing literary and artistic activity of the period – to which I have not had the opportunity to do full justice here – is well illustrated by, e.g., Henry and Marsh-Micheli's 'Century of Irish illumination' and Henry's *Irish art in the Romanesque period*. The so-called twelfth-century reform of the church – a largely superficial transformation – has been well documented in Gwynn's various studies, though useful counters to his excessively pious approach have been offered by Bethell's 'English monks and Irish reform' and Ó Corráin's 'Dál Cais – church and dynasty'. Likewise, Ó Fiaich's 'The church of Armagh under lay control' is nicely balanced by a more recent study from Dorothy Africa, 'St. Malachy the Irishman: kinship, clan, and reform' and Candon's articles. The *New History of Ireland*, vol. 1, will contain a number of contributions which should revise the older thinking on the period. For the relations between the Viking town of Dublin and the Norse kingdom of Man, see Seán Duffy, 'Irishmen and Islesmen in the kingdoms of Dublin and Man, 1052–1171' in *Ériu*, xliii (1992), pp. 92–133, and Benjamin Hudson, 'Knútr and Viking Dublin' in *Scandinavian Studies*, lxvi, pt. 3 (Summer 1994). pp. 319–35.

The transition period of the late twelfth century and after has been curiously neglected by Irish historians, mainly because students of early Irish history have tended to draw the line at AD1172, while historians of the later period have, in their turn, tended to ignore the earlier centuries as a rather exotic and slightly distasteful prelude to the centuries of 'civilization'. This pattern has not yet been broken, though Katherine Simms's *Kings to warlords* is a bold attempt to straddle the two periods. Flanagan's *Irish society, Anglo-Norman settlers* has some interesting points to make and is better than Otway-Ruthven's *Medieval Ireland*, which paid no attention to native sources. Frame's *English lordship in Ireland* leads off with the fourteenth century, which leaves Orpen's *Ireland under the Normans* as far and away the best survey still of the period after 1169. George Cunningham, *The Anglo-Norman advance into the south-west midlands of Ireland 1185–1221* (Roscrea 1987) is a pioneering study that combines historical, archaeological, and geographical approaches in an interesting way.

BIBLIOGRAPHY

Abrams, Lesley and Carley, James (eds) (1991), *The archaeology and history of Glastonbury Abbey. Essays in honour of the ninetieth birthday of C.A. Ralegh Radford* (Woodbridge).

Adamson, Ian (1974), *The Cruthin. A history of the Ulster land and people* (Belfast).

Adamson, Ian (1979), *Bangor, light of the world* (Belfast).

Adriaen, Marc (ed.) (1969), *Ecloga quam scripsit Lathcen filius Baith de Moralibus Iob quas Gregorius fecit* in *CCSL*, cxlv (Turnhout).

Africa, Dorothy (1985), 'St. Malachy the Irishman: kinship, clan, and reform' in *Harvard Celtic Colloquium*, x, pp. 103–27.

Ahlqvist, Anders (ed.) (1982), *The early Irish linguist* (Helsinki).

Ahlqvist, Anders (1983), Review of Law (1982), in *Cambridge Medieval Celtic Studies*, vi, pp. 100–1.

Alenstam-Petersson, Brita (1951–52), 'Irish imports into south Sweden' in *Bulletin de la Société Royale des Lettres de Lund*, pp. 233–42.

Alexander, J.J.G. (1978), *Insular manuscripts 6th to the 9th century* (Survey of manuscripts illuminated in the British Isles, i) (London).

Almqvist, Bo and Greene, David (eds) (1976), *Proceedings of the Seventh International Viking Congress* (Dublin).

Anderson, Alan O. and Anderson, Marjorie O. (eds) (1961), *Adomnan's Life of Columba* (Edinburgh).

Anderson, W.B. (ed.) (1963), *Sidonius, poems and letters* (2 vols), Loeb Classical Library (Cambridge, Mass. and London).

Andersson, T. and Sandred K.I. (eds) (1978), *The Vikings* (Acta Universitatis Upsaliensis, viii) (Uppsala).

Andrews, J.H. (1985), *Plantation acres: an historical survey of the Irish land surveyor and his maps* (Belfast).

Anton, Hans Hubert (1982), 'Pseudo-Cyprian: *De duodecim abusivis saeculi* und sein Einfluss auf den Kontinent, insbesondere auf die karolingischen Fürstenspiegel' in Löwe (1982), ii, pp. 568–617.

Armstrong, E.R.C. and Macalister, R.A.S. (1920), 'Wooden book with leaves indented and waxed found near Springmount Bog, Co. Antrim' in *Journal of the Royal Society of Antiquaries of Ireland [JRSAI]*, l, pp. 160–6.

Atsma, Hartmut (1983), 'Kloster und Mönchtum in Auxerre' in *Francia*, xi, pp. 1–96.

(Pseudo-)Augustinus Hibernicus, *De mirabilibus sacrae scripturae* in *MPL*, xxxv, cols 2149–200.

Bagnall, Roger S. (1982), 'Religious conversion and onomastic change in early Byzantine Egypt' in *Bulletin of the American Society of Papyrologists*, xix, pp. 105–24.

Bailie, M.L.G. (1980), 'Dendrochronology – the Irish view' in *Current Archaeology*, lxxiii, pp. 62–3.

Bannerman, John (1974), *Studies in the history of Dalriada* (Edinburgh).

Bardy, Gustave (ed.) (1950a), *Saint Germain d'Auxerre et son temps* (Auxerre).

Bardy, Gustave (ed.) (1950b), 'Constance de Lyon, biographe de saint Germain d'Auxerre' in Bardy (1950a), pp. 88–108.

Barley, M.W. and Hanson, R.P.C. (eds) (1968), *Christianity in Britain, 300–700* (Leicester).

Barlow, Claude (1969), *Iberian Fathers (2): Braulio of Saragossa, Fructuosus of Braga* (The Fathers of the Church, a new translation, lxiii) (Washington, D.C.).

Barlow, Frank (1994), review of Flanagan (1989) in *Peritia*, viii, pp. 237–9.

Barrow, G.W.S. (1981), *Kingship and unity: Scotland 1000–1306* (The New History of Scotland, ii) (London).

Barry, John (ed.) (1974), *Historical Studies*, ix (Belfast).

Bately, Janet, Brown, Michelle and Roberts, Jane (eds) (1993), *A palaeographer's view: Selected writings of Julian Brown* (London).

Becker, Gustav (1885), *Catalogi bibliothecarum antiqui* (Bonn).

Beeson, Charles H. (1932), 'Insular symptoms in the commentaries on Vergil' in *Studi Medievali*, 3rd Series, v, pp. 81–100.

Berg, Dieter (1987), *Die Anglo-Normannen und das Kontinent: Studien zur auswärtigen Politik der anglonormannischen Könige im 11. und 12. Jahrhundert* (Bochum).

Bergin, Osborn (1914), 'What brought the Saxons to Ireland' in *Ériu*, vii, pt. ii, p. 244.

Bergin, Osborn (1930), 'The mythology of Lough Neagh' in *Béaloideas*, ii, pp. 246–52.

Bergmann, Werner (1993), 'Dicuils *De mensura orbis terrae*' in Butzer and Lohrmann (1993), pp. 525–37.

Bernt, Günter, Rädle, Fidel and Silagi, Gabriel (eds) (1989), *Tradition und Wertung: Festschrift Franz Brunhölzl* (Sigmaringen).

Bersu, Gerhard (1947), 'The rath in townland Lissue: report on the excavations in 1946' in *Ulster Journal of Archaeology*, x, pp. 30–58.

Best, R.I. (1915), 'The St. Gall incantation against headache' in *Ériu*, viii, pt. 1, p. 100.

Best, R.I. and Bergin, Osborn (eds) (1929), *Lebor na hUidre, the Book of the Dun Cow* (Dublin).

Best, R.I., Bergin, Osborn, O'Brien, M.A. and O'Sullivan, Anne (eds)

(1954–83), *The Book of Leinster, formerly Lebar na Núachongbála* (6 vols) (Dublin).

Bethell, Denis (1971), 'English monks and Irish reform in the eleventh and twelfth centuries' in *Historical Studies*, viii, pp. 111–35.

Bethell, Denis (1981), 'The originality of the early Irish church' in *JRSAI*, cxi, pp. 36–49.

Beyerle, Fritz (ed.) (1947), *Die Gesetze der Langobarden* (Weimar).

Bieler, Ludwig (1950), 'The humanism of St Columbanus' in *Mélanges Columbaniens* (Paris), pp. 95–102.

Bieler, Ludwig (ed.) (1952) *Libri epistolarum Sancti Patricii episcopi* (Dublin) [repr. Dublin 1993].

Bieler, Ludwig (1954), 'The island of scholars' in *Revue du Moyen Age Latin*, viii, pp. 213–34.

Bieler, Ludwig (ed.) (1963a), *The Irish penitentials* (Scriptores Latini Hiberniae, v) (Dublin).

Bieler, Ludwig (1963b), *Ireland, harbinger of the middle ages* (London).

Bieler, Ludwig (ed.) (1974), 'Muirchu's Life of St Patrick as a work of literature' in *Medium Aevum*, xliii, pp. 219–43.

Bieler, Ludwig (1979), *The Patrician texts in the Book of Armagh* (Scriptores Latini Hiberniae, x) (Dublin).

Binchy, D.A. (ed.) (1936), *Studies in early Irish law* (Dublin).

Binchy, D.A. (1938a), 'Bretha Crólige' in *Ériu*, xii, pp. 1–77.

Binchy, D.A. (1938b), 'Sick-maintenance in Irish law' in *Ériu*, xii, pp. 78–134.

Binchy, D.A. (ed.) (1941), *Críth Gablach* (Medieval and Modern Irish Series, xi) (Dublin).

Binchy, D.A. (1952), 'The saga of Fergus mac Léti' in *Ériu*, xvi, pp. 33–48.

Binchy, D.A. (1954), 'Secular institutions' in Dillon (1954), pp. 52–65.

Binchy, D.A. (1955a), 'Bretha Nemed' in *Ériu*, xvii, pp. 4–6.

Binchy, D.A. (1955b), 'Coibnes uisci thairidne' (Irish law tracts re-edited, i) in *Ériu*, xvii, pp. 52–85.

Binchy, D.A. (1956), 'Some Celtic legal terms' in *Celtica*, iii, pp. 221–31.

Binchy, D.A. (1962a), 'Patrick and his biographers, ancient and modern', in *Studia Hibernica*, ii, pp. 7–173.

Binchy, D.A. (1962b), 'The passing of the old order' in Ó Cuív (1962), pp. 119–32.

Binchy, D.A. (1966), 'Bretha Déin Chécht' in *Ériu*, xx, pp. 1–66.

Binchy, D.A. (1968), 'Mellbretha' in *Celtica*, viii, pp. 144–54.

Binchy, D.A. (1970), *Celtic and Anglo-Saxon kingship* (Oxford).

Binchy, D.A. (1971), 'An archaic legal poem' in *Celtica*, ix, pp. 152–68.

Binchy, D.A. (1973a), 'Distraint in Irish law' in *Celtica*, x, pp. 22–71.

Binchy, D.A. (1973b), 'A text on the forms of distraint' in *Celtica*, x, pp. 72–86.

Binchy, D.A. (1975–76), 'Irish history and Irish law (I, II)' in *Studia Hibernica*, xv, pp. 7–36; xvi, pp. 7–45.

Binchy, D.A. (ed.) (1978), *Corpus Iuris Hibernici* (6 vols) (Dublin).

Binchy, D.A. (1982), 'Brewing in eighth-century Ireland' in Scott (1982), pp. 3–6.

Bischoff, Bernhard (1934), 'Die alten Namen der lateinischen Schriftarten' in *Philologus*, lxxxix, pp. 461–5 [repr. Bischoff (1966–67, 1981), i, pp. 1–5].

Bischoff, Bernhard (1954), 'Wendepunkte in der Geschichte der lateinischen Exegese im Frühmittelalter' in *Sacris Erudiri*, vi, pp. 189–279 [repr. in Bischoff (1966–67, 1981), i, pp. 206–73].

Bischoff, Bernhard (1955), 'Theodulf und der Ire Cadac-Andreas' in *Historisches Jahrbuch*, lxxiv, pp. 91–8 [repr. in Bischoff (1966–67, 1981), ii, pp. 19–25].

Bischoff, Bernhard (1957a), 'Die Kölner Nonnenhandschriften und das Skriptorium von Chelles' in *Karolingische Kunst. Werden, Wesen, Wirkung* (Wiesbaden), pp. 395–411 [repr. in Bischoff (1966–67, 1981), i, pp. 16–34].

Bischoff, Bernhard (1957b), 'Il monachesimo irlandese nei suoi rapporti col continente' in *Settimane di Studi del Centro Italiano di Studi sull' Alto Medievo*, iv, pp. 121–38 [repr. in Bischoff (1966– 67, 1981), i, pp. 195–205].

Bischoff, Bernhard (1958), 'Eine verschollene Einteilung der Wissenschaften' in *Archives d'histoire doctrinale et littéraire du moyen âge*, xxv, pp. 5–20 [repr. in Bischoff (1966–67, 1981), i, pp. 273–88].

Bischoff, Bernhard (1961) 'Die europäische Verbreitung der Werke Isidors von Sevilla' in *Isidoriana. Estudios sobre San Isidoro de Sevilla en el XIV centenario de su nacimiento* (Léon), pp. 317–44 [repr. in Bischoff (1966–67, 1981), i, pp. 171–94].

Bischoff, Bernhard (1966–67, 1981), *Mittelalterliche Studien: Ausgewählte Aufsätze zur Schriftkunde und zur Literaturgeschichte* (3 vols) (Stuttgart).

Bischoff, Bernhard (1977), 'Irische Schreiber im Karolingerreich' in *Jean Scot Érigène et l'histoire de la philosophie* (Actes des Colloques Internationaux du CNRS, Laon 1975) (Paris), pp. 47–58 [repr. in Bischoff (1966–67, 1981), iii, pp. 39–54].

Bischoff, Bernhard (1990), *Latin palaeography: antiquity and the middle ages* (Cambridge).

Bischoff, Bernhard (1988 [1991]), 'Die "Zweite Latinität" des Virgilius Maro Grammaticus und seine jüdische Herkunft' in *Mittellateinisches Jahrbuch*, xxiii, pp. 11–16.

Bischoff, Bernhard and Bieler, Lugwig (1956), 'Fragmente zweier mittelalterlichen Schulbücher aus Glendalough' in *Celtica*, iii, pp. 216–20.

Bischoff, Bernhard and Löfstedt, Bengt (eds) (1992), *Anonymus ad Cuimnanum, Expossitio Latinitatis* in *CCSL*, cxxxiii D (Turnhout).

Bitel, Lisa M. (1990), *Isle of the saints. Monastic settlement and Christian community in early Ireland* (Ithaca and London).

Blair, Peter Hunter (1939), 'Olaf the White and the Three Fragments of Irish annals' in *Viking: Tidskrift for nørron arkeolgi*, iii, pp. 1–27 [repr. in Lapidge and Blair (1984), chapter 1].

Blindheim, Charlotte (1978), 'Trading problems in the Viking age' in Andersson and Sandred (1978), pp. 166–76.

Bloch, Marc (1966), *French rural history* (Berkeley and Los Angeles).

Bloch, Marc (1967a), *Land and work in medieval Europe: Selected papers* (London).

Bloch, Marc (1967b), 'The advent and triumph of the watermill' in Bloch (1967a), pp. 136–68.

Blume, Clemens (ed.) (1908), *Hymnodia Hiberno-Celtica* (Analecta Hymnica, li) (Leipzig).

Bøe, Johannes (1940), 'Norse antiquities in Ireland' in Shetelig (1940–54), iii, pp. 12–25.

Boll, Franz (ed.) (1909–20), *Vorlesungen und Abhandlungen* (3 vols) (Munich).

Bollandus, Iohannes (ed.) (1643–), *Acta Sanctorum quotquot toto orbe coluntur*, etc.

Bonner, Gerald (ed.) (1976), *Famulus Christi: Essays in commemoration of the 13th centenary of the birth of the Venerable Bede* (London).

Borgolte, Michael and Spilling, Herrad (eds) (1988), *Litterae medii aevi: Festschrift für Johanne Autenrieth zu ihrem 65. Geburtstag* (Sigmaringen).

Borst, Arno (ed.) (1974), *Mönchtum, Episkopat und Adel* (Vorträge und Forschungen, 20) (Darmstadt).

Bourke, Cormac (1991), 'The Blackwater shrine' in *Dúiche Néill*, Journal of the O Neill Country Historical Society, No. 6, pp. 103–6.

Bourke, Cormac (1993), *Patrick: the archaeology of a saint* (Belfast).

Bowman, Alan K. (1983), *The Roman writing tablets from Vindolanda* (London).

Bradley, John (ed.) (1984), *Viking Dublin exposed: the Wood Quay saga* (Dublin).

Bradley, John (1987), 'Recent archaeological research on the Irish town' in Jäger (1987), pp. 321–70.

Bradley, John (ed.) (1988a), *Settlement and society in medieval Ireland: Studies presented to Francis Xavier Martin O.S.A.* (Kilkenny).

Bradley, John (1988b), 'The interpretation of Scandinavian settlement in Ireland' in Bradley (1988a), pp. 49–78.

Bradley, John (1991), 'Excavations at Moynagh Lough, County Meath' in *JRSAI*, cxxi, pp. 5–26.

Breatnach, Liam (1984), 'Canon law and secular law in early Ireland: the significance of *Bretha Nemed*' in *Peritia*, iii, pp. 439–59.

Breatnach, Liam (1989), 'The first third of *Bretha Nemed toísech* in *Ériu*, xl, pp. 1–40.

Breatnach, Pádraig A. (ed.) (1977), *Die Regensburger Schottenlegende–Libellus de fundacione ecclesiae Consecrati Petri* (Münchener Beiträge zur Mediävistik und Renaissanceforschung, xxvii) (Munich).

Breatnach, Pádraig A. (1984), Review of Law (1982) in *Celtica*, xvi, pp. 182–6.

Brown, C. Gaskell and Harper A. (1984), 'Excavations on Cathedral Hill, Armagh, 1968' in *Ulster Journal of Archaeology*, xlvii, pp. 109–61.

Brown T.J. (1975), 'An historical introduction to the use of classical Latin authors in the British Isles from the fifth to the eleventh century' in *Settimane di studio del Centro Italiano di Studi sull' alto medioevo*, xxii, pp. 237–99 (Spoleto) [repr. in Bately, Brown and Roberts (1993), pp. 141–77].

Brown, T.J. (1982), 'The insular system of scripts to circa AD850' in Löwe (1982), i, pp. 101–19 [repr. in Bately, Brown and Roberts (1993), pp. 201–20].

Brundage, James A. (1987), *Law, sex, and Christian society in medieval Europe* (Chicago).

Brunhölzl, Franz (1988), 'Die sogenannten Afrikaner. Bemerkungen zu einem paläographisch-überlieferungsgeschichtlichen Problem' in Borgolte and Spilling (1988), pp. 17–26.

Bugge, Alexander S. (1900), *Contributions to the history of the Norsemen in Ireland* (Christiania [Oslo]).

Bugge, Alexander S. (1904–06), *Vikingerne* (2 vols) (Copenhagen and Christiania [Oslo]).

Bu'lock, J. (1956), 'Early Christian memorial formulae' in *Archaeologia Cambrensis*, cv, pp. 133–41.

Burn, A.E. (ed.) (1909), *Facsimiles of the Creed from early manuscripts* (Henry Bradshaw Society Publications, xxxvi) (London).

Bury, J.B. (1905), *The life of St. Patrick and his place in history* (London).

Butzer, Paul and Lohrmann, Dietrich (eds) (1993), *Science in western and eastern civilization in Carolingian times* (Basel).

Byrne, Francis John (1958), 'Éoganacht Ninussa' in *Éigse*, ix, pp. 18–19.

Byrne, Francis John (1965), 'The Ireland of St Columba' in McCracken (1965), pp. 37–58.

Byrne, Francis John (1967), 'Seventh-century documents' in *Irish Ecclesiastical Record* [*IER*], 5th Series, cviii, pp. 164–82.

Byrne, Francis John (1971a), 'Tribes and tribalism in early Ireland' in *Ériu*, xxii, pp. 128–66.

Byrne, Francis John (1971b), 'Ireland before the Norman invasion' in Moody (1971), pp. 1–15.

Byrne, Francis John (1973), *Irish kings and high-kings* (London).

Byrne, Francis John (1974) '*Senchas*: the nature of Gaelic historical tradition' in Barry (1974), pp. 137–59.

Byrne, Francis John (1979), *1000 years of Irish script* (Exhibition catalogue) (Oxford).

Byrne, Francis John (1980), 'Derrynavlan: the historical context' in *JRSAI*, clx, pp. 116–26.

Byrne, Francis John (1982a), 'Varia III, 2 (*cadessin*)' in *Ériu*, xxxiii, pp. 167–9.

Byrne, Francis John (1982b), 'Chronology (B) 432–1169' in Moody, Martin and Byrne (1982), viii, pp. 16–71.

Byrne, Francis John (1984), 'Genealogical tables' in Moody, Martin and Byrne (1984), ix, pp. 16–71.

Calder, George (ed.) (1917), *Auraicept na n-Éces. 'The scholar's primer'* (Edinburgh).

Cahill, Michael (1994), 'Is the first commentary on Mark an Irish work?' in *Peritia*, viii, pp. 35–45.

Callahan, Philip S. (1984), *Ancient mysteries, modern visions: the magnetic life of agriculture* (Kansas, Missouri).

Campbell, Alistair (ed.) (1938), *The Battle of Brunanburh* (London).

Campbell, Alistair (ed.) (1967), *Aethelwulf's 'De abbatibus'* (Oxford).

Campbell, James (1973), 'Observations on the conversion of England' in

Ampleforth Journal, lxxviii, pp. 12-26 [repr. in Campbell (1986a), pp. 155–70].

Campbell, James (1986a), *Essays in Anglo-Saxon history* (London).

Campbell, James (1986b), 'Observations on English government from the tenth to the twelfth century' in Campbell (1986a), pp. 155–70.

Campbell, James (1986c), 'The significance of the Anglo- Norman state in the administrative history of western Europe' in Campbell (1986a), pp. 171–89.

Candon, Anthony (1988), 'Muirchertach Ua Briain, politics and naval activity in the Irish Sea' in Mac Niocaill and Wallace (1989), pp. 397–415.

Candon, Anthony (1991), 'Barefaced effrontery: secular and ecclesiastical politics in early twelfth century Ireland' in *Seanchas Ardmhacha*, xiv, pp. 1–25.

Cappuyns, Maieul (1933), *Jean Scot Érigène, sa vie, son oeuvre, sa pensée* (Louvain).

Carley, James and Dooley, Ann (1991), 'An early Irish fragment of Isidore of Seville's *Etymologiae*' in Abrams and Carley (1991), pp. 135–61.

Carney, James (1955), *Studies in Irish literature and history* (Dublin).

Carney, James (1967), *Medieval Irish lyrics* (Dublin).

Carney, James (1973), *The Problem of St. Patrick* (Dublin).

Carney, James (1978–79), 'Aspects of archaic Irish' in *Éigse*, xvii, pp. 417–33.

Casey, P.J. (ed.) (1979), *The end of Roman Britain* (British Archaeological Reports, British Series, lxxi) (Oxford).

Chadwick, Nora K. (ed.) (1958a), *Studies in the early British church* (Cambridge).

Chadwick, Nora K. (1958b), 'Early culture and learning in North Wales' in Chadwick (1958a), pp. 29–120.

Chadwick, Nora K. (1962), 'The Vikings and the western world' in Ó Cuív (1962), pp. 13–42.

Charles, B.G. (1934), *Old Norse relations with Wales* (Cardiff).

Charles-Edwards, Thomas (1971), 'The heir-apparent in Irish and Welsh law' in *Celtica*, ix, pp. 180–90.

Charles-Edwards, Thomas (1972a), 'Kinship, status, and the origin of the hide' in *Past and Present*, lvi, pp. 3–33.

Charles-Edwards, Thomas (1972b), 'Note on common farming' in Hughes (1972a), pp. 61–4.

Charles-Edwards, Thomas (1980), Review of Binchy (1978) in *Studia Hibernica*, xx, pp. 141–62.

Charles-Edwards, Thomas (1984), 'The church and settlement' in Ní Chatháin and Richter (1984), pp. 167–75.

Charles-Edwards, Thomas (1993a), 'Palladius, Prosper, and Leo the Great: mission and primatial authority' in Dumville (1993), pp. 1–12.

Charles-Edwards, Thomas (1993b), *Early Irish and Welsh kinship* (Oxford).

Charles-Edwards, T., Owen, M. and Walters, D. (eds) (1986), *Lawyers and laymen: Studies in the history of law presented to Dafydd Jenkins on his seventy-fifth birthday* (Cardiff).

Chavanon, Jules (ed.) (1897), *Ademar de Chabannes, Chronique* (Paris).

Christiansen, Rheidar T. (1962), 'The people of the north' in *Lochlann*, ii, pp. 137–64.

Clanchy, M.T. (1974), 'Law, government, and society in medieval England' in *History*, lix, No. cxcv, pp. 73–8.

Clarke, H.B. (1977), 'The topographical development of early medieval Dublin' in *JRSAI*, cvii, pp. 29–51.

Clarke, H.B. and Brennan, Mary (eds) (1981), *Columbanus and Merovingian monasticism* (British Archaeological Reports, International Series, cxiii) (Oxford).

Clarke, H.B. and Simms, Anngret (eds) (1985), *The comparative history of urban origins in non-Roman Europe: Ireland, Wales, Denmark, Germany, Poland and Russia from the ninth to the thirteenth century* (British Archaeological Reports, International Series, cclv) (Oxford).

Clemoes, Peter and Hughes, Kathleen (eds) (1971), *England before the Conquest: studies presented to Dorothy Whitelock* (Cambridge).

Colgan, John (1645), *The 'Acta sanctorum Hiberniae' of John Colgan* (Louvain 1645; repr. 1947 Dublin).

Colgrave, Bertram (ed.) (1927), *The Life of Bishop Wilfrid by Eddius Stephanus* (Cambridge).

Colgrave, Bertram (1940), *Two 'Lives' of Saint Cuthbert* (Cambridge).

Colgrave, Bertram and Mynors, R.A.B. (eds) (1969), *Bede's 'Ecclesiastical History of the English people'* (Oxford Medieval Texts) (Oxford).

Cone, Polly (ed.) (1977), *Treasures of early Irish art, 1500 BC to 1500 AD* (New York).

Connolly, Seán and Picard, Jean-Michel (1987), 'Cogitosus's *Life of St Brigit*, content and value', *JRSAI*, cxvii, pp. 5–27.

Conrat (Cohn), Max (1908), 'Ein Traktat über romanischfränkisches Ämterwesen' in *Zeitschrift der Savigny-Stiftung*, Germ. Abt., xxix, pp. 239–60.

Contreni, John J. (1978), *The cathedral school of Laon from 850 to 930, its manuscripts and masters* (Münchener Beiträge zur Mediävistik und Renaissanceforschung, xxix) (Munich).

Contreni, John J. (1982), 'The Irish in the western Carolingian empire (according to James F. Kenney and Bern, Burgerbibliothek 363)' in Löwe (1982), ii, pp. 758–98.

Coplestone-Crow, B. (1981–82), 'The dual nature of the Irish colonization of Dyfed in the Dark Ages' in *Studia Celtica*, xvi–xvii, pp. 1–24.

Corish, Patrick (1971), 'The pastoral mission in the early Irish Church' in *Léachtaí Cholm Cille*, ii, pp. 14–25.

Cosgrove, Art (ed.) (1985), *Marriage in Irish society* (Dublin).

Cramp, Rosemary (1993), 'A reconsideration of the monastic site at Whitby' in Spearman and Higgitt (1993), pp. 64–73.

Crawford, Barbara E. (1987), *Scandinavian Scotland* (Scotland in the Early Middle Ages) (Leicester).

Crump, C.G. and Jacob, E.F. (eds) (1926), *The legacy of the middle ages* (Oxford).

Cubitt, Catherine (1989), 'Wilfrid's "usurping bishops": episcopal elections in Anglo-Saxon England, *c*.600–*c*.800' in *Northern History*, xxv, pp. 18–38.

Curtis, Edmund (1921), 'Murchertach O'Brien, high king of Ireland, and his Norman son-in-law, Arnulf de Montgomery, circa 1100' in *JRSAI*, xx, pp. 116–24.

Curwen, E.C. (1944), 'The problem of early water-mills' in *Antiquity*, xviii, pp. 130–46.

Darmon, Pierre (1985), *Trial by impotence: virility and marriage in pre-Revolutionary France* (London).

Davies, R.R. (1979), 'Kings, lords and liberties in the Marches of Wales, 1066–1276' in *Transactions of the Royal Historical Society*, xxix, pp. 41–61.

Davies, Wendy (1982a), *Wales in the early middle ages* (Leicester).

Davies, Wendy (1982b), 'The Latin charter-tradition in western Britain, Brittany and Ireland in the early medieval period' in Whitelock, McKitterick and Dumville (1982), pp. 258–80.

Davies, Wendy and Fouracre, Paul (eds) (1986), *The settlement of disputes in early medieval Europe* (Cambridge).

De Paor, Liam (1976), 'The Viking towns of Ireland' in Almqvist and Greene (1976), pp. 29–37.

De Paor, Liam (1986), *The peoples of Ireland from prehistory to modern times* (London).

De Paor, Liam (1987), 'The high crosses of Tech Theille (Tihilly), Kinnitty, and related sculpture' in Rynne (1987), pp. 131–58.

De Paor, Liam (1993), *Saint Patrick's world. The Christian culture of Ireland's apostolic age* (Dublin).

Díaz y Díaz, Manuel C. (ed.) (1972), *Liber de ordine creaturarum. Un anónimo irlandés del siglo VII* (Monografías de la Universidad de Santiago de Compostela, x) (Santiago de Compostela).

Dickins, Bruce (1952), *The place-names of Cumberland*, iii (Cambridge).

Dill, Samuel (1926) *Roman society in Gaul in the Merovingian age* (London).

Dillon, Myles (1936), 'The relationship of mother and son, of father and daughter, and the law of inheritance with regard to women' in Binchy (1936), pp. 129–79.

Dillon, Myles (1946), *The cycles of the kings* (London).

Dillon, Myles (1951), 'The taboos of the kings of Ireland' in *Proceedings of the Royal Irish Academy [PRIA]*, liv C 1, pp. 1–36.

Dillon, Myles (ed.) (1954), *Early Irish society* (Radio Éireann, Thomas Davis Lecture Series) (Dublin).

Dillon, Myles (1960), 'Laud Misc. 610' in *Celtica*, v, pp. 64–76.

Dillon, Myles (ed.) (1962), *Lebor na Cert, the Book of Rights* (Irish Texts Society, xlvi) (Dublin).

Dillon, Myles (1977), 'The Irish settlements in Wales' in *Celtica*, xii, pp. 1–11.

Dinneen, Patrick S. (ed.) (1906[1908]), *The history of Ireland by Geoffrey Keating* (Irish Texts Society, ix) (London).

Dinneen, P.S. and O'Donoghue, T. (eds) (1909), *Dánta Aodhagáin Uí Rathaille* (Irish Texts Society, iii) (London).

Doherty, Charles (1982), 'Some aspects of hagiography as a source for Irish economic history' in *Peritia*, i, pp. 300–28.

Doherty, Charles (1985), 'The monastic town in Ireland' in Clarke and Simms (1985), pp. 55–63.

Doherty, Charles (1991), 'The cult of St Patrick and the politics of Armagh in the seventh century' in Picard (1991), pp. 53–94.

Dooley, Ann and Stoclet, Alain (1989), 'Autour du sacre de Pépin' in *Le moyen âge*, xcv, pp. 129–34.

Drew, Katherine Fischer (1949), *The Burgundian Code. Book of Constitutions or Law of Gundobad: additional fragments* (Philadelphia).

Drew, Katherine Fischer (1967), 'The barbarian kings as lawgivers and judges' in Hoyt (1967), pp. 7–29 [repr. in Drew (1988), Chapter II].

Drew, Katherine Fischer (1973), *The Lombard laws* (Philadelphia).

Drew, Katherine Fischer (1977), 'The law of the family in the Germanic barbarian kingdoms: a synthesis' in *Studies in Medieval Culture*, xi, pp. 17–26 [repr. in Drew (1988), Chapter VIII.

Drew, Katherine Fischer (1988), *Law and society in early medieval Europe: Studies in legal history* (Variorum Collected Studies Series, cclxxi) (London).

Driscoll, S.T. and Nieke, M.R. (eds) (1988), *Power and politics in early medieval Britain and Ireland* (Edinburgh).

Duft, Johannes (1956), 'Iromanie–Irophobie' in *Zeitschrift für Schweizerische Kirchengeschichte*, l, pp. 241–62.

Duft, Johannes (1982), 'Irische Handschriftenüberlieferung in St. Gallen' in Löwe (1982), ii, pp. 916–37.

Dugmore, C.W. and Duggan, C. (eds) (1964), *Studies in Church History*, i (London).

Duignan, Michael V. (1944), 'Irish agriculture in early historic times' in *JRSAI*, lxxiv, pp. 128–45.

Dümmler, Ernst (ed.) (1884), *MGH, Poetae Latini aevi Carolini [PLAC]*, II (Hannover and Leipzig).

Dümmler, Ernst (ed.) (1902–25), *Monumenta Germaniae Historica [MGH]*, *Epistolae Karolini aevi*, II, III, IV (Hannover and Leipzig).

Dumville, David N. (1979a), 'Kingship, genealogies and regnal lists' in Sawyer and Wood (1979), pp. 72–104.

Dumville, David N. (1979b), 'The Ætheling: a study in Anglo-Saxon constitutional history' in *Anglo–Saxon England*, viii, pp. 1–33.

Dumville, David N. (1984), 'Some British aspects of the earliest Irish Christianity' in Ní Chatháin and Richter (1984), pp. 17–24.

Dumville, David N. (ed.) (1993), *Saint Patrick,* AD493–1993 (Woodbridge).

Dutton, Paul (1984), 'The uncovering of the *Glosae super Platonem* of Bernard of Chartres' in *Mediaeval Studies*, xlvi, pp. 192–221.

Düwel, Klaus, Jankuhn, Herbert, Siems, Harold and Timpe, Dieter (eds) (1987), *Untersuchungen zur Handel und Verkehr der vor- und frühgeschichtlichen Zeit in Mittel- und Nordeuropa*, iv, 'Der Handel der Karolinger- und Wikingerzeit' in *Abhandlungen der Akademie der Wissenschaften in Göttingen*, phil.–hist. Kl., 3. Folge, clvi (Göttingen).

Eckhardt, Karl August (ed.) (1969), *Lex Salica* in *MGH, Leges nationum Germanicarum*, iv, pt. 2 (Munich).

Edwards, R. Dudley (1938), 'Anglo-Norman relations with Connacht, 1169–1224' in *Irish Historical Studies*, i, pp. 135–53.

Ekwall, Eilert (1910), *The Scandinavians and Celts in the north-west of England* (Lund).

Enright, Michael J. (1985), *Iona, Tara and Soissons. The origin of the royal anointing ritual* (Arbeiten zur Frühmittelalterforschung, xvii) (Berlin).

Erichsen, Johannes and Brockhoff, Evamaria (eds) (1989), *Kilian, Mönch aus Irland, aller Franken Patron, 689–1989*, (Veröffentlichungen zur Bayerischen Geschichte und Kultur, xix) (2 vols) (Würzburg).

Esposito, Mario (1907), 'An unpublished astronomical treatise by the Irish monk Dicuil' in *Proceedings of the Royal Irish Academy* [*PRIA*], xxvi C 15, pp. 378–445.

Esposito, Mario (1910), 'Conchubrani Vita Sanctae Monennae' in *PRIA*, xxviii C 12, pp. 202–51.

Esposito, Mario (1919), 'On the pseudo-Augustinian treatise *De mirabilibus sacrae scripturae*' in *PRIA*, xxxv C 2, pp. 189–207.

Esposito, Mario (1920), 'The sources of Conchubranus's Life of St. Monenna' in *English Historical Review*, xxxv, pp. 71–8.

Esposito, Mario (1956), 'The Patrician problem and a possible solution' in *Irish Historical Studies*, x, pp. 131–55.

Esposito, Mario (1961), Review of Walker (1957) in *Classica and Medievalia*, xxi, pp. 184–203.

Etchingham, Colmán (1991), 'The early Irish church: some observations on pastoral care and dues' in *Ériu*, xlii, pp. 99–118.

Evans, D. Ellis, Griffith, John G. and Jope, E.M. (eds) (1986), *Proceedings of the Seventh International Congress of Celtic Studies, Oxford, 1983* (Oxford).

Ewald, Paul and Hartmann, Ludo M. (eds) (1887–99), *Gregorii I papae Registrum epistolarum*. Libri i–vii, viii–xiv (2 vols) (Berlin).

Ewig, Eugen (1974), 'Bemerkungen zu zwei merowingischen Bischofs-privilegien und einem Papstprivileg des 7. Jahrhunderts für merowingische Kloster' in Borst (1974), pp. 215–49.

Fahy, Edward M. (1956), 'A horizontal mill at Mashanaglass, Co. Cork' in *Journal of the Cork Historical and Archaeological Society*, lxi, pp. 13–57.

Fairley, James (1981), *Irish whales and whaling* (Belfast).

Ferrari, Mirella (1972), 'In Papia conveniant ad Dungalum' in *Italia medioevale e umanistica*, xv, pp. 1–52.

Finberg, H.P.R. *et al.* (eds) (1967–), *The agrarian history of England and Wales* (8 vols) (London) [in progress].

Flanagan, Deirdre (1969), 'Ecclesiastical nomenclature in Irish texts and place-names: a comparison' in *Proceedings of the 10th International Congress of Onomastic Sciences* (Vienna) pp. 379–88.

Flanagan, Deirdre (1980), 'Place-names in early Irish documentation: structure and composition' in *Proceedings of the 12th International Congress of Onomastic Sciences* [= *Nomina*, iv] (Vienna), pp. 41–5.

Flanagan, Deirdre (1984), 'The Christian impact on early Ireland: place-names evidence' in Ní Chatháin and Richter (1984), pp. 25–51.

Flanagan, Marie-Therese (1989), *Irish society, Anglo-Norman settlers, Angevin kingship: interactions in Ireland in the late twelfth century* (Oxford).

Flower, Robin (1926), *Catalogue of the Irish manuscripts in the British Musuem*, ii (London).

Flower, Robin (1947), *The Irish tradition* (Oxford).

Foote, P.G. and Wilson, David (1970), *The Viking achievement. The society and culture of early medieval Scandinavia* (London).

Ford, Patrick K. (ed.) (1983), *Celtic folklore and Christianity: essays for W.W. Heist* (Santa Barbara).

Fox, Sir Cyril and Dickins, Bruce (eds) (1950), *The early cultures of north-west Europe (H.M. Chadwick memorial studies)* (Cambridge).

Frend, W.C.H. (1968), 'The Christianization of Roman Britain' in Barley and Hanson (1968), pp. 37–49.

Frend, W.H.C. (1979), 'Ecclesia Britannica: prelude or dead end?' in *Journal of Ecclesiastical History*, xxx, pp. 129–44.

Funaioli, G. (1930), *Esegese Virgiliana antica* (Milan).

Gailey, Alan and Fenton, Alexander (eds) (1970), *The spade in northern and Atlantic Europe* (Belfast).

Ganshof, François Louis (1968), *Frankish institutions under Charlemagne* (Providence, Rhode Island).

Ganz, David and Goffart, Walter (1990), 'Charters earlier than 800 from French collections' in *Speculum*, lxv, pp. 906–32.

Gerriets, Marilyn (1983), 'Economy and society: clientship according to the Irish laws' in *Cambridge Medieval Celtic Studies*, vi, pp. 43–61.

Gerriets, Marilyn (1987), 'Kingship and exchange in pre-Viking Ireland' in *Cambridge Medieval Celtic Studies*, xiii, pp. 39–72.

Goedheer, A.J. (1938), *Irish and Norse traditions about the Battle of Clontarf* (Haarlem).

Goody, Jack (1966), *Succession to high office* (Cambridge).

Gougaud, Louis (1909), 'Le témoignage des manuscrits sur l'oeuvre littéraire du moine Lathcen' in *Revue Celtique*, xxx, pp. 37–46.

Gougaud, Louis (1932), *Christianity in Celtic lands* (London) [repr. Dublin 1993].

Gradara, Carlo (1915), 'I "pueri Aegyptiaci" di Alcuino' in *Roma e l'Oriente*, ix, pp. 83–7.

Graham-Campbell, James (1976), 'The Viking-Age silver hoards of Ireland' in Almqvist and Greene (1976), pp. 39–74.

Greene, David (ed.) (1955), *Fingal Rónáin and other stories* (Medieval and Modern Series, xvi) (Dublin).

Greene, David (1968), 'Some linguistic evidence relating to the British church' in Barley and Hanson (1968), pp. 75–86.

Greene, David (1976), 'The influence of Scandinavian on Irish' in Almqvist and Greene (1976), pp. 76–7.

Greene, David (1977), 'Archaic Irish' in Schmidt (1977), pp. 11–33.

Grimm, Jacob and Grimm, Wilhelm (1984), *Kinder- und Hausmärchen gesammelt durch die Brüder Grimm* (Munich).

Grosjean, Paul (1945), 'Notes chronologiques sur le séjour de S. Patrice en Gaule' ('Notes d'hagiographie celtique, vii') in *Analecta Bollandiana*, lxiii, pp. 73–92.

Grosjean, Paul (1955), 'Sur quelques exégètes irlandais du VIIe siècle' in *Sacris Erudiri*, vii, pp. 67–98.

Gwynn, Aubrey (1941a), 'Lanfranc and the Irish church' in *IER*, lvii, pp. 481-500; lviii, pp. 1–15 [repr. in Gwynn (1992), pp. 68–83].

Gwynn, Aubrey (1941b), 'Gregory VII and the Irish church' in *IER*, lviii, pp. 97–109 [repr. in Gwynn (1992), pp. 84–98].

Gwynn, Aubrey (1952), 'The continuity of the Irish tradition at Würzburg' in *Herbipolis Jubilans: 1200 Jahre Bistum Würzburg* (Festschrift zur Säkularfeier der Erhebung der Kiliansreliquien) (Würzburg), pp. 57–81.

Gwynn, Aubrey (1964), 'The Irish Missal of Corpus Christi College, Oxford' in Dugmore and Duggan (1964), pp. 47–68 [repr. in Gwynn (1992), pp. 17–33].

Gwynn, Aubrey (1978), 'Brian in Armagh (1005)' in *Seanchas Ardmhacha*, ix, pp. 35–50.

Gwynn, Aubrey (1992), *The Irish church in the eleventh and twelfth centuries* (Dublin).

Gwynn, E.J. (ed.) (1903–35), *The Metrical Dindsenchas* (5 vols) (Royal Irish Academy, Todd Lecture Series, viii–xii) (Dublin).

Gwynn, E.J. (1926), 'Sén dollotar Ulaid' in *Ériu*, x, pp. 92–4.

Gwynn, E.J. (1942), 'An Old-Irish treatise on the privileges and responsibilities of poets' in *Ériu*, xiii, pp. 1–60, 220–36.

Hagen, Hermann (1861–67), 'Scholia Bernensia ad Vergili Bucolica atque Georgica' in *Fleckeisens Jahrbücher für classische Philologie*, Supplement iv (Leipzig), pp. 673–1014.

Hagen, Hermann (ed.) (1897), *Augustinus, Beda, Horatius, Ovidius, Servius, alii Codex Bernensis 363* (Codices Graeci et Latini photographice depicti duce Scatone de Vries, Bibliothecae Universitatis Leidensis Praefecto, ii) (Leiden).

Haliday, Charles (1881), *The Scandinavian kingdom of Dublin* (Dublin).

Hamlin, Ann and Lynn, Chris (eds) (1988), *Pieces of the past: archaeological excavations by the Department of the Environment for Northern Ireland 1970–1986* (Belfast).

Hanson, R.P.C. (1970), 'The church in fifth-century Gaul: the evidence of Sidonius Apollinaris' in *Journal of Ecclesiastical History*, xxi, pp. 1–10.

Harrison, Kenneth (1984), 'A letter from Rome to the Irish clergy, AD640' in *Peritia*, iii, pp. 222–29.

Harvey, Anthony (1987), 'Early literacy in Ireland: the evidence from ogam' in *Cambridge Medieval Celtic Studies*, xiv, pp. 1–15.

Harvey, Anthony (1992), 'Latin, literacy and the Celtic vernaculars around the year AD500' in McLennan (1992), pp. 11–26.

Hayes-McCoy, G.A. (ed.) (1976), *Historical Studies*, x (Galway).

Healy, John (1900), 'Early national synods in Ireland', *IER*, 4th Series, 7, pp. 385–99.

Healy, John (1905), *The life and writings of St. Patrick* (Dublin).

Heist, William W. (ed.) (1965), *Vitae sanctorum Hiberniae ex codice olim Salmanticensi nunc Bruxellensi* (Subsidia Hagiographica, xxviii) (Brussels).

Hellmann, Siegmund (ed.) (1909), *Ps.-Cyprianus De xii. abusiuis saeculi* (Texte und Untersuchungen, xxxiv) (Leipzig).

Henry, Françoise (1970), *Irish art in the Romanesque period, 1020–1170 AD* (London).

Henry, Françoise and Marsh-Micheli, Genevieve (1962), 'A century of Irish illumination (1070–1170)' in *PRIA*, lxii C 5, pp. 101–64.

Herbert Máire (1988), *Iona, Kells, and Derry* (Oxford).

Herity Michael (1989), 'The antiquity of *an Turas* (the Pilgrimage Round) in Ireland' in Lehner and Berschin (1989), pp. 95–143.

Herren, Michael (ed.) (1974, 1987), *The Hisperica Famina, I, II* (2 vols) (Pontifical Institute of Mediaeval Studies, Studies and Texts, xxxi, lxxxv) (Toronto).

Herren, Michael (1980), 'On the earliest Irish acquaintance with the works of Isidore of Seville' in James (1980), pp. 243–50.

Herren, Michael (1982), 'Insular Latin C(h)araxare (craxare) and its derivatives' in *Peritia*, i, pp. 273–80.

Herren, Michael (1983), Review of Law (1982) in *Peritia*, ii, pp. 312–16.

Hillgarth, J.N. (1984), 'Ireland and Spain in the seventh century' in *Peritia*, iii, pp. 1–16.

Hogan, James (1920), 'The trícha cét and related land-measures' in *PRIA*, xxxviii C 7, pp. 148–235.

Holder, Alfred (1907), 'Altirische Namen im Reichenauer Codex CCXXXIII' in *Archiv für Celtische Lexikographie*, iii, pp. 266–7.

Holder-Egger, Oswald (ed.) (1887), 'Ex miraculorum S. Vedasti libro II. auctore Ulmaro aliisque', in *MGH, Scriptores*, xv, pp. 399–402 (Hannover and Leipzig).

Holm, Poul (1986), 'The slave trade of Dublin, ninth to twelfth centuries' in *Peritia*, v, pp. 317–45.

Holm, Poul (1994), 'Between apathy and antipathy: the Vikings in Irish and Scandinavian history', in *Peritia*, viii, pp. 151–69.

Holtz, Louis (ed.) (1977a), *Murethach (Muridac), Ars Grammatica* in *Corpus Christianorum* [*CC*], *Continuatio Medievalis* [*CM*], xl (Turnhout).

Holtz, Louis, (1977b), 'Grammairiens irlandais au temps de Jean Scot, quelques aspects de leur pedagogie' in *Jean Scot Érigène et l'histoire de la philosophie* (Actes des Colloques du CNRS, Laon 1975) (Paris), pp. 69–78.

Holtz, Louis (1981a), 'Irish grammarians and the continent in the seventh century' in Clarke and Brennan (1981), pp. 135–52.

Holtz, Louis (1981b), *Donat et la tradition de l'enseignement grammatical. Étude sur l'Ars Donati' et sa diffusion (IVe–IXe siècle) et édition critique* (Paris).

Holtz, Louis (1983), 'Les grammairiens Hiberno-Latins, étaient–ils des Anglo-Saxons?' in *Peritia*, ii, pp. 170–84.

Howlett, David (1989), 'Ex saliva oris meae' in Ó Corráin, Breatnach and McCone (1989), pp. 86–101.

Howlett, David R. (ed.) (1994), *The book of letters of Saint Patrick the bishop* (Dublin).

Hoyt, Robert S. (ed.) (1967), *Life and thought in the early middle ages* (Minneapolis).

Hübner, Aemilius (ed.) (1876), *Inscriptiones Britanniae Christianae* (Berlin and London).

Hudson, Ben (1979), 'The family of Harold Godwinson and the Irish Sea province' in *JRSAI*, cix, pp. 92–100.

Hudson, Benjamin T. and Ziegler, Vickie (eds) (1991), *Crossed paths: methodological approaches to the Celtic aspect of the European middle ages* (Lanham, Maryland).

Hughes, Kathleen (1966), *The church in early Irish society* (London).

Hughes, Kathleen (1968), Introduction to Otway-Ruthven (1968), pp. 1–33.

Hughes, Kathleen (ed.) (1972a), *Early Christian Ireland: introduction to the sources* (The Sources of History: Studies in the Uses of Historical Evidence) (London).

Hughes, Kathleen (1972b), Review of Ó Corráin (1972) in *Studia Hibernica*, xii, pp. 1992–3.

Hughes, Kathleen (1973), 'Sanctity and secularity in the early Irish church', in *Studies in church history*, pp. 21–37.

Hull, Vernam (1966), 'Cáin Domnaig' in *Ériu*, xx, pp. 151–77.

Hunt, R.W. (ed.) (1961), *Saint Dunstan's 'Classbook' from Glastonbury (Oxford, Bodleian Library, MS. Auct. F.4/32* (Umbrae Codicum Occidentalium, iv) (Leyden).

Hurley, Vincent (1982), 'The early church in the south-west of Ireland: settlement and organisation' in Pearce (1982), pp. 297–332.

Hyde, Douglas (1899), *A literary history of Ireland from earliest times to the present day* (London) [repr. Dublin 1980].

Jackson, Kenneth (1950), 'Notes on the ogam inscriptions of southern Britain', in Fox and Dickins (1950), pp. 199–213.

Jackson, Kenneth (1953), *Language and history in early Britain: a chronological survey of the Brittonic languages 1st to 12th c. AD* (Edinburgh).

Jackson, Kenneth (1956), 'The Pictish language' in Wainwright (1956), pp. 129–66.

Jackson, Kenneth (1962), 'The Celtic languages during the Viking period' in Ó Cuív (1962), pp. 3–11.

Jackson, Kenneth (1964), *The oldest Irish tradition: a window on the Iron Age* (The Rede Lecture) (Edinburgh).

Jacobsen, Peter (1982), 'Carmina Columbani' in Löwe (1982), i, pp. 434–67.

Jäger, Helmut (ed.) (1987), *Stadtkernforschung* (Cologne and Vienna).

James, Edward (ed.) (1980), *Visigothic Spain: new approaches* (Oxford).

James, Edward (1982), *The origins of France: from Clovis to the Capetians, 500–1000* (London).

James, M.R. (1921), *A descriptive catalogue of the Latin manuscripts in the John Rylands Library at Manchester* (2 vols) (Manchester).

Jäschke, Kurt-Ulrich (1974), 'Frühes Christentum in Britannien' in *Archiv für Kulturgeschichte*, lvi, pp. 91–123.

Jeauneau, Édouard (1986), 'Pour le dossier d'Israël Scot' in *Archives d'Histoire doctrinale et littéraire du moyen âge*, xxxiv, pt.5 (1986), pp. 7–71.

Jenkins, Dafydd (ed.) (1973), *Celtic law papers introductory to Welsh medieval law and government* (Studies presented to the international Commission for the History of Representative and Parliamentary Institutions, xlii) (Brussels).

Jenkins, Dafydd (1981), 'The medieval Welsh idea of law' in *Tijdschrift voor Rechtsgeschiednis*, xlix, pp. 323–48.

Jenkins, Dafydd (1986), *The Law of Hywel Dda. Law texts from Medieval Wales translated and edited*. The Welsh Classics (Llandysul).

Jenkins, Dafydd (1982), 'Agricultural co-operation in Welsh medieval law' in *Amgueddfa Werin Cymru* (Amgueddfa Genedlaethol Cymru) (Aberystwyth).

Jenkins, Dafydd (1988), Review of Davies and Fouracre (1986) in *Cambridge Medieval Celtic Studies*, xv, pp. 89–92.

Jenkins, Dafydd and Owen, Morfydd (eds) (1980), *The Welsh law of women: studies presented to Prof. D.A. Binchy* (Cardiff).

Jenkins, Geraint (ed.) (1969), *Studies in folk-life: essays in honour of Iorwerth C. Peate* (London).

Jeudy, Colette (1977), 'Israël le grammairien et la tradition manuscrite du commentaire de Rémi d'Auxerre à l'*Ars minor* de Donat' in *Studi Medievali*, 3rd Series, xviii, pp. 187–248.

John, Eric (1970), 'Social and political problems of the early English church' in Thirsk (1970), pp. 39–63.

Jones, Charles W. (ed.) (1943), *Bedae opera de temporibus* (Medieval Academy of America Publications, xli) (Cambridge, Massachusetts).

Jones, Charles W. (1975), 'Carolingian aesthetics: why modular verse?' in *Viator*, vi, pp. 309–40.

Jones, Charles W. (ed.) (1976a), *Bedae Liber de natura rerum* in *CCSL*, cxxiii A (Turnholt).

Jones, Charles W. (1976b), 'Bede in medieval schools' in Bonner (1976), pp. 261–85.

Jones, Glanville R.J. (1983–84), 'The ornaments of a kindred in medieval Gwynedd' in *Studia Celtica*, xviii–xix, pp. 135–46.

Kaster, Robert (1986), 'Islands in the stream: the grammarians of Late Antiquity' in *Historiographia Linguistica*, xiii, pp. 323–42.

Kaster, Robert (1988), *Guardians of language: the grammarian and society in Late Antiquity* (Berkeley).

Kelleher, John V. (1963), 'Early Irish history and pseudo-history' in *Studia Hibernica*, 3, pp. 113–27.

Kelleher, John V. (1979), *Too small for stove wood, too big for kindling* (Dublin).

Kelly, Fergus (1973), 'A poem in praise of Columb Cille' in *Ériu*, xxiv, pp. 1–23.

Kelly, Fergus (1975), 'Tiughraind Bhécáin' in *Ériu*, xxvi, pp. 66–98.

Kelly, Fergus (ed.) (1976a), *Audacht Morainn* (Dublin).

Kelly, Fergus (1976b) 'The Old Irish tree-list' in *Celtica*, xi, pp. 107–24.

Kelly, Fergus (1986) 'An Old Irish text on court procedure' in *Peritia*, v, pp. 74–106.

Kelly, Fergus (1988) *A guide to early Irish law* (Early Irish Law Series, iii) (Dublin).

Kelly, Fergus and Charles-Edwards, Thomas (eds) (1983), *Bechbretha: an Old Irish law-tract on bee-keeping* (Early Irish Law Series, i) (Dublin).

Kelly, Joseph F. (1978), 'Pelagius, pelagianism and the early Irish' in *Medievalia*, iv, pp. 99–124.

Kelly, Joseph F. (1988–90), 'A catalogue of early medieval Hiberno-Latin biblical commentaries' in *Traditio*, xliv, pp. 537–71; xlv, pp. 393–434.

Kenney, James F. (1929), *The sources for the early history of Ireland*, i Ecclesiastical (New York [repr. Dublin 1993]).

Kerlouégan, François (1968–69), 'Essai sur la mise en nourriture et l'éducation dans les pays celtiques d'après le témoignage des textes hagiographiques latines' in *Études Celtiques*, xii, pp. 101–46.

Ker, W.P. (1904), *The Dark Ages* (London [repr. New York, 1958]).

Keynes, Simon and Lapidge, Michael (eds) (1982), *Alfred the Great* (Penguin Classics) (Harmondsworth).

Kiesel, Georges and Schroeder, Jean (eds) (1989), *Willibrord, Apostel der Niederlande, Gründer der Abtei Echternach. Gedenkgabe zum 1250. Todestag des angelsächsischen Missionars* (Echternach).

King, P.D. (1972), *Law and society in the Visigothic kingdom* (Cambridge Studies in Medieval Life and Thought, 3rd Series, v) (Cambridge).

Kissane, Noel (1977), '*Uita metrica sanctae Brigidae*' in *PRIA*, lxxvii C 3, pp. 57–192.

Klingshirn, William (1985), 'Charity and power: Caesarius of Arles and the ransoming of captives in sub-Roman Gaul' in *Journal of Roman Studies*, lxxv, pp. 183–203.

Klotz, A. (1953), *Scaenicorum Romanorum fragmenta, i, Tragicorum fragmenta* (Munich).

Knoch, August (1936), 'Die Ehescheidung im alten irischen Recht' in Binchy (1936), pp. 235–68.

Knox, Ronald (1950), *Enthusiasm. A chapter in the history of religion* (Oxford).

Körntgen, Ludger (1993), *Studien zu den Quellen der frühmittelalterlichen Bußbücher* (Quellen und Forschungen zum Recht im Mittelalter, vii) (Sigmaringen).

Krusch, Bruno (ed.) (1880), *Studien zur christlich-mittelalterlichen Chronologie [i]: Die 84-jährige Ostercyklus und seine Quellen* (Leipzig).

Krusch, Bruno (ed.) (1902a), 'Vitae Columbani abbatis discipulorumque eius libri duo auctore Iona' in *MGH, SRM*, iv, pp. 1–152 (Hannover and Leipzig).

Krusch, Bruno (ed.) (1902b), 'Vita Galli auctore Walahfrido' in *MGH, Scriptores Rerum Merovingicarum [SRM]*, iv, pp. 280–337.

Krusch, Bruno (ed.) (1905), 'Ionae vitae sanctorum Columbani, Vedastis, Iohannis', in *MGH, SRM in usum scholarum* (Hannover and Leipzig).

Krusch, Bruno (ed.) (1937, 1941–42), 'Gregorii Episcopi Turonensis Historiarum Libri X' in *MGH, SRM*, i (Hannover and Leipzig).

Laing, Lloyd (1985), 'The Romanization of Ireland in the fifth century' in *Peritia*, iv, pp. 261–78.

Laistner, M.L.W. (1931), *Thought and letters in western Europe, AD500 to 900* (Ithaca, New York).

Lambert, Pierre Yves (1984), Review of Ó Cróinín (1981) in *Études Celtiques*, xxi, pp. 367–8.

Lanoë, Guy (1984), 'Les évêques en Angleterre (597–669)' in *Le Moyen Age*, lxxxix, pp. 333–55.

Lapidge, Michael (1977), 'The authorship of the Adonic verses "Ad Fidolium" attributed to Columbanus' in *Studi Medievali*, 3rd Series, xviii, pp. 249–314.

Lapidge, Michael (1985), 'Columbanus and the Antiphonary of Bangor' in *Peritia*, iv, pp. 104–16.

Lapidge, Michael (1986), 'Latin learning in Dark Age Wales: some prolegomena' in Ellis Evans, Griffith and Jope (1986), pp. 91–107.

Lapidge, Michael (ed.) (1988), *Latin learning in medieval Ireland* (Aldershot).

Lapidge, Michael (ed.) (1990), *Irish books and learning in medieval Europe* (Aldershot).

Lapidge, Michael (1992), 'Israel the grammarian in Anglo-Saxon England' in Westra (1992), pp. 97–114.

Lapidge, Michael and Blair, Peter Hunter (eds) (1984), *Anglo-Saxon Northumbria* (London).

Lapidge, Michael and Dumville, David N. (eds) (1984), *Gildas: new approaches* (Studies in Celtic History, v) (Woodbridge).

Lapidge, Michael and Sharpe, Richard (1985), *Bibliography of Celtic Latin literature 400–1200* (RIA, Dictionary of Medieval Latin from Celtic Sources, Ancillary Publications, i) (Dublin).

Law, Vivien (1981), 'Malsachanus reconsidered' in *Cambridge Medieval Celtic Studies*, i, pp. 83–97.

Law, Vivien (1982), *The Insular Latin grammarians* (Studies in Celtic History, iii) (Woodbridge).

Law, Vivien (1985), 'Linguistics in the earlier middle ages: the Insular and Carolingian grammarians' in *Transactions of the Philological Society*, lxxxv, pp. 171–93.

Law, Vivien (ed.) (1993), *History of linguistic thought in the early middle ages* (Studies in the History of the Language of Science, lxxi) (Amsterdam/ Philadelphia).

Lawlor, H.C. (1925), *The monastery of St Mochaoi of Nendrum* (Belfast).

Lehmann, Paul (ed.) (1918), *Mittelalterliche Bibliothekskataloge Deutschlands und der Schweiz*, i (Munich).

Lehmann, Paul (1925), 'Fuldaer Studien' in *Sitzungsberichte der Bayerischen Akademie der Wissenschaften*, philos.-philol. u. hist. Kl. 1925, iii (Munich), pp. 1–53.

Lehner, Albert and Berschin, Walter (eds) (1989), *Lateinische Kultur im VIII. Jahrhundert. Traube Gedenkschrift* (St Ottilien).

Levison, Wilhelm (1904), 'Bischof Germanus von Auxerre und die Quellen zu seiner Geschichte' in *Neues Archiv der Gesellschaft für ältere deutsche Geschichtskunde*, xxix, pp. 95–175.

Levison, Wilhelm (1946), *England and the continent in the eighth century* (Oxford).

Lindsay, W.M. (1910), *Early Irish minuscule script* (St Andrew's University Publications, ix) (Oxford).

Lindsay, W.M. (1936), Review of Funaioli (1930) in *American Journal of Philology*, lvii, pp. 336–8.

Llewelyn, Morgan (1980), *Lion of Ireland: the legend of Brian Boru* (London).

Löfstedt, Bengt (1965), *Der hibernolateinsiche Grammatiker Malsachanus* (Uppsala).

Löfstedt, Bengt (1976), 'Zur Grammatik des Asper Minor' in O'Meara and Naumann (1976), pp. 132–40.

Löfstedt, Bengt (ed.) (1982a), *Ars Ambrosiana e codice Mediolan. Bibl. Ambros. L. 22 Sup.* in *CCSL*, cxxxiii C (Turnhout).

Löfstedt, Bengt (1982b), 'Miscellanea grammatica' ('Zur grammatischen Schwindelliteratur') in *Rivista di cultura classica e medioevale*, xxiii, pp. 159–64.

Loth, Joseph (1924), 'Les noms et les variétés du froment chez les Celtes insulaires' in *Revue Celtique*, xli, pp. 193–203.

Lowe, E.A. (1926), 'Handwriting' in Crump and Jacob (1926), pp. 197–226.

Lowe, E.A. (1935–71), *Codices Latini Antiquiores: A palaeographical guide to Latin manuscripts prior to the ninth century* (11 vols + Supplement) (Oxford).

Löwe, Heinz (1981), 'Columbanus und Fidolius' in *Deutsches Archiv*, xxxvii, pp. 1–19.

Löwe, Heinz (ed.) (1982), *Die Iren und Europa im früheren Mittelalter* (2 vols) (Stuttgart).

Lucas, A.T. (1953), 'The horizontal mill in Ireland' in *JRSAI*, lxxxiii, pp. 1–36.

Lucas, A.T. (1953–54), 'Two recent bog-finds: (1) Kilbennan Bog, Co. Galway; (2) Roebuck, Co. Cavan' in *Galway Archaeological and Historical Society Journal*, xxv, pp. 86–9.

Lucas, A.T. (1955), 'A horizontal mill at Ballykilleen, Co. Offaly' in *JRSAI*, lxxxv, pp. 111–13.

Lucas, A.T. (1956), '*An fhóir:* a straw-rope granary' in *Gwerin*, i, pp. 2–20.

Lucas, A.T. (1957), 'Local tradition, III: Irish folk life' in Meenan and Webb (1957), pp. 196–206.

Lucas, A.T. (1958a), '*An fhóir:* a straw-rope granary: further notes' in *Gwerin*, ii, pp. 68–77.

Lucas, A.T. (1958b), 'Cattle in ancient and medieval Irish society' in *O'Connell School Union Record, 1937–1958* (Dublin), pp. 75–87.

Lucas, A.T. (1960), 'Irish food before the potato' in *Gwerin*, iii, pp. 8–43.

Lucas, A.T. (1966), 'Irish-Norse relations: time for a reappraisal?' in *Journal of the Cork Historical and Archaeological Society*, lxxi, pp. 62–75.

Lucas, A.T. (1967), 'The plundering and burning of churches in Ireland, 7th to 16th century' in Rynne (1967), pp. 172–229.

Lucas, A.T. (1969a), 'A horizontal mill at Knocknagranshy, Co. Limerick' in *North Munster Antiquarian Journal*, xii, pp. 12–22.

Lucas, A.T. (1969b), 'Sea sand and shells as manure' in Jenkins (1969), pp. 184–205.

Lucas, A.T. (1970), 'Paring and burning in Ireland: a preliminary survey' in Gailey and Fenton (1970), pp. 99–147.

Lucas, A.T. (1971), 'Conjoined rough-outs for wooden bowls from Derrybrick, Co. Fermanagh' in *Journal of the Cork Historical and Archaeological Society*, lxxvi, pp. 134–6.

Lucas, A.T. (1975), A stone-laid trackway and wooden troughs, Timoney, Co. Tipperary' in *North Munster Antiquaries Journal*, xvii, pp. 13–20.

Lucas, A.T. (1978), 'History from garbage: excavations in Dublin city 1962–1976' in *O'Connell School: 150 years 1828–1978* (Dublin), pp. 51–66.

Lucas, A.T. (1989), *Cattle in ancient Ireland* (Studies in Irish Archaeology and History) (Kilkenny).

Lutz, Cora (1956), 'Remigius' ideas on the origins of the seven liberal arts' in *Medievalia and Humanistica*, x, pp. 32–49.

Lynch, C.H. (1938), *Saint Braulio of Saragossa (631–651): his life and writings* (Catholic University of America Studies in Medieval History, New Series, ii) (Washington, D.C.).

Lydon, James F. (1972), *The lordship of Ireland in the middle ages* (Dublin).

Lynn, Chris (1982), 'The Dorsey and other linear earthworks' in Scott (ed.) (1982), pp. 121–8.

Lyons, F.S.L. (1982), *Culture and anarchy in Ireland 1890–1939* (Ford Lectures) Oxford.

Mabillon, Jean (ed.), *Annales Ordinis Sancti Benedicti* (6 vols, Paris, 1668–1701).

Mac Airt, Seán (ed.) (1951), *The Annals of Inisfallen (MS. Rawlinson B. 503)* (Dublin).

Mac Airt, Seán (1953, 1955–56, 1958–59), 'Middle-Irish poems on world kingship' in *Études Celtiques*, vi, pp. 255–80; vii, pp. 18–45; viii, pp. 98–119.

Mac Airt, Seán (1958), 'The churches founded by Saint Patrick' in Ryan (1958), pp. 67–80.

Macalister, R.A.S. (ed.) (1945, 1949), *Corpus inscriptionum insularum Celticarum* (2 vols) (Dublin).

Mac Cana, Proinsias (1970), 'The three languages and the three laws' in *Studia Celtica*, v, pp. 62–78.

Mac Carthy, Bartholomew (1892), *The Codex Palatino-Vaticanus No. 830* (RIA, Todd Lecture Series, iii) (Dublin).

McCarthy, Daniel (1994), 'Origin of the *latercus* paschal cycle of the Insular Celtic church' in *Cambrian Medieval Celtic Studies*, xxviii, pp. 25–49.

McCarthy, D.P. (1994), 'The origin of the Latercus Paschal cycle of the Insular Celtic churches' in *Cambrian Medieval Celtic Studies*, xxviii, pp. 25–49.

McCone, Kim (1982), 'Brigit in the seventh century: a saint with three lives?' in *Peritia*, i, pp. 107–45.

McCone, Kim (1986a), 'Dubthach maccu Lugair and a matter of life and death in the pseudo-historical Prologue to the *Senchas Már*' in *Peritia*, v, pp. 1–35.

McCone, Kim (1986b), 'Werewolves, cyclopes, *díberga*, and *Fianna*: juvenile delinquency in early Ireland' in *Cambridge Medieval Celtic Studies*, xii, pp. 1–22.

McCone, Kim (1990), *Pagan past and Christian present in early Irish literature* (Maynooth Monographs, iii) (Maynooth).

McCormick, Finbar (1983), 'Dairying and beef production in early Christian Ireland: the faunal evidence' in Reeves-Smith and Hammond (1983), pp. 253–68.

McCracken, J.L. (ed.) (1965), *Historical studies: papers read to the Sixth Irish Conference of Historians* (Belfast).

McCurtain, Margaret and Ó Corráin, Donnchadh (eds) (1978), *Women in Irish society: the historical dimension* (Dublin).

MacDonald, Aidan (1984), 'Aspects of the monastery and monastic life in Adomnán's Life of Columba' in *Peritia*, iii, pp. 271–302.

MacDonald, Aiden (1985), 'Iona's style of government among the Picts and Scots: the toponymic evidence of Adomnán's Life of Columba' in *Peritia*, iv, pp. 174–86.

Mac Eoin, Gearóid (1982), 'The early Irish vocabulary of mills and milling' in Scott (1982), pp. 13–19.

Mac Eoin, Gearóid (1983), 'The death of the boys in the mill' in *Celtica*, xv, pp. 60–4.

McGrail, Seán (1987), *Ancient boats in N.W. Europe: the archaeology of water transport to AD 1500*. (Longman Archaeology Series) (London).

McKitterick, Rosamond (1985), 'Knowledge of canon law in the Frankish kingdoms before 789: the manuscript evidence' in *Journal of Theological Studies*, xxxvi, pp. 97–117.

McKitterick, Rosamond (1989), *The Carolingians and the written word* (Cambridge).

McKitterick, Rosamond (ed.) (1990), *The uses of literacy in early medieval Europe* (Cambridge).

McLennan, Gordon (ed.) (1992), *Celtic languages and Celtic peoples* (Proceedings of the 2nd North American Congress of Celtic Studies) (Halifax, Nova Scotia).

McLeod, Neil (1982), 'The concept of law in ancient Irish jurisprudence' in *Irish Jurist*, New Series xvii, pp. 356–67.

McLeod, Neil (1986–87), 'Interpreting early Irish law: status and currency' in *Zeitschrift für Celtische Philologie [ZCP]*, xli, pp. 46–65; xlii, pp. 41–115.

McLeod, Neil (1992), *Early Irish contract law* (Sydney Series in Celtic Studies, i) (Sydney).

McManus, Damian (1986), 'Ogam: archaizing, orthography and the authenticity of the manuscript key to the alphabet' in *Ériu*, xxxvii, pp. 1–31.

McManus, Damian (1991), *A guide to ogam* (Maynooth Monographs, iv) (Maynooth).

MacMullen, Ramsey (1982), 'The epigraphic habit in the Roman Empire' in *American Journal of Philology*, ciii, pp. 233–46.

MacMullen, Ramsey (1984a), *Christianizing the Roman Empire (AD100–400)* (Yale).

MacMullen, Ramsey (1984b), 'Notes on Romanization' in *Bulletin of the American Society of Papyrologists*, xxi, pp. 161–77 [repr. in MacMullen (1990), pp. 56–66].

MacMullen, Ramsey (1990), *Changes in the Roman Empire: Essays in the ordinary* (Princeton).

McNally, Robert E. (ed.) (1968), *Scriptores Hiberniae Minores* in *CCSL*, cviii B (Turnhout).

McNamara, Jo-Ann and Wemple, Suzanne (1976), 'Marriage and divorce in the Frankish kingdom' in Stuard (1976), pp. 95–124.

McNamara, Martin (1975), *The apocrypha in the Irish church* (Dublin).

McNamara, Martin (1984), 'Tradition and creativity in early Irish psalter study' in Ní Chatháin and Richter (1984), pp. 283–328.

Mac Neill, Eoin (1909), 'Notes on the distribution, history, grammar, and import of the Irish ogham inscriptions' in *PRIA*, xxvii C 15, pp. 329–70.

Mac Neill, Eoin (1911–12), 'Early Irish population- groups: their nomenclature, classification, and chronology' in *PRIA*, xxix C 7, pp. 59–114.

Mac Neill, Eoin (1919), *Phases of Irish history* (Dublin).

Mac Neill, Eoin (1921), *Celtic Ireland* (Dublin) [repr. Cork 1988].

Mac Neill, Eoin (1922), 'A pioneer of nations' in *Studies*, xi, pp. 13–28; 435–46.

Mac Neill, Eoin (1923), 'Ancient Irish law: the law of status or franchise' in *PRIA*, xxxvi C 16, pp. 265–300.

Mac Neill, Eoin (1926), 'The native-place of Saint Patrick' in *PRIA*, xxxvii c 6, pp. 118–40.

Mac Neill, Eoin (1928), 'Dates of texts in the Book of Armagh relating to Saint Patrick' in *JRSAI*, lviii, pp. 85–101 [repr. in Ryan (1964), pp. 137–57].

Mac Neill, Eoin (1929), 'The mythology of Lough Neagh' in *Béaloideas*, ii, pp. 115–21.

Mac Neill, Eoin (1930), 'The Vita Tripartita of St. Patrick' in *Ériu*, xi, pp. 1–41.

Mac Neill, Eoin (1931), 'Beginnings of Latin culture in Ireland' in *Studies*, xx, pp. 39–48; 449–60.

Mac Neill, Eoin (1935), *Early Irish laws and institutions* (Dublin).

Mac Niocaill, Gearóid (1968), 'The "heir designate" in early medieval Ireland' in *Irish Jurist*, New Series, iii, pp. 326–9.

Mac Niocaill, Gearóid (1970–71), 'A propos du vocabulaire social irlandais du bas moyen âge' in *Études Celtiques*, xii, pp. 512–46.

Mac Niocaill, Gearóid (1971), 'Jetsam, treasure trove and the lord's share in medieval Ireland' in *Irish Jurist*, New Series, vi, pp. 103–10.

Mac Niocaill, Gearóid (1972), *Ireland before the Vikings* (Gill History of Ireland, i) (Dublin).

Mac Niocaill, Gearóid (1981), *Irish population before Petty: problems and possibilities* (O'Donnell Lecture) (Galway).

Mac Niocaill, Gearóid, and Wallace, Patrick F. (eds) (1988), *Keimelia. Studies in medieval archaeology and history in memory of Tom Delaney* (Galway).

McTurk, Rory (1976), 'Ragnarr Lodbrók in the Irish annals?' in Almqvist and Greene (1976), pp. 93–124.

Madoz, José (ed.) (1941), *Epistolario de S. Braulio de Zaragoza* (Biblioteca de Antiguas Escritores Cristianos Españoles, i) (Madrid).

Magnusson, Magnus and Palsson, Hans (1972), *Njal's Saga* (Penguin Classics) (Harmondsworth).

Maierù, A. (ed.) (1987), *Grafia e interpunzione del latino nel medioevo* (Rome).

Manitius, Max (1911–31), *Geschichte der lateinischen Literatur des Mittelalters* (3 vols) (Munich).

Manning, Conleth (1991), 'Toureen Peakaun: three new inscribed slabs' in *Tipperary Historical Journal*, 1991, pp. 209–14.

Marstrander, Carl (1911), 'Lochlann' in *Ériu*, v, pp. 250–1.

Marstrander, Carl (1915), *Bidrag til det norske sprogs historie i Irland* (Oslo).

Marstrander, Carl, Bergin, Osborn, Dillon, Myles and Quin, E.G. (eds) (1913–76), *Royal Irish Academy Dictionary of the Irish Language [DIL]* (Dublin).

Matthews, John (1975), *Western aristocracies and imperial court, AD364–425* (Oxford).

Maund, K.L. (1991), *Ireland, Wales, and England in the eleventh century* (Studies in Celtic History, xii) (Woodbridge).

Meehan, Denis (ed.) (1958), *Adamnan's 'De locis sanctis'* (Scriptores Latini Hiberniae, iii) (Dublin).

Meenan, James and Webb, David A. (eds) (1957), *A view of Ireland: twelve essays on different aspects of Irish life and the Irish countryside* (Dublin).

Meyer, Kuno (1901), 'The Expulsion of the Dessi' in *Y Cymmrodor*, xiv, pp. 101–35.

Meyer, Kuno (ed.) (1906), *The triads of Ireland* (RIA, Todd Lecture Series, xiii) (Dublin).

Meyer, Kuno (1907a), 'The Expulsion of the Déssi' in *Ériu*, iii, pp. 135–42.

Meyer, Kuno (1907b), 'Colman's farewell to Colman' in *Ériu*, iii, pp. 186–9.

Meyer, Kuno (1908), 'Irish mirabilia in the Norse *Speculum Regale*' in *Ériu*, iv, pt. 1, pp. 1–16.

Meyer, Kuno (1909), *The instructions of King Cormac mac Airt* (RIA, Todd Lecture Series, xv) (Dublin).

Meyer, Kuno (1912), 'The Laud genealogies and tribal histories' in *ZCP*, viii, pp. 292–338.

Meyer, Kuno (1917), *Miscellanea Hibernica* (University of Illinois Studies in Language and Literature, ii) (Urbana, Illinois).

Meyvaert, Paul (1971), 'Bede's text of the *Libellus Responsionum* of Gregory the Great to Augustine of Canterbury' in Clemoes and Hughes (1971), pp. 15–33.

Mitchell, G.F. (1986), *The Shell guide to reading the Irish landscape* (Dublin).

Mitchell, G.F. (1987), 'Archaeology and environment in early Dublin' (RIA, Medieval Dublin Excavations 1962–81) in *PRIA*, lxxxvii C 1.

Moisl, Hermann (1983), 'The Bernician royal dynasty and the Irish in the seventh century' in *Peritia*, ii, pp. 103–26.

Momigliano, Arnaldo (1955), 'Cassiodorus and Italian culture of his time' in *Proceedings of the British Academy*, xli, pp. 207–45.

Momigliano, Arnaldo (ed.) (1964), *The conflict between paganism and Christianity in the fourth century* (Oxford).

Momigliano, Arnaldo (1966), *Studies in historiography* (London).

Mommsen, Theodor (ed.) (1892), 'Prosperi Tironis epitoma de chronicon' in *MGH, Auctores Antiquissimi* [*AA*], ix, *Chronica Minora*, i, pp. 384–499.

Mommsen, Theodor (ed.) (1898), 'Laterculus imperatorum Romanorum Malalianus ad a. DLXXIII' in *MGH, AA*, xii, *Chronica Minora*, iii, Berlin, pp. 424–37.

Moody, T.W. (ed.) (1971), *Irish historiography 1936–70*, Irish Committee of Historical Sciences (Dublin).

Moody, T.W. (ed.) (1978), *Nationality and the pursuit of national independence* [= *Historical Studies*, xi] (Belfast).

Moody, T.W., Martin, F.X. and Byrne, F.J. (eds) (1976–), *A new history of Ireland* (Oxford).

Moore, Walter (1989), *Schrödinger, life and thought* (Cambridge).

Moran, Dermot (1989), *The philosophy of John Scottus Eriugena. A study of idealism in the middle ages* (Cambridge).

Most, William G. (1946), *The syntax of the Vitae Sanctorum Hiberniae* (Catholic University of America, Studies in Medieval and Renaissance Latin Language and Literature, xx) (Washington, D.C.).

Mulchrone, Kathleen (1936), 'The rights and duties of women with regard to the education of their children' in Binchy (1936), pp. 187–205.

Mulchrone, Kathleen (ed.) (1939), *Bethu Phátraic, the Tripartite Life of Patrick* (Dublin).

Munier, Charles (ed.) (1963), *Conciliae Galliae a. 314 – a. 506, CCSL*, cxlviii (Turnhout).

Murphy, Gerard (1928), '*Scotti peregrini*: the Irish on the continent in the time of Charles the Bald' in *Studies*, xvii, pp. 39–50, 229–44.

Murray, Hilary (1983), *Viking and early medieval buildings in Dublin* (British Archaeological Reports, British Series, cxix) (Oxford).

Mytum, Harold (1992), *The origins of early Christian Ireland* (London).

Nash-Williams, V.E. (1950), *The early Christian monuments of Wales* (Cardiff).

Nees, Lawrence (1993), 'Ultán the scribe' in *Anglo-Saxon England*, xxii, pp. 127–46.

Netzer, Nancy (1994), 'The origin of the beast canon tables in the Book of Kells reconsidered' in O'Mahony (1994), pp. 322–32.

Newton, Robert R. (1972), *Medieval chronicles and the rotation of the earth* (Baltimore, Maryland).

Ní Bhrolcháin, Muireann (1982), 'A possible source for Keating's Foras Feasa ar Éirinn' in *Éigse*, xix, pp. 61–81.

Ní Chatháin, Próinséas, (1980), 'The liturgical background of the Derrynavlan altar service' in *JRSAI*, cx, pp. 127–48.

Ní Chatháin, Próinséas, and Richter, Michael (eds) (1984), *Irland und Europa/Ireland and Europe: Die Kirche im Frühmittelalter/The early Church* (Stuttgart).

Ní Chatháin, Próinséas, and Richter, Michael (eds) (1987), *Irland und die Christenheit/Ireland and Christendom: Bibelstudien und Mission/The Bible and missions* (Stuttgart).

Nicholls, Kenneth (1982), Review of Frame, Cosgrove and McNeill in *Peritia*, ii, pp. 370–403.

Nyberg, Tore (ed.) (1985), *History and heroic tale: a symposium* (Odense).

O'Brien, George (1923), *Advertisements for Ireland* (Dublin).

O'Brien, M.A. (ed.) (1962), *Corpus genealogiarum Hiberniae* (Dublin).

O'Brien, M.A. (1973), 'Old Irish personal names' in *Celtica*, x, pp. 211–36.

Ó Buachalla, Liam (1952), 'Contributions towards the political history of Munster' in *Journal of the Cork Historical and Archaeological Society*, lvii, pp. 67–86.

Ó Cathasaigh, Thomás (1984), 'The Déisi and Dyfed' in *Éigse*, xx, pp. 1–33.

Ó Cíobháin, Breandán (1987–88), Review of Andrews (1985) in *Peritia*, vi–vii, pp. 364–6.

O'Connor, Frank (1967), *The backward look: a survey of Irish literature* (London).

Ó Corráin, Donnchadh (1971), 'Irish regnal succession: a reappraisal' in *Studia Hibernica*, xi, pp. 7–39.

Ó Corráin, Donnchadh (1972), *Ireland before the Normans* (Gill History of Ireland, ii) (Dublin).

Ó Corráin, Donnchadh (1973), 'Dál Cais – church and dynasty' in *Ériu*, xxiv, pp. 52–63.

Ó Corráin, Donnchadh (1976), 'A handlist of publications on early Irish history' in Hayes-McCoy (1976), pp. 177–203.

Ó Corráin, Donnchadh (1978a) 'Women in early Irish society' in McCurtain and Ó Corráin (1978), pp. 1–13.

Ó Corráin, Donnchadh (1978b), 'Nationality and kingship in pre-Norman Ireland' in Moody (1978), pp. 1–35.

Ó Corráin, Donnchadh (1979), 'High-kings, Vikings, and other kings' in *Irish Historical Studies*, xxi, pp. 283–323.

Ó Corráin, Donnchadh (1980), Review of Byrne (1973) in *Celtica*, xiii, pp. 150–68.

Ó Corráin, Donnchadh (1981a) 'The early Irish churches: some aspects of organization' in Ó Corráin (1981b), pp. 327–41.

Ó Corráin, Donnchadh (ed.) (1981b), *Irish antiquity: essays and studies presented to M.J. O'Kelly* (Cork).

Ó Corráin, Donnchadh (1982), 'Foreign connections and domestic politics: Killaloe and the Uí Briain in twelfth-century hagiography' in Whitelock, McKitterick and Dumville (1982), pp. 213–31.

Ó Corráin, Donnchadh (1983), 'Some legal references to fences and fencing in early historic Ireland' in Reeves-Smith and Hammond (1983), pp. 247–51.

Ó Corráin, Donnchadh (1984), 'Irish law and canon law' in Ní Chatháin and Richter (1984), pp. 157–66.

Ó Corráin, Donnchadh (1985a), 'Marriage in early Ireland' in Cosgrove (1985), pp. 5–24.

Ó Corráin, Donnchadh (1985b), 'Irish origin legends and genealogy: recurrent aetiologies' in Nyberg (1985) pp. 51–96.

Ó Corráin, Donnchadh (1987), 'Irish vernacular law and the Old Testament' in Ní Chatháin and Richter (1987), pp. 284–307.

Ó Corráin, Donnchadh (1989), 'Early Irish "nature" poetry' in Ó Corráin, Breatnach and McCone (1989), pp. 251–67.

Ó Corráin, Donnchadh, Breatnach, Liam and Breen, Aidan (1984), 'The laws of the Irish' in *Peritia*, iii, pp. 382–438.

Ó Corráin, Donnchadh, Breatnach, Liam and McCone, Kim (eds) (1989), *Sages, saints and scholars: Celtic studies in honour of James Carney* (Maynooth).

Ó Cróinín, Dáibhí (1981), 'The oldest Irish names for the days of the week?' in *Ériu*, xxxii, pp. 95–114.

Ó Cróinín, Dáibhí (1982a), 'Mo-Sinu maccu Min and the computus at Bangor' in *Peritia*, i, pp. 281–95.

Ó Cróinín, Dáibhí (1982b), *The Irish 'Sex Aetates Mundi'* (Dublin).

Ó Cróinín, Dáibhí (1982c), 'A seventh-century Irish computus from the circle of Cummianus' in *PRIA*, lxxxii C 11, pp. 405–30.

Ó Cróinín, Dáibhí (1982–83), Review of Law (1982) in *Studia Hibernica*, xxii–xxiii, pp. 149–56.

Ó Cróinín, Dáibhí (1983a), 'Early Irish annals from Easter-tables: a case restated' in *Peritia*, ii, pp. 74–86.

Ó Cróinín Dáibhí (1983b), 'The Irish provenance of Bede's computus' in *Peritia*, ii, pp. 229–47.

Ó Cróinín, Dáibhí (1984), 'Rath Melsigi, Willibrord, and the earliest Echternach manuscripts' in *Peritia*, iii, pp. 17–49.

Ó Cróinín, Dáibhí (1985), ' "New heresy for old": Pelagianism in Ireland and the papal letter of 640' in *Speculum*, lx, pp. 505–16.

Ó Cróinín, Dáibhí (1986), 'New light on Palladius' in *Peritia*, v, pp. 276–83.

Ó Cróinín, Dáibhí (1988), *Evangeliarium Epternacense (Universitätsbibliothek Augsburg, Cod. I.2.4°2* (Codices Illuminati Medii Aevi, ix) (Munich).

Ó Cróinín, Dáibhí (1989a), 'Early Echternach manuscript fragments with Old Irish glosses' in Kiesel and Schroeder (1989), pp. 135–43.

Ó Cróinín, Dáibhí (1989b), 'Cummianus Longus and the iconography of the apostles in early Irish literature' in Ó Corráin, Breatnach and McCone (1989), pp. 268–79.

Ó Cróinín, Dáibhí (1989c), 'The date, provenance, and earliest use of the works of Virgilius Maro Grammaticus' in Bernt, Rädle and Silagi (1989), pp. 13–22.

Ó Cróinín, Dáibhí (1993), 'The Irish as mediators of antique culture on the continent' in Butzer and Lohrmann (1993), pp. 41–52.

Ó Cuív, Brian (ed.) (1962), *The impact of the Scandinavian invasions on the Celtic-speaking peoples c. 800–1100AD* (Proceedings of the [First] International Congress of Celtic Studies) (Dublin).

Ó Cuív, Brian (1986), 'Aspects of Irish personal names' in *Celtica*, xviii, pp. 151–84.

Ó Cuív, Brian (1988), 'Personal names as an indicator of relations between native Irish and settlers in the Viking period' in Bradley (1988a), pp. 79–88.

Ó Cuív, Brian (1990), 'The Irish marginalia in Codex Palatino-Vaticanus No. 830' in Éigse, xxiv, pp. 45–67.

O Daly, Máirín (1952), 'A poem on the Airgialla' in Ériu, xvi, pp. 179–88.

O'Doherty, J.F. (1933), 'Rome and the Anglo-Norman invasion of Ireland' in IER, xlii, pp. 131–45.

O'Doherty, J.F. (1937), 'St. Laurence O'Toole and the Anglo-Norman invasion' in IER, 5th Series, l, pp. 449–77, 600–25; li, pp. 131–46.

O'Doherty, J.F. (1938–39), 'The Anglo-Norman invasion of 1167–71' in Irish Historical Studies, i, pp. 154–7.

Ó Fiaich, Tomás (1969), 'The church of Armagh under lay control' in Seanchas Ardmhacha, iii, pt. 1, pp. 75–127.

O'Grady, Standish H. (1889), 'The last kings of Ireland' in English Historical Review, iv, pp. 286–303.

O'Grady, Standish H. (ed.) (1892), Silva Gadelica: a collection of tales in Irish (2 vols) (London).

Ó hUiginn, Ruairí (1989), 'Tongu do dia toinges mo thuath and related expressions in Ó Corráin, Breatnach and McCone (1989), pp. 332–41.

O'Keeffe, J.G. (1934), 'Frithfholaith Chaisil' in Irish Texts, i, pp. 19–21.

Olsen, Magnus (1954), 'Runic inscriptions in Great Britain, Ireland and the Isle of Man' in Shetelig (1940–54), vi, pp. 151–232.

O'Mahony, Felicity (ed.) (1994), The Book of Kells: Proceedings of a conference at Trinity College Dublin, 1992 (Dublin).

O'Meadhra, Uaininn (1979, 1987), Early Christian, Viking, and Romanesque art: motif-pieces from Ireland (Theses and Papers in North European Archaeology) (2 vols) (Stockholm).

O'Meadhra, Uaininn (1988), 'Skibe i ranveigs Skrin' in Tidsskriftet Skalk, v, pp. 3–5.

O'Meara, J.J. (1951), The first version of the Topography of Ireland by Giraldus Cambrensis (Dundalk).

O'Meara, J.J. and Naumann, Bernd (eds) (1976), Latin script and letters, AD400–900: Festschrift presented to Ludwig Bieler on the occasion of his 70th birthday (Leiden).

Ó Murchadha, Domhnall and Ó Murchú, Giollamuire (1988), 'Fragmentary inscriptions from the West Cross at Durrow, the South Cross at Clonmacnois, and the Cross of Kinnitty' in JRSAI, cxviii, pp. 53–66.

Ó Néill, Pádraig (1981), 'The background to the Cambrai Homily' in Ériu, xxxii, pp. 137–47.

Ó Néill, Pádraig (1984), 'Romani influences on seventh-century Hiberno-Latin literature' in Ní Chatháin and Richter (1984), pp. 280–90.

O'Rahilly, Cecile (1924), Ireland and Wales, their historical and literary relations (London).

O'Rahilly, T.F. (1926), 'A note on the "Culmen" ' in Ériu, x, p. 109.

O'Rahilly, T.F. (1946), Early Irish history and mythology (Dublin).

Ó Riain, Pádraig (1973), 'The "crech ríg" or "royal prey" ' in Éigse, xv, pp. 23–30.

Ó Riain, Pádraig (1984), 'Finnian or Winniau?' in Ní Chatháin and Richter (1984), pp. 52–7.

Ó Riain, Pádraig (ed.) (1985), *Corpus genealogiarum sanctorum Hiberniae* (Dublin).

Ó Riain, Pádraig (1986), 'Celtic mythology and religion' in Schmidt (1986), pp. 241–51.

Ó Riain, Pádraig (1989), 'Conservation in the vocabulary of the early Irish Church' in Ó Corráin, Breatnach and McCone (1989), pp. 358–66.

Ó Riain, Pádraig (1990), 'A misunderstood annal: a hitherto unnoticed cáin' in *Celtica*, xxi, pp. 561–6.

Ó Riain, Pádraig, (1993), *Anglo-Saxon Ireland: the evidence of the Martyrology of Tallaght* (H.M. Chadwick Memorial Lectures, iii) (Cambridge).

Ó Riain-Raedel, Dagmar (1982), 'Aspects of the promotion of Irish saints' cults in medieval Germany' in *ZCP*, xxxix, pp. 220–4.

Ó Riain-Raedel, Dagmar (1984), 'Irish kings and bishops in the *memoria* of the German *Scottenklöster*' in Ní Chatháin and Richter (1984), pp. 390–404.

Ó Riain-Raedel, Dagmar (ed.) (1992), *Das Nekrolog der irischen Schottenklöster* in *Beiträge zur Geschichte des Bistums Regensburg*, xxvi, pp. 7–119.

Orpen, G.H. (1911–20), *Ireland under the Normans, 1169–1333* (4 vols) (Oxford [repr. 1968]).

Oskamp, H.P.A. (1977), 'A schoolteacher's hand in a Florentine manuscript' in *Scriptorium*, xxxi, pp. 191–7.

Oskamp, H.P.A. (1978), 'The Irish material in the St. Paul Irish Codex' in *Éigse*, xvii, pp. 385–91.

Otway-Ruthven, A.J. (1965), 'The character of Norman settlement in Ireland' in McCracken (1965), pp. 75–84.

Otway-Ruthven, A.J. (1968), *A history of medieval Ireland* (London).

Parkes, Malcolm (1982), *The scriptorium of Wearmouth–Jarrow* (Jarrow Lecture) (Jarrow) [repr. in Parkes (1991), pp. 93–120].

Parkes, Malcolm (1987), 'The contribution of Insular scribes of the seventh and eighth centuries to the "Grammar of Intelligibility"' in Maierù (1987), pp. 15–29 [repr. Parkes (1991), pp. 1–18].

Parkes, Malcolm (1991), *Scribes, scripts and readers: studies in the communication, presentation and dissemination of medieval texts* (London).

Payer, Pierre J. (1984), *Sex and the penitentials: the development of a sexual code 550–1150* (Toronto).

Pearce, Susan M. (ed.) (1982), *The early church in western Britain and Ireland* (British Archaeological Reports, British Series, cii) (Oxford).

Pelteret, David (1981), 'Slave raiding and slave trading in Anglo-Saxon England' in *Anglo-Saxon England*, ix, pp. 99–114.

Pertz, George H. and Kurze, F. (eds) (1895), *Annales regni Francorum inde ab A. 741 usque ad A. 829* in *MGH, SRM in usum scholarum* (Hannover and Leipzig).

Petersen, Jan (1940), 'British antiquities of the Viking period found in Norway' in Shetelig (1940–54) v.

Petrie, George (1837), 'The history and antiquities of Tara Hill' in *Transactions of the Royal Irish Academy*, xviii, pp. 25–206.

Phillimore, Egerton (ed.) (1888), 'The *Annales Cambriae* and Old-Welsh genealogies from *Harleian MS*. 38591' in *Y Cymmrodor*, ix, pp. 141–83.

Picard, Jean-Michel (1982), 'The purpose of Adomnán's *Vita Columbae*' in *Peritia*, i, pp. 160–77.

Picard, Jean-Michel, (ed.) (1991), *Ireland and northern France, AD600–850* (Dublin).

Plummer, Charles (ed.) (1896), *Venerabilis Baedae opera historica* (2 vols) (Oxford) [repr. 1969].

Plummer, Charles (ed.) (1910), *Vitae sanctorum Hiberniae* (2 vols) (Oxford).

Plummer, Charles (ed.) (1922), *Bethada náem nÉrenn, lives of Irish saints* (2 vols) (Oxford).

Plummer, Charles (1926), 'On the colophons and marginalia of Irish scribes' in *Proceedings of the British Academy*, xii, pp. 11–44.

Plummer, Charles (1928), 'Notes on some passages in the Brehon Laws, IV' in *Ériu*, x, pp. 113–14.

Polara, Giovanni (ed.) (1979), *Virgilio Marone Grammatico Epitomi ed Epistole* (Nuovo Medioevo, ix) (Naples).

Polara, Giovanni (1993), 'A proposito delle dottrine grammaticali di Virgilio Marone' in *Historiographica Linguistica*, xx, pp. 205–22.

Pollock, Frederick (1893), 'Anglo-Saxon law' in *English Historical Review*, viii, pp. 239–71.

Price, Liam (1941), 'The placenames of the barony of Arklow, County of Wicklow' in *PRIA*, xlvi C 5, pp. 237–86.

Prinz, Friederich (1965), *Frühes Mönchtum im Frankenreich. Kultur und Gesellschaft in Gallien, den Rheinlanden und Bayern am Beispiel der monastischen Entwicklung (4. bis 8. Jahrhundert)* (Kempten/Allgäu) [2nd rev. ed. Darmstadt 1988].

Prinz, Friedrich (1973), 'Die bischöfliche Stadtherrschaft im Frankenreich vom 5. bis zum 7. Jahrhundert' in *Historische Zeitschrift*, ccxvii, pp. 1–35.

Proudfoot, V.B. (1961), 'The economy of the Irish rath' in *Medieval Archaeology*, v, pp. 94–122.

Raby, F.J.E. (1932), 'Some notes on Virgil, mainly in English authors, in the middle ages' in *Studi Medievali*, 3rd Series, v, pp. 359–71.

Rädle, Fidel (1982), 'Die Kenntnis der antiken lateinischen Literatur bei den Iren in der Heimat und auf dem Kontinent' in Löwe (1982), i, pp. 484–500.

Radner, Joan (ed.) (1978), *Fragmentary annals of Ireland* (Dublin).

Radner, Joan (1983), 'The significance of the Threefold Death in Celtic tradition' in Ford (1983), pp. 180–200.

Rahtz, Philip and Bullough, Donald (1977), 'The parts of an Anglo-Saxon mill' in *Anglo-Saxon England*, vi, pp. 15–37.

Rees, Brian R. (1988), *Pelagius, a reluctant heretic* (Woodbridge).

Reeves, William (1861), 'On Augustin, an Irish writer of the seventh century' in *PRIA*, vii, pp. 514–22.

Reeves-Smith, Terence and Hammond, Fred (eds) (1983), *Landscape archaeology in Ireland* (British Archaeological Reports, British Series, xvi) (Oxford).

Richards, Jeffrey (1980), *Consul of God. The life and times of Gregory the Great* (London).

Richards, Melville (1960), 'The Irish settlement in south-west Wales – a topographical approach' in *JRSAI*, xc, pp. 133–52.

Richardson, Hilary (1980), 'Derrynavlan and other early church treasures' in *JRSAI*, cx, pp. 92–115.

Richter, Michael (1974), 'The first century of Anglo-Irish relations' in *History*, lix, pp. 195–210.

Richter, Michael (1988), *Medieval Ireland, the enduring tradition* (New Gill History of Ireland, i) (Dublin).

Richter, Michael (1991), 'The English link in Hiberno-Frankish relations' in Picard (1991), pp. 95–118.

Riggs, Charles H. Jr (1963), *Criminal asylum in Anglo- Saxon law* (University of Florida Monographs, Social Sciences, xviii) (Gainseville, Florida).

Rittmueller, Jean (1983), 'The gospel commentary of Maél Brigte Ua Maéluanaig and its Hiberno-Latin background' in *Peritia*, ii, pp. 185–214.

Rittmueller, Jean (1984), 'Postscript to the Gospels of Maél Brigte' in *Peritia*, iii, pp. 215–18.

Robinson, J. Armitage (1923), *The times of Saint Dunstan* (Oxford).

Round, J.H. (1899a), *The commune of London and other studies* (London).

Round, J.H. (1899b), 'The Inquest of Sheriffs (1170)' in Round (1899a), pp. 125–36.

Round, J.H. (1899c), 'The conquest of Ireland' in Round (1899a), pp. 137–70.

Round, J.H. (1899d), 'The Marshalship of England' in Round (1899a), pp. 302–20.

Ryan, John (1931), *Irish monasticism, origins and early development* (Dublin) [repr. Dublin 1993].

Ryan, John (1938), 'The Battle of Clontarf' in *JRSAI*, lxviii, pp. 1–50.

Ryan, John (1941, 1942–43), 'The O'Briens in Munster after Clontarf' in *North Munster Antiquaries Journal*, ii, pp. 141–52; iii, pp. 1–152, 189–202.

Ryan, John (ed.) (1958) *Saint Patrick* (Dublin).

Ryan, John (ed.) (1964), *Saint Patrick* (Dublin).

Ryan, John (1967), 'Brian Boruma, King of Ireland' in Rynne (1967), pp. 355–74.

Ryan, Kathleen (1987), 'Parchment as faunal record' in *MASCA, University of Pennsylvania Journal*, iv, pp. 124–38.

Ryan, Kathleen (1987–88), 'Holes and flaws in medieval Irish manuscripts' in *Peritia*, vi–vii, pp. 243–64.

Rynne, Colin (1992), 'Milling in the 7th century – Europe's earliest tide mills' in *Archaeology Ireland*, vi, pt. 2 pp. 22–3.

Rynne, Etienne, 'The impact of the Vikings on Irish weapons' in *Atti del Congresso Internazionale delle Scienze Preistoriche e Protoistoriche*, iii, pp. 181–4 (Rome).

Rynne, Etienne (ed.) (1967), *North Munster studies: Essays in commemoration of Mgr Michael Moloney* (Limerick).

Rynne, Etienne (ed.) (1987), *Figures from the past: Studies on figurative art in Christian Ireland in honour of Helen M. Roe* (Dublin).

Salis, Ludwig Rudolf von (ed.) (1892), *Lex Burgundionum* in *MGH, Leges nationum Germanicarum*, ii, pt. 1 (Hannover).

Sawyer, P.H. (1982), *Kings and Vikings. Scandinavia and Europe* AD 700–1100 (London and New York).

Sawyer, P.H. and Wood, Ian (eds) (1977), *Early medieval kingship* (Leeds).

Schindel, Ulrich (1975), 'Die lateinischen Figurenlehren des 5. bis 7. Jahrhunderts und Donats Vergilkommentar' in *Abhandlungen der Akademie der Wissenschaften zu Göttingen*, phil.–hist. Kl., 3. Folge, ix (Göttingen).

Schmidt, Karl Horst (ed.) (1977), *Indogermanisch und Keltisch* (Wiesbaden).

Schmidt, Karl Horst (ed.) (1986), *Geschichte und Kultur der Kelten* (Heidelberg).

Scott, B.G. (ed.) (1982), *Studies on early Ireland: Essays in honour of M.V. Duignan* (Belfast).

Searle, William G. (ed.) (1899), *Anglo-Saxon bishops, kings and nobles. The succession of the bishops and the pedigrees of the kings and nobles* (Cambridge).

Selmer, Carl (1950), 'Israel, ein unbekannter Schotte des 10. Jahrhunderts' in *Studien und Mitteilungen zur Geschichte des Benediktinerordens*, lxii, pp. 69–86.

Selmer, Carl (ed.) (1956), *Navigatio Sancti Brendani abbatis* (Notre Dame, Indiana).

Severin, Tim (1978), *The Brendan Voyage* (London).

Sharpe, Richard (1982a), '*Vitae S. Brigitae*: the oldest texts' in *Peritia*, i, pp. 81–106.

Sharpe, Richard (1982b), 'St Patrick and the See of Armagh' in *Cambridge Medieval Celtic Studies*, iv, pp. 33–59.

Sharpe, Richard (1984a), 'Some problems concerning the organization of the church in early medieval Ireland' in *Peritia*, iii, pp. 230–70.

Sharpe, Richard (1984b), 'Armagh and Rome in the seventh century' in Ní Chatháin and Richter (1984), pp. 58–72.

Sharpe, Richard (1992), 'An Irish textual critic and the *Carmen paschale* of Sedulius: Colmán's letter to Feradach' in *Journal of Medieval Latin*, ii, pp. 44–54.

Shearman, John F. (1879), *Loca Patriciana: an identification of localities, chiefly in Leinster, visited by Saint Patrick* (Dublin).

Sheldon-Williams, I.P. (1956), 'An epitome of Irish provenance of Eriugena's *De diuisione naturae*' in *PRIA*, lviii C 1, pp. 1–20.

Sheldon-Williams, I.P. and Bieler, Ludwig (eds) (1968–81), *Iohannis Scotti Eriugenae Periphyseon (De diuisione naturae)*. Libri I–III (3 vols) (Scriptores Latini Hiberniae, vii, ix, xi) (Dublin) [in progress].

Shetelig, Haakon (ed.) (1940–54), *Viking antiquities in Great Britain and Ireland* (6 parts) (Oslo).

Shetelig, Haakon (1954a), 'The Viking graves' in Shetelig (1940–54), vi, pp. 65–111.

Shetelig, Haakon (1954b), 'The Norse style of ornamentation in the Viking settlements' in Shetelig (1940–54), vi, pp. 113–50.

Simms, Katharine (1987), *From kings to warlords. The changing political structure of Gaelic Ireland in the later middle ages* (Studies in Celtic history, vii) (Woodbridge).

Sims-Williams, Patrick (1978), 'Thought, word and deed: an Irish triad' in *Ériu*, xxix, pp. 78–111.

Sisam, Kenneth (1953), 'Anglo-Saxon royal genealogies' in *Proceedings of the British Academy*, xxxix, pp. 287–348.

Smit, Johannes W. (1971), *Studies in the language and style of Columba the Younger (Columbanus)* (Amsterdam).

Smyth, Alfred P. (1974–75a), 'The Húi Néill and the Leinstermen in the Annals of Ulster, 131–516 AD' in *Études Celtiques*, xiv, pp. 121–43.

Smyth, Alfred P. (1974–75b), 'Húi Failgi relations with the Húi Néill in the century after the loss of the Plain of Mide' in *Études Celtiques*, xiv, pp. 503–23.

Smyth, Alfred P. (1975–79), *Scandinavian York and Dublin. The history and archaeology of two related Viking kingdoms* (2 vols) (Dublin).

Smyth, Alfred P. (1982), *Celtic Leinster: towards an historical geography of early Irish civilization AD500–1600* (Dublin).

Smyth, Alfred P. (1984), *Warlords and holy men. Scotland AD80–1000* (New History of Scotland, i) (London).

Sommerfelt, Alf (1958), 'On the Norse form of the name of the Picts and the date of the first Norse raids on Scotland' in *Lochlann*, i, pp. 218–22.

Southern, R.W. (1963), *Saint Anselm and his biographer* (Cambridge).

Spearman, R. Michael and Higgitt, John (eds) (1993), *The age of migrating ideas. Early medieval art in northern Britain.* (Proceedings of the Second International Conference on Insular Art) (Edinburgh).

Stacey, Robin Chapman (1991), 'Law and order in the very old West: England and Ireland in the early middle ages' in Hudson and Ziegler (1991), pp. 39–60.

Stacey, Robin Chapman (1994) *The road to judgement: From custom to court in medieval Ireland and Wales* (Philadelphia).

Stancliffe, Clare (1982), 'Red, white and blue martyrdom' in Whitelock, McKitterick and Dumville (1982), pp. 21–46.

Stanford, W.B. (1946), *Faith and faction in Ireland now* (Dublin and Belfast).

Stanley, E.G. (ed.) (1990), *British Academy papers on Anglo-Saxon England* (Oxford).

Steenstrup, J.C.H.R. (1876–82), *Normannerne* (4 vols) (Copenhagen).

Stenton, F.M. (1947), *Anglo–Saxon England* (Oxford).

Stern, Ludwig Christian (ed.) (1910), *Epistolae beati Paulae glosatae glosa interlineali* (Halle).

Stevenson, Jane (1989), 'The beginnings of literacy in Ireland' in *PRIA*, lxxxix C 6, pp. 127–65.

Stevenson, Jane (1990), 'Literacy in Ireland: the evidence of the Patrick dossier in the Book of Armagh' in McKitterick (1990), pp. 11–35.

Stevenson, W.H. (1904), *Asser's Life of Alfred* (Oxford).

Stewart, James (1970–71), 'The death of Turgesius' in *Saga-book of the Viking Society for Northern Research*, xviii, pp. 64–83.

Stockmeier, Peter (1981), 'Bemerkungen zur Christianisierung der Goten im 4. Jahrhundert' in *Zeitschrift für Kirchengeschichte*, xcii, pp. 315–24.

Stokes, Whitley (1890), 'Old-Norse names in the Irish annals' in *The Academy*, No. 959 (20 Sept. 1890), pp. 248–9.

Stokes, Whitley (ed.) (1895–8), 'The Annals of Tigernach' in *Revue Celtique*, xvi, pp. 374–419; xvii, pp. 6–33, 119–263, 337–420; xviii, pp. 9–59, 150–303, 374–91.

Stokes, Whitley (1897), 'Cuimmín's poem on the saints of Ireland' in *ZCP*, i, pp. 59–73

Stokes, Whitley (ed.) (1905), *Félire Oéngusso Céli Dé, the Martyrology of Oengus the Culdee* (Henry Bradshaw Society Publications, xxix) (London).

Stokes, Whitley and Strachan, John (ed.) (1901–3), *Thesaurus Palaeohibernicus: a collection of Old Irish glosses, scholia, prose and verse* (2 vols) (Cambridge).

Strecker, Karl (ed.) (1914), *MGH, PLAC*, ii, pt. 2, *Rhythmi aevi merovingici et Carolini* (Berlin).

Stroheker, Karl F. (1948), *Der senatorische Adel im spätantiken Gallien* (Tübingen).

Stuard, Susan Mosher (ed.) (1976), *Women in medieval society* (Philadelphia).

Stubbs, William (1874), *Memorials of St Dunstan* (London).

Swan, D.L. (1985), 'Monastic proto-towns in early medieval Ireland: the evidence of aerial photography' in Clarke and Simms (1985), pp. 77–102.

Szövérffy, Joseph (1957–60), 'The Anglo–Norman conquest of Ireland and St Patrick: Dublin and Armagh in Jocelin's Life of St Patrick' in *Repertorium Novum*, ii, pp. 6–16.

Thilo, Georg (1860), 'Beiträge zur Kritik der Scholiasten des Virgilius' in *Rheinisches Museum*, xv, pp. 119–52.

Thirsk, Joan (ed.) (1970), *Land, church, and people: Essays presented to H.P.R. Finberg* (Reading).

Thomas, Charles (1971), *The early Christian archaeology of North Britain* (Oxford).

Thomas, Charles (1972), 'The Irish settlements in post-Roman western Britain: a survey of the evidence' in *Journal of the Royal Institution of Cornwall*, New Series, vi, pp. 251–74.

Thomas, Charles (1979), 'Saint Patrick and fifth-century Britain: an historical model explored' in Casey (1979), pp. 81–101.

Thomas, Charles (1981) *Christianity in Roman Britain to AD500* (Berkeley and London).

Thompson, Darcy Wentworth (1945), 'Sesquiuolus, a squirrel, and the *Liber de mirabilibus s. scripturae*' in *Hermathena*, lxv, pp. 1–7.

Thompson, E.A. (1964), 'Christianity and the northern barbarians' in Momigliano (1964), pp. 56–78.

Thompson, E.A. (1966), *The Visigoths in the time of Ulfila* (Oxford).

Thompson, E.A. (1985), *Who was Saint Patrick?* (Woodbridge).

Thorpe, Lewis (transl.) (1969), *Einhard and Notker the Stammerer: Two Lives of Charlemagne* (Penguin Classics) (Harmondsworth).

Thurneysen, Rudolf (1923), 'Das Unfrei-Lehen' (Aus dem irischen Recht, I) in *ZCP*, xiv, pp. 335–94.

Thurneysen, Rudolf (1924a), 'Das Frei-Lehen' (Aus dem irischen Recht, II, 2) in *ZCP*, xv, pp. 238–60.

Thurneysen, Rudolf (1924b), 'Das Fastem beim Pfändungsverfahren' (Aus dem irischen Recht, II, 3) in *ZCP*, xv, pp. 260–76.

Thurneysen, Rudolf (1925), 'Die falschen Urteilssprüche Caratnia's' (Aus dem irischen Recht, III, 4) in *ZCP*, xv, pp. 302–76.

Thurneysen, Rudolf (1926), 'Cóic Conara Fugill, Die fünf Wege zum Urteil, ein altirischer Rechtstext' in *Abhandlungen der Preußischen Akademie der Wissenschaften*, Jahrg. 1925, phil.–hist. Kl., 7 (Berlin).

Thurneysen, Rudolf (1927), 'Zu den bisherigen Ausgaben der irischen Rechtstexte' (Aus dem irischen Recht, IV) in *ZCP*, xvi, pp. 167–230.

Thurneysen, Rudolf (1928), 'Die Bürgschaft im irischen Recht' in *Abhandlungen der Preußischen Akademie der Wissenschaften*, Jahrg. 1928, phil.–hist. Kl., 2 (Berlin).

Thurneysen, Rudolf (1930), 'Zu Gúbretha Caratniad' (Aus dem irischen Recht, V, 7) in *ZCP*, xviii, pp. 353–408.

Thurneysen, Rudolf (1933), 'Colmán mac Lénéni und Senchán Torpéist' in *ZCP*, xix, pp. 193–207.

Thurneysen, Rudolf (1936), '*Cáin Lánamna*' in Binchy (1936), pp. 1–80.

Thurneysen, Rudolf (1949), *Old Irish reader* (Dublin).

Tierney, J.J. (ed.) (1967), *Dicuili 'Liber de mensura orbis terrae'* (Scriptores Latini Hiberniae, vi) (Dublin).

Todd, James H. (ed.) (1867), *Cogadh Gaedhel re Gallaibh (The War of the Gaedhil with the Gaill or The invasions of Ireland by the Danes and other Norsemen)* (Rolls Series) (London).

Traube, Ludwig (1892), 'O Roma nobilis' in *Abhandlungen der königlichen Bayerischen Akademie der Wissenschaften*, phil.–philol. Kl., xix, pt. 2.

Traube, Ludwig (ed.) (1896), 'Sedulii Scotti carmina' in *MGH, PLAC* iii (Berlin).

Traube, Ludwig (1900), 'Perrona Scottorum. Ein Beitrag zur Überlieferungs-geschichte und zur Paläographie des Mittelalters' in *Sitzungsberichte der Königlichen Bayerischen Akademie der Wissenschaften*, phil.–hist. Kl., iv, pp. 469–537 [repr. in Boll (1909–20), iii, pp. 95–119].

Travis, James (1973), *Early Celtic versecraft: origin, development, diffusion* (Shannon).

Ussher, James (ed.) (1632), *Veterum epistolarum Hibernicarum sylloge* (Dublin).

Van Dam, Robert (1985), *Leadership and community in Late Antique Gaul* (Berkeley).

Vogt, H. (1896), *Dublin som Norsk By* (Christiania, Oslo).

Vollrath, Hanna (1985), *Die Synoden Englands bis 1066* (Paderborn).

Waddell, Helen (1927), *The wandering scholars* (London).

Waddell, Helen (1929), *Medieval Latin lyrics* (London).

Wailes, Bernard (1982), 'The Irish "royal sites" in history and archaeology' in *Cambridge Medieval Celtic Studies*, iii, pp. 1–29.

Wainwright, F.T. (1948), 'Ingimund's invasion' in *English Historical Review*, lxiii, pp. 145–69.

Wainwright, F.T. (ed.) (1956), *The problem of the Picts* (Edinburgh).

Wainwright, F.T. (ed.) (1962), *The Northern Isles* (Studies in History and Archaeology) (London).

Walker, G.S.M. (ed.) (1957), *Sancti Columbani opera* (Scriptores Latini Hiberniae, ii) (Dublin).

Wallace, Patrick F. (1982), 'The origins of Dublin' in Scott (1982), pp. 129–43.

Wallace, Patrick F. (1984), 'A reappraisal of the archaeological significance of Wood Quay' in Bradley (1984), pp. 112–33.

Wallace, Patrick F. (1985a), 'The archaeology of Viking Dublin' in Clarke and Simms (1985), pp. 103–45.

Wallace, Patrick, F. (1985b), 'The survival of wood in tenth to thirteenth century Dublin' in *Waterlogged wood-study and conservation* (Proceedings of the 2nd ICOM waterlogged woodgroup conference) (Grenoble)), pp. 81–7.

Wallace, Patrick F. (1987a), 'The layout of later Viking Age Dublin: indications of its regulation and problems of continuity' in *Proceedings of the Tenth Viking Congress* (Universitets Oldsaksamlings Skrifter, Ny Rekke, ix) (Oslo), pp. 271–85.

Wallace, Patrick F. (1987b), 'The economy and commerce of Viking Dublin' in Düwel, Jankuhn, Siems and Timpe (1987), pp. 200–45.

Wallace, Patrick F. (1988), 'Archaeology and the emergence of Dublin as the principal town of Ireland' in Bradley (1988a), pp. 123–60.

Wallace, Patrick F. (1992), *The Viking-Age buildings of Dublin.* (RIA Medieval Dublin Excavations 1962–81) (2 vols) (Dublin).

Wallace-Haddrill, J.M. (1971), *Early Germanic kingship in England and on the continent* (Oxford).

Walsh, A. (1922), *Scandinavian relations with Ireland during the Viking period* (Dublin).

Walsh, John and Bradley, Thomas (1991), *A history of the Irish Church 400–700 AD* (Dublin).

Walsh, Maura and Ó Cróinín, Dáibhí (eds) (1988), *Cummian's letter 'De controuersia paschali' together with a related Irish computistical tract 'De ratione conputandi.* (Pontifical Institute of Mediaeval Studies, Studies & Texts, lxxxvi) (Toronto).

Wamers, Egon (1983), 'Some ecclesiastical and secular Insular metalwork found in Norwegian Viking graves' in *Peritia*, ii, pp. 277–306.

Ward, Alan (1973), ' "Will" and "testament" in Irish' in *Ériu*, xxiv, pp. 183–5.

Warner, Richard (1976), 'Some observations on the context and importation of exotic material in Ireland, from the first century BC to the second century AD' in *PRIA*, lxxvi C 15, pp. 267–92.

Warner, Richard (1982), 'The Broighter hoard: a reappraisal, and the iconography of the collar' in Scott (1982), pp. 29–38.

Warner, Richard (1988), 'The archaeology of early historic Irish kingship' in Driscoll and Nieke (1988), pp. 47–68.

Warren, F.E. (ed.) (1879), *The manuscript Irish missal belonging to the President and fellows of Corpus Christi College, Oxford* (London).

Wasserschleben, Hermann (ed.) (1874, 1885), *Die irische Kanonensammlung* (Gießen).

Watkins, Calvert (1976), 'Sick-maintenance in Indo-European' in *Ériu*, xxvii, pp. 21–5.

Watkins, Calvert (1978), 'Varia III, 2 (*'In essar dam do á?'*) in *Ériu*, xxix, pp. 161–5.

Wemple, Suzanne Fonay (1985), *Women in Frankish society: marriage and the cloister 500 to 900* (Philadelphia).

Westra, Haijo Jan (ed.) (1992), *From Athens to Chartres. Neoplatonism in medieval thought* (Leiden).

White, Gilbert (1977), *The natural history of Selbourne* (Penguin English Library) (Harmondsworth).

White, Newport J.D. (ed.) (1905), *Libri Sancti Patricii, the Latin writings of St. Patrick* (Dublin).

Whitelock, Dorothy (ed.) (1979), *English historical documents*, i (London).

Whitelock, Dorothy, McKitterick, Rosamond and Dumville, David N. (eds) (1982), *Ireland in early medieval Europe: essays in memory of Kathleen Hughes* (Cambridge).

Wickham, Chris (1981), *Early medieval Italy, central power and local society 400–1000* (London).

Williams, Hugh (1912), *Christianity in early Britain* (Oxford).

Wilson, David (1976), 'Scandinavian settlement in the north and west of the British Isles – an archaeological point of view' in *Transactions of the Royal Historical Society*, xxvi, pp. 95–113.

Winterbottom, Michael (1976), 'Columbanus and Gildas' in *Vigiliae Christianae*, xxx, pp. 310–17.

Woodman, Peter (1992), 'Irish archaeology today: a poverty amongst riches' in *The Irish Review*, No. 12, pp. 34–9.

Wormald, Patrick (1976), Review of Matthews (1975) in *Journal of Roman Studies*, lxvi, pp. 217–26.

Wormald, Patrick (1977), 'Lex scripta and verbum regis: legislation and Germanic kingship' in Sawyer and Wood (1977), pp. 105–38.

Wright, David (1963), 'The tablets from the Springmount Bog: a key to early Irish palaeography', in *American Journal of Archaeology*, lxvii, p. 219.

Young, J.I. (1950), 'A note on the Norse occupation of Ireland' in *History*, xxxv, pp. 11–33.

Youngs, Susan (ed.) (1989), *The work of angels: Masterpieces of Celtic metalwork 6th–9th centuries AD* (British Museum Exhibition catalogue) (London).

Zeumer, Karl (ed.) (1902), *Leges Visigothorum*, in *MGH, Leges nationum Germanicarum*, i.

Zückmayer, Carl (1966), *Als wär's ein Stück von mir* (Vienna).

INDEX